A DICTIONARY OF
ECONOMICS AND COMMERCE

By the Same Author

A TEXTBOOK OF ECONOMICS
ECONOMICS FOR STUDENTS
MONETARY THEORY AND PRACTICE
AN OUTLINE OF MONETARY THEORY
THE STRUCTURE OF MODERN COMMERCE

A DICTIONARY OF ECONOMICS AND COMMERCE

J. L. HANSON
M.A., M.Ed. (Leeds), Ph.D., B.Sc.(Econ.) (London)
*Formerly Senior Lecturer in charge of Economics
at the Huddersfield College of Technology
(now Huddersfield Polytechnic)*

FIFTH EDITION

MACDONALD AND EVANS

MACDONALD AND EVANS LTD.
Estover, Plymouth PL6 7PZ

First published 1965
Reprinted 1965
Reprinted 1966
Second Edition 1967
Reprinted 1968
Third Edition 1969
Fourth Edition 1974
Reprinted 1975
Fifth Edition 1977
Reprinted 1979
Reprinted 1984

©

J. L. HANSON
1977

ISBN 0 7121 0424 0 (home edition)
ISBN 0 7121 0446 1 (export edition)

This book is copyright and may not be reproduced in whole or in part (except for purposes of review) without the express permission of the publishers in writing.

To
E. H.

PRINTED AND BOUND IN ENGLAND BY
HAZELL WATSON AND VINEY LIMITED
MEMBER OF THE BPCC GROUP
AYLESBURY, BUCKS

PREFACE TO THE FIFTH EDITION

Most of the entries in this Dictionary of Economics and Commerce—of which there are over 5,000—refer to principles of economic theory and applied economics. Many items of current interest have been included as these are the ones that are so often the most difficult to trace. There are also many entries from economic history where these have a bearing on economics, as well as a number of items from cognate aspects of the social sciences. To add to the general usefulness of the Dictionary brief definitions of some of the more important commercial terms have also been included. In an age when initials are often preferred to words —or chosen to form barbaric and grotesque combinations of letters without meaning or claim to etymology—it has been thought necessary to include only abbreviations of this kind that are in general use. Following the practice of the compilers of the Oxford Dictionary, entries are listed in strict alphabetical order.

The purpose of the Dictionary is to enable the reader to find quickly and expeditiously an explanation—not merely a definition—of some matter of economic interest without having to seek for it among the mass of material in a number of textbooks. An attempt, therefore, has been made to give entries concerning pure and applied economics as full treatment as necessary for an understanding of their meaning and significance. Thus, it should be of particular value to the student who has as yet made little headway with the subject and who constantly finds himself coming up against difficulties which impede his progress. It is hoped therefore that most items of economic importance have been included. It has been possible, however, to include only a selection of entries relating to topics on the fringe of economics, chosen on the basis of their importance and relevance to the main purpose of the Dictionary. Of necessity these entries have been given the briefest possible treatment.

As a work of reference, more especially perhaps for recent developments, it is hoped that the book will be found useful to men and women in many professions, especially accountants, bankers, civil servants, secretaries, and others engaged in commerce and industry. Not least it is hoped that it may prove of service to the general reader who has little or no knowledge of economics and yet finds himself constantly coming up against economic affairs in his ordinary life and in his interest in current events, in which economic matters have so important a place at the present day.

I would like to express my thanks to Mr D. Symes of the publishers' editorial department for his invaluable assistance. I am greatly indebted to him for his many helpful suggestions.

J. L. H.

Northedge,
Huddersfield,
August 1977

A

A1 at Lloyd's. For a long time the first class in Lloyd's Register of Shipping (*q.v.*). The higher the class the lower is the rate of premium. By extension the term A1 is used to describe anything that is of high quality.

A.A.R. Abbreviation of Against All Risks—the most comprehensive type of marine insurance policy.

Abandonment. Goods that have been insured may be abandoned (i) if their actual loss appears to be unavoidable; or (ii) if the cost of repairing the damage will exceed their value. In such cases the insured will inform the insurers that he wishes to abandon the goods as a Constructive Total Loss (*q.v.*).

Abbey National Building Society. Founded in 1849, it is the second largest building society in Great Britain and was formed by the amalgamation of the Abbey and the National Societies. Like the Halifax it has branches (as distinct from agencies) throughout Great Britain. *See* Building Societies.

A.B.C.C. Abbreviation of Association of British Chambers of Commerce (*q.v.*).

ABC Code. *See* Codes.

Ability to Pay. A principle of taxation—that the amount of tax payable by a person should depend on his ability to pay. In applying the principle the difficulty is to decide what exactly is to be understood by ability to pay. Both the proportional and the progressive systems of taxation are based in varying degrees on the ability to pay. *See* Taxation.

Able-bodied Poor. The Poor Law made a distinction between the able-bodied poor and the aged poor. It was a recognised principle that, though the aged poor might be treated more generously, any assistance given to the able-bodied poor should not make them any better off than 'the independent labourer of the lowest class'.

'Above-the-line.' A term used during 1949–64 in the Chancellor of the Exchequer's Financial Statement. Though the terms 'above-the-line' and 'below-the-line', did not precisely distinguish between current and capital expenditure and revenue, most current items appeared above the line and most capital items below. Some items shown below-the-line were not included at one time in the Budget at all. Though the term is no longer employed in the Financial Statement the term is still sometimes used to distinguish current from capital items of expenditure. *See* Budget.

Abrasion. With reference to coins, this is the loss of weight resulting from wear while they are in circulation. When gold coins were in circulation the making good of abrasion was an expensive business.

Absenteeism. This term is generally restricted to mean frequent voluntary absence from work for which no satisfactory reason is given, though sometimes it is also used of frequent absence as a result of sickness. If absenteeism is high it has a deleterious effect on the efficiency of a firm, and of course it reduces output. Absenteeism is a serious problem in times of full employment in occupations where there is a shortage of labour. It occurs most frequently where the work is of an unpleasant nature, especially if wage-rates are relatively high. The 'pay-as-you-earn' system of collecting income tax tends to encourage absenteeism since tax falls most heavily on marginal earnings, with the result that a half-day's absence from work reduces the tax payable for that week by an amount considerably above the average rate paid on a full week's earnings. Particularly where work is of a disagreeable kind and where the risk of losing one's job is slight, a worker who has worked part of a week may feel that leisure is to be preferred to further income. In such circumstances to raise wages with a view to attracting more labour to an industry where there is a shortage may in fact result in less labour being supplied, that is, in fewer 'man-hours' being worked on account of an increase in absenteeism, thus providing an example of a Regressive Supply Curve (*q.v.*).

Absentee Landlord. A landowner who does not reside in the country in which he owns land; the term is applied particularly to English owners of land in Ireland.

Absolute Monopoly. If the entire output of a commodity or service, for which there is no substitute of any kind, were in the hands of a single producer or supplier absolute monopoly would occur. This never occurs in actual conditions since there are alternatives for most things. The production of electricity in Great Britain, undertaken by the Central Electricity Generating Board, is often regarded as monopolistic, but the C.E.G.B. does not possess an absolute monopoly since coal, gas, and oil are all possible alternatives to electricity. *See* Monopoly.

Absorption. When a small company amalgamates with a large one it may completely lose its identity and become merely part of the larger company by which it has been absorbed. *See* Amalgamation.

Abstinence Theory. Also known as the Agio Theory of interest, the Abstinence Theory asserts that interest is a payment for abstaining from current consumption. Some people have so strong a preference for present than for future consumption that they are willing to pay interest on a loan in order to enjoy this privilege. Loanable funds become available to such borrowers because other people prefer future to present consumption, especially if they are paid interest as a reward for their abstinence.

Abstract of Title. A summary of all matters affecting title to a piece of property. Before purchasing property it is of great importance, therefore, that the buyer should be sure that the seller has a good title to it and so is in fact entitled to sell it.

A.C.A. Designatory initials of an Associate of the Institute of Chartered Accountants in England and Wales. *See* Chartered Accountant.

A.C.A.S. Abbreviation of Advisory Conciliation and Arbitration Service, set up under the Employment Protection Act (*q.v.*).

A.C.C.A. Designatory initials of an Associate of the Association of Certified Accountants. *See* Certified Accountant.

Accelerated Depreciation. A practice whereby for tax purposes a firm is permitted to depreciate a new machine over a shorter period than that for which it is likely to be employed, with possibly a much larger allowance for the first year than for subsequent years.

Acceleration Principle. Where the demand for one commodity is derived from another, as with capital goods, the demand for which is derived from the demand for consumers' goods, a change in the demand for one will bring about a change in the demand for the other, though not necessarily a proportionate change. Thus, changes in the demand for consumers' goods bring about even wider variations in the production of the appropriate capital goods. This is known as the Acceleration Principle. Suppose, for example, that the demand for Commodity Y, a capital good, is derived from the demand for Commodity X, a consumers' good. Let us further assume that when demand is steady an annual production of 20 units of Y will meet the requirements of producers of X. Let us also assume that Y has a life of seven years. Then, in any given year there will be in use 20 units of Y aged one year, 20 units aged two years, 20 units aged three years, and so on for each year up to seven, as shown under Year 1 in the table below. If now a temporary increase takes place in the demand for X this will be transmitted to Y, and an increase in the output of this commodity will be required, but only for one year. If demand for X returns to its previous level, then the production of Y will need to be curtailed until its supply has been reduced to its previous level. This can be seen more clearly from the table.

Age-distribution of Commodity Y

Year	Ages of Y							Total stock	No. produced annually
	1 yr	2 yrs	3 yrs	4 yrs	5 yrs	6 yrs	7 yrs		
I	20	20	20	20	20	20	20	140	20
II	40	20	20	20	20	20	20	160	40
III	0	40	20	20	20	20	20	140	0
IV	20	0	40	20	20	20	20	140	20
V	20	20	0	40	20	20	20	140	20

From the table it can be seen that at first in this industry an annual output of 20 units of Y will maintain an even age-distribution of this type of capital, but the effect of the *temporary* increase in demand is to introduce a *permanent* cyclical irregularity into its annual output. It was formerly thought by some economists that in such fluctuations in the output of capital goods industries the trade cycle had its origin, the Acceleration Principle being responsible, therefore, for one of the real as distinct from monetary causes of the cycle. The Acceleration Principle shows that there is a functional relationship between consumption and investment, an increase in consumption bringing about a greater increase in the demand for machines to make consumers' goods, so that fluctuations are greater in capital producing industries than in consumers' goods industries. Contrast the concept of the Multiplier, which indicates the effect of a given amount of investment on consumption and incomes.

Accelerator. *See* Acceleration Principle.

Acceptance. After a bill of exchange has been drawn by the drawer (the creditor) it must be accepted by the drawee (the debtor), the bill being then known as an Acceptance. For a fee an Acceptance House will often add its own acceptance to a bill, thereby making it more negotiable. *See* Bill of Exchange.

Acceptance Credit. This is a method of payment in international trade. Accepting Houses (*q.v.*) maintain agents in the chief commercial centres of the world, their business being to make themselves acquainted with the credit-worthiness of foreign traders. If, for example, the credit standing of an Argentine import merchant is regarded as satisfactory the Accepting House will open an acceptance credit for him in London. A purchase from a British exporter will then be financed by a bill drawn on the Accepting House, and such a bill will be easily discounted in the London money and discount market.

Acceptance for Honour. When a bill of exchange has been dishonoured it may be accepted by someone who has no interest in the bill in order to safeguard the good name of the drawee. This is known as Acceptance for Honour.

Accepting Houses. Also known as merchant bankers, these institutions specialised in accepting bills of exchange when they were the usual means of payment in foreign trade. Accepting foreign bills developed out of the business of merchants who specialised in trade with particular parts of the world where they maintained their agents. On account of their special knowledge of the financial standing of traders in these areas they were able to guarantee payment of bills of exchange drawn on them. This was done by accepting these bills, for which a service fee had to be paid, and so making them more negotiable in the London money and discount markets where possibly few people knew the foreign traders on whom the bills were drawn. In course of time the financial business of the merchants outgrew their trading activities and they became primarily merchant bankers. London being the commercial and financial centre of the world, they transferred their head offices there. Merchant bankers who established themselves in London included such well-known firms as the Rothschilds (who came from Frankfurt-am-Main), Barings, Schroder, Kleinwort, and Lazard. The decline of the bill of exchange as a means of payment, both in internal and in foreign trade, brought about a severe decline in acceptance business, with the result that the merchant bankers, most of whom still operate as partnerships or private companies, have had to develop other banking activities.

Acceptor. Before any value attaches to a bill of exchange it must be accepted by the person who is to make the payment, that is, the person on whom it is drawn. Thus the acceptor of a bill is also the drawee, that is, the debtor.

Access. The credit card issued jointly by Lloyds Bank, the Midland Bank, the National Westminster Bank, the Royal Bank of Scotland, Clydesdale Bank and the Ulster Bank. Access is linked with the American Interbank Master Change and Eurocard. *See* Credit Card.

Accommodation Bill. This is a bill of exchange to which a person known as an accommodation party has given his name, thereby accepting liability as drawer, acceptor, or endorser.

Accord and Satisfaction. A term used of a contract which has been discharged by mutual agreement of the parties concerned. If neither party has carried out his undertaking under the original contract no further consideration is required, but if one party has done so the other will have to give some new consideration.

Account. A stock exchange term, it refers to the period during which transactions take place, at the end of which settlement must be made. Ordinarily each account is of a fortnight's duration, except when it includes a Bank Holiday, in which case the account is extended to three weeks.

Accountant. A person qualified in bookkeeping and cognate subjects. In addition to specialist firms of accountants who act as auditors and tax consultants to other firms, many large companies employ their own accountants. Manufacturers also generally require the services of a cost accountant whose function is to calculate the cost of the firm's product. *See* Certified Accountant; Chartered Accountant; Cost Accountant.

Accountant and Comptroller General. The title of the head of the accounts department of the inland revenue or customs and excise.

Account Day. A stock exchange term, it is Tuesday week after the end of an account. It is the day on which settlement has to be made for transactions made during the previous account. It is also known as Settlement Day or Pay Day.

Account (or A/c) Payee Only. If a cheque is crossed in this way it can be paid only into the account of the payee named on the cheque and, therefore, cannot be transferred by endorsement to someone else as is the case with a simple crossing. *See* General Crossing; Special Crossing.

Account Sales. A document supplied to his principal by an agent who has been engaged to sell a quantity of goods. It gives full details of the transaction—the amount sold, the price obtained, the expenses incurred, and the agent's commission.

Accrued Interest. Interest on a security which has accumulated up to a certain time.

A.C.C.S. Designatory initials of an Associate of the Corporation of Secretaries (*q.v.*).

Accumulating Society. A type of friendly society (*q.v.*) which is centrally organised in contrast to the locally independent affiliated orders (*q.v.*). The accumulating societies offer a wider range of benefits than other friendly societies and resemble insurance companies. The Hearts of Oak Benefit Society is the largest friendly society of this kind.

Accumulation, Capital. *See* Capital Formation.

Accumulation Units. A type of unit trust where the interest is re-invested, the aim being to maximise capital growth.

A.C.G.I. Designatory initials of an Associate of the City and Guilds Institute of London.

A.C.I.B. Designatory initials of an Associate of the Corporation of Insurance Brokers (*q.v.*).

'Acid-test' Ratio. A term used to describe the ability of a firm to meet its obligations in the short-run, the only items taken into account in calculating this ratio being easily realised assets such as cash in hand, payments due from customers, and current liabilities.

A.C.I.I. Designatory initials of an Associate of the Chartered Insurance Institute (*q.v.*).

A.C.I.S. Designatory initials of an Associate of the Institute of Chartered Secretaries and Administrators (*q.v.*).

A.C.M.A. Designatory initials of an Associate of the Institute of Cost and Management Accountants. *See* Cost Accountant.

A.C.P. Abbreviation of African, Caribbean and Pacific States, comprising mainly former colonies of European powers. In 1975 they entered into the Lomé Agreement (*q.v.*) with the E.E.C.

Acronym. An artificial word formed from the initial letters of the words comprising the title of an organisation, *e.g.* EFTA, UNESCO, BACIE, etc.

Active Balance of Payments (or Trade). An alternative term for Favourable Balance of Payments or Trade (*q.v.*).

Active Circulation. That part of the note issue of the Bank of England which is in circulation at a given time. It is shown in the weekly Bank Return for the Issue Department as 'Notes in Circulation', the remainder of the note issue being held in reserve in the Banking Department.

Active Market. A stock exchange term for a particular stock or share in which there are frequent and regular dealings, so that buyers can obtain reasonably large amounts at any time.

Act of God. In law this term denotes any occurrence that cannot be ascribed to human agency and, therefore, could not be foreseen, such as storms, floods, etc.

Actual Total Loss. A term used in marine insurance to denote goods that have become a total loss, as when goods are completely destroyed by fire or when a ship sinks after a collision, or when goods have been rendered unusable, as for example by sea water, so that they are totally unfit for the purpose for which they were originally intended. *See also* Constructive Total Loss.

Actuary. One of the chief executive officials of an assurance company. His main responsibilities are the calculation of premiums and matters connected with pension funds. To qualify as an actuary in England it is necessary to pass the examinations of the Institute of Actuaries.

Addison Scheme. A housing scheme introduced by an Act of 1919, Dr C. (later Lord) Addison (1869–1951) being Minister of Health at the time. Local authorities were to build houses to let at rents which the tenants could afford to pay. As a result of the cessation of house building during the First World War there was a serious shortage of houses to rent.

Addressograph. A machine for printing addresses where regular communication has to be made with clients, etc.

Ademption. A term used of a clause in a will which becomes void when a bequest refers to something that no longer exists.

Adjudication Order. A Court order declaring the debtor to be a bankrupt and putting his property under the control of a Trustee in Bankruptcy. *See* Bankruptcy.

Adjustable Peg. A type of flexible exchange rate (*q.v.*) where the rate is permitted to vary but only within very narrow limits.

Administered Prices. A term used by Lord Keynes for prices charged by a monopolist and therefore determined by considerations other than marginal cost.

Administrator. When no testators have been appointed under a will or where those named are not prepared to act the Court will appoint an administrator to administer the estate.

Adulterine Gild. A medieval gild that had not obtained a charter. Such gilds often continued to function by paying an annual fine to the king. *See* Gild.

Ad Valorem. Taxes on commodities are calculated in two ways, either according to quantity or according to value. In the case of a specific tax, the amount of the tax to be paid depends on the *amount* of the commodity bought. In the case of an *ad valorem* tax the amount to be paid is proportionate to the *value* of the commodity. Many stamp duties also are *ad valorem*.

Advancement. A legal term, it refers to money advanced to a beneficiary under a will or settlement to promote his interest as, for example, to enable him to set up in business for himself.

Advances to Customers. Loans and overdrafts to industry and commerce and personal loans appear under this heading in the balance sheet of a commercial or joint-stock bank. Together with Investments, Advances to Customers form the two less liquid assets of a bank, in Great Britain forming approximately 28% of a bank's total assets. Advances are generally loans to provide industry with its circulating capital, since it is rare for British banks to provide fixed capital. It is usual for bank advances and investments to vary inversely. When advances are in great demand, the banks sell some of their investments. Since bank advances create purchasing power the British monetary authorities seek to influence the level of bank advances in order to implement their monetary policy. Thus in a times of inflation it may be thought necessary to restrict bank advances, whereas in a time of recession the aim might be to encourage their expansion.

Advantages, Non-monetary. One of the reasons why wages in some occupations are less than in others is that such occupations often possess some non-monetary advantages. These include such things as more congenial working conditions, security of tenure, a greater degree of independence, shorter or more convenient hours of work, longer holidays, prestige of the job. The principal effect of non-monetary advantages to an occupation is to increase its attractiveness and, therefore, the supply of labour offering itself for employment. This greater supply in relation to demand tends to keep down the level of wages in such occupations. In some occupations in addition to money-wages employees sometimes receive other benefits such as the allowance of free coal to coalminers, free travel to and from work for transport workers, uniform for many kinds of workers, board and lodging for some hotel workers, etc. Such benefits, however, are better regarded as payments in kind (*q.v.*) rather than as non-monetary advantages. *See also* Non-monetary Advantages and Disadvantages.

Adverse Balance. As applied to the balance of trade or the balance of payments it means an excess of payments over receipts, that is, a debit balance. Such a balance is sometimes described as an unfavourable or passive balance. *See* Balance of Payments.

Advertising. Selling costs are those costs that a producer, wholesaler, or retailer incurs in order to stimulate sales. A certain amount of advertising is of an informative kind, the aim simply being to let consumers know what goods and services are available—'consumer education' as it is sometimes called. There is no economic objection to purely informative advertising. Most advertising, however, is of the persuasive or competitive kind, the aim of which is to persuade people to buy one thing rather than something else. Advertising is a selling cost particularly associated with imperfect competition, since under perfect competition there would be no advertising of a competitive kind, the products of all producers of a commodity being considered to be homogeneous in those conditions, although an industry as a whole might advertise. Advertising is particularly associated with oligopoly and to a lesser degree with monopolistic competition. In the sale of branded goods, a clear example of imperfect oligopoly, advertising is essential in order to try to impress on consumers that one maker's brand is superior to all others, although in fact the only difference between brands may sometimes be in their trade marks and labels. Any producer with some degree of monopoly, however slight, will generally find it more advantageous to advertise his product widely and at considerable expense rather than cut his prices. In such cases advertising becomes an alternative to price-cutting. Any advantages accruing to price-cutting are likely to be only temporary, since after a time other producers also will cut their prices, the eventual result being a reduction in all producers' profit margins. Thus, the aim of advertising is to influence the demand for a commodity so that a greater quantity of it is bought without having to reduce its price.

Advertising can take many forms, though advertising in newspapers, magazines, and trade journals accounts for 60% of total expenditure on advertising. Circulars, leaflets, catalogues, or free samples may be distributed. The cinema, commercial radio, and television offer opportunities to the advertiser, and for a long time advertising on street hoardings has been supplemented by increasingly elaborate electric street signs at night. Other forms of advertising include both the exterior and interior of buses, the exterior of traders' and manufacturers' own vans, exhibitions and window displays. A popular recent method of advertising has been the issue of coupons entitling the holder to a temporary reduction in the price of a specified commodity. Expenditure on advertising has reached enormous proportions in some countries, especially in the United States, where it now exceeds $10,000 million p.a. Although advertising in Great Britain costs only one-tenth of that sum it is, nevertheless, a serious cost of production, though the amount varies very considerably between different industries, in patent medicines being as high as 45% of the total cost.

Selling costs are regarded by economists as one of the wastes of imperfect competition, and so competitive advertising is condemned as a waste of economic resources which otherwise might be employed on the production of other goods. To the individual manufacturer advertising is clearly of great advantage as a means of increasing his sales at the expense of his rivals, but from the point of view of the community as a whole it simply leads to a misdirection of economic activity. It is said too that it interferes with the free choice of consumers. Nevertheless, large numbers of consumers actually prefer to buy goods that are widely advertised. Advertising may be used to stimulate demand generally and in the affluent society (*q.v.*) it may be used to create wants of which consumers were previously quite unaware. Even if the State decided to prohibit competitive advertising this would be difficult to enforce since it is not possible to make a clear distinction between the two types of advertising. Much competitive advertising also aims at supplying consumers with information just as also much informative advertising contains a little at least of a persuasive element.

Advertising Standards Authority. An independent body set up in 1962 by all sides of the advertising industry. It aims to promote and enforce high standards in advertising as set out in the British Code of Advertising Practice.

Advice Note. A note to a person to inform him that a certain transaction has been carried out. More particularly it refers to a commercial document despatched by the supplier of a quantity of goods, such as a manufacturer or a wholesaler, to a purchaser informing him of the date on which the listed goods were despatched and of the means of transport employed. When goods are sent by railway the advice note is usually sent by post the same day so that it reaches the purchaser ahead of the goods, thus serving to warn him that they are on the way and also giving him details of the goods to be expected.

'Advise Fate.' A term used in connection with cheques. If it is required to know whether the drawer of a cheque has a sufficient balance in his current account to meet it the receiving banker may ask for this information to be telegraphed to him, that is, to be advised of the 'fate' of the cheque in question.

A.E.A. Abbreviation of Atomic Energy Authority (*q.v.*).

Aer Lingus. The airline of the Irish Republic.

Aeroflot. The Russian airline.

A.E.U. Abbreviation of Amalgamated Engineering Union. With over a million members, it is the second largest industrial union in Great Britain.

A.F.A. Designatory initials of an Associate of the Faculty of Actuaries.

Affiliate. A firm which is associated with another, generally as its subsidiary.

Affiliated Orders. A type of friendly society (*q.v.*) such as the Independent Order of Oddfellows, in which small, but independent, local lodges are organised in federations.

Affluent Society. A term used to denote the high standard of living achieved in many countries in Western Europe and the United States in the 1960s. The phrase was popularised by Professor J. K. Galbraith with particular reference to the United States in *The Affluent Society*, a book devoted to a study of the economic and social problems these new conditions have produced. With the rising real income of the great mass of people and the virtual abolition of poverty a time arrives when most of them can satisfy their basic wants and still have money with which to buy other things. When this stage is reached wants do not originate with the individual. The high level at which it is thought necessary to maintain production makes it constantly necessary to stimulate—indeed, often actually to create—demand by advertising and other means. If wants are not urgent, says Prof. Galbraith, then production is not urgent. Human experience of affluence, he says, is very brief, and the economic ideas still current are those developed in a world where most people lived in poverty in conditions of inequality and insecurity. Today we are concerned with production, not primarily to satisfy the real wants of consumers, but to provide employment. Since the standards of many people are not very high much of production is devoted to the satisfaction of trivial wants. On the other hand, expenditure on public services has lagged behind private expenditure, especially in the United States, where services provided even by many of the large cities have not kept pace with the rise in individual standards of living, the result, as Prof. Galbraith puts it, being 'private affluence amid public squalor'. If this lack of balance between privately produced goods and the supply of public services, worsened as it often is by the effects of inflation, could be remedied, Prof. Galbraith thinks that production would be less dependent on changes of consumers' demand and, therefore, greater stability would be given to the economy.

Afghani. The currency unit of Afghanistan. One afghani is equal to 100 puls.

A.F.L. Abbreviation of American Federation of Labor ($q.v.$).

After Date. A term used on a bill of exchange to indicate the date from which the period of the bill is to be calculated.

After Sight. A term used on a bill of exchange to indicate that the period for the bill is to be calculated from the date on which it is presented to the drawee for acceptance.

A.G. Abbreviation of Aktiengesellschaft, the German equivalent of limited company. *See also* GmbH.

Age-distribution of Capital. *See* Acceleration Principle.

Aged Poor, Royal Commission on (1893). This Commission was set up by Parliament in 1893 to consider what should be done to improve the lot of people who were unable to maintain themselves. Consideration was given to the possibility of granting them old-age pensions ($q-v.$).

Ageing Population. Since 1890 there has been a gradual increase in the percentage of old people in Great Britain. In 1891 almost half the people in Britain were under the age of 21, whereas by 1975 the number of young people under this age had fallen to 30%. In 1891 only 7% of the people were over 60 years of age, but by 1970 this percentage had increased to 18. In 1970 there were 6·5 million people over the age of 65. There are two main reasons for the increase in the proportion of older people: (i) the fall in the birth-rate from 34·2 per thousand in 1880 to 13·0 per thousand in 1974; and (ii) the rise in the expectation of life in the twentieth century. *See* Population Problem.

Agency Shop. A type of closed shop permitted under the Industrial Relations Act, 1971 ($q.v.$).

Agent. In law a person who is given authority by some other person to enter into a contract on his behalf, the authority of the agent being limited to the power given him by his principal. Where the buyer requires to have expert knowledge, as on most of the highly organised produce exchanges, it is usual for the principal—a wholesaler or a manufacturer—to employ an agent or broker who is a specialist buyer of the commodity concerned. Also, where a special procedure has to be followed in the selling of goods as, for example, in a wholesale market where the method of sale is the auction, the seller, usually an import merchant, engages an agent or broker to act on his behalf. A *del credere* agent is one who guarantees payment to his principal for goods sold on his principal's behalf.

Agents of Production. An alternative term for Factors of Production ($q.v.$).

Age-specific Mortality Rate. A refinement of the crude death rate ($q.v.$) for a country, showing the number of deaths each year per thousand persons in each of the main age groups.

Aggregates. Some of the most important modern problems of economics are concerned with aggregates such as the general price level rather than with individual items such as the price of a particular product. To the branch of economic theory dealing with individual prices, wages, saving, etc., the name micro-economics has been given. Lord Keynes saw that micro-economics failed to explain the great problem of his own day, which could be considered only in terms of aggregates such as the volume of investment, saving, consumption, employment, the national income, since what is true of the individual is not always true of the community as a whole. Thus, it may be to the interest of the individual to save at a period when it is not so for the community as a whole, as for instance in a time of heavy unemployment. An individual may increase his personal income by a purchase of (say) £100 of a new issue of Government stock, but from the point of view of the community this is simply an increase in Government debt, adding nothing to the real national income. With the increasing interest taken by Governments in economic policy greater attention has had to be paid to aggregates since a Government of necessity is concerned with the welfare of the whole community and not with particular individuals. Since it accepted responsibility for the maintenance of full employment the British Government has had to take an interest in such aggregates as the level of employment, investment, saving, consumption, production, and trade and, because of its concern to check inflation, the level of prices. To the branch of economics devoted to a study of aggregates the name macro-economics has been given.

Agio. 1. An alternative name for the Abstinence Theory of interest (*q.v.*).
2. A charge made for exchanging the currency of one country for that of another. When a currency has depreciated, perhaps as a result of inflation, or in the case of coins because they have lost weight due to wear, the agio represents the difference between the nominal and the actual value of the currency.

Agiotage. Speculation in foreign exchange or stock exchange securities.

A.G.M. Abbreviation of Annual General Meeting.

Agorot. A unit of the currency of Israel, there being 100 agorots to the pound.

Agrarian Revolution. The improvements in farming that took place in England mainly during the second half of the eighteenth century. One of the most important changes was the abolition of the fallow field, the four-course system of crop rotation replacing the former three-field system. Fields previously left fallow were given up to the cultivation of turnips and other root crops, thus providing winter food for cattle and other animals, so that it was no longer necessary to kill off most of them at the onset of winter. As a result fresh meat replaced salted meat in the winter months with beneficial effects on the health of the people. At the same time improved methods of breeding raised the quality of both sheep and cattle. The enclosure of the common lands made for more efficient farming, although it resulted in large numbers of independent yeomen having to accept employment as hired labourers.

Agreed Charges. At one time British railways imposed standard charges for the carriage of goods. In order to enable them to compete more effectively against road operators the Road and Rail Traffic Act of 1933 permitted them to make special terms with individual traders, subject to the approval of the Railway Rates Tribunal.

Agricultural Bank. A bank specially established to assist agricultural development by granting loans of longer duration than is customary with commercial banks. Each of the states of Australia has a bank of this type. *See also* Agricultural Mortgage Corporation.

Agricultural Committees, County. War Agricultural Committees were established during the Second World War with power to give directions to farmers regarding the crops they should grow. After the war these committees were succeeded by County Agricultural Committees, representing landowners, farmers, and farm workers, to give advice to farmers.

Agricultural Fluctuations. When the demand for a commodity is inclined to be inelastic and when also supply is slow to adjust itself to changes in demand, as is the case with most agricultural products, violent fluctuations in output are liable to occur. Thus, the immediate effect of an increase in demand is a steep rise in price, because in the short run supply is fixed. On account of this high price producers tend to be over-optimistic and expand production by a greater amount than is justified by the increase in demand. Then, when this additional supply comes on to the market the price of the commodity falls steeply, and because this makes producers over-pessimistic they reduce production to too great an extent. Again price rises and the whole cycle of fluctuating production is set in motion once again. Such extreme fluctuations in output are most likely to occur with agricultural products because such commodities are most inclined to fulfil the two necessary conditions of inelastic demand and slow responsiveness of supply. *See* Cobweb Theorem.

Agricultural Marketing Act (1931). This Act made possible the setting up of a Marketing Board for any agricultural commodity where the producers of a large proportion of the total output of the commodity were in favour of such a scheme. The Milk Marketing Board was the first to be established.

Agricultural Mortgage Corporation. This is one of a number of finance corporations set up for the purpose of making loans to industry —in this case, agriculture—for longer periods than those for which the commercial banks lend. The Agricultural Mortgage Corporation was established under the Agricultural Credits Act (1928) the share capital being provided by the Bank of England and the English commercial or joint-stock banks. The Corporation also initially received from the Ministry of Agriculture and Fisheries a loan equal in amount to its share capital. In addition the Ministry (now the Ministry of Agriculture, Fisheries and Food) has made regular annual contributions towards its working expenses. The Corporation obtains further funds by the issue of debentures which are marketable on the stock exchange. The Corporation serves farmers in England and Wales—for Scottish farmers there is the Scottish Agricultural Securities Corporation— who are desirous of obtaining credit and who through this institution can mortgage their land up to two-thirds of its current value for periods up to sixty years. The commercial banks act as agents of the Corporation, and so farmers seeking loans can transact their business through their bank managers.

Agricultural Rates. By an Act of 1896 local rates on agricultural property were reduced to half, by an Act of 1923 to a quarter, and finally in 1929 complete relief was given. *See also* De-rating.

Agricultural Support Subsidies. *See* Farm Subsidies.

Agricultural Wages Board. Body responsible for negotiating the wages of agricultural workers.

Agriculture Act (1947). The aim of this Act was to offer British farmers guaranteed prices and assured markets for their products in order to give British agriculture greater stability of output and prices. The preamble to the Act states that its aim was to encourage the British farming industry to produce 'such part of the nation's food as in the national interest it is desirable to produce' and at 'minimum prices consistent with proper remuneration and living conditions for farmers and workers in agriculture, and an adequate return on the capital invested.' Each year the Government decides what shall be the guaranteed prices for such things as milk, potatoes, livestock, etc. The Act also contained provisions for maintaining a high standard of farming in Great Britain, including the dispossession of farmers who failed to reach the required minimum standard of efficiency.

Agriculture, Annual Review of.

A Government statement of the guaranteed prices for certain agricultural products for the ensuing year, published in accordance with the Agriculture Act of 1947 (*q.v.*).

Agriculture, Fisheries and Food, Ministry of. The Government department which is responsible for all matters appertaining to the agricultural and fishing industries and, since 1955, food. The department is generally under a minister of cabinet rank.

A.I.A. Designatory initials of an Associate of the Institute of Actuaries. *See* Actuary.

A.I.A.C. Designatory initials of an Associate of the Institute of Company Accountants.

A.I.B. Designatory initials of an Associate of the Institute of Bankers. *See* Institute of Bankers.

A.I.C.S. Designatory initials of an Associate of the Institute of Chartered Shipbrokers.

A.I.D. Abbreviation of Agency for International Development, a U.S. institution established in 1961 to centralise most of the Government's foreign aid.

Aids (or **Ancillaries**) **to Trade.** In the study of commerce it is usual to divide commerce into seven or eight main branches—the four branches of trade (retail, wholesale, import, export) and four aids to trade (transport, banking, insurance, and advertising).

A.I.M.T.A. Designatory initials of an Associate of the Institute of Municipal Treasurers and Accountants. *See* C.I.P.F.A.

Air Canada. The principal international airline of Canada. The Canadian Pacific also operates a number of international routes.

Air France. The principal French airline.

Air Letter. Letter form, purchasable at post offices, with impressed stamp, for sending by air mail.

Air Mail. The first air mail service was between London and Paris, opened in 1919. A year later air mail services to Brussels and Australia were started. At the present day there are air mail services between all the principal countries of the world.

Air Mail Transfer. An alternative means to the Bank Draft and Telegraphic Transfer for making a payment abroad.

Air Transport. The first regular British air service for passengers and mail was between London and Paris, inaugurated in 1919. Between the two World Wars development was slow, but after 1945 a huge expansion took place. Air services are now operated between all the important commercial cities of the world. Large countries like the United States have developed extensive internal systems of air transport, but in Great Britain, where distances are relatively short, internal routes are limited to connections between the larger cities and services between the mainland and the outlying islands—the Shetlands, Orkneys, Hebrides, Isle of Man, and the Scilly Isles. The main British airline is the State-owned British Airways, formed in 1973 by a merger of B.E.A. and B.O.A.C. In addition there are a number of independent lines, the largest being British Caledonian. The outstanding advantage of air transport is its speed, and its main disadvantage is the high operational cost in relation to the load carried. Nevertheless, one of the greatest developments of recent years has been the expansion of freight services and a huge increase in the total load of freight carried. Airlines now compete against both ocean-going liners and railways.

Airway Letters. As a result of an agreement between the Post Office and British Airways letters can be accepted at certain airports for conveyance by air.

Airways Board. Set up under the Civil Aviation Act (1971) to manage British Airways (*q.v.*).

A.L.A. Designatory initials of an Associate of the Library Association (*q.v.*).

Alexanders Discount Co. Ltd. One of the nine public companies carrying on discount business in the

London money market, it was founded in 1810.

'A' and 'B' Licences. Under the Traffic Act of 1933 road hauliers were divided into three categories —A, B, and C, the aim being to regulate traffic on the roads. The Transport Act (1968) (*q.v.*) abolished this licensing system, 'A' and 'B' licences being replaced by the 'O' licence (*q.v.*). *See also* Geddes Report (2).

Alitalia. The Italian State airline.

Allen Report (1965). The report of a Committee appointed in 1963 to consider 'the impact of rates on households', it found rates in effect to be an *ad valorem* tax on dwellings and generally regressive.

Allied Irish Banks Ltd. An Irish commercial bank established in 1966 as a result of the amalgamation of three Irish banks—the Munster & Leinster Bank, the Provincial Bank of Ireland, and the Royal Bank of Ireland.

Allonge. A slip of paper attached to a bill of exchange to provide additional space for endorsements where the reverse side of the bill has already been fully covered. In the days when a bill of exchange might pass freely from hand to hand, as at one time in the Manchester district, an allonge might be necessary. It is rarely required nowadays.

Allotment Letter. When a company makes a public offer of shares applicants are informed by means of allotment letters of the number of shares that have been allotted to them. If the issue has been oversubscribed it will be necessary to allot to some applicants fewer shares than they have applied for.

Allowances. For Income Tax (*q.v.*) purposes each taxpayer is allowed a certain sum as untaxed income, a certain amount for a single person, a greater amount for a married couple, with additional allowances for other dependent relatives.

Allowance System. The system of supplementing wages out of parish funds, first adopted in 1795 at Speenhamland in Berkshire, and more often known as the Speenhamland System (*q.v.*).

'All-up' Service. A term used of the practice now adopted by the Post Office of sending all mail to Europe by air if this will ensure earlier delivery than other means of transmission.

Alpine Routes. The Alps for a long time proved to be an almost insurmountable obstacle to transport, most of the roads over the high passes being closed for long periods in winter. Railway tunnels were constructed under the Mont Cenis, Simplon, St Gotthard and Arlberg passes, and two road tunnels were opened in 1964–65—the Mont Blanc and the Great St Bernard. Other road tunnels have been planned, including a St Gotthard tunnel.

Alternative Cost. An alternative term for Opportunity Cost (*q.v.*).

Alternatives. The basic principle of modern economic theory is that all things are scarce relative to the demand for them. Consequently consumers must choose between alternatives, since to have more of one thing necessitates having less of another. The reason why all things are scarce is that the supply of economic resources, that is, the factors of production, is limited, so that a choice has to be made as to how they shall be employed. This choice may be made by consumers through the price mechanism (*q.v.*) in a free economy or by the State in a State-planned economy. Thus, economic decisions resolve themselves into choices between alternatives.

Amalgamation. When two firms, previously independent, coalesce to form one new business an amalgamation or merger takes place. When this type of merger occurs the old firms completely lose their identity in the new organisation. If two limited companies amalgamate, shares in the old companies will be exchanged for shares in the new company at an agreed ratio. Businesses can expand either by natural growth or by amalgamation. For example, the English commercial banks have reached their present size partly by natural expansion—opening new branches—and partly by the amalgamation of banks. When two companies of approximately equal importance amalgamate, the new company may take a name that combines the two old names or they may select an entirely new name. If a very large company amalgamates with a small one the well-known name of the large company will probably be retained, the small company in effect being absorbed by the large. Nowadays mergers of well-known companies are more usually effected through the formation of a holding company so that the old names with the goodwill they bear, can be retained. There are two main motives for the amalgamation of firms: (i) to secure economies associated with large-scale production, or (ii) to obtain a larger share of the total market for a commodity. *See* Combine; Holding Company.

A.M.B.I.M. Designatory initials of an Associate Member of the British Institute of Management (*q.v.*).

A.M.C. Abbreviation of Agricultural Mortgage Corporation (*q.v.*).

American Account. After the withdrawal of convertibility of sterling in 1947, convertibility was restored in stages. At one period there were three groups of countries, sterling being freely convertible within each group, with only limited convertibility between the groups. One group comprised the Sterling Area, the second group being the area of the Transferable Account, and the third being the area of the American Account. The members of the American Account were the United States, Canada, and some countries in Central America. *See also* Sterling Area; Transferable Account.

American Airline. A U.S. domestic airline, it ranks third in the world for the number of passenger-miles it operates.

American Bankers' Association. Founded in 1875, it is the American counterpart of the Institute of Bankers in Great Britain, though inclined to be more active in directly providing courses in banking subjects for employees in banking throughout the United States. In addition it is responsible for running a Graduate School of Banking at the university at New Brunswick, New Jersey.

American Express Co. An American travel agency which also runs a bank and credit card business. *See* Credit Card. *See also* Amex Bank.

American Federation of Labor (A.F.L.). This federation of American trade unions, comprising mainly those whose members were skilled workers, was established in 1881. It was not until 1935 that the large industrial unions of the United States formed a rival federation known as the Congress of Industrial Organisations (C.I.O.). For many years the two federations were bitterly antagonistic to one another, but in 1955 they amalgamated together. The combined federation comprises over one hundred national unions, over five hundred local unions and a number of independent individual members, and represents a total of over 14 million trade unionists. Neither of the federations has ever been as powerful as the various unions affiliated to it. The individual unions retain complete independence of action over their own affairs. It is useful at times, however, as with the Trades Union Congress in Great Britain, to have a single body representing labour. Since 1955 the organisation has been known as the American Federation of Labor and Congress of Industrial Organisations (A.F.L.–C.I.O.).

American Loan. *See* Washington Loan Agreement (1945).

American Plan. Sometimes known as the White Plan after the U.S. Secretary to the Treasury, this international currency scheme was put forward by the U.S. Treasury immediately before the Bretton Woods Conference of 1944. Like the Keynes Plan it aimed at increasing world trade through stable exchange rates and freely convertible currencies. Both Plans favoured the establishment of an international institution such as the International Monetary Fund. *See* Bretton Woods Agreement; Keynes Plan.

American System. A system of taxation in which a tariff is the main source of revenue, so called because after securing independence the Government of the United States found it difficult to impose direct taxes or excise duties on account of the resentment aroused by British attempts to tax the American colonists.

Amex Bank Ltd. A subsidiary of American Express (*q.v.*). In 1975 it acquired Rothschilds International Bank Ltd.

A.M.I.Ex. Designatory initials of an Associate Member of the Institute of Export (*q.v.*).

A.M.Inst.T. Designatory initials of an Associate Member of the Institute of Transport (*q.v.*).

Amortisation. The provision for the gradual extinction of a debt by means of a sinking fund. A portion of the debt may be repaid at intervals along with the interest. Until recent times this method was adopted for the gradual reduction of the British National Debt. In the case of a wasting asset, such as a mine, a portion of income may be set aside each year to provide a fund to cover the capital which will eventually have been used up. This practice also is known as amortisation.

'Amounts Differ.' A term used of a cheque, payment of which has been refused because the amounts in words and figures do not agree.

Amro. Abbreviation of Amsterdam–Rotterdam Bank (*q.v.*).

Amsterdam. The financial centre of the Netherlands.

Amsterdam–Rotterdam Bank. Founded in 1871, it is the largest commercial bank in the Netherlands, undertaking slightly over 10% of the total banking business of that country. It has an interest in the Banque Européenne de Crédit à Moyen Terme (*q.v*).

Amtrak. The semi-public Railroad Corporation created in 1971 to operate railway services in the United States, it reduced inter-city passenger services from 300 to 184.

Andes Agreement (1957). The agreement by which the British-owned railways of Argentina were sold to that country.

Angel. A former English gold coin, first issued in 1465 and worth £0·33 at that time. Gradually its value rose, so that in 1661 it was worth £0·58. During the period of circulation of the angel there were also issued angelets (half-angels), and in 1544 and from 1560 to 1661 quarter angels.

Angelet. A former English coin, a half angel, and originally worth £0·16. *See* Angel.

Anna. A former Indian or Pakistani coin equal in value to one-sixteenth of a rupee.

Annates. A feudal tax. *See* First Fruits.

Annual Abstract of Statistics. A publication of the Central Statistical Office which gives statistics compiled by the Central Statistical Office on matters of economic importance, such as population, the distribution of labour among different occupations, foreign trade, prices, banking, and finance, etc.

Annual Return. A limited company must by law draw up each year a summary of its capital and shares, together with an up-to-date list of directors and members, with their names, addresses, occupations, and the number of shares held, the names of those who have ceased to be members since the previous Return, a statement showing the indebtedness of the company and a copy of its last balance sheet. This information has to be supplied to the Registrar of Companies.

Annuity. A sum of money received annually, in one or more instalments, for a period of time. In the case of a *life* annuity payment continues until the death of the person to whom it has been awarded. Such annuities can be purchased from insurance companies and, until 1962, from the Government. For over 150 years the British Government had sold life annuities to private individuals, but the demand for them had declined, mainly owing to better terms being obtainable from insurance companies. Annuities *certain* continue for an agreed period of time, when they are said to be *terminable*, or they may even be *perpetual*. Some insurance companies issue terminable annuities that continue to be paid to the annuitant's dependents until the end of an agreed period if he dies within that period. The National Debt Commissioners hold a large sum in terminable annuities, the money having been received by them for investment from the savings banks. Government debt to the Bank of England (*see* Bank Return) is in the form of perpetual annuities. An *immediate* annuity is one that commences immediately after it has been purchased, whereas a *deferred* annuity starts at an agreed future date. The cost of an annuity depends in the first place on the rate of interest prevailing at the time of the purchase. In the case of a life annuity the purchase price also depends on the age and sex of the annuitant, the price being higher for women than for men for annuities of equal amount. Some assurance companies now issue annuities linked to unit trusts as a safeguard against the falling value of money.

Antedate. To date a document earlier than the actual date on which it was drawn up.

Anticipated Prices. Since prices over a period of time tend to fluctuate, this influences consumers' demand. If it is thought that prices are likely to rise this tends to increase demand, but if prices are expected to fall consumers may postpone some of their purchases, so that a decrease in demand occurs. Expected changes in taxes such as purchase tax or value added tax will have the same effect. When planning his output an entrepreneur has to take account of what he expects the market price of the commodity to be at the time it will begin to flow on to the market.

Anticipation. In a free economy much of production takes place in anticipation of demand, the fact that conditions of demand may change in the interval giving rise to uncertainty (*q.v.*).

Anti-Corn Law League. A movement started in Manchester in 1838, its leading supporters being John Bright and Richard Cobden, to work for the repeal of the Corn Laws, which had been imposed to protect British farmers against foreign competition, but which made bread dear to the poor. The movement was strongly supported by northern manufacturers who thought that if bread were cheaper demands for higher wages would be checked. Lower costs to manufacturers, it was argued, would result in an expansion of British exports of manufactured goods. The Corn Laws were repealed in 1846, after which the League was disbanded. This was the first great step taken by Great Britain towards free trade.

Anti-Trust Laws. A series of Acts passed by the Federal Government of the United States to check and control the formation of trusts (*q.v.*). The first was the Sherman Anti-Trust Act of 1890. Under this Act two trusts—the Standard Oil Company and the Tobacco Trust—were dissolved. Both, however, were reconstituted shortly afterwards in such a way as to keep within the law. In 1914 the Clayton Act was passed to check the development of monopolies by prohibiting the amalgamation of firms producing a large proportion of the total output of a commodity. Though not very successful in achieving their objects these acts indicate the concern of the American Government to check the growth of monopolies.

A.O.B. Abbreviation of 'Any Other Business', as an item on the agenda of a meeting.

Application for a Quotation. See Quotation.

Applied Economics. The branch of economics devoted to a study of practical problems with the help of the principles and tools of analysis provided by Pure Economics. See Economics.

Appraiser. A professional valuer of property. He must be licensed unless already licensed as an auctioneer or estate agent.

Appreciation. An increase in the value of something: (i) of stocks and shares when their prices rise on the stock exchange; (ii) of a currency when its value increases in terms of other currencies; (iii) of stocks held by manufacturers and merchants in a period of rising prices. When exchange rates are free to fluctuate an appreciation of a country's currency occurs if the value of its exports increases relatively to the value of its imports. As a result its exports become dearer to other countries and its imports become cheaper, and in consequence the volume of its exports tends to fall and the volume of its imports to increase. In this way equilibrium is restored to its balance of payments.

Apprenticeship. The system whereby a young person wishing to learn a trade is employed under the supervision of a skilled worker for an agreed number of years. It had its origin in the Middle Ages when the beginner in a trade had to serve for a period under a master who was a member of the appropriate gild. Before becoming a journeyman and a member of the gild the apprentice had to satisfy the gild of his skill by producing an example of his work, known as his 'masterpiece'. For a long time the period of apprenticeship was seven years. At one time apprentices were unpaid during the period of their apprenticeship and in some cases a premium had to be paid. Trade unions of skilled workers (craft unions) have often insisted on unnecessarily long periods of apprenticeship in order to make it more difficult to enter an occupation.

Appropriation Account. After the net profit of a business has been calculated an Appropriation Account is drawn up to show how this profit is to be apportioned between dividend, reserve, pension fund, etc.

Appropriation Act. An Act passed by Parliament giving authority for payments to be made from the Consolidated Fund for the purposes for which it has been voted.

Appropriation-in-aid. Each Government department has to prepare Estimates for the next financial year for presentation to Parliament in February of each year. Any department which earns revenue from sales of goods or services to the public shows this as an Appropriation-in-aid, which is deducted from its estimated gross expenditure to show net expenditure, that is, the actual amount required of the Exchequer.

Approved Societies. A term first used in the National Insurance Act of 1911. This Act was at first regarded with some apprehension by the friendly societies, trade unions and assurance companies until it was decided to administer the section concerned with health insurance through 'approved societies'. In the end all types of friendly society came to be approved for this purpose. See Friendly Society.

Aptitude Tests. These are tests set to try to discover the potentialities of people for certain kinds of work, especially of young people entering industry and commerce from school.

A.R. 1. Abbreviation of Advice of Receipt.

2. Abbreviation of Annual Return.

3. Abbreviation of Australian Registered (with reference to shares).

Arbitrage. A form of speculation more particularly found in foreign exchange markets, where it is sometimes possible to purchase currency in one centre and immediately sell it at a profit in another. Arbitrage in foreign currencies is possible only because of the ease and speed of telegraphic transfers between commercial centres throughout the world.

Thus an operator in London might buy French francs in Amsterdam and sell them a few minutes later in New York. The effect of arbitrage is to iron out differences in the rates of exchange of currencies in different centres, thereby creating a single world market in foreign exchange.

Arbitration. In disputes, as, for example, between employers and trade unions, where agreement cannot be reached and a deadlock has occurred, it may be decided to submit the matter to arbitration. In such cases an arbitrator will then be appointed, subject to the approval of both parties to the dispute, the person chosen generally being a judge or a leading barrister who has no direct interest in the matter. Each side appoints a representative to state its case in as favourable a light as possible. After hearing both sides the arbitrator sums up the evidence as in a court of law and after due consideration gives his decision. Unless both parties to the dispute agree in advance to accept the verdict of the arbitrator, whether favourable to them or otherwise, arbitration is pointless. During wartime, when loss of production as a result of strikes cannot be tolerated, arbitration in industrial disputes is often made obligatory. A weakness of arbitration where wage claims are in dispute is that, since arbitrators are generally inclined to compromise, granting the employees less than they are asking for but more than the employers have been prepared to offer, the trade unions put in claims for much greater increases than they know they have any hope of receiving so that as a result of the compromise they may obtain the amount they really want. In Great Britain arbitration in industrial disputes was first placed on a legal footing by the Conciliation Act of 1896. This Act was supplemented by the Industrial Courts Act of 1919. *See* A.C.A.S.; Industrial Courts.

Arbitration, Rules of. The procedure which a Court of Arbitration must follow is defined in the Acts of 1889–1934, the aim being to devise a procedure somewhat similar to that of a court of justice, with counsel representing each side in the dispute. In support of this aim it is usual to appoint as Arbitrator a person highly qualified in law.

Arc Elasticity. The average degree of elasticity between two points on either a demand curve or a supply curve.

ARCRU. A unit of account based on twelve Arab currencies, agreed June 1974.

Arithmetic Mean. The ordinary average, calculated by dividing the total of the items concerned by the number of such items. *See also* Geometric Mean; Mode.

Arithmetic Progression. A series of numbers, the difference between each being equal, as, for example, the series 5, 7, 9, 11, 13, 15, . . . Malthus used it in contrast to Geometric Progression to indicate the slower expansion of food production as compared with the increase in population. *See* Geometric Progression; Malthusian Theory of Population.

A.R.S.A. Designatory initials of an Associate of the Royal Society of Arts.

Articled Clerk. A condition of entry to some professions as, for example, those of chartered accountant and solicitor, is a period of service as articled clerk to a practising member of the profession. During the period of his 'articles' the clerk may receive only a nominal salary or none at all. Somtimes a premium has to be paid before articles are entered into. In some cases the period of service as an articled clerk may be reduced for people who have attended a university and taken a degree.

Articles of Association. The procedure for the establishment of a new limited company laid down in the Companies Acts includes among other things the drawing up of a Memorandum of Association (*q.v.*) and Articles of Association. The purpose of the Articles of Association is to prescribe a set of rules to govern the internal working of the company. They cover such things as the issue and transfer of the company's shares, the procedure to be followed in calling general meetings, shareholders' voting rights, and many other matters. Articles of Association require to be registered with the Registrar of Companies. Unless this is done the Registrar will assume that the company has adopted the articles set out in Table A of the Companies Act (1948).

Articles of Partnership. A written agreement setting out the terms of partnership (*q.v.*). *See also* Deed of Partnership.

Artisans and Labourers Act (1868). This Act enabled local authorities to condemn property not regarded as fit for human habitation and, if it could not be repaired, to demolish it—the first attempt at slum clearance.

Artisans' Dwellings Act (1875). An Act passed giving powers to local authorities to deal with slums.

As. A Roman copper coin, it remained the unit of account even when silver coins were struck.

'A' Shares. *See* Non-voting Shares.

Asian Development Bank. Established in 1966 on the recommendation of the United Nations Economic Commission for Asia and the Far East. A total of 32 countries participated in its formation including a number of countries outside the region such as the U.S.A., Great Britain, and Switzerland. The main purpose of the bank is to provide financial aid to the developing countries of Asia.

A.S.L.E.F. Abbreviation of Associated Society of Locomotive Engineers and Firemen.

Assaying. Determining the proportion of precious metal in an alloy. In the Middle Ages this was the duty of the goldsmiths' gilds. There are now four assay offices in Great Britain at London, Birmingham, Sheffield and Edinburgh. Each office is under the control of a local board of guardians, not all of whom nowadays are goldsmiths or silversmiths. Each office has its own hall-mark. Formerly there were assay offices at Chester, Exeter, Glasgow, Newcastle upon Tyne, Norwich and York.

Assembly Line. A system of production where the article under construction is passed through the workshop by a conveyor belt along a line of workers, each of whom performs a single operation to it when it reaches him, a technique highly developed in the motor-car industry. It enables division of labour by process to be carried to the greatest possible extent.

Assented. A term used in connection with stocks and bonds, dealt in on the stock exchange, the holder of which has agreed voluntarily to some change in the terms or conditions of issue. The term is more particularly used of stocks which have been issued by foreign governments which for some reason—the effects of war or revolution or simply bad faith—find it impossible to meet their obligations as defined in the terms of the original issue. In such cases when a holder is confronted by a choice of receiving less than the amount to which he feels himself entitled or of receiving nothing at all he will generally 'assent' to the new terms offered.

Assessed Taxes. A term used of taxes imposed in the eighteenth century on carriages, racehorses, men-servants, windows, etc., these taxes being assessed by Surveyors of Taxes.

Assessment. 1. A statement showing a person's liability for tax and how it has been calculated.

2. For the purpose of local rates property is assessed at what is called its rateable value. *See* Rates.

Assessor. In insurance the assessor estimates the extent of the loss suffered by the insured person when a claim against the insurer has been made.

Asset. When the balance sheet of a business is drawn up everything which it owns at the time that has a money value is listed as an asset. Its fixed assets will include such tangible things as factory buildings, machinery, etc., and intangible items like goodwill. Current assets will include stock, bills receivable, and cash.

Assets of a Bank. The most important assets of a commercial or joint-stock bank in order of declining liquidity are: (i) coin, notes, and balances at the Bank of England; (ii) money at call and short notice; (iii) bills discounted; (iv) Special Deposits (if any) at the Bank of England; (v) investments; (vi) advances to customers. All these items are of economic importance. In addition there are the bank's premises. Items (i) to (iii) are known as the more liquid assets, and items (v) and (vi) as the less liquid assets. *See* Liquidity Rules, Bank.

Assignat. A bond issued during the French Revolution representing confiscated land, formerly the property of the clergy, the king or emigré nobles, and assigned to the holders of the bonds. There was a gross overissue of the bonds, which were used to supplement coins, and a steep rise in prices occurred, the value of the bonds eventually declining almost to nothing. In 1796 they were exchanged at a rate of 300 francs in assignats for one franc in gold.

Assignment. The making over of property such as an insurance policy, copyright, patent rights, trade marks, by one person to another.

Assistance Board. *See* Unemployment Assistance Board.

Associated Companies. Two or more companies with interlocking directorates, that is with some directors who are members of two or more boards to enable the companies to pursue a common policy. It is thus an alternative to a complete amalgamation or the setting up of a holding company.

'Association Clause.' The clause in the Memorandum of Association of a limited company which states that the subscribers wish to form a company and are prepared to take up the number of shares stated written opposite their names.

Association for Consumer Research. An organisation established to protect the interests of consumers. *See* Consumers' Associations; Consumer Protection; Research Institute for Consumers' Affairs.

Association of British Chambers of Commerce. An organisation to which over a hundred Chambers of Commerce in Great Britain, together with a few British Chambers of Commerce in foreign countries, are affiliated. *See* Chamber of Commerce.

Association of Stock and Share Dealers. Licensed dealers in stocks and shares who are not members of a stock exchange, they are better known as 'Outside Brokers' (*q.v.*).

Assumptions. In every science theory is built up from certain assumptions by logical reasoning. In the case of a social science like economics these assumptions refer to the behaviour of individuals. For example, it is assumed that in his economic activity everyone behaves in a perfectly rational manner, whereas in actual life this is not always so, but without this assumption it would be impossible to build up any theory of economics at all. Another assumption is that entrepreneurs always seek to maximise their profit, whereas at times some entrepreneurs are influenced by other considerations. Again, in order to isolate the economic aspect of a problem it may be necessary to assume that 'all other things remain equal', whereas in actual life this is never so.

Assurance. At one time this term was restricted to the provision of cover against some eventuality which must occur at some time in the future such as, for example, the death of a person, the only uncertainty in this case being the date of the occurrence of the event. Insurance on the other hand provides cover against eventualities such as fire, burglary, etc., which may never occur. Consequently, it is usual to speak of life assurance but of fire insurance. It is increasingly common, however, to

find the term 'insurance' being used as a general term to include all kinds of both assurance and insurance. See Insurance.

A.T.I.I. Designatory initials of an Associate of the Institute of Taxation.

Atkin Committee on Women in Industry. Appointed in September 1918, this Committee published its report in the following April. It was mainly concerned with reviewing the rates of pay of men and women in different occupations. Although in May 1920 the House of Commons accepted a resolution in favour of equal pay in the Civil Service, this was not implemented for nearly 40 years. See Equal Pay.

Atlantic Charter. An agreement between President Roosevelt of the United States and Winston Churchill, the British Prime Minister, signed on a warship in the Atlantic in August 1941 during the Second World War. Only one of the eight clauses—the fifth—concerned economic matters. It stated that it was their desire to bring about the fullest collaboration between all nations with the object of securing for all improved labour standards, economic advancement, and social security.

Atlantic International Bank. A bank consortium formed in 1969 in London, it comprises four U.S. banks and four European banks.

Atomic Energy Authority (A.E.A.). A public corporation set up in 1954 to take charge of the entire production of nuclear power for industrial and commercial purposes in the United Kingdom. A number of nuclear stations for the production of electricity have been built and a number of others have been planned.

'At Sight.' A term used on a bill of exchange to indicate that it is payable on its being presented. In contrast to other bills of exchange it does not require to be accepted. Such a bill is known as a 'Sight' bill. Legally a cheque is a bill of exchange of this kind.

Attendance Money. Also known as 'Fall-back' Pay, it is a payment made to workers such as dockers, who, after the decasualisation of dock work, became entitled to such payment for turning up at the docks when no work was required of them.

Attestation. Before a will is valid there must be a formal witnessing of the signature of the testator by two persons who have no interest in the will. This is known as attestation.

Attorney, Power of. See Power of Attorney.

Auction. When a commodity is sold by auction bids are made by prospective buyers, the commodity being sold to the person making the highest bid. This is the usual method of sale on organised commodity markets or produce exchanges, such as those for wool, tea, fish, etc., where the commodity cannot easily be graded. Prior to the sale the seller, usually a broker acting on behalf of an import merchant, arranges for the commodity to be made available for inspection and sampling by prospective buyers who, because of the high degree of skill required, generally employ their own specialist buyers, brokers, or agents. The bids of the buyers are thus influenced by their own personal estimate of the quality of the commodity offered for sale. Commodities that can be fairly accurately graded, such as wheat and cotton, are more usually sold by private treaty ($q.v.$). Auctions are not so common at the retail stage, though rare consumers' goods, such as works of art and antiques, are frequently sold by auction. Valuable paintings, jewellery, and antiques are sold at the well-known London auctions of firms like Sotheby's. Houses are sold either by auction or by private treaty. In a Dutch auction ($q.v.$) the reverse procedure is adopted, the commodity being offered for sale at successively lower prices.

Audit. The examination of a firm's books of accounts by a person qualified to do so to check whether they have been properly kept. Under the Companies Acts this is compulsory for public companies.

Ausgleich. The name given to the treaty of 1867 which set out the economic relations between Austria and Hungary—at that time associated together in the dual monarchy.

Austrian School. The concept of marginal utility had its origin in Austria, and writers on economics who helped to develop this concept are regarded as belonging to the Austrian school of thought. The leaders of this school were Karl Menger, Stanley Jevons of Manchester University, and Leon Walras in France, all of whom were writing during the later years of the nineteenth century. *See* Marginal Utility.

Autarchy (or Autarky). Economic self-sufficiency. The term acquired prominence after the First World War when many of the new countries of Central Europe attempted as far as possible to make themselves economically independent of their neighbours.

Authorised Banks. Those banks listed by the Exchange Control Act (1947) as empowered to deal in foreign exchange.

Authorised Capital. When a new company is formed its application for registration is accompanied by a statement indicating the amount of capital with which it proposes to be registered. This is known as its nominal, registered, or authorised capital. The actual amount issued may be less than this, and so the company will be able to increase its capital at a later date up to the full amount authorised without further application to the Registrar of Companies.

Authorised Clerk. An employee of a stockbroker who is entitled to enter a stock exchange and act on behalf of his employer.

Automatic Saving. When a person's income after payment of tax is so large that he can reasonably spend only part of it, the unspent portion is regarded as being 'automatically' saved since it has involved no sacrifice on the part of the saver. Much of the saving of the well-to-do in England before 1914, when direct taxation of high incomes was very low, was of this kind. Since then income tax, together with surtax, has become increasingly progressive, the rate of tax on the highest incomes reaching no less than 19s. 6d. (£0·975) in the £ during 1939–45, and though since then the rate of tax has been slightly reduced. This, together with steeply progressive capital transfer tax, has resulted in there being now very little, if any, automatic saving today.

Automatic Selling. The sale of goods by means of coin-operated vending machines. Such automatic machines have been in use for a long time for the sale of sweets and cigarettes, but in recent years their use has been extended to a much wider range of products, especially food and drink.

Automatic Termination of Cover. A new principle adopted by Lloyd's underwriters in 1959 to terminate a policy of marine insurance immediately on the outbreak of war, whether declared or not. Previously marine insurance policies could be cancelled only after 48 hours' notice.

Automation. The early years of the Industrial Revolution were characterised by outstanding technical progress. Periodically since then there have been periods of rapid technical progress. The present day is such a period. To recent technical developments the term 'automation' has been applied. Automation implies more than the invention of new machines. New features associated with automation are machines with automatic control over their performance, machines linked together in such a way that one process automatically follows another, and the use of electronic computers which enable masses of calculations to be carried out in a very short time. The effect of automation is ultimately likely to be an expansion of production greater than anything that has as yet been known. It also increases the demand for skilled workers and reduces the demand for the unskilled and semi-skilled. In time it may reduce the total volume of labour employed in industry, thereby releasing labour for the expanding service occupations.

Auto-Teller. An improved form of cash dispenser (*q.v.*) introduced in 1975 by Barclays Bank Ltd. Not only does it dispense Bank of England notes but it also accepts customers' deposits. *See also* Cashpoint.

Auxiliary Capital (or **Instrumental Capital**). Terms used by Alfred Marshall for all goods that aid labour in production—tools, machines, raw materials, means of transport, *i.e.* all things which nowadays would be called capital goods, or simply capital.

Average. 1. There are four types of average for statistical purposes—arithmetic mean, geometric mean, median, and mode (*qq.v.*).

2. A stock exchange term. If, after an investor has bought (say) one hundred shares in a company at £1·20 per share, the price of the shares on the market falls to £1·00 he may decide to purchase a further hundred shares at this lower price. If he does so, he is said to be averaging, since the average price at which he has bought his two hundred shares will now be £1·10. Thus a 'bull', who eventually expects the price to rise, will buy more after a fall in price in order to reduce the average price he has paid. On the other hand a 'bear' who eventually expects the price to fall will sell more, if he can, in order to increase the average price of his sale.

3. A term used in marine insurance. *See* General Average; Particular Average.

Average cost. The total cost of production of a commodity incurred by a firm during a period divided by the number of its units of output. When calculating total cost in conditions of either perfect competition or monopoly it is usual to include normal profit (*q.v.*). *See* Cost.

Average Cost/Marginal Cost Relationship. When average cost is falling marginal cost, although rising, is always less than average cost. When, however, average cost is rising marginal cost is greater than average cost. Average cost and marginal cost are equal when average cost is at a minimum. Consider the following cost schedule of a firm:

Output units	Total cost (£)	Average cost (£)	Marginal (cost £)
20	250	12·5	—
30	320	10·7	7
40	400	10·0	8
50	500	10·0	10
60	630	10·5	13
70	790	11·3	16

This can be shown diagrammatically:

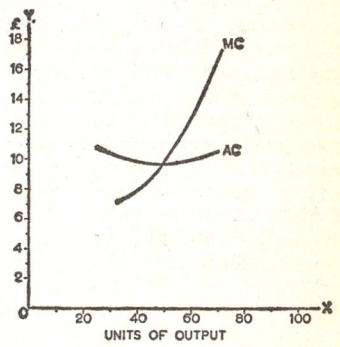

MC = MARGINAL COST   AC = AVERAGE COST

Average Revenue. The total receipts accruing to a firm during a period divided by the number of units of output. If the entire output has been sold at the same price, then clearly average revenue is equal to the price.

B

B.A. Abbreviation for Bachelor of Arts. At a number of English universities the B.A. degree can be taken with Honours in Economics.

B.A.C.I.E. Abbreviation of British Association for Commercial and Industrial Education.

Backing a Bill. A term used in connection with bills of exchange. When a person backs a bill by endorsing it he is guaranteeing that it will be met.

'Back Door.' A term used of Bank of England transactions involving the purchase of Treasury bills by the bank from the discount market. Such operations take place through the bank's own broker in the market at the prevailing market rate of discount as a means of assisting discount houses in temporary difficulties when bank rate is very high and 'front door' transactions in consequence very expensive.

Backing. Support for a country's note issue. It may consist of gold or securities. That part of a note issue which is not backed by gold is known as the fiduciary issue (*q.v.*).

Back-to-back Credit. An alternative name for Countervailing Credit (*q.v.*).

Backwardation. A payment made by a speculator on the stock exchange who is unable to deliver stock to the buyer on the required date.

Backward Integration. The expansion of a business which takes the form of acquiring control over firms supplying it with its raw materials.

Bad Debt. A debt that it is difficult or impossible to collect. *See* Factoring Company.

Bad Money. 1. A debased coinage; 2. An alternative term for Hot Money (*q.v.*).

'Bad Money Drives Out Good.' A tendency often designated as Gresham's Law (*q.v.*).

Baht. The standard unit of the currency of Thailand, it is subdivided into 100 satang.

Bailment. A legal term referring to the temporary transfer of property, including cash, from the owner (or bailor) to some other person, often an employee (the bailee), to be employed for a specific purpose.

Balanced Bond. An alternative term for a Managed Bond (*q.v.*).

Balance of Payments. International trade and other financial dealings between countries make it necessary for them to make payments to one another. The balance of payments shows the relationship between one country's total payments to all other countries and its total receipts from them. It is thus a sort of statement of income and expenditure on international account. Payments and receipts on international account are of three kinds: (i) the visible balance of trade; (ii) invisible items; and (iii) capital transfers. The chief payments and receipts arise from trade in goods, payment having to be made for imports and being received from the sale of exports. Together these items account for more than 60% of all Great Britain's payments and receipts. This is the balance of trade, now also known as the visible balance. Services provided by one country for another also give rise to payments and receipts, and the relation between these provides the invisible balance. For a long time Great Britain has relied on a credit invisible balance to offset a debit trade balance. Invisible items in the balance of payments include receipts and payments for shipping, financial services, and income from investment abroad. Shipping was formerly a much more important invisible item for Great Britain than it is today. At one time Great Britain had almost a monopoly of the carrying trade of the world, but in 1960 Britain actually paid out more than it received for shipping services. Banking and insurance, however, are still important credit items. Though investments abroad were greatly reduced as a result of two World Wars these are still an important source of income to Great Britain, although offset to an increasing extent by payments abroad of dividends derived from foreign investments in this country. Foreign travel, whether for business or pleasure, is another invisible item, and this has been very nearly self-balancing in recent years, although British travellers continue to spend a little more abroad than foreign visitors spend in Great Britain. When both visible and invisible items are taken together we have the Balance of Payments on Current Account. The balance of payments is also affected by capital movements. Income from foreign investments, as we have just seen, is a receipt, but when the investment was originally made it would be a payment. Capital transfers take place for purposes of investment or when one country makes a loan to another or capital may be transferred from one centre to another for greater safety, such capital being known as 'hot money' (*q.v.*) or refugee capital. Hot money can have a disturbing effect on a country's balance of payments. During the severe inflation of 1973–6 huge debits occurred in the British balance of payments, covered mainly by borrowing from abroad.

Information on the balance of trade is published monthly. Twice each year White Papers are published, and annually a *Pink Book*, showing the current British balance of payments. The following table shows how the debit in the balance of trade is generally offset on current account by a credit in the invisible balance. A debit balance of payments is often described as being unfavourable or adverse or passive, a credit balance being considered as favourable or active. Since, however, every payment to one country is a receipt to another all countries clearly cannot achieve favourable balances every year. In one sense

Date	Balance of trade (visible items) (£ million)	Invisible items (£ million)	Balance of payments (£ million)
1950	−133	+433	+300
1952	−120	+258	+138
1954	−186	+364	+178
1956	− 55	+292	+237
1958	+120	+335	+455
1960	−406	+141	−265
1962	−102	+214	+112
1964	−519	+124	−395
1966	− 73	+116	+ 43
1968	−634	+324	−319
1970	+ 3	+576	+579
1972	+114	+677	+791
1973	−2,375	+1,210	−1,165
1974	−5,234	+1,566	−3,668

each country's balance of payments must balance each year, for a debit or credit balance must be covered in some way. In the case of a debit balance the deficit may be covered in any one of the following ways: (i) by borrowing; (ii) by assistance from the International Monetary Fund; (iii) by selling investments abroad; (iv) by importing on credit; (v) by gifts from abroad; (vi) by exporting gold. A credit balance can be used to increase investment abroad or to add to a country's gold reserve.

Balance of Trade. Known also as the visible balance, this is the relationship between a country's payments for imports of goods and its receipts from the export of goods. Because of its generally favourable invisible balance, Great Britain has for a long time had a deficit in its trade balance, except for the years 1956, 1958 and 1971. This debit balance is known as the Trade Gap. *See* Balance of Payments.

Balance Sheet. A statement showing the assets and liabilities of a business at a certain date.

Balance Sheet of a Bank. The chief items in the balance sheet of a bank are:
Liabilities:
  Deposits: (*a*) on current account;
  (*b*) on deposit account.
Assets:
  Coin, notes, and balance with the Bank of England;
  Money at call and short notice;
  Bills discounted:
    (*a*) Treasury bills;
    (*b*) other bills;
  Special deposits;
  Investments;
  Advances to customers.

The structure of a bank's balance sheet is of considerable importance. The most profitable activity of a commercial bank is lending to customers, but every time a bank increases its lending it increases the possibility of withdrawals in cash. British banks, therefore, maintained two liquidity rules: (i) a ratio of 8% between the cash they hold (coin, notes, and balance with the Bank of England) and their total deposits—the cash ratio; and (ii) a ratio of 28% between their more liquid and their total assets, their less liquid assets being cash, call money, and bills discounted. In 1971 the Bank of England recommended that $12\frac{1}{2}\%$ of a commercial bank's assets should be comprised by its three more liquid assets together with its holding of Government stocks within one year of maturity and a proportion of eligible commercial bills. *See* Bank Advances; Money at Call; Special Deposits.

Balboa. The standard unit of the currency of the Republic of Panama, it is divided into 100 centesimos.

Balfour Committee on Industry and Trade (1927). A report of this Committee favoured the consolidation of industry as a more 'rational' means of reducing excess capacity than free competition. *See* Rationalisation.

Baltic Exchange. Abbreviated name of the Baltic, Mercantile and Shipping Exchange. Situated in the City of London, it was formerly a produce exchange concerned with products from the Baltic countries. Although it still deals in imported cereals, its main business now is with the chartering of ships, its members being merchants, brokers, shipowners, and shipbrokers. Most shipbroking business, however, is now done by telephone and not on the floor of the exchange.

Banca di Napoli. A commercial bank with branches throughout Italy and also in New York and Buenos Aires. Founded in 1539, it is one of the oldest banks in Europe.

Banca d'Italia. The central bank of Italy, it was founded in 1893. Since 1926 it has been the only bank in the country with the right to issue bank-notes. Since 1959 its shares have all been held by other Italian banks and insurance companies, most of these being State-owned. Its head office is in Rome. It has a small number of branches.

Banca Nazionale Del Lavore. The largest Italian commercial bank, with its head office in Rome. It has an interest in the Banque Européenne de Crédit à Moyen Terme (*q.v.*)

Banco do Brazil. The principal bank of Brazil, it was in 1977 the eighth largest in the world.

Bancogiro. The transfer of a credit from the account of one customer to that of another of the same bank. *Cf.* the Postal Giro.

Bancor. For the international monetary conference at Bretton Woods (1944) the British delegation under Lord Keynes worked out a plan for international monetary co-operation which proposed an international currency with the bancor as unit. *See* Bretton Woods Agreement; International Monetary Fund.

Bandesco. A Spanish development bank formed by Barclays and six other European and American banks.

Bani. A sub-unit of the currency of Romania, 100 bani being equal to one leu.

Bank. A comprehensive term for a number of institutions carrying on certain kinds of financial business. Several types of bank are to be found in England: (i) savings banks, which accept deposits; (ii) commercial (or joint-stock) banks which do most kinds of banking business—accepting deposits, allowing customers the use of cheques, granting credit by loan or overdraft, discounting bills of exchange, foreign exchange transactions, acting as agents for customers in the sale or purchase of stock exchange securities, acting as executors or trustees, and providing safe custody for valuables; (iii) merchant banks which still to a considerable extent specialise in business connected with bills of exchange, especially the acceptance of foreign bills; (iv) central banks, the main business of which is to carry out a country's monetary policy. There are also (v) investment banks, but these have never been popular in Great Britain. They acquire shares in limited companies on their own account and not merely as agents for their customers. Sometimes banks are established to undertake specialised banking functions for particular industries, as in France, where there are Agricultural Banks, a Bank for Building and Public Works, a Cotton Bank, and several others. There are also a number of firms which describe themselves as Industrial Bankers and although most of them undertake some ordinary banking business, they are primarily finance houses whose main concern is with the financing of hire purchase. In some countries, as for example the United States, the finance of house purchase by mortgage is undertaken by banks, but in Great Britain such business is mainly in the hands of specialist building societies. *See also* Banking; Bank of England; 'Big Four'; Central Bank; Commercial Bank; Investment Bank; Merchant Banks; Trustee Savings Banks.

Bank Acceptance. A bill of exchange that has been accepted by a bank, then known as a bank bill. *See* Bill of Exchange.

Bank Account. There are several types of bank account—Deposit Accounts, Current Accounts, Loan Accounts (*qq.v.*).

Bank Advances. An item in the balance sheet of a commercial bank showing the extent of its lending to customers by loan or overdraft. Businesses in all branches of industry and commerce borrow working or circulating capital from the banks, which also lend to professional men and private borrowers. Bank Advances form one of the less liquid assets of a bank and, together with Investments, comprise about 72% of the total assets of a bank. When desirable borrowers are to be found Advances tend to increase at the expense of Investments, but when industry is depressed Investments increase at the expense of Advances. Since increases in these two assets also increase bank deposits (*see* Credit) a restrictive monetary policy aims at checking bank lending. Apart, however, from temporary checks of this kind Bank Advances have increased steadily in recent times.

BankAmericard. The credit card (*q.v.*) issued by the Bank of America, it was the first bank credit card to come into use. By 1968 over 8 million had been issued in California. In addition, through the Bank of America Service Corporation, banks in other states of the U.S.A. can be licensed to issue these cards, licences having been given to banks in 38 states by 1969. There are reciprocal facilities for holders of the Barclaycard (*q.v.*).

Bank Bill. A bill of exchange which has been accepted by an accepting house or merchant bank or by a commercial bank.

Bank Chain. Branch banking in the United States is limited to only a few states. Two ways have been found for circumventing state legal restrictions on bank expansion: (i) by means of interlocking directorates, and (ii) by the formation of holding companies. The former has led to the development of bank chains, and the latter to the growth of bank groups. In general the bank chains are smaller than the bank groups.

Bank Charges. Commission charged by a bank to a customer for the management of his account. Usually no charge is made if a satisfactory credit balance is maintained.

Bank Charter Act (1826). The three main provisions of this Act were: (i) The establishment of joint-stock banks in England was permitted provided that they were situated outside a radius of 65 miles from London; (ii) The Bank of England was to be allowed to open branches outside London; (iii) The issue of banknotes for denominations under £5 was prohibited in England, but the Act expressly exempted the Scottish banks, which were to be allowed to continue to issue notes.

Bank Charter Act (1833). The most important provision of this Act was the removal of the limitation of the rate of interest to 5% on bills of exchange for periods of up to three months, which in effect made it possible for bank rate to be raised above this rate. Bank of England notes were made legal tender in England and Wales for amounts over £5.

Bank Charter Act (1844). One of the most important Acts of Parliament affecting banking in England. It was passed by the Government of Sir Robert Peel because of a demand for Parliament to control the issue of bank-notes after a series of banking crises during 1825–37, which it was thought were due mainly to the overissue of bank-notes by many banks. Before the Act was passed there was keen controversy between two schools of thought—the Currency School, which favoured a rigid control of the note issue, and the Banking School, which considered that a flexible note issue was required for an expanding economy. The Act showed the influence of the Current School. It divided the work of the Bank of England into two parts, an Issue Department and a Banking Department. The Issue Department was to be solely concerned with the note issue. A balance sheet—the Bank Return—had to be published each week. A small fiduciary issue was permitted to the Bank of England, but apart from that all notes had to be fully backed by gold or to a limited extent by a small amount of silver. The note issues of other banks of issue were not to exceed their average circulation during the twelve weeks immediately before the passing of the Act. No new bank was permitted to issue notes at all, and a bank was to lose its right to issue notes if it opened a branch in London or amalgamated with another bank. If any bank lost its right to issue notes the Bank of England was to be allowed to increase its fiduciary issue, but only up to two-thirds of the value of the lapsed issue. The eventual result of this clause was to make the Bank of England the sole bank of issue in England, though this did not happen till 1921. The Bank Charter Act of 1844 has never been repealed but an increase in the note issue has been achieved by a huge expansion in the fiduciary issue of the Bank of England which, with the permission of the Treasury, the Act of 1928 made possible. *See* Currency and Bank Notes Act (1928).

Bank Consortium. A banking group, usually international in character, formed to make funds available for medium-term lending on the scale required to meet the needs of large, international concerns. The funds usually take the form of Eurodollars. One of the first bank consortia to be established was the Midland and International Bank (M.A.I.B.L.) (*q.v.*), dating from 1964.

Bank Credit. Banks lend by granting loans or overdrafts to customers, or lend to the Government by the purchase of Government stocks. When banks increase their lending this also increases their deposits. Unlike other lenders a bank does not require to possess what it lends. Since about 80% of the money used in Great Britain today consists of bank deposits, an increase in bank credit is an increase in purchasing power. *See* Credit.

Bank Credit Transfer. *See* Credit Transfer.

Bank Custody. *See* Safe Custody.

Bank Deposits. The amount standing to the credit of the customers of a bank. Deposits become the property of the banker but must be repaid when asked for. Deposits are not held in trust but are borrowed from customers. Accepting deposits is the oldest function of a bank, and deposits still form the principal liability of a bank. British commercial banks accept deposits from their customers either on current account or on deposit or savings account, these terms in the United States being respectively demand and time deposits.

Bank Deposits

Date	£ million
1844	50
1865	200
1894	600
1900	734
1913	962
1938	2,277
1945	4,692
1955	6,400
1960	7,236
1965	9,454
1967	10,129
1969	10,650
1971	12,055
1973	16,187
1975	22,783
1977	24,613

Bank deposits on current account are of great economic importance, since they can be transferred by cheque from one person's account to another's and so serve as a means of payment. Bank deposits are the most important type of money today. In calculating the total of this kind of money it is usual to add together the deposits on both current and deposit accounts at the commercial banks, on the ground that transfers can easily be made from deposit to current accounts, but deposits with trustee savings banks are excluded. Over the past twenty-five years bank deposits have increased enormously in all countries. The table shows the increase in the deposits of the London Clearing Banks.

Bank Disclosure. Only when required to do so by a court of law is a bank compelled to supply information regarding a customer's accounts, except that all banks are required to inform the Inland Revenue authorities of the amount of interest credited to customers' deposit or saving accounts when the amount exceeds £25.

Bank Draft. A cheque drawn on a bank. When a creditor is unwilling to accept a personal cheque in payment a bank draft can be used. Being drawn on a bank it is safer than a cheque, the debtor having paid the bank for it in advance.

Banker, The. A journal devoted to topics of interest to those employed in banking.

Banker and Customer. At law the relationship between these two parties is that of debtor and creditor, bank deposits not being held in trust for the depositor but borrowed by the banker. In the collection of a customer's cheques the relation of banker and customer is that of principal and agent.

Bankers' Bank. One of the functions of a central bank. *See* Bank of England.

Banker's Card. An alternative term for Cheque Card (*q.v.*).

Bankers' Clearing House. *See* Bankers' Provincial Clearing Houses; London Bankers' Clearing House.

'Bankers' Club.' A popular term for the meetings at Basle of the Bank for International Settlements (B.I.S.) and the Group of Ten (*qq.v.*).

'Banker's Dilemma.' The name sometimes given to the compromise that a banker has to make between his concern for the liquidity of his assets on the one hand and his desire for profit-earning assets on the other, since the more liquid an asset the less profit it earns.

Bankers' Industrial Development Company. Founded 1930, its share capital was subscribed by the Securities Management Trust, a subsidiary of the Bank of England which has a controlling interest, the commercial banks and the merchant banks. The company was established to provide assistance to industry for longer periods than was the usual banking practice at a time when even some of the older and larger firms were feeling the strain of the Great Depression.

Banker's Inquiry. *See* Banker's Reference.

Banker's Lien. A lien is the right to retain property which has been deposited by a borrower as security for a loan. Thus, a banker has a right to retain collateral deposited as security against a loan if the loan is not repaid, but a banker's lien does not cover securities left with the bank for safe custody.

Bankers' Provincial Clearing Houses. Formerly there were Clearing Houses in most large cities, but now the only Provincial Clearing House is at Liverpool.

Banker's Reference (or **Opinion**). A trader who desires credit from his supplier may be asked for references. As one of his references he can give the name of his banker. Such a reference cannot be taken up directly as inquiry must be made through the supplier's own banker. A report by a banker on a customer is given in very general terms.

Bank for International Settlements. A bank established in 1930 at Basle by representatives of the leading central banks, primarily to facilitate reparations payments under the Young Plan (*q.v.*). It came near to being liquidated on the establishment of the I.M.F. but it has shown a remarkable capacity for adapting itself to changing circumstances, and it has proved itself to be a useful international banking institution. In 1948 it became banker to the Organisation for European Economic Co-operation, in 1950 to the European Payments Union, and in 1954 to the European Coal and Steel Community. Its importance increased very considerably during 1961–68 when it became the centre for central bank co-operation and the Group of Ten (*q.v.*), so that it appears to have fully justified its continued existence. It also acted as agent to the gold pool. It assists 'swap' transactions between central banks. (*See* Swap Facilities.) Regular monthly meetings are held at its office in Basle, at which the U.S.A. also is represented.

Bank Giro Credit. A system of credit transfer, it is a useful means of making payment through a bank especially by a person who has no current account. It is somewhat similar to a Credit Transfer. It is necessary for the payer to know the name of the payee's bank, and usually his account number. *See* National Giro.

Bank Group. *See* Bank Chain.

Bank Holiday. By an Act of 1871, sponsored by Sir John Lubbock, bank holidays were established. There are now seven bank holidays in England and Wales, New Year's Day being added in 1974, six in Scotland, and seven in Northern Ireland. Bills due on these days are payable on the next working day, except in the case of Good Friday and Christmas Day, when they fall due the previous day.

Banking. In England banking had its origin with the London goldsmiths who in the seventeenth century began to accept deposits from merchants and others who, unlike the goldsmiths, had no place for the safe keeping of money and other valuables. The next stage in the development of banking came when the receipts for these deposits began to be used as a means of payment, later being superseded by the issue of bank-notes. The goldsmiths also became lenders, at first of money and later of their own bank-notes. Banking, at first merely a sideline to other business, expanded so much that it had to be hived off from the ordinary business of the goldsmith to become a separate business in its own right.

The Bank of England (*q.v.*) was founded in 1694, principally for the purpose of lending money to the Government, though it undertook some ordinary banking business also. At an early date it became the only bank in London with the right to issue bank-notes, and until 1826 it was also the only joint-stock bank in England, all the others being private banks. Outside London banking developed as a sideline to the businesses of merchants or manufacturers, but there was little expansion of banking outside London until the Industrial Revolution. In 1821 there were 62 banks in London and 781 'country' banks, all private except the Bank of England. Joint-stock banks, apart from the Bank of England, were not permitted to be established in London until 1833. During the years 1815–30 there were over 200 bank failures in England, but very few in Scotland, where many joint-stock banks in addition to the Bank of Scotland (founded 1695) had been established. The joint-stock banks proved themselves better able to withstand financial crises, and this led to a great expansion of joint-stock banking in England. By 1836 there were 99 joint-stock banks in England.

Large-scale banking developed in two ways: (i) by the opening of new branches, and (ii) by the amalgamation of existing banks. During the half century 1840–90, the number of private banks in England fell from 321 to 155, though still outnumbering the joint-stock banks. Branch banking developed slowly. In 1865 the London and County Bank had 127 branches, but at that date there were only two other banks with more than 30 branches. In 1890 nine banks each had over 50 branches, these banks together having over 900 branches. Before 1913 bank amalgamations were mostly small affairs (*a*) between small country banks, (*b*) between private banks and joint-stock banks, and (*c*) between London banks and country banks, even though to have a branch in London often meant that a country bank had to sacrifice its right to issue bank-notes. By 1913 branch banking was well established, thirty-seven joint-stock banks having between them a total of over 6,000 branches. Although at that date there were still sixty private banks, these had a total of only 400 branches. It was during the years immediately after the First World War that the 'Big Five' were created as a result of further amalgamations among the larger banks. A Treasury Committee recommended that no further amalgamations should take place without its prior approval. The first important amalgamation after this was that of the National Provincial and the District in 1962. Then in 1968 the National Provincial and the Westminster merged to form the National Westminster, and Barclays took over Martins. This reduced the 'Big Five' to the 'Big Four'. The 'Big Four' control three of the four Scottish banks, the Bank of Scotland being the only independent commercial bank in Scotland. In 1958 each of the large English banks acquired an interest in a hire-purchase finance company. Each of the 'Big Four' has between 1,000 and 2,000 branches. The feature of the British banking system is a small number of banks, each with branches all over the country. *See* Bank; Branch Banking.

Banking Act (1945). An Australian Act which empowered the Commonwealth Bank of Australia (now the Reserve Bank of Australia) to compel each of the Australian Trading Banks (that is, the Australian commercial banks) to maintain such deposits with it in a Special Account as it might require.

Banking Department. One of the two departments into which the work of the Bank of England was divided by the bank Charter Act (1844), the other being the Issue Department. *See* Bank Return.

Banking School. During 1825–37 a number of banking crises occurred in England, and these led to a demand for parliamentary intervention to control the issue of bank-notes. There were two schools of thought, the Currency School (*q.v.*) and the Banking School, the former believing that strict measures were needed to restrict the note issues of the banks, whereas the members of the Banking School believed that the note issue should not be so restricted but should be flexible and made to suit the needs of business at the time. Though the Bank Charter Act of 1844 showed the influence of the Currency School, neither group foresaw the future development of the use of cheques, a more flexible monetary medium than the banknote.

Bank Money. Bank deposits used as money, that is, deposits in an account where they are subject to withdrawal by cheque. *See* Bank Deposits.

Bank-note. A note issued by a bank for a sum of money which it promises to pay the bearer on demand. At the present time notes of only four denominations are issued by the Bank of England—£1, £5, £10, and £20. The Scottish banks also issue £100 notes. Before 1940 notes of higher denominations were issued by the Bank of England, the only bank in England now with the right to issue notes. Bank-notes had their origin in England in the receipts issued by goldsmiths when money was deposited with them. At first banknotes were really only substitutes for money, their value being dependent on their being able to be exchanged on demand for gold coin of equivalent value. It was not until 1931, when English bank-notes became inconvertible, that bank-notes really became money in their own right. They can serve as money only so long as confidence in them is maintained. *See* Bank of Issue; Convertibility; Inconvertible Banknotes.

Bank of America. One of the few states in the United States which permits branch banking is California, but in no case are U.S. banks allowed to have branches in more than one state. The Bank of America with over 1,000 branches is the largest bank in the world and, although it has over 100 branches abroad, all its American branches, in spite of its name, are in the state of California. It has, however, a wholly owned subsidiary—Bank of America (International Service) in New York. Its associate, Banca di America e Italia, has 85 branches in Italy. It also has an interest in the Société Financière Européenne. The Bank of America was the first bank in the world to issue credit cards. *See* BankAmer card.

Bank of Canada. The central bank of the Dominion of Canada, it was established in 1934. Since 1935 it has been the sole bank of issue in that country. It was nationalised in 1938. It is located at Ottawa.

Bank of England. Founded in 1694 by a group of City of London merchants for the purpose of lending money to William III, it was only gradually that it developed as a central bank. It differed in two ways from other British banks of the time in being a joint-stock company and having the privilege of limited liability. At first its business differed from that of its contemporaries in only one respect, namely that it was banker to the Government, although in consequence its prestige stood higher than that of other banks. Slowly it developed into a powerful central bank with control over the policy of the other banks. Even within a hundred years of its foundation Adam Smith was able to say of it: 'It acts, not only as an ordinary bank, but as a great engine of state.' Its slow development as a central bank is not surprising when it is remembered that the first attempt to formulate a set of principles of central banking was not made until 1877 when Bagehot published his book, *Lombard Street*.

During the eighteenth century it continued to function very much like the other banks, and it was not until a succession of financial crises in the nineteenth century that it began to take to itself functions which we now regard as those of a central bank. Excessive lending by the smaller banks, mainly in the form of over-issues of bank-notes, brought on the crises of 1825 and 1837, and resulted in many bank failures. In 1825 the Bank of England did nothing to relieve the crises, but in 1837 it began to act for the first time as lender of last resort. These crises led to a demand for legislation to control the note issues of the banks, the result being Peel's Bank Charter Act of 1844. The aim of this Act was to restrict the note issue. It divided the work of the Bank of England into two departments: the Issue Department and the Banking Department. The Issue Department was to concern itself solely with the note issue. The Bank was permitted a fiduciary issue of £14 million, but all notes issued in excess of this amount were to be fully backed by gold or, up to 20% of the total value, by silver. Other banks of issue, of which there were seventy-two in 1844, were not to exceed their average circulation during the twelve weeks immediately before the passing of the Act. No new bank was permitted to issue notes, and a bank was to lose this right if it opened a branch in London or amalgamated with another bank. The ultimate effect of this was to make the Bank of England the only bank in the country with the right to issue bank-notes. The Act of 1844 also compelled the Bank of England to publish a weekly balance sheet, the Bank Return (*q.v.*). In the financial crises of the later years of the nineteenth century the Bank of England became more of a central bank and began to use its bank rate as an instrument of monetary policy. In the crises of 1847 and 1957 the Bank acted as lender of last resort, the Government agreeing to indemnify it if in doing so it contravened the Act of 1844. By the end of the century the Bank of England was actively controlling the credit policy of the commercial banks.

The functions of the Bank of England can be briefly summarised: (i) It is now the sole bank of issue in England, though some Scottish and Northern Ireland banks retain the right to limited issues of notes; (ii) It is the Government's bank, and manages the national debt; (iii) It is the bankers' bank, the commercial banks maintaining balances with it; (iv) It acts as lender of last resort—an essential function of a central bank—that is, it is willing to lend to certain members of the money market when the commercial banks are unwilling to lend to them; (v) In collaboration with the Chancellor of the Exchequer and the Treasury, it is responsible for carrying out the country's monetary policy; (vi) It acts as agent for the Treasury in many matters affecting Great Britain's monetary relations with other countries through the Exchange Equalisation Account, the International Monetary Fund and the International or World Bank; (vii) The country's gold reserves are stored at the Bank of England. It still continues to do a little ordinary banking business.

Through a number of subsidiaries the Bank of England gives assistance to industry. The Bank of England has a large shareholding in United Dominion Trust. Through its subsidiary, the Securities Management Trust, it has a controlling interest in the Bankers' Industrial Development Company. It also has an important shareholding interest in Finance for Industry (*q.v.*). In 1946 the Bank of England was nationalised. It has branches in Birmingham, Bristol, Leeds, Liverpool, Manchester, Newcastle upon Tyne, Southampton and the Law Courts (London).

Bank of England Quarterly Bulletin. A quarterly survey of the current economic situation of the United Kingdom, first published in December 1960. It provides up-to-date statistics and articles on banking, monetary, and other financial matters.

Bank of England's Minimum Lending Rate (M.L.R.). The rate at which the Bank of England acts as 'lender of last resort', until 1972 known as bank rate (*q.v.*).

Bank of France. *See* Banque de France.

Bank of Ireland. The oldest bank in Ireland, established in 1783, it never developed into a central bank. The Currency Act of 1927 set up a Currency commission to supervise its note issue, this commission being dissolved in 1942 when the Central Bank of Eire was established.

Bank of Issue. A bank possessing the right to issue bank-notes. This was a privilege which all early banks desired. Since 1921 the Bank of England has been the only bank of issue in England, and though some Scottish banks and some banks in Northern Ireland still retain this privilege the extent of these issues is strictly limited.

Bank of Italy. *See* Banca d'Italia.

Bank of London and Montreal. A bank established in 1958, with its head office in Nassau in the Bahamas, to explore banking possibilities in the West Indies. It is a fully owned subsidiary of Lloyds International Bank (*q.v.*).

Bank of Montreal. The largest commercial bank of Canada, it has over 950 branches at home and abroad, including branches at London, Paris, and Dusseldorf.

Bank of New York. Founded in 1784 by Alexander Hamilton, it is the oldest bank in New York.

Bank of Scotland. The oldest bank in Scotland, founded in 1695, the year after the establishment of the Bank of England. In spite of its name it has never acted as a central bank. At first it issued notes only to the value of £100 and £5, but later began to issue £1 notes. It still issues its own notes, but the issue has to be fully backed by Bank of England notes of equivalent value. In 1958 it acquired an interest in North West Securities Ltd., a finance house. In 1969 it merged with the British Linen Bank to form the Bank of Scotland Group in which Barclays Bank has a 35% interest.

Bank Post Bills. A device introduced in 1738 and formerly employed to defeat highwaymen. Not being payable until seven days after sight such bills could not be cashed immediately like bank-notes, and so banks could be warned to stop payment.

Bank Rate. The minimum rate at which the Bank of England, acting in its capacity as 'lender of last resort', is prepared to discount—or, more accurately, rediscount—first-class or bank bills of exchange, brought to it by members of the London money market. Bank rate, however, is of much greater importance than this, since it is the oldest instrument of monetary policy employed by the Bank of England, and many other rates of interest—for example, the rate charged by commercial banks on loans and overdrafts to customers, and also the rate on deposit accounts—move up and down with bank rate. Some other financial institutions also find it necessary to vary their rates of interest with changes in bank rate—the deposit rate of Finance Houses, the rate of interest on mortgage loans of municipal corporations, and both the borrowing and deposit rates of building societies, though not necessarily with every change in bank rate. During the latter part of the nineteenth century the Bank of England employed bank rate in conjunction with open-market operations (*q.v.*) in order to expand or contract the supply of money, a high bank rate discouraging borrowing and a low rate encouraging it. In carrying out its monetary policy at that time the Bank of England regarded its bank rate as its principal instrument of policy, open-market operations being employed, so it was said, only 'to make bank rate effective'.

After 1931 it was argued that bank rate was not an effective instrument of monetary policy, a low rate not necessarily encouraging lending in a severe depression, and so not stimulating recovery. As a result bank rate fell into disuse. Between 1932 and 1951, when bank rate was revived, it remained unchanged at 2%, except for a brief period on the declaration of war in 1939. Since 1951 there have been wide variations in bank rate which on occasion has been raised to 8%. There is still a wide difference of opinion regarding the effectiveness or otherwise of bank rate. Those who oppose the use of bank rate as an instrument of monetary policy point out that since its revival in 1951 it has always been accompanied by other instruments of policy—variations in hire purchase regulations, changes in purchase tax, the Treasury directive at first and Special Deposits more recently—the so-called 'package deal' (q.v.). Some of those who favour the use of bank rate point out, however, that it may be slow to take effect, as during the Great Depression of the early 1930s. It is said too that it has an important psychological effect as an indication of the intentions of the monetary authorities. Whether or not bank rate is effective for the internal situation, it appears to be of some importance in the external sphere. Faced by an adverse balance of payments bank rate may be raised to check an outflow of foreign funds or to encourage an inflow of such funds from abroad. The introduction of Base Rate (q.v.) in 1971 reduced the importance of Bank Rate, and in 1972, after 270 years as the regulator of interest rates in the U.K., it was abolished. Since October 1972 the minimum lending rate of the Bank of England has been the average rate of discount for Treasury bills in the market and thus is determined by the market itself and is not by the monetary authorities. This is the rate charged by the Bank of England as 'lender of last resort'. *See* Minimum Lending Rate.

Bank Reconciliation Statement. *See* Reconciliation Statement, Bank.

Bank Restriction Act (1797). Until the Napoleonic Wars the Bank of England had continuously maintained the convertibility of its notes into gold on demand. The heavy drain on the Bank's resources, however, during that war compelled it to cease payment in gold, permission to do so being granted by an Order in Council. Bank-notes in denominations of £2 and £1 were issued, the Act of 1797 making them legal tender. Cash payments were not resumed until 1821.

Bank Restriction Period. The period 1796–1819 during which Bank of England notes were not convertible for gold on demand.

Bank Return. The weekly balance sheet which the Bank of England has been compelled to issue by the Bank Charter Act of 1844. It is published every Wednesday, and in accordance with the above Act it is issued in two parts, one for the Issue Department and the other for the Banking Department. It takes the form shown in the illustration on page 36.

The return for the Issue Department shows the extent of the note issue, the value of the notes in circulation and the reserve of notes held in the Banking Department. The assets of the Issue Department consist mainly of securities. Government debt comprises loans made to the Government by the Bank of England during the first hundred and fifty years of its existence, generally in return for a renewal of its charter. Government securities are Government bonds and Treasury bills. Other securities are other first-class securities such as bank bills and fine trade bills. These securities, together with coin other than gold, provide the backing for the fiduciary issue (q.v.). Only a small amount of gold is now held in the Issue Department, most of the country's gold now being held by the Exchange Equalisation Account (q.v.).

The principal liabilities of the Banking Department are (i) capital, a sum equal to the capital subscribed by the stockholders when the Bank of England was a public limited company; (ii) The Rest, the Bank's reserve, accumulated out of undistributed profits; (iii) Public de-

Wednesday, 15th October 1975

I. Issue Department

	£ million		£ million
Notes issued:			
In circulation	5,839	Government debt	11
In Banking Department	36	Government securities	5,261
		Other securities	603
		Coin	1
	5,875	Fiduciary issue	5,875

II. Banking Department

	£ million		£ million
Capital	14½	Government securities	1,268
Rest	3½	Other securities	85
Public deposits	21	Discounts and advances	249
Bankers' deposits	245	Notes	36
Special deposits	381	Coin	1
Other accounts	977		
	1,639		1,639

posits, the balance standing to the credit of Government accounts; (iv) Bankers' deposits, the balances of the commercial banks; (v) Special deposits (if any), compulsory deposits of the English and Scottish commercial banks demanded by the Bank of England in carrying out the country's monetary policy; (vi) Other accounts, the balances of Commonwealth and foreign banks and ordinary customers. The main assets of the Banking Department comprise: (i) Government securities, mainly Government stocks, Treasury bills and 'Ways and Means' advances; (ii) Other securities, mostly securities acquired by the Bank in the open market; (iii) Discounts and advances, the amounts lent by the Bank to members of the London money market; (iv) Notes, the reserve of bank-notes; (v) Gold and silver coin, nowadays almost entirely silver, held like the notes to meet a demand from the commercial banks for cash.

Bankruptcy. If a debtor is unable to meet his commitments his creditors may file a bankruptcy petition, provided the sum involved exceeds £50. The petition asks for a receiving order to be made and if this is done the official receiver, an official of the Board of Trade, will temporarily take charge of the debtor's affairs. Then the official receiver will call a meeting of creditors and if they so desire the debtor can be formally declared bankrupt. Either an individual or a company can be adjudged bankrupt, the company in such circumstances going into liquidation. When the debtor's assets have been realised, the creditors will receive a dividend. An undischarged bankrupt cannot serve as director of a limited company or take an active part in its management without the consent of the Court. If he continues to trade he is not allowed to incur credit in excess of £10 unless he informs his creditor of the fact that he is a bankrupt. As an alternative to bankruptcy a debtor may effect a composition with his creditors, if they are agreeable, to pay (say) £0·50 in the £.

Bank Statement. *See* Statement.

Banque d'Affaires. A type of French bank mainly concerned with investment banking. The largest is the Banque de Paris et des Pays Bas.

Banque de Bruxelles. The second largest commercial bank in Belgium, it has a network of 950 branches covering the whole country with branches also in Luxembourg. It is an associate of Barclays Bank Ltd.

Banque de Commerce d'Anvers. One of the smaller banks of Belgium, it is an associate of Barclays Bank Ltd. In 1965 the Chase Manhattan Bank of New York also acquired an interest in it.

Banque de France. Established by Napoleon in 1800. As early as 1803 it acquired the sole right to issue notes in Paris, and since 1848 it has been the sole bank of issue in France. It is one of the oldest central banks on the continent of Europe. It undertakes a great deal more ordinary banking business than the Bank of England and has over 260 branches distributed throughout France. It was nationalised in 1945.

Banque de la Société Générale. The largest commercial bank in Belgium.

Banque Européenne de Crédit à Moyen Terme. An international bank consortium established in 1967 with headquarters in Brussels, for the provision of medium-term credit to industry. All the participating banks are European—the Midland and Samuel Montagu (British), Credit Lyonnais and Société Générale (French), Deutsche Bank (German), Amsterdam–Rotterdam Bank (Dutch), Société Générale de Banque (Belgian), and the Banca Nazionale del Lavore (Italian). The head office is in Brussels. *See* Medium-term Credit.

Banque Nationale de Belgique. The National Bank of Belgium, it is that country's central bank. It was founded in 1850 with its head office in Brussels and with branches in Antwerp, Liege, and Luxembourg. It is the sole bank of issue in Belgium.

Banque Nationale de Paris. Formed in 1966 by the amalgamation of two nationalised French banks— Banque Nationale pour le Commerce et l'Industrie and Comptoir Nationale d'Escompte de Paris. It joined in 1968 with a number of other banks to form the Société Financière Européenne. It is the largest commercial bank in France. The British & French Bank is its London affiliate. It has over 2,000 branches in 62 countries.

Banque Occidentale. Established in Paris in 1969 by the Société Générale Française and the Central National Bank of Cleveland, U.S.A.

Banque Populaire. A type of bank found in the smaller French towns. They are now linked together through a Caisse Centrale.

Barclaycard. A credit card offered by Barclays Bank. Reciprocal facilities are available to holders of this card and BankAmericard (*q.v.*) in the United States and with Carte Bleu in France (*q.v.*). *See also* Credit Card.

Barclays Bank. One of the 'Big Four', this bank developed from a private bank run by John Freame, a London goldsmith, in the eighteenth century, whose son-in-law, James Barclay, later joined the family business. By amalgamations with other banks and by the opening of new branches it increased in size, but it was not until 1896 that it became a limited company on the amalgamation of twenty private banking firms, for some time having been the leading member of this group. Amalgamations with other banks followed. In 1968 it acquired Martins Bank. It has over 3,000 branches. It also controls the Bank of Scotland. Its subsidiary, Barclays Bank London & International has branches abroad. It also has interest in the Banque de Bruxelles, the Banque de Commerce d'Anvers, the Canadian Bank of Commerce, and a Spanish Bank—Banco del Desarrollo Económico Español. It controls Barclays Overseas Development Corporation, Crédit Congolais, Barclays Bank (California), and it has interests in the Bank of London and Montreal and the finance company, the United Dominion Trust (a hire purchase finance company), and in the Société Financière Européenne. It ranks as the twelfth largest bank in the world. It was the first British bank to offer its own credit card—the Barclaycard. Also in the Barclays Group is Barclays Unicorn, a unit trust company.

Barclays Bank International. A subsidiary of Barclays Bank, it was formerly known as Barclays D.C.O. (Dominions, Colonial and Overseas). It is the leading British overseas bank and has over 1,500 branches.

Barclays Bank Review. A quarterly publication of Barclays Bank Ltd., it contains articles on current economic and monetary matters.

Bar Council. In full, the General Council of the Bar, it is the representative body of the English Bar. It acts in an advisory capacity on matters affecting the profession and has disciplinary powers.

Bargain. A transaction on the stock exchange. The number of bargains 'marked' on any day is merely the number of transactions for the sale or purchase of securities recorded for that day. All 'bargains', however, are not recorded.

Bargaining. *See* Haggling; Collective Bargaining.

Bargaining Theory of Wages. The theory that wages in an occupation are determined by the relative strength of the trade union and employers' association concerned. *See* Wages.

Baring Crisis. In 1890 Baring's, one of the oldest merchant banks in the City of London found itself in serious financial difficulties. The firm was heavily involved in Argentina, where a financial crisis had occurred, and, though sound, Baring's had insufficient liquid assets to meet all calls on them and there was a danger that payment would have to be suspended. However, with the help of the Bank of England the firm was able to overcome the crisis and it met all its liabilities in full. It was reconstituted as a limited company five years later. It is still active in London.

Barlow Report (1940). The Report of the Royal Commission (Sir Montague Barlow being Chairman) on the *Distribution of the Industrial Population*, published 1940. Two-fifths of the population of Great Britain, the report pointed out, lived in seven great conurbations, each with a population of over a million, with London as the outstanding example of urban congestion. The report described these huge urban areas as 'sprawling agglomerations of humanity', which it was considered had strategic, economic, and social dangers to the country's life and development. It was recommended that the Government should take definite action to remedy the situation, and that a new central authority to plan the location of industry should be set up. The planning and development of New Towns was one result of the Barlow Report.

Barter. The exchanging of goods for goods without the use of money. It has three serious drawbacks: (i) it is dependent on two people mutually being able to satisfy one another's wants; (ii) a rate of exchange has to be determined before a transaction can take place; (iii) the exchange of large for small commodities is difficult. The use of a medium of exchange overcomes the difficulties of barter.

Base Rate. A new concept, introduced in 1971, it replaced Bank Rate as the basis for other interest rates, e.g. bank loans, bank deposits. *See* Bank Rate.

Base Stock Method. When the value of money is falling rapidly the valuation of current assets presents a problem. The 'Base Stock' method is one way of attempting to surmount this difficulty. Where a certain amount of raw material is always being employed it is treated in the firm's accounts as basic stock and always valued at the price at which it was originally purchased.

Base Year. The year selected as a base for an index number series and usually given the index number 100. For example, for the Index of Retail Prices the base year has been changed from time to time, 1914, 1947, 1952,

1956, and 1962 all having at different times served this purpose. *See* Cost-of-living Index; Index of Retail Prices.

Basic Rate. It was formerly known as Standard Rate. With reference to income tax, the rate charged on all income above a certain level of income (depending on the allowances of individual taxpayers), the lower branches of taxable income being taxed at lower rates. On high incomes surtax is additional to tax at the standard rate in some countries.

Basing-point System. A method of standardising freight charges to all their customers irrespective of the distance the goods have to be carried, adopted by some producers in the United States.

Basle Arrangements. A meeting in March 1961 at the Bank for International Settlements, Basle, of the Group of Ten (*q.v.*), called to consider the run on sterling that followed the revaluation of the German mark. As a result of these Basle arrangements Switzerland made a loan to Great Britain. In 1968 the Group of Ten offered Great Britain a substantial credit to support the sterling balances (*q.v.*).

Basle Club. *See* Bankers' Club.

B.A.T. Abbreviation of British American Tobacco Co. Ltd.

Batch. *See* Economic Batch Quantity.

Bazaar. In Eastern countries the term is used to mean an open market. In this country it is sometimes used to mean a fixed-price shop that sells a variety of goods. For example, before 1914 there were Penny Bazaars in Great Britain, shops with open access from the street selling a variety of articles at one penny each. Between the wars the larger fixed-price stores sold only goods priced at threepence and sixpence. Since 1945 the severe fall in the value of money and the rise in the general standard of living have together caused the disappearance of the fixed-price stores, which now sell goods over a much wider range of prices.

B.C.A. Abbreviation of British Caledonian Airways (*q.v.*).

B.C.I. Abbreviation of Banca Commerciale Italiana, a large Italian commercial bank with its head office in Milan. It has an interest in the Banque Européenne de Crédit à Moyen Terme.

B.Com. (or **B.Comm.**). Abbreviation of Bachelor of Commerce, a degree awarded by a number of British universities. Courses of study usually include economics, economic history, commercial geography, accountancy, commercial law, and cognate subjects.

B.Com.Sc. Abbreviation of Bachelor of Commercial Science, a university degree similar to B.Com. (*q.v.*).

B/d. Abbreviation of Brought Down.

B/Dft. Abbreviation of Bank Draft (*q.v.*).

B/E. Abbreviation of Bill of Exchange (*q.v.*).

Bear. The name given to a speculator on a market, more particularly on the stock exchange, who sells stock or shares in anticipation of a fall in their prices.

Bearer. A term applied to cheques and bonds, the possession of which gives a right to payment without formality. A cheque payable to bearer, unless crossed, can be cashed over the counter of the issuing bank without having to be endorsed by the person presenting it. Bank-notes are always payable to bearer.

Bearer Bonds. Bonds which can be transferred from one person to another without the new ownership having to be registered, the legal owner being the holder.

B.E.C. Abbreviation of Business Education Council (*q.v.*).

Bedaux System. A bonus system of wage payment invented in New York in 1911 by Charles Bedaux, it was introduced into England in 1926. It attempts to apply a uniform system of bonus payments to work of differing degrees of difficulty, each type of work being analysed and, according to the strain involved, a proportion of time being allowed for rest. For all kinds of work there is a standard unit of time, known as a 'B' unit, these standard times being supplied by experts employed by the Bedaux company. The bonus is then calculated as a percentage (usually 75%) of the hourly rate for the time saved, and this is paid in addition to the time rate for the actual time taken.

Beeching Plan. A scheme outlined by Dr (now Lord) Beeching after a detailed examination under his direction of British Railways at the request of the Minister of Transport. The Report was published in March 1963. Lord Beeching's aim was to re-shape the British railway system to suit the needs of the present day. For some time British Railways had experienced an increasing annual deficit. On many routes the decline in both passenger and freight traffic had been very considerable as a result of severe competition from road haulage, public passenger road transport, internal airlines, and above all from the private motor car, which affected both suburban traffic and passenger travel to holiday resorts.

The main recommendations made in the Report were: (i) Non-remunerative branch lines and their stations should be closed to passenger traffic or entirely closed to all traffic; (ii) Stopping trains on many lines should be abolished, and intermediate stations closed, and only fast services provided between many towns. By 1962 the railways enjoyed only 10% of a declining demand for short journeys for which stopping trains were run, and yet such trains provided 40% of the total train mileage. Over 95% of all railway traffic was dealt with by only half the total of 7,000 stations, the average distance between stations being only 2½ miles; (iii) Speedier and regular 'liner' freight service should be provided, freight to be distributed by road from a smaller number of railheads. For example, it suggested that coal should be distributed from a few modernised loading centres instead of from the existing 3,750 loading points; (iv) Higher fares should be charged to suburban travellers (so-called 'commuters'), owing to the excessively high cost of meeting the intensive peak period demand; (v) Even some main lines should be closed where there were alternative routes between the same towns, a relic of the days of independent competitive railways. For example, it suggested that the old Great Central line between London and the North and the old Midland line between Leeds, Carlisle, and Edinburgh should be closed; (vi) Many lines serving the smaller holiday resorts should be closed. To meet peak demand for holiday traffic was unremunerative in spite of the low marginal cost of running additional trains, since two-thirds of the coaches required for these services were idle for the rest of the year, and their earning formed only a fraction of the cost of their maintenance. As a result of these changes the labour force on the railways would have to be reduced, but redundancies would not be excessive, since to carry out all the changes recommended would take time during which wastage due to death, retirement or leaving the service would reduce the number employed and recruitment would be kept to a minimum.

There was opposition to the Report from all classes of people adversely affected by it, and in some quarters it was suggested that the railways should be deliberately run at a loss as 'a service'. If fully implemented the Report would leave large areas of the country without railways—Central Wales, parts of north and west Scotland, the seaside resorts of North Devon and Cornwall, the smaller resorts of North Wales, and the coastal areas of Lincolnshire and parts of East Anglia and the Yorkshire coast. Suburban traffic would be almost confined to London and Glasgow. The aim, however, was to make use of the railways for the sort of traffic for which they were most suited. It was hoped that 'if the plan was implemented with vigour, much of the railways' deficit would be eliminated by 1970', though it might take as long as ten years to make the 'liner' freight system fully operative. Before any line is closed objectors have to be heard and any decision by B.R. to close a line can be vetoed by the Secretary of State for the Environment if he thinks fit. *See* British Rail.

'Beggar-my-neighbour' Policy. A term used to describe the policy adopted by many countries during the Great Depression of the 1930s. On account of the severity of the trade depression a country might be led to adopt a policy which it hoped would be of some benefit to itself irrespective of the harm it might do to the economies of other countries. These policies included extreme forms of exchange control, multiple exchange rates, competitive devaluation of currencies, restriction of imports, bilateral trade agreements. The overall effect of these measures was a gradual strangling of international trade from which all countries suffered.

'Below-the-line.' A term used during 1949–64 in the Financial Statement for income and expenditure on capital account. Though the terms 'above-the-line' and 'below-the line' did not precisely distinguish between current and capital expenditure and revenue, most current items appeared above the line and most capital items below. *See* Budget.

Beneficial Rates (or **Remunerative Rates**). Terms used by Alfred Marshall for local rates where the money is spent on such things as lighting, drainage, etc., the services so provided being regarded as a net benefit to the people paying the rates, in contrast to Onerous Rates which yield no compensating benefits to the ratepayer.

Benefit Society. A type of Friendly Society (*q.v.*).

Benefit Theory. With reference to taxation, the view that people should be charged by the Government for services according to the benefit received. The same argument is sometimes put forward as a basis for the payment of rates to local authorities. If this principle were adopted it would mean that taxation would be regressive since the State provides services which are more for the benefit of people with low incomes.

Benelux. The name given to the customs union between Belgium, the Netherlands, and Luxembourg, established shortly after the Second World War. A closer economic union between the three countries was established in 1958. *See* Customs Union.

Benevolence. A compulsory loan first levied by Edward IV. Although Parliament in 1484 declared such loans to be unlawful they continued to be levied in Tudor times, but they were again declared illegal in 1628 and 1689.

Bentley's Code. *See* Codes.

Berne Convention (1886). An international agreement on copyright, it was superseded by the U.N.E.S.C.O. Agreement of 1952. *See* Copyright.

Berne Union. An international association, known as the Union d'Assurance des Credits Internationaux, established in 1934, to assist credit insurance in international trade, the British Government Export Credits Guarantee Department being a founder member.

Betterment. A charge on local rates to cover local improvements. The term was also used of the tax levied by the Land Commission (*q.v.*) on the development value of land.

Betting Duties. A tax on betting through bookmakers imposed by the Finance Act of 1926. It was repealed in 1930. In 1947 a tax on football pools was imposed, the tax being levied on the whole pool and not on individual winnings. Most forms of betting have been taxed since 1966.

Beveridge Report. A *Report on Social Insurance and Allied Services* made by Lord (then Sir William) Beveridge in 1942 at the request of the British Government; its conclusions are sometimes referred to as the Beveridge Plan. Its principal recommendations were: (i) the establishment of a comprehensive health service, providing sickness benefit for those too ill to work, medical, dental attention; (ii) the payment of family allowances; (iii) more generous unemployment benefit; (iv) widows' pensions; (v) a higher rate of retirement pension; (vi) maternity benefit; (vii) funeral grants. To provide all these benefits higher contributions would have to be paid. The Report formed the basis of the comprehensive system of national insurance introduced in 1947 (*see* National Insurance). In 1944 Lord Beveridge independently published his *Report on Full Employment in a Free Society*. *See* Full Employment.

B/f. Abbreviation of Brought Forward. A balance in a statement or ledger brought forward from the previous page. *See also* c/f.

B.I.B. Abbreviation of Brazilian Investment Bank (Banco de Investimento do Brasil).

B.I.C.C. Abbreviation of British Insulated Callenders Cables Ltd.

Bid. 1. At an auction sale an offer to purchase the commodity put up for sale at a stated price.

2. An offer to purchase the whole or a large fraction of the capital of a company. *See* Take-over Bid.

Bid Price. Two prices are quoted for stocks and shares, the lower or bid price being the price at which the broker or agent will purchase the security from the investor. *See also* Offer Price.

'Big Four.' The four large English commercial banks are known as the 'Big Four'. They are Barclays, Lloyds, the Midland, and the National Westminster. Together they have upwards of 10,000 branches. *See* Banking.

Bilateral Flow. With reference to Government expenditure and revenue, a bilateral flow occurs when goods produced by the private sector of the economy are sold to the Government, payment then being made by the Government to the private sector. The term is used in contrast to a unilateral flow where payments are made to the Government, as in the case of most taxes.

Bilateralism. *See* Bilateral Trade.

Bilateral Monopoly. This occurs when there is only one buyer of a commodity or service and only one supplier. Such a condition might exist in the case of a nationalised industry which has a complete monopoly of some form of production and so becomes the sole employer of a particular kind of specific labour, the suppliers of which are all without exception members of a craft union. Discussion between employers and employees would then be between two monopolists.

Bilateral Trade. This occurs when each country attempts to balance its payments and receipts separately and individually with every other country. Such a system is very similar to barter. Its effect would be to reduce the total volume of trade of all countries taking part in it, since it would reduce the trade between each pair of countries to the lesser amount that one wished to purchase from the other. Multilateral trade is necessary if the total volume of world trade is to be raised to its maximum amount.

Bilateral Trade Agreement. A trade agreement between two countries. *See* Bilateral Trade.

Bill. 1. A bill of exchange (*q.v.*).

2. American term for a bank-note.

Bill Broker. A small firm engaged in discount business on the London money market. *See* Discount House.

Billingsgate. The most important wholesale fish market in London, it is the oldest London market.

Billion. In American usage 1,000 million but in Great Britain generally taken to mean a million million, though increasingly used in the American sense.

Bill Market. An alternative term for Discount Market (*q.v.*).

Bill of Entry. Particulars of all goods imported into the country are required by the Customs at the port of entry, these particulars being given on a form known as a Bill of Entry.

Bill of Exchange. As legally defined, 'an unconditional order in writing, addressed by one person to another, signed by the person giving it, requiring the person to whom it is addressed to pay on demand or at a stated future date a sum of money to a certain person or to the order of that person or to bearer.' Most bills of exchange are drawn for three months after date, except cheques, which in effect are 'sight' bills. An example of an inland bill of exchange is illustrated:

cheque generally being preferred. Bills of exchange, whether inland or foreign, arising out of trade transactions are known as trade bills. *See also* Acceptance; Foreign Bills of Exchange; Treasury Bill.

Bill of Exchequer. *See* Exchequer Bill.

Bill of Health. When a ship leaves port its captain receives a Bill of Health which gives particulars of the state of health at that port.

Bill of Lading. A document used in foreign trade, it gives the name of

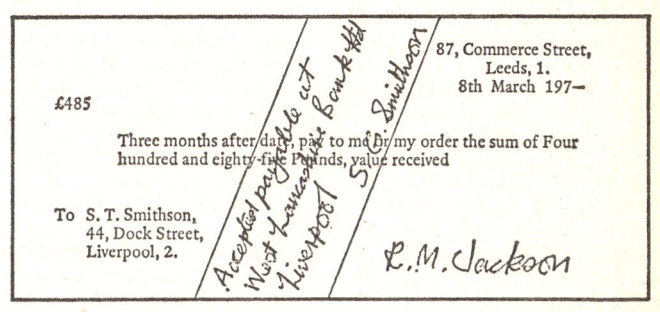

```
                                              87, Commerce Street,
                                                    Leeds, 1.
                                                8th March 197—
 £485

         Three months after date, pay to me or my order the sum of Four
         hundred and eighty-five Pounds, value received

 To S. T. Smithson,
    44, Dock Street,
    Liverpool, 2.                              R. M. Jackson

 (Accepted payable at West Lanark Bank Ltd
  Liverpool   S. Smithson)
```

Jackson, the drawer of the bill, has agreed to accept payment from Smithson by a three-months bill. Jackson is also the payee, and Smithson the drawee of the bill. The bill falls due for payment three months and three days after date, the extra three days being known as 'days of grace.' Before the bill has any value it requires to be accepted by the drawee. It is then often known, especially among bankers, as an Acceptance. Once the bill has been accepted three courses are open to Jackson: (i) he can hold it himself until it is due for payment; (ii) he might be able to discount it with a bank, that is receive payment at once, less interest for the outstanding period and the bank's fee for the service; (iii) he might be able to use it, after he has endorsed it, to pay a creditor of his own, if the creditor is willing to be paid in this way. At one time bills of exchange were commonly used as means of payment in inland trade, but nowadays they are rarely used for this purpose, the

the ship and full particulars of the goods—the quantity, their type, the special markings on the packing cases (if any), any other important details, together with the names of the ports of embarkation and disembarkation. A Bill of Lading is made out in triplicate, one copy being retained by the exporter of the goods, another being handed to the Master of the ship carrying the goods, and the third being despatched to the importer in the country to which the goods are being consigned. The copy—or sometimes, an additional copy—is sent to the importer by a different route from that taken by the ship carrying the goods, nowadays usually by air mail. A Bill of Lading is a document of title, giving the holder a right to possession of the goods to which it refers.

Bill of Sale. A method of raising a loan on the security of one's possessions—furniture, stock-in-trade, etc. —a bill of sale is a document formally transferring legal ownership of the property to the lender, the borrower retaining possession of the goods until the debt is repaid, it being a condition of the agreement that the goods shall then be re-assigned. Thus, a bill of sale is a kind of mortgage. An absolute bill of sale, however, transfers property absolutely from one person to another. To be valid a bill of sale must comply with certain legal formalities and requires to be registered.

Bill of Sight. A document used in the import trade and given to the customs officer when a full description of the goods cannot be provided, to enable the goods to be landed. A full description of the goods must be given later.

Bill of Store. A document giving permission to re-import dutiable British goods, exported within the previous five years, without payment of duty.

Bill Rate. The discount rate on bills of exchange, it varies according to the quality of the bill, being lower on Treasury bills than on first-class (bank) bills, and lower on the latter than on fine trade bills.

Bills Discounted. An item in the Balance Sheet of a Bank (q.v.), it shows the total value of bills held by a bank at a particular date.

Bills in a Set. A term used when more than one copy of a bill of exchange is drawn up. Foreign bills of exchange are drawn up in triplicate and are known respectively as the First, Second, and Third of Exchange, the aim being to reduce the risk of loss in transit.

Bills Retired. A term used, mainly in the United States, of bills of exchange that have been withdrawn from circulation or taken up before due.

B.I.M. Abbreviation of British Institute of Management (q.v.).

Bi-metallism. At one time most monetary systems were based on a silver standard, and later on gold. A bi-metallic standard is one based on two metals, the belief being that such a monetary standard would be less liable to fluctuations in the value of the currency than single-metal standards. If, however, coins composed of different metals—for example, gold and silver—were minted so that each contained its face value in metal, difficulties would arise as soon as any change took place in the relative value of the two metals. If the price of silver rose while that of gold remained unchanged, the silver coins would become worth more than their face value, and would tend to be driven out of circulation, in accordance with Gresham's Law. However, during 1878 unsuccessful efforts were made to introduce a bi-metallic standard into Europe. In the United States bi-metallism was an important item at the presidential elections of 1896 and 1900, but in 1900 the United States adopted the gold standard and the controversy died down.

Birmingham Municipal Bank. Founded in 1919, it is the only municipally owned bank in Great Britain.

Birth-rate. The crude birth-rate is the number of births per thousand of the population during a period, usually of one year. The birth-rate of the United Kingdom fell continuously from 34·2 in 1880 to 14·7 in 1940. Since 1945 it has been more variable but during the period 1955–64 it rose from 15·4 to 18·7, then fell to 13·2 in 1974. Changes in the birth-rate are studied in connection with the population problem, but changes in the average family size are probably of greater importance than the birth-rate.

B.I.S. Abbreviation of Bank for International Settlements (q.v.).

B/L. Abbreviation of Bill of Lading (q.v.).

'Black.' A colloquial trade union term for goods or activities that are to be boycotted.

Black-Bourse. A black market in foreign exchange. See 'Black' Exchange Rates.

'Black' Exchange Rates. Unauthorised exchange rates when exchange rates are controlled—similar to the 'Black Market' when retail prices are controlled. Traders doing business at 'black' exchange rates are generally liable to heavy penalties.

Blackleg. A pejorative term used during a strike of those who continue to work in defiance of instructions from the trade union concerned or of those who volunteer to work in order to try to break a strike.

Black List. A list of traders to whom it is risky to allow credit, compiled by Status Inquiry Agents (*q.v.*), so that they can inform subscribers when required.

'Black Market.' When the price of a commodity is controlled by the State and rationing introduced, demand for the commodity at the controlled price will be greater than the available supply. As a result some people will be prepared to offer a much higher price than the controlled price in order to try to obtain greater amounts of the commodity than they are permitted to have as their rations. Since such a black market is illegal, heavy penalties are usually imposed on both buyers and sellers when caught contravening the rationing laws in force at the time.

'Black Year.' A term applied to the year 1879, a particularly bad year in Great Britain for agriculture on account of exceptionally bad weather following a succession of poor seasons. Migration from the country to the towns was accelerated. It led to the appointment of a Royal Commission which recommended a reduction of local rates payable by landowners.

Blank Cheque. A cheque which the drawer has signed but deliberately left the amount blank for someone else to complete. As a safeguard he may add 'Under £-.' The term is often confused with Open Cheque (*q.v.*).

Blanketeers. Cotton workers who gathered in St Peter's Field, Manchester, in March 1817 prior to marching to London to draw attention to their grievances, carrying blankets so that they could sleep in the open on the journey—hence their name. The arrest of the leaders, however, led to the demonstration being called off.

Blind Alley. A term used of occupations which offer no future prospects to employees. In many cases, school-leavers entering such occupations are dismissed on reaching a certain age. These jobs are often better paid at first than those with better prospects.

B.L.M.C. Abbreviation of former British Leyland Motor Corporation. *See* British Leyland.

Blocked Accounts. When a restrictionist system of exchange control is operated payments for imports may be credited to blocked accounts in the names of the foreign exporters, who may be prohibited—at least, for a time—from drawing on them other than in the country where they are located. When Germany introduced exchange control on leaving the gold standard in 1931 payments at the time due to foreign merchants were transferred to blocked accounts, some of which were released later at a rate of exchange disadvantageous to the foreign holders. During the Second World War Great Britain was unable to earn much foreign currency by exports, and so it was impossible currently to pay for imports. Foreign exporters, therefore, were credited with the amounts due to them in blocked accounts. This was simply a method of buying on credit, but it was impossible to release the entire amount of sterling in blocked accounts at the end of the war, as by that time the amount involved was much too great. However, after 1945 holders were allowed to draw on blocked accounts gradually.

Blocked Balances. An alternative term for Blocked Accounts (*q.v.*).

Block Grant. Services provided by the State fall heavily on Local Authorities which, since these are to a large extent national services, the Government helps to finance by making grants to Local Authorities. At one time these grants were earmarked for particular purposes, so much for education, so much for roads, etc. The system was abolished in favour of the general or block grant, the division of which among the various services to be provided was left to the Local Authority, though the Local Authority's choice was severely restricted by the fact that by law certain minimum services had to be provided.

Block Offer. The offer at one time of a large number of units by a unit investment trust. Although units can be purchased—and sold—at any time it appears that many investors prefer to respond to a block offer.

Block Vote. At the meetings of some trade unions and of the Trades Union Congress delegates vote not as individuals but according to the number of members they represent. This is known as a Block Vote.

Blue Book. An official publication of the British Government, published by the Central Statistical Office, so called on account of its blue covers. Blue Books are usually larger than White Papers, often being reports of Royal Commissions which may run to hundreds of pages. The Report of the Radcliffe Committee was published as a Blue Book. In March of each year it is usual for a White Paper to be published giving a preliminary estimate of National Income and Expenditure for the previous calendar year, this being followed in August or September by a more detailed account in the form of a Blue Book.

'Blue Button.' A term used of an authorised clerk of the London Stock Exchange, so-called because he wears a blue badge in the lapel of his coat. *See also* Pink Button.

Blue Chip. A term of American origin used to describe the shares of progressive, soundly run public limited companies which are not likely to be seriously affected by temporary trade recessions.

Blue Collar Workers. A term sometimes used of technicians and other manual workers to distinguish them from white collar workers (*q.v.*).

B.N.E.C. Abbreviation of British National Export Council (*q.v.*).

Board of Directors. A Committee elected by the shareholders of a limited company to be responsible for the policy of the company. Sometimes full-time functional directors are appointed, each being responsible for some particular branch of the firm's work.

Board of Guardians. Under the Poor Law Amendment Act of 1834 parishes were grouped together in unions which had to provide workhouses, their administration being placed under Boards of Guardians. During the Great Depression the administration of the Poor Law placed a great strain on areas of high unemployment and eventually led to a complete reorganisation of the administration of relief. In 1929, therefore, the Boards of Guardians were abolished as few people were willing to offer themselves for election, and their functions transferred to Public Assistance Committees of local authorities.

Board of Trade. A former Government department. In 1970 it was merged with the Department of Trade and Industry and in 1974 it again became separate as the Department of Trade. *See* Trade, Department of.

B.O.C. Abbreviation of British Oxygen Co.

BOLAM. Abbreviation of Bank of London and Montreal (*q.v.*).

Bolivar. The standard unit of the currency of Venezuela, it is divided into 100 centimos.

Boliviano. Formerly the standard unit of the currency of Bolivia, it has been replaced by the peso.

Bond. 1. Goods are said to be in bond when they are stored in a bonded warehouse (*q.v.*) until customs duty is paid.

2. An alternative name for a stock or security. Many Government stocks are known as bonds, for example, the various issues of Savings Bonds, Defence Bonds, Premium Bonds, etc. The issue of bonds is a method of borrowing adopted by most governments, local authorities and some other institutions. Government bonds are usually due to be

redeemed at some future date. *See* Government Stocks.

3. A type of investment including a measure of life assurance, usually for a limited period. *See* Insurance Bond, Managed Bond.

Bonded Warehouse. Customs duty is payable on many commodities on their arrival at the port. If the duty is not to be paid at once special precautions must be taken to ensure that goods are not removed without payment of duty. At the ports bonded warehouses are provided where such goods can be stored until the duty is paid, goods being transferred from the ship and released from 'bond' only under the supervision of customs officers. Bonded warehouses are of particular importance to importers of commodities like tobacco where the duty is very heavy. The first bonded warehouses were introduced by Walpole in 1724 for tea and coffee.

Bond Washing. The practice, now illegal, of selling securities cum dividend at a high price and purchasing them back later ex-dividend at a lower price.

Bon Marché. A Paris department store, opened as a small shop in 1852, and generally regarded as the first shop of this kind to be established.

Bonus. A payment in addition to an amount contracted for. 1. In the case of life assurance those policies described as being 'with profits' receive an annual addition, known as a bonus, depending on the amount of profit made by the company during the year.

2. Bonuses are often added to wages. Modifications of simple piece-rate systems of wage payment have been devised to provide employees with a bonus to encourage them to put forward greater effort. The best known are the Premium Bonus systems. Sometimes a group bonus is paid where the work of individual employees cannot be measured. Some firms, including some commercial banks, set aside a certain fraction of their profits to provide an annual bonus for their employees. *See* Premium Bonus System; Task Bonus System.

Bonus Share. A limited company may decide to finance expansion from its reserves which have been built up out of undistributed profits. Then, in order to bring its issued capital into line with the capital it employs, it may decide to issue bonus shares to existing shareholders to the value of this additional capital, each shareholder receiving a number of bonus shares proportionate to his original holding as, for example, one for three or two for five, etc. After a period of inflation a firm's real capital may have appreciated in value in terms of money, and in such a case bonus shares may be issued to bring the two into line. The issue of bonus shares does not necessarily make a shareholder any better off financially than he would otherwise have been. If a company made exactly the same profit after the issue of bonus shares as before, and if it decided to distribute exactly the same amount of profit to shareholders as before, the rate of dividend would fall proportionately to the new issue, and shareholders would receive exactly the same amount of dividend as before.

Book-keeping. The systematic keeping of business accounts. Limited companies in Great Britain are compelled by the Companies Acts to keep books, and public limited companies have to submit to the Registrar of Companies an audited copy of their balance sheets. Failure to keep proper books is a possible cause of bankruptcy, and in such cases the bankrupt is liable to be penalised.

Booksellers' Association. An association of booksellers in the United Kingdom whose main object is to ensure the carrying out of the Net Book Agreement, whereby members agree not to sell books below the prices attached to them by the publishers. In 1962 the Restrictive Practices Court found that this agreement was not a restrictive practice under the Restrictive Trade Practices Act (1956) and therefore should be allowed to continue. The Booksellers' Association also concerns itself with all matters affecting the book trade.

Book Tokens. Vouchers purchaseable at booksellers and valid for purchases of books at other booksellers. First suggested in 1926, they were introduced in 1932, being issued by Book Tokens Ltd., a subsidiary of the Booksellers' Association.

Book Trade Improvement Co. A company established to make loans to booksellers, it is associated with Book Tokens Ltd.

Book Value. In its balance sheet a company may value assets in the form of investments at the prices shown in its books, namely the prices at which they were purchased, even though their current price on the stock exchange may be higher or lower.

Boom. A term used to describe a period when business activity is at a high level. During the nineteenth century booms and depressions succeeded one another with great regularity, the average time interval between one boom and the next being about seven or eight years. During a boom production expands, prices and wages rise, and unemployment declines. After full employment has been reached a boom will, unless checked, become inflationary in character. *See* Trade Cycle.

Boon-work. Additional work required of villeins at harvest-time by the lord of the manor in medieval times.

Bootlegging. The illegal sale of illicit liquor, as during the period when Prohibition was in force in the United States.

Bordar. A worker on a medieval manor who held a smaller amount of land than a villein.

Borrowing (Control and Guarantees) Act (1946). The renewal of an Act passed during the Second World War to control investment. All issues of capital in excess of £50,000 (reduced to £10,000 in 1956) in any period of one year had to have the prior permission of the Capital Issues Committee of the Treasury, which had to decide whether the issue was in 'the public interest.' During the post-war period the Act was used to assist the Government in carrying out a policy of planned location of industry, consent to the raising of new capital often being made conditional on a firm setting up in one of the Development Areas.

B.O.T. Abbreviation of Board of Trade (now the Department of Trade *q.v.*).

Bottomry Board. A shipping term. If the captain of a ship finds it necessary to incur expenditure, such as for the repair of his ship, he may give a bond mortgaging his ship as security for a loan obtained to cover this expenditure. Loss of the ship would extinguish the mortgage.

Bought Day Book. A book-keeping term, it contains a list of all items purchased by a business.

Bought Note. When a broker has been employed to make a purchase on the stock exchange or on a produce exchange he will supply his principal with a statement, known as a Bought Note, giving details of the transaction.

'Bounce.' A colloquial term applied to a dishonoured cheque. *See* Dishonour.

Bounty. A subsidy paid by the Government to the exporters of certain commodities in order to enable them to be sold more cheaply abroad, thereby stimulating the export of such goods. Bounties, like tariffs, are contrary to the Principle of Comparative Cost, the basis of the theory of international trade. *See* Export Incentives.

Bourse. The Paris stock exchange. The term is also used in some other European countries.

Bowmaker Ltd. A finance house in which Lloyds Bank Ltd. has an interest, its head office being in Bournemouth. It is a member of the Finance Houses Association and the International Credit Union.

Bowyers' Company. One of the 82

Guilds or Livery Companies of the City of London, its existence dates back to medieval times.

Boycott. Refusal to have commercial relations with a trader or a country. For political reasons one country might impose a boycott on another country, for a time prohibiting all imports from that country.

B.P. Abbreviation of British Petroleum Ltd. (in which since 1914 the British Government has had a substantial interest); one of the leading British oil refining and distributing companies, it is a holding company with over 200 subsidiaries.

B/P. Abbreviation of Bill(s) Payable.

B.R. Abbreviation of British Rail (*q.v.*).

B/R. Abbreviation of Bill(s) Receivable.

'Brain Drain.' A colloquial term for the drift of scientists, doctors, and technologists from Europe to the United States. As a percentage of the number of graduates in these branches of study the European countries most seriously affected have been Switzerland, Norway, and the Netherlands, with Great Britain suffering a loss of only about half of these countries.

Branch Banking. A banking system with a small number of banks each with a large number of branches, as in the British banking system and in the banking systems of some other countries, in contrast to the system of unit banks which prevails over most of the United States. The main advantage of branch banking lies in the greater stability of such banks compared with unit banks. This was clearly seen during the Great Depression of the 1930s when large numbers of American banks failed although not a single British bank had to close its doors.

Branded Goods. Goods sold under a brand name registered in accordance with the Trade Marks Act of 1938. The aim is to distinguish one manufacturer's product from similar products of other manufacturers. The goods are then widely advertised in an attempt to impress this differentiation on the minds of consumers. Such goods are produced and sold in conditions of imperfect oligopoly—a few producers of a commodity which is not homogeneous. Since the degree of monopoly is only slight, competition will be keen between producers of different brands of the same commodity. This may take the form of price-cutting or more probably advertising wars, if manufacturers insist on resale price maintenance. Branded goods are often distributed by manufacturers direct to retailers in order to ensure for their goods the maximum number of selling points. To the retailer branded goods have the advantage of being uniformly packed. They are easy to handle and can be ordered from the manufacturer without previous inspection. The consumer has the advantage of knowing exactly what he is buying. The great disadvantage to the retailer is that, if he is to try to please all his customers, he will have to stock a great many varieties of the same commodity.

Brassage. Also known as Mintage, it is a charge made by a mint for the minting of coins. The Royal Mint makes no such charge, the cost of coinage being defrayed from the profit from minting token coins.

Break-even. Carrying on business so that neither profit nor loss is made. Most of the Nationalisation Acts passed between 1946 and 1951 included clauses which stated that the aim of the industry concerned should be to make neither a large profit nor a loss.

Break-up Value. The value at current stock exchange prices of the stocks and shares held by an investment trust or unit trust.

Bretton Woods Agreement (1944). An international conference which met at Bretton Woods, New Hampshire, U.S.A., in 1944 to consider the international monetary system to be operated after the end of the Second World War. Experience of restrictionist practices during the 1930s had clearly only led to a reduction of world trade, and therefore the conference condemned all such devices as multiple exchange rates, blocked accounts, bilateral trade agreements, and all forms of exchange control, although it was accepted that during the immediate post-war period a degree of exchange control would have to be tolerated. What was desired was a system that would encourage the development of multi-lateral trade, and for this purpose stable exchange rates and free convertibility of currencies were considered necessary. It was hoped to work out a scheme that would have the advantages of the gold standard without its rigidity.

To achieve these objectives two new international institutions were proposed—the International Monetary Fund and the International (or World) Bank. Prior to the meeting at Bretton Woods the British Treasury under the lead of Lord Keynes and the American Treasury under Mr White had each prepared a scheme. In general principles the two plans were remarkably similar to one another, though there were important differences. The British and American representatives finally agreed on a compromise scheme, which, however, leaned more to American than British ideas, and this was then put to the conference and accepted. The final act of the conference was to recommend the establishment of the I.M.F. and the World Bank. *See* International Monetary Fund; World Bank.

Bridgewater Canal. The first canal to be built in Great Britain, it was constructed during 1759–61 to carry coal from the Duke of Bridgewater's colliery at Worsley to Manchester, the Duke financing the project and James Brindley being the engineer in charge.

Bridging Loan. Borrowing to make a purchase ahead of receiving payment for a sale as, for example, buying a new house before selling an old one.

Bridlington Rules. A set of rules drawn up by the T.U.C. at its meeting at Bridlington in 1939 to restrain 'poaching' between trade unions, that is, competition for members.

Britannia Building Society. Formed in January 1975 by a merger of the Leek and Westbourne Building Society and the Eastern Counties Building Society.

British Airports Authority. A body set up in 1965 to manage certain airports in Great Britain—Heathrow, Gatwick, Stansted, Prestwick and Edinburgh.

British Airways. The State-owned U.K. airline, formed in 1972 by the merger of B.E.A. and B.O.A.C.

British Airways Board. The controlling body for British Airways.

British & French Bank. The London affiliate of the Banque Nationale de Paris.

British Association. In full, the British Association for the Advancement of Science, it was founded in York in 1831 and it meets annually in different cities of Great Britain. There are thirteen sections, one being for Economics, and at the meetings paper are read to the members of the various sections.

British Broadcasting Corporation (B.B.C.). A public corporation established by Royal Charter in 1926, governed by five persons nominated by the Prime Minister. It took over from the British Broadcasting Company which had been formed in 1922. It was one of the earlier public corporations, established at a time when an attempt was being made to work out a suitable constitution for State-controlled bodies. It is financed by revenue obtained from licences.

British Caledonian Airways. The largest independent British airline, it was formed in 1970 by a merger of Caledonian and British United Airways.

British Consular Service. *See* Consul.

British Cotton-Growing Association. A body set up in 1902 to encourage the production of raw cotton in the Commonwealth. The Cotton

Famine during the American Civil War had shown the disadvantage of relying on one area for supplies.

British Electricity Authority. The name of the body set up under the Electricity Act (1948), which nationalised the electricity undertakings of Great Britain. The Electricity Reorganisation Act (1954) changed the name to the Central Electricity Authority (later known as the Central Electricity Generating Board). *See* Electricity Council; Central Electricity Generating Board.

British Electricity Stocks. Stocks issued by the Central Electricity Generating Board to finance expansion, or to provide compensation for the previous owners of electricity generating stations, not municipally owned, on the nationalisation of the industry. The stocks issued by nationalised industries are guaranteed by the Government, and so rank with gilt-edged stocks. British Electricity Stocks issued comprise 3% 1974–77, $4\frac{1}{4}$% 1974–79, and $3\frac{1}{2}$% 1976–79. Expansion is no longer financed in this way, capital being provided direct by the Government or out of revenue.

British Employers' Confederation. A body representative of British employers, it amalgamated with the British Industries Confederation in 1965 to form the Confederation of British Industry (*q.v.*).

British Export Board. *See* British National Export Council.

British Funds. Often referred to simply as the 'Funds' they comprise British Government stocks or 'gilt-edged' securities (*q.v.*).

British Gas Corporation. Successor to the Gas Council, it is directly responsible to Parliament for the gas industry. The regional gas boards were then abolished.

British Gas Stocks. Stocks issued by the Gas Council, at first to compensate the previous owners of gas undertakings on their nationalisation in 1949, and then later to finance expansion. British Gas Stocks comprise 4% 1969–72, $3\frac{1}{2}$% 1969–71, and 3% 1990–95, these stocks being guaranteed by the Government and so ranking with gilt-edged securities. Nationalised industries no longer raise additional capital in this way, expansion being financed either out of revenue or by direct loans from the Government.

British Industries Fair. A fair held annually with the purpose of promoting British trade. It was formerly held in two sections, one in Birmingham and one in London, but since 1947 it has been held only in Birmingham, where the responsibility for its organisation is in the hands of the Birmingham Chamber of Commerce.

British Institute of Management. A body established to promote management and education in management studies in Great Britain. In co-operation with the Department of Education and Science courses are held at senior Technical Colleges and examinations are held leading to the qualification of Associate Member of the Institute.

British Leyland. Formed in 1968 by the merger of the Leyland Motor Co. Ltd. with the British Motor Corporation. In 1975 the State acquired an interest in the company.

British Market Research Bureau. A body specialising in market research which can supply general information on the buying habits of particular groups of consumers and the effect on them of different means of advertising.

British National Export Council. Founded in 1964 to co-ordinate arrangements for stimulating exports, it is a non-political body sponsored by the D.T.I., the C.B.I., the T.U.C. and the Association of British Chambers of Commerce. It operates through ten area councils. In 1971 its functions were taken over by the British Export Board.

British Productivity Council. The concern of this body is to increase productivity. It is supported by the Trades Union Congress and the Confederation of British Industry, the chairmanship being taken in turn by a representative of each of these bodies. The council also receives help from Chambers of Commerce, the National Association of British Manufacturers, and the nationalised industries.

British Rail. Under the Transport Act (1947) the four large railway groups, formed in 1922, were amalgamated and nationalised along with British Waterways, London Transport, and railway-owned hotels under the newly-established British Transport Commission. As with other nationalised means of transport, the railways were given a degree of independence and placed under the direct control of the Railway Executive. The Transport Act (1953), however, brought all nationalised transport undertakings under the direct control of the British Transport Commission and abolished the Executives. The Transport Act (1963) transferred the assets and functions of the British Transport Commission to a number of boards, the British Railways Board taking over the operation of British Rail. Public transport was further reorganised by the Transport Act (1968) (*q.v.*) to deal with a declining railway system in consequence of the continued expansion of road transport and private motoring. The British Railways Board was brought directly under the Ministry of Transport and a National Freight Corporation was created. In general, British Rail was expected 'to break even' financially, but the Government undertook to subsidise certain routes if these could be shown to be 'socially necessary.' Even so British Rail continued to show a loss. *See also* Beeching Plan.

British Road Services. The Transport Act of 1947 nationalised most forms of inland public transport in Great Britain, including road haulage and road passenger services, though the latter was never carried out. Each form of transport was put under the direct control of its own Executive under the general control of the British Transport Commission. Thus British Road Services, established to undertake road haulage except for goods carried in their own vans by manufacturers, wholesalers or retailers, became the Executive for road transport. At the time road haulage was in the hands of over 20,000 firms, mostly small and with an average of between two and three vehicles each. British Road Services were given powers to acquire road haulage undertakings by individual bargaining with the firms concerned. Road transport was denationalised by the Transport Act of 1953 which also abolished the various Transport Executives and brought all nationalised transport under the direct control of the British Transport Commission. Fear of re-nationalisation made many people unwilling to re-enter the road haulage industry, and in consequence only 54% of the vehicles were returned to private operators, the Transport (Disposal of Road Haulage Property) Act of 1956 enabling the British Transport Commission to retain 15,000 vehicles. From 1953 to 1968, therefore, British Road Services were in competition with independent road hauliers. After the passing of the Transport Act of 1968 the member companies of British Road Services were organised in seven autonomous regional companies.

British Savings Bonds. First issued in 1968 bearing interest at 6% to replace National Development Bonds and Defence Bonds (*q.v.*).

British Standards Institution. A body which lays down what it regards as minimum standards in engineering, building, chemical, and textile products, etc., over 3,000 commodities being assessed. Its certification mark is the 'kite'.

British Steel Corporation. A body established under the Iron and Steel Act (1967) which re-nationalised the steel industry. It replaced the Iron and Steel Board (*q.v.*) set up in 1953. Under it are four operational groups.

British Sugar Corporation. Formed in 1936 by the amalgamation of the existing fifteen British producers of beet sugar in order to develop more effectively the production of beet sugar in Great Britain.

British Tourist Authority. Set up in 1969, it took over the functions of the British Travel Association. Its aims are to encourage visitors to the United Kingdom and to encourage the provision of tourist amenities in this country. It co-operates with the Tourist Boards of England, Scotland, Wales and Northern Ireland.

British Transport Commission. The Act of 1947 which nationalised inland transport in Great Britain set up the British Transport Commission under the Ministry of Transport to take over the railways, docks and inland waterways, road transport, London Transport, and hotels previously owned and operated by the railways. An Act of 1953 de-nationalised road transport, but only about 54% of the Transport Commission's vehicles were returned to private enterprise, the remainder continuing to be operated by British Road Services for the Transport Commission. The Act of 1953 also provided for the abolition of the separate Executives for the Railways, Waterways, Road Services, Hotels, etc., all these services being brought under the direct control of the British Transport Commission. The Transport Act of 1962 replaced the British Transport Commission by four boards—the British Railways Board, the London Transport Board, the British Waterways Board, and the British Transport Docks Board. To these bodies the functions and property of the British Transport Commission were transferred.

British Transport Docks Board. One of the Transport Boards set up under the Transport Act (1962) to operate all State-owned docks and harbours. *See* Transport Act (1968).

British Transport Stocks. The first British Transport Stock was issued to compensate the shareholders of the railway companies and other transport undertakings at the time of their nationalisation. Later stocks were issued to finance the modernisation of the railways. British Transport Stocks comprise 3% 1968–73, 4% 1972–77, and 3% 1978–88. Nationalised industries no longer raise additional capital in this way, but instead borrow direct from the Government. These stocks are guaranteed by the Government, until January 1963 being known as British Transport Guaranteed Stock, and so they rank with gilt-edged securities.

British Travel Association. *See* British Tourist Authority.

British Wagon Co. Ltd. A finance house with its head office in Rotherham and in which the Royal Bank of Scotland has an interest. Its name dates from the time when its main business was the financing of the private ownership of railway wagons, a practice ended by the Transport Act of 1947. It is a member of the Finance Houses Association.

British Waterways Board. The Transport Act of 1947 which nationalised railways, canals, etc. established the British Transport Commission which delegated its powers so far as canals and other inland navigable waterways were concerned to the British Waterways Executive. The Transport Act of 1953, however, brought all nationalised transport under the direct control of the British Transport Commission. The Transport Act of 1963 transferred the functions and property of the British Transport Commission to a number of boards, British waterways coming under the control of the British Waterways Board. *See* Transport Act (1968).

Broker. Generally an agent acting on behalf of a principal, except in the case of the bill broker, who usually acts on his own account. Brokers are found on most markets, both as buyers and sellers. They are employed by other people on account of their knowledge of market conditions and procedure and because of their expert knowledge of the commodity dealt in. Brokers are found on all highly organised markets. In the case of the stock exchange only brokers and jobbers are permitted to do business on the exchange. On the produce exchanges importers employ special brokers to sell the commodities and the buyers may employ independent brokers or their own specialist buyers. Brokers are usually paid commission for their services, known as brokerage, proportionate to the value of the transaction in which they have been engaged. *See also* Insurance Broker; Pawnbroker; Shipbroker.

Brokerage. Commission charged by brokers to clients on whose behalf they have carried out transactions on one of the organised markets.

Brougham Commission (1818). Appointed by the Government to inquire into the state of trusts established for charitable purposes which it was no longer possible to fulfil. Many later inquiries have been made into this problem. Funds can generally be diverted to purposes other than those intended by the benefactors with the consent of the courts.

Brussels Conference (1920). Called to consider the currency chaos after the First World War it recommended that every country having a currency of its own should have a central bank.

B.S. Abbreviation of Bill of Sale (*q.v.*).

B.S.A. Abbreviation of 1. Birmingham Small Arms Co. Ltd.; 2. Building Societies Association (*q.v.*).

B.S.C. Abbreviation of 1. British Steel Corporation (*q.v.*); 2. British Sugar Corporation (*q.v.*).

B.Sc. (Econ.). Bachelor of Science in the Faculty of Economics. Several English universities award this degree. Courses of study usually include a basic group of subjects including economics and economic history, after which students are generally permitted to specialise in some branch of economics, economic history, geography, government, or law.

B.Sc. (Soc.). Bachelor of Science in the Faculty of Sociology or Social Science, a degree offered by the University of London.

B.S.I. Abbreviation of British Standards Institution (*q.v.*).

B.S.O. Abbreviation of Business Statistics Office (*q.v.*).

B.T.A. Abbreviation of British Tourist Authority (*q.v.*).

B.T.C. Abbreviation of British Transport Commission (*q.v.*).

Bubble. A term for excessive speculation in the shares of an unsound company, as a result of which the prices of the shares are pushed up to an extremely high level that bears no relation to their real value. *See* South Sea Bubble.

'Bubble' Act (1720). After the collapse of the South Sea Bubble (*q.v.*) this Act was passed to put difficulties in the way of the formation of joint-stock companies, and aimed at restricting their activities to undertakings where a large amount of capital was required. The Act was repealed in 1825.

Buchanan Report (1963). This report suggested means by which large towns should prepare to deal with the expected future increase in the number of motor vehicles in Great Britain.

'Bucket Shop.' A colloquial term of American origin used in connection with share-pushing (*q.v.*) or speculation in shares.

Budget. An estimate of Government expenditure and revenue for the ensuing financial year, usually presented to Parliament by the Chancellor of the Exchequer early in April each year. Occasionally, in times of financial crisis, interim budgets have been introduced later in the year to increase taxation or reduce expenditure. Occasionally, too, there have been slight modifications of taxation through the Regulator (*q.v.*) at other times without the formality of drawing up a revised budget. During 1949–64 the budget was presented in two parts, one known as 'above-the-line', for ordinary Government expenditure and revenue, and the other 'below-the-line', mainly for items of a capital nature, although this distinction between current and capital items was not precisely maintained. The reason for this division is that the budget has now become an important instrument of economic and monetary policy, and therefore it is necessary to know whether all Government expenditure is covered by revenue. In framing a budget to suit the economic needs of the country at the time the Chancellor of the Exchequer is helped by the publication of a number of White Papers shortly before budget day—the *Economic Survey* (or *Report*), *National Income and Expenditure*, and the *Balance of Payments*. The budget is also used to reduce inequality of personal incomes through steeply progressive income tax. To fight inflation the Chancellor aims at budgeting for a large surplus. To check a trade recession taxation would be reduced and if necessary he might deliberately budget for a deficit.

Budget Account. A system of credit trading operated by some shops, especially department stores, the customer agreeing to pay a certain sum per month which enables credit up to eight times that amount to be obtained. A service charge is levied on all purchases.

Budgetary Control. A business term, it is the checking of the actual results against what had been originally planned.

Budgeting, Personal. The way in which an individual distributes his income and expenditure.

Buffer Stocks. Stocks built up to iron out fluctuations of supply, and therefore of price, in industries producing primary products capable of being stored. Stocks are accumulated when supply is plentiful usually by a Government-sponsored body and released to the market when supply is less plentiful.

Building Societies. Institutions which accept deposits and then use their funds to lend on mortgage to people who wish to buy their own houses. The earliest building societies were terminating societies, a group of people contributing to a fund which was used to purchase houses for them, these activities ceasing when the last member of the group had bought a house. During the nineteenth century permanent societies came to be established, a number of them still retaining the word 'Permanent' in their titles today. These societies are willing to accept deposits from anyone wishing to invest money in this way. By arrangement with the Inland Revenue building societies pay income tax in an agreed lump sum, and so interest on deposits is not subject to ordinary income tax, but where applicable the grossed-up interest is liable to higher rates of income tax. In addition building societies offer paid-up shares which yield a slightly higher rate of interest than deposits, these being more like deposits than shares since they can be withdrawn on notice being given. Most societies also offer subscription shares at a rate of interest slightly higher than that on paid-up shares. Income from these shares also is not liable to income tax. Investment in building societies is, therefore, attractive to people who pay the standard rate of income tax. Rates of interest offered by building societies have to be at a level that will attract sufficient funds for their lending business, and so the rates rise and fall with the prevailing rate of interest, but are not subject to adjustment for every change of bank rate. Most of the lending of building societies is to owner-occupiers of property. Loans are repaid in monthly instalments spread over a period of years. During 1968–70 several building societies began to offer life assurance linked to building society investment.

There has been relatively little amalgamation among building societies, most of them being local institutions, the larger ones having expanded mainly by opening branches. There are a few national societies in Great Britain with branches or agencies throughout the country, the largest being the Halifax and the Abbey National, both of which have expanded both by opening branches and by amalgamation. In 1967 both these societies had assets in excess of £1,000 million—more than double those of the third largest society. The earliest building societies were formed under the Friendly Societies Act of 1829, but existing building societies are incorporated under the Building Societies Act of 1874. A Registrar of Building Societies maintains a general surveillance over building societies, and if he is not satisfied with the way a society is managed he can compel it to cease its activities until its affairs have been investigated. *See also* Financial Intermediaries.

Building Societies Acts. 1. **1834.** This Act extended the Friendly Societies Acts to cover building societies.

2. **1874.** Under this Act building societies became corporate bodies, and a Registrar of Building Societies was to be appointed.

3. **1962.** A consolidating Act, it also laid down further regulations for the operation of building societies.

Building Societies Association. An association which includes in its membership most British building societies, its members pursuing a common policy with regard to rates of interest on mortgages.

Built-in Stabilisers. With reference to the business cycle, a term used for sources of purchasing power which are unaffected by a depression, for example, retirement pensions, a high rate of unemployment pay.

Bulk Buying. Buying in large quantities. This is the normal practice of wholesalers and large-scale retailers. During the Second World War the term was generally taken to mean buying in bulk by the Government.

'Bull.' A speculator on the stock exchange who buys securities in expectation of a rise in their prices. A market is said to be 'bullish' when buyers predominate over sellers.

Bullion. A country's gold reserves may be held in gold coin or bullion. In Great Britain gold bullion is in the form of gold bars each weighing 400 oz.

Bullion Committee (1810). In its report this Committee supported the view that there was an excessive issue of paper money, a view strongly put forward by Ricardo in a series of letters to the *Morning Chronicle*, and by Cobbett in his *Political Register*.

Bullock Report (1976). Set up to inquire into industrial democracy, it recommended that workers should elect representatives to the boards of companies employing more than 2,000 people, although the committee was not unanimous in its recommendations.

Buoyancy. A term applied to the revenue from taxation in an inflationary period. Government expenditure tends to exceed the budget estimate, but because wages and prices have been rising the returns from income tax and value added tax also increase, the revenue then being said to be buoyant.

Burden. The economic effect on the community of taxation or the National Debt. With reference to the National Debt, its total or the annual interest payment can be calculated per head of the population, or as a percentage of the national income. In all these cases, for comparison between one period and another allowance must be made for changes in the value of money. To the extent that the National Debt is an internal debt it does not make a country any poorer, since interest payments are only transfer payments from taxpayers to holders of Government securities and there is certain to be considerable overlapping, the highest taxpayers being most likely to be those holding most Government stock. It is a different matter with that part of the National Debt which is owing to other countries since the interest payments adversely affect the balance of payments.

Burial Society. A type of friendly society established during the eighteenth and nineteenth centuries for the purpose of life assurance, usually on a small scale, to provide a sum of money sufficient to cover the funeral expenses of the deceased where otherwise such an expense might be a serious drain on the resources of a poor family.

Burnham Scales. The salary scales for teachers in England and Wales. They are negotiated by the Burnham Committee, of which Lord Burnham was the first chairman in 1919. The committee comprises representatives of local authorities and of teachers' organisations.

Business Cycle. An American term for the Trade Cycle (*q.v.*).

Business Economics. An old-fashioned term for Commerce as a subject of study.

Business Education Council (BEC). A body set up by the Department of Education and Science to formulate a unified rational system of non-degree courses and examinations for students employed in business and public administration. There are three levels of award with courses starting in 1978—the BEC General Award, the BEC National Award and the BEC Higher National Award. These replaced the former National and Higher National Certificates and Diplomas in Business Education.

Business Enterprise. *See* Firm.

Business Names Registration Act (1916). A person can carry on business in his own name without formality, but if he wishes to use some other name such as, for example, The Astoria Dyeing Company, the name must be registered with the Registrar of Business Names. In such a case the name or names of the persons actually running the business must be given on the firm's notepaper and its commercial documents. *See also* Company Titles.

Business Reply Service. A firm wishing to obtain replies from clients without putting them to the expense of paying postage can supply them with printed reply cards or envelopes or gummed labels which do not require to be stamped. Before a firm can supply such cards to its clients a licence to do so must be obtained from the Post Office, and a sum to cover postage deposited in advance. *See also* Freepost.

Business Savings. The undistributed profits of a limited company or other type of business. *See* Saving.

Business School. A department (usually of a university) for the study of high-level management problems. *See* Franks Report.

Business Statistics Office. A department of the Central Statistical Office responsible for the collection of business statistics.

Business Studies. Under the auspices of the Council for National Academic Awards (*q.v.*) institutions for further education other than universities can offer degree courses in Business Studies. *See* National Certificates and Diplomas in Business Education.

Business Wealth. Capital goods such as factory buildings, raw materials, partly-finished goods, machinery, means of transport. These things all possess the atributes of wealth, although they do not yield satisfaction for their own sake, being wanted merely to assist the production of other forms of wealth.

Butler Act. The Education Act of 1944. *See* Education Acts.

'Butty' System. An example of sub-contracting whereby an employer puts out a certain amount of work to one man (a 'butty') who then engages labour to assist him to accomplish it.

Butut. A unit of the currency of Gambia, 100 Bututs being equal in value to one Dalasi.

Buyers' Market. A condition in a market where demand is low relative to supply, so that prices tend to be low, and therefore to the advantage of buyers. When conditions are changing from boom to recession markets tend to become more favourable to buyers. *See also* Sellers' Market.

Buyer's Surplus. An alternative term for Consumer's Surplus (*q.v.*).

Buying Indent House. A firm which acts as agent for a foreign buyer, it often takes responsibility for payment.

By-product. It is often impossible to produce one product without also producing another. Thus coke is a by-product of gas production. In the case of a very small firm a by-product, produced in very small quantities, may be regarded merely as waste. One of the advantages of large-scale production is that use can be made of such waste, which then becomes a by-product.

C

© Abbreviation of copyright (*q.v.*).

C.A. 1. Designatory initials of a Chartered Accountant (Scotland). See also A.C.A.
2. Abbreviation of Crown Agents (*q.v.*).

Cable and Wireless Act (1946). This Act compulsorily transferred all the shares of Cable and Wireless Ltd. to nominees of the Treasury, thus bringing the activities of the company under State ownership. A new public company, Cable and Wireless (Holdings) Ltd., was formed as an investment trust company.

Cabotage. The carriage of passengers or freight between ports in the same country. *See also* Coasting Trade.

C.A.C. Abbreviation of Central Arbitration Committee, set up under the Employment Protection Act (*q.v.*).

C.A.C.M. Abbreviation of Central American Common Market.

Caisse Nationale de Crédit Agricole. A French bank that provides credit for agriculture. It is the largest bank in France and in 1977 it was the third largest in the world.

Caisse Nationale d'Épargne. The French State savings bank, it is a branch of the Ministry of Posts. The other French savings banks, of which there are 560 with 4,700 branches, are attached to the Ministry of Finance.

Caledonian Canal. A canal, constructed by the State, Telford being the engineer, to link the lochs of the Great Glen and so provide a route for shipping between the east and west coasts of Scotland less hazardous than that round the north of Scotland. It was completed in 1847, but it has never carried much traffic.

Call. When the shares of a limited company are not fully paid at the time of issue the company may call for payment of the amount outstanding or a portion of it, if and when it requires additional capital. *See* Called-up Capital.

Callable Stocks. An American term for fixed interest stocks such as debentures which the company can redeem and re-issue at a lower rate of interest should prevailing interest rates fall.

Called-up Capital. A company with issued capital of £200,000 in £1 shares may perhaps have required shareholders to pay only (say) 10s. (£0·50) for each £1, the balance of 10s. per share remaining as a reserve to be called up later if the company should need it. In such a case the called-up capital would be £100,000.

Call Money. *See* Money at Call and Short Notice.

Call Option. A stock exchange term, it means the right to buy a stated security during a specified future period, generally of three months, at the price ruling at the time the bargain is struck plus an amount between $1\frac{3}{4}\%$ and 2% of that price.

'Calorie' Wages. During the great inflation in Hungary in 1946 workers received, in addition to a basic wage, a supplementary allowance sufficient to purchase food of a value of 14,000 to 16,000 calories per week together with 5,000 calories for each of their dependants.

Cambridge School. The followers of Alfred Marshall, Professor of Economics at the University of Cambridge in the late nineteenth century, who accepted and developed his ideas into a systematic body of economic thought, which still forms the basis of much of modern economic theory.

Canals. It was during the eighteenth century that the British canal system was mainly built up, links being provided between (i) the rivers Thames, Severn, Trent, and Mersey;

(ii) the Lancashire and Yorkshire industrial areas; and (iii) the rivers Clyde and Forth. Eventually one-third of the canals came under the control of the railways, but faced by competition from other means of transport the canal-owners showed a complete lack of any progressive spirit, except the owners of the Manchester Ship Canal, which was not opened until 1894. The Transport Act of 1947, which nationalised inland transport, placed the canals and navigable inland waterways under the control of the British Waterways Executive, but in 1953 they came directly under the control of the Transport Commission. Since 1962 they have been operated by the British Waterways Board. The great drawback to canals is that they provide a very slow means of transport, although at the time of their construction they were regarded as speedy. In hilly districts passage through tiers of locks still further reduces their efficiency. Carriage by water is, however, cheaper than by other means, especially for relatively cheap, bulky goods, such as coal and clay, where speed is of little consequence. Many of the British canals could be used to a much greater extent than they are, and their chief drawback is to be found in the system itself. Another serious drawback is their lack of uniformity of depth, width, and the size of locks. The belief that they were an out-of-date mode of transport gave the companies no stimulus to improve the system.

Canals and Inland Navigations, Royal Commission on (1906). A Commission appointed to look into the condition of the British canals. Its report stressed the lack of progress shown by the canal-owners, and recommended that four main canal routes between the rivers Thames, Severn, Mersey, and Humber should be developed.

C. & f. Abbreviation of cost and freight (*q.v.*).

Canons of Taxation. According to Adam Smith, a good tax system should be based on four principles or canons: (i) the amount of tax to be paid should be proportional to the taxpayer's income; (ii) the amount to be paid should be known and not left, as in the days when taxes were farmed out, to the discretion of the tax collector; (iii) the time for payment of taxes should be as convenient as possible for taxpayers; (iv) taxes should not be imposed where the cost of collection would be excessive.

Capacity. With reference to a firm or industry it means the maximum output it is capable of producing at a given time with its existing stock of factors of production. A firm or industry can increase its capacity up to a point by introducing more modern forms of capital or by varying the proportion in which the factors of production are combined. *See* Excess Capacity.

Capital. One of the factors of production, it has been defined as wealth used in the production of further wealth. All wealth, however, cannot be used in this way. A country may be wealthy in the sense of having many fine buildings, though it may have little of the type of wealth we call capital, which consists of machinery, tools, factory buildings and all kinds of industrial plant, raw materials, partly-finished goods, and means of transport. Some writers regard unsold stocks of consumer's goods, still in the hands of wholesalers and retailers, as capital. Real capital has to be produced, factors of production having to be employed for this purpose, and Karl Marx in *Das Kapital* argued that capital consisted merely of labour that had been employed in the past. The accumulation of modern forms of capital, however, requires the employment of all the factors of production. Land, though clearly a form of wealth that assists production, is regarded by most economists as a separate factor of production. It is useful to be able to refer to the factors of production by name, but the difficulty of composing entirely satisfactory definitions of them is that economically their similarity is more important than their differences.

For business purposes capital generally has to be considered in terms of money. In monetary terms capital can be regarded as the money value of real assets. The capital of a company is the money that has to be raised to purchase the real capital required for starting up the business. In this sense, the word capital is often used as if it were synonymous with money. Any calculation of the capital of a business must be in terms of money, as that is the only measure available for adding together a heterogeneous mass of capital assets. Thus, the capital of a business is taken to be its net worth, that is, the value of its assets less the amount owing to creditors.

Capital Accumulation. *See* Capital Formation.

Capital Budget. At one time it was usual for the budget in most countries to cover mainly items of current revenue and expenditure, so that often there was considerable expenditure, and perhaps also a little revenue, not shown in the budget. During the 1930s many economists were of the opinion that current and capital items should be separated from one another and two budgets compiled, one for current items and one as a capital budget. For many years Sweden has followed this practice. From 1949 to 1964 it was customary in Great Britain for the budget to be divided into two parts, known respectively as 'above-the-line' and 'below-the-line' (*qq.v.*), items of a capital expenditure being shown below the line.

Capital Consumption. If a country fails to make good its capital depreciation, that is, if its output of new capital is insufficient to replace worn-out or out-of-date capital, then its total stock of capital will decline and it will be said to be consuming capital. Clearly, a country cannot permit capital consumption to continue for very long. In a modern state it is most likely to happen in time of war when for a short time a country's efforts may be concentrated on the production of goods to assist the prosecution of the war, the country gambling on winning the war before the consumption of capital reduces production.

Capital Duty. Stamp duty on the share issue of a limited company.

Capital Element. That part of an annuity payment regarded as a repayment of capital and therefore not subject to tax.

Capital Formation. Also known as Capital Accumulation, it means increasing a country's stock of real capital. Since every country possesses only a limited supply of factors of production, to increase the production of capital goods necessitates a smaller production of consumers' goods. Consumers, therefore, are required to sacrifice some present consumption—that is, they are required 'to save'—in order to set free factors of production to make capital goods. In any case, some capital is wearing out all the time and must be replaced if the existing amount of capital is to remain intact. Capital formation, then, requires new capital production to be in excess of the amount required to replace worn-out or out-of-date capital. Economic progress depends on the rate of capital formation, but in the early stages of a country's development capital formation is likely to be slow and will involve considerable sacrifice. A country which is poor in its productive resources will find it extremely difficult to accumulate any capital at all. Once, however, the initial stage of capital formation has been overcome the further accumulation of capital becomes progressively easier, since the more capital a country possesses the easier it is to increase output. This is the economic basis for the more economically advanced countries giving assistance to the under-developed countries.

Capital Gain. The gain when a capital asset—a house or other property or stock exchange securities—is sold at a higher price than was paid for it. Until 1962 (*see* Capital Gains Taxes) capital gains were not taxed in the United Kingdom unless obtained in the ordinary course of business as in the case of jobbers on the stock exchange. There are three types of capital gain: (i) gains arising from the natural growth of a business, the shares of a company increasing in value because the earning power of the company has increased; (ii) gains arising from a fall in the prevailing rate of interest, the prices of many fixed interest securities then rising; (iii) in a period of inflation the money value of real assets may rise in proportion to the fall in the value of money, so that in terms of what the money will buy there is no real change in their value. It would seem inequitable, therefore, to tax capital gains of the third type, though in practice it may not always be possible in the short run to distinguish between the three types.

Capital Gains Tax. First introduced in Great Britain in 1962, it is a tax on the increase in value of a capital asset from 5 April 1965 or the time of its acquisition to its resale. In addition to stock exchange securities other assets liable to tax include land, houses purchased as investments for letting, works of art in excess of £1,000 in value. Since 1969 gilt-edged securities have been exempt from the tax. Liability to tax can be off-set by capital losses, any excess loss being carried forward to future years.

Capital Goods. An alternative name for Producers' Goods, they comprise all goods not wanted for their own sake but only because they assist in the production of other goods.

Capital Intensive. A form of production in which a large amount of capital is employed relative to other factors. *Cf.* Labour Intensive.

Capitalisation Issue. An alternative term for a rights issue (*q.v.*).

Capitalisation of Reserves. A company may decide to use some of its reserves to finance further expansion, thereby increasing the capital of the business. The company will then issue bonus shares to its existing shareholders in proportion to the number of shares already held. *See* Bonus Shares.

Capitalised Value. The value of an asset on its current earnings in relation to the prevailing rate of interest. For example, if the prevailing rate of interest were 5% and the current annual earnings of an asset were £200 its capital value would be twenty times its earnings, that is, £4,000.

Capitalism. A political and economic system where private ownership of real capital is permitted, so that people are generally free to engage in production to meet demand, one of its basic principles being that consumers have freedom of choice. It is alternatively known as free or private enterprise (*qq.v.*). In all countries today the State intervenes to protect the workers and in most also undertakes some economic activity.

Capital Issues Committee. The Borrowing (Control and Guarantee) Act (1946) continued the control of investment instituted during the Second World War. The function of the Committee was to consider applications for raising new capital in excess of £50,000 (reduced to £10,000 in 1956) and to decide whether such an issue was in 'the public interest'. Control of private investment came to an end in 1958.

Capitalistic Production. A method of production where the maximum amount of real capital is employed, the greater the amount of capital the more capitalistic the method of production. The term would, therefore, be equally applicable to a communist as to a capitalist system.

Capital Levy. A tax on privately owned wealth. Though there was some agitation in favour of such a tax during the First World War, a capital levy has never been imposed in this country, though the 'once-for-all' Special Contribution imposed on British industry in 1948 was somewhat similar to a capital levy, as also was the surtax surcharge imposed on 'unearned' incomes in 1968, since at the highest level of income it brought the total tax rate on income to over 100%.

Capital, Marginal Efficiency of. Defined by Lord Keynes in his *General Theory of Employment, Interest and Money*, published in 1935, as 'the relation between the prospective yield of one more unit of a type of capital and the cost of producing that unit'.

Capital Market. In contrast to the money market, which is the market for very short-term loans, the capital market is the market for medium-term and long-term loans. The money market, too, serves the needs of the discount market, whereas the capital market serves the need of industry and commerce, Governments and local authorities. Business firms often borrow their circulating capital from the commercial banks, but raise their fixed capital by an issue of shares or from their own reserves, the shares being taken up by individuals, insurance companies, investment trusts and unit trusts. Limited companies also go to the capital market to borrow by means of debentures, the Government, or a local authority, by the issue of a new stock. Most stocks are redeemable at a specified future date—ten, fifty, or more years ahead. A few Government stocks are perpetual, that is, they have no date for redemption, and some others are redeemable *after* a certain date, which in practice may turn these also into perpetual stock.

Capital Movements. A term used in connection with the movement of capital from one country to another. Such movements are of two kinds: (i) for the purpose of investing abroad, and (ii) speculative short-term capital movements. When capital is *exported* for foreign investment it has the same effect on the balance of payments of the country it leaves as payment for *imports* of goods or services, but interest and dividends paid on such investment provide 'invisible' income to the country from which the capital was exported. The aim of short-term capital movements may be to obtain a higher rate of interest or to safeguard the capital from currency depreciation. The great objection to these short-term capital movements is that capital is withdrawn from a country whenever that country is faced with difficulties with its balance of payments, thereby aggravating the situation. Such short-term capital is often described as 'hot money' or 'refugee capital'. After the balance of payments on current account has been calculated, capital movements must be allowed for to obtain the balance of payments on current and capital account. *See* Balance of Payments.

Capital of a Company. The feature of a company is that its capital is divided into stock or shares. These may consist entirely of ordinary shares (*q.v.*) or partly of ordinary shares and partly of deferred (*q.v.*) or preference shares (*q.v.*), of which there are several types. In addition the company may have borrowed from the capital market by issuing debentures. In such a case the interest due on the debentures will be paid before any distribution is made to shareholders. The amount due on the preference shares will next be paid, and what is left will be distributed among the ordinary shareholders, except for any sum put into reserve. The amount received by the ordinary shareholders will vary according to the amount of profit earned by the company. *See* Authorised Capital; Issued Capital; Paid-up Capital.

Capital Owned. This is the excess value of the assets of a business over the value of its liabilities.

Capital-saving Inventions. New inventions can be classified as labour-saving or capital-saving, the former causing some frictional unemployment, whereas the latter, being a substitution of one kind of real capital for another, would not have this effect on the demand for labour. Most new inventions, however, have some labour-saving effect, very few being entirely capital-saving.

Capital Transfers. *See* Capital Movements.

Capital Transfer Tax. Introduced in 1974 to replace Estate Duty, it covers gifts made during the taxpayer's lifetime as well as those made at death. The tax is on a graded scale, gifts up to £15,000 being exempt, the rate of tax after that varying from 10% to 75%. All gifts between husband and wife, during their lifetime or at death, are exempt.

Capitation Tax. Similar to a poll tax, a certain sum per head having to be paid. *See* Poll Tax.

Cardwell's Act (1854). This Act (i) forbade a railway to give one customer preference over another; (ii) ordered the railways to provide facilities for through traffic. Restrictions on the further building of wide gauge lines had been imposed in 1846, but it was not until 1868 that the Great Western Railway (*q.v.*) began to convert its wide gauge to the 'standard' gauge.

Carey Street. The former address of the office of the Official Receiver (*q.v.*). The phrase, *To be in Carey Street*, therefore means *To go bankrupt*.

Car Ferries. These are available for the crossing of many rivers where tunnels or bridges have not been constructed. Larger car ferries now operate across narrow stretches of the sea such as the English Channel, the Adriatic, and between Denmark, Germany, Sweden, and Norway.

Cargo Liners. Liners carrying goods which ply regularly between two ports according to a pre-arranged time-table.

Carifta. An acronym for Caribbean Free Trade Area, it includes Jamaica and some other islands of the West Indies.

Carr. Fwd. (or Cd. Fwd.). Abbreviation of Carriage Forward (*q.v.*).

Carriage Forward. A price quotation for goods which does not include carriage, which will have to be paid for by the person to whom the goods are consigned.

Carrier's Risk. An alternative term for Company's Risk (*q.v.*).

Carrying Cost. A term used by Lord Keynes and others. It refers to the fact that assets, other than money, decline in value with the passage of time, and this is their carrying cost.

Carrying Trade. In connection with world trade, this refers to the share of the total carriage of goods enjoyed by a country's shipping, and this can be greater or less than that country's own share of world trade. In the sixteenth and seventeenth centuries countries often attempted to limit the carriage of imports to their own ships or those of the country from which the goods had been exported. Some countries, however, possess advantages as carriers which others lack. Both Great Britain and the Netherlands have enjoyed a large share of the world's carrying trade, Great Britain's share at one time during the nineteenth century reaching as much as 80% of the world total. Revenue from this trade is a valuable 'invisible' export and, therefore, of great advantage to a country's balance of payments. The two World Wars not only restricted Great Britain's share of the carrying trade but also stimulated the building of merchant shipping by other countries unable to have the use of British ships at those times. Since 1914 Great Britain's share of the carrying trade of the world has declined to little more than 25%, although the tonnage of British merchant shipping has increased. Not only are there more nations engaged in the carrying trade today than ever before, but in addition there has been a huge expansion in air freight traffic. There has too been a very considerable increase in the number of ships flying 'flags of convenience,' that is, ships registered in countries where taxation is less onerous than elsewhere. As a result of these developments shipping services no longer provide Great Britain with as substantial an 'invisible' export they formerly did.

Carry-over. A stock exchange term, it refers to carrying over, that is, postponing settlement until the next stock exchange account. *See* Contango.

Carte Bleu. A French credit card linked with Barclaycard. *See* Credit Card.

Carte d'Or. A French credit card.

Cartel. A monopolistic type of organisation of German origin established originally for the purpose of restricting the output of member firms in order to keep up the price of their product. The cartel first made its appearance in the Ruhr. A central selling organisation is established, the member firms, however, retaining their independence, except in so far as they agree to restrict their output. In the German cartels a code of rules was drawn up and the member firms agreed to abide by them, fines being imposed on those who broke them. Voluntary cartels are likely to break up in the long run as their policy is not permanently to the advantage of the more efficient firms. The British agricultural marketing boards (*q.v.*) are cartels compulsorily established by the State when a majority of the producers of a commodity desire one, but their policy has not generally been to restrict output, though there has always been restriction on the entry of new producers.

Cascade. A term used of some turnover tax systems. Cascade (or Cumulative) taxes are assessed on the total value of an article each time it is the object of a commercial transaction. *Cf.* Value-added Tax.

Case Study. A technique used mainly in courses on management. The students are given details of problems that might be met with in actual business conditions for study, followed by discussions on how these problems might be tackled.

Cash. Strictly, money in the form of bank-notes and coin. A bank regards as cash its balance at the Bank of England since withdrawals in cash can be made from it at any time. Similarly, a business firm regards its balance at the bank as cash. *See* Money.

Cash Bond. The use of this type of bond—Bon de Caisse or Kassa-obligation—is a feature of Swiss banking and they are also used in some other European countries. Issued in denominations of 500, 1,000, and 5,000 Swiss francs, they are for periods of from two to ten years, bearing interest slightly higher than the rate paid on ordinary deposits.

Cash Deposits Scheme. A scheme agreed in 1968 between the Bank of England and the non-clearing banks as an alternative to Special Deposits (*q.v.*) which were not regarded as being appropriate to banks as diverse as these as a means of controlling their credit policy. When requested to do so, these banks will make cash deposits with the Bank of England calculated as a percentage of their sterling deposit liabilities.

Cash Discount. A deduction from a price charged if payment is made before a certain date—an inducement to pay promptly offered especially by wholesalers to retailers.

Cash Dispenser. A mechanical means for supplying cash used in some hotels, airports, railway stations, as well as banks. To obtain cash a customer of the bank inserts a plastic card with his personal code and receives the required cash immediately. It is essentially a labour-saving device. *See also* Auto-Teller; Cashpoint.

Cash Flow. The total of the retained profits of a business after tax, together with the amount set apart for depreciation is known as the *net cash flow*.

Cash on Delivery (C.O.D.). A service provided by the Post Office to assist mail-order business, the purchaser paying the postman who delivers the goods.

Cashpoint. A cash dispenser which permits customers of a bank to withdraw sums from their accounts, usually in one pound or five pound

Bank of England notes, on the insertion of a card and after dialling the card number and the amount of money required. *See also* Auto-Teller; Cash Dispenser.

Cash Ratio. The relation between a bank's reserve of cash and its total deposits. Since a bank must always be able to pay cash on demand to those of its customers entitled to ask for it, a certain amount of cash has to be held for this purpose. The greater the extent to which people make payments in cash the greater the cash reserve required; the greater the use made of cheques as means of payment the smaller the cash reserve required. With the development of banking bankers learned from experience how much cash they required to meet ordinary demands on them, no bank being able to withstand a run on it whether rumours regarding its soundness were justified or not. British bankers in general have if anything erred well on the side of safety. In the early days of banking a fairly large cash reserve would be necessary, but by the beginning of this century it had become an accepted principle of British banking that a cash ratio of 10% was sound policy. The English commercial banks have always regarded as cash, in addition to the amount in the tills of their branches, their balances at the Bank of England, and although these are simply book entries, they are justified in doing so, since withdrawals from these balances can always be made in cash. Between the two World Wars the English banks found that a cash ratio of 8% gave them an ample margin of safety, and although they continued to show a ratio of 10% in their monthly statements and half-yearly balance sheets, by means of a practice generally known as 'window-dressing' (*q.v.*), between times they maintained a ratio of only 8%. Shortly after its nationalisation in 1946 the Bank of England recommended that the commercial banks should desist from this practice, and this advice was followed. In contrast to some other countries, there is no legal cash ratio imposed on British banks. Nevertheless in evidence before the Radcliffe Committee it was stated that the Bank of England would insist if necessary on the present cash ratio being maintained. In the United States the cash ratio varies between different cities and also between demand (current account) and time (deposit account) deposits. Also the Federal Reserve authorities have power to vary these cash ratios whenever they think such a course necessary.

The maintenance of a known cash ratio is of vital importance to control by the central bank of the credit policy of the commercial banks. By means of open-market operations the central bank can reduce or increase the cash reserves of the commercial banks, and this then affects the cash ratio of these banks, compelling them, in the case of a reduction, to curtail their lending in order to reduce their deposits so that their cash ratio can be maintained. Perhaps more important than the cash ratio, however, is the second liquidity rule of the banks—to keep liquid assets to a value of 28% of their total. If the cash ratio falls below 8% it is fairly easily restored by the banks' calling in some of their loans to the money market, but this would not restore the liquid assets to the required 28% level. To maintain the 28% ratio requires more drastic action—the curtailment of a bank's lending. In 1971 the Bank of England proposed that the commercial banks should maintain a ratio of $12\frac{1}{2}\%$ between the total of their cash, money at call, Treasury bills, some commercial bills and Government stocks within one year of maturity and their total assets.

Casual Labour. The employment of workers for a brief period. Employment at docks was formerly on these terms, the number of workers employed each day depending on the amount of work available, the men having to turn up each morning to see whether there was work for them. In these circumstances there was a tendency for the number of workers generally to exceed the demand for them, the supply of labour being sufficient to cope with periods of peak activity. This was an important cause of unemployment, and in his policy for full employment Lord Beveridge stressed that labour should not be employed on these terms. Since then the conditions of employment for most dock workers in Great Britain have been greatly improved, most of them now receiving a guaranteed minimum payment. *See* Devlin Report.

Cattle. At one time used as money. The earliest forms of money were always things which were regarded as being valuable for their own sake, and which, therefore, were generally acceptable. At one time in some countries—for example, Greece in the time of Homer, and among the Anglo-Saxons—cattle served this purpose. Obvious drawbacks to cattle as money were: (i) lack of divisibility for small payments; (ii) lack of homogeneity; (iii) lack of durability; (iv) lack of easy portability. *See* Commodity Money.

Caveat Emptor. A Latin legal term, meaning literally 'Let the buyer beware.' When making a purchase it is up to the buyer to examine what he is buying and make sure that it is of the standard required for his purpose. Nevertheless, the Sale of Goods Act (1893), the Trade Descriptions Acts (1968 and 1972) and the Supply of Goods (Implied Terms) Act (1973) protect the buyer against wrongful representation, such as a salesman asserting that an article is new when in fact it is not.

C.B.I. Abbreviation of Confederation of British Industry (*q.v.*).

Cd. *See* Cmnd.

C.d. Abbreviation of Cum. Div. (*q.v.*).

C/d. Abbreviation of Carried Down.

C.D.C. Abbreviation of Commonwealth Development Corporation (*q.v.*).

Cedel. One of the clearing systems for Eurobonds, the other being Euroclear (*q.v.*).

Cedi. The standard unit of the currency of Ghana, it is subdivided into 100 pesewa.

Ceiling Prices. Maximum prices imposed under a system of price control.

Census. To take a count of something. 1. *Population*. With the exception of the year 1941, a census of the population of the United Kingdom has been taken every tenth year since 1801. It has been proposed that (from 1966) a census should be taken every five years. Estimates of the population are also made twice each year. It is of great economic importance to know (i) the rate at which the total population is increasing; (ii) what changes (if any) are taking place in the distribution of population between the different age groups.

2. *Production*. On a number of occasions the Board of Trade has undertaken a Census of Production for this country. This shows the output of each industry—the quantity of coal, steel, wheat, barley, potatoes, sugar beet, milk, motor vehicles, boots and shoes, cotton cloth, woollen cloth, chemicals, etc.

3. *Distribution*. In 1951, 1957, 1961, 1966 and 1971 the Board of Trade undertook a Census of Distribution. Not only do these show the number of shops in each branch of retail trade—the number of grocers, butchers, confectioners, chemists, etc.—and the shares of retailing enjoyed by multiple shops, department stores, co-operative societies, and sole traders, but also the value of their turnover and their profit margins.

Cent. From Latin *centum*, one hundred. In countries which have adopted a decimal coinage the standard unit of the currency is divided into 100 units known by various names indicating a fraction of one-hundredth—cent in the United States, Canada, Australia, New Zealand, Bermuda, the Bahamas, Hong Kong, and other countries which use the dollar, centime in France, Belgium and Switzerland, centimos in Spain, centesimi in Italy, centavos in Portugal, Brazil and most other countries in Latin America, and centesimos in Chile.

Central African Customs and Economic Union (U.D.E.A.C.). This union developed out of the Equatorial Customs Union (*q.v.*) in order to carry co-ordination further by harmonisation of the members' tax and investment policies, with free movement of labour between them. Membership is open to all independent African states.

Central Bank. The principal function of a central bank is to carry out the monetary policy of a country, and this requires that it should work closely with the Government and must have some means of controlling the commercial banks. Many central banks, like those of Great Britain and France, are nationalised institutions, but even where the central bank has not been nationalised it must work with the State.

Few countries today are without central banks, though this is a fairly recent development. The Bank of England began to take to itself some of the functions of a central bank, such as acting as lender of last resort, about the middle of the nineteenth century. The Federal Reserve System, which undertakes central banking in the United States, was established in 1913. Both France and Germany also had central banks in the nineteenth century, but Canada did not have one until 1935. The acceptance by Governments of responsibility for the maintenance of full employment has made it more than ever necessary for a Government to have some measure of control over monetary policy. It is now generally agreed that complete independence of a central bank is undesirable.

When Great Britain was on the gold standard down to 1914 it was easier for the Bank of England to carry out its central banking functions as a private institution. Things became more difficult between the two Wars and during this period the Bank of England and the Chancellor of the Exchequer developed a habit of regular consultation. Since 1945 Government responsibility for economic affairs has led to a closer partnership between the Bank and the Government, with the Government as the senior partner. The introduction of new non-banking instruments of monetary policy has lessened the importance of the central bank, which in many countries today can be regarded as only one of the agents for carrying out a Government's policy. In addition to its control over the credit policy of the commercial banks and acting as lender of the last resort it is desirable that a central bank should act as banker to the Government, holding the Government's account and managing the National Debt, but it is not thought advisable for a central bank to compete with the commercial banks and, therefore, it should not engage in ordinary banking business, though the Bank of France with over 250 branches does so. *See* Bank of England.

Central Bank Co-operation. Co-operation between central banks has been traditional since the days of the gold standard. Between the two World Wars the central banks of Great Britain, France, and the United States frequently helped one another in times of difficulty. The Bank for International Settlements (*q.v.*) at Basle was established, not only to deal with the problem of reparation payments, but also to provide an institution with facilities for European central bankers to meet to consider some of the problems with which they were faced. When the European Payments Union was set up procedure was worked out by the central banks of the countries concerned and the B.I.S. became banker to the Union. Since 1945 there have been many examples of co-operation between central banks, perhaps one of the most important occasions being the one resulting in the Basle Arrangements (*q.v.*). It was largely due to American influence, where there is still an important anti-banking interest, that the International Monetary Fund, unlike the B.I.S., has not been operated by central banks.

Central Bank of Central Banks. A term sometimes used of the Bank for International Settlements (B.I.S.) (*q.v.*).

Central Electricity Board. A public corporation established in 1927 by the Electricity (Supply) Act to co-ordinate the supply of electricity in Great Britain at a time when the generation of electricity was in the hands of a large number of relatively small producers. The Board was responsible for the establishment of the 'grid' system which linked together the more efficient plants, as a result of which it became possible when necessary to spread the load, but distribution was left in private hands. Production was concentrated at a number of conveniently situated, modern power plants. On the nationalisation of the industry in 1948 its functions were taken over by the British Electricity Authority, as it was then called.

Central Electricity Generating Board. In 1948 the electricity generating industry was nationalised under the control of a body known as the British Electricity Authority, the name later being changed to Central Electricity Authority. The Central Electricity Generating Board is responsible for the production of electricity in Great Britain.

Central Health Services Council. A body established under the National Health Service Act (1946) to advise the Minister of Health on matters connected with the National Health Service.

Central Office of Information. A Government department under the administrative control of the Treasury which supplies information and undertakes publicity for other departments by means of films, leaflets, exhibitions, etc. It also organises schemes for the sales of books in developing territories of the Commonwealth.

Central Planning. The determination by the State of what shall be produced, the State allocating factors of production among different employments accordingly, in contrast to free enterprise where consumers through their demand mainly decide what shall be produced. Under a communist system there is the maximum amount of central planning, but in all countries, especially since Governments accepted responsibility for the maintenance of full employment, the amount of central planning has tended to increase. This is true even of countries like Great Britain and the United States that are most inclined to free enterprise. In 1962, for example, Great Britain set up a National Economic Development Council (*q.v.*) to assist and advise the Government on the planning of production.

Central Statistical Office. A Government department established to centralise a good deal of the statistical work of other departments.

Certificate in Secondary Education. An examination instituted in 1965 for pupils aged about 16 in England and Wales.

Certificate of Deposit. A negotiable instrument issued in London, first in terms of U.S. dollars in 1966 and then in 1968 in sterling. *See* Sterling Certificates of Deposit.

Certificate of Incorporation. When a new limited company is in process of formation, and all the formalities have been complied with to the satisfaction of the Registrar of Companies, he will issue a Certificate of Incorporation, which in effect gives the company legal existence.

Certificate of Origin. A document signed by a customs officer of the exporting country to show from which country the goods have been exported. This document is of particular importance when the importing country has a preferential tariff applicable only to certain countries.

Certificate of Posting. For a nominal fee the Post Office will give a certificate to prove that an unregistered letter or postal packet has been posted at a particular post office.

Certificate of Pratique. A document issued by the British customs authorities to a ship from overseas which has entered a British port and been inspected by an official of the Customs Waterguard Service, the ship then being allowed to proceed.

Certificate of Tax Deposit. Introduced in 1975 as a successor to Tax Reserve Certificates (*q.v.*) which were withdrawn in 1973.

Certified Accountant. A member of the Association of Certified Accountants who has passed the qualifying examinations (A.C.C.A.). *See also* Chartered Accountant.

C.E.T. Abbreviation of Common External Tariff (*q.v.*).

Ceteris Paribus. Latin for 'Other things being equal.' This is one of the assumptions most frequently made in economic theory, in order to study a particular aspect of a problem with all other disturbing influences removed.

C.F. Abbreviation of Compensation Fee. *See* Compensation Fee Parcels.

C/f. Abbreviation of Carried Forward, a balance in a statement or ledger carried forward to the next page. *Cf.* B/f.

C.G.T. 1. Abbreviation of Capital Gains Tax (*q.v.*).
2. Abbreviation of Confédération Générale du Travail (*q.v.*).

Chain Stores. A term mainly used in the United States, though perhaps increasingly used also in Great Britain, for Multiple Shops (*q.v.*).

Chamberlain Act (1923). A Housing Act promoted by Neville Chamberlain to subsidise houses built by private enterprise down to October 1925. If they wished, local authorities could reduce rents by a further subsidy from the rates. It was modified by the Wheatley Act (1924).

Chamber of Commerce. Almost every industrial town in Great Britain has a Chamber of Commerce, a body established to represent local industry and guard its interests. The members are manufacturers and merchants. Their interests are nationally represented by the Association of British Chambers of Commerce. The largest British Chamber of Commerce is the London Chamber of Commerce, which also acts as an examining body in commercial subjects. Chambers of Commerce are also to be found in many other countries. *See also* Junior Chamber of Commerce.

Chamber of Shipping. A body representing British ship-owners' associations.

Chamber of Trade. A body representing the retail traders of a locality, established to watch their interests and to enable them to discuss problems of common interest.

Chancellor of the Exchequer. Cabinet minister responsible for carrying out the country's monetary policy. Not only is he now responsible for presenting the budget statement to Parliament, but since the Government accepted responsibility for the maintenance of full employment, in co-operation with the Treasury and the Bank of England he is responsible for all aspects of monetary policy affecting problems such as inflation and the level of employment. No change in bank rate occurs nowadays without his prior agreement though its announcement is left to the Bank of England. Nor would the Bank of England call for or release Special Deposits unless at his request. When the Treasury directive was employed the Chancellor of the Exchequer in effect issued direct instructions to the commercial banks regarding their lending policy, but in general his direct influence is now restricted to taxation changes.

Changes in Demand. A change in demand occurs when a greater or smaller quantity of a commodity or service is demanded without any change in price having taken place. It should not be confused, therefore, with different quantities being demanded at different prices, which is the usual condition of demand, merely indicating movement up and down the *same* demand curve, whereas a change in demand requires a *new* demand curve over at least part of a range of prices. The following are some of the main causes of change in demand: (i) change of taste or fashion; (ii) more up-to-date commodities coming on to the market and replacing older things; (iii) changes in the amount of money in a country; (iv) changes in real incomes; (v) changes in the distribution of income between different groups of people; (vi) population changes, which may bring about a change in the distribution between the various age groups; (vii) changes in the prices of other goods, since the demand for all things is to some extent competitive, though this will have greater effect where the goods are close substitutes for one another; (viii) expectations of the future trend of trade will have a great effect on the demand for producers' goods; (ix) expectations of future changes of prices, demand tending to increase if prices are expected to rise; (x) taxation changes.

Changes in Supply. A change in supply occurs when a greater or smaller quantity of a commodity or service is supplied without any change having taken place in the market price of the commodity. Without any change in the condition of supply more of a good will be supplied the higher its market price, this being nothing more than the usual condition of supply, as the typical supply curve shows. A change of supply requires a new supply curve over at least a portion of a range of prices. Some of the principal causes of change of supply are: (i) changes in the technique of production; (ii) changes in the cost of production; (iii) effects of the weather in the case of agricultural commodities; (iv) taxation, either by means of a purchase tax, which is equivalent to an increase in cost, or by a profits tax, which increases the risk inherent in production.

Changes in the Value of Money. *See* Value of Money.

Channel Tunnel. For a long time there has been agitation for a tunnel under the English Channel between Kent and North France. Plans for such a tunnel were rejected on strategic grounds, but in 1963 it was decided that a Channel tunnel should be built. In 1968 the British and French Governments appointed a banking consortium to build the tunnel. New developments in transport—drive-on ferries, container ships, hovercraft, larger aircraft—led an increasing number of people to believe that the tunnel was no longer necessary, and in 1975 it was indefinitely postponed.

Chapman. An old term for pedlar (*q.v.*).

Charge. When a farmer borrows from a bank he may offer as security for a loan what is known as a charge on his agricultural assets, including livestock. This may be either a fixed charge or a floating charge (*q.v.*).

Charge Account. An American term for a Monthly Account (*q.v.*).

Charging What the Traffic Will Bear. A form of differential charges arising out of conditions where some degree of monopoly exists. It can take several forms. It is best known as the basis of railway charges when a higher rate is charged for the carriage of more expensive goods than for the carriage of cheaper things. *See* Discriminating Monopoly.

Charity Commissioners. A permanent body set up under the Charitable Trust Act (1853) and mainly concerned with ensuring that charitable trusts are devoted to the purposes the testators desired, and to sanction modifications suggested by the trustees in cases where it is no longer possible to carry out the original intentions of the testators.

CHARTAC. Abbreviation of Chartered Accountant (*q.v.*).

Chartered Accountant. A member of the Institute of Chartered Accountants in England and Wales (I.C.A.E.W.) or of the Institute of Chartered Accountants of Scotland (I.C.A.S.) who has qualified in accountancy and auditing as a result of (i) serving a specified period articled to a qualified member of the appropriate Institute, and (ii) passing the required examinations. Members of the English Institute comprise Associates (A.C.A.) and Fellows (F.C.A.). The designatory initials of a member of the Scottish Institute are C.A. Since 1968 the Institute of Chartered Accountants in England and Wales has been working in close cooperation with the Institute of Municipal Treasurers and Accountants, the Association of Certified Accountants and the Institute of Cost and Management Accountants (*q.q.v.*)

Chartered Bank. *See* Standard Chartered Bank.

Chartered Companies. The earliest companies to be established in Great Britain received royal charters granting them certain specified rights and privileges of trade. Chartered companies of this type were the Hudson's Bay Company and the British East India Company, and at a later period the British East Africa Company. Such companies were often the forerunners of British politicial rule over the areas concerned.

Chartered Insurance Institute. A professional body established 'to provide and maintain a central organisation for the promotion of efficiency, progress, and general development among persons engaged or employed in insurance'. Its members comprise Associates (A.C.I.I.) and Fellows (F.C.I.I.), admission to both grades of membership being by examination. The Institute itself provides postal tuition, both for its own examinations and for general courses. It also supports a College of Insurance. It publishes a journal.

Chartered Municipal Treasurer. The title of an Associate or Fellow of the Institute of Municipal Treasurers and Accountants (*q.v.*).

Charter Party. A contract by which a ship or aircraft is temporarily leased by the owners to another person or firm who is said then to have chartered it. The period may be for a definite journey or a definite period of time. A ship may be chartered for the carriage of cargo or for the carriage of passengers.

Chartism. A movement, mainly supported by working men, taking its name from the People's Charter, drawn up in 1838. This charter set forth their aims which were to secure political power for working men, as this was regarded as an essential prerequisite to an improvement in their standard of living. Only a few of the Chartists wished to resort to physical force, the majority favouring constitutional action. They offered no support to the Anti-Corn Law League, which was active about the same time, as they thought that cheap bread—the aim of the League—would merely result in lower wages, thereby bringing no benefit to them. The Corn Laws were repealed in 1846 and the great Chartist demonstration, planned for 1848, turned out to be a fiasco, after which the movement rapidly declined.

'Chartist.' A colloquial term of American origin for a person who makes use of graphs of economic trends to forecast future price trends of stock exchange securities.

Chase Manhattan Bank. The third largest commercial bank in the United States and in 1977 fourth largest in the world with its head office and 150 branches in New York, it has branches throughout the world. It has an interest in the Standard Bank (*q.v.*), and several of banks in South America and Belgium are affiliated to it, including the Banque de Commerce d'Anvers (*q.v.*).

Chattels. *See* Property.

Cheap Jack. A term used of an itinerant salesman who sells his wares at very low prices—usually because they are of poor quality.

Cheap Money. A term used to describe a situation where bank rate and other rates of interest are low. A policy of cheap money may be adopted in a time of industrial depression to try to stimulate recovery. After 1932 Great Britain adopted such a policy and continued it during the Second World War to enable the Government to borrow more cheaply. In the totally different circumstances of inflation after 1945 it was pursued in an extreme form until 1951 in the belief that bank rate is not an effective instrument of policy and so, in the interests of institutional borrowers like the Government and local authorities, it was felt that it should be kept as low as possible. The ultra-cheap money policy came to an end in 1947 with the failure of the issue of the unredeemable $2\frac{1}{2}\%$ Treasury Stock. The maintenance of a cheap money policy after 1945 required constant intervention in the market by the Government broker.

Cheap Trains Act (1844). This Act compelled British railway companies to run at least one train per day each way on every line with enclosed accommodation for third-class passengers who were to be carried at a rate of not more than one penny per mile.

Checkweighman. When coalminers are paid piece rates their union is permitted to appoint a checkweighman to ensure that the worker is credited with the full amount of work to which he is entitled.

Cheque. The Bills of Exchange Act of 1882 defines a cheque as 'a bill of exchange drawn on a banker payable on demand'. It is an order, written by the drawer, to a banker to pay on demand a specified sum of money to the person or persons named as payee on the cheque. Since February 1971 cheques have been exempt from stamp duty. In order to be able to draw a cheque the drawer must maintain a current account with the bank on which his cheques are to be drawn. The drawer completes the cheque by inserting the name of the payee, the amount he is to be paid, and then dating and signing it. The cheque may be made payable to the payee or order, or to the payee or bearer. It may be either open or crossed. If it is open it can be cashed at the branch of the bank on which it has been drawn, but if it has been crossed it must be paid into a banking account. In the case of a bearer cheque no endorsement is required, but endorsement of an order cheque is required unless it is paid directly into the payee's own account. By endorsing an order cheque the payee can renounce his interest in it and use it to pay a debt of his own to another person. Restrictions can be placed on the negotiability of cheques by means of special crossings (*q.v.*). The cheque has almost ousted the inland bill of exchange. The increased use of cheques and the advantages they give to banks in the creation of credit has easily compensated the English commercial banks for their loss of the right to issue bank-notes. *See* Cheques Act (1957).

Cheque Card. Also known as a Banker's Card, it is issued by several British banks. These cards permit the holders to cash personal cheques for sums up to £50 at any one of the branches or a specified bank or group of banks or to make payments by cheque, the issuing bank guaranteeing to meet cheques up to this amount. The card contains a specimen signature of the holder who must sign his cheque in the presence of the payee. The Cheque Card is a useful alternative to the Credit Card (*q.v.*) for small amounts for people not requiring credit.

Cheques Act (1957). Previous to this Act all order cheques had to be endorsed. This Act made it no longer necessary to endorse an order cheque if it was paid directly into the payee's own account. This Act also stated that a cheque was proof of payment of a debt, and as a result many firms have ceased to issue receipts for payments made by cheque, though a receipt must always be supplied if requested. This was often quite wrongly taken to mean that when such a receipt was supplied on request it no longer required a twopenny stamp for amounts of £2 or over. However, stamp duty on cheques has now been abolished and is no longer payable.

Chicago School. A group of writers on economics attached to the University of Chicago, their leader being Prof. Friedmann, and their followers. They attach great importance to the money supply as an influence on inflation.

Child Benefit. *See* Family Allowances.

Children and Young Persons Act (1933). An Act restricting the employment of children. With certain minor exceptions no child under the age of thirteen was to be employed at all. Children of school age were not to be employed during school hours in term time, nor earlier than 6 a.m. or after 8 p.m., nor for more than two hours on school days or Sundays.

Children and Young Persons Act (1963). This Act raised the age of criminal responsibility in the case of children from 8 to 10 years of age.

Children, Employment of. The employment of children is restricted by the Children and Young Persons Act (1933) (*q.v.*).

Chose in Action. A legal term, it refers to the ownership of a right as distinct from ownership of a thing, as, for example, performing rights in gramophone records or patent rights. *See also* Chose in Possession.

Chose in Possession. A legal term, it refers to the ownership of actual goods and chattels as distinct from the ownership of a right. *See also* Chose in Action.

Christie's. A London auction especially renowned for the sale of works of art—paintings, jewellery, and *objets d'art* generally.

Christmas Club. *See* Club Trading.

C.i.f. Abbreviation of Cost, insurance and freight (*q.v.*).

Cigarettes as Money. Not only did commodities serve as the earliest acceptable media of exchange but their use as money has been revived in more recent times: (i) when there has been a shortage of conventional money, as among the early settlers in Virginia when tobacco served this purpose; (ii) when inflation or a complete breakdown of an economic system has occurred, as in Germany after its defeat in 1945 when cigarettes for a time served as money. *See* Commodity Money.

C.I.O. Abbreviation of Congress of Industrial Organisations, merged in 1955 with the American Federation of Labor (*q.v.*).

C.I.P.F.A. Abbreviation of Chartered Institute of Public Finance and Accounting, formerly Institute of Municipal Treasurers and Accountants (*q.v.*).

Circular Letter of Credit. These are issued by banks for the use of people who intend to travel abroad, and therefore in some ways they are similar to travellers' cheques, except that travellers' cheques are issued in relatively small denominations between £5 and £50, whereas a Circular Letter of Credit covers one large sum, usually up to a maximum of £5,000. A Letter of Credit is an instruction to a bank's agents abroad authorising them to honour 'sight' drafts drawn on the issuing bank up to a certain amount stated in the Letter. As with travellers' cheques the customer pays the full amount when the Letter is issued to him. The amounts as drawn are entered on the reverse side of the Letter. For greater safety the customer is also given a Letter of Indication, on which he has previously given a specimen of his signature, which has to be produced whenever payment is required from a foreign bank.

Circulating Capital. Also known as Working or Floating Capital, the circulating capital of a retail business comprises the stock, cash in hand and any debts owing to it. Where the rate of turnover is rapid, as in greengrocery, the amount of circulating capital required will be small, but where the rate of turnover is slow, as in the case of a jeweller or furniture dealer, a large amount of circulating capital will be required. A retailer who grants credit or who himself finances hire purchase transactions for his customers will require much more circulating capital than a retailer who sells only for cash. The circulating capital of a manufacturing business will comprise mainly raw materials, work in progress (partly finished goods) and cash in hand.

Circulation. *See* Currency Circulation; Velocity of Circulation.

Citibank. Popular name of the First National City Bank of New York (*q.v.*).

City. A generic term for the various financial institutions of the City of London—the Bank of England, the head offices of the commercial banks, the merchant banks, branches of many foreign banks, discount houses, the stock exchange, insurance companies, etc., Lloyds, the gold and foreign exchange markets, commodity markets, etc.—all situated within a single square mile. The financial services provided by the 'City' for foreign customers are an important source of 'invisible' income to the British balance of payments.

Civil Aeronautics Board. A U.S. body representing American airlines, it negotiates with the owners of other international airlines such matters as fares, etc.

Civil Aviation Act (1971). This Act set up (1) the Civil Aviation Authority to control civil aviation in the U.K. and (2) an Airways Board to manage B.E.A. and B.O.A.C.

Civil Service Commission. A Government body which since 1855 has been responsible for examining candidates seeking appointments in the British Civil Service. Though retaining its independence it now forms part of the Civil Service Department, established 1968.

Civil Votes. A term used in the budget statement for one of the main groups of items of Government ordinary expenditure. It covers estimated expenditure on education, pensions, the health service, and other social services and also includes the cost of tax collection.

Clad. A term used in the United States of coins made from metal alloys.

Classical School. The economists who wrote during the period 1750–1850, often known as the classical economists, who formulated a systematic body of economic principles for the first time. The principal members of the School were Adam Smith, Malthus, Ricardo, Nassau Senior, James Mill, John Stuart Mill, and Bentham. In general they supported the idea of *laissez-faire* in opposition to the mercantilism (*q.v.*) prevalent in the early part of the period.

Class Struggle. The Marxist doctrine that in any system in which the means of production are privately owned there is a constant struggle between the owners of capital and the proletariat.

Clayton Anti-Trust Act (1914). An Act passed by the Congress of the United States to prohibit the amalgamation of large companies which would result in their producing so large a proportion of the total output of a commodity as to give them a high degree of monopoly power.

Clean. As applied to a Bill of Lading it refers to goods 'in apparent good order and condition'. If this condition is not fulfilled the Bill of Lading is said to be 'foul'.

Clean Bill. In foreign trade, a bill without documents attached to it, in contrast to a Documentary Bill (*q.v.*).

Clearing Agreement. The system of exchange control introduced by Germany in 1931–32 was so severe that it would have led to a complete loss of its foreign trade. To make trade possible bilateral trading agreements, known as Clearing Agreements, were made between Germany and countries such as Sweden and Switzerland. In the case of Great Britain an improved type of agreement, known as a Payments Agreement, was made. The feature of these agreements was that all payments between the countries concerned had to be made through their central banks, though the actual buying and selling were conducted through the ordinary trade channels.

Clearing Bank. A bank which is a member of the London Bankers' Clearing House, the term is often used merely to mean a commercial or joint-stock bank.

Clearing House. An institution where mutual indebtedness between undertakings can be settled. When 'through' tickets are issued by transport undertakings the fare may have to be divided between several of them. At a clearing house debts between the members may be largely cancelled out and differences paid. When there were many railways in Great Britain a Railways Clearing House was established to undertake this work. The best-known clearing house is the London Bankers' Clearing House (*q.v.*).

Clearing the Market. At the equilibrium price the total supply offered to a market will be sold, the demand at the price being for neither more nor less than this quantity. *See* Equilibrium.

Close Company. A company under the control of five or fewer persons (or families), such a company being compelled to distribute at least 60% of its profits in dividends. First used in the Finance Act (1965), the term was given legal status by the Companies Act (1967). Most private companies are of this type. *See also* Private Company.

Close Corporation. An American term for a company, the shares of which are held entirely by a small group of people such as a family.

Closed-end Trust. An American term for an investment trust company, as distinct from an Open-end Trust, the term used in the United States for a unit trust. *See* Investment Trust.

Closed Indent. Foreign orders are known as indents, the term being more particularly used of orders placed through agents. A Closed Indent names the manufacturer from whom the foreign buyer wishes the goods to be bought.

Closed Shop. A condition of employment where only members of the appropriate trade union are permitted to work, employers agreeing to employ only members of the union.

Closed System. In developing some aspects of economic theory it is an advantage to make an assumption that the economy under consideration is self-sufficient, so that it has no commercial relations of any kind with any other economy, the theory then being worked out under these simplified conditions.

Closed Union. A term of American origin for a trade union which restricts its membership partly—like a craft union—to maintain a certain standard of skill among its members, but also often for undesirable reasons such as to restrict numbers in order to keep up wages.

Clothing Club. An organisation collecting regular payments to enable people who have subscribed a sufficient amount to make purchases of clothing from a given list of shops. The extension of hire purchase to a wider range of goods has tended to reduce the activities of such clubs. *See* Club Trading.

Clothworkers' Company. One of the twelve more important companies of the 82 Guilds or Livery Companies of the City of London, many of which date their existence from the gilds of medieval times. The Clothworkers' Company did not come into existence and receive its charter until 1528 on the amalgamation of two older companies. It ranks twelfth in order of civic precedence.

Club Cheques. *See* Club Trading; Shopping Cheques.

Club Trading. Some shops organise clubs, the members of which pay regular contributions on which interest may be paid and which periodically can be withdrawn in order to make purchases at the shops. Some shops run clubs only for Christmas purchases, but others operate them all the year round. Sometimes clubs are run independently but members may be offered special terms at certain specified shops. *See also* Clothing Clubs; Shopping Cheque.

Clydesdale and North of Scotland Bank Ltd. The third largest of the Scottish commercial banks, it has over 340 branches; it is affiliated to the Midland Bank Ltd. (*q.v.*).

Cmnd. Abbreviation of Command, used in connection with the printing of official Government Papers. *See* Command Papers.

C.N. Abbreviation of Credit Note (*q.v.*).

C.N.A.A. Abbreviation of Council for National Academic Awards (*q.v.*).

Coal Consumers' Councils. Bodies set up to watch the interests of consumers of coal, both domestic and industrial.

Coal Mines Act (1930). An Act which regulated the output of coal and fixed minimum prices. It also recommended the amalgamation of coal-mining companies in Great Britain in order to achieve economies of large-scale operation. Few firms took advantage of this, the owners of the more efficient mines being unwilling to combine with less efficient firms.

Coal Mines Nationalisation Act (1946). The Act which nationalised the coal-mining industry of Great Britain, it placed the industry under the control of the National Coal Board, a public corporation, which acquired 1,500 coal mines. Some 400 mines, each employing fewer than thirty underground workers, were excluded from nationalisation, although they had to be licensed by the National Coal Board. The Act declared the policy of the National Coal Board to be the provision of coal in such quantities and at such prices as would 'further the public interest'.

Coasting Trade. A considerable amount of the internal trade of the United Kingdom is carried on by ships which ply between the country's many ports. Coasting trade and the use of navigable rivers were the only means of carrying bulky goods before the development of canals and railways. The coasting trade retains its importance because the carriage of goods by water is cheaper than by any other form of transport, especially in the case of relatively cheap, bulky goods, such as coal and raw materials. Large quantities of coal, for example, are carried by sea to London from the North-East, and from South Wales to the South Coast.

Cobden Treaty (1860). A commercial treaty between Great Britain and France, by which both countries agreed to a reduction of their import duties on one another's goods. The treaty emphasised the more liberal trade policy that Napoleon III was trying to develop in Europe at that time.

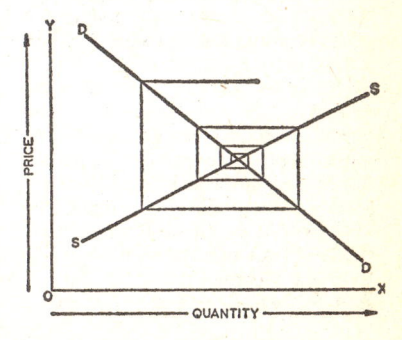

Cobweb Theorem. In any industry where supply is slow to adjust itself to changes of demand violent fluctuations in output are likely to occur. This is particularly the case with agriculture, where a considerable period of time must elapse between the taking of a decision to change production and the effect of this decision on the market. For example, an increase in demand will immediately result in a sharp rise in price, since in the short run there can be no increase in supply. This high price may, however, make producers increase their output to a greater extent than is justified by the increase in demand. Consequently, when this increased supply comes on to the market there will be a sharp fall in price, which may then result in a reduction in output to a greater extent again than is justified. The result is that violent changes in output succeed price changes, and that each successive change is greater than the one that preceded it. When represented diagrammatically this produces the 'cobweb theorem': see p. 77 Without doubt the cobweb theorem grossly exaggerates the situation.

C.O.D. Abbreviation of Cash on Delivery (q.v.).

Codes. To reduce the cost of cablegrams, which can be expensive, codes have been devised for the use of merchants and others, single words representing long phrases or even complete sentences. There are several codes in use, and so it is necessary to specify which is employed, the best known being the ABC Code and Bentley's.

Coding. Under the P.A.Y.E. system for the payment of income tax employers have to deduct tax weekly or monthly from the pay of their employees, each employee being given a code number by the tax authorities based on the tax allowances appropriate to that person, without these having to be declared to the employer.

Coffee Institute of Brazil. A body established by the Government of Brazil as the sole exporter of coffee from that country, all coffee growers being compelled to sell to it at prices fixed by the Government. As a result the Institute is able to exercise a high degree of monopoly power in the world market for coffee, the 'monopoly profit' thus accruing to the State.

Cohen Committee. See Council on Prices, Productivity and Incomes.

C.O.I. Abbreviation of Central Office of Information (q.v.).

Coinage. The precious metals, more especially silver, superseded other commodities in use as money on account of their greater convenience, being more easily divisible and portable, more durable and homogeneous. To facilitate making payments it was an advantage to have the metal weighed out in advance—though it would still be necessary to allow the seller to check the weight on his own scales—and from this it was a short step to the issue of coins of known weight and fineness. The first coins to be used in Europe were minted in Greece nearly 3,000 years ago. Coins of many different shapes have been struck, but the circular coin has proved to be the most popular, the only one not of this shape to be minted in Great Britain being the twelve-sided threepenny piece before decimalisation and the seven-sided Fifty New Pence coin after decimalisation. In time coinage came to be regarded as the special prerogative of the State. Coins may be either of full face value, as was the gold sovereign, or they may be merely tokens, as are all the British coins in circulation at the present day.

Coinage, British. Few countries have had such a variety of coins as Great Britain. The oldest English coin is the penny (q.v.), first minted in 764 A.D., soon followed by the halfpenny (q.v.). In 1257 a gold twentypenny piece was struck. Later came the groat, the farthing, the florin and the noble (qq.v.). Then during the Tudor period there came the testoon or shilling, the crown, half-crown, sovereign, half sovereign, double and triple sovereigns, the sixpence and the threepenny piece, three halfpence, three farthings, ryal, double noble, angel, half angel or angelot (qq.v.). Under the Stuarts even more coins were issued—the unite, double crown, thirty-shilling and fifteen-shilling pieces, the laurel, with half and quarter laurels, the guinea, half guinea, two guineas, five guineas (qq.v.). In Victorian times there came a revival of the fourpenny piece and the florin, the crown, double florin, and these coins circulated alongside the sovereign, half sovereign, shilling, sixpence, threepenny piece, penny, halfpenny, farthing and for a time the half farthing. Until the decimalisation of the coinage in 1971 (q.v.) the only new coin of the 20th century was the twelve-sided threepenny piece introduced in the 1930s.

Coinage Acts. 1. The Act of 1774 provided for the recoinage of worn gold coins—at that time, guineas. When coins worth their full face value are in circulation it becomes necessary from time to time to withdraw worn coins which no longer contain the required amount of metal.

2. The Act of 1816 provided for the free coinage at the Royal Mint of gold of the required degree of fineness at £3 17s. 10½d. per oz. This Act also made the gold sovereign the standard unit of currency for this country instead of the guinea.

3. The Act of 1891 made it compulsory for the Royal Mint to exchange on demand worn gold sovereigns and half sovereigns for new coins of full weight, it having been discovered that 46% of the gold coins in circulation were below the required weight.

4. The Act of 1920 reduced the silver content from 92% to 50% of British silver coins, the higher price of silver having made new silver coins worth more than their face value.

Coin Clipping. At one time before coins were given a milled edge clipping was of common occurrence. It was regarded as a serious offence and those found guilty of this practice were severely punished.

Collateral Security. Banks generally require some kind of collateral security from the people to whom they lend by loan or overdraft (even though they regard the personal integrity of the borrower as ranking first in importance) since in the case of a loan not being repaid the security can then be disposed of. The collateral security may take the form of an assurance policy or marketable securities like stocks and shares, bills of lading, warehouse warrants, or deeds of property. In effect, what a bank does is to turn an illiquid security, such as shares in a company, into purchasing power. The amount of collateral security might then be regarded as one of the limitations on the power of a bank to create credit, were it not for the fact that the amount of such security depends on what the banks regard as eligible. By varying their standard of eligibility they can vary the amount of available security. Then, in the case of many sound borrowers, their good names may be regarded as sufficient.

Collective Bargaining. A term applied to negotiations between associations representing employers and trade unions representing employees in an industry. By himself the employee is in a weak bargaining position, but when he combines with other workers in a trade union he can bargain more effectively. Employers too prefer collective bargaining, as individual bargaining with each employee would take to much time. Collective bargaining depends for its success on the willingness of the members of each organisation to accept whatever agreement is made on their behalf by their representatives. Unofficial strikes, undertaken against the advice of the union concerned, are therefore contrary to the principle of collective bargaining.

Collective Farms. Farms in a communist state owned collectively by the groups of people working on them, in contrast to individual ownership of farms in non-communist countries. They were formed by grouping together individual holdings of peasants in order to form larger units which could be worked more efficiently.

Collective Goods. A term used by Alfred Marshall for goods not in private ownership but owned by the community as a whole—roads, parks, libraries, etc. Such things are often termed social wealth.

Collectivism. An economic system where the State owns most real capital and undertakes the planning of production, as in a communist state.

Colombo Plan. A scheme for providing assistance to the underdeveloped nations of South-east Asia formulated at Colombo in 1950.

Assistance has been given by the United States, Great Britain and the more economically advanced members of the Commonwealth, and Japan.

Colon. The Spanish form of the name Columbus, it is the standard unit of currency of the Central American republics of Costa Rica and El Salvador.

Colonialism. *See* Old Colonial System.

Colonial Stock Act (1900). This Act declared that stocks issued by colonial governments should be regarded as trustee stock, thereby enabling these colonies to borrow on the London market at a lower rate of interest.

Colwyn Committee. The most important section of the Report of this Committee, published in 1927, is that which asserts that income taxes have no economically adverse directional effects, so that income taxes do not affect the relative prices of goods and services or the quantities of them that are produced.

Combination Acts (1799 and 1800). These Acts reinforced the common law under which trade unions, regarded as conspiracies were illegal. Fear of the spread of revolutionary ideas from France was mainly responsible for their enactment. They were repealed in 1824, largely as a result of the efforts of Francis Place and Joseph Hume, but they were restored in a modified form a year later. Though after 1825 a trade union of itself was no longer illegal, their organisers and members were in danger of prosecution for conspiracy, the authorities being particularly severe in cases where an oath was administered to members. It was this that led to the prosecution of the Tolpuddle agricultural workers in 1834.

Combination of Producers. *See* Combine.

Combine. The association in temporary or permanent form of two or more firms. Amalgamations, mergers, and trusts are examples of permanent combines; cartels may be either temporary or permanent associations of firms, depending on whether the cartel is formed voluntarily or State-inspired. Combines may be (i) horizontal, where the constituent firms are all at the same stage of production, e.g. cartels; or (ii) verticle, where the firms are at different stages of production, e.g. trusts.

Combined Demand and Supply Curve. In some markets the same people may at different times be buyers or sellers. The higher the price the more likely they are to sell; the lower the price the more inclined they may be to buy. This is true of speculators on the stock exchange and on some commodity markets. Thus, it becomes possible to construct a Combined Demand and Supply Schedule such as the following:

Price £	Quantity bought or sold + = Bought − = Sold
£0·80	+ 1,000
£0·85	+ 450
£0·90	+ 250
£0·95	+ 100
£1·00	—
£1·05	− 50
£1·10	− 200
£1·15	− 400
£1·20	− 700

This can be represented diagrammatically as follows:

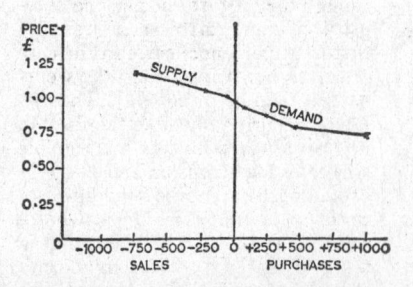

Both Supply and Demand for this commodity are represented by a single curve, thus supporting the

Comecon. Abbreviation of Council for Mutual Economic Assistance, a body representing the U.S.S.R., the other European communist countries (except Albania and Yugoslavia) together with Mongolia. In 1971 it was agreed to create a joint convertible currency backed by gold—perhaps the first step towards a single exchange rate within the Soviet bloc. *See* Transferable Rouble.

COMEX. Abbreviation of Commodity Exchange Inc., New York's metal exchange. It deals in silver, copper, mercury and (since 1974) gold.

Command Papers. Official Government publications which are given Command numbers and published by H.M. Stationery Office. The first series were numbered with the prefix Cd., the second series prefix Cmd., and the present or third series with Cmnd.

Commerce. A comprehensive term for all forms of trade—wholesale, retail, import, export, entrepôt—and all services which assist the carrying on of trade, such as banking, insurance, and transport.

Commerce, Education for. British universities offer courses leading to degrees in economics or commerce (*qq.v.*). Advanced courses in economics, commerce, and management studies are provided by some Colleges of Commerce, commerce departments of regional and area Technical Colleges, Colleges of Technology, Polytechnics and Universities. More elementary commercial education is provided by Technical Colleges and Evening Institutes. Many secondary schools, including comprehensive schools now include some commercial teaching in their curricula.

Commerce, University Degrees in. The degree of B.Com. (or B.Com.Sc.) is awarded by the universities of Leeds, Liverpool, Manchester, and Edinburgh. Southampton university awards a B.Sc. (Soc. Sci.) in commercial subjects. Strathclyde and Herriot-Watt universities offer a B.A. in Commerce. *See also* Degrees in Economics.

Commercial Bank. A bank which undertakes all kinds of ordinary banking business. *See* Joint-stock Bank.

Commercial Banking Co. of Sydney. The fourth largest trading bank in Australia, it has 600 branches.

Commercial Banking School. A term used in the United States of those economists who stress that the lending policy of the banks should pay particular attention to the banking principles of liquidity and adequacy of reserves.

Commercial Bank of Australia. With its head office in Melbourne, it is the third largest of the Australian trading banks. It has over 800 branches.

Commercial Bill. *See* Bill of Exchange.

Commercial Intelligence Department. A department of the Board of Trade established in 1900, its function being to provide information for traders. *See* Board of Trade.

Commercial Law. That branch of law concerning matters appertaining to commerce such as contract, ownership and transfer of goods, agency, etc.

Commercial Sale Rooms. A produce exchange in London which deals mainly in such commodities as sugar, tea, coffee, cocoa, spices, copra.

Commercial Treaty. A trade agreement made between two or more countries, often dealing with reciprocal tariff or other trade privileges.

Commercial Union Assurance Co. One of the largest insurance companies in the United Kingdom. It was formed by the merger of 12 previously independent companies.

Commission Agent. A merchant who buys and sells goods on commission.

Commission for New Towns. *See* New Towns, Commission for.

Commission Manufacturer. A manufacturer who undertakes a single process of production on behalf of other firms which either do not carry out that particular process themselves or are at the time too busy with other orders.

Committee of Inspection. In bankruptcy proceedings, a committee appointed by the creditors to supervise the performance of the trustee and to watch their interests.

Commodity. Not only are there many varieties of many things, such as potatoes, cigarettes and tobacco, fruit, motor cars, etc., but the economic importance of a thing does not depend solely on its physical characteristics, but also on its location and on the time when it is available. Oil in the Middle East is not the same as oil in London; strawberries in June are not the same as strawberries in December. It is, therefore, very difficult to define a commodity with precision. The assumption in perfect competition that a commodity is homogeneous is very far from reality.

Types of Commodity. Commodities can be classified as Consumers' Goods—goods that have reached the people who actually want them in the form in which they wish to have them—and Producers' Goods —goods which are not wanted for their own sake, but only for the assistance they give to further production. Commodities can also be classified as Primary Products—raw materials and foodstuffs—and Secondary Products—that is, manufactured goods. The term 'tertiary products' has been given to the provision of direct or personal services.

Commodity Control Schemes. There are two types of scheme: (i) Those to encourage an expansion of exports by selling a commodity more cheaply in foreign markets than at home. At one period before 1939 Great Britain operated such a scheme for coal, France for wheat and Australia for butter. (ii) Those aiming at restriction of output. Attempts to keep up prices by restricting output can be organised only if the number of individual producers is small or if the scheme has the backing of the Governments of the principal producing countries. It is in times of trade depression that Governments are inclined to encourage or sponsor commodity control schemes. During the Great Depression of 1929-35 there were commodity control schemes for rubber, coffee, tin, sugar. On its own account the Government of the United States organised a scheme for the curtailment of the production of cotton in that country, the United States at that time producing a large proportion of total world output. Schemes for the restriction of output all depend for their success (from the point of view of the producers) on the elasticity of demand for the commodity. Only when demand is fairly inelastic will the total revenue of producers increase as a result of a restriction of output. Unless too all producers of the commodity join the scheme there will be every encouragement for producers outside to expand their output in order to take advantage of the higher price, as happened with cotton. A serious drawback to restriction schemes is that they tend to favour the less efficient producers at the expense of the more efficient.

Commodity Market. *See* Organised Markets.

Commodity Money. To overcome the difficulties of barter a medium of exchange came to be used. Whatever was chosen had to be generally acceptable to the people concerned. It would have to be useful or ornamental since it was necessary for it to be valuable for its own sake, so that it could be put to some other use if for any reason it ceased to serve as money. Thus, the earliest things used as money were ordinary commodities. At different times and in different places many different commodities have been used as money, as, for example, cattle in

Ancient Greece and sheep in the early days of Rome, rice in Japan, tea in China, and salt in Arabia. All these commodities have their own disadvantages—some are not very durable or not easily divisible, others are not homogeneous or not easily portable. The precious metals soon superseded commodities such as these as money, at first being used as commodity money, but later in the form of coins.

Commodity Paper. A term sometimes used, more particularly in the United States, for promissory notes and bills of exchange arising out of trade transactions, especially documentary bills with bills of lading or warehouse warrants attached.

Common Carrier. A term used of a transport undertaking as, for example, railways, which were compelled by law to carry any goods offered to them (except dangerous articles) at a reasonable charge to any destination to which the undertaking operated a service.

Common Employment. The doctrine that an employer is not responsible for an injury to one of his employees due to the negligence of another employee. The courts, however, often refuse to apply this doctrine, as it may be a means by which an employer might seek to avoid his responsibilities.

Common External Tariff. A feature of the foreign trade of the E.E.C., all members of which agreed to impose the same rates for duties on imports.

Common Market. *See* European Common Market.

Common Stock. An alternative name (used particularly in the United States) for Ordinary Shares (*q.v.*).

Commonwealth Bank Act (1953). An Act which set out the main functions of the Reserve Bank of Australia (at that time known as the Commonwealth Bank of Australia *q.v.*), thereby confirming its powers as a central bank. It is laid down in the Act, for example, that 'it shall be the duty of the Commonwealth Bank within the limits of its powers to pursue a monetary and banking policy directed to the greatest advantage of the people of Australia, and to exercise its powers under this Act and the Banking Act of 1945 in such a manner as, in the opinion of the Bank, contributes to (*a*) the stability of the currency of Australia; (*b*) the maintenance of full employment in Australia; (*c*) the economic prosperity and welfare of the people of Australia.'

Commonwealth Bank of Australia. Former name of the central bank of Australia, now known as the Reserve Bank of Australia (*q.v.*).

Commonwealth Development Corporation. A body established in 1947 to assist the economic development of the dependent territories of the Commonwealth, it was known until 1963 as the Colonial Development Corporation. Assistance takes the form of loans from the Treasury on which no interest is payable during the first seven years. The loans can be employed to finance all kinds of economic projects.

Commonwealth Development Finance Co. Established 1953 with authorised capital of £15 million, the shares being divided into two categories—'AA' shares, held by leading industrial companies, and 'B' shares, held by the Bank of England. Its purpose is to provide medium-term capital for firms in the Commonwealth in the same way that Finance for Industry does for firms in Great Britain.

Commonwealth Immigration Act (1962). An Act to control the flow of immigrants into Great Britain.

Commonwealth Liaison Committee. One of two committees—the other being the Sterling Area Statistical Committee—set up to provide opportunities for discussion of common problems of members of the Sterling Area.

Commonwealth Sugar Agreement. Under this agreement the United Kingdom contracts to buy sugar from Commonwealth suppliers at prices agreed annually. The sugar is then re-sold to the Sugar Board (*q.v.*).

Commonwealth Trading Bank. With over 1100 branches, it is the largest commercial bank in Australia. Its head office is in Sydney. It is owned by the Commonwealth of Australia.

Communism. A political and economic system in which the State makes the major economic decisions, owning the bulk of the capital assets and being responsible for production and distribution.

Community Land Act (1975). The purpose of this Act was to enable local authorities more easily to buy land for development. *See also* Development Land Tax.

Commuter. A colloquial term for people who live in one place and travel regularly to and from work in another, especially those travelling into and out of London daily. There is a tendency for the word—of American origin—to be wrongly made synonymous with traveller.

Compagnie Internationale de Crédit à Moyen Terme. A banking consortium formed in Switzerland in 1967 by Bankers Trust and 14 other British, European, and American banks for the provision of medium-term credit (*q.v.*).

Companies Acts. *See* Company Law.

Company. A group of persons associated together for the purpose of carrying on a business of some kind. Many partnerships engage in business under names which include the word company. The term nowadays is generally taken to mean a joint-stock or limited company. Some companies have been incorporated by royal charter, others by Act of Parliament, but most companies nowadays are established in accordance with the Companies Acts and registered with the Registrar of Companies. *See* Capital of a Company; Close Company; Formation of a Company; Joint-stock Company; Private Company; Public Company.

Company Director. A person elected by the shareholders to act with the other directors in the running of a company. A director may have no specialist function, merely sharing with other directors responsibility for the general policy of the company, or he may be a functional director, in which case, in addition to acting as a general director, he has full-time responsibility for a particular branch of a firm's activities as, for example, sales.

Company Law. A body of law, consolidated in the Companies Acts, covering the formation, registration, and operation of companies and setting out legal requirements regarding the appointment of directors, the issue of shares and debentures, etc. The Companies Act (1948) said that a company's balance sheet should show a true record of a company's financial position. The Companies Act (1967) still further amended the law relating to companies. It abolished the exempt private company and introduced the close company (*q.v.*), and compelled all companies to make more of their affairs public. The Board of Trade was given greater powers to investigate companies. The Companies Act (1976) tightened up still further the law relating to limited companies, especially the activities of the directors of such companies.

Company Promotor. A person who undertakes to form a new company and who carries out all the preliminary work in connection with its establishment as a going concern.

Company's or **Carrier's Risk.** When goods are so consigned the carrier undertakes to make good any loss.

Company Taxation. *See* Corporation Tax.

Company Titles. The Companies Act (1948) made the consent of the Board of Trade (now the Department of Trade) necessary when a new company wishes to choose a name under which it intends to operate. Titles including the words 'Royal', 'National', 'Imperial', 'International', and many others are no longer permitted, though some were adopted before 1948. Nor must the title be so nearly like that of an existing company as to cause confusion. Before 1948 many new companies, especially small private companies, used to seek glamorous titles. The Department of Trade prefers for small companies such names as A. B. Smith (Leeds) Ltd. or A. & B. Smith (Chemists) Ltd. *See also* Business Names Registration Act.

Comparability, Principle of. A basis for the determination of wages, more particularly in service occupations. Wages, in these occupations, it is said, should be comparable with those paid in similar occupations. This principle was invoked by the Priestley Commission (1955) in its inquiry into the pay of civil servants, by the Guillebaud Committee (1960) in the case of railway workers, the Pilkington Commission (1960) which inquired into the remuneration of doctors and dentists, and the Franks Committee (1965) which considered the pay of higher civil servants. The difficulty in applying this principle is that no two occupations are exactly alike, so that it is extremely difficult to compare different kinds of work. Further, if wages are based on this principle it makes it more difficult to redistribute labour between different kinds of employment. If lower rates of pay are the lot of employees in declining occupations they are thereby encouraged to move to expanding industries if rates of pay are higher there.

Comparative Advantage, Principle of. Both the individual and the community will benefit if each person specialises in that occupation in which he has the greatest comparative advantage over others, that is, if division of labour is carried to the greatest possible extent. For example, from the standpoint of economics alone it would be better for a successful barrister to employ a gardener than to work in his garden himself, however good a gardener he may be, if to do so means that he would have to decline a brief.

Comparative Cost, Principle of. The basic principle underlying the Theory of International Trade, it is an extension of the principle of division of labour to the international field. The greatest total output of all kinds of goods and services for the world as a whole will be achieved only if each country specialises in the production of those things for which it has the greatest comparative advantage over other countries. During the latter part of the nineteenth century Great Britain specialised in manufacturing, because it had the greatest advantage over other countries in this kind of production, even though it meant neglecting its farming, since labour could not be employed in both types of production at the same time. For non-economic reasons a country may decide not to allow the principle free play. Customs unions and areas of free trade will benefit the member countries economically only if the breaking down of tariff barriers enables greater specialisation to be introduced and the Principle of Comparative Cost given free play. It should be stressed that it is real cost in terms of the factors of production employed to which the Principle refers. *See also* International Trade.

Compensated Dollar Plan. A scheme to promote price stability. Irving Fisher suggested that the gold dollar should vary in weight in accordance with an index number of prices, the country's gold reserves being revalued accordingly and the issue of gold certificates suitably adjusted.

Compensating Payment. A term sometimes used of the increase in income a buyer in a market would require to restore his demand to its level before an increase in price took place.

Compensating Wage Differentials. Differences in wages due to the disadvantage of certain occupations—dangerous work, awkward hours of work, unpleasant conditions, etc.

Compensation. An amount payable to someone who has suffered injury.

To some extent injuries at work are covered by the National Insurance (Industrial Injuries) Act of 1946, but it is still possible for an employee to sue his employer in court under the Employers' Liability Act of 1880, the amount of the compensation a court will award being based on the extent of the injured person's loss of physical or mental powers.

Compensation Fee Parcels. A new service introduced in 1972 by the Post Office to replace the registration of parcels providing compensation against loss or damage in the post. The fee payable depends on the amount of compensation required. The sender must complete a certificate of posting.

Compensation Stocks. During 1945–50 a programme of nationalisation was carried out in Great Britain. When an industry was nationalised the shareholders in the firms taken over were generally given compensation in the form of British Government Guaranteed Stocks such as British Transport Stock, British Electricity Stock, British Gas Stock, etc. The basis of compensation was generally an amount of stock that would produce approximately the same income as the yield on the shares at a date near to the date of nationalisation.

Compensation Trade. A modern form of barter, one country agreeing to accept a certain quantity of another's goods in exchange for a specified quantity of exports, the transaction not affecting the balance of payments of either country.

Competition. A term used to indicate the environment in which production and distribution are carried on. The two extreme environments are perfect competition and monopoly, both being theoretical conditions which do not exist in actual life. Between these two extremes are the actual conditions of varying degrees of imperfect competition, ranging from nearly perfect competition to near-monopoly. In studying production it is usual to consider the theoretical extremes of perfect competition and monopoly because they can both be precisely defined and analysed, before going on to study imperfect competition, regarding which generalisation is more difficult. In a more general sense competition between suppliers was regarded by the classical economists, and is still so regarded by many, as a spur to efficiency.

The conditions necessary for perfect competition are: (i) the commodity produced must be homogeneous so that the buyer has no preference for the product of any particular seller; (ii) there must be a large number of both buyers and sellers, none of whom is buying or selling a large enough proportion of total output to enable him appreciably to influence total supply by varying his output or his demand, the result being that all must take the price of the commodity as fixed; (iii) all buyers and sellers must be in easy and immediate contact with one another, so that all are fully aware at all times of what is happening in the market; (iv) there must be no preferential treatment—by tariffs, bounties, taxes, or other means—of any suppliers or buyers.

When these conditions are not fulfilled there is imperfect competition of which the following main types may be distinguished: (i) monopolistic competition, where although there are many suppliers, the commodity or service is not homogeneous; (ii) perfect oligopoly, where the commodity is homogeneous but there are few suppliers; (iii) imperfect oligopoly where there are only a few suppliers with differentiation of product, competition often being of the type described as cut-throat competition (*q.v.*); (iv) duopoly, where there are only two producers. Differentiation can be slight; it may be nothing more than a distinctive brand name. Whereas in perfect competition there can be only one price for a commodity at any particular time, a feature of imperfect competition is price differentiation.

Competition and Credit Control. A document, published in 1971 by the Bank of England, outlining new rules for the control of credit in the United Kingdom, including a new liquidity rule (*q.v.*), greater control of the finance houses and discount houses.

Competitive Advertising. Advertising undertaken to attract demand for a particular product as distinct from informative advertising which aims primarily at disseminating information. Competitive advertising is particularly associated with oligopoly and cut-throat competition. *See* Advertising.

Competitive Demand. When two commodities are fairly close substitutes for one another, an increase in the demand for one of them will result in a fall in the demand for the other. To some extent all things are in competitive demand with one another, since, people's resources being limited, to have more of one thing necessitates their having less of some other. When, however, two things serve more or less the same purpose, then there is a more direct relation between the change in demand for one and the change in demand for the other. This occurs in the case of commodities like butter and margarine which are close substitutes, as also with different brands of the same commodity, where the difference, if any, is very slight. The following diagram shows the effect of an increase in the demand for Commodity A which is assumed to be in competitive demand with Commodity B. The increased demand for Commodity A raises its price and increases the quantity supplied, while the resulting fall in demand for Commodity B reduces both the price and the quantity supplied of that commodity.

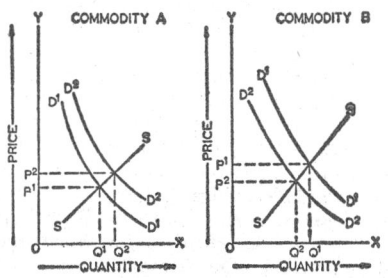

Competitive Firm. In conditions of perfect competition with long-run equilibrium no firm will receive more than normal profit, the minimum amount required to keep an entrepreneur in a particular line of production. This being so, and normal profit being regarded as a cost of production, the total costs of the firm will be equal to its total revenue. In the short run profit may be above or below normal, but when equilibrium is established profit will return to normal as a result, in the first case, of an increase in the number of firms and, in the second, as a result of a decrease in the number of firms. *See* Normal Profit; Perfect Competition.

Competitive Supply. Since the supply of factors of production is limited, an increase in the employment of factors on one form of production will reduce the supply of factors available for other purposes. Therefore, in conditions of full employment to increase the output of one commodity may in the short run require curtailment of the output of another. This is especially true of farming in Great Britain. Milk and wheat production are in competitive supply, since to increase the amount of grazing land for the rearing of cattle will reduce the amount of land for wheat growing. On a wider scale farming and manufacturing compete for labour, and so farm products and manufactured goods are in competitive supply.

Complementarity. The relation between the demand for two goods which are in complementary or joint demand. The extent of this complementarity may vary from goods which will always be demanded in the same proportion to goods where the proportion can be varied to some extent.

Complementary Demand. Often known as Joint Demand, this occurs when two commodities are jointly demanded, one by itself giving little satisfaction. Examples of complementary or joint demand usually quoted are such pairs of things as tea and sugar, strawberries and cream, shoes and shoe-laces, pens and ink. In such cases changes in demand tend to affect each commodity proportionally, so that an increase in the demand for one brings about a similar increased demand for the other. Clearly, in many cases the proportions can be varied. Where the demand for one is the result of the demand for the other, as in the case of motor cars and petrol, this is really an example of Derived Demand (*q.v.*). In the following diagram it is assumed that Commodities A and B are in complementary demand and are required always in the same proportion, the effect then of an increase in demand being:

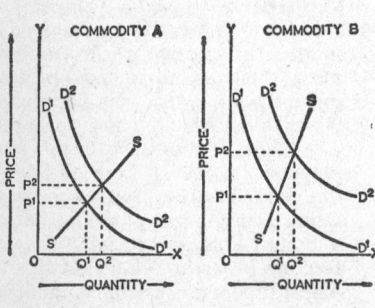

In the case of both commodities the increase in demand results in a rise in price and an increase in the quantity supplied, but since there must be proportionate increases in quantity the extent of the rise in prices depends on the relative elasticities of supply. Thus, the supply of B being more inelastic than the supply of A, the price of B rises more than the price of A.

Complementary Factors. Factors of production are in general in competition with one another, since it is often possible to substitute a little of one for a little of another, but if some form of production requires certain specific factors an increase in the demand for one will increase the demand for the others. Thus, an increase in the demand for motor cars will increase the demand both for skilled automobile engineers and for steel.

Composite Demand. When a commodity can be used for more than one purpose, the demand for it may vary as a result of a change in demand for any one of these purposes. Raw wool is required for making cloth and carpets, steel is required in the manufacture of motor cars, for shipbuilding, structural engineering, etc. An increase in the demand for steel for one purpose will reduce the amount available in the short run for other purposes, with the result that the price of steel will rise, and the amount of steel demanded for these other purposes may be expected to fall.

'Composite' Office. A term sometimes used of an insurance company undertaking insurance business—fire, burglary, accident, etc.—other than or in addition to life assurance.

Composition. A debtor who finds himself in financial difficulties may, as an alternative to filing a petition in bankruptcy, effect a composition with his creditors, whereby he may agree to pay (say) £0·625 in the £. For this course to be followed creditors for at least three-quarters of the amount must be agreeable. To be valid a composition arrangement must be by a registered deed. There is then no need for the debtor to be made a bankrupt. *See also* Deed of Arrangement.

Compound Arbitrage. Also known as Indirect Arbitrage, it refers to dealings in foreign currencies involving more than one centre when a free foreign exchange market exists. *See* Arbitrage.

Compounding. Calculating the effect at some future date of a constant rate of growth; it might refer to capital accumulation or the growth of the national income or to an individual's savings.

Comptroller and Auditor-General. The Head of the Exchequer and Audit Department.

Compulsory Liquidation. The winding up of a company as a result of a Court order. *Cf.* Voluntary Liquidation.

Compulsory Purchase. Public authorities in Great Britain have powers to purchase land or property even though the owners are opposed to it when such land is required for a public project, such as a school, motorway, nuclear power station, etc. There is always the right of appeal against a decision of compulsory purchase, and in some cases public inquiries must be held.

Computer. An electric calculating machine capable of a mass of work at great speed.

Concealed Unemployment. In times of extreme labour shortage (over-full employment) firms may retain labour for which they have no immediate demand and which in other circumstances would have been laid off.

Concentration. With reference to location of industry, it means the localisation of an industry in a particular area. During the period of the Industrial Revolution many British industries became highly localised—the cotton industry in South Lancashire, the wool textile industry in West Yorkshire, shipbuilding in North-east England and on Clydeside, the tinplate industry in South Wales, pottery manufacture in North Staffordshire, etc. In all these cases the principal localising factor was nearness to coal, which was required to produce steam power, coal being a commodity which, at that time especially, was very expensive to transport. There are many advantages accruing to highly concentrated industries—the development of subsidiary and service industries, special marketing facilities, etc. There is also one very serious drawback in that a decline in the basic industry, due to a change in demand or foreign competition, will result in a very high level of unemployment in the area even though the rest of the country continues to enjoy full employment. This can be avoided only if industries are more widely dispersed. *See* Location of Industry.

Conciliation. The Conciliation Act (1896) empowered the Board of Trade (later the Department of Employment) to inquire into the causes of industrial disputes and to attempt to bring the two sides together where negotiations had broken down and on the application of one of them to appoint a conciliator or, if both sides were agreeable, an arbitrator. *See* Arbitration.

Condores. A fractional unit of the currency of Chile (also known as centesimos), 100 condores being equal to one escudo.

Confédération Générale du Travail (C.G.T.). The French equivalent of the British Trades Union Congress. It was founded in 1895 and comprises 58 trade unions.

Confederation of British Industry (C.B.I.). A body formed in 1965, it combines the work previously undertaken by the British Employers' Confederation, the Federation of British Industry (F.B.I.) and the National Association of British Manufacturers. It acts for British industry as a whole, as, for example, in relations with the Government. Its members comprise companies, trade associations, employers' federations, and commercial associations.

Confederazione Generale Italiana del Lavoro (C.G.I.L.). The largest Italian trade union, it has nearly four million members.

Confirmed Credit. A credit opened at a London bank by a British importer in favour of a foreign seller and which the bank has confirmed.

Confirmed Letter of Credit. A letter of credit, payment of which has been confirmed by the paying bank. *See* Letter of Credit.

Confirming House. An agent that acts on behalf of a foreign buyer, paying the exporting manufacturer promptly and often helping with the shipment of the goods.

Conglomerate. A term of American origin for a large company or group of companies with a wide variety of interests.

Congress of Industrial Organisations. *See* American Federation of Labor.

Conjuncture. A term which Alfred Marshall suggested should be revived to describe the conditions giving rise to consumer's surplus (*q.v.*).

'Conscience Money.' A voluntary payment by an anonymous person of a sum of money to cover non-payment in the past of tax which in some way he was able to evade. *See* Tax Avoidance; Tax Evasion.

Conseils de Prud'hommes. Councils, set up in France by Napoleon I, on which there were representatives of both employers and employees, for the purpose of considering industrial disputes.

Consideration. 1. A legal term. Except when drawn up under a deed, a contract, according to English law, is not valid unless the gain to one party is balanced by some benefit (known as consideration) to the other party.

2. A stock exchange term. It is the amount paid for the purchase of a security excluding stamp duty and brokerage.

Consignment. A term used in foreign trade. Goods may be exported in response to definite orders or a whole cargo may be consigned to a foreign importer with instructions to sell for the best price he can obtain. Commodities such as tea and wool are generally exported to Great Britain on consignment and then sold by auction in London.

Consignment Note. A document supplied by a carrier when goods are to be dispatched from one place to another. It gives details of the goods, the number of packages and their weight, the name and address of the sender and also of the consignee. It states whether the goods are being sent Carriage Paid or Carriage Forward, Free on Rail, etc., and also whether they are to be at Owner's Risk or Company's (or Carrier's) Risk. The document, after being completed by the sender, is handed to the carrier, and signed by the consignee on the delivery of the goods, thus providing proof of delivery.

Consolidated Fund. Formed in 1786 by the consolidation of several Government funds, it is maintained in the Exchequer Account (Public Deposits) at the Bank of England by the Government. Taxes are paid into the Consolidated Fund and Government expenditure is paid out of it.

Consolidated Loan. A Government stock due for redemption after 1957 and bearing interest at 4%, the total amount issued being £377 million. The name of the stock is usually abbreviated to 4% Consols, but it should not be confused with 'old' $2\frac{1}{2}$% Consols (*q.v.*).

Consolidated Stamp Act (1891). This Act distinguished three types of stamp duty: (i) *ad valorem* duties on the conveyance of property and on share transfers; (ii) the stamp duty on cheques and receipts (at that time one penny in each case); (iii) specific duties on other deeds.

Consols. Abbreviation for Consolidated Stock, created in 1750 by Henry Pelham who was then prime minister. Throughout the nineteenth century Consols formed the main part of the National Debt but now, with a total nominal value of £276 million, they form only a small fraction of it. Consols now carry $2\frac{1}{2}$% interest (though there is also a 4% issue) and have no redemption date.

Consortium. A group of firms working together on a project too large or too complex for a single firm to undertake.

Constant Marginal Cost. If as the output of a firm expands the cost of adding one more unit to total output is always the same, there will be constant marginal cost. This would occur only where there were constant returns to scale (*q.v.*).

Constant Returns to Scale. If, without varying the proportions in which the factors of production are combined, there is an increase in output proportionate to the increase in the total quantity of factors employed then constant returns to scale occur—a condition unlikely to be met with under modern industrial conditions. In a small-scale craft industry, where each man carried out the entire production of the product and where every process had to be carried out by hand, over a limited range of output there may have been constant returns to scale. *See* Returns, Laws of.

Constructive Total Loss. A term used in connection with marine insurance. If a ship is lost at sea, or if the cargo is completely destroyed, this is known as Actual Total Loss. If, however, the cargo is not actually lost but is so seriously damaged as to make the goods no longer of any use for the purpose for which they were originally intended, or if the ship itself has to be abandoned, then Constructive Total Loss occurs.

Consul. A Government official, resident in a foreign country, whose duties are primarily commercial in character. For example, he has to send back an annual report on trading conditions in his area.

Consular Invoice. A document used in foreign trade, it is an invoice that has been signed by a consul of the country to which the goods are to be consigned.

Consumer Behaviour. The way in which consumers react to certain situations in the market as, for example, rising or falling prices, rising real incomes, etc. The standard of living to which a people have become accustomed is an important influence on consumer behaviour. The study of consumer behaviour is a branch of market research (*q.v.*).

Consumer Council. A body established by the Government in 1963, its aim was to provide protection for consumers, but it had little authority and in 1971 it was abolished. *See* Consumer Protection.

Consumer Credit. This can take the form of hire purchase or be in the form of a personal loan from a bank. Hire purchase is still the principal method by which consumers obtain credit, but in recent years there has been a considerable increase in borrowing from banks for the purchase of consumer's goods. Hire purchase is largely financed by finance companies, and though British banks do not finance hire purchase directly most of them have hire purchase companies as subsidiaries and in addition lend to such companies. Since 1950 consumer credit has expanded enormously in Great Britain. *See* Crowther Report (2).

Consumer Credit Act (1974). This Act gave further protection to consumers by introducing a system of licensing for traders offering hire purchase transactions.

Consumer Durables. *See* Durable Goods.

Consumer Education. *See* Advertising.

Consumer Groups. These are small groups of people who make a study of prices and the quality of goods sold in their own locality and who then make recommendations to their members. Such groups have been formed because national groups cannot take account of local variations in prices. One of the first consumer groups to be formed was one in the Manchester area.

Consumer Price Index (C.P.I.). 1. An index to measure annual changes in the purchasing power of the £ compiled by the Central Statistical Office. *Cf.* the General Index of Retail Prices (RPI) compiled monthly by the Department of Employment.

2. The U.S. index of retail prices. The weighting of the index reflects the high standard of living.

Consumer Protection. In spite of a number of Acts of Parliament affecting weights and measures, purity of food, etc., it has still been felt that consumers were not effectively protected against manufacturers of goods of inferior quality, or against the more unscrupulous methods of some firms offering goods on hire purchase. The Molony Committee considered in detail this problem of consumer protection, one section of it dealing with hire purchase regulations. It recommended the abolition of the £300 limit imposed by the Act of 1954. In 1963 the Government established a Consumer Council, but this was abolished in 1971. For some time the Consumers' Association has been conducting tests of commodities. Another body —the Research Institute for Consumer Affairs—undertakes tests of services. All these bodies aim at making consumers aware of the quality of goods or service of different producers. Further protection was given to consumers by the Fair Trading Act (1973) (*q.v.*), which set up the Consumer Protection Advisory Committee and the Office of Fair Trading, and the Consumer Credit Act (1974) (*q.v.*). A Department of Prices and Consumer Protection was set up in 1974 with a wide range of functions for the protection of the consumer. A number of bodies exist, therefore, to watch over the interest of consumers. There is also the British Standards Institution (*q.v.*). Acts of Parliament lay down minimum standards and regulations for the handling of food.

Consumers' Associations. Where associations have been formed for the protection of consumers' interests they have generally met with little success owing to the difficulty of persuading a large enough proportion of consumers to take concerted action, such as restraining their demand for commodities regarded as being too dear. Greater success has attended the efforts of the Consumers' Association, which conducts tests of the brands of different producers of various commodities and publishes the results in its monthly journal *Which?*

Consumers' Co-operative Societies. The first societies were established by working men to protect themselves against what they regarded was the high cost of distribution. The earliest retail co-operative societies survived only for a few years until the establishment in 1844 of the society at Rochdale by twenty-eight weavers. Progress was still slow until 1880. Between 1880 and 1914 the number of retail societies increased from 871 to 1,385 and their membership from just over half a million to over three million, the total turnover of these societies increasing by six times during this period. By 1960 the total membership exceeded twelve million, though the number of societies, mainly as a result of amalgamations, had fallen to 875. At that date there were still 168 societies each with fewer than 1,000 members, though at the other extreme there were nineteen with over 100,000 members, the largest being the London society with over one and a quarter million members. Co-operative societies bear some resemblances to joint-stock companies, but are more democratically controlled. The Industrial and Provident Societies Acts of 1852 and 1862 gave co-operative societies similar protection to that enjoyed by friendly societies and gave member-shareholders limited liability.

Members are usually required to pay an entrance fee of one pound and are usually allowed to purchase only one share each, though they may invest in the society up to £1,000. At meetings each member has only one vote irrespective of the amount of his investment in the society. The members elect a Committee of Management or Board of Directors to be responsible for general policy and the appointment of paid officials. Profits are distributed in the form of a dividend based on the value of each member's purchases. In recent years dividends have been very small. In 1967 a complete reorganisation of retail co-operative societies was announced. Shops were to be modernised and a single brand symbol was to be adopted for all the products of the C.W.S., and more attention was to be paid to staff training. It was proposed too that the number of societies should be reduced by amalgamation to about fifty regional societies (the Gaitskell Report had suggested 300). During 1960–69 the number of societies was reduced from 875 to 480, and the number of shops too was reduced. At the Census of Distribution (1971) their share of total retail business was 7% and the number of shops was 15,413. Co-operative societies are now to be found in over forty countries. *See also* Co-operation; Co-operative Retail Services; Co-operative Wholesale Society.

Consumers' Goods. These are goods in the form in which consumers wish to have them, as distinct from producers' goods which are wanted only because they assist in the production of consumers' goods in the future. Some consumers' goods, such as foodstuffs, are quickly consumed, whereas some others, such as furniture, are durable and possess some of the qualities of capital goods.

Consumer's Preference. *See* Scales of Preference.

Consumers' Sovereignty. The concept that under a system of free enterprise it is consumers who decide what goods and services shall be produced and in what quantities. Thus, under this system, every time a consumer makes a purchase he is in effect voting for the continued production of that commodity. An increase in consumers' demand for a commodity will raise its price and so encourage producers to increase their output of it. If consumers' demand declines prices will fall and producers will reduce output. Since consumers' demand determines the quantity of a commodity that can be sold at a price, it is said that even a monopolist is subject to the sovereignty of the consumer since, though he can either fix the price of his product or decide how much he will produce, he cannot do both of these things at the same time.

Consumer's Surplus. Also known as Buyer's Surplus. The Theory of Diminishing Marginal Utility shows that after a point each successive increment one obtains of a commodity yields less utility or satisfaction than the preceding increment. (*See* Diminishing Marginal Utility.) Thus, if a person buys three units of a commodity at £1 per unit, the first poundsworth of the commodity yields him more satisfaction than a second poundsworth, and a second poundsworth yields more satisfaction than a third. Since it is assumed that he would not have bought the third unit for £1 unless he had considered that it would yield him that amount of satisfaction, it can be argued that the first and second units each yielded him more than a poundsworth of satisfaction, this additional satisfaction being considered to be consumer's surplus. This concept can also be applied to the purchase of a single article. If a reader would have been willing, if necessary, to pay £3 for a book which, in fact, he was able to buy for £2 it could be said that he obtains one poundsworth of surplus satisfaction. When discriminating prices can be charged consumers' surplus can be reduced to a minimum.

Consumption. The total volume of production (that is, the national income) comprises consumers' goods and producers' goods, together with armaments and services. The term 'consumption' is sometimes taken to mean the total output of consumers' goods during a period, in contrast to investment, which is the total output of capital or producers' goods. Regarded from another angle consumption represents the total quantity of goods brought and consumed by consumers during a period, that is, it is the expression of total consumer demand. The concept of consumption is therefore important to the theory of income and employment. The level of employment depends on the combined influence of investment and consumption, consumption itself being independent on income. *See* Income Determination.

Consumption Capital. A term used by Alfred Marshall for consumers' goods, the term 'auxiliary capital' being used for producers' or capital goods.

Consumption Goods. An alternative name for consumers' goods (q.v.).

Consumption Line. A term sometimes used of a line on a graph covering all possible choices between two commodities for a person with a given amount of money to spend. In the following diagram AB is the Consumption Line. If the individual concerned spends all his money on Commodity A he can buy the quantity of it OA and he will of course have to forgo Commodity B completely; if he spends all his money on Commodity B he can purchase the quantity of it OB and go completely without Commodity A. By taking any point (say X) on the axis OA and reading from the line AB we find that for the same total expenditure he can have quantity OX of Commodity A + quantity OY of Commodity B. Similarly, for the same total expenditure any other combination of Commodity A and Commodity B can be read off from the line AB.

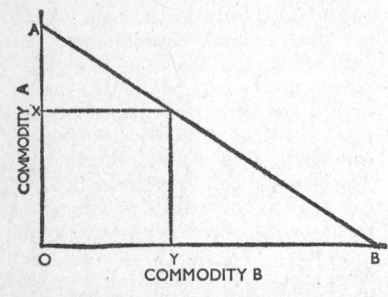

Contango. A stock exchange term meaning carry-over. A broker who wishes to postpone settlement of a transaction to the following account may do so on payment of interest on the sum due. The term 'contango' is also used to mean the extra payment itself.

Continental Banking Services. A banking consortium comprising Barclays Bank, the Chartered Bank, Lloyds & BOLSA International Bank and the Australia & New Zealand Bank.

Continental System. The prohibition by Napoleon in 1806 of the purchase of British goods by countries under his control or in alliance with him in an attempt to ruin British export trade.

Contingent Liability. A liability which may arise only in certain circumstances. For example, a person may have acted as guarantor in order to enable another to obtain a loan. If the loan is not repaid by this borrower the guarantor will have to accept liability for it.

Contours. The drawback to most diagrams used in illustration of economic theory is that they are two-dimensional and so can show only two variable quantities: for example a range of prices and a range of quantities, as in diagrams used to illustrate supply and demand. The only way to show a third variable is by the geographical device of contours. By the use of contours for one of the variables it is possible to produce a diagram showing the range of outputs that would result from the employment of different amounts of labour and different amounts of capital. For such a diagram it would be most convenient to show quantities of labour and capital on the vertical and horizontal axes and represent increasing output by contours A, 2A, 3A, etc. Thus, the employment of OL of labour + OC of capital will yield an output of quantity 3A of the product.

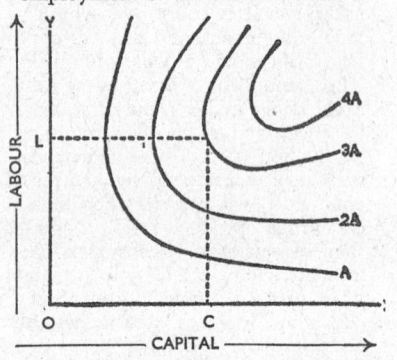

Contract. A legal agreement between two parties. To be valid a contract must fulfil the following requirements: (i) a definite offer must have been made by one party to the other; (ii) the offer must have been unconditionally accepted; (iii) there must be consideration, that is, the benefit to one party must be balanced by a benefit to the other; (iv) those entering into it must have contractual capacity; (v) it must be undertaken for a legal purpose; and (vi) it must be possible to carry it out. If a contract involving no consideration is desired it must be embodied in a deed. To be valid some types of contract must always be in writing, as for example hire-purchase contracts.

Contract In/Out. A term used more especially in connection with the deduction of a political contribution from a trade union subscription. Before the passing of the Trades Disputes Act (1927) members of a trade union who were unwilling to pay a political contribution had to 'contract out'. The Act of 1927 reversed the practice, so that those who wished to pay had to 'contract in'. The Act was, however, repealed in 1947, so that again those unwilling to pay a political contribution had to 'contract out'.

Contract Note. A document sent by a stockbroker to his client stating the terms on which he has bought or sold stocks or shares on his behalf. It also shows the stockbroker's commission, or brokerage, and the amount of stamp duty and any other charges payable.

Contracts of Employment Acts.
1. **1963.** This Act declared that workers with six months' to two years' service with a firm should be entitled to one week's notice with pay, those with two years' service to two weeks' notice with pay and those with five years' service to four weeks' notice with pay. *See* Notice.

2. **1972.** Considerable changes were made by the Industrial Relations Act (1971) to the contract of employment previously defined in the Act of 1963. These changes were codified in the Act of 1972 and subsequently modified by the Trade Union and Labour Relations Act in 1974. This code laid down that a contract of employment should include *inter alia* details of the employee's job, to whom he is responsible, his rights with regard to his joining a trade union, grievance procedure, length of notice required to terminate his employment, terms and conditions of employment, circumstances which can lead to his suspension or dismissal.

Contractual Payment. A fixed amount payable, as by an entrepreneur, irrespective of his output or profit, for example, wages. After all contractual payments have been made to the other factors of production the entrepreneur receives a residual payment.

Contractual Saving. Money saved as a result of agreed deductions from one's pay. In 1969 the Save as You Earn (S.A.Y.E.) (*q.v.*) scheme for regular savers was introduced in Great Britain.

Contributory Negligence. Until 1945 an employee injured at work who could be shown to have been himself partly to blame for an accident would at common law have been unable to recover any damages at all from his employer. Under the Law Reform (Contributory Negligence) Act (1945), however, the effect of contributory negligence is simply to reduce the amount of damages according to the extent to which the court regards the plaintiff as being to blame. *See* Workmen's Compensation Acts.

Contributory Pension. Many pension schemes are in operation where the employee and his employer contribute to a fund during the employee's working life so that on retirement he becomes entitled to a pension based on the length of the period of contribution and his average salary during the last few years he was employed. Unless transferable, as in the case of local government officers and teachers, who may move from one authority to another, contributory pensions tend to have the economic disadvantage of making labour less mobile. The term 'contributory pension' is sometimes used to distinguish the contributory pension under the National Insurance Acts from non-contributory pensions awarded under the Old Age Pensions Act (1908).

Controlling Interest. One company is said to have a controlling interest in another when it holds shares in it carrying over 50% of the voting rights.

Control of Investment. When the demand for factors of production is in excess of the available supply, as occurs especially in time of war; it becomes necessary to ensure that resources are made available for those purposes which are regarded as being 'in the public interest'. In the post-war years immediately after the Second World War, owing to the supply of most things having fallen to a very low level while at the same time demand was excessively high, competition for the available factors of production would have pushed up their prices to an enormous extent with the result that many forms of investment, regarded by the State as important, would have failed to secure the necessary resources. In those years too the Government was anxious to carry out a policy of planned location of industry and this also required control of investment. Although control of investment means the control of real investment—that is, the actual production of capital goods—control had to be exercised by financial means. A Capital Issues Committee (*q.v.*) of the Treasury was set up to consider applications for the raising of new capital in excess of £50,000 (reduced to £10,000 in 1956), so that each application could be considered from the point of view of 'the national interest'. For example, industries producing for export or producing capital goods had little difficulty in securing permission to go ahead, whereas applications to produce some kinds of consumers' goods were refused. In other cases permission might be dependent on the applicant's agreeing to set up in one of the Development Areas.

Controls, Government. In a communist state there is the maximum amount of Government control in both political and economic fields. Complete freedom from control is not possible, and in all countries there has been increasing Government control during the past half century. Even in the days of *laissez-faire* the State had to intervene to protect the weak, as for example by Factory Acts. In modern times Government controls have taken many new forms—restrictions on imports by tariffs or quotas, control of investment, exchange control, controlled location of industry, Treasury directives to banks, town and country planning regulations, and, during both World Wars and for nearly ten years after the Second World War, price control and rationing of a great many consumers' goods and of some producers' goods. See*e also* Rationing.

Conurbation. A term invented by Prof. C. B. Fawcett for large urban areas where towns are so close together that they merge into one another, so that it is impossible to see where one town ends and the next begins. The term is now used with reference to problems of population distribution, and in the population census of Great Britain seven conurbations are now recognised: Greater London, the West Midlands, West Yorkshire, South-east Lancashire, Merseyside, Tyneside, and Clydeside. Nearly 40% of the total population of the United Kingdom live in these conurbations.

Convenience, Flags of. See Flags of Convenience.

Convenience Goods. A term sometimes used of non-durable consumers' goods, especially cheap goods in wide and regular demand and food (frozen, canned or freeze-dried). Frozen foods in particular have changed patterns of shopping and consumption.

Convention of Stockholm. Also known as the Treaty of Stockholm, it established E.F.T.A., the European Free Trade Association (*q.v.*), which came into being in May 1960.

Conversion. If a Government stock carrying a high rate of interest is due for redemption at a time when there is a lower prevailing rate of interest it provides the Government with an opportunity to borrow at the lower rate by the issue of a new 'conversion' stock in order to repay the maturing stock. When the rate of interest was low in the 1930s it gave Mr N. Chamberlain, Chancellor of the Exchequer at the time, an opportunity to convert several stocks issued at a high rate of interest during the First World War, and which were due for redemption, to a lower rate of interest, thereby considerably reducing the cost of the National Debt. It was the greatest conversion operation ever undertaken.

Conversion Rights. Debentures giving the holder the right within a specified period to convert them into ordinary shares of the company on specified terms are said to carry conversion rights.

Conversion Stock. The name of several Government stocks, some of which have already matured. The name indicates that the stock has been offered to holders of a stock that was due for redemption, but this is also true of many other stocks —Treasury, Exchequer, Funding— and so the name now has no special significance.

Convertibility. 1. When used of bank-notes or other paper money it means that they can be exchanged on demand for coin of full face value. Bank of England notes enjoyed this degree of convertibility down to 1914 except for the years 1797–1821 during and immediately after the Napoleonic Wars. During the years 1925–31, the period of the revived gold standard, Bank of England notes had only a restricted degree of convertibility, since they could be exchanged for gold only in large amounts—the amount equivalent in value to a gold bar weighing 400 oz.

2. When used in connection with foreign exchange a currency is said to be convertible when it can be readily exchanged for other currencies. It may be fully convertible, when it can be exchanged in all circumstances; it may enjoy non-resident convertibility, as in the case of sterling since January 1959, when it became freely convertible to all holders resident outside the United Kingdom. Convertibility of currencies is essential if multilateral trade is to be developed.

Convertibility Crisis (1947). Under the Washington Loan Agreement of December 1946 sterling had to be made freely convertible by July 1947. When sterling acquired by current transactions was made freely convertible in 1947 (the sterling balances accumulated during the Second World War continuing to remain blocked) there were such heavy demands from European countries for American goods that most of the sterling they acquired was immediately exchanged for U.S. dollars. This was equivalent to Great Britain having to pay for all its imports in U.S. dollars. The drain on Great Britain's reserves was so heavy that after only five weeks convertibility of sterling had to be suspended. At the time of the Washington Loan Agreement the American Government had greatly underestimated the effects of the War on Great Britain and overestimated this country's powers of recovery. The result was the generous American scheme of assistance known as Marshall Aid (*q.v.*).

Convertibility of Sterling. Great Britain's failure to maintain the convertibility of sterling in 1947 made the British monetary authorities reluctant to risk a second failure, and convertibility was restored in easy stages. For a time after 1947 sterling was convertible only among members of the Sterling Area. Gradually, two other areas of convertibility were developed—the area of the American Account and the area of the Transferable Account. The former group of countries comprised the United States, Canada, and some of the countries of Central America. The area of the Transferable Account comprised the rest of the world, and countries were admitted to it by individual agreements, but by 1955 it included almost the whole of the world outside the Sterling Area and the area of the American Account. Within each of these three areas sterling was convertible, but not until 1959 did it become freely convertible between members of different areas.

Convertible Debentures. *See* Convertible Loan Stock.

Convertible Loan Stock. A debenture stock which can be converted into ordinary stock at a stated future date. Conversion may be at the option of the holder.

Cook, Thomas Ltd. The oldest British tourist agency, established in 1841 when Thomas Cook organised the first railway excursions. It merged with the Compagnie Internationale des Wagons-Lits. It was taken over by the British Government in 1940 to prevent its assets falling into enemy hands. In 1972 it was returned to private enterprise, a consortium consisting of the Midland Bank, Trust Houses Forte Ltd. and the Automobile Association purchasing it from the Government. In 1976 T.H.F. disposed of its share.

Co-operation. During the early nineteenth century the ideal of co-operation was put forward as an alternative to competition. The earliest attempt at co-operation in production to achieve a measure of success was that of Robert Owen (1771–1858) at New Lanark. Producers' co-operatives, however, have had little success in England, at the present day the Co-operative Productive Federation having fewer than thirty firms in membership. Producers' co-operatives have been more successful on the continent of Europe, especially in Denmark. (*See* Farm Co-operatives.) The early consumers' co-operatives were generally short-lived. The success of the retail co-operative society really dates from the formation of the society of the Rochdale Pioneers in 1844 but it is only since 1880 that the movement has become firmly established, progress having been rapid after that date. (*See* Consumers' Co-operative Societies.) A Co-operative Party has been established to propagate co-operative principles and it puts up candidates at parliamentary elections, working in close alliance with the Labour Party. Co-operative societies use some of their funds for 'education', that is, the propagation of co-operative principles.

Co-operative Bank. In 1970 it became a separate limited company.

Co-operative Building Society. *See* Nationwide Building Society.

Co-operative Commercial Bank. The merchant banking division of the Co-operative Bank.

Co-operative Farming. The farmers of Denmark were the first to form co-operative organisations to enable them to enjoy the advantages of large-scale buying and selling. Co-operative farming has spread to other countries such as New Zealand and the Republic of Ireland where farming is mainly a small-scale industry.

Co-operative Productive Federation. An association of firms, mainly manufacturing boots and shoes, which have applied the co-operative principle to production. Most of their output is purchased by retail co-operative societies.

Co-operative Retail Services Ltd. A company established by the Co-operative Wholesale Society and the Scottish Wholesale Society to undertake retailing by the establishment of retail societies in areas where this could not be accomplished as a result of local effort or by taking over existing societies, generally those that have found themselves in difficulties. In 1960 Co-operative Retail Services had thirty-five branches each with its own chain of shops.

Co-operative Union. A body, established in 1869, representing co-operative interests in Great Britain—retail and wholesale societies, the

Co-operative Permanent Building Society, the Co-operative Insurance Society, and the British producers' co-operatives. It gives advice to local co-operative societies on legal and financial matters. Much of its activity is devoted to education and it organises examinations for co-operative employees and runs a residential college. In 1972 it took the first steps towards a trading alliance with the co-operative societies of the E.E.C.

Co-operative Wholesale Society Ltd. Established as their wholesale supplier by the English retail societies (the Scottish societies setting up the Scottish Co-operative Wholesale Society). The C.W.S. was established in 1863 because of the difficulties experienced by many retail societies in obtaining supplies through the normal channels. The capital was provided by the retail societies, which share the profits in proportion to their purchases in the same way as they distribute profits among their own members. However, unlike the retail societies where each member has only one vote, the members of the C.W.S. have votes in proportion to their purchases, so that control is largely in the hands of the larger retail societies. The C.W.S. is also engaged in production and operates over two hundred factories in addition to owning tea and other plantations abroad. In 1973 a merger of the C.W.S. and the S.C.W.S. was proposed.

Coopers' Company. One of the 82 Guilds or Livery Companies of the City of London whose existence dates back to medieval times.

Co-ordination. With reference to factors of production, it means deciding in what proportions to combine them in order to achieve the output the entrepreneur desires. *See also* Substitution.

Co-ordination of Transport. The organisation of all transport services, both for passenger and goods, so that the various means of transport supplement rather than compete against one another, each being employed for the type of service it can best perform.

Co-partnership. Attempts have been made to secure the loyalty of employees by setting aside a portion of a firm's profits for distribution among them, often in proportion to their ordinary wages or salaries. Many firms in Great Britain operate such profit-sharing schemes. In other cases employees are given shares in the company or permitted to buy them on favourable terms.

Copyright. The sole right to reproduce a literary work or a musical composition, it gives the owner a monopoly of a particular piece of property, which like other property can be assigned, in return for payment to another person or persons. Literary copyright continues until fifty years after the death of the author whereas musical copyright continues until fifty years after the publication of the work. Copyright was considered at international conferences at Berne in 1886 and 1911, at Stockholm in 1958 and at Paris in 1972. In Great Britain the law of copyright was codified in the Copyright Act (1956). An attempt was made in 1976 to amend this Act to take account of Public Lending Right (*q.v.*) but it failed.

Cordoba. The standard unit of the currency of Nicaragua, it is divided into 100 centavos.

Cordwainer's Company. One of the 82 Guilds or Livery Companies of the City of London whose existence dates back to the gilds of the Middle Ages. The members of the company were originally workers in leather, including shoemakers.

Corner. A term of American origin applied to the action of a dealer in a commodity market who has obtained possession of almost the entire supply of a commodity available at a particular time.

Corn Exchanges. Highly organised wholesale markets dealing in cereals and kindred products and sometimes responsible for the grading of the product. In addition to the corn exchange in London there are several in the provinces, the most important of these being the one at Liverpool. *See* Corn Trade Association.

Corn Trade Association. A body which undertakes, among other things, to grade wheat before it is sold on the London and other corn exchanges. Graded commodities are then usually sold by private treaty, those not capable of being so graded being generally sold by auction.

Corporate Income Tax. An American term for Corporation Tax (*q.v.*).

Corporate Saving. A good deal of saving comes from the undistributed profits of limited companies. This is known as Corporate Saving and it is used to finance capital expansion. *See* Saving.

Corporation. Legally, a group of persons associated together for some particular purpose, such a corporation being known as a corporation aggregate. A corporation can be established (i) by Royal Charter, as in the case of chartered companies, local government corporations, educational establishments such as universities and professional bodies; (ii) by Act of Parliament, as with the early railway companies, and the modern public corporations set up to operate the nationalised industries; (iii) under the Companies Acts, the method by which limited companies are now established. The term is used of limited companies in the U.S.A. and of some large companies in Great Britain. *See also* Public Corporation.

Corporation Aggregate. *See* Corporation.

Corporation of Insurance Brokers. A professional body which watches over the interests of insurance brokers, its members being known as Incorporated Insurance Brokers.

Corporation of Secretaries. A professional body which offered membership to those who passed its qualifying examinations. Members, who included Associates (A.C.C.S.) and Fellows (F.C.C.S.), were described as certified secretaries. In 1971 it merged with the Institute of Chartered Secretaries and Administrators (*q.v.*).

Corporation Sole. A legal fiction which enables an office held from time to time by different individuals to be regarded as a corporation. Examples of corporations sole are incumbents of church livings and certain public officials, such as the public trustee. *See* Corporation.

Corporation Stocks. Securities carrying a fixed rate of interest with redemption usually at some time between two stated dates, issued by British local authorities. Many local authorities also borrow for short periods of 2, 3, 5, or 7 years directly from the public at the prevailing rate of interest.

Corporation Tax. A tax on company profits, first imposed in the U.K. in 1965. Under this system distributed profits were taxed twice, the company paying Corporation Tax and the shareholder paying income tax. From April 1973 this was eliminated by the introduction of the imputation system. Companies will make advance payments of Corporation Tax equal to $\frac{3}{7}$ of dividends, this to be offset against their total tax for the period. Shareholders receive a dividend and a tax credit equal to the standard rate of income tax. *See* Profits Taxes.

Corporative State. Government by a body representing employers and employees of the various industries, with some representation also of the main political party, as with the dictatorships of Mussolini in Italy, Franco in Spain and Salazar in Portugal.

Correspondent Bank. A bank which acts as a clearing agent for another which is not a member of the country's clearing system. Thus, in England the Yorkshire Bank, not being a member of the London Clearing House, has to maintain a balance with one of the clearing banks. The term is also used of a foreign agent of a bank in a town where the bank itself has no foreign branch of its own.

In the United States where branch banking is limited correspondent banks play a more important role in banking than they do in Great Britain.

Corvée. Forced labour in lieu of taxation as, for example, in the making or maintenance of roads.

Cosmopolitan Wealth. A term used by Alfred Marshall to cover wealth which is common to all nations as, for example, the oceans.

Cost. The cost of producing a certain output of a commodity is the sum of all the payments to the factors of production engaged on the production of that commodity. The term 'cost of production' has meaning only when it is related to output. The cost of producing a motor car depends on whether the manufacturer is turning out 50, 100, 500, etc., per week. The term 'cost' is ambiguous since it has several different meanings. For a given output it may be total cost, whereas for one unit of output—a single motor car, for example—it is clearly average cost that is being considered. If a firm is already producing 500 motor cars per week and it decides to increase its weekly output to 501, the cost of producing one more motor car per week will probably be much less than the average cost, though in other cases it might be more than average cost. This is the marginal cost of the commodity. In other lines of production—for example, coalmining—marginal cost may exceed average cost. As output increases marginal cost may increase, decrease, or remain constant.

A firm's costs can be divided into fixed and variable costs, or into prime and supplementary costs. Fixed costs are those that remain the same over a wide range of output, whereas variable costs are those that increase or decrease with every change of output. Prime costs include all the variable costs together with the cost of administration, which only in the short run is to be regarded as a fixed cost, supplementary costs then being the remainder of the fixed costs. In a trade depression a firm might be expected to close down if its income fails to cover its prime costs, the term 'shutdown cost' sometimes being used in this connection. Supplementary costs are frequently spoken of as overhead costs. Real or opportunity cost (*q.v.*) is the alternative forgone in order to produce or consume a commodity. The importance of cost in economics lies in its influence on supply, a rise in cost tending to curtail supply and a fall in cost tending to bring about an increase in supply (*q.v.*).

Cost Accountant. A person qualified in cost accountancy, usually as a result of passing the qualifying examinations of the Institute of Cost and Management Accountants and becoming an Associate of that body (A.C.M.A.). Firms employ cost accountants to work out the unit cost of their finished products, taking into account not only variable costs but also a proportionate amount of the fixed costs. *See also* Chartered Accountant.

Cost and Freight (c. & f.) A quotation of a price for goods on these terms means that the charge covers the price ex-warehouse, delivery to the docks, dues, and carriage as far as the port to which the goods are to be consigned, but excluding insurance and delivery from the docks to the purchaser's premises.

Cost/Benefit Analysis. A technique for the evaluation of an existing situation whereby the social cost is considered in relation to the benefit it confers on the community. This technique might be used in considering the site for a new airport or the line of a new motorway.

Cost Curve. A diagrammatic representation of cost. Curves can be drawn to show average cost and marginal cost over a range of output. The diagram on p. 102 shows that average cost and marginal cost are equal when average cost is at a minimum, the marginal cost curve cutting the average cost curve at the lowest point on the average cost curve. Before this point is reached average cost exceeds marginal cost; after this point marginal cost exceeds average cost.

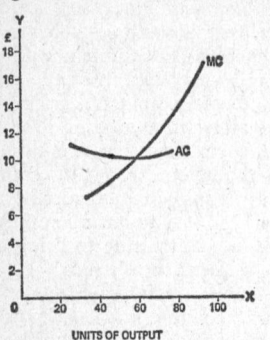

Graph: vertical axis £ from 0 to 18, horizontal axis UNITS OF OUTPUT from 0 to 100, showing MC (marginal cost) rising curve and AC (average cost) U-shaped curve. MC = MARGINAL COST, AC = AVERAGE COST.

Cost, Insurance, and Freight (c.i.f.). A quotation of a price for goods covering the price ex-warehouse, and including delivery to the docks, dock dues, carriage, and insurance as far as the port to which the goods are to be consigned, but excluding delivery from the docks to the purchaser's premises.

Cost Ladder. With reference to differences in costs of production between different firms in the same industry, the cost ladder is said to be steep if firms are evenly distributed over a wide range of cost. If the cost ladder is nearly horizontal it means that there is little difference between the costs of one firm and another. The concept is useful to an understanding of the effects of a decline in demand on the contraction of an industry, contraction being more easily achieved when the cost ladder is steep since the firms to drop out will be those with highest costs. It is less easy to predict what will happen in the case of an industry where the cost ladder is nearly horizontal since the effect of a fall in price will make all firms unprofitable so that excess capacity results.

Cost-of-living Bonus. An addition to basic pay dependent on the Index of Retail Prices. Thus, if the cost of living, as indicated by the Index of Retail Prices, rises by an agreed amount—so many points as measured by the Index—an increase in the cost-of-living bonus automatically follows. During both World Wars many groups of workers were awarded such bonuses, which later were consolidated into the basic pay scale. Unless the index is based on a similar standard of living to that of the workers concerned it is a very arbitrary method of compensating them for a rise in the cost of living. Some trade unions have secured agreements whereby the wages of their members are calculated according to a sliding scale varying with the Index of Retail Prices. If rigidly adhered to such a scheme might guarantee workers a certain standard of living, wages rising and falling with prices, but it would not give them a rising standard of living as the real national income increases, unless, as generally happens, adjustments are made to the basic pay from time to time.

Cost-of-living Index. An attempt by means of index numbers to measure changes in the cost of living of people within a particular income range. The method is to select a group of commodities and weight them according to the extent to which the members of the group as a whole make use of them. A base year is then chosen and assigned the index number 100. A rise in prices of 1% will then give a new index number of 101, just as a fall in price will give an index number of 99. The first cost-of-living index number to be calculated in Great Britain—and the only one to be given that name—was the one calculated by the Ministry of Labour which took July 1914 as its base. In 1904 a survey had been taken of the working classes at that time with the result that food was given a weight of 60%, rent and rates 16%, fuel and light 8%, clothing and footwear 12%, and a few miscellaneous items covered the remaining 4%. The index was introduced at an unfortunate time, the First World War breaking out shortly afterwards. By 1921 this index stood at 240, but by 1929 it had fallen back to 100 and by 1933 to 85, though it rose again to 96 by 1939. The heavy weighting of food indicates a rather low standard of living, and by 1945 it was very much out of date, people's distribution of expenditure having changed very greatly since the time of the survey of 1904. Since 1947 an Index of Retail Prices has superseded the cost-of-living index, although the older term is popularly often applied to it. *See* Index of Retail Prices.

Cost of Production Theory of Value. The theory that the price of a commodity depends on its cost of production, taking account of the services of all factors required in its production—a refinement of the labour theory of value which took account only of the labour cost. The modern theory of value relates the value of a commodity, as shown by its price, to the interaction of the forces of supply and demand, cost in so far as it affects supply being only one of the two influences on price. In the long run a producer must clearly cover his costs or he will be driven out of business, but in the short run the price of a commodity may be quite independent of its cost of production. For example, if a speculative builder put up a house at a total cost of £4,000 he would be able to obtain this price only if he could find someone willing to pay it, for once the house has been built the demand for houses of this type will decide its price, though clearly if the builder is unable to cover his costs he will curtail his output.

Cost-of-service Principle. With reference to taxes and local rates the principle that taxpayers and ratepayers should pay taxes and rates in proportion to the extent to which they benefit from the services provided by the State and local authority. To base taxation on this system is quite impracticable apart from the fact that it would often mean that those least able would have to pay most.

'Cost Plus' Principle. A method of fixing prices often adopted in wartime and the immediate post-war years, each producer or supplier being permitted to add a prescribed percentage to what the commodity has cost him. The great drawback to this system is that the greater the cost of production of a commodity the greater will be the profit percentage to the producer, inefficiency thus being encouraged and the more efficient firms penalised.

Cost-push. A term used to describe an inflation induced by rising prices due to increasing costs of production, especially increased wages. *See* Inflation.

Cost Schedule. A table showing total cost, average cost, marginal cost, fixed and variable cost, or any one of these, at a series of outputs. Such schedules form the basis of cost curves.

Cottage Industry. This occurs when people make goods at home for sale. It still survives in some countries. *See also* Domestic System.

Cotton Board. A body representing the cotton industry, established 1948, it was superseded in 1967 by the Textile Council (*q.v.*).

Cotton Famine. During the American Civil War (1861–65) the cotton industry was short of raw cotton, resulting in severe unemployment in Lancashire.

Cotton Industry Act (1959). The purpose of this Act was to reduce the total capacity of the cotton industry to make it more efficient. Compensation was to be paid to firms willing to scrap old machinery, thereby assisting the modernisation of the industry.

Council for National Academic Awards (C.N.A.A.). Successor to the Hives Committee (*q.v.*), it was established by royal charter in 1964. It is empowered to award degrees to students in institutions of higher education other than universities. All courses for such degrees have to be comparable in standard to those offered by universities and have to be approved by the Council. The degrees at present offered by the C.N.A.A. are B.A. and B.Sc. as first degrees,

M.A. and M.Sc. for postgraduate study, and M.Phil. and Ph.D. for research. In addition to courses in technological subjects, degree courses are now available in business studies. These require a study of basic subjects such as economics and accountancy, followed by a study of more specialised subjects such as marketing, business finance, etc.

Council for Scientific and Industrial Research. See Department of Scientific and Industrial Research.

Council of Associated Stock Exchanges. An association representing the separate stock exchanges in 21 of the larger provincial towns of Great Britain. See Stock Exchange.

Council of Members. The administrative institution of the E.E.C. to which problems, first considered by the Economic Commission of the Community, are submitted.

Council on Prices, Productivity and Incomes. A small committee of experts, known also as the Cohen Committee, set up in 1957 to report periodically on economic matters, more especially on the subjects mentioned in its title. Like the later National Incomes Commission it failed to secure the support of the trade unions.

Counterfoil. A detachable portion of a cheque, dividend warrant, or postal order which can be retained as a record of a payment or receipt.

Countervailing Credit. If a foreign exporter, A, sells goods through a British intermediary, B, to a merchant, C, in a third country, B may obtain a Countervailing Credit to cover payment from C if A has obtained a Confirmed Credit covering the transaction.

Countervailing Duty. An import duty imposed to protect a home industry against what is regarded as unfair foreign competition.

Country Bank. In England a bank without a branch in London. In the early nineteenth century there were many such banks, before 1826 these all being private banks. With the establishment of joint-stock banks banking began to increase in scale and amalgamations became frequent, so that the number of banks declined. Country banks found it to their advantage to amalgamate with banks that had branches in London, and so the number of country banks declined still further. In the United States banks are classified in three categories—central reserve city banks, reserve city banks, and country banks—for the purpose of the cash ratio which varies according to a bank's classification.

Country Clearing. One of the divisions of the clearing at the London Bankers' Clearing House (q.v.). All cheques drawn on banks outside London are dealt with at the country clearing.

County Bank. A merchant bank, a member of the National Westminster group.

Coupon. 1. A detachable certificate sometimes used for the payment of interest on bonds, debentures, and similar fixed interest securities. Coupons are issued in sheets and numbered in the order in which they are to be detached for payment.

2. A synonym for the rate of interest, a high coupon investment being one carrying a high rate of interest.

3. Used in the rationing of consumer goods (q.v.).

Coutts & Co. One of the smaller London clearing banks, it is now controlled by the National Westminster Bank (q.v.).

Covenant, Deed of. An undertaking to make a regular contribution to a charitable institution for a period of seven years. It is of benefit to the recipient since it enables income tax on the contribution to be reclaimed, so that in effect contributions are increased by the amount of the tax.

Covenanted Subscriptions. Non-profit-making organisations are exempt from income tax. In consequence contributions to these societies, if the donor agrees in advance to contribute a regular sum each year for at least seven years, are tax-free, the society being able to claim a refund of the tax the donor would otherwise have had to pay.

Covent Garden Market. The chief wholesale fruit, vegetable, and flower market in London. In 1974 it moved from Covent Garden to a new site at Nine Elms in South London.

Cover. A term used of the earnings of limited companies, it indicates how many times greater is the total profit than the distributed profit.

Cover Note. Temporary insurance cover to enable the insured to enjoy the benefits of a policy while it is being prepared.

Cowrie Shells. In some of the islands of the Pacific and countries bordering on that ocean cowrie shells at one time served as money. They were generally acceptable as they had value as ornaments. *See* Commodity Money.

C.P.A. Abbreviation of Calico Printers' Association.

C.P.I. Abbreviation of Consumer Price Index (*q.v.*).

C.P.R. Abbreviation of Canadian Pacific Railway.

C.R. Abbreviation of Company's (or Carrier's) risk (*q.v.*).

Cr. Abbreviation of Creditor.

Craft Gild. *See* Gild.

Craft Unions. These are small unions of skilled workers as distinct from the large industrial unions which include in their membership all grades of workers in an industry. The craft unions are the oldest trade unions. They are particularly concerned with the enforcement of apprenticeship regulations in order to restrict entry to the occupation. *See* Closed Union.

Crawling Peg. A type of flexible exchange rate (*q.v.*), allowing only a small movement of the rate per year.

Credit. 1. *Trade Credit.* This occurs when the seller permits the buyer to pay for goods received after an agreed interval of time. Its economic importance lies in the fact that the receiver of the credit is being helped to provide capital for the running of his business by another firm, while the granter of the credit has to forgo the use of the capital which he allows his customers to have. Many small retailers would find it difficult to carry on without receiving credit from wholesalers.

2. *Bank Credit.* When a bank makes an advance to a customer, whether by overdraft or loan account, the result is an increase in total purchasing power. Bank loans bring about an increase of equal amount in bank deposits: if a borrower has only a small balance to the credit of his account and he obtains an overdraft of £200 he can draw a cheque for this amount, and pay it to a creditor who will then deposit it in his own account. The creditor's account will have increased by £200, but the borrower's account can only show a debit for this amount. In the combined banks' balance sheets Advances and Deposits will both have increased by £200. This power of the banks to create credit is of great economic importance, and it is essential, therefore, that the monetary authorities should have power to control it, according to the monetary policy they wish to pursue. Banks have always restricted their expansion of credit by their cash ratio, as it was in their own interests to do so. The traditional instruments of control exercised by the Bank of England were by open market operations and changes in bank rate. Since 1945 other instruments of policy have been tried by the British monetary authorities—the Treasury Directive (a definite instruction to the banks), and Special Deposits (compelling the banks to deposit at the Bank of England a certain fraction of their deposits when it has been desired to curtail bank credit). *See* Monetary Policy.

Credit Bank. An alternative name for a commercial or joint-stock bank.

Credit Card. A card enabling the holder to obtain goods and services on credit at specified suppliers, including travel, meals, and hotel accommodation, up to an agreed maximum amount, payment being made monthly to the issuer of the card. Cards are issued, after the applicant's creditworthiness has been considered. The main advantage of credit cards is that they economise the use of cash. They can, however, be used to obtain credit up to the holder's limit. The banks issuing credit cards expect to cover their administrative costs from the interest they charge on the credit facilities they offer. Credit cards, which in their modern form date only from 1964, are of American origin and are more widely used in the United States than elsewhere though their use in Great Britain is increasing. Most credit cards are issued by banks. In the United States, where banks generally are small the Interbank (Master Charge) card is issued by 3,000 banks. The first British bank to issue its own card was Barclays (Barclaycard). The other three of the 'Big Four'— Lloyds, the Midland and the National Westminster—combined with some other banks to issue Access. Credit cards have become international in scope, the Barclaycard, for example, being linked in the United States with BankAmericard as well as having European connections, including a link with the French Carte Bleu. Access is linked in Europe with Eurocard and with the United States with Interbank Master Charge. *See also* Cheque Card.

Credit Clearing. A section of the London Bankers' Clearing House (*q.v.*), only opened in 1960, to deal with the settlement of credit transfers (*q.v.*).

Crédit Congolais. A bank with branches in Central Africa, it is an associate of Barclays Bank Ltd.

Crédit Export. A Belgian institution which assists traders and manufacturers to finance exports.

Crédit Foncier. In France a number of specialist institutions exist for the provision of credit to industry. The Crédit Foncier provides this service for the building industry.

Crédit Hotelier. One of the specialist institutions established in France for the provision of credit to particular industries, the Crédit Hotelier providing this service for the hotel and catering industry.

Credit Insurance. Insurance against bad debts. This form of insurance has been successfully provided only since it became the practice for the insured to accept liability for an agreed portion of the debt, as otherwise there is little inducement for the creditor to harry the debtor.

Credit, Letter of. *See* Circular Letter of Credit; Letter of Credit.

Crédit Lyonnais. The second largest commercial bank of France and in 1977 sixth largest in the world. Though nationalised it operates under its old name. It has an interest in the Banque Européenne de Crédit à Moyen Terme (*q.v.*).

Credit Note. A document, usually printed in red, used in commerce to inform one party to a transaction that a certain sum has been credited to his account. A credit note would be employed if inadvertently an overcharge had been made, or if goods which had been charged for had to be returned for some reason (not as ordered or if received in a damaged condition), or when packing cases are returned. The next statement will show a corresponding credit item.

Creditor Nation. A nation which has a greater income from foreign investment and loans to other nations than the amount of interest and dividends it has to pay out to other nations and foreign investors. By the end of the nineteenth century Great Britain, as a result of a succession of favourable balances of payment on current account, had become the greatest creditor nation in the world. The two World Wars greatly weakened Great Britain's position.

Credit Rating. *See* Credit Status.

Credit Rationing. This occurs when banks discriminate between borrowers, lending to some and refusing to lend or restricting their lending to others. Banks may do this voluntarily if, for example, they wish to limit lending for speculative purposes, or this policy may be forced on them by the monetary authorities by a Treasury Directive (*q.v.*), or when a demand for Special Deposits by the Bank of England reduces their liquidity ratio.

Credit Slip. An alternative term of Paying-in Slip (*q.v.*).

Credit Squeeze. A popular term for a policy of credit restriction by the monetary authorities such as occurred in 1955, 1961, 1965–66, and 1968–69.

Credit Status. Before granting credit to a new customer a trader will usually want to know something about his credit-worthiness. He may ask for trade and bank references or he may apply to a Status Inquiry Agent, a firm which specialises in acquiring information regarding the credit standing of business firms.

Credit Theory of the Trade Cycle. An attempt to explain the trade cycle in terms of changes in the volume of bank credit. It is asserted that there is a tendency for banks periodically to over-expand credit, mainly the result of banks being in competition with one another and advances to customers being their most profitable asset. After a time, it is asserted, the banks become alarmed and so tend then to contract credit unduly with the result that ups and downs of business activity follow variations in bank credit. Against this theory it has been pointed out that changes in bank credit follow and do not precede changes in the level of business activity, banks not expanding credit until recovery from a boom is already under way and not contracting credit until the peak of a boom has passed.

Credit Transfer. A means by which one or a number of accounts can be paid through a bank, the Clearing Banks operating a Credit Clearing similar to their cheque clearing system. Not only is the service open to a bank's customers but also to others on payment of a small fee. Credit transfers are payments made on instructions to a bank to credit customers of the same or other banks. To make use of this method of payment the debtor must know the name of his creditor's bank. The advantage of this system lies in the saving it effects in stationery, stamp duty, and postage. *See* Bank Giro Credit.

Creeping Inflation. An alternative term for Persistent Inflation. *See* Inflation.

Crofters (Scotland) Act (1955). An Act empowering the Treasury to make loans to crofters.

Cross Act (1875). An Act giving power to local authorities to carry out schemes of slum clearance.

Cross-elasticity of Demand. Where two commodities, which are close substitutes for one another, are in competitive demand, an increase in the price of one will increase demand for the other. The effect of this change of price of one commodity on the quantity demanded of the other is the cross-elasticity of demand. If a rise of 5% in the price of butter results in a 10% increase in the quantity demanded of margarine, then the cross-elasticity can be numerically calculated as follows:

$$\frac{\frac{100}{5}}{\frac{100}{10}} = \frac{100}{5} \times \frac{10}{100} = 2$$

Cross-elasticity is equal to 2 because the price change of one commodity produces twice as great a change in the quantity demanded of the other.

Crossing. This means drawing two parallel lines across the face of a cheque, the effect of which is to make it necessary to pay it into a banking account. There are several types of general and special crossing which can be used to place restrictions on the negotiability of a cheque. *See also* General Crossing; Special Crossing.

Cross Rate. Also known as Indirect Parity, it is the rate of exchange between currencies as calculated through a third centre. Thus the purchase of French francs for German marks in Zurich might yield a rate of exchange different from the rate in Paris, and so give rise to Arbitrage (*q.v.*).

Crown. A coin in circulation in a number of countries at different periods. The English crown first appeared in the reign of Henry VIII, made of an alloy of gold and silver, but in the reign of Edward VI it was made of silver. On account of its weight and size it was little used, few ever being minted. No provision has been made for a coin of this value in the British decimal coinage system. The earliest coin of this name was probably the French *couronne*, issued in the fourteenth century. Before 1914, the crown was the standard unit of currency in the Austro-Hungarian Empire. In the form *krone* it is the standard unit of the Norwegian and Danish currencies, and as *krona* of the Swedish.

Crown Agents, Office of. An organisation which acts as financial and commercial agent for over 200 overseas government and public authorities. In 1833 colonial governors, who had previously appointed individual agents as purchasing and investment officers in London, established a single body for this purpose. At first known as the Agents-General for the Colonies, the name was recently changed to the Crown Agents for Overseas Governments and Administrations. It has offices in many parts of the world. Since some former colonies on becoming independent (*e.g.* Ghana) have set their own offices in London its business recently has declined a little.

Crown of the Double Rose. A former English gold coin, first issued in 1526 and worth £0.25.

Crown of the Rose. A former English gold coin, first issued in 1526 and worth £0.22½.

Crowther Reports. 1. **1959.** The report of the Central Advisory Council for Education (England), Sir Geoffrey Crowther being chairman, it recommended that the school leaving age should be raised to 16 by 1968 and that this should be followed by the establishment of County Colleges for compulsory part-time education for young people aged 16 to 18.

2. **1971.** A report on consumer credit, its principal recommendations being: (i) Hire purchase regulations should not be used as an instrument of economic policy; (ii) Expansion of credit facilities should be allowed; (iii) Hire purchase should be free from controls regarding the initial deposit or the period of repayment.

C.R.S. Abbreviation of Co-operative Retail Services Ltd. (*q.v.*).

Crude. With reference to the birth and death rates it means the actual number per 1,000 of the population.

Cruzeiro. The standard unit of the currency of Brazil, it is divided into 100 centavos.

C.S.E. Abbreviation of Certificate in Secondary Education (*q.v.*).

C.S.I.R. Abbreviation of Council for Scientific and Industrial Research.

Cum Distribution. Similar to cum dividend but with reference to units trusts.

Cum Dividend (Cum Div.). A stock exchange term meaning including dividend. The purchaser of a stock quoted 'cum div.' will be entitled to receive the next dividend when due.

Cum. Pref. Abbreviation of Cumulative Preference Shares (*q.v.*).

Cum Rights. When a stock or share is quoted in this way on the stock exchange it means that a current purchaser is entitled to a 'rights' issue which has probably already been announced.

Cumulative Preference Shares. If in a previous year the interest on these shares has not been paid the holders are entitled to receive it in a later year before any dividend is paid on the ordinary shares if profit is available.

Cunliffe Report (1918). The report of a committee appointed to inquire into the English banking and monetary system, and to consider the restoration of the gold standard. In the course of its Report it gave a descriptive account of the working of the gold standard before 1914, showing that when gold was exported it reduced the amount of gold available for internal purposes, so that the note issue had to be reduced, this being supported by a contraction of credit. An inflow of gold on the other hand would lead to an opposite sequence of events, the gold standard in either case working 'automatically' to restore equilibrium to the country's balance of payments. The required changes were assisted by raising bank rate when credit was to be contracted in order to check borrowing, and reducing bank rate when an expansion of credit was desired in order to encourage borrowing. No one doubts today that this was a much oversimplified account of the working of the gold standard even before 1914, and bank rate was credited with a greater influence than it probably ever had. Not unnaturally, the Committee recommended a return to the gold standard when the time was ripe. The Committee considered that the Bank Charter Act (1844), even though in time of crisis it had to be suspended, had fulfilled its purpose in preventing an over-issue of bank-notes. The Cunliffe Committee also recommended that the Bank of England should absorb the Treasury notes issued during the First World War. As a result of the Report Great Britain returned to the gold standard in 1925, and in 1928 the Currency and Bank Notes Act transferred the Treasury Issue to the Bank of England.

Cupro-nickel Coinage. This replaced silver in Great Britain in 1946. The metal used is an alloy consisting of 75% copper and 25% nickel.

Currency. In a narrow sense it may be limited to cash—coin, notes, and bank deposits subject to withdrawal by cheque. In a wider sense it may be taken to include bills of exchange and, perhaps, money orders and postal orders. For a list of units of foreign currency see Monetary Unit.

Currency and Bank Notes Act (1928). This Act made provision for the withdrawal from circulation of the £1 and 10s. Treasury notes issued during the First World War, and their replacement by the issue of Bank of England notes of similar denominations, the Bank being allowed to increase its fiduciary issue of £260 million. The new notes were declared to be legal tender up to any amount. For future changes in the fiduciary issue the consent of the Treasury was required. Actually the Act empowered the Treasury to sanction a change in the issue in the first place for six months only, although such sanction was to be renewable for up to two years. Particulars of proposed changes had to be laid before Parliament, and any extension of the period beyond two years required Parliament's approval. One effect of the Act was to make seasonal changes in the note issue possible, but the many changes since 1939 have made alterations to the fiduciary issue a mere formality. The Act also declared that in future the entire profits of the Issue Department of the Bank of England should go to the Treasury.

Currency and Bank Notes Act (1939). This Act empowered the Bank of England to revalue its gold weekly according to the price ruling in the market. This would have meant that that part of the note issue backed by gold could be increased when the price of gold rose, but reduced if the price of gold had fallen. Soon afterwards the Second World War broke out and this new development ceased to be of importance as almost the entire stock of gold of the Bank of England was transferred to the Treasury's Exchange Equalisation Account, and since then the note issue has been almost entirely fiduciary in character.

Currency and Bank Notes Act (1954). This Act gave the Bank of

England power to issue notes of any denomination it pleased. It also gave the fiduciary issue as £1,575 million, subject to variation only with the consent of the Treasury. Since the Act was passed not a year has gone by without an increase in the fiduciary issue (q.v.).

Currency Appreciation. A rise in the value of a currency in terms of others on the foreign exchange market. The term is used more particularly of a foreign exchange system where currencies are free to fluctuate on the market in response to changes in supply and demand. Thus, an excess of exports (visible and invisible) will reduce the supply of a country's currency on the market and so cause it to appreciate. In consequence imports will become cheaper but to foreigners its exports will be dearer, with the result that imports will tend to increase and exports to decline until equilibrium is again established.

Currency Circulation. The value of the Bank of England notes in circulation as shown in the weekly Bank Return for the Issue Department of the Bank of England, the balance of the note issue being held in reserve in the Banking Department. For over twenty-five years the amount of currency in circulation has tended to increase, this being partly due to inflation and partly the result of increasing production and a rising standard of living. There are seasonal increases in the amount of currency in circulation shortly before Christmas and again in the summer, due to the public's increased demand for cash.

Currency Depreciation. A fall in the value of a currency in terms of others on the foreign exchange market. The term is particularly used of a system of foreign exchange where currencies are free to fluctuate on the market in response to changes in supply and demand. Thus, an excess of imports over exports will increase the supply of a country's currency on the market and cause it to depreciate. As a result imports will become dearer and so be checked while exports being cheaper to other countries will be encouraged and in consequence equilibrium will be restored.

Currency Notes. *See* Treasury Notes.

Currency School. A number of banking crises occurred in England during 1825–37, due mainly, it was thought, to an excessive issue of notes by some banks. As a result a demand arose for the issue of bank-notes to be controlled by Parliament. A keen controversy developed between those people, like the members of the Currency School, who wished the issue of notes to be rigidly controlled by law, and those, like the members of the Banking School, who desired a more flexible note issue to meet an expanding economy. The more extreme members of the Currency School thought that the entire note issue should be fully backed by gold, but if a fiduciary issue was permitted they thought that it should be small and that any increases in the note issue should be fully backed by gold. The Currency School tended to over-emphasise the dangers associated with an over-issue of notes. The Bank Charter Act of 1844 clearly showed the influence of the Currency School. *See* Bank Charter Act.

Currency Stabilisation. Fixing the value of a currency in terms of a particular assortment of goods in order to stabilise its purchasing power.

Current Account. The type of bank account required if a customer wishes to make payments by means of cheques.

Current Assets. Very liquid or short-term assets.

Current Balance. A term used in connection with the balance of payments (q.v.) for the balance of visible and invisible items, but excluding capital movements.

Current Liabilities. Debts that must be paid in the short-term.

Current Ratio. Also known as the 'Acid-test' Ratio, it is the relation between the current assets and the current liabilities of a business.

Curriers' Company. One of the 82 Guilds or Livery Companies of the City of London whose existence dates back to medieval times.

Custom. A factor to be taken into account when considering the behaviour of consumers in the market. It shows that consumers are not perfectly rational when consideration is being given to a change of price. People often become accustomed to buying certain things and may continue to do so to the same extent as previously even after a rise in price.

Customer Service. Imperfect competition arises in retailing as a result of (i) the different locations of shops (every shop being more conveniently situated than others for some people), and (ii) the variation in the services the retailer provides for his customers. These services include free delivery, the granting of credit, willingness to exchange goods, etc.

Customs and Excise, Commissioners of. A department of the Inland Revenue responsible since 1671 for the collection of customs duties (*q.v.*), and since 1908 excise duties also.

Customs Drawback. When customs duty has been paid on goods that later are to be re-exported it is possible to claim a refund of duty, known as Customs Drawback.

Customs Duties. Taxes on imports. One of the oldest forms of tax, they date back in England to the time of King John, probably being imposed in the first place to cover expenditure on docks and harbours and the cost to the State of defending shipping against pirates. For a long time customs duties were imposed to provide revenue for specific purposes, but later they became one of a number of general sources of revenue. During the period 1846–72, as a result of the influence of the free trade movement, many hundreds of import duties were withdrawn. Since that time customs duties have been imposed for the protection of home industries. The McKenna Duties of 1915 comprised taxes on imported motor cars, pianos, and a few other commodities. In 1932 Great Britain adopted a comprehensive tariff of protection, the 'free list' comprising mainly food and raw materials. Even so the protective duties only yield 12% of the total revenue from customs duties. The Ottawa Trade Agreement resulted in the Import Duties Act (1932) which provided for preferential duties on goods imported from Commonwealth countries. Economic theory shows that duties on imports are contrary to the Principle of Comparative Cost (*q.v.*), and therefore restrict the full development of international trade. In 1976 a new distinction was made between customs and excise duties, customs duties being imposed for non-revenue purposes and excise duties for revenue. *See also* Excise Duties.

Customs Specification. A document required by the British authorities who are responsible for recording the value of imports and exports, this information being required for the calculation of the balance of trade. The document shows the value (f.o.b.) of the goods exported and the country to which they have been consigned.

Customs Union. A group of countries with a common external tariff. A well-known example was that of 1833 between Prussia and some of the smaller German states, a forerunner of the political union of these states. In 1922 Belgium and Luxembourg formed a customs union, and after the Second World War this was enlarged to include the Netherlands and came to be known as Benelux. The success of the European Iron and Steel Community, which comprised the three countries of Benelux together with France, West Germany, and Italy, led to the formation of the O.E.E.C. (the Organisation for European Economic Co-operation) and other regional areas of free trade such as E.F.T.A. (the European Free Trade Association) and L.A.F.T.A. (the

Latin American Free Trade Area). The economic basis of these associations is to be found in the Principle of Comparative Cost, which shows that total output and trade are likely to increase if hindrances to international trade such as tariffs are removed or reduced. *See also* Comparative Cost, Principle of; European Common Market.

Customs Waterguard Service. A branch of the British Customs service whose duty it is to intercept every ship from overseas entering a British port in order to inspect its cargo and inquire of the state of health of the passengers (if any) and crew.

Cutlers' Company. One of the 82 Guilds or Livery Companies of the City of London whose existence dates back to the gilds of medieval times.

Cut-throat Competition. An extreme form of competition, most likely to occur in conditions of duopoly where there are only two producers or of imperfect oligopoly where there are only a few producers, the product of each being differentiated from the products of the others, often by little more than a distinctive brand name. Cut-throat competition may take the form of a price war, in an extreme case carried to the point where the weakest producer is driven out of business—hence the term 'cut-throat'. Since, however, a price war may have serious consequences for all taking part in it, only the first to cut prices achieving a short-lived gain until his rivals follow suit, in more recent times cut-throat competition has more often taken the form of advertising wars for the purpose of maintaining, and if possible increasing, sales without reducing prices. An advertising war might be accompanied by some measure of price cutting.

C.W.S. Abbreviation of Co-operative Wholesale Society (*q.v.*).

Cybernetics. The science of systems of control and communications, one of the subjects of study in courses of Management studies

Cycle, Business (or **Trade**). *See* Trade Cycle.

Cyclical Fluctuations. *See* Trade Cycle.

Cyclical Unemployment. Unemployment associated with the downswing of the trade or business cycle, which was a pronounced feature of economic activity during the hundred and twenty years before 1914. The main characteristic of cyclical unemployment is that it is associated with a general depression, so that nearly all forms of production are affected, although even at such times a few expanding industries may be less seriously affected than others. On account of its widespread nature it is the most serious cause of unemployment, since it produces mass unemployment, and to prevent its occurrence was the first aim of Lord Beveridge's policy of full employment.

D

Dai-Iohi Kangyo. The chief bank of Japan, it was in 1977 the ninth largest in the world.

Dalasi. Standard unit of the currency of Gambia, it is equal in value to 100 Bututs.

Damages. Compensation awarded by a court of law to a plaintiff who has suffered loss as a result of an act of the defendant. In addition a plaintiff may receive exemplary damages if the defendant's act has caused hurt to his feelings or his prestige. Nominal damages are awarded where it is clear that no material loss has been suffered although legally the defendant has been at fault.

Dangerous Trades. Elaborate regulations have been framed for the protection of workers in dangerous trades, the Home Secretary having power if he thinks fit to add further trades to the list of those to which the regulations already apply.

Danmarks Nationalbank. The central bank of Denmark, it has its head office in Copenhagen and five branches in other cities. Since its establishment in 1818 it has been the only bank in Denmark with the right to issue bank-notes.

Danske Landmandsbank. The leading Danish commercial bank, its head office is in Copenhagen and it has branches throughout Denmark.

Datel. Services provided by the Post Office for the transmission of punched tape data.

Dawes Plan. A scheme formulated in 1924 by a committee under the chairmanship of C. G. Dawes, whereby financial assistance was given to Germany after the collapse of the mark to enable that country to continue to pay reparations, although at a reduced rate. It gave way to the Young Plan (*q.v.*) in 1929.

Days of Grace. Unless there is an express statement to the contrary bills of exchange, except 'sight' bills, fall due for payment three days, known as 'days of grace', after the period for which the bill has been drawn. Thus, a three-months bill, dated 8th January, will fall due for payment on 11th April.

D.C.L. Abbreviation of Distillers Company Ltd., producers of 70% of the whisky of the U.K.

D.E. Abbreviation of Department of Employment. *See* Employment, Department of.

'Dead Book.' A colloquial term for the Register of Defunct Companies.

Dead Letter Office. The department of the Post Office which deals with letters and postal packets which for some reason cannot be delivered.

Dead Stock. Unsaleable goods or any form of capital not in use.

Deadweight Debt. A debt not covered by any real asset. Most of the British National Debt is of this type, the greater part of it having arisen in the financing of wars, so that what was borrowed was spent on materials of war that were consumed at the time.

Dear Money. A period when rates of interest are high, so that borrowing is expensive.

Death Benefit. One of the benefits under the National Insurance (Industrial Injuries) Act (1946), where an employee suffers death as a result of an accident at work. It is not to be confused with Funeral Expenses (*q.v.*).

Death Duties. A direct tax on the estate of a deceased person, more correctly known as Estate Duty, and since 1975 incorporated in Capital Transfer Tax (*q.v.*).

Death Grant. Also known as a funeral grant, it is one of the benefits provided by the early friendly societies as well as by Burial Societies established specifically to make provision for funeral expenses. A death grant (Funeral Benefit) is provided under the National Insurance Scheme.

Death-rate. The number of deaths in a year per thousand of the population, this being known as the crude death-rate. The death-rate is influenced by (i) changes in expectation of life, and (ii) the distribution of the population among the different age groups. Thus, a country with a large proportion of old people may have a high crude death-rate, although expectation of life may have increased in that country. During the past two hundred years there has been an almost continuous decline in the death-rate in the United Kingdom and many other countries. For the year 1800 it has been estimated at 25 per thousand for the United Kingdom; at the present day it is less than half that rate. For the second of the two reasons given above the death-rate of the U.K. has increased slightly since 1953, so that over the past 25 years it has shown very little change. It was the persistent fall in the death-rate that was the main cause of the large increase in the population of the U.K. during the nineteenth century, the birth-rate remaining almost unchanged until 1880.

Debasement of the Coinage. Coins can be debased by the issuing authority or by others. For a long time coins were expected to be of full face value, but there was always the danger that the issuing authority might make them of less weight than they were reputed to be. The issue of coins being from early times the special prerogative of the State, monarchs in financial straits were often tempted to debase the coinage for the sake of the gain accruing to themselves from this practice. Henry VIII was responsible for the debasement of the English coinage during the years 1543–51, the amount of silver in the coins eventually being only one-seventh of what it should have been. Debasement on this scale could not pass unnoticed and the consequence was a fall in the value of the coins, shown by a steep rise in prices. In those days merchants who had the slightest doubt about the weight of precious metal in coins would again have recourse to the older practice of weighing them as metal. Debasement of the coinage by clipping has always been regarded as a serious offence.

Debenture Stock. In addition to raising capital by the issue of shares a company may borrow by the issue of debentures, these forming loan capital, and the holders being creditors of the company. Debentures rank, therefore, ahead of all types of shares for payment of the interest due on them. They carry a fixed rate of interest, usually a little lower than that on preference shares. Generally, they are redeemable at par at some future date, but irredeemable debentures are sometimes issued. *See also* Mortgage Debentures; Secured Debentures; Simple Debentures; Unsecured Debentures.

Debit Note. A document similar to an invoice in that it shows the sum owed by the purchaser to the supplier of the goods. It may be issued to supplement an invoice when an item has been omitted or on which an error of undercharge has been made.

Debt. Legally described as a chose in action (*q.v.*) it can be transferred by the creditor to some other person, provided that the transfer is in writing and that the whole and not merely a part of the debt is so assigned. Assignable debts are usually those that have been embodied in special legal form as negotiable instruments.

Debt Conversion. The issue of a new Government stock at a lower rate of interest in exchange for a stock to be redeemed. Often a Government has to borrow when the prevailing rate of interest is high, but if a stock bearing a high rate of interest falls due for redemption at a time when the prevailing rate of interest is low the Government will take advantage of this to reduce the cost of its borrowing.

Debt, Imprisonment for. Strictly this is imprisonment for 'contempt of court' since imprisonment can now occur in Great Britain only when a debtor has failed to comply with a court order for payment.

Debt Management. Now an important instrument of monetary policy. Opportunities for debt management are provided for the monetary authorities when Government stocks reach their date of maturity or when new issues are made, and they are assisted by the fact that Government departments—especially the Issue Department of the Bank of England—with funds at their disposal, can be asked to take up stocks. The Government broker may intervene on the stock exchange to buy or sell securities. The authorities also operate in Treasury bills. Government policy in the management of the National Debt aims at influencing the prevailing rate of interest, either to keep it as low as possible in pursuance of a cheap money policy, or to keep it up in order to make investment more attractive.

Debts, Inter-Allied. During the First World War Great Britain lent large sums of money to its European allies, but in order to do so had itself to borrow from the United States. A number of European countries also borrowed directly from the United States. Eventually most of the debts were funded except the Russian debt to Great Britain. The payment of interest and repayment of principal in connection with these debts was one of the causes of the balance of payments difficulties of European countries which had suffered so severely as a result of the war, and international payment on this scale was one of the main causes of failure to maintain the gold standard after its revival in the early 1920s. Matters were still further aggravated by the Great Depression, as a result of which many countries repudiated their debts. Though Great Britain did not repudiate its debt to the United States only a token payment was made in 1933 and no further payments were made. During the Second World War the introduction of the 'Lease-Lend' system by President Roosevelt prevented war debts arising between Great Britain and the United States.

Decasualisation. A term used by Lord Beveridge for the replacement of a system of casual labour by one of regular employment, as happened in 1967 with dock workers.

Decentralisation. In the case of any large-scale organisation it is not always possible for every aspect of the undertaking's activities to be organised from the centre, so that a certain amount of decentralisation becomes necessary. The larger the undertaking usually the greater is the extent of decentralisation. For example, both the Gas Council and the Central Electricity Generating Board found it necessary to set up regional boards.

Decimal Coinage. A system of coinage in which the standard unit is divisible into 100 minor units. On account of its simplification of monetary calculations many countries have adopted decimal coinage. A drawback to the system is that divisibility by 100 does not give a very wide range of value between the highest and lowest units. If a small standard unit is chosen high prices will be represented by very large numbers. Decimalisation of the coinage was advocated as long ago as 1682 by Sir William Petty. The United States, however, was the first country to adopt the system in 1792, followed by France in 1793. In Great Britain a first step towards decimalisation was taken, it was thought, when the florin was revived in 1849. Then a Select Committee in 1853 recommended decimalisation with the pound as unit, divided into 1,000 mils. Further consideration was given to the question in 1856 and 1868, and then in 1918 a Royal Commission decided against it. During the late 1950s and early 1960s many new states, formerly British possessions, adopted a decimal coinage on achieving independence, as also did South Africa. Both Australia and New Zealand decimalised their coinage with the dollar as standard units equal in value to £0·50. In 1961 the British Government appointed the Halsbury Committee to advise on 'the most convenient and practical form which a decimal coinage might take' if adopted by Great Britain. By a majority the Committee favoured the retention of the £1 divided into 100 new pence. Decimalisation of the coinage took place in the United Kingdom in February 1971.

Declining Population, Effects of, Until fairly recently it was expected that the population of Great Britain and some other West European countries would begin to decline in the not too distant future. During the 1920s, for example, there was talk in Great Britain of race suicide. Recent population trends appear to have refuted this view, though the present tendency for population to increase may in time be reversed. One effect of a declining population would be to alter the distribution within the various age groups, with an increase in the number of older people (*See* Ageing Population.) A decline in population might mean a falling off in demand and so a tendency for unemployment to increase. This might check economic growth. Structural unemployment is likely to increase because of the greater difficulty of redistributing labour among different occupations, reducing labour in declining industries and increasing labour in expanding ones. Redistribution is easier if industries are declining only relatively to others and not absolutely. Similarly, unemployment arising from technical progress is easier to overcome with an increasing population. The burden of the National Debt and the cost of the social services would fall more heavily on those of working age if the population were to decline. *See also* Increasing Population; Population Problem.

Decreasing Marginal Cost. This occurs when the cost of producing each successive unit of output is less than the cost of producing the previous unit. Over the range of output where this occurs there will be increasing returns to scale. Sooner or later, however, marginal cost will begin to increase and diminishing returns will set in.

Decreasing Returns. *See* Diminishing Returns, Law of.

Deductive Method. One of the two methods—the other being the inductive method—by which a body of theory is built up. Starting from a given hypothesis—some generally accepted fact of everyday experience—in certain defined conditions logical deductions are made. From these deductions laws are then formulated. This is the traditional method of pure economics.

Deed. Technically this is a specialty contract, a document which has been signed, sealed, and delivered, though nowadays the sealing of the document is a formality. The purpose of a deed is to impress on the parties to it the seriousness of the contract to which it refers. Certain transactions always require a deed, among them being the conveyance of property, and contracts where no consideration is involved.

Deed of Arrangement. An agreement made by a debtor with his creditors in order to avoid bankruptcy. *See also* Composition.

Deed of Assignment. *See* Assignment.

Deed of Covenant. An arrangement whereby a contributor undertakes to make an annual subscription for seven years to a society approved by the Inland Revenue, the society then being allowed to re-claim the tax paid by the contributor on this subscription and thereby obtaining additional income.

Deed of Gift. *See* Gifts *Inter Vivos*.

Deed of Partnership. A document drawn up to clarify the respective positions of the partners in a business. It should be sufficiently detailed and explicit to regulate every matter affecting the partners that is likely to arise during the continuation of the partnership or on its dissolution, the aim being to obviate disputes. The provisions of the Deed can be varied subsequently only by agreement of the partners.

Defence Aid. After the United States had terminated large-scale aid to Europe, known as Marshall Aid, it continued to give specific assistance for defence purposes, this being known as Defence Aid. For some years it gave assistance to the British balance of payments, in 1952 amounting to £121 million, though by 1956 it had fallen to £23 million.

Defence Bonds. A National Savings security introduced in 1939. They were superseded by in 1964 National Development Bonds, these in turn being replaced in 1968 by British Savings Bonds (*q.v.*).

Deferred Annuity. An annuity arranged to start at a stated future date, payment being made over an agreed period prior to the date on which the annuity payments are to start.

Deferred Payments. One of the functions performed by money is serving as a means for making deferred payments, this arising out of its function as a medium of exchange. Undertakings to make payments at some future date will be entered into only if it is accepted that the value of money is likely to remain stable during the interval which elapses between the incurring of the debt and its settlement.

Deferred Shares. A type of share which, when issued, ranks after Ordinary Shares, which then carry a fixed rate of dividend, the Deferred Shares taking the residue of distributed profit. It is rare now for this type of share to be issued.

Deficiency Payment. Under the Agriculture Act (1947) British farmers are guaranteed certain prices for many farm products. When the actual market prices of these products are below the guaranteed prices the State makes up the difference by 'deficiency payments' to the farmers.

Deficit Financing. Deliberately budgeting for a deficit. Fiscal policy through the Budget is now a recognised adjunct to monetary policy. To check inflation the aim has often been to obtain a large budget surplus to reduce the volume of purchasing power in the hands of consumers. Faced by a trade depression and serious unemployment it has been suggested that a budget deficit should be deliberately incurred, taxes being reduced in order to make more purchasing power available as a stimulus to demand.

Definitions of Economics. *See* Economics, Definitions of.

Deflation. A policy aiming at reducing the quantity of money in order to check inflation. On the gold standard the Bank of England used to adopt a deflationary policy in order to check an outflow of gold. In these circumstances bank rate would be raised and open-market operations undertaken to reduce the balances of the commercial banks at the Bank of England in order to compel them to curtail their advances and thereby reduce their deposits. During the nineteenth century deflationary action of this kind was generally on a small scale, but during the period of the revived gold standard, 1925-31, a policy of deflation was first required in order to establish the high parity of sterling with the American dollar that had been chosen and then again deflation had to be adopted to check the serious outflow of gold during 1930-31. In the nineteenth century only a small degree of deflation had been required but it was thought that this had its effect in restoring equilibrium to the balance of payments (i) by stimulating exports by reducing their prices and (ii) by checking imports by reducing incomes at home. In the twentieth century the main effect of deflation was to increase unemployment in consequence of the fall in demand, and when in 1931 it was thought necessary to have further deflation at a time when unemployment was already a serious problem, the term deflation became popularly synonymous with depression and unemployment. Consequently, since 1945 mildly deflationary policies have often been described as disinflationary.

Deflationary Gap. A certain volume of investment, public and private, will give full employment. If full employment is not achieved the deflationary gap is the amount of additional investment required to restore employment to the level of full employment.

Defunct Company. A limited company which has been wound up and ceased to function. Such companies are listed in the Register of Defunct Companies, known colloquially as the 'Dead Book' (*q.v.*).

Degrees in Economics. Most universities nowadays offer degrees in economics. In some cases it is an alternative subject of study for a B.A. degree and in others it takes the form of a B.Sc.(Econ.) (Bachelor of Science in Economics) degree or B.Com. (*qq.v.*).

Delaware Company. In the United States company law varies between one state and another. In the state of Delaware (one of the smallest in size) the law is more favourable to companies than in the rest of the country. Consequently a high proportion of American corporations —and some British companies too— are registered there.

***Del Credere* Agent.** An agent who, in return for a higher rate of commission, guarantees that his principal will receive payment for the goods he has sold on his behalf.

Delegation of Authority. The ability to delegate authority is one of the essential attributes of the entrepreneur. Even in a small business some delegation of authority is necessary if the entrepreneur is to find time to weigh policy and make decisions. The larger the business the greater must be the extent to which delegation of authority is carried. A characteristic of a good manager is his ability to select suitable people to whom he can delegate authority.

Delixery Note. A document which usually accompanies the delivery of goods, providing the consignee with a list of items in that particular consignment. Its purpose is to enable the consignment to be checked.

Delivery Order. A document issued by the owner of goods stored in a warehouse entitling the person whe name appears on it to collect the goods specified. In the case of goods stored in a bonded warehouse customs duty will have to be paid before the goods can be removed.

Delivery, Terms of. Methods of indicating whether the sender or the consignee shall pay the delivery charges on a consignment of goods or whether the charge shall be divided between them. When Goods are despatched Carr. Fwd. (Carriage Forward) the consignee pays the delivery charge, but if they are sent Carr. Pd. (Carriage Paid) the sender will pay. Other terms of delivery include c.&f.; c.i.f.; ex-warehouse; ex-works; f.o.b.; f.o.r.; franco; loco (*qq.v.*).

Demand. By demand is meant the quantity of a commodity that will be bought at a particular price and not merely the desire for a thing. This is sometimes described as effective demand to distinguish it from need. Generally at a high price less will be bought than at a low price. This does not mean, however, that a change in demand has taken place, for it is simply the expression of the behaviour of buyers when their demand is at a certain intensity. *See* Changes in Demand; Changes in Supply; Demand Curve; Equilibrium (i); Supply.

Demand Curve. If the quantities of a commodity that would be bought over a range of prices at a particular time were known this information could be represented in graphical form by means of a Demand Curve. There is a typical Demand Curve on p. 119. The curve DD represents the state of demand at a particular time. OY is the price scale and OX the quantity scale. The diagram shows that at the price *OP* the quantity *OQ* will be demanded. In a similar way the amounts that would be demanded at other prices can be read from the graph, which clearly shows that at a price higher than *OP* a smaller quantity would be demanded, and at a price lower than *OP* a greater quantity would be demanded.

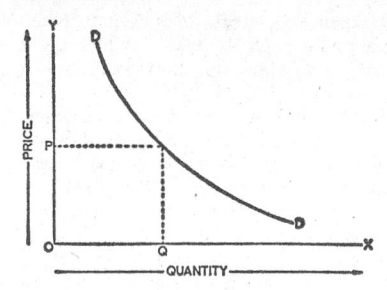

Demand Deposits. A term used in the United States of deposits on current account, that is, withdrawable on demand by cheque.

Demand Draft. An alternative term for a bill of exchange payable at sight.

Demand for Labour. An example of derived demand the demand for labour being derived from the demand for the goods and services the labour is required to produce. The demand for labour can be increased by stimulating a great demand for goods and services by an expansion of purchasing power.

Demand for Money. This means the demand to hold money as an alternative to investing it. Lord Keynes distinguished three motives for holding money: (i) the transactions motive, (ii) the precautionary motive, and (iii) the speculative motive. Everyone requires a certain amount of money to cover ordinary, everyday expenditure on such things as housekeeping, newspapers, tobacco, gas and electricity bills, rates, etc. Few people would limit the amount of money they hold to what was only just sufficient for this purpose, but would prefer to keep a little extra in reserve to cover unforeseen expenditure caused by sickness (though the existence of a National Health Service makes this less necessary than formerly), household breakages or expenses in connection with any kind of emergency. The amount of money held for purposes (i) and (ii) will depend largely on custom and habit and the social and financial position of the people concerned. It will also depend on the length of the interval between one payday and the next, for those in receipt of monthly salaries will require to hold more than weekly wage-earners but less than those who are paid quarterly. The total amount held for these two purposes, therefore, will not vary much in the short period unless prices are rising very steeply, as in a period of inflation, when clearly more money will be required to pay for a given quantity of goods and services. Therefore, if the total amount of money held by the community as a whole varies very much it will be for the third—the speculative—motive. To hold money involves a loss of the interest it would otherwise have earned, and so it costs money to hold money. If, however, the prevailing rate of interest is expected to rise in the near future the loss of interest may be more than balanced by the gain from the purchase of a security at a lower price. By holding money instead of investing it there will be a loss of interest but a gain of a lower price. Thus, the main influence on holding money, that is, on the demand for money, is expectation of the future trend of the rate of yield on securities. When people prefer to hold money to investing it their liquidity-preference is said to be high. Thus, the demand for money depends on liquidity-preference.

Demand, Law of. *See* Supply and Demand, Laws of.

Demand Price. The quantity of a good demand at a price. For example, in the demand schedule shown on p. 120 at a Demand Price of £1·30 the quantity demanded is 58,000.

Demand-pull. A term used to describe an inflation induced by increased demand due to increased incomes. *See* Inflation.

Demand Schedule. This shows the amount of a commodity that will be demanded in the same state of demand at each of a range of prices. Demand schedule can be compiled either for individuals or for all buyers in a market, but in either case the schedule is purely hypothetical since it is impossible to compile statistics to show how much of a commodity will de demanded at different prices at the same moment of time. The following is a specimen market demand schedule:

Price of commodity	Quantity of commodity demanded per month (kg)
£	
1·60	40,000
1·50	45,000
1·40	51,000
1·30	58,000
1·20	66,000
1·10	76,000
1·00	89,000

From a market demand schedule a demand curve (*q.v.*) can be constructed.

Demarcation Dispute. In some industries, such as shipbuilding and building, workers in different trades are employed and disputes sometimes occur between the trade unions concerned as to which workers should undertake particular jobs, the members of one union perhaps going on strike because work which they regarded as theirs was being done by members of another union.

Demise Charter. A form of Charter Party where the charterer of a ship makes all the arrangements for working it, so that in effect for a period it is owned by him.

Demography. The study of birth-rate and death-rate trends and their effect on population changes. *See* Birth-rate; Death-rate; Population Problems.

Demonetisation. This occurs when a metal such as gold or silver used as a monetary standard ceases to be so used.

Demurrage. A term used in connection with Charter Party, it is an extra charge the charterer has to pay per day for exceeding the period of charter originally agreed upon, and detaining the vessel beyond that time. The term is also used by railways which also make a charge if their wagons are detained beyond a certain time or if parcels are not collected within a stated time.

Denationalisation. Returning a nationalised industry back to free enterprise as occurred in Great Britain with the iron and steel industry in 1953 and to a partial extent with road haulage also in 1953.

Department Store. The distinguishing feature of this type of retail business is that it is really a group of shops all under one roof and one management, each department dealing in a particular branch of retail trade. The department store had its origin in France, and it is well established both in that country and the United States. Clearly, very large premises are required and these are often quite palatial in appearance. For this type of business a large turnover is essential, and so department stores are to be found only in large cities which serve as shopping centres for extensive areas, such as London, Leeds, Manchester, Birmingham, Edinburgh, and other places. Their development has been greatly assisted by improvements in transport. In England many department stores developed out of drapery businesses, and in the smaller ones the drapery department is often the main department of the concern. Department stores vary considerably in size, the largest having over three hundred departments and the smallest fewer than ten. The distinctive feature of the organisation is that each department is under its own manager, generally known as a buyer since the purchase of stock for his department is one of his principal functions. By this standard many large provincial shops, selling a variety of goods, with strong resemblances to the department store, and often regarded as such, fail to comply with this definition.

Dependant's Benefit. One of the benefits under most schemes of social security, an additional amount being payable to a beneficiary for a wife and/or children.

Dependence Effect. A term used by J. K. Galbraith. In an affluent society, he says, 'wants are increasingly created by the process by which they are satisfied.' This he calls the Dependence Effect. *See* Affluent Society.

Depopulation. *See* Declining Population, Effects of.

Deposit. In connection with hire purchase, it is the amount the customer is required to pay as his first instalment. By increasing or decreasing the legal deposit for goods bought on hire purchase a Government can encourage or discourage buying, according to whether it thinks that the economy requires a stimulus or a check. Together with variations in the length of the period of repayment it has become one of the modern instruments of monetary policy for influencing the level of demand.

Deposit Account. An account with a bank, withdrawals from which usually require a period of notice to be given, and on which interest is paid.

Deposit Bank. An alternative term for a commercial bank (*q.v.*).

Deposit Insurance. The American practice, compulsory for all commercial banks in the United States, of insuring bank deposits (at present up to a maximum of $10,000 for any one account) against loss. The business is carried on by the Federal Deposit Insurance Corporation (*q.v.*), established in 1933 at a time when most American banks had been compelled to suspend payments. The aim is to check a run on a bank by small depositors.

Deposit Reserves. *See* Cash Ratio.

Deposits, Bank. *See* Bank Deposits.

Deposit Society. A type of friendly society which encourages saving by allowing members to open deposit accounts which can be used to suplement the insurance benefits in case of prolonged need. On retirement members are entitled to repayment of the amounts standing to their credit.

Depreciation, Accelerated. *See* Accelerated Depreciation *and also* Depreciation Allowance.

Depreciation Allowance. A tax allowance to businesses on the amount paid for new machinery spread over a period of time, generally rather shorter than the expected life of the machine.

Depreciation of a Currency. Off the gold standard on a system where exchange rates are free to fluctuate (or 'float'), the rate of exchange depends on the supply of a currency in the foreign exchange market in relation to the demand for it in that market. The demand for a country's currency is derived from the demand for that country's exports; the supply of its currency depends on its demand for imports, both visible and invisible. If, therefore, the demand for a currency in the foreign exchange market is large in relation to the supply it will bring about an appreciation of that currency in terms of others, but if the supply of it is large in relation to the demand for it, then that currency will depreciate. The effect of the depreciation of a currency is to make imports dearer and exports cheaper until a balance in the balance of payments is achieved. After sterling was allowed to float in 1972 it began to depreciate on the foreign exchange market, and by 1976 it had lost one-third of its foreign exchange value.

Depreciation of Capital. In time all capital wears out and has to be replaced. Even if some types of capital prove to be exceptionally durable they become out-of-date, and it is economically desirable that such capital should be replaced by more up-to-date capital. A certain amount of production, therefore, must each year be devoted to replacing worn out or obsolescent capital.

Depressed Areas. A term used of those parts of Great Britain with exceptionally high levels of unemployment during the Great Depression of 1929–35, the unemployment rate being over 35% of insured workers in these areas as compared with only 6% in some southern counties. The Depressed (or Distressed) Areas comprised mainly the centres of heavy industry—South Wales, Durham, West Cumberland, Clydeside, South Lancashire. The Acts of 1934 and 1937 re-named these districts 'Special Areas' (*q.v.*) and gave the Government power to assist them. In 1945 they became Development Areas (*q.v.*). *See also* Location of Industry.

Depression. A term used to describe a period of heavy unemployment and stagnation of business activity. During the nineteenth century booms and depressions succeeded one another with great regularity, the average time interval between one depression and the next being about seven years. The period between the two World Wars was characterised by the longest and most severe depression experienced down to that time. In a depression nearly all industries are affected, though some to a greater extent than others. Both the nineteenth-century depressions and the Great Depression of 1929–35 were world-wide in their effects. Since 1945 there have been several brief periods when business activity has declined a little below the level necessary to give full employment, these generally being described as recessions. The most serious recession of recent times occurred during 1974–77, many countries being affected, Great Britain seriously so.

Depression of Trade (1886), Commission on. This Commission noted the perseverance and enterprise shown by the Germans in developing their foreign trade, with the result that Germany was becoming a serious rival to Great Britain in the markets of the world.

Depth Interview. A type of interview conducted by a market research interviewer who tries to learn as much as he can about a respondent's background as a means of discovering why he has bought a particular brand of a commodity since few people can say directly and precisely why they prefer one brand to another.

De-rating. A local rating system whereby some classes of property, such as agricultural property and business premises, are rated at a lower rate than other property. For example, the Rating Valuation (Apportionment) Act of 1928 reduced the liability of business premises and abolished rates on agricultural land, the aim being to assist production. The de-rating of industrial and commercial premises was abolished in 1963. *See also* Agricultural Rates.

Derivation of Demand. *See* Demand; Demand Curve; Demand Schedule; Diminishing Marginal Utility, Law of.

Derived Demand. Where the demand for one commodity is the direct result of the demand for another. The term is particularly applicable to factors of production, since the demand for land, labour, and capital is derived from the demand for the goods on the production of which these factors are employed. The demand for capital goods is derived from the demand for the consumers' goods in the production of which they assist. The demand for petrol can be regarded as being derived from the demand for motor cars.

Derived Value. A term used by Alfred Marshall for the value of a commodity the demand for which is derived from the demand for another commodity. Thus, the value of capital is derived from the value of things the capital is to assist in making.

D.E.S. Abbreviation of Department of Education and Science (*q.v.*).

Descriptive Economics. An elementary study of economics devoted merely to a description of the working and functions of economic institutions such as the banking system, the International Monetary Fund, etc. *See* Economics.

Design Council. The Council for Industrial Design was set up in 1944 by the Board of Trade (now the Department of Trade) to promote improvement in the design of British products.

Deutsche Bank. The principal commercial bank of West Germany and the largest commercial bank on the continent of Europe. It has an interest in the Banque Européenne de Crédit à Moyen Terme (*q.v.*) and a majority holding in Daimler-Benz. In 1977 it was the fifth largest bank in the world.

Deutsche Bundesbank. The central bank of West Germany. Between 1948 and 1957 West Germany had a federal central banking system, each region having its own Landeszentralbank, with the Bank Deutscher Länder as lender of last resort and sole bank of issue. (*Cf.* the Federal Reserve System of the United States.) In 1957 these regional banks were merged with the Berliner Zentralbank to form the Deutsche Bundesbank in order to provide the West German Republic with a unitary central bank. Its head office is at Frankfurt-am-Main.

Deutsche Mark. The name of the standard unit of the currency of West Germany adopted after the Second World War to replace the Reichsmark which had become worthless. It is divided into 100 Pfennig.

Deutscher Generschaftsbund (D.G.B.). A group of sixteen German trade unions whose membership comprises 88% of all trade union membership in the country.

Devaluation. Reducing the value of a currency in terms of the monetary metal or in terms of another currency. Devaluation requires deliberate action on the part of the monetary authorities whereas depreciation occurs as a result of market forces on the foreign exchange market. On any system of foreign exchange, such as the gold standard or the Bretton Woods system, where fixed rates of exchange are in operation, a country with a fundamental disequilibrium in its balance of payments might devalue its currency in order to stimulate its exports (cheaper to foreigners after devaluation) and to discourage imports (foreign goods now being dearer), thereby restoring equilibrium to its balance of payments. Clearly, devaluation is not a remedy that can be applied whenever a country is experiencing difficulty with its balance of payments. Repeated devaluation can only result in other countries completely losing confidence in a currency. Devaluation is not, therefore, to be regarded as a normal means of stimulating exports by reducing their prices in terms of other people's currencies. During 1931–39, however, there were several instances of devaluations of this kind. Competitive devaluation of currencies, if persisted in, can only lead to complete loss of confidence in the currencies concerned, their eventual ruin, and stagnation of world trade.

Competitive devaluation of currencies was one of the undesirable currency practices condemned by the Bretton Woods conference (1944). It was realised, however, that in certain circumstances devaluation might be desirable, as for example, whenever a country has a fundamental disequilibrium in its balance of payments, since this is the result of a currency being given a greater value in terms of others than its real worth. Under the Bretton Woods scheme, therefore, although currency parities were generally to be regarded as fixed, member countries agreed to consult the International Monetary Fund if a devaluation of over 10% was contemplated, and for a devaluation of over 20% the prior consent of the I.M.F. was required. Devaluation, in any case, was to be permitted only if there was a fundamental disequilibrium in the balance of payments of the country concerned.

The theory of devaluation is that by making imports dearer and exports cheaper equilibrium will be restored to a country's balance of payments. If, however, there is an inelastic demand for imports—as for food and raw materials in the case of Great Britain—and if in conditions of full employment higher prices of imports lead to wage increases there is likely to be little check to imports, with the result that in these circumstances the devaluation of a currency is unlikely to achieve its objective. Any gain from devaluation is likely to be only temporary unless it is accompanied by severe wage restraint. This was clearly shown on the devaluation of sterling in 1949 and in the difficulties the British Government had to face with its prices and incomes policy after the devaluation of 1967.

Devaluation of Sterling. 1. **(1949).** The parity of sterling with the U.S. dollar adopted in 1945 was bound to be to a large extent arbitrary since there was no means of precisely assessing the relative values of the two currencies. It was recognised that sterling had been weakened by the war, and so sterling was given a slightly lower value in terms of dollars than the 1939 rate. Even so, the effect of the war on Great Britain was grossly underestimated, especially in the United States, as was clearly shown by the Convertibility Crisis of 1947. There were definite advantages to Great Britain in sterling's being over-valued in the immediate post-war years, since (i) at that time it was necessary for this country to import on a large scale and over-valuation would reduce the cost of imports, and (ii) there was at that time a seller's market for our exports, and so the fact that over-valuation made them dearer had little or no effect on their sale. By 1949, however, things had changed somewhat. The first post-war recession, though mild, had occurred in the United States, and this led to a questioning of the advisability of continuing Marshall Aid to Europe, the idea gaining ground in the United States that so long as Great Britain could rely on American assistance little serious effort would be made to bring the British balance of payments into balance, the cause of the disequilibrium being of the kind described as fundamental. It appeared to Americans that the British people were unwilling to make the necessary sacrifice. The growing expectation, however, that sterling sooner or later would have to be devalued led to American importers temporarily holding off buying from Great Britain, and the resultant worsening of the condition of the British balance of payments finally made the devaluation of sterling unavoidable.

2. **(1967).** Throughout the period since 1945, and in spite of the devaluation of 1949, Great Britain had recurring difficulties with its balance of payments. In general the invisible credit balance had not kept pace with the visible debit balance. Sterling too as an international reserve currency was from time to time subjected to severe strain. The sterling crises of 1964–65 and 1966–67 were particularly severe. In addition to taking full advantage of the drawing rights to which it was entitled from the I.M.F., Great Britain received assistance from other central banks —the Group of Ten—and the Bank for International Settlements at Basle. The internal measures taken by the British Government in 1965 were inadequate to meet the crisis, and the more severe July measures in 1967 also proved to be unavailing. As a result there was a growing feeling both at home and abroad that Great Britain was suffering from a fundamental disequilibrium in its balance of payments which could be remedied only by a change in the exchange rate, that it, by a devaluation of sterling. This in the end made devaluation inevitable,

since it caused a run on the country's reserves of gold and convertible currencies, and in November 1967 the value of sterling in terms of the U.S. dollar was reduced from $2.80 to $2.40 to the £. On the devaluation of sterling in 1949 the other members of the sterling area and most other countries in Western Europe also devalued (though not all to the same extent), so that what really happened was a revaluation of the U.S. dollar. In 1967, however, only a few other countries—Bermuda, Malta, Spain, Denmark, New Zealand—devalued their currencies. By 1972 the advantages of the 1967 devaluation had been completely eroded by the steep rise in wages and prices that occurred during 1969–72.

Devaluation of the U.S. Dollar. The ultimate effect of the Bretton Woods Agreement (1944) was to provide a dollar standard for the signatories. In the early years there was a dollar 'shortage', but gradually as other countries recovered from the effects of the war on their economies this 'shortage' disappeared. The U.S. dollar joined sterling as an international reserve currency. In fulfilling this role sterling had to face many crises, but the dollar remained strong until 1971. In supplying the world with dollars the United States year after year suffered an adverse balance of payments which depleted its gold stocks. In 1971 the U.S. Government took measures to check this drain on gold including withdrawing the convertibility of the dollar for gold. By the Smithsonian Agreement (q.v.) new parities were then agreed between the U.S. dollar and other leading currencies which were revalued in varying degrees in relation to the dollar which in effect meant that there was a general devaluation of the dollar.

Developing Nations. Those countries which for some reason have been backward in developing their economic resources with the result that their peoples have a much lower standard of living than that enjoyed in the more economically advanced countries of Europe and America. Since 1950 both the United Nations and the more advanced countries individually have given considerable assistance to the under-developed nations. *See also* Colombo Plan.

Development and Road Improvement Funds Act (1909). The increasing number of motor vehicles made it necessary to improve the roads which outside the towns had become neglected. The Act of 1909 set up roads boards which were empowered to build new roads and to assist other road authorities to do so.

Development Areas. The regions so designated by the Distribution of Industries Act (1945), or later designated as such by the Board of Trade, in which new firms were to be encouraged to set up. They were mostly areas of highly localised heavy industry which had suffered severe unemployment between the two World Wars, and the aim was to give them greater variety of industry. The first four regions to be recognised as Development Areas were the pre-1939 Special Areas, generally with enlarged boundaries —(i) the North-East, mainly Durham with contiguous parts of Northumberland and the North Riding of Yorkshire; (ii) West Cumberland; (iii) South Wales and Monmouthshire; (iv) Clydeside and the Lanarkshire coalfield. To these were added: (v) South-east Lancashire; (vi) the Wrexham district; (vii) Merseyside; (viii) Inverness and district; (ix) North-east Lancashire. The Local Employment Act (1959) abolished the Development Areas as such and empowered the Government to assist in similar fashion any part of the country where unemployment was above the national average. The Industrial Development Act (1966) revived the Development Areas which were to absorb the Development Districts. The new Development Areas are much wider in extent than were the earlier ones.

Development Corporations. Bodies established to develop the New Towns established under the New Towns Act (1946), the Government making loans to the corporations to enable them to finance the building of houses, factories, etc. *See also* New Towns, Commission for.

Development Councils. Bodies set up in a number of non-nationalised industries to permit joint consultation between employers and the trade unions concerned.

Development Districts. Districts so designated under the Act of 1960 became eligible for Government assistance to reduce unemployment on similar terms to those offered to Development Areas. They were much smaller in area than the Development Areas (*q.v.*). In 1966 the Development Districts were absorbed into the Development Areas.

Development Land Tax. A tax on the development of land by private interests, introduced in 1976 by the Development Land Tax Act.

Deviation. The taking of an unusual course by a ship, unless to render assistance to the crew and passengers of a ship in distress, is known as a deviation, and this relieves the insurers of their liability.

Devise. To dispose of real property by will.

Devlin Report (1965). The report of a committee under the chairmanship of Lord Devlin on conditions in Great Britain's docks. The report declared that inefficiency was widespread and due to many causes—inefficient management, restrictive practices, conditions of employment, and trouble-makers among the dockers. The inefficient employers were mainly the smaller firms, and so the report, like the Rochdale Committee, recommended the licensing of employers, with licences restricted to efficient firms. The report also declared that strikes, both official and unofficial, were too frequent, and recommended decasualisation (*q.v.*) of dock labour. *See also* Rochdale Report.

Dictum meum pactum. Latin for 'My word is my bond', the motto of the London Stock Exchange, where much business on the floor of the exchange is done verbally, written agreements being made out later.

Difference. A stock exchange term. Purchases or sales of securities take place at the prices prevailing on the day of the transaction, speculators often preferring on Settlement Day merely to pay or receive the difference between the price then and the price on the day the transaction took place.

Differential. With reference to wage rates it is the difference between the wages of one class of workers and another, as for example between the skilled and the unskilled. The term too is used of differences in wages between employees in different industries, or between different grades of employees in the same occupation, as for example in teaching between graduates and non-graduates. Trade unions generally aim at reducing differentials, but these are necessary to induce a sufficient number of workers to accept responsibility or undertake courses of study to obtain qualifications necessary for certain kinds of work. Since 1945 there has been a tendency for wage differentials to be reduced.

Differential Duty. *See* Discriminating Duty.

Differentiation. Any means by which a producer attempts to distinguish his product from similar products made by rival producers, the most common method of differentiation being by means of trade marks and brand names. Differentiation is one of the causes of imperfect competition. Where it is practised commodities are no longer perfect substitutes for one another.

Digest of Statistics. A publication of the Central Statistical Office, issued monthly, giving the latest statistics of population, employment and unemployment, production, banking, trade, etc. An *Annual Abstract of Statistics* is also published.

Dilution. Increasing the supply of a particular type of labour in response to an increased demand for it by employing people who do not possess what have previously been regarded as the minimum qualifications for it, as for example may occur in wartime in some branches of engineering.

Diminishing Marginal Utility, Law of. The marginal utility of a commodity is the amount of satisfaction to be derived from having a little more of it. The more of a thing a person possesses the less satisfaction he will derive from having a little more of it. Each successive increment that is added to one's supply of a commodity yields less satisfaction than the previous unit until eventually satiety is reached. This Law of Diminishing Marginal Utility, however, begins to operate only after a point known as the origin, since a minimum quantity of a good must be acquired before effective use can be made of it. Diminishing Marginal Utility is the basis of the demand curve.

Diminishing Returns, Law of. One of the Laws of Returns, it arises as a result of varying the proportions in which factors of production are combined. If one factor of production is fixed and increasing quantities of the other factors are combined with it, then the average physical output in relation to the fixed factor will eventually diminish. Alternatively, it can be said that for each addition to the variable factor or factors the addition to total output declines. Consider the following table:

applicable whichever of the factors is fixed. Clearly, as output increases the average output per man declines as also do the additions to total output. If stated as the Law of Eventually Diminishing Returns it becomes applicable to all forms of production. See Returns, Laws of.

Diminishing Substitution, Law of. This law is closely akin to the Law of Diminishing Marginal Utility. If a person with limited resources has a choice between only two commodities or services he may be willing to give up a little of one in exchange for a little of the other. Let A and B be the two commodities concerned. If he has a large quantity of A and none of B he may be prepared to give up a fairly large amount of A in exchange for a little of B; if he continues to exchange some of A for some of B he will be prepared to give up successively smaller amounts of A in exchange for equal additional amounts of B. The Law of Diminishing Substitution explains the shape of Indifference Curves ($q.v.$).

Dinar (Din). The standard unit of currency of a number of countries—Yugoslavia, Algeria, Libya, Tunisia, Iraq, Kuwait, Bahrain, Jordan. The Yugoslav dinar is divided into 100 paras, the Tunisian dinar into 1,000 millimes, the Kuwait, Iraqi, and Jordanian dinars each into 1,000 fils. In Iran the standard unit of the currency is the rial and this is divided into 100 dinars.

Diners' Club. A credit card company in which the National Westminster Bank has an interest. See Credit Card.

No. of men	Units of land and capital	Output (units)	Additions to output	Average physical product per man
4	10	100	—	25
5	10	120	20	24
6	10	132	12	22
7	10	140	8	20
8	10	146	6	18

The law was first applied to land as the fixed factor, but it is equally

Dingley Tariff Act (1897). An American Act passed by the McKinley Government, Dingley being responsible for seeing it through Congress. The feature of the Act was a highly protective tariff for the United States. *See* McKinley Tariff.

Direct Arbitrage. Also known as Simple Arbitrage, it refers to dealings in foreign currencies when these are confined to one centre. *See* Arbitrage.

Direct Cost. An alternative term for Prime Cost (*q.v.*).

Direct Debit. This occurs when a bank debits a customer's account in response to a standing order or an instruction from the payer.

Directional Effects. The disadvantage of using variations of purchase tax as an instrument of monetary policy, it is said, is the fact that only the industries producing commodities subject to these taxes feel the effects of changes in the rates of tax. If it is thought necessary, for example, in a period of inflation to check demand by increasing the rates of purchase tax it will reduce the quantity demanded only of goods subject to the tax and not check demand generally. A Sales Tax (*q.v.*), being applicable to all retail sales, would not have directional effects.

Direction of Labour. One method of overcoming immobility of labour is for the State compulsorily to direct people to industries where it is desired to expand production from those where production is to be reduced. Direction of labour can be employed in a fully planned economy as a means of redistributing labour, but in a democratic country it is likely to be vigorously opposed as an infringement of individual liberty except in very exceptional circumstances such as times of national crisis. During the Second World War the Ministry of Labour used its powers of direction to deploy labour among industries to the greatest advantage of the British war effort. In a time when men and women are being conscripted into the armed forces, workers are more prepared to accept direction of labour, but when the Government again obtained powers of direction during 1947–50 it made little use of them.

Directive, Treasury. An instrument of monetary policy employed in Great Britain by the monetary authorities on several occasions after 1951. Treasury directives took the form of requests to the commercial banks to adopt a more selective or more restrictive lending policy, the aim being to check the expansion of credit or to reduce it. The early directives were qualitative in character, that is, banks were asked to restrict loans to purposes that could be regarded as in the country's economic interest. The later directives were quantitative, that is, the banks were definitely requested to reduce the volume of their lending. As an alternative to the directive the Bank of England, for the first time in 1960, requested the commercial banks to make Special Deposits with it, the aim being to reduce the cash basis of the commercial banks and thereby check their lending. In 1965–66 the directive was employed in conjunction with Special Deposits.

Director. *See* Company Director.

Direct Orient Express. A train that formerly ran from Calais and Paris to Milan with through coaches, two days per week to Athens and two days per week to Istanbul. Like the former Simplon Orient Express (*q.v.*) its traffic had diminished by the expansion of air travel.

Directors, Institute of. A body which concerns itself with matters affecting directors of public and private companies, it was founded in 1903 and granted a Royal Charter in 1906. Since 1960 it has interested itself in education for business and management, endowing a fellowship at Balliol College, Oxford, and a chair at the University of Warwick. In addition to a journal it publishes booklets on subjects of special interest to directors and businessmen.

Direct Production. When a person

satisfies his wants entirely by his own efforts, as would be the case if there was no division of labour.

Direct Selling. A chain of distribution (*q.v.*) between the producer and the consumer which by-passes the wholesaler or both wholesaler and retailer.

Direct Services. A term used in connection with the classification of occupations for all personal services unconnected with the distribution of goods. In this category there is a great variety of occupations—doctors, dentists, teachers, clergy, solicitors, judges, civil servants and local government officers, entertainers of all kinds, hotel employees, police, the armed forces, and many others. In an advanced economy there are many non-material wants to be satisfied, and as a result a large number of people are required to provide direct services. With economic progress the proportion of people engaged in work of this kind tends to increase.

Direct Taxation. Direct taxes are taxes on income as distinct from taxes levied on goods and services. Since direct taxes can be more closely related to ability to pay—as with progressive income tax, and death duties—they are generally regarded as being more equitable than indirect taxes. Since, however, many direct taxes act as disincentives to work or saving, they may have the undesirable effect of adversely affecting the total volume of production. In any case, the total revenue required by a modern state is too great for it to be covered entirely from direct taxation. The result in most countries is that a compromise has had to be made between direct and indirect taxation.

Dirham. The standard unit of the currency of Morocco, it is divided into 100 centimes.

Disablement Benefit. One of the benefits under the British scheme of social security. *See* Industrial Injury Benefit.

Disablement Pension. One of the benefits under the National Insurance (Industrial Injuries) Act (1946) in cases where injury suffered at work has been so severe as to make it impossible for the person concerned to follow his normal employment.

Discharge. With reference to a bill of exchange, it means that all rights attaching to the bill have been extinguished, payment in due course being the usual method by which the discharge of a bill is effected.

Disclosure, Bank. *See* Bank Disclosure.

Discount. 1. An inducement offered by a creditor to debtors to pay promptly. (Cash discount.)

2. A deduction from the catalogue price of an article generally allowed by a wholesaler to a retailer, that is, trade discount.

3. With reference to bill of exchange, to discount a bill means to acquire it by purchase for a sum less than its face value, the amount of this discount depending partly on the length of the unexpired term of the bill, and partly on the amount of risk involved.

4. When a recently issued stock falls below its issue price it is said to stand at a discount.

Discounted Cash Flow. A method of assessing and so comparing alternative capital projects. Comparison is made of the present values of the flows of cash that can be expected from each capital project during the course of its existence.

Discount House. 1. A financial institution which specialises in discounting bills of exchange. The London Discount Houses Association comprises twelve large and twelve small firms engaged in discount business. The largest firms are Alexanders, the National Discount Company, and the Union Discount Company of London. *See* Discount Market.

2. An alternative term for Discount Store (*q.v.*).

Discount Market. A market in which the principal business has to do with bills of exchange. Although the London Money Market and the

Discount Market can be separably defined—the money market as the market for very short-term loans, and the discount market as the market concerned with the discounting of bills of exchange—they are so intimately linked that the two terms are often regarded as synonymous. The members of these markets comprise the commercial banks, the London agents or branches of some foreign banks, the Bank of England in its capacity as 'lender of last resort', the discount houses and the accepting houses or merchant banks. The 'commodity' coming on to this market is the bill of exchange, which at one time was not only the principal means of foreign trade payment in but also widely used internally. Unless the acceptor of a bill is widely known and his credit-worthiness generally recognised, it cannot easily be discounted. The accepting houses specialised in accepting bills of exchange and, being bankers of international standing, the discount houses readily discounted bills that had been so accepted. The discount houses normally borrowed 'at call or short notice' from the commercial banks, but they enjoyed the unique privilege of being able to borrow from the Bank of England as 'lender of last resort' when the commercial banks were unwilling to lend. The discount houses held the three-month bills, they had discounted for one month arranging them in 'parcels' falling due at the same date, and then re-discounting them with the commercial banks. The character of the discount market changed as a result of the decline in the use of bills of exchange for trade payments and the huge increase in the issue of Treasury bills. The result has been a decline in acceptance business, and in consequence the accepting houses have had to expand their ordinary banking business. Treasury bills do not require to be arranged in 'parcels' since they can be dated for any day of the week following their issue. However, the commercial banks do not tender for Treasury bills direct, thereby in effect permitting the discount market to continue to function. The existence of a money market between the central bank and the commercial banks is a unique feature of the English banking system. As a result the commercial banks in this country do not borrow directly from the central bank, as is the case in most other banking systems, but instead call in some of their loans to the discount market, thereby forcing the market 'into the bank'.

Discounts and Advances. One of the assets of the banking department of the Bank of England, it shows the extent of borrowing of members of the money and discount markets from the Bank of England as 'lender of last resort'. The Bank of England lends to the discount houses either by re-discounting bills of exchange that conform to its eligibility rule at bank rate or lending at a somewhat higher rate than bank rate with bills of exchange as collateral security. Thus, this item increases whenever the market is 'in the bank'.

Discount Stores. Also known as Discount Houses, these are stores and supermarkets which sell a great variety of goods and offer their customers a substantial discount on their purchases. They are able to do this by cutting their overheads to a minimum and by buying their stock in bulk. They are very popular in the United States. Their development in Great Britain was encouraged by the modifications in the law affecting resale price maintenance by the Restrictive Trade Practices Act (1956).

Discretionary Income. The amount of a person's income that remains after all his basic needs and commitments have been met, i.e. after he has paid for food, clothing, shelter, rates, and taxes. A wider choice is open to him in the disposal of his discretionary income.

Discriminating Duty. An import duty which varies according to the country of origin of the imported goods such as preferential duties imposed by Great Britain in favour of Commonwealth countries by the Ottawa Agreement of 1932.

Discriminating Monopoly. This means the charging of different prices to different groups of buyers. It is possible only if the various markets can be kept separate from one another, so that the commodity or service cannot be transferred from the cheaper to the dearer market. It is profitable to charge discriminating prices only if the elasticity of demand for the commodity differs between one market and another. The demand curve for a good shows that different groups of people would be willing to pay different prices for it, a few being willing to pay a high price, a larger number a rather lower price, and perhaps a huge number of people would buy the goods only at a low price. A monopolist could maximise his revenue if he was able to charge every buyer the maximum price the buyer was willing to pay. This is, of course, impracticable, but a new book may be published at £2·50, issued later in a cheaper edition at £1·25 and possibly finally as a paperback at perhaps £0·35. With personal services it is easier to keep the markets separate, as used to be the case when doctors had various scales of charges to suit the pockets of different patients. *See also* Charging What the Traffic Will Bear.

Discriminatory Prices. *See* Discriminating Monopoly.

Discriminatory Taxation. Taxes on the products of certain industries in order to enable some other industry to compete more favourably against them. Suggestions have been made that oil should be taxed more heavily in Great Britain in order to encourage the use of coal for power and heating.

Diseconomy. An increase in the scale of production after a point may bring certain diseconomies; administration, for example, may become more complex and so more expensive. *See also* Distributive Costs.

Disequilibrium. In conditions of equilibrium in an economic situation there is a tendency for things to remain as they are. If these conditions are disturbed, causing disequilibrium, forces are set in motion to restore equilibrium. Thus, if the equilibrium price prevails in a market and then unexpectedly there occurs a large increase in supply, disequilibrium will persist until the forces of supply and demand have brought about a new position of equilibrium, probably at a lower price. With reference to the balance of payments, disequilibrium occurs when receipts from all sources are not exactly equal to all payments that have to be made, that is, when the balance is 'favourable' or 'unfavourable', though more often restricted to the latter case. When disequilibrium in the balance of payments is the result of the currency of the country concerned being either undervalued or overvalued it is said to be a fundamental disequilibrium.

Disguised Unemployment. Also known as Hidden Unemployment, it can take several forms: (i) working short-time which does not give rise to application for unemployment benefit; (ii) employers retaining on their books a greater number of men than they require so that they may have sufficient labour when what they believe to be a temporary recession ends.

Dishoarding. When money is hoarded by a miser it is taken out of the economic system, and dishoarding will bring it back into it. It can also be applied to goods. Fear of inflation may lead to the hoarding of precious metals, especially gold, or goods might be hoarded in excess of people's demand for them in times of shortage or due to fear of shortage, dishoarding taking place when the cause of the hoarding has passed away.

Dishonour. A bill of exchange is dishonoured when the drawee has insufficient funds to discharge it when it falls due for payment. (*See* Protest.) Similarly, a cheque is dishonoured when the drawer has insufficient funds to meet it.

Disinflation. A mild form of deflation. A policy adopted to check inflation by restricting demand, the term came to be used because of the pejorative meaning that the term, deflation, had acquired during the 1930s when it came to be associated with restriction of credit and a high level of unemployment.

Disinvestment. A term used by Lord Keynes for the sale of an investment, a practice to which he sometimes referred as negative investment. For an expansion of output new investment must exceed disinvestment. Disinvestment occurred during the Second World War when many British investments abroad had to be sold to provide foreign currency with which to pay for imports.

'Dismal Science.' A term applied to economics by Thomas Carlyle, not because he regarded it as a disagreeable subject of study but because of the dismal results, forecast by Malthus and his followers, of the consequences of a rapidly increasing population in relation to the Law of Diminishing Returns, which seemed to show that by the end of the nineteenth century there might be a severe fall in the standard of living in Great Britain.

Displaced Persons. People who have had to leave their countries owing to political or racial persecution. During 1933–39 many Germans and Austrians came to Great Britain for these reasons, though the term was not used of such movements of peoples until the Second World War. As a result of that war large numbers of Poles, Letts, Latvians, and Estonians settled in Great Britain, and later some Hungarians became displaced persons.

Disposable Income. The income of an individual or a community after all direct taxes have been deducted. *Cf.* Discretionary Income.

Dis-saving. A term used by Lord Keynes. Dis-saving occurs when an individual is living on past savings. In an inflationary period some people, finding that with the fall in the value of money their incomes no longer provide them with the standard of living to which they have become accustomed, prefer to draw on past savings rather than suffer a reduction in their standard of living.

Distress Committees. Set up by the Government to give assistance to people who had become unemployed on the outbreak of war in 1914.

Distressed Areas. An alternative term for Depressed Areas (*q.v.*).

Distribution. 1. One of the main divisions of economics, it is concerned with the principles underlying the sharing out of the national income among the owners of the factors of production. Income received by the factors of production is variously known as rent, wages, interest, and profit according to its origin. The marginal productivity theory of distribution asserts that it is the marginal productivity of a factor that determines its share of total output. Another approach applies the principles of the market to the determination of the rewards of the factors. For each factor there is a supply and this in relation to the demand for its services determines the price entrepreneurs will pay for it—the pricing of the factors of production.

2. The movement of raw materials to the places of manufacture and of finished goods to consumers. *See* Distribution, Commercial.

3. A term used in connection with unit investment trusts for what would be described as dividend in the case of a limited company.

Distribution, Census of. *See* Census of Distribution.

Distribution, Commercial. This refers to the channels by which goods are taken from their place of production to the people who actually want to make use of them. There are several channels of distribution, depending on such things as whether the goods are home produced or imported, whether they are manufactured goods or farm produce, whether there are a large number of producers or only a few, whether the goods are distinguished by trade marks or brand names. The most usual route by which goods pass from the producer to the consumer is still by way of wholesaler and retailer, though in the case of many branded goods the manufacturer supplies them direct to the retailer. In some cases the manufacturer may open his own shops in order to bypass both wholesaler and retailer. The more complicated the distribution, as with imported goods, the greater the number of wholesalers or middlemen between producer and retailer. The greater too the amount of specialisation introduced into distribution the greater will be the number of middlemen employed. Similarly, the increased specialisation of production with concentration of production of particular commodities in particular places leads to an increasing proportion of the working population being engaged in commercial distribution.

Distribution of Incomes. When the total national incomes of countries were small, differences in personal income were often enormous, a few people having extremely high incomes and the great mass of people being extremely poor. With increases in the national income and the rise of a middle class the proportion of people of moderate income tended to increase. It was not, however, until the early years of the twentieth century that Governments made definite efforts to reduce inequality of income by progressive taxes on income and inheritance. The huge increase in the national income in recent times, combined with steeply progressive tax systems, has greatly reduced inequality of income.

Distribution of Industries Act (1945). An Act which made the Board of Trade responsible for the location of industry. Development Areas were designated, the Board of Trade being empowered to add to the number if circumstances warranted it. *See also* Development Areas; Development Districts.

Distribution of Property. Although over the years there has been a very considerable reduction in inequality of income, there is still a wide difference in the amount of property in its widest sense held by different groups of people. Property in the form of houses and other buildings, land, stocks and shares, or personal possessions is acquired either by inheritance or by saving. Steeply progressive capital transfer taxes have made it more difficult for large amounts of property to be inherited, and steeply progressive income taxes have made it increasingly difficult to save. As a result ownership of property has become much more widespread. Although a few people in Great Britain at the present day still own very large amounts of property, an increasing amount of property nowadays is held by the middle classes, mostly in moderate amounts, and the number of such people is increasing.

Distributive Costs. The cost of distributing goods from the place of production to the people who want them. Increasing specialisation and regional division of labour make the cost of distribution more expensive, and this is one of the diseconomies that has to be set against the gains from large-scale production. Selling costs—mainly advertising—also increase the cost of distribution.

Distributive Trades Alliance. A body which represents the interests of multiple shops and department stores, it includes in its membership most of the best known multiple retailers and some of the department stores. It is opposed to offering trading stamps to customers.

Distributor. A term used in some trades, as for example the motor car trade, for a wholesaler or middleman.

Disutility. Since utility means the amount of satisfaction to be derived from a commodity or service, disutility can be regarded as a loss of satisfaction resulting from having too much of a thing. After a point the marginal utility of a commodity diminishes as one's supply of it increases until a point is reached when an extra increment would yield no further satisfaction, and further addition to one's supply may actually yield some disutility. Additional increments of food to a hungry man would yield diminishing marginal utility until, his hunger completely assuaged, he desired no more, after which a further increment might cause discomfort or yield disutility.

Diversification. 1. The provision of greater variety of industry to an area, especially one mainly dependent on a highly localised industry, aims to make employment less dependent on the fortunes of one particular industry since, where an industry which is highly localised declines, a pocket of serious unemployment can occur even when the country as a whole is enjoying full employment. One of the three main conditions laid down by Lord Beveridge for the maintenance of full employment was planned location of industry, the aim of which he considered to be to give greater variety of industry to all industrial areas. It is extremely difficult—in many cases probably impossible—to disperse old-established heavy industry, and the most that can be done in the areas where such industries are situated is to attract new light industries.

2. The term is also used of a firm which produces a wide range of different products. This may take the form of producing by-products from what would otherwise be waste, or the aim may be to make a firm independent of the vagaries of the market for a single product. A fall in demand for the product of a single-product firm could put it in difficulties, but where a variety of products is produced the effect of a change in demand for one of them will be much less serious. For example, both the Imperial Tobacco Co. and the British-American Tobacco Co., fearing a future decline in the demand for tobacco, have diversified their interests by taking over companies producing widely different products.

Dividend. 1. In the case of limited companies, the rate of dividend is the amount of distributed profit as a percentage of the nominal value of the share capital to which it relates. For example, if a limited company with issued ordinary share capital of £100,000 in £1 shares declares a dividend of 10% a shareholder will receive £0·10 (10% of £1) for each share he holds, but if a shareholder paid £2 each for these £1 shares the yield to him would be only 5%. Dividends are usually declared annually, but many companies pay something on account as an interim dividend.

2. With reference to co-operative societies, the rate of dividend is the amount of surplus (*i.e.* profit), to be returned to members in proportion to their purchases. Thus, a dividend of £0·03 in the £ would mean that a member who during the period to which it relates had made purchases to the value of £40 would receive a dividend of £1·20.

Dividend Limitation. During periods when attempts have been made to check inflation by asking for restraint on wage increases there has been a strong request at the same time, in order to placate the trade unions, to companies not to increase their dividends. This occurred during the 'wage freeze' of 1950–51, during the 'wage pause' of 1961–62 and the 'wage freezes' of 1966–67 and 1972–73.

Dividend, National. An alternative term for National Income (*q.v.*).

Dividend Warrant. A draft issued by a limited company and made payable to a shareholder for the amount of dividend due to him for a stated period. *See* Interest Warrant.

Dividing Society. A type of small friendly society, so called because it periodically returns part of its funds to its members, the amount generally varying inversely with the amount of sickness benefit received by the member during the period, a practice which tends to reduce malingering.

Division of Labour. The first stage in the division of labour occurred when men began to specialise in particular crafts instead of doing everything for themselves. The term is, however, more particularly applied to specialisation of processes where the production of a commodity is divided into a number of separate processes each of which is performed by a different man. Adam Smith was very much impressed by the effect of division of labour on output. Even though no more or no different capital is employed the introduction of division of labour into a workshop results in a huge increase in output. The reasons for this are that men acquire greater skills when they specialise in single operations, and it obviates the waste of time that occurs when men have to change from one process to another. Division of labour too paved the way for the introduction of machinery, the early machines being single process machines. Disadvantages of division of labour are that the work becomes more monotonous, a decline in craftsmanship occurs, and specialists find it more difficult to obtain work if they become unemployed. The effect of division of labour and specialisation is to increase the complexity of the distribution of the product. The extent to which division of labour can be carried is limited by the extent of the market for the commodity. Division of labour, combined with the use of ever more efficient capital, has led to the mass production of many commodities for which a wide demand has developed. A third stage in the division of labour occurs when industries become highly localised, so that entire firms can specialise in single processes, this being known as regional or territorial division of labour. Finally, the theory of international trade shows that if division of labour is carried into the international field, countries specialising in the production of those commodities for which they have the greatest comparative advantage over others, the total output for the world as a whole will be increased. Division of labour at all stages is based on the principle of Comparative Advantage (*q.v.*) or, as it is known in the theory of international trade, the principle of Comparative Cost (*q.v.*).

D.L.O. Abbreviation of Dead Letter Office (*q.v.*).

DM. Abbreviation of Deutsche Mark (*q.v.*).

Dock Labour Board. An agency set up under the Dock Labour Scheme *(q.v.)*.

Dock Labour Scheme. Introduced in 1947, the aim of the scheme was to provide dock workers with a regular wage to replace earnings by casual employment, long the custom among dock workers. Under the scheme a Dock Labour Board was set up with powers to direct men to one employer or another, the dock worker becoming entitled to a payment, known as 'fall-back pay' if he failed to obtain work.

Dock Landing Account. A document issued to the Master of every ship on its arrival at a British port. The ship is given a reference number, and information has to be supplied regarding the cargo—the marks and numbers of packages, together with particulars of any damaged goods. This is independent of the customs examination.

Dock Warrant. A receipt for goods stored in a warehouse, it entitles the holder to take possession of the goods. It can be transferred by endorsement to another person.

Documentary Bill. A bill of exchange which has attached to it a document of title to goods, such as a bill of lading.

Documentary Credit. A method of payment in foreign trade. The importer opens a credit in favour of the exporter at a bank in the exporter's country. A documentary bill is then drawn by the importer in favour of the exporter. The development of this method of payment in foreign trade has greatly reduced the importance of the acceptance business of the London merchant banks.

Documents of Title. These are documents such as bills of lading, dock warrants, warehouse warrants, which entitle the holders to claim possession of the goods named on them.

Doit. An alternative name for the Groat (q.v.).

Dole. A colloquial term for Unemployment Benefit (q.v.).

Dollar. The English form of the German *thaler*, it is best known as the standard unit of the currency of the United States. The dollar is also used in a number of other countries —Canada, Australia, New Zealand, Bermuda, the Bahamas, Malaya, Hong Kong, Ethiopia, the West Indies. In all these cases the dollar is subdivided into 100 cents.

Dollar, Devaluation of. *See* Devaluation of the U.S. dollar.

Dollar Diplomacy. An American term for the policy of President Taft (1908–13), which aimed at encouraging American investment abroad.

Dollar Gap. A term used during the period 1945–58 for the excess of British imports from the United States and other members of the dollar area over its exports to those countries. Other countries, in Western Europe, had similar difficulties. The problem arose immediately after the Second World War when the United States was almost the only country able to supply Western Europe, especially with the goods required for rebuilding its economy. The problem of the Dollar Gap receded as Western Europe gradually recovered from the effects of the war.

Dollar Pool. In the years before 1959 the countries of the sterling area pooled their dollars, all dollars earned by members being paid into the common dollar pool, held by Great Britain. Though there were no precise restrictions on withdrawals members were expected to exercise restraint. *See* Sterling Area.

Dollar Premium. On account of exchange control restrictions on the purchase by British people of U.S. and Canadian dollar securities and because in general purchases are possible only where the sellers of the stocks are also British investors, the demand for such securities usually outruns the supply, the dollar premium being the amount by which the prices on the London Stock Exchange exceed the prices that day in New York or Montreal. The premium has generally varied between $12\frac{1}{2}\%$ and 40% but in April 1975 it was 100%. *See* Investment Dollars; Property Dollars.

Dollar Stocks. U.S. and Canadian stocks and shares.

Domestic System. The system which preceded the factory system, the workers doing their work at home and being supplied with the necessary raw materials by merchants who travelled round to collect the finished products. It was prevalent in the woollen industry of the West Riding of Yorkshire and some other industries in the seventeenth century. In Great Britain it survived to more recent times in the boot and shoe industry.

Dong. Standard unit of the currency of both North and South Vietnam.

Donovan Report (1968). The Report of the Royal Commission on Trade Unions and Employers' Associations (1965–68). One of its principal recommendations was that local agreements between employers and employees should replace national agreements and be registered with the Department of Employment and Productivity. The Commission, however, rejected suggestions that agreements should be made legally enforceable. Inadequate conduct of industrial relations at company and plant level was blamed for the large and increasing number of 'unofficial' strikes. It was proposed that an Industrial Relations Commission should be set up to consider the problems of particular industries and factories and to supervise the registration of agreements. Workers should be protected against unfair dismissal. The Commission rejected suggestions that the 'closed shop' should be prohibited and that there should be a ballot before any 'unofficial' strike was declared. It was considered too that more mergers of unions were necessary in order to ensure that there was only one union for each grade of work in a factory. *See* Industrial Relations Act (1971).

Dormant Partner. An alternative term for a Sleeping Partner (*q.v.*).

Dormitory Towns. The new urban areas that developed between the two World Wars on the fringe of London as residential areas with little or no industrial activity, the residents therefore having to travel to other parts of London to work. A feature of the New Towns planned after the Second World War was that there should be work in them for the people who live there.

Dose. A term used by Alfred Marshall for an increment of a factor or a commodity. Thus, it is possible to speak of additional doses of labour or capital in connection with a fixed supply of land.

Double Counting. One of the dangers to be avoided when calculations are made of the total volume of production or national income. Thus, the value of partly finished goods should not be included as well as the value of the final products.

Double Cropping. An intensive type of farming where the climate and nature of the soil enable two crops of a product to be obtained in a single season, or where two different crops can be grown on the same piece of land in one season.

Double Crown. A British coin issued in the Stuart period. *See* Crown.

Double Eagle. A former U.S. gold coin, it had a value of $20.

Double Entry. The system in bookkeeping whereby every transaction that has to be recorded gives rise to two entries, the one a credit and the other a debit, so that total credits always equal total debits.

Double Florin. A British silver coin first issued in 1887 and worth £0·20.

Double Napoleon. A former French coin worth 40 francs.

Double Noble. A former English coin. *See* Noble.

Double Option. This gives the holder the right either to buy or to sell a specified security at a certain date. *See* Option.

Double Pricing. The practice of showing two prices on goods displayed for sale, the higher price being cancelled to indicate a price cut, as an inducement to buyers. It has been subject to much criticism.

Double Ryal. Former English gold coin, first issued in 1489 with a value at that time of 20*s*. It eventually came to be known as the sovereign.

Double Sovereign. A former English gold coin, first issued in 1489 and worth £2. Later it became to be issued only on special occasions such as coronations and jubilees of the reigning monarch. *See* Sovereign.

Double Standard. When two metals, such as gold and silver, are jointly used as the monetary standard, the aim being to give greater stability to the value of the currency. The fundamental difficulty of a double standard is that, with different conditions of both supply and demand for the two metals, their relative value is liable to fluctuate. *See* Bimetallism.

Double Taxation Relief. A reciprocal arrangement between Great Britain and a number of other countries whereby holders of securities in each other's countries are relieved of having to pay tax in both countries on income from the same investment.

Doubloon. A former Spanish gold coin, a double pistole.

Douglas Theory. *See* Social Credit.

Dow Jones Index. An American index number showing the yield on industrial shares. Dow Jones & Co. were owners of the Wall Street Journal.

Down Payment. A deposit in connection with a hire purchase transaction (*q.v.*).

Downswing (or **Downward Swing**). *See* Downward Phase.

Downward Phase. With reference to the trade cycle, the period during which business activity is falling, prices are declining, and unemployment is rising. During the nineteenth century the downward phase of the cycle lasted on average about three or four years.

Dow Theory. An American theory that the main trend of stock exchange prices is indicated in advance by the daily and medium-term trends of prices of a selected group of securities. The main difficulty in applying the theory is for the investor to decide which are the main and which the minor movements of prices.

D.P. Abbreviation of Displaced Person (*q.v.*).

Dr. Abbreviation of: 1. Debtor; 2. Drachma (*q.v.*).

Drachma. The standard unit of the currency of Greece, it is divided into 100 lepta.

Drage Return. A White Paper, published annually 1920–39 giving a return of expenditure on the social services, the chief source of information on the subject during that period.

Drapers' Company. One of the more important of the Guilds or Livery Companies of the City of London whose existence dates back to the gilds of the Middle Ages, ranking third in order of civic precedence. The company is known to have been in existence in the twelfth century and it received its charter in 1364. Until the seventeenth century it enjoyed a monopoly of the woollen cloth trade. Its energies are now mainly devoted to charity.

Drawback. A repayment, when goods are to be re-exported, of customs duty which has been paid on them.

Drawee. A person or institution on which a bill of exchange is drawn. In the case of a bill of exchange the drawee is the debtor and acceptor of the bill, but in the case of a cheque the drawee is the bank on which the cheque is drawn.

Drawer. The person responsible for drawing a document. In the case of a bill of exchange it is the creditor, whereas for a cheque the drawer is the debtor.

Drawing Rights. The amount a member country is entitled to purchase of a foreign currency in exchange for its own from the International Monetary Fund. *See also* Special Drawing Rights.

Drawings. 1. With reference to Government stocks *see* Drawn Bonds.

2. In the case of Premium Bonds the interest is pooled and numbers are drawn, as in a lottery, prizes then being given to the lucky numbers so drawn.

3. A term used in bookkeeping, *e.g.* the drawings of partners in a firm.

4. Borrowing from the International Monetary Fund (*q.v.*).

Drawn Bonds. Bonds redeemable by drawings at intervals. This has never been a popular practice in Great Britain, but 4% Victory Bonds 1920–76 are being gradually redeemed in this way.

Drought Reserve. An Australian term for the expansion of the central bank's gold reserves in good years for use later, *i.e.* in years of low rainfall.

D.S.I.R. Abbreviation of Department of Scientific and Industrial Research (*q.v.*).

D.T.I. Abbreviation of the former Department of Trade and Industry. *See* Industry, Department of; Trade, Department of.

Ducat. A gold coin issued by a number of European countries, the ducat of Venice being perhaps the best known, and which from the twelfth to the sixteenth century circulated generally in Europe. Some states issued silver ducats.

Due Course, Holder in. *See* Holder in Due Course.

Due Date. The date on which a bill of exchange is due for payment. If drawn for three months the number of days in the calendar month concerned would be of no account, all months being regarded as equal for this purpose. Three days of grace are added to the period for which a bill of exchange has been drawn.

'Dummy' Dollars, London. The prices of U.S. and Canadian securities until 1971 were quoted on the London Stock Exchange at a fictitious rate of £1 = $5, these being known as London 'Dummy' Dollars.

Dumping. Selling goods abroad at a lower price than is charged for them in the home market; it is an example of discriminating monopoly. If the monopolist covers all his fixed costs in the home market he can add to his total profit even if the price he charges to foreign buyers is little more than sufficient to cover his marginal cost. For dumping to be practised a protective tariff is required to prevent foreign buyers reselling on the monopolist's home market. Not unnaturally, dumping gives rise to strong protests from producers of similar goods in the country in which goods are dumped, with demands for protection against foreign producers who, they claim, are selling their products 'below cost'.

Duopoly. A form of imperfect competition where there are only two producers of a commodity. Such a situation can give rise to cut-throat competition of a particularly virulent type, and to prevent both parties being ruined by it they may agree to share the market, perhaps on a territorial basis, each agreeing not to compete against the other in its share of the market. *See* Oligopoly.

Duopsony. A condition in a market where there are only two buyers for a commodity or service.

Durable Goods. Durability is a quality possessed by many types of producers' goods such as machinery, factory buildings, etc., and also by some consumers' goods, such as furniture, etc. The fact that durable goods require to be replaced only at intervals tends to create fluctuations in their production, and thus could be one of the real causes of the trade cycle or of periodic recessions in business activity.

Durlacher Oldham Mordaunt & Co. One of the two large firms of jobbers on the London stock exchange.

Dutch Auction. An auction where the first bid is a large one and each succeeding bid progressively smaller.

Dynamic Economics. A theory of economics which attempts to take account of the fact that change is a feature of all actual conditions, as distinct from static economics which, for the purposes of theory, assumes that no disturbing changes take place. No theory of profit would be possible in static theory since pure profit arises from dynamic conditions.

Dynamic Function of Money. The passive functions of money derive from the use of money as a medium of exchange. Nowadays money has a dynamic function to perform in the economy, since control over the supply of money is one of the means by which a Government, having accepted responsibility for the maintenance of full employment, attempts to influence the level of production and the rate of industrial expansion.

E

Eagerness to Buy. This is one of the two main influences on the price of a commodity, the other being the eagerness of sellers to sell. Eagerness to buy (coupled with ability to do so) is the basis of demand. The influence of eagerness on price is most clearly exemplified at an auction sale. Stock exchange prices too provide a good example of eagerness to buy or to sell on the part of the same investors or speculators.

Eagle. A former U.S. gold coin worth $10.

E. & O.E. Abbreviation of Errors and Omission Excepted, used on such documents as invoices and statements of account to safeguard the creditor against loss from such mistakes.

Early Closing. With reference to the permitted hours for the opening of retail establishments, *see* Shops (Early Closing) Act (1920–21).

Early Closing Act (1904). This Act granted a weekly half-holiday to shop assistants.

Earmarked. Set aside for a particular purpose. With reference to taxation it means that the proceeds of a certain tax are to be devoted entirely to a particular purpose. For example, the tax on whisky imposed in 1890 was to be devoted to the provision of secondary school education. Similarly, the revenue from the road fund licences of motor vehicles was originally intended to be used for the improvement, maintenance, and building of roads. The earmarking of taxes is bad in principle. Taxes are imposed to raise revenue and so far as indirect taxes are concerned it is generally accepted that the net should be spread as widely as possible. The revenue so raised should then be allocated according to the needs of the services that are to be provided. There could be no worse form of taxation than a system whereby the amount to be spent on a particular service should depend on the yield of a particular tax.

Earned Income. Apart from gifts and other windfalls all income is earned in that it is payment for economic services to production and distribution. A person who holds Government stock is paid interest for his service of lending to the Government. The term *earned income* however, is used by the Inland Revenue authorities to mean income derived from paid employment, whether as an employee or as a self-employed person, as distinct from *unearned income* which, for tax purposes, is income derived from interest and dividends. Most tax authorities tax earned income more leniently than investment income. *See* Income Tax.

Earnest Money. Also known as a Token Payment, it is a payment made to make binding a verbal agreement.

Earning Assets. Assets that yield income to a bank. Their earning assets are Money at Call and Short Notice, Bills Discounted, Investments, and Advances. The principal non-earning assets of British banks are their Coin, Notes, and Balances at the Bank of England.

Earnings. With reference to the wages of an employee it means the total amount of money he receives for a week or some other period for his services. It is clearly of greater importance than the wage-rate, which takes no account of either overtime or short-time working. In a period of over-full employment earnings will for most people be much greater than the basic wage, because to this payment must be added the additional pay at a higher rate for overtime. Demands for shorter hours are mainly inspired by a desire for more hours to count as overtime, thereby increasing earnings without raising the weekly wage-rate. When, however, employment is below the level of full employment weekly wage earnings will often be below the wage-rate if short-time is being worked, though in some occupations there may be a guaranteed minimum wage. Some salaried workers increase their earnings by taking on additional employment in their spare time, such as evening school teaching.

Earnings Yield. The total profit of a limited company in relation to its ordinary share capital after all prior charges have been met. *See* Cover.

Easement. A legal term. A class of rights over someone else's land, for example, a right of way. *See* Profits à Prendre.

East India Company. The British East India Co. was chartered in 1600 by Queen Elizabeth I for the purpose of trading with India and the East Indies, the Dutch already having founded a company for a similar purpose. In return for payments of money successive Parliaments renewed the privileges of the company. In its early days the company built fortresses in India and by the eighteenth century it had become a ruling power, though after 1773 the appointment of a Governor-General for India had to be sanctioned by the British Government. It was not until after the mutiny in 1857 that the British Government took over entirely the political government of India.

East Midland Educational Union. A body with headquarters in Nottingham which organises examinations in commercial and technical subjects for part-time students in evening institutes and technical colleges.

Easy Money Policy. An American term for cheap money (*q.v.*).

E.B.I. Abbreviation of European Investment Bank (*q.v.*).

E.B.I.C. Abbreviation of European Banks International Corporation, a group of associated banks comprising the Amsterdam-Rotterdam Bank, Banca Commerciale Italiana, Kreditstalt-Bankverein, Deutsche Bank, the Midland Bank, Société Generale de Banque and the Société Generale.

E.C. Abbreviation of Eurocheque (*q.v.*).

E.C.A.F.E. Abbreviation of Economic Conference for Asia and the Far East.

E.C.G.D. Abbreviation of Export Credits Guarantee Department (*q.v.*).

Econometrics. The employment of mathematical and statistical methods in the testing of economic theories. In econometrics the aim is to obtain quantitative information regarding economic problems.

Economic. Any action or proposal that has to do with the production or distribution of economic goods (*q.v.*). One method of production is said to be more economic than another if it is more efficient, that is, if for the production of the same output a smaller total quantity of factors of production—land, labour, and capital—is required. Economic matters have to do with all these problems, with foreign trade, and with the financial problems that arise in connection with them. Parliaments nowadays give great attention to the economic as well as the social and political aspects of problems.

Economica. The quarterly journal of the London School of Economics and Political Science of the University of London.

Economic Affairs, Department of (D.E.A.). A Government department that functioned 1964–69, it took over some of the economic business previously undertaken by the Treasury. The department had four main divisions: (i) Regional policy; (ii) Problems of economic growth, and prices and incomes policy; (iii) Industrial policies, including the promotion of industrial efficiency; (iv) Economic planning. Much of the department's work was in conjunction with other departments. It produced a National Plan (*q.v.*) for the period 1965–70, but restrictions on credit made it impossible for it to achieve its objectives, and in 1969 it was abolished as a separate department.

Economic Affairs, Institute of. *See* Institute of Economic Affairs.

Economic and Social Committee. One of the administrative institutions of the European Economic Community (E.E.C. or Common Market) which considers the social aspects of new proposals brought before the Economic Commission of the Community.

Economic and Social Research, National Institute of. *See* National Institute of Economic and Social Research.

Economic Batch Quantity. The amount of work in a department of a firm which allows the longest possible run of a standardised product of that department consistent with the total amount of work being undertaken by the firm.

Economic Commission. One of the administrative institutions of the European Economic Community (E.E.C. or Common Market) to which problems of members have first to be submitted before being considered by the Council of Members and the Political or Parliamentary Body.

Economic Conflict. It is sometimes suggested that economic conflict exists between the interests of buyers and sellers. Since, however, all people gain from specialisation, the adoption of which makes exchange necessary, there is in effect no such conflict, for both parties to an exchange benefit from it, each gaining more satisfaction from the commodity or service he receives than the loss of satisfaction resulting from whatever he gives in exchange. This is clearly the basis of a barter transaction, but it is also the basis of all exchange, including international trade, although the use of money often tends to hide this community of interest between buyer and seller.

Economic Continuity. The view that in spite of political changes, such as changes of Government, an economic policy should be continued, and the efforts of sectional interests to influence the Government of the day ignored.

Economic Decisions. These mainly resolve themselves into making a choice between alternatives since all things are limited in supply. Individuals have to make decisions as to how to spend their limited amounts of income, or how much to spend and how much to save. Entrepreneurs have to decide what to produce, how much to produce, and what method of production to adopt, and in what proportions to employ factors of production. To an increasing extent Governments have to make entrepreneurial decisions.

Economic Determinism. The theory that all historical development is determined solely by economic forces.

Economic Development Committees. These were established as sub-committees of the N.E.D.C. (*q.v.*). By January 1966 nineteen committees had been established including those for the machine tool industry, the chemical industry, electronics, the distributive trades, the Post Office, hotels and catering, etc. Together these committees covered two-thirds of the private sector of industry, the only committee dealing with matters in the public sector being the one for the Post Office.

Economic Freedom. A term used by Alfred Marshall for Free or Private Enterprise.

Economic Friction. This occurs when non-economic considerations prevent the easy working of economic principles. The term is used most frequently with regard to unemployment. If there was a change in demand from one commodity to another there would be no unemployment if all the labour rendered redundant in one industry could be immediately transferred to the other. Since labour comprises human beings and there is not complete mobility of labour, there is at least some temporary unemployment in the declining industry. Such unemployment is often described as frictional. Unemployment resulting from technical progress too is generally frictional.

Economic Good. Any commodity or service which, directly by the individual or indirectly by the community as a whole, must be paid for, in money in a monetary economy or in terms of the employment of factors of production in a non-monetary economy. The subject-matter of economics is concerned only with the problems associated with the production and distribution of economic goods because these problems arise out of the scarcity of such goods. A free good in unlimited supply would present no economic problems. Economic goods can be classified as consumers' goods and producers' goods.

Economic Growth. The rate of expansion of the national income or total volume of production of goods and services of a country. For a long time, though progress was very uneven, the average rate of expansion in Great Britain was between 2% and 3%, but great efforts are being made at the present time to increase the rate of progress, largely because some other nations have shown in recent years a much greater percentage rate of growth than Great Britain. However, to compare the economic growth of countries according to the percentage increase in their total output over a brief period of time is not a very reliable basis of comparison. For an advanced country a small *percentage* increase represents a much greater *absolute* increase than does a large percentage increase for a less well-developed country. The importance of the rate of economic growth is that it determines the rate at which the real standard of living of a people increases. During the period 1955-65 many countries achieved extraordinary economic growth, Japan leading the way with a growth rate average of over 9% per year, followed by West Germany with 7%, and France with 4·9%. The average rate of economic growth for both Great Britain and the United States was under 3%. Many people in Great Britain thought the British rate of growth too slow. In 1963 this was ascribed to the Government's 'stop-go' (*q.v.*) policies since 1950. During 1963-64 for the first time the British Government gave economic growth priority over the need to check inflation, and the result was a huge deficit in the balance of payments. In an attempt to restore equilibrium deflationary policies had to be adopted. Nevertheless the National Plan of 1965 (*q.v.*) aimed at a growth rate of 3·8% per year for the five years 1965-70. These hopes came to nothing in consequence of a succession of sterling crises and the continued necessity to pursue deflationary policies, culminating in the devaluation of sterling in 1967. Even after devaluation further bouts of deflation had to be imposed, and so the years 1964-71 were a period of slower economic growth than before. A greater rate of economic growth was achieved in Great Britain during 1972-73 but only at the cost of increased inflation, a serious depreciation of the pound and an adverse balance of payments. *See also* National Income.

Economic Indicators. In recent years great developments have taken place in attempts to reduce entrepreneurial risk. In addition to market research, the entrepreneur aiming at looking as far into the future as possible will watch such economic indicators as: (i) the Wholesale Price Index; (ii) the Retail Price Index; (iii) the Index of Industrial Production; (iv) the White Papers and Blue Book on National Income and Expenditure, and other White Papers such as the Balance of Payments and the Economic Survey (or Report); (v) whether the number of bankruptcies is increasing or decreasing, and also the distribution of bankruptcies among different occupations; (vi) the extent to which overtime is being worked in the more important industries; (vii) unemployment trends; (viii) Government policy with regard to indirect taxation; (ix) the trend of production and employment in those industries concerned with the manufacture of capital goods and durable consumers' goods, since changes in the general level of economic activity are felt earlier, for better or worse, in these industries.

Economic Institutions. Production, exchange, and distribution, and all forms of economic activity are assisted by the existence of economic institutions such as banks, discount houses, finance houses, costing and personnel departments of firms, and highly organised markets, such as the stock exchange, etc.

Economic Journal. The official journal of the Royal Economic Society of Great Britain. It is an important means by which economists put forward new theories and new ideas on economics in the form of articles, which are subject to criticism by other leading economists. It also contains reviews of new books on economics, especially more advanced works.

Economic Laws. It is generally pointed out that economics possesses all the characteristics of a science, being based on the observation of facts—certain aspects of human behaviour—the selection and classification of relevant material, and then making use of this as a basis for generalisations. Thus, economic laws can be formulated which are universally true—like all scientific laws—under the conditions specified. Examples of economic laws are the Law of Diminishing Returns, the Law of Diminishing Marginal Utility, the Laws of Supply and Demand.

Economic Man. A fiction of the early English writers on economics—a person motivated in all his actions by purely economic considerations. They believed that their theory of economics required such a concept. It is, of course, quite unreal and has been discarded. Nevertheless, economists today find it essential to much of economic theory to make the assumption that Man is perfectly rational in all his economic activity, and yet as everyone knows most persons at some time or other, to a lesser or a greater extent, behave irrationally. Without some such assumptions the building up of a body of economic theory would be impossible.

Economic Maturity. With reference to a country the condition of being economically fully developed. Whether or not a country is economically mature shows clearly in the character of its balance of payments. An immature country will generally have to borrow heavily from abroad, and so on invisible items it will show a large deficit, which should be covered by its surplus on visible items, whereas a mature country will generally have a deficit on visible items, paying for its surplus of imports by its credit balance on 'invisibles', as does Great Britain.

Economic Method. Both the deductive and the inductive methods are employed in the study of economics (*qq.v.*).

Economic Motives. Conduct inspired entirely by economic considerations. *See also* Economic Man.

Economic Nationalism. The aim to make a nation economically independent of others. *See* Self-sufficiency.

Economic Paradoxes. Some statements made by economists appear to be paradoxical. Two examples of such statements are: (i) A bumper harvest may yield a lower income to a farmer than a poor harvest (*see* Monopoly); (ii) An increase in saving by some individuals in a period of depression may reduce the total savings of the community. *See* Saving and Investment. *See also* Gibson Paradox; Paradox of Value.

Economic Planning. Deciding how the factors of production of a country shall be allocated among different industries, thereby deciding how much of all kinds of goods and services shall be produced in the ensuing period. Though it can refer to the planning of the individual entrepreneur, the term is more often restricted to State planning. This is found to its maximum extent in a communist country, but in all capitalist countries there has been in recent years an increase in State planning. Although in Great Britain it has been the Labour Party that has been most favourable to State planning, nevertheless it was under a Conservative Government in 1962 that the N.E.D.C. (*q.v.*) was established. *See also* National Plan.

Economic Planning Regions. In 1965 ten economic planning regions were designated: (i) Scotland, with Edinburgh as its regional capital; (ii) Northern England with Newcastle upon Tyne as capital; (iii) Yorkshire and Humberside with Leeds as capital; (iv) North-west England with Manchester as capital; (v) the East Midlands with Nottingham as capital; (vi) the West Midlands with Birmingham as capital; (vii) Wales and Monmouthshire with Cardiff as capital; (viii) Southwest England with Bristol as capital; (ix) East Anglia with Norwich as capital. For London and the South-East there was to be special treatment. For each of these regions there have now been set up Regional Economic Planning Boards and Regional Economic Planning Councils (*qq.v.*). Their function is to co-ordinate the work of different Government departments in the regions.

Economic Policy. The following are some of the principal aims of Government economic policy, some of which might be adopted concurrently though some might conflict with one another: (i) to maintain full employment; (ii) to maintain as high a rate of economic growth as possible in order to raise the standard of living of the people; (iii) to increase economic welfare through some redistribution of wealth, by progressively taxing the well-to-do and providing services or even money payments for the poorer sections of the community; (iv) to maintain stability of the monetary unit, that is, to keep inflation in check. Economic policy is often very closely related to social policy where matters such as social security or improvement of living conditions are concerned.

Economic Pressures. Attempts on the part of sectional interests to persuade the Government of the day to change its policy or to pursue a particular policy to the advantage of the group concerned but not necessarily to the advantage of the community as a whole.

Economic Progress. Increasing the average output of goods and services per head of the population and at the same time reducing the inequality of their distribution. Economic progress has been brought about by making better use of existing factors of production, increasing their quality and sometimes also their quantity. Land has been improved in quality by irrigation and other means; by education and training both labour and management have become more efficient; but probably the greatest single factor responsible for the huge increase in the average output per worker has been the vast increase in the quantity of capital employed and the really stupendous improvement in its quality. For a long time, even in the more economically advanced countries, economic progress was extremely slow. Since the early eighteenth century it has become more rapid. Though for the past hundred years the average rate of progress for Great Britain, judged by the increase in the national income, has been between 2% and 3%, progress has been very irregular, expansion being by fits and starts. The Industrial Revolution was one of the periods of rapid progress, that is, in comparison with previous periods, and there are indications that the second half of the twentieth century is likely to be another period with a rate of progress well above the average. In recent years Governments have attached more importance to the question of economic progress and nowadays make great efforts to increase the rate of expansion, if only to maintain parity of progress with other nations. With increasing industrial expansion an increasing percentage of the working population will be given up to the provision of services.

Economic Quantities. The amount of a commodity produced or consumed, the volume of employment or unemployment. These are economic quantities, but now more commonly referred to as aggregates (*q.v.*).

Economic Rent. A term sometimes used to indicate the sense in which the word, rent, is used in economics, to distinguish it from rent in the ordinary sense. The term is now rarely used, the word, rent, being generally preferred. See Rent.

Economic Report. A British White Paper, published annually in March, or early April, it gives a survey of the economy for the previous year, together with prospects for the current year. It provides up-to-date information on personal income and expenditure, production, investment and saving, costs and prices, Government income and expenditure, employment, foreign trade and the balance of payments. More detailed information on national income and expenditure and on the balance of payments is provided in separate White Papers. Since the Government accepted responsibility for the maintenance of full employment and the budget became an important instrument of economic policy, it has been necessary for the Chancellor of the Exchequer to have the latest economic information at his disposal before he frames his budget. The various White Papers published shortly before the budget statement is due give an indication of the economic situation of the country and the type of economic policy required to deal with it, though it is left to the Government and the Chancellor of the Exchequer to decide on the details of how this shall be done.

Economic Review. The journal of the National Institute of Economic and Social Research, it is published bi-monthly.

Economics. It is usual for books on economics to open with a discussion of the inadequacy of concise definitions of the subject. (*See* Economics, Definitions of.) Though it may be difficult to agree on a satisfactory, concise definition of economics, its subject matter presents less difficulty. Since nowadays most people earn their living by specialising in relatively narrow fields of activity, almost any ordinary business transaction involves many branches of the subject. Specialisation makes an exchange of goods and services necessary, and this is helped by the use of money as a medium of exchange. Economics is concerned with many problems of production, but not with the technique of production. Some problems of production fall within the province of the technician. Economics is concerned with such problems as the scale of production, whether firms carry out the production of a commodity from start to finish or whether they undertake only single processes. Economics has to do with production as a whole, that is, the national income. Another important branch of the subject is devoted to problems associated with the distribution of the national income. This involves a study of money and the determination of prices.

If certain assumptions are made regarding the economic behaviour of people a set of economic principles can be built up by logical reasoning. Economic theory may often appear to be unrelated to the problems of the actual world, but it provides the principles and tools of analysis required for a study of the actual economical problems of the real world, this being the field of applied economics. Yet another branch of economics is devoted to a description of the working and functions of economic institutions such as central and commercial banks, the stock exchange, etc. Most practical problems can be regarded from many different angles, the economic aspect being only one of them. Economics is a social science because it concerns itself with an aspect of human behaviour. As such it formed at one time a branch of philosophy. With the expansion of the subject, due to the increasing complexity of production and distribution following upon the Industrial Revolution, it became a separate subject of study.

Economic Sanctions. *See* Sanctions, Economic.

Economics, Definitions of. On account of the difficulty of framing a concise definition of economics there are many definitions of the subject. The earliest definitions were usually in terms of wealth, Adam Smith giving his great work the title: *An Inquiry into the Nature and Causes of the Wealth of Nations*. Later, J. S. Mill defined economics as 'the practical science of the production and distribution of wealth', and this was the definition of economics adopted by the *Concise Oxford Dictionary*. Although the problems of production and distribution form an important part of economics at least as much attention is paid nowadays to problems of price determination. Davenport emphasised this important aspect of the subject when he described economics as 'the science that treats phenomena from the standpoint of price'. Prof. Pigou stressed the human as distinct from the material aspect of the subject by defining economics in terms of welfare. Marshall considered economics to be 'a study of mankind in the ordinary business of life', then going on to say that economics 'examines that part of individual and social action connected with the attainment of the material requisites of well-being', the subject being 'on the one side a study of wealth; on the more important, a part of the study of man'. The most generally accepted modern definition of economics is that of Lord Robbins. Since all things are scarce in the sense of being limited in supply economic decisions resolve themselves into the making of choices. Economics then becomes 'the science which studies human behaviour as a relationship between ends and scarce means which have alternative uses'. Thus, economics is a study of a particular kind of economising. This definition covers all kinds of economic activity, but unfortunately it gives little indication of the subject-matter of economics. *See* Economics.

Economic Statistics. In Great Britain the Government Statistical Service makes itself responsible for the compilation of statistics both for its own use and for the use of industry. At the centre of the statistical service is the Central Statistical Office (C.S.O.). In addition there is the Business Statistics Office (B.S.O.). *The Monthly Digest of Statistics*, *Economic Trends* and *Financial Statistics* are monthly publications of the Central Statistical Office. Annual publications include *The Annual Abstract of Statistics*, the *Blue Book of National Income and Expenditure* and the *Balance of Payments Pink Book*.

Economic Survey. *See Economic Report*.

Economic System. Broadly speaking there are three types of economic system, the main difference between them being who undertakes the entrepreneurial function, and who owns the means of production. In a capitalist system there is private ownership of capital, and consumers, through the attempt of entrepreneurs to satisfy their demands, really decide what shall be produced and in what quantities. In a communist system decisions regarding production and the actual production itself are undertaken by the State. In most of the so-called capitalist countries today the entrepreneurial function is divided between individual entrepreneurs and the State, this often being known as the 'middle way'.

Economic Theory. A body of economic principles built up as a result of logical reasoning, it provides the tools of economic analysis and it is pursued irrespective of whether it appears likely to be of any practical advantage or not.

Economic Thought. The branch of economics which concerns itself with the development of economic ideas through the writings of the great economists of each period.

Economic Trends. A monthly publication of the Central Statistical Office, giving in a more simplified form much of the information to be found in the *Monthly Digest of Statistics*.

Economic Warfare, Ministry of. A Government department established for the duration of the Second World War to take charge of such matters as the economic blockade of enemy countries.

Economic Welfare. Defined by Prof. Pigou as 'that part of social welfare that can be brought directly or indirectly into relation with the measuring rod of money', it means more than just material well-being. In the first place the economic welfare of people depends on the size of the national income, that is, the total volume of production, but since production includes the provision of services as well as the manufacture of goods, an increase in the economic welfare of an individual may mean either that he has command over a greater quantity of goods than before or that he is able to enjoy to a greater extent than before the services of other people such as musicians and actors. In the second place, economic welfare depends on how the total volume of goods and services is distributed among the members of the community. In general the more equal the distribution the greater will be the economic welfare of the community as a whole, unless the achievement of greater equality reduces the total volume of production.

Economies of Scale. Throughout the past two hundred years there has been a tendency for the scale of production to increase, one of the main features of industrial development during this period being the increasing size of the business unit in most lines of production. The reason for this development has been mainly to take advantage of some of the economies associated with large-scale production, although in more recent times there has often been the additional motive of attempting to obtain a larger share of the market for a commodity and thereby some degree of monopoly power. Economies of scale may be of two kinds —internal and external. Internal economies are those which any single firm by its own organisation and effort can enjoy, external economies being open only to a whole industry. External economies are associated with localisation of industry (*q.v.*). Some of the principal internal economies of scale are as follows: (i) economies in the use of factors of production, since to expand output by a given amount does not require a proportionate increase in the quantities of the factors of production employed. To double output twice the amount of land will not be required, nor is it likely to be necessary to double the labour force. Greater division of labour and specialisation will be possible, and more specialised capital can be employed as can units of capital too large for a small firm to make effective use of; (ii) there will also be economies in administration, since it is unlikely that to double its output a firm will require to double its office staff. The large firm too can make use of office machinery, only extremely large firms having sufficient work to make it worthwhile to employ the latest electronic computers; (iii) marketing economies are possible—both in the form of lower prices for buying raw materials in bulk and in the selling costs of the firm; (iv) on the financial side it is often cheaper for a large firm to borrow, whether from the bank or by an issue of debentures, than for the small firm; (v) only the large firm can undertake research work on its own account. See also Large-scale Production.

Economist, The. A weekly journal, published in London and founded in 1843, mainly, but not exclusively, devoted to consideration of current problems of economic interest. It has been noteworthy for the high calibre of its editors, who have included such well-known economists as Walter Bagehot (appointed 1877), Lord Layton (1922–38), and Lord Crowther (1938–56).

Economist-Extel Indicator. An index of 50 industrial share prices published by *The Economist*, with the average of mid-monthly prices in 1953 as its base. Each year the constituents of the index are reviewed, some being deleted and replaced by others when this course is considered necessary. See also Stock Exchange Indices.

Economy of High Wages. The belief that higher wages will increase the efficiency of the worker to an extent sufficient to compensate the employer for the greater cost of labour. Where workers have previously been insufficiently fed, ill-clad, and badly housed an increase in wages will clearly improve their efficiency. It was true in Great Britain over the greater part of the nineteenth century and it still holds good for many under-developed countries.

E.C.S.C. Abbreviation of European Coal and Steel Community (*q.v.*).

E.C.U. Abbreviation of European Currency Unit, it is a unit of account linked to the currencies of the six original members of the E.E.C.

E.D.C. 1. Abbreviation of European Defence Community.

2. Abbreviation of Economic Development Committee (*q.v.*).

Edge Act (1919). An American Act which permitted U.S. banks to establish subsidiaries to engage in foreign banking. Many of these subsidiaries have their headquarters in New York.

Edinburgh Gazette. An official Government publication similar to the London Gazette (*q.v.*).

EDITH. An acronymic abbreviation of Estate Duties Investment Trust Ltd. (*q.v.*).

Education. One of the principal factors influencing the quality of a country's labour force is education. Formerly individuals were educated primarily for the benefit to be derived from it by the individual himself, in developing his character, mental capacity and potentialities, and the fuller life it enabled him to lead. Though many educationalists have always regarded these aims of education as of paramount importance, some education has always been considered as a means to particular kinds of employment where a high level of education was necessary and where special educational and professional qualifications had to be obtained. It was a long time before Governments regarded vocational education from the economic point of view as a means of raising the quality of labour, and thereby increasing its efficiency and output. In recent years Governments have begun to vie with one another in turning out large numbers of university graduates, especially in highly specialised branches of science and technology for no other reason than to provide the highly qualified labour that the modern economy requires. In Great Britain three aspects of education and training are recognised: (i) general education up to the age of sixteen; (ii) technical education to provide a study of the background subjects of a chosen career, leading to professional qualifications, and often being continued at universities or colleges of technology; (iii) training within industry, where firms undertake the training of their employees for the type of work on which they are actually engaged. It is now realised that efficiency of production does not depend entirely on the efficiency of the three factors of production— land, labour, and capital, and courses are run nowadays at universities and colleges of technology in management studies for young executives and for those likely to reach posts of responsibility. On occasions courses are offered to those who have already reached managerial status, the highest grade of this kind of work being conducted by the Business School of Harvard University in the United States, and London and Manchester Universities in England.

Education Acts. Outstanding Education Acts include the following: (i) 1870. *See* Elementary Education Act (1870). (ii) 1902. This Act abolished School Boards, whose duties were taken over by committees of local authorities. (iii) 1918. (The Fisher Act) The school-leaving age was raised to 14 but many of the recommendations of the Act were never carried out. (iv) 1944. (The Butler Act) The school-leaving age was raised immediately to 15, and in 1973 to 16. It also proposed the establishment of county colleges. There was to be 'secondary' education for all children in Secondary Modern, Secondary Technical or Secondary Grammar Schools.

Education and Science, Department of. A Government department formed in 1964 by a merger of the Ministry of Education and the Department of Science. The first Government department for education was the Board of Education, established in 1899, its name being changed to Ministry of Education in 1944. All aspects of education in England and Wales fall within the purview of the Secretary of State who is generally a member of the Cabinet. Contact with local authorities is maintained through H.M. Inspectors. A separate education department is responsible for education in Scotland.

Education, Colleges of. Colleges for the training of teachers, formerly known as Teacher Training Colleges.

Education for Commerce. *See* B.A.C.I.E.; Commerce, Education for.

Edwards Report (1969). Appointed to inquire into air transport in the 1970s, its main recommendations were: (i) the establishment of a new Airways Board to be responsible for both B.E.A. and B.O.A.C.; (ii) the possibility should be considered of licensing other airlines to compete with B.E.A. and B.O.A.C. on scheduled routes; (iii) a Civil Aviation Authority should be set up to replace the Air Transport Licensing Board and the Air Registration Board.

E.E.C. Abbreviation of European Economic Community (*q.v.*).

Effective Demand. Demand for a commodity backed up by the ability to purchase it. In economic theory demand is always taken to mean effective demand, and so this term is really superfluous.

Effective Tax Rate. A person with a very high income in Great Britain pays tax at possibly £0·83 in the £ on his marginal income. He is, however certain to be entitled to some tax-free allowances (either as a single or married person), and after these have been deducted from his gross income, successive levels of his taxable income are taxed at progressively higher rates, so that the average rate of tax on his gross income, that is, his effective rate of tax, will be much lower than £0·83, possibly no more than £0·50 in the £.

Efficiency Audit. If a nationalised industry is to be run deliberately at a loss 'as a service' it loses the economic test of its efficiency. In such a case the profit test would have to be replaced by some kind of 'efficiency audit'.

Efficiency, Economic. The maximum average output per employee. This in turn depends on the quality, not only of labour, but also of the other factors of production, including capital and the entrepreneur, which must be combined in the optimum proportion. Thus, economic efficiency is a much wider term than technical efficiency, which applies only to the efficiency of one

factor of production, namely capital. Indeed it is possible for a machine to be highly efficient in a technical sense and yet, for some reason, it may not be economically efficient—perhaps because a firm is not large enough to make sufficient use of it.

Efficiency Unit. A unit of measurement, suggested by Prof. Joan Robinson, for use in connection with supply curves of factors of production. If two portions of a factor have the same physical productivity they would be equal to the same number of efficiency units.

Efficient Demand. A term used by A. Marshall to signify the demand of a person when the price he is willing to offer reaches that at which others are willing to sell. It is similar to Effective Demand.

E.F.T.A. Abbreviation of European Free Trade Association (q.v.).

Egalitarianism. Belief in equality of income or at least that inequality of income should be as low as possible consistent with economic progress and economic welfare. As Professor Pigou pointed out, a reduction in equality of income will increase economic welfare provided that it does not at the same time reduce the national income.

Egg Marketing Board. One of the marketing boards set up under the Agriculture Act (1947) but replaced by the Egg Authority in 1971. *See* Agriculture Marketing Act, Marketing Boards.

E.I.B. Abbreviation of European Investment Bank (q.v.).

Eight Hours Act (1908). This granted an eight-hour day to mine workers.

E.I.S. Abbreviation of Educational Institute of Scotland.

Elasticity. The degree of responsiveness of demand or supply to a change of price. If a small change of price results in a large change in demand or supply, then demand or supply respectively is elastic; if, on the other hand, a large change in price has only a slight effect on demand or supply, then demand or supply respectively is inelastic. If a change in price has no effect whatever on the quantity of a commodity that is demanded or supplied, then demand or supply is perfectly inelastic; and if a change in price has an infinite effect on the quantity demanded or supplied, then supply or demand is perfectly elastic—a rather unrealistic situation. Between the extremes of perfect elasticity and perfect inelasticity there are varying degrees of elasticity, and for most commodities or services demand is fairly elastic at one extreme and fairly inelastic at the other. Where a change of price results in a proportionate change in the quantity of a commodity that will be demanded or supplied, then elasticity of demand is said to be equal to unity ($\varepsilon = 1$). The symbol ε is used to represent elasticity. When demand is perfectly inelastic, then elasticity is equal to zero ($\varepsilon = 0$), and when demand is perfectly elastic, then elasticity is equal to infinity ($\varepsilon = \infty$). When demand is fairly elastic, elasticity is said to be greater than unity (> 1), and when demand is fairly inelastic, then elasticity is said to be less than unity (< 1). Similar terms can be used with regard to supply. Degrees of elasticity can be calculated by comparing a change in price with its effect on the quantity that will be demanded or supplied. Thus, if a 50% increase in price results in only a 20% fall in the quantity demanded, then the following fraction can be used to show the degree of elasticity:

$$\frac{\% \text{ change in quantity}}{\% \text{ change in price}} = \frac{20}{50} = 0.4$$

Thus, the degree of elasticity is clearly less than unity. If, however, a 25% increase in price results in 40% fall in the quantity demanded, we have:

$$\frac{\% \text{ change in quantity}}{\% \text{ change in price}} = \frac{40}{25} = 1.6$$

The degree of elasticity in this case is clearly greater than unity. *See also*

Cross-elasticity of Demand; Elasticity of Demand; Elasticity of Supply.

Elasticity of Demand. The responsiveness of demand to changes of price. (*See* Elasticity.) Elasticity determines the shape of the demand curve. If demand is perfectly elastic the demand curve will be a horizontal straight line, and if perfectly inelastic a vertical straight line as shown in the diagrams above. The less steep the curve the more elastic will be the demand, provided that the curves to be compared are drawn to identical scales. Most demand curves show different degrees of elasticity over different parts of their length as shown in the third diagram. This shows that at prices below OP^1 demand is fairly inelastic, at prices between OP^1 and OP^2 demand is fairly elastic, but at prices higher than OP^2 demand is very elastic.

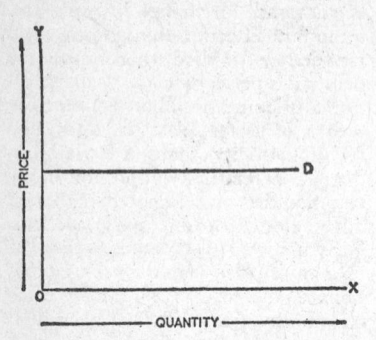

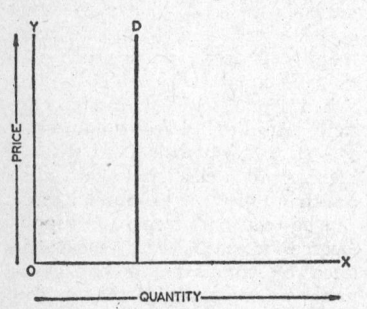

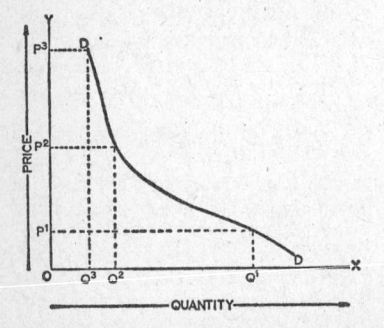

Influences on Elasticity of Demand.

(i) Time. In the short period a change of price may have little influence on demand, since it may be some time before all consumers become aware of the change of price, or it may be thought that in the case of a fall in price this may merely be the first stage in a more prolonged fall. With durable goods the effect of a fall in price may be slow to take effect since consumers may be reluctant to replace such goods if they are still in good condition.

(ii) The possibility of substitution. The closer the substitutes for a commodity the more likely is the demand for it to be elastic.

(iii) The degree of necessity. The possibility of substitution is of greater importance than the degree of necessity. Nevertheless, the greater the degree of necessity the more likely is the demand for a commodity to be inelastic, at least over a moderate price range.

(iv) The size of consumers' incomes. The poorer a person the more elastic is likely to be his demand for most things.

(v) Habit. People's purchases are to some extent determined by habit, with the price that for small changes of price their demand is fairly inelastic. In the case of tobacco even quite large increases in price have had little effect on demand, which has proved to be very inelastic for this commodity.

Effect of Elasticity of Demand on Price Changes. If demand is elastic an increase in supply will greatly increase the quantity supplied but will have little effect on price:

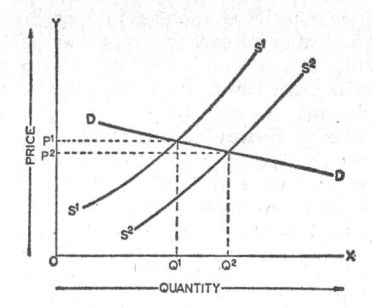

If, however, demand is inelastic an increase in supply will have little effect on the quantity demanded, but a considerable effect on price:

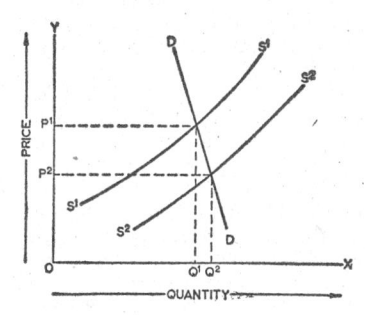

Elasticity of Demand and Total Income. If the demand for a commodity is very elastic a slight rise in price will decrease the income of the seller. Consider the following diagram:

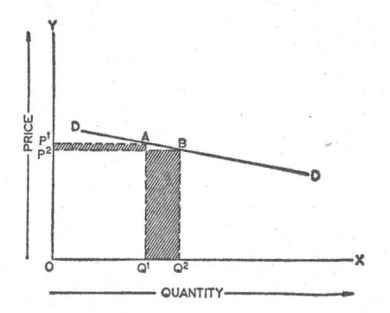

This diagram shows that the price has risen from OP^2 to OP^1 but the quantity demanded has fallen from OQ^2 to OQ^1. The income of the seller is represented by the rectangle OP^2BQ^2 (price × quantity demanded) before the rise in price took place. After the rise in price the seller's income is shown by the rectangle OP^1AQ^1 which is obviously smaller than the previous one, representing his income before the rise in price. If, on the other hand, demand is very inelastic the seller's income will increase considerably as a result of a rise in price. Consider now the next diagram. In this case the seller's income before the rise in price was shown by the rectangle OP^2BQ^2, which is clearly smaller than the rectangle OP^1AQ^1, the rectangle representing his income after the rise in price.

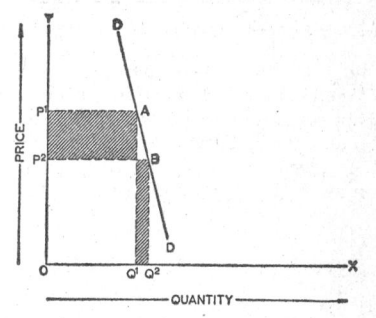

Elasticity of Substitution. The extent to which one good can be substituted for another. Elasticity of demand is a mixture of elasticity of substitution and income elasticity of demand (*q.v.*). Perfect elasticity of substitution would occur if two commodities were perfect substitutes for one another, which would mean that they were really one and the same commodity. The other extreme would occur if there were no substitute at all for a commodity. Elasticity of substitution is the determinant of the shape of an individual's indifference curve. *See* Elasticity.

Elasticity of Supply. The responsiveness of supply to a change of price. (*See* Elasticity.) Elasticity determines the steepness of the slope of the supply curve, the steeper the slope the more inelastic the supply, provided the curves to be compared are drawn to identical scales. If supply is perfectly inelastic it will be represented diagrammatically by a vertical straight line, and if perfectly elastic by a horizontal straight line. For most commodities the degree of elasticity of supply will lie between these two extremes. The greatest influence on supply is time. For some things supply may be permanently inelastic, as in the supply of paintings by deceased great masters, but for many things supply is fixed in the short period because it often takes time to increase supply, as for example with agricultural products. Elasticity of supply, therefore, depends on the length of time it takes supply to adjust itself to new conditions. Supply can be increased by new firms entering an industry and by existing firms increasing their output. The more inelastic the supply the greater will be its effect on the price of the commodity. An increase in the demand for works of art will increase their price enormously, but an increase in the demand for most things will be met, at least in the long run, by an increase in the supply and eventually the price may be little higher than before, or even in some cases lower. *See also* Changes in Supply.

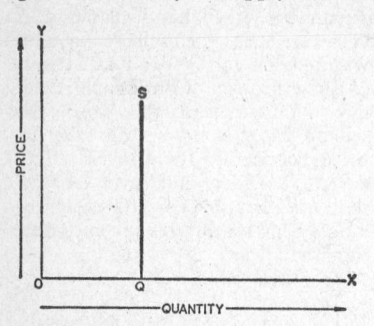

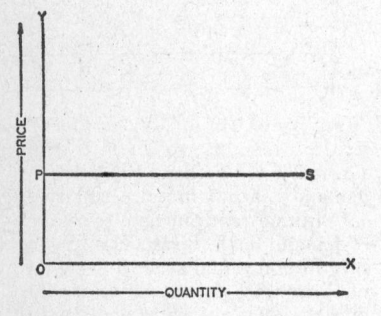

Elderly, Employment of the. At one time people worked just as long as they were physically capable of doing so, since the payment they received for their work was generally their only source of income. During the past two hundred years not only has the expectation of life, both for men and women, increased, but they have retained their physical and mental capacities to a greater age. When the first British National Insurance Scheme was introduced after the Act of 1911 it seemed reasonable that men could not be expected to work beyond the age of 65, but nowadays a large proportion of men are still capable of undertaking many kinds of work, even though at that age they are entitled to a retirement pension if they cease working. It can no longer be said that the employment of men over this age is prevented by their lack of efficiency, though in some cases this may be true. The employment of the elderly depends on other factors, such as the general state of economic activity at the time. When there is serious unemployment there is a tendency to look askance at the employment of men of pensionable age, or even actively to resist their employment. In times of full, or more particularly, over-full employment, the approach to the employment of the elderly is quite different. Shortages of labour in many fields of activity make employers readier to employ older men. In such circumstances the Government may actively encourage people not to retire if they are physically and mentally capable of going on working, and those who have already retired may be encouraged to return to work. Since, however, the pension under the national insurance scheme is intended to be a retirement pension, those in receipt of it have to suffer some reduction if they earn more than a stated amount in any week. At the age of 70 there are no such reductions to pensions.

Another problem arises in connection with the extended employment of people in high executive positions in that they tend to delay the promotion of promising younger men, who as a result may pass their prime before reaching such positions. Another factor in the situation since 1945 has been that over the greater part of the period there has been at least full employment, with the result that people on fixed incomes, which include mainly the elderly, have suffered a decline in their real incomes, and this fact encourages many of the elderly to continue at work longer than they otherwise would have cared to do. The Reports of the Watkinson Committee on the Employment of Older Men and Women had little to recommend to aid a solution of this problem. Nor did the suggestion of the Phillips Committee (1954) that the pensionable age for men should be raised from 65 to 68 meet with much enthusiasm.

Electricity Consultative Councils. Bodies set up to watch the interests of consumers of electricity and make recommendations to the Electricity Boards.

Electricity Council. Under the Electricity Act (1957) the Central Electricity Authority was dissolved and replaced by the Electricity Council and the Central Electricity Generating Board. The obligations of the former Central Electricity Authority with regard to outstanding British Electricity Stocks were transferred to the new Electricity Council. The Electricity Council is responsible for policy with regard to the provision of electricity in Great Britain, whereas the Central Electricity Generating Board is the owner and operator of all the generating power stations in England and Wales.

Electronic Computer. An electronically operated machine capable of carrying out complicated calculations with great rapidity. There are two types—the analogue and the digital. A programme of instructions has to be prepared and 'fed' into the machine. Such computers are one of the great aids to automation, but clearly only a very large firm with a mass of work of the necessary kind can fully employ one of these machines, which are extremely costly to purchase. Firms with a large number of branches—such as banks—can employ them if they concentrate the appropriate kind of work at one office. Alternatively, some firms which can find sufficient work for these machines only for a part of the week often offer them on hire to other firms for short periods.

Elementary Education Act (1870). This Act set up School Boards in those places where there were insufficient schools to accommodate all the children of the district, each School Board having to make good the deficiency in its own area by building new schools known as Board Schools. Only when sufficient accommodation had been provided was education made compulsory for all children.

Eligibility Rule. With reference to the Bank of England in its capacity as 'lender of last resort', the Bank of England performing this service for the members of the London Discount Market. When requested it will re-discount only bills which satisfy its rule of eligibility, that is bank bills and fine trade bills.

Eligible Paper. Negotiable instruments—bills of exchange, etc.—bearing names of sufficiently high standing to make them acceptable to banks.

Elsie Mackay Fund. Established in 1929 in memory of their daughter by Lord and Lady Inchcape, this Fund was to be allowed to accumulate for 50 years and then applied to a reduction of the National Debt. *See* National Fund.

E.M.A. Abbreviation of European Monetary Agreement (*q.v.*).

Embargo. With reference to the import trade, the prohibition by a

Government, or possibly by a docker's or other trade union, of the import of certain classes of goods or goods coming from a particular country with the policy of which there is strong disagreement.

Embezzlement. The appropriation to his own use by an employee of money rightfully belonging to his employer.

Emerson Bonus System. A system of wage payment whereby a certain output per man is regarded as the standard for each worker, who receives a small bonus even if he only achieves two-thirds of this amount, the bonus increasing progressively as the standard is approached. It is claimed that this system, where the 'task' is more easily achieved, gives the workers a greater incentive to increase production than many other bonus systems where the 'task' is more severe, even though in such cases the bonus may be much larger.

E.M.I. Abbreviation of Electric and Musical Industries Ltd., a holding company controlling 85 other companies, concerned *inter alia* with the manufacture of gramophones, gramophone records, radio, television and, more recently, medical electronic equipment.

Emigration. Though economists often stress the lack of mobility of labour in the geographical sense of the term, throughout the world's history down to the present day there has been considerable migration of peoples. Even today there are large numbers of nomads who, because of the poverty of the soil in the regions they inhabit, are compelled to move from one place to another as their flocks consume the vegetation. Emigration, however, is generally restricted to the movement of people from one country to another. There have been two main reasons for emigration: (i) economic; (ii) fear of religious or political persecution. The emigration of Scots and Irish has been mainly of an economic character, as also has been the immigration of people from the West Indies and Pakistan into Great Britain in recent times. In earlier days both French and Flemings emigrated to Great Britain because of religious persecution in their own countries, and many British settlers emigrated to the United States for similar reasons, though in some cases, as with the Royalists in the seventeenth century, there were political motives also. Since 1935 there has been considerable emigration from Europe to Great Britain, the United States, and other parts of the world for political reasons, and in the case of the Jews on account of racial persecution. Within Great Britain there has been considerable migration from the Highlands of Scotland to the Lowlands, and from Scotland as a whole to England. Over-populated countries sometimes encourage emigration, just as under-populated countries encourage immigration. For some time now the United States has placed restrictions on immigration. Whether emigration or immigration should be encouraged on economic grounds depends on whether a country already has a population greater or less than its optimum.

Emigration Societies. Societies established for the purpose of encouraging emigration to Commonwealth countries.

Empire Marketing Board. A body set up in 1926 to stimulate demand in Great Britain for Empire products. *See* Imperial Preference.

Empiricism. A method of studying a subject whereby knowledge is acquired as a result of actual experience.

Employee Motivation. An American term. *See* Incentives.

Employee Rating. Also known as Merit Rating. A large firm requires to have some method of assessing the quality of its employees. Not only is this a necessary pre-requisite for determining rates of pay for some jobs, but it is of even more vital importance when the question of promotion has to be considered. Most managers prefer to promote on merit; most trade unions, however, prefer promotion to depend on seniority. For merit rating a firm might draw up an Employee Rating Chart for each employee, marks or points being awarded to each for such qualities as skill, capacity, initiative, willingness to co-operate with others, dependability or any other quality which the firm may regard as relevant to the job in question. The value of the chart clearly depends on the skill and reliability of the persons who are responsible for making the various assessments, and greater reliability will be achieved the greater the number of persons who have to make the different assessments of the workers' ability and character. If the various ratings are left entirely to the foremen or supervisors there is a danger of too much attention being paid to personal likes and dislikes. If an Employee Rating Chart is to be used as a basis for promotion it must be seen to be fair to all employees concerned, and if so it is clearly a more efficient guide to promotion than mere seniority. Promotion can be made to depend on a number of factors, the Employee Rating Chart being in such a case only one of them.

Employee Rating Chart. A system whereby the ability and character of employees are assessed by awarding them marks or points, subject to periodic revision, for certain selected attributes. *See* Employee Rating.

Employer and Employee. Usually referred to as the Law of Master and Servant (*q.v.*). Employment by an employer of an employee implies a contract between them even if there is not written agreement. The National Insurance (Industrial Injuries) Act (1946) replaced the Workmen's Compensation Acts, the State accepting responsibility for this type of injury, and weekly premiums being added to the National Insurance payments, of both employer and employee. Consideration of injury at work is now the responsibility of the Health and Safety Executive of the Department of Employment, under the Health and Safety at Work, etc., Act (1974). Where compensation is payable the accident must have arisen in the course of the claimant's employment, a fact which constantly gives rise to litigation. Compensation is based on the extent to which the person injured has suffered a loss of physical or mental capacity. Cases are considered on their merits, but an injured person, if not satisfied with their decision, has the right to appeal to a special tribunal. *See also* Employers' Liability Act (1880).

Employers' Association. An association of the employers in an industry. In general, their purpose is twofold: (i) to provide a means for discussing problems common to the industry; (ii) to enable collective bargaining to take place with the appropriate trade unions representing the employees. Often, as in the wool textile industry, there are separate employers' associations for each of the main branches of the industry, these being linked together in the Wool (and Allied) Textile Employers' Council. At the national level most employers' associations are affiliated to a national body—the Confederation of British Industry.

Employers' Liability Act (1880). At common law it is recognised that every employer owes a duty to his employees not to cause them injury. Thus, an employee is entitled to claim damages from his employer under this Act, although any negligence on his own part will reduce the amount of the damages the court will award. If the work is known to be of a dangerous character by the employee he will usually be paid more than for less dangerous work of a similar kind ('danger money' (*q.v.*)) and this may mean that in case of injury he may have to depend on National Insurance benefit for compensation, though in certain cases he may still be able to claim damages from his employer. There is also the doctrine of 'common employment' (*q.v.*) which applies to cases where there has been negligence on the part of the employer. The courts, however, are often reluctant to apply this principle if they fear that an employer is merely trying to take advantage of it to reduce his own liability. With regard to the dismissal of employees each is entitled to a reasonable period of notice which may vary in length according to what is regarded as customary in a particular occupation, and an employee can sue his employer where insufficient notice has been given. *See also* 'Golden Handshake'; Redundancy Payment.

Employment Act (1946). An American Act of Congress which in effect commits the United States to pursue a policy of full employment.

Employment Appeals Tribunal. Set up under the Employment Protection Act (1975) it replaced the National Industrial Relations Court (*q.v.*).

Employment, Department of. Until 1968 known as the Ministry of Labour and then until 1970 as the Department of Employment and Productivity, the new title was intended to emphasise the Government's incomes policy with wage increases related to increases in productivity. The expansion of the work of the Labour Department of the Board of Trade led to this department being transferred in 1916 to a new ministry, now known as the Department of Employment, then the Ministry of Labour. Its functions include the administration of employment exchanges and the Youth Employment Service, the provision of vocational training for disabled persons, the administration of the Factory Acts, and matters concerning wages and conditions of employment. It is concerned with industrial relations through its conciliation service and its appointment of arbitrators and courts of inquiry. The Department undertakes surveys in connection with index numbers of retail prices and compiles the index. After 1939 it also became responsible for registration for service in the armed forces and for a time, therefore, it was known as the Ministry of Labour and National Service.

Employment Exchange. An institution, with branches in all the larger towns, established by the Labour Exchanges Act (1909), and formerly known as labour exchanges, to bring employers requiring labour into contact with people who are unemployed. They are administered by the Department of Employment (formerly the Ministry of Labour). The duties of the exchanges increased after the passing of the National Insurance Act (1911). Employers report vacancies to the local employment exchange, which also pay unemployment benefit there. Since 1952 it has been compulsory for most jobs to be filled through employment exchanges.

Employment, Full. *See* Full Employment.

Employment Function. As defined by Lord Keynes in his *General Theory of Employment, Interest and Money*, it is the mathematical relationship between effective demand, measured in terms of the wage-unit, and the amount of employment.

Employment Multiplier. *See* Multiplier.

Employment of Children. The Children and Young Persons Act (1933) restricts the employment of children of school age. Children under the age of 13 cannot be employed at all, with certain minor exceptions. No child of school age can be employed during school hours, before 6 o'clock in the morning or generally after 8 o'clock in the evening. There are also some other restrictions on the employment of children.

Employment of Older Men and Women, Reports of Watkinson Committee on (1953 and 1955). Two reports were issued by this committee, but they did little more than recommend that the employment of elderly people depended on a change of attitude to the question among employers. *See* Elderly, Employment of.

Employment Policy, White Paper on (1944). Described by Lord Beveridge in a Postscript to his *Full Employment in a Free Society*, as epoch-making, this White Paper set out the policy of the Government with regard to employment. Its outstanding feature was that it indicated that the British Government for the first time in its history accepted responsibility for the maintenance of full employment. When, it says, private investment is insufficient to provide full employment, then public investment must be undertaken to fill the gap. Like Lord Beveridge himself, the White Paper regards controlled location of industry as an essential pre-requisite to the success of any full employment policy.

Employment, Primary. Employment resulting directly from a given amount of investment. *See* Multiplier.

Employment Protection Act (1975). An Act consolidating the law relating to the employment of labour after the repeal of the Industrial Relations Act (1971) (*q.v.*). The aim was to establish a new legal framework for collective bargaining and to list for workers a series of statutory rights on pay and job security.

Employment Rate. The percentage of workers who at a given time are in employment. It is more usual to consider this rate, as it were, negatively, as the Unemployment Rate. After 1856 the trade unions began to calculate the numbers of their members who were out of work. The introduction of National Insurance made a more accurate estimate possible, based on the number of insured workers who were unemployed and in receipt of unemployment pay. These returns are now compiled monthly by the Department of Employment. The widening of the scope of the National Insurance scheme since 1947 has made the calculation of the employment rate even more accurate, though still not quite complete. It is, of course, the Unemployment Rate that attracts most attention, as this is an important indicator of the economic trend of the period when it has been seasonally adjusted. *See* Unemployment Rate.

Employment, Secondary. In addition to the direct or primary employment created by a given amount of investment, additional employment, known as secondary employment, will be created as a result of the increased spending of the people drawn into primary employment.

Employment Theory, Classical. The employment theory of the classical economists was based on the assumption of full employment. Involuntary unemployment, where aggregate supply exceeds aggregate demand, was either not considered to any serious degree by the classical economists or its possibility actually denied. At an equilibrium wage, it was thought, there would always be work for all those who desired it, whereas the Great Depression showed all too clearly that full employment was far from being inevitable. The view of Say, that supply created its own demand, was generally accepted. This view was, however, queried by one or two economists even in the early nineteenth century, but it was not until the Great Depression and the writings of Lord Keynes that it was seriously questioned. *See* Income Determination.

Employment Volume. The actual number of people in employment at a given time. Since 1945 the labour force of Great Britain has increased in size very considerably for a number of reasons: (i) the greater proportion of married women going out to work, both young and middle-aged; (ii) the tendency of many men to go on working beyond the normal retirement age, a tendency encouraged by the falling value of money during an inflationary period; (iii) the reduction in the numbers in the armed forces; (iv) the tendency of many people who would not otherwise go out to work to take part-time jobs; and (v) in recent years the immigration into this country of displaced persons from Europe, and more recently of coloured people from the West Indies, Pakistan, and India. Then there has been the normal factor of natural increase.

E.M.U. Abbreviation of European Monetary Union (*q.v.*).

Encashment Credit. A permit to a person who has a bank account in one town to enable him to draw cheques on his account at a branch of the same or another bank in another town up to an agreed maximum amount per month or for any other specified period.

Enclosure. Parliamentary permission to enclose a piece of land—grazing land, woodland, or wasteland—formerly regarded as common to the inhabitants of a village. There were many enclosures in the sixteenth century, but the great period of enclosures was the late eighteenth century. The result was that the poorer people in these places were debarred from rearing a few animals and access to fuel, and poor but independent yeomen were turned into poor labourers who had to work for the larger landowners. On the other hand, the enclosures of the eighteenth century made possible the new developments in agriculture of which only the larger landowners could take full advantage.

Endogenous Change. A change arising from within, that is, for economic reasons. *Cf.* Exogenous Change.

Endorsement (or **Indorsement**). It is a signature, generally but not always on the reverse side of a document (hence the name), given to transfer the rights to which the document gives rise to some other person or party. Endorsement of bills of exchange and cheques is in certain circumstances compulsory. Until the passing of the Cheques Act (1957) all cheques made payable to '. . . or Order' required to be endorsed, but since then this has been no longer necessary when the payee pays such a cheque into his own banking account at the branch where he maintains his account. An 'Order' cheque requiring a bank to pay cash to the payee, even if drawn in favour of himself, still requires endorsement.

Endowment Assurance. Really a combination of life assurance and investment. The assured person takes out a policy for a specified number of years or until he reaches a certain age, and during the whole of that period his life is assured for an agreed sum. If the assured survives to the end of the period of the assurance he receives the agreed capital sum (if the policy is 'without profits') or this sum together with the annual bonuses that have been added. Endowment assurance is a convenient and profitable way of preparing to meet some future financial commitment, such as for the education of children, old age, etc.

End Product. An alternative term for Final Product. It is the final stage to which a particular firm carries the production of a commodity.

Ends. In his definition of economics Lord Robbins used this term for the many purposes for which factors of production can be employed, his main point being that ends are many and various in relation to the limited means at the disposal of entrepreneurs for achieving them, and therefore a choice has to be made at any particular period of time as to which ends to pursue.

Enfaced. With reference to foreign bonds, an alternative term for 'assented' (*q.v.*).

Engels' Law. According to this law the smaller a person's income the greater the proportion of it that he will spend on food. This is borne out by the weighting of the indexes of retail prices published in Great Britain and based on surveys of family expenditure. For the original Cost of Living Index, first issued in 1914, food was given a weight of 60%, whereas the Index of Retail Prices with 1962 as its base gave food a weight of only 35%, the reduction of the weight being the result of the great rise in the standard of living in the intervening half century.

English Equivalent. The London Stock Exchange equivalent of the prices of U.S. and Canadian securities. It is calculated by multiplying the American price by 5 (the fictitious 'Dummy' Dollar (*q.v.*) rate of exchange between dollars and sterling) and dividing by the actual rate for the day.

Engrossing. The buying up of a large proportion of the supply of a commodity in order to push up its price, a practice generally condemned in the Middle Ages as being contrary to the idea then prevalent of a 'just price'.

Enquiry Agent. *See* Status Inquiry Agency.

Entail. Where succession to a piece of land is laid down by law and which the existing owner cannot change.

Enterprise. As a factor of production an alternative name for the entrepreneur. Also it is used as an alternative name for a firm. For the use of the term for a type of economic system *see* Free Enterprise.

Enterprise, Free. *See* Free Enterprise.

Enterprise, Private. *See* Free Enterprise.

Enterprise, Public. When the production of a commodity or service is in the hands of the State (nationalised industries) or a Local Authority (for example, a public library). This is known as the public sector of the economy.

Entertainments Duty. An excise duty first imposed in 1916 on most forms of entertainment—concerts, theatres, sport. It was removed in easy stages. In most cases the removal of the tax was for economic reasons and occurred where the entertainment industry in question was itself declining. The imposition of VAT in 1973 again brought entertainment within the range of taxation.

Entrepôt Trade. Re-export trade. Ports which are conveniently situated as distributing centres for wide areas import large quantities of goods, in addition to those for home consumption, to re-export to neighbouring countries. London, Rotterdam, Le Havre, Singapore all have a considerable amount of entrepôt trade. For example, most of the tea imported into Europe is first brought to London, just as most coffee for continental Europe comes in by way of Le Havre. If customs duty has been paid on goods which are to be re-exported it can be reclaimed as Customs Drawback (*q.v.*).

Entrepreneur. A term used to denote the organising factor in production. The entrepreneur is responsible for such economic decisions as determining what to produce and how much to produce. He must also decide what method of production to adopt and in what proportions to combine his resources of land, labour, and capital. On the combined decisions of entrepreneurs depends, then, the assortment of goods that will be available to consumers, but in a free economy entrepreneurs will try to anticipate the demand of consumers. Consequently, the bearing of uncertainty is regarded as the primary function of the entrepreneur. Risks which can be insured against form no part of the function of the entrepreneur, uncertainty comprising those risks against which it is not possible to insure. Much of production is carried on in anticipation of demand, and modern methods of production have become so complex that the time interval between the decision to produce and the commodity coming on to the market has considerably lengthened, and this greatly increases the risk of production—the risk that demand in the interval may change, or that other producers may enter the market.

The entrepreneur is also responsible for the management of business. Many economists recognise the entrepreneur as a fourth factor of production in addition to land, labour, and capital, though some refuse to distinguish between labour and the entrepreneur. They argue that a certain amount of organising is required of all labour, though more in some cases than others, the only difference, they say, being the proportion of time devoted to organising. However, the organising undertaken by the entrepreneur is not only on a wider scale than that of labour, but also different in kind, the entrepreneur not merely being responsible for organising how a particular small piece of work shall be done since his responsibility extends to organising the work of others, the people he employs. Also the decisions he has to make are of a much more far-reaching character. The great difficulty is in locating the entrepreneurial factor in the principal forms of modern business enterprise. In the case of the sole proprietor the entrepreneurial function is clearly undertaken by one person who accepts the entire risks of the enterprise and is solely responsible for its management. In a partnership the function is equally clearly divided between the partners, but in the public limited company the two main functions of the entrepreneur are divided, the shareholders bearing the risk while the board of directors take responsibility for policy and decision making. Similarly, with public enterprise, the risk of a municipally owned undertaking lies with the ratepayers, but the decision-making with a committee of the council, and in the case of a nationalised industry the taxpayers bear the risk while decisions are left to Parliament or some authority to which Parliament has delegated its powers.

Entry for Free Goods. A document employed at the port of entry when imported goods are not subject to customs duty. It gives full particulars of the goods. The customs officer at the port of entry compares the particulars given on this form with those on the Ship's Report, and inspects the cargo before releasing the goods.

Entry for Home Use. A document employed at the port of entry for use in connection with goods liable to customs duty when the duty is to be paid immediately. After payment of duty the goods can then be removed by the importer.

Entry for Warehousing. A document used at the port of entry for goods which are liable to customs duty where the duty is not to be paid immediately, such goods being removed under the supervision of customs officers to a bonded warehouse, which must be named on the form. Goods can then be removed from the bonded warehouse only after payment of duty on the consignment of goods to be removed and under the supervision of the customs authorities.

Environment. A term used by A. Marshall as an alternative to Conjunction to indicate the condition that makes it possible for a person to enjoy Consumer's Surplus (*q.v.*).

Environment, Department of. Formed in 1970 by merging three ministries—Housing and Local Government, Transport, Public Building and Works, its responsibilities include local government, housing, pollution, roads and transport, conservation.

E.P.T. Abbreviation of Excess Profits Tax (*q.v.*).

E.P.U. Abbreviation of European Payments Union (*q.v.*).

Epunit. A name sometimes given to the unit of account of the European Payments Union which had a gold value equal to that of the U.S. dollar.

Equal Advantage, Principle of. *See* Equi-marginal Principle.

Equal Cost Lines. A graph showing

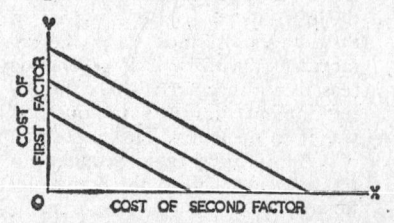

lines which represent equal total cost of the factors of production employed over a range of outposts. To show three factors would require a three-dimensional diagram.

Equalisation. All holders of units in a unit trust receive equal distributions per unit even though some may have been held only for a short time and others for the full period since the previous distribution. On the units not held for the full period only part of the distribution comprises dividend the remainder—the equalisation—being regarded as a return of capital.

Equalisation Grant. *See* Exchequer Equalisation Grant.

Equality of Saving and Investment. A concept first put forward by Lord Keynes in 1935 in his *General Theory of Employment, Interest and Money*. Previously, Keynes and others had believed that it was differences between saving and investment that were responsible for the booms and depressions of the trade cycle: when saving exceeded investment (that is, real capital production) it was thought that a depression would occur; when investment exceeded saving there would then be a danger of an inflationary boom. However, in his most famous book, named above, Keynes declared that saving and investment were always equal to one another. He demonstrated this in the following manner. Regarding the national income as the total of all incomes derived from economic activity, some of this will be spent on consumers' goods (consumption) and some will be saved, so that

Saving = Income − Consumption

The national income can also be regarded as the value in terms of money of the total volume of goods and services produced, and since some goods are consumers' goods and others are producers' goods (that is, investment or capital goods), it follows that

Investment = Income − Consumption

Since, then both saving and investment are equal to the difference between income and consumption it follows that they must be equal to one another. Therefore, saving, said Lord Keynes, must always be equal to investment.

One difficulty presented by the theory is that saving is undertaken by one group of people, individuals as well as some entrepreneurs, whereas real investment is entirely the responsibility of entrepreneurs. It would appear, therefore, that the saving of individuals depends on considerations quite different from those which influence entrepreneurs, and so saving can either exceed or fall short of investment. The reply to this is that people may *attempt* to save more than the amount of investment but that economic influences prevent their doing so. An individual may increase his rate of saving, but if entrepreneurs are unwilling to increase their rate of investment, the fact that more saving means less spending will have the effect of reducing other people's incomes by exactly the same amount, since all spending is at the same time income to those who receive payment. The result is that, although a particular individual's saving has increased, that of the community as a whole has not. Considering the problem from another angle, it is investment that is primarily responsible for the generation of income, and so an increase in investment brings about an increase in income and, therefore, in saving. Thus, whether saving increases relatively to investment, or vice-versa, influences are set in motion that affect income, and the effect on income is to bring saving and investment into equality.

For a generation this new concept of Lord Keynes's caused great controversy, which has only recently subsided, as a result of efforts to reconcile the apparently irreconcilable statements (i) that saving and investment are not necessarily always equal and (ii) that saving and investment must always be equal. Sir Dennis Robertson put forward what he called the period analysis, money which may be earned in one period being available for spending or saving in the next, so that the saving and consumption of one period depend on the income of the previous period, and in consequence although forces tend to bring saving and investment into equality, they are not necessarily equal in the same period. Somewhat similar explanations have been elaborated by Professor B. Ohlin of the Scandinavian School and Sir Ralph Hawtrey. The Scandinavians regard the situation from two positions—*ex ante* and *ex post*, the *ex ante* corresponding to Robertson's first period and *ex post* to the period immediately following. *Ex ante* saving and *ex ante* investment are unlikely to be equal to one another, but because of the economic forces brought into play, *ex post* saving is likely to be equal to *ex post* investment, though the amount of *ex post* saving may not be the same as was *ex ante* intended. Hawtrey uses the terms 'designed' or 'active' for the amount of saving people as a whole plan to undertake, and the terms 'undesigned' or 'passive' for the amount actually achieved by the community as a whole as a result of the amount of investment undertaken.

Equality of Taxation. A term used by Adam Smith to mean taxation *proportionate* to income.

Equal Pay. A term referring to equal pay for men and women for 'work of equal value'. In the civil service and the professions where it is easier to determine what is equal work, there has been equal pay for some time. Where men and women are engaged on similar work the argument in favour of equal pay appears to be logical. In industry fewer women do similar work to the men, and where the work is different it is likely to be thought, at least by the trade unions dominated by men, that the work done by the women is less skilful or less exacting. There still remains something of the traditional belief that women in any case require less pay than men. The fact that large numbers of women are married and, therefore, not entirely dependent on their own earnings tends to keep down their wages, and in industries like textiles where it was for long customary for husband and wife to work in the mill it tended to keep down the men's wages too. Another factor was that trade union organisation was less well developed among women than among men. Many girls used to look upon the period of employment after leaving school merely as a temporary interval before marriage, and so were unwilling to equip themselves to make their jobs a career, but this factor has been modified by the increasing tendency for women, especially those with professional knowledge or skills, to return to employment later in life after their children have grown up. The principle of equal pay is now generally accepted in the more advanced countries. It was laid down by the E.E.C. in the Treaty of Rome (1957) and by the I.L.O.

The aim of the Equal Pay Act (1970) was to remove discrimination between men and women with regard to pay and conditions of employment. The Act made it illegal after 1975 to have lower rates of pay for women for 'work of equal value' —a condition not easy to define. In 1972 women in Great Britain employed as manual workers in industry received on average only 60% of the rate for men, the differential being much less in most other West European countries. For the reasons given above most women tend to be concentrated in the less well-paid occupations such as catering and shop work. In all countries where equal pay has been legally imposed there have been attempts to segregate women into different (and lower-paid) jobs from men. In 1975 the Sex Discrimination Act (*q.v.*) was passed.

Equal Pay, Royal Commission on (1946). Majority and Minority reports were published. The former favoured differentiation on the ground that men have greater physical strength and are generally more efficient than women, that women are more likely than men to absent themselves from work, and are in general less ambitious and show less initiative. The Minority Report had to admit the point about physical strength, but it was claimed that in other respects women are equally as efficient as men, their failure to secure promotion in the past being mainly the result of the prejudice of employers and the jealousy of male workers.

Equal Product Curve. A curve showing the same amount of production obtained by the employment of different quantities of two factors, (say) x and y:

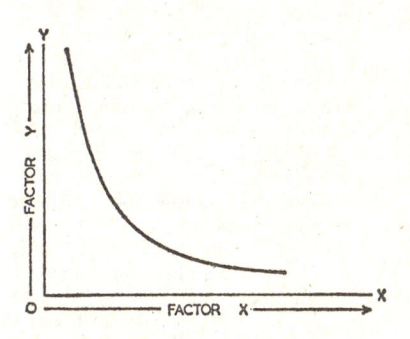

See also Contours.

Equal Sacrifice Theory. A theory that taxation should involve equal sacrifice for all, the less the sacrifice the greater the amount to be paid by the taxpayer. The great difficulty is the inability to measure with any degree of accuracy the amount of sacrifice involved in tax payments by different people.

Equation of Exchange. The equation employed to illustrate the Quantity Theory of Money, as modified by Irving Fisher. It is expressed as follows:

$$MV = PT$$

The symbol M represents the total amount of money in existence at a certain time, the total value of all bank-notes and bank deposits and coin. Sometimes the total quantity of money is represented as $M + M'$, where M stands for cash and M' for bank deposits, though it is not really necessary to make this distinction. The symbol V represents the velocity of circulation, a variable difficult to calculate, although the total value of all the cheques passing through the bankers' clearing houses in relation to the total quantity of money at the time gives some indication of it. The total MV, therefore, represents the total amount of money employed during a period. The symbol P represents a very difficult concept—the general price level, a sort of general average of the prices of all kinds of goods and services, producers' goods as well as consumers' goods. Finally, the symbol T represents the total of all transactions that have taken place for money during the period. The equation of exchange above shows that the price level and, therefore, the value of money, can be influenced not only by M, the quantity of money, but also by V, the rate at which money circulates, and T, the output of goods and services and the number of trade transactions that take place. Thus, P, the general price level, can be influenced by any one of these variables, and it is possible for a change in one of them to be offset to a greater or a less extent by a change in one of the others.

There is no doubt that the four variables, M, V, P, and T are all related to one another, though perhaps not in so precise a manner as the Equation of Exchange implies. Criticism of the Equation of Exchange is criticism of the Quantity Theory of Money, and is best considered under the heading. *See therefore* Quantity Theory of Money.

A second equation of exchange has been constructed as follows:

$$p = \frac{M}{kR}$$

In this case M as before represents the total of all kinds of money. The symbol k represents the total of the country's income held in the form of money, and the symbol R represents the total of goods and services—the country's real income. Finally, p represents the general level of prices for consumers' goods, being represented by a small letter to distinguish it from P in the first equation, which represents the general level of all prices. There is clearly some similarity between the two equations, for k, representing the demand to hold money, is very much related to V of the first equation, for the greater the proportion of money held the lower will be the velocity of circulation. In other words, V of the first equation varies inversely with k of the second equation.

Equatorial Customs Union (U.D.E.). Comprising the four equatorial countries of the Central African Republic, Chad, Congo, and Gabon, the U.D.E. (Union Douanière Equatoriale) was established in 1959 to form these countries into a customs union and to enable them to have a common monetary system and central bank. In 1961 Cameroon became an associate member.

Equilibrium. A situation in which economic forces, as they exist at the time, have no tendency to change. Sometimes a distinction can be made between short period and long period equilibrium, a short period equilibrium being established in the conditions of a given time whereas in the long run other circumstances will have to be taken into account to produce a long period equilibrium situation. Equilibrium theory states that if a position of equilibrium is disturbed by some outside influence forces will be immediately set in motion to bring about a new position of equilibrium. The following are some examples of the concept of equilibrium:

(i) *Equilibrium Price.* In price theory the equilibrium price is one where the quantity demanded of a commodity is exactly equal to the quantity supplied; this can be a short-period equilibrium in a market on perhaps one particular day, price perhaps being high because at that moment supply is small, or it may be a long-period equilibrium after supply has had time to adjust itself to the condition. A change in either supply or demand will upset the equilibrium price, but immediately forces will be set in motion to restore equilibrium, perhaps at first in the short run, and later in the long run.

(ii) *Equilibrium Distribution of an Individual's Resources.* This occurs when a consumer so distributes his expenditure among a group of commodities that he could gain no additional satisfaction by foregoing a small amount of one in order to be able to buy a little more of another. Equilibrium will be achieved when he assesses the money value of the marginal utility of each commodity he purchases at its prevailing price. A change in the price of one or more of these commodities would temporarily upset this distribution of the individual's resources, but a redistribution of his expenditure would restore equilibrium.

(iii) *Equilibrium of a Firm.* A firm is said to be in equilibrium when the entrepreneur has no motive to change its organisation or its scale of production. In such circumstances he will not wish to change the proportion in which the factors of production are combined or to change output as either will result in a smaller profit, for his average cost per unit of output will be at a minimum. Two conditions must be fulfilled: (i) marginal cost must be equal to marginal revenue; and (ii) the marginal cost curve must cut the marginal revenue curve from below.

(iv) *Equilibrium of an Industry.* An industry is regarded as being in equilibrium when there is no tendency for the size of the industry to change, that is, when no firms wish to leave it and no new firms are being attracted into it, the marginal firm in the industry just making 'normal' profit, neither more nor less. If in conditions of perfect competition every firm in the industry was just making normal profit it could be said to be in perfect equilibrium.

(v) *Equilibrium Wage*. With regard to wages a condition of equilibrium would exist if an industry were able at the prevailing wage to obtain just as much labour as it required, neither more nor less. *See also* Particular and General Equilibrium.

Equi-marginal Principle. If a consumer has a certain amount of money to spend, and by means of it purchases various quantities of (say) five commodities, he will derive maximum satisfaction from his total expenditure if as a result he has just so much of each commodity that its marginal utility to him in money terms is equal to its price. In such circumstances to give up one unit of one commodity in exchange for one unit of another of the five would mean a greater loss of satisfaction from a reduction in his supply of the first commodity than the amount of satisfaction he gains from an additional unit of the second commodity. An Indifference Curve (*q.v.*) shows all the possible combinations of two commodities, usually distinguished as *x* and *y*, which yield an equal satisfaction to the individual whose preferences it represents. When a consumer is considering whether to buy a commodity offered for sale he has to consider the marginal utility of the commodity concerned in relation to the marginal utility of the money he will have to pay for it. If the marginal utility of money to him at that time is greater than the marginal utility of the commodity he will not buy it, but if the marginal utility of the commodity exceeds the marginal utility to him of money, then he will buy just so much of it as to bring the marginal utilities of the commodity and money into equality.

Equi-marginal Returns. *See* Equi-marginal Principle.

Equitable Interest. A legal term. Some property has legal interests (that is, subject to the common law) and some has equitable interests (subject to equity). Since the Act of 1873 common law and equity have both been administered in the same courts, but the two systems still remain, though where they conflict equitable interests always prevail over legal interests. For example, an interest which confers rights in a piece of land to some other person on the death of the present holder is now an equitable interest.

Equitable Life Assurance Co. Ltd. Established in 1762, it is one of eight British insurance companies founded before 1800.

Equitable Mortgage. An agreement that an equitable interest in a specified property shall be transferred to the mortgage as security for a debt. A bank requires written evidence to support its possession of deeds as security for a loan.

Equities. A popular alternative term for Ordinary Shares (*q.v.*).

Equity. 1. A legal term, it refers to that branch of English law which developed separately from the common law, early common law being administered in the King's Court and equity in the Chancellor's. The distinction was abolished by the Judicature Acts of 1873 and 1875, so that common law and the rules of equity are now applied to any case in any court. In a sense equity covered deficiencies in the common law, especially where the common law worked harshly. *See also* Equitable Interest.

2. As applied to taxation, it implies that taxation as a whole should be imposed in as equitable a manner as possible, this being interpreted in various ways as equally of sacrifice, a preference for direct as against indirect taxation, a proportional system of taxation (Adam Smith) or more recently as a progressive system of taxation. The main point is that a system of taxation must be considered as a whole, and individual taxes should not be considered independently.

Ergonomics. The study of the relationship between a worker's capabilities and the work he does, the aim being to suit his work to his capacity. Ergonomics is one of the subjects of study in courses on management (*q.v.*). *See also* Time and Motion Study.

E.R.P. Abbreviation of European Recovery Programme (*q.v.*).

Escheat. When a person dies intestate and no relatives of his can be found, however distant, his estate reverts to the State.

Escudo. The standard unit of the currency of Portugal and Chile, being divided into 100 centavos in Portugal and 100 centesimos in Chile.

E.S.O.M.A.R. Abbreviation of European Society for Opinion and Market Research.

E.S.R.O. Abbreviation of European Space Research Organisation.

Essay on the Principle of Population. The principal work of the Rev. T. R. Malthus, it was first published in 1798. The purpose of his essay was to refute the current belief that conditions of life were gradually moving towards an earthly paradise. At the time of the publication of the first edition it was clear that the population of Great Britain was increasing more rapidly than ever before, such a growth of population being something quite new in the history of any country, and Malthus was led to speculate on its possible consequences. He related the growth of population to the Law of Diminishing Returns and this led him to forecast a decline in the standard of living in Great Britain before the end of the nineteenth century unless the expansion of population was checked. His book aroused great controversy among his contemporaries, and he revised it no fewer than five times. *See* Malthusian Theory of Population; Population Problems.

Essential Work Orders. Used more especially in time of war, though they can be employed in other times of crisis, to ensure that labour is distributed among different occupations to the greater economic benefit of the State in the light of the conditions of the time. *See also* Direction of Labour.

Establishment Charges. In a department store each department in calculating its profit must bear a share of the overhead and general expenses of the business, such as the rent (if any), rates, taxes, heat and light, and the cost of running the non-selling departments. These establishment charges are usually apportioned among the various selling departments in proportion to the turnover of each. In general each selling department is expected to pay its way, unless it is being deliberately run as a 'loss leader' (*q.v.*), in which case its losses will be regarded as an establishment charge.

Estate. A person's interest in land or other property.

Estate Agent. A person engaged mainly in the buying, selling, or letting of property—houses, shops, etc. —his payment usually being a commission based on the price at which the deal takes place. Estate agents also often undertake the collection of rents for landlords.

Estate Duties Investment Trust Ltd. Known as EDITH, it was a subsidiary of the Industrial and Commercial Finance Corporation Ltd., being established in 1953 to assist executors and shareholders in family businesses and sometimes also small companies when the payment of Estate Duty (now Capital Transfer Tax) might otherwise mean selling large blocks of shares and possibly losing control of the business.

Estate Duty. A tax on inherited property. Though in some form Estate Duty had been in existence as Legacy Duty and Succession Duty for over two hundred years it really dates back to 1894. In 1975 gifts made during a person's lifetime were added to Estate Duty and incorporated in the Capital Transfer Tax (*q.v.*).

Estimate. A statement of the price at which a firm agrees to undertake a piece of work. Usually an estimate is no more than an approximation of the actual cost and is subject to variation in certain specified circumstances, thus differing from a tender or quotation which states the exact amount to be paid.

Estimates, Select Committee on. An all-party parliamentary committee which considers the estimates of expenditure for the coming financial year put forward by the various Government departments. As early as October the Treasury requests the departments to prepare estimates which, after long discussion, are introduced to Parliament each February, where they are first considered by the House of Commons sitting as a Committee of Supply. The Select Committee on Estimates often examines selected items in great detail, its aim being to see if public money can be saved. It is, nevertheless, an important element in parliamentary procedure for the control of Government expenditure.

Estoppel. A legal term, it means that a person is precluded from acting in a certain way on account of a previous act of his. For example, in the case of a written contract it is assumed that the parties are fully aware of the conditions set down. A contract cannot be repudiated simply because one of them was not fully aware of what was involved when it was reasonable for the other party to assume that he was, provided, of course, there was no misrepresentation. In such a case a person is said to be 'estopped' from denying his liability.

Ethics. The study of morals and conduct. Like economics and politics it was at one time studied along with these other subjects as part of the discipline of philosophy. The increasing complexity of economics from the eighteenth century onwards made it necessary to separate these subjects into separate studies. In more recent times, however, the increasing study of problems of applied economics, and the greater time devoted by Parliament to economic questions, has tended to bring these various subjects into closer relationship with one another again. The economic theorist, that is, the student of pure as distinct from applied economics, finds it necessary for clarity of thought to separate purely economic considerations from other aspects of problems. As a result of this, he will state in his consideration of demand theory that it is only the demand for the commodity in question and its economic implications that interest him, not being concerned, as a pure economist, with any moral or ethical principles that may be involved. Even if a commodity is harmful in some way to consumers, this aspect of the question is outside the scope of the work of the pure economist, but as an applied economist or politician or even as an ordinary citizen, he must take account of all aspects of a problem where a practical course is involved.

E.T.U. Abbreviation of Electrical Trades Union.

E.U.A. Abbreviation of European Unit of Account which is pegged into the European 'snake'. *See* 'Snake in the Tunnel'.

Euratom. Abbreviation of European Atomic Energy Community (*q.v.*).

Eurobonds. These bonds developed out of the Eurodollar market (*q.v.*) to provide longer term loans than was usual with Eurodollars. They are generally issued by a consortium of banks and issuing houses, usually comprising some of the London merchants banks and the French, German, and Italian commercial banks, though not the British commercial banks. Eurobonds have proved to be particularly useful to American firms wishing to establish branches or subsidiaries in Europe, especially since the U.S. Government tried to restrict foreign investment by American firms. Other attractions of Eurobonds are that they are bearer bonds and paid without deduction of any withholding tax.

Eurocard. A European credit card especially strongly established in Scandinavia. It is linked with the Access card. *See* Credit Card.

Eurocheque (E.C.). A facility whereby cheques drawn on British banks can be cashed at banks in Europe, such banks carrying the sign *E.C.*

Euroclear. One of the systems for clearing Eurobonds, the other being Cedel (*q.v.*).

Euro-Co-op. Established in 1962, it is the co-ordinating body representing the co-operative societies of the E.E.C.

Eurocurrency Market. The name by which the Eurodollar Market is coming to be known since other expatriate currencies in addition to the U.S. dollar came to be used. *See* Eurodollar Market.

Eurodollar Market. Eurodollars are claims to U.S. dollars held by banks, business firms, etc., outside the United States. The market in Eurodollars dates from 1957, by which time U.S. dollars were becoming more plentiful in Europe. The decline in the use of sterling as an international currency was accompanied by an increasing use of the dollar. The persistent adverse balance in recent years in the U.S. balance of payments, largely due to investment abroad and foreign aid, made an increasing volume of dollars available to other countries, and during 1960–67 the Eurodollar market expanded rapidly. Though London is still the main centre for this market other centres in Europe and elsewhere now deal in them. The Eurodollar market has become one of the largest international markets for short-term funds, for in addition to U.S. dollars it also deals in other convertible currencies. In all cases transactions take place outside the country whose currency is being dealt in, and the success of the market owes a great deal to the fact that it is outside the control of any national authority. The main operators in the market are banks, and to obtain a share in its expanding business U.S. banks have opened branches in London and other European centres. The development of the Eurodollar market has also led to the formation of international groups of banks. Deals are usually for very large amounts, mostly used to finance foreign trade, and loans are generally for short periods—three months or less, Eurobonds (*q.v.*) being employed for longer-term loans. Since other expatriate currencies began to be employed in addition to the U.S. dollar the market is coming to be known as the Eurocurrency Market.

Euromarket. An alternative name for the European Economic Community (*q.v.*).

Europa. Name proposed by the European Monetary Union (*q.v.*) for its unit of account.

Europartners. A banking consortium comprising Banco di Roma, Banco Hispano Americano, Commerzbank, Crédit Lyonnais. The group has over 4,000 branches in Europe.

European Advisory Committee. A group of associated banks comprising the Midland Bank of the United Kingdom, the Amsterdam–Rotterdam Bank of the Netherlands, the Banque de la Société Générale de Belgique of Belgium and the Deutsche Bank of Germany.

European Agricultural Guidance and Guarantee Fund. A body established by the European Economic Community to assist farming in member countries, especially in the modernisation of farms and farming methods. It obtains its funds from levies imposed on farm products imported into the E.E.C. *See* Target Prices.

European–American Banking Corporation. A bank consortium formed in 1968 by the Midland Bank, the Amsterdam–Rotterdam Bank, the Deutsche Bank and the Société Générale de Banque.

European Atomic Energy Community. Established under the Treaty of Rome (1957) concurrently with the European Economic Community. Its purpose is to enable the members of the E.E.C. to pool their resources in the development of atomic energy for peaceful purposes. Control of Euratom was transferred in 1967 to the E.E.C.

European Coal and Steel Community. An institution establishing a common market in coal, iron, and steel, established in 1953, largely due to the efforts of M. Schuman, the French Foreign Minister at the time. The members comprised France, West Germany, Belgium, the Netherlands, Italy, and Luxembourg, the original members also of the European Economic Community. One of the difficulties of the location of the coal and iron resources of western Europe was that they were crossed by political boundaries. The High Authority, which in certain matters has power to override the Governments of the member countries of the Community, is located in the city of Luxembourg. Although Great Britain was not a member it was an 'associate', as are several other states. The success of the E.C.S.C. was an important factor in the establishment of the E.E.C. Control of the E.C.S.C. was transferred in 1967 to the E.E.C.

European Common Market. The name by which the European Economic Community (*q.v.*) is generally known in Great Britain.

European Court of Justice. Established by the European Economic Community, its function is to deal with any complaints of unfair trading practices or other matters affecting trade between members of the E.E.C.

European Development Fund. A Fund established by the European Economic Community to provide aid to overseas countries that have been admitted as members of the E.E.C.

European Economic Community (E.E.C.). The theory of International Trade shows that tariffs and other interferences with the free flow of trade reduce the volume of international trade. For their own reasons, however, countries have generally preferred protection. In 1947 the United Nations Organisation set up G.A.T.T. (General Agreement on Tariffs and Trade) for the purpose of persuading members to reduce their tariffs, and it has enjoyed a greater measure of success than previous attempts of a similar character. It has long been realised that on a regional basis free trade can be beneficial. This was shown by the success of the German *Zollverein* which formed an important stage in the political unification of Germany in the nineteenth century. Since 1945 several groups of countries have formed free trade areas, the best known being the European Economic Community. Immediately after the Second World War Belgium, the Netherlands, and Luxembourg formed a customs union under the name of Benelux. Then, in 1952 France, West Germany, and Italy joined Benelux to form the European Coal and Steel Community, one of the great difficulties of the coal, iron, and steel industries of Europe being that the economic boundaries of the areas of the raw material did not coincide with the political boundaries. It was largely because of the success achieved by Benelux and the European Coal and Steel Community that the six countries concerned determined to go a stage further and establish the European Economic Community, with free trade between them within ten years as their main objective. Since in the past many economic associations had led to political union this also was stressed as one of the ultimate objectives of the E.E.C.

By the Treaty of Rome (1957) the European Economic Community came into existence, the treaty containing provisions whereby other countries with similar ideas might be admitted as members. Already considerable reductions of tariffs have taken place between the members, the aim being eventually to have a common tariff, but not necessarily a high one, against the rest of the world. From the start Great Britain was interested in the E.E.C., but this country's special problems with regard to farming products, including especially those from members of the Commonwealth, and perhaps in the early days the political aspect of the association, all hindered this country's efforts to join. The failure of Great Britain's early efforts to join the E.E.C. led to the formation of the European Free Trade Association (*q.v.*). During the first five years of its existence the E.E.C. countries as a whole enjoyed a much greater rate of economic growth than Great Britain, the United States and other non-members. This fact naturally made membership appear all the more attractive. Some less well-developed countries have been admitted as associated members, for example the former French colonies of West Africa.

The United Kingdom resumed negotiations with the E.E.C. in 1970 and by late 1971 agreement had been reached on most issues—the interests of New Zealand, Jamaica and other Commonwealth countries, fishing rights and agricultural policy. In 1972 the United Kingdom, along with Denmark, and the Republic of Ireland, were admitted as members of the E.E.C. In 1976 an application for membership of the E.E.C. by Greece was considered, and Portugal applied in 1977. A further application is expected from Spain.

European Free Trade Association (E.F.T.A.). After Great Britain had found unacceptable the terms offered to it for joining the European Common Market in 1959, a group of seven European countries comprising Great Britain, Denmark, Norway, Sweden, Switzerland, Austria, and Portugal formed in 1960 the European Free Trade Association, a purely economic association without political implications, but otherwise similar in its aim to the European Common Market in that it was proposed gradually to reduce the tariff barriers between them and so produce an area of regional free trade. This was achieved for manufactured goods by 1 January 1967. The members of E.F.T.A. were sometimes referred to as the 'Outer Seven' (though Finland became an associate member in 1961 and Iceland in 1970) in contrast to the more homogeneous location of the 'Six', the members of the E.E.C. In 1972 E.F.T.A. lost two of its members when the United Kingdom and Denmark were admitted to membership of the E.E.C. *See* European Economic Community.

European Investment Bank (E.I.B.). Established in 1958, with headquarters at Brussels, by the European Economic Community to assist economic development within the Community, especially the less developed areas of the Community. Though all six countries have received assistance most so far has gone to southern Italy.

European Monetary Agreement (1958) (E.M.A.). When sterling and other West European currencies became convertible in January 1959, the European Monetary Agreement dealt with the outstanding debits and credits of the former E.P.U. (*q.v.*). Eventually debits were settled in gold.

European Monetary Union (E.M.U.). A proposed unification of the currencies of the E.E.C. It has been suggested that the E.M.U. should start with a unit of account to be known as Europa.

European Payments Union (E.P.U.). A payments scheme introduced in 1950 to encourage multilateral trade between the countries of Europe. In effect it was an attempt to put into practice on a regional basis the scheme worked out in 1944 at Bretton Woods. The United States provided the E.P.U. with an initial reserve of $350 million. Each member of the E.P.U. was assigned a quota based on its share of world trade. There were fifteen member countries, and accounts against one another were presented monthly, indebtedness being offset at the Bank for International Settlements at Basle. An interesting aspect of the operations of the E.P.U. was that all transactions took place in units of account, each of which was equal to one U.S. dollar. When sterling and other West European currencies became convertible in January 1959 the E.P.U. ceased to function.

European Productivity Agency. Established by the O.E.E.C. (Organisation for European Economic Co-operation) to consider means for raising productivity and, thereby, the standard of living in Western Europe.

European Recovery Programme. The official name, usually abbreviated to E.R.P., given to the scheme better known in Europe as Marshall Aid. The failure of Great Britain to maintain the convertibility of sterling in 1947 convinced the United States that the damage done by the war to the economies of Great Britain and other countries of Western Europe was much greater than anyone in that country had realised. As a result the American Secretary of State, G. C. Marshall, set up the Organisation for European Economic Co-operation to work out the needs of each country, as a basis for American assistance to Europe. *See* Marshall Plan.

European Social Fund. A body established by the European Economic Community to assist the movement of redundant workers to other jobs or to other areas in the E.E.C.

Eurosyndicat Index. An index number for European stock exchange securities.

Evaluation. A term used in connection with the assessment of the ability and capacity for promotion of employees. *See* Employee Rating.

Ever-normal Granary. A term for the policy introduced in the U.S.A. by the Agricultural Adjustment Acts of 1933. These Acts attempted to stabilise prices and production by fixing quotas for a number of agricultural commodities, which American farmers had not to exceed. Farmers were often compensated by money payments to persuade them to reduce the output of certain commodities.

Eviction. Being compulsorily turned off land or other property, as, for example, for non-payment of rent.

Ex-ante. The position before some occurrence takes place. The term is used particularly with reference to saving-investment theory, when the saving or investment of one period (the ex-ante saving or investment) is being related to the saving or investment of the period immediately following (the ex-post saving or investment). Ex-ante refers to what was expected before certain events took place, and ex-post to the actual situation which arises. Ex-post saving is always equal to ex-post investment, but ex-post saving is not necessarily equal to ex-ante saving, that is, the amount people expected saving to be. *See* Equality of Saving and Investment.

Ex-capitalisation. A stock exchange term indicating that the price quoted for a share does not include any capital distribution or issue of bonus shares recently made or about to be made.

Ex-cathedra. An official or authoritative statement.

Exception Principle. A principle of management of American origin which states that only exceptions to what the firm regards as 'normal' should be brought to the notice of a departmental manager.

Excess Capacity. The result of a serious falling off in the demand for a commodity. It becomes a particularly serious problem where highly specific heavy capital is employed, and if, as is so often the case, the industry is highly localised, a pocket of high unemployment may arise even though most of the rest of the country is enjoying conditions of full employment. Sometimes when there is an increase in the demand for a commodity, additional capacity may be provided, only to find later that the increase in demand is of a temporary nature. The case or difficulty of contracting an industry to meet a fall in demand depends largely on the cost structure of the industry, that is, on the steepness or otherwise, of the 'cost ladder'. If the cost ladder of the industry is steep, with only a few firms at each level of cost, contraction will be easier, the few high-cost firms dropping out as a result of the fall in price following upon the reduction in demand for the commodity. If, however, there is little difference between the costs of the various firms contraction of the industry will be more difficult, and excess capacity, with most firms earning less than normal profit, may tend to persist.

Excess Capacity in the Retail Trade. There are many varieties of imperfect competition, one type being known as monopolistic competition. In this case, although differentiation between firms exists there is a large number of producers. The retail trade is the best example of monopolistic competition. Where an element of monopoly exists there is a strong tendency for prices to be higher than they would otherwise have been. In monopolistic competition there is an even greater tendency for the condition to result in excess capacity. Differentiation is strong because consumers do not regard all shops in the same branch of trade as being exactly alike. In addition to differences in the quality of the service, there is the fact that almost every shop is more conveniently situated for some people than other shops. Another factor is that retailing is now one of the few remaining types of business which it is possible for the person with only a little capital to enter. The small shop too finds it possible to cope with peak periods by temporarily calling on the services of other members of the family. Further, some people run small shops merely as sidelines to their ordinary occupations, the wife taking over while the husband is at work. Excess capacity in retailing tends to keep up prices, and this has been encouraged in the past by resale price maintenance, which prevented the more efficient retailers selling many commodities at lower prices than their less efficient competitors. The effect of the Restrictive Trade Practices Act (1956) and the abolition in most trades of resale price maintenance (1964) may eventually reduce excess capacity in the retail trade, but any artificial restriction on the number of shops would be more likely to increase the element of monopoly.

Excess Demand. If the price of a commodity is below the equilibrium price, demand will exceed supply. This may be due to Government control of the price. Rationing in some form is then inevitable. *See* Equilibrium (i).

Excess Liquidity. This occurs when banks maintain, voluntarily or otherwise, a greater degree of liquidity than is customarily regarded as necessary according to sound banking principles. After the First World War American banks had excess reserves; after the Second World War the British banks found themselves with their more liquid assets at a higher level than was customary. This made it difficult for the monetary authorities to restrict credit and so other means than the traditional instruments of policy had to be adopted such as the Treasury Directive. *See also* Excess Reserves.

Excess Profits Levy. A tax on profits imposed in Great Britain between 1952 and January 1954. *See* Excess Profits Tax.

Excess Profits Tax. A tax imposed by the British Government during both World Wars. In general, economists do not favour taxes of this type. Not only are they taxes on enterprise, but there is the additional difficulty of deciding on what basis the excess shall be calculated. In time of war, however, the taxation of high profits, perhaps largely resulting from conditions induced by the war itself, appears to be justified. During both World Wars the rate of E.P.T. was 100% at its highest point, the basis on which the excess was calculated generally being the rate of profit earned by a firm before the war. In January 1946 E.P.T. was reduced to 60%, and in December of the same year it was abolished. After

Excess Reserves. both wars a portion of the tax was refunded on condition that the money was used to finance either capital replacement or expansion. An attempt was made in 1952 to reintroduce a tax on excess profits known as an Excess Profits Levy, but it was repealed a year later. Such a tax in peacetime is all to the advantage of the firm which has made large profits in the base year, but clearly to the disadvantage of any firm which was struggling to establish itself at that time.

Excess Reserves. A term applied more particularly to American banking. It occurs when a bank or banking system maintains a higher proportion of cash, as a percentage of its total assets, than is customary or legally necessary. Thus it makes it more difficult for the central bank to impose restrictions on the lending policy of the commercial banks, since open-market operations, though reducing the cash basis of the commercial banks, do not compel them to take action to reduce their deposits. One of the great problems of American banking during the years 1930–33 was that of excess reserves. The eventual solution to the problem was to give the Federal Reserve System power to vary the cash ratios of the commercial banks to meet the needs of the situation, depending on whether a policy of credit restriction or expansion was called for. After the Second World War the British banks for a time faced a somewhat similar problem of excess liquidity (*q.v.*).

Excess Shares. A shareholder in a public limited company may be offered a 'rights' issue, a certain number of new shares being provisionally allotted to him. These additional shares he may accept or decline as he wishes. Sometimes, in addition to the shares provisionally allotted to him he may be given the opportunity to apply for excess shares which other shareholders have declined to take up.

Excess Supply. According to Say's Law, generally accepted by the early English economists, supply creates its own demand, and therefore excess supply, except temporarily for very brief periods, is impossible. Both Mills and Ricardo accepted this theory, and the opposition of Malthus made little impression. According to the theory effective demand is never deficient and so there could never be overproduction or excess supply. It was not until the onset of the Great Depression that this doctrine was effectively challenged by Keynes.

Exchange. Although traditionally the subject matter of economics was divided into three main sections—production, exchange, and distribution—nevertheless the basis of the greater part of economic study is exchange. Specialisation is the characteristic of all forms of economic activity today, and the corollary of specialisation is exchange, and this gives rise to most of the problems of production and distribution as well as the monetary problems of economics.

Exchange Broker. An agent who operates on the foreign exchange market on behalf of others on a commission basis.

Exchange Clearing. The system of exchange control—a severely restrictionist type—introduced by Germany after 1931 was in danger of bringing to a standstill all trade between that country and others. One feature of the German system of control was the blocking of payments due to foreign merchants in accounts in Germany, which could not be drawn on outside that country. To protect themselves from further losses other countries insisted that all payments due to Germany should be made through their own central banks. As a result a series of bilateral Clearing Agreements were made between Germany and a number of other countries, including Sweden, Switzerland, and Great Britain, though in the case of Great Britain there were some important differences of detail and the scheme was known as a Payments Agreement (*q.v.*). Under these Clearing Agreements payments were made only through the central banks of the countries concerned. Whatever form they took all Clearing Agreements had the disadvantage of replacing multi-lateral trade by bilateral trade, with a consequent reduction in the volume of international trade.

Exchange Control. When the gold standard broke down in the early 1930s there was a general unwillingness to return to freely fluctuating exchange rates. Both these systems had their drawbacks: the gold standard's rigidity, with the possibility of a country having to deflate at a time when it was suffering from severe unemployment, together with the uneven world distribution of monetary gold; and the danger, experienced to an extreme degree by many countries, of a runaway inflation, due to an unwillingness to take unpopular monetary measures, when exchange rates are free to fluctuate. In the case of Germany, to leave the gold standard in 1931 for freely fluctuating exchange rates only a few years after a runaway inflation, would almost certainly have brought on a second runaway inflation. Some means, therefore, had to be devised for controlling exchange rates. Broadly, there are two main types of exchange control, though these can to some extent be combined.

Exchange restriction occurs when the inhabitants of a country are permitted to obtain foreign currency only after application to the central bank and if the central bank, carrying out Government policy, approves of the purpose for which the foreign currency is required. Germany was the first country to adopt this system of exchange control, under which an official rate of exchange is maintained. After 1931 the acquisition of foreign currency by German nationals for private purposes was almost certain to be refused, and even importers were allowed foreign currency only for the payment for goods which the German Government thought necessary to the country's economy, and after 1933 this meant goods likely to further re-armament. Foreigners to whom German traders owed money had to accept credits in blocked accounts in German banks, an action which caused a severe shrinkage in trade with Germany. (*See* Exchange Clearing.) To obtain foreign currency Germany offered a more favourable rate of exchange to foreign tourists, and this led to the adoption of multiple exchange rates, that is, different rates for different purposes, according to its importance in the eyes of the German Government.

Exchange intervention was an alternative system of exchange control, although in the form operated by Great Britain before 1939, it hardly deserved to be called control. All that happened was that the monetary authorities of a country—in the case of Great Britain the Treasury's Exchange Equalisation Account (*q.v.*)—intervened in the foreign exchange market in order to influence the rate of exchange by buying or selling their own or foreign currencies. On the outbreak of war in 1939 Great Britain adopted a restrictionist type of exchange control, and this was continued with decreasing severity until January 1959, when most West European currencies became convertible for most purposes except investment abroad. Between 1945 and 1959 and again in 1966–69 however, British residents were allowed only limited amounts of foreign currency for their own private purposes, additional amounts for business purposes being obtainable only if their applications were sanctioned by the Bank of England. Since January 1959 there has been non-resident convertibility of sterling, and since then exchange control regulations have been at a minimum (except during 1966–70). In the foreign exchange market, however, the Bank of England until 1972 continued to intervene, to keep the value of sterling in U.S. dollars within the agreed limits of its variability.

Exchange Economy. An economic system where specialisation has been introduced, so that an exchange of products is necessary. For the smooth working of such a system money must be employed.

Exchange Equalisation Account. Established in 1932 by the Treasury for the purpose of carrying out the British system of exchange control. This system was of the interventionist type, that is, the Account intervened on the foreign exchange market to buy foreign currency for sterling or to sell sterling for other currencies. When Great Britain left the gold standard in 1931 the pound was for a time left to find its own level, that is, this country went over to freely fluctuating exchange rates, the rate depending on the supply of and the demand for sterling in the foreign exchange market, and by March 1932 sterling had fallen to about 30% below its value on the gold standard. It was at this point that the Exchange Equalisation Account was set up, at first, at least, with the intention of stabilising the exchange rate. Thus, the monetary authorities tended to act in a manner opposite to the general tendency in the market by buying sterling when others were selling it, and selling sterling when others wished to buy it. To buy sterling required resources in other currencies or gold; to sell sterling merely required the issue to the Account of Treasury bills. The moment of intervention was, however, well chosen, for by March 1932 the demand to sell sterling, heavy at the time of leaving the gold standard, had almost dried up, and instead there was beginning to develop a demand to buy sterling at its new lower price. Consequently, for some considerable time after the Exchange Equalisation Account began its operations it was building up a supply of foreign currency in exchange for the sterling it was selling. Any temporary demands later on the part of other countries to sell sterling, therefore, could easily be met.

The establishment and operation of the Exchange Equalisation Account was a new departure in British monetary history (apart from the brief period of the First World War), the Bank of England previously being responsible for any action that had to be taken in connection with foreign exchange, whereas the Exchange Equalisation Account was a department of the Treasury and the Bank of England only its agent. An important aim of the Exchange Equalisation Account was to try to offset the effect of short-term capital movements which had a disturbing effect on the foreign exchange market and on trade. The great difficulty, however, was to distinguish purely speculative movements of capital. Where it was felt that changes in the exchange rate for sterling might be due to the ordinary influence of foreign trade transactions it was at first the intention of the authorities to permit the rate to fluctuate, but in time they came to aim at stabilisation of the rate, since a stable rate of exchange is of great advantage to foreign trade. At first the British Exchange Equalisation Account operated in U.S. dollars, the dollar being a gold standard currency, but when the United States temporarily left gold in 1933 the British Account switched to French francs, another gold standard currency, but when France left the gold standard in 1936, the British Account immediately exchanged any supplies of foreign currency it obtained for gold. As a result the Account acquired a stock of gold, and so became a joint holder with the Bank of England of the country's stock of gold. In 1939 almost the entire stock of gold held by the Bank of England was transferred to the Account, and since that date the country's stock of gold has been held by the Treasury in its Exchange Equalisation Account.

In 1936 both France and the United States established similar exchange equalisation accounts, and in that year these three countries made the Tripartite Agreement, whereby they agreed to buy for gold any of their own currency held by either of the other two countries. Other countries joined the scheme and a sort of modified, more flexible regional gold standard came to be operated. The British Account continues to intervene on the foreign exchange market to maintain the parity of sterling with the U.S. dollar within the agreed range of variability.

Exchange Equation. *See* Equation of Exchange.

Exchange, Foreign. *See* Foreign Exchange.

Exchange Intervention. Intervention by the monetary authorities of a country in the foreign exchange market to buy or sell their own or foreign currencies. *See* Exchange Control.

Exchange Management. Any form of interference by the monetary authorities of a country to prevent the free working of a foreign exchange system like the gold standard, the carrying out of the 'rules' of which is essential to its successful operation, or of a system like freely fluctuating exchange rates, where without outside interference the rates of exchange depend on the market forces of supply and demand, which in their turn are determined by a country's exports and imports. On the gold standard there was after 1919 often a strong desire not to carry out either the rule to deflate when gold is flowing into the country or to inflate when gold is flowing out. To avoid having to inflate, the higher prices of home-produced goods being bad for the country's export trade, the United States 'sterilised' gold, that is, prevented its influencing the monetary system and causing an expansion of credit. In this sense the gold standard after 1919 was a managed standard. Exchange management can also take any of the forms of exchange control (*q.v.*), such as exchange intervention and exchange restriction.

Exchange of Shares. One of the methods by which two companies can combine, an exchange of shares taking place in order to give shareholders, especially those with a controlling interest or a particularly large block of shares, holdings in each company.

Exchange, Produce. *See* Produce Exchange.

Exchange Rate. The rate at which one currency can be exchanged for another. When two countries are on the gold standard the exchange rate will vary only between very narrow limits. On a system of Freely Fluctuating Exchange Rates the rate varies from day to day. Under a system of exchange control of the restrictionist type, there may be an official fixed rate of exchange and different rates of exchange between the same two currencies according to the purpose for which the foreign currency is required, that is, there may be multiple exchange rates. Special rates of exchange have been frequently offered to foreign tourists since Germany first adopted this idea in the middle 1930s.

Exchange Restriction. A system of exchange control whereby the Government of the country concerned restricts the amounts of foreign currency its people are allowed to purchase, or restricts the purposes for which foreign currency can be obtained. *See* Exchange Control.

Exchange Stabilisation Fund. The American equivalent of the British Exchange Equalisation Account (*q.v.*).

Exchange Telegraph Company. One of the services provided by this company for investors is to supply, through stockbrokers, up-to-date statistical information regarding companies whose shares are dealt in on the stock exchange.

Exchequer. The name derives from the fact that in Norman times the accounts were calculated on a chequered cloth. *See* Exchequer, Chancellor of the; Treasury.

Exchequer Bill. A security issued by the British Government as a means of borrowing. Exchequer bills, first issued in 1696, were current for five years, and the interest could be varied each six months, but none has been issued since 1897. For short-term borrowing the Government now issues Treasury bills, and for longer term funded stocks including Exchequer Stock (*q.v.*).

Exchequer, Chancellor of the. Cabinet Minister at the head of the Treasury department. Formerly he was responsible only for securing sufficient revenue to cover Government expenditure, but now he bears the political responsibility for economic policy and for the framing of a budget to suit it. The monetary authorities of Great Britain nowadays comprise the Chancellor of the Exchequer, with advice from the experts at the Treasury, and the Bank of England. The Governor of the Bank and the Chancellor of the Exchequer meet regularly to discuss monetary and other economic matters.

Exchequer Equalisation Grant. These were Government grants to Local Authorities under the Local Government Act (1948). Grants were weighted according to the number of children in the area under the age of 15 years, and in county areas there was an allowance where the population density is low. The aim was to assist authorities which otherwise would have had expenditure per head of their population in excess of the average for the country as a whole. Since 1959 Rate Deficiency Grants (*q.v.*) have taken the place of Exchequer Equalisation Grants.

Exchequer Returns. The inflow and outflow of Government revenue and expenditure for a period as compared with the Budget estimate and the similar period of the previous year.

Exchequer Stock. The name given to some Government stocks as, for example, $13\frac{1}{4}\%$ Exchequer Stock 1996.

Excise Duties. Taxes on home produced goods to raise revenue, as distinct from customs duties which are taxes on imports not primarily imposed to raise revenue. Excise duties may be imposed either to raise revenue or to check the consumption of the commodities on which they are imposed.

Excise Licences. Imposed for certain services, they include television licences, motor vehicle licences, motor vehicle driving licences, licences to keep dogs or to possess guns, game licences, etc.

Excise Tax. *See* Excise Duties.

Exclusive Contract. A particularly undesirable method of attempting to achieve some degree of monopoly power. Such contracts bind the retailer not to sell similar products made by other manufacturers. Formerly a common American practice, it has been declared illegal under the anti-trust laws.

Ex-distribution. Similar to ex-dividend but with reference to unit trusts. *See* Ex-div.

Ex-dividend (Ex-div.). With reference to quotations on the stock exchange it means that the price quoted does not entitle the purchaser to the next dividend which is due for payment usually within the ensuing five weeks.

Executive. A person whose employment includes some degree of responsibility for ensuring that a certain branch or aspect of a firm's work is carried out. At a high level there are executive directors with functional responsibilities, but nowadays the term is often employed of persons whose work involves only a relatively small amount of responsibility.

Executives. The Act of 1947 which nationalised inland transport established a number of Executives to which the Transport Commission delegated its powers for the operation of each of its main activities. Thus, Executives were established for the railways, waterways, road haulage, hotels, and London Transport. An Act of 1953, abolished the

Executor. continued — Executives and brought the whole of nationalised transport directly under the control of the Transport Commission. An Act of 1963 transferred the assets and functions of the Transport Commission to a number of Boards.

Executor. A person or institution appointed to ensure that the provisions of a will are carried out according to the testator's wishes. When drawing up a will it is usual to name one or more persons as executors. Most banks are prepared to perform this function.

Exempted Dealers. Dealers so described under the Prevention of Fraud (Investments) Act were permitted to buy and sell securities on their own behalf, and include banks, insurance companies, and independent pension funds.

Exempt Private Company. A private company which was not obliged to include in its annual return to the Registrar of Companies a copy of its balance sheet. It was abolished by the Companies Act (1967).

Ex-factory. As a price quotation it is the amount payable at the factory, that is, excluding the cost of delivery from the factory to the buyer's premises.

Exhibition. An organised display of goods to promote trade, sometimes of one industry as in the case of the British Motor Show or the Toy Fair, or for industry in general as in the case of the British Industries Fair. Wholesalers often arrange small exhibitions for the benefit of retailers. Occasionally national or international exhibitions on a very large scale are held, though not very frequently, the countries taking part making an extensive show of their main products. The first was the Great Exhibition of 1851, followed in 1855 by the Paris Exposition. Other exhibitions of this type were those held at Wembley in 1924–25, Brussels in 1961, New York 1964, and Montreal 1967.

Eximbank. Abbreviation of Export–Import Bank (*q.v.*).

'Exit Interview.' A term used of an interview by the personnel officer of a firm with an employee who is about to leave in order to try to discover the reasons for his dissatisfaction.

Exogenous Change. A non-economic change affecting economic conditions, such as an exceptionally severe winter as in Great Britain in 1946–47 and 1962–63, or a rise in population due to a fall in the death rate as a result of the spread of medical knowledge. Exogenous change is in contrast to endogenous change which is economic in origin.

Exor(s). Abbreviation of executor(s) (*q.v.*).

Expansionist Policy. A policy designed to encourage an increase in the volume of production or national income by the appropriate instruments of monetary policy and other adjuncts to monetary policy—a lower bank rate to provide cheaper money to encourage borrowing from the banks, a relaxation of hire purchase regulations, a reduction in taxation, and a release of Special Deposits by the Bank of England. Such a policy would be adopted if the economic situation was such as to need a stimulus to restore full employment. *See* Monetary Policy.

Expansion of a Firm. This can take place either by natural growth (ploughing back profits into the business) or by amalgamation with other firms, or by a combination of these two methods. *See* Large-scale Production.

Expectational Cycle. The psychological influence on the trade cycle—the fluctuations in expectations regarding future business conditions, the alternation of the optimistic with the pessimistic outlook, which appears to some to be a feature of the behaviour of business men. *See* Trade Cycle, Causes of.

Expectation of Life. The actuarial calculation of the number of years a particular group of people may expect to live from a given moment in time. Tables for men and women and people in particular occupations are compiled and regularly revised, and form the basis of life assurance premiums. The outstanding feature of Expectation of Life is the extent to which it has been increased for both men and women during the past hundred years. For example, at the present time the expectation of life for a man aged 20 is 50·6 years and for a woman of that age 55·9 years; for a man aged 65 it is 12 years and for a woman of the same age it is 15·3 years.

Expectations. One of the psychological influences considered by Lord Keynes in his Employment Theory. An important influence on the amount of investment in capital goods at any time is the expectations of business men with regard to the future trend of business activity. Optimism regarding the future leads to a high level of investment, but pessimism regarding the future leads to caution in renewing existing capital and expanding productive capacity with the result that a smaller amount of investment is undertaken. The level of investment is the key influence on the level of employment. Keynes related expectations to the prospective yield of capital, the amount of investment in a period depending on whether entrepreneurs expected the yield from capital investment to exceed the prevailing rate of interest.

Expenditure Curves (or **Lines**). Lines drawn on a diagram to represent the different assortments of two commodities that can be bought with the same amount of money. For example, if x and y are two commodities, the line AB represents all the possible combinations of x and y for a given outlay. See Indifference Curves.

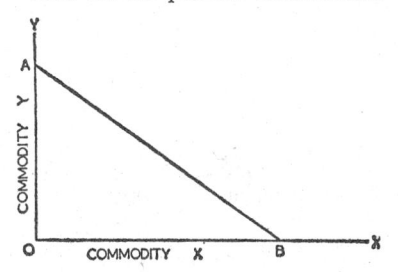

Expenditure, Government. See Expenditure of the State.

Expenditure of the State. At the present day the expenditure of the British Government is mainly devoted to: (i) Interest on and management of the National Debt; (ii) Defence; (iii) Social and welfare services and the maintenance of law and administration of justice; (iv) Agricultural subsidies; (v) Grants to local authorities; (vi) General administration. These items fall under the heading of Government Ordinary Expenditure. In addition there is expenditure on loans to New Towns, nationalised industries, etc. See Budget.

Expenditure, Public. See Expenditure of the State; Budget.

Expenditure Taxes. These comprise such taxes as Value-added Tax (V.A.T.), purchase taxes, general sales taxes, and all taxes on outlay as distinct from taxes on income. See Indirect Taxes.

Expense Account. See Expenses.

Expenses. For income tax purposes an individual is allowed to deduct from his taxable income any expenses necessarily incurred in carrying out his employment. This generally excludes travelling expenses to and from work but the representative of a firm who has to travel to visit customers or clients of the firm will be entitled to claim travelling expenses. A clergyman will be able to claim for the upkeep of his study, an author for the salary he pays to his secretary (if he employs one) and so on. In all cases the Inland Revenue authorities have to be satisfied that the expenses are incurred in the actual carrying out of the person's employment. Large firms often pay a sum additional to salary, known as an expense account, to some of their senior employees to cover their expenses, and members of parliament are allowed to charge an additional sum for their expenses.

Expenses of Production. See Cost.

Exploitation. In its pejorative sense, exploitation results from circumstances brought about by the violation of some economic principle, such as artificial restriction of output by a monopolist, who does it for his own advantage which is contrary to that of consumers. In another sense, the term has been used with a bad—but often quite unjustified—implication, to mean the opening up to greater economic advantage of a land not previously fully economically developed.

Expo. Abbreviation of exposition, *i.e.* exhibition.

Export Agent. An agent who acts abroad, where he maintains offices, for manufacturers who do not have export departments of their own.

Export Bounty. *See* Bounty.

Export Commission Houses. Firms which act as agents for manufacturers whose businesses are not large enough to warrant their having export departments of their own. Unlike the export merchant they do not own the goods in which they deal, but as agents are paid commission for their services. They receive orders from abroad and place them with the manufacturers concerned in the case of closed indents, or with whatever manufacturer they please if they receive open indents.

Export Credits Guarantee Department. A department of the Department of Trade, it offers British exporters, in return for a fee, insurance against bad debts incurred as a result of sales to foreign buyers. For this purpose the Department of Trade has opened a number of offices in London and other cities in the U.K. It is one of the methods by which the Department of Trade attempts to encourage exports.

Exporter. A merchant who either purchases goods produced in his home country for sale abroad, or who acts as an agent for home producers, arranging for the despatch of their produce to an importer in a foreign country for sale there for the best price the importer can obtain. In the latter case the exporter will be paid a commission for his services.

Export-Import Bank. An American institution established at Washington, D.C., by the Government of the United States, its purpose being to encourage by means of loans trade between the United States and other countries.

Export Incentives. Concessions to exporters in order to enable them to compete more effectively in foreign markets. One method is for a Government to pay bounties (*q.v.*) to exporters. Another method, adopted by Germany in the late nineteenth century, was to offer reduced freight rates on State-owned railways from inland manufacturing areas to the ports. In 1965 British exporters were offered rebates of taxes on oil, motor vehicles and raw materials to the extent that these taxes affected their costs of production.

Export Industries, Fluctuations in. One of the difficulties of maintaining full employment in a country like Great Britain which requires a high level of exports is that the widest fluctuations in demand are experienced in those industries producing mainly for export, these fluctuations more often depending on domestic problems in countries of the export market, and so generally outside the control of the Government of the exporting country.

Export, Institute of. A professional body established in 1935, its principal aim being to promote 'the development of British export trade by assisting British exporters to improve their knowledge and to develop their experience of the practice of exporting'. To be admitted to membership it is necessary to be engaged in some branch of the export trade and generally to have passed the Institute's qualifying examination. There are two grades of members—corporate members (M.I. Ex.) and associate members (A.M.I. Ex.). The institute publishes a journal.

Export Intelligence. A department of the Department of Trade which offers advice and information to British exporters.

Export Licence. Sometimes goods can be exported only under licence, the issue of which is the responsibility of the Department of Trade.

Export Merchant. A term nowadays applied to a merchant who is usually responsible only for the marketing of the goods, but formerly used of a merchant who was also responsible both for the packing, shipping and transport of the goods and the financial aspects of the transaction. The export merchant differs from the export agent in that he actually buys and for a time owns the goods in which he deals.

Export Packer. A firm which specialises in the packing of goods for export in a manner suitable to the type of goods concerned, their destination, and the mode of transport to be employed.

Export Quotas. The amount of a commodity a country is permitted to export under an international agreement. For example, the U.N. International Coffee Agreement of 1962 restricted the export of coffee by coffee-producing countries and allotted export quotas to Brazil, Colombia, and other producers.

Export Rebates. A scheme introduced in 1964 to repay to exporters some amounts of specified indirect taxes entering into costs of production such as purchase tax, petrol tax, motor vehicle licences, as a means of stimulating exports.

Exports, Invisible. *See* Balance of Payments; 'Invisibles'.

Export Surplus. A rather ambiguous term, it may be taken to mean an overall surplus in the balance of payments, the doctrine of the mercantile system, or a surplus of visible exports over visible imports. On account of the damage done by two World Wars to Great Britain's income from invisible items, it has been necessary since 1945 to reduce the deficit on visible items by expanding the export of goods, and because the country's reserves of gold and convertible currencies have been inadequate to modern requirements, the aim has been to secure an export surplus in order to build up investment abroad and so later increase invisible income to the benefit of the balance of payments. Immature economic systems tend to have export surpluses of goods in order to pay the interest on foreign loans raised to assist the development of their economies. In a mature economic system one would generally expect to find a deficit in visible items and a credit balance in invisibles, though the United States has often had credit balances on current account in both visibles and invisibles, its difficulties in its balance of payments being due to capital movements, including assistance to under-developed nations.

Exports, Visible. *See* Balance of Payments; Visible Items.

Export Trade. Selling the products of a country abroad. Exports are of two main kinds, goods and services, the former being known as visible items and the second as invisibles. Over a period of time the total value of exports should balance with the total value of imports. An excess of exports over imports, the basis of the mercantilist system, is impossible for the world as a whole. A country like Great Britain, which would find it impossible with its large population to be self-sufficient, must import both some foodstuffs and raw materials for its manufacturing industries. One complication of the export trade is that each country has its own independent currency system; and another is that countries often impose customs duties or other restrictions on imports.

The first consideration of an exporter is his method of quoting prices. The price quoted for a commodity by a merchant in (say) Great Britain to a merchant in some other country may include their basic ex-warehouse price, together with the cost only of carrying the goods to the port of embarkation, or also include the dock dues and other charges for loading the ship, the freight charge for transporting the goods from the home port to the foreign port, insurance of the goods while in transit, and finally the transport charge for carrying the goods from the foreign port to the buyer's premises. (*See* c. & f., c.i.f., f.o.b., franco.)

To obtain orders from abroad past customers may be circularised, travellers or commission agents may be employed, a firm with a large amount of export business may employ an export agent or an export commission house or open offices of its own abroad. International trade exhibitions are sometimes held to attract foreign orders. The order from abroad may come in the form of an indent from a foreign importer, a closed indent specifying the name of the firm from whom the goods have to be obtained, an open indent allowing the exporter to whom it has been sent to choose his own supplier. The indent will state how the goods have to be packed and the special markings to be employed on the packing cases, and if there is more than one these will be numbered. A number of documents will have to be drawn up, the principal ones being the Shipping Advice Note, Bills of Lading, a certified invoice where required, a freight note, a certificate of insurance, a certificate of origin and a customs specification. For the financing of foreign trade *see* Financing of Foreign Trade.

Exposition. *See* Exhibition.

Ex-Post. The position after some occurrence has taken place. The term is used especially in connection with the period analysis of the saving-investment theory of Lord Keynes. For example, the amount of saving achieved ex-post may differ from the amount of saving planned ex-ante. *See* Equality of Saving and Investment.

Express Letter. There are a number of means provided by the Post Office for speeding up the delivery of letters and other postal packets. The simplest is the express letter which is dealt with immediately at the office of posting, being despatched by the next ordinary mail, and again given priority of sorting at the post office of its destination and then generally being delivered by special messenger. A postal packet can also on request be conveyed all the way by special messenger, or by special messenger to the nearest railway station to be despatched by the first train and then delivered by special messenger from the destination station. Additional charges are payable for these services.

Ex-quay. Goods sold on this condition must be taken charge of by the purchaser after they have been landed from the ship.

Ex-rights. A stock exchange term, indicating that the price quoted for a share excludes any 'rights' issue that has just been or is about to be made. *See* 'Rights' Issue.

Ex-ship. A price quoted for goods at the port of arrival and excluding costs of unloading and delivery to the purchaser's premises.

Extel. Abbreviation of Exchange and Telegraph Co. Ltd.

Extended Credit. Permission granted, through his own bank, by the Bank of England to a British exporter who wishes to offer a foreign customer a period of credit in excess of six months.

Extended Unemployment Benefit. During the Great Depression, especially the years 1929–35, some of the unemployed were entitled to receive standard unemployment pay for which they were qualified under the National Insurance Scheme, but many others had been unemployed for so long a period that they had 'exhausted' their rights under the scheme; however their right to receive unemployment pay was extended, subject to a 'means test' (*q.v.*).

Extensive Cultivation. This occurs where small amounts of labour and capital are employed on a large area of land, usually where land is cheap and population small, as in the early days of the development of the United States and many other new countries. Under this type of cultivation the average output of the crop per acre will be small. In densely populated countries with advanced economies, such as Great Britain, Belgium, and Holland, cultivation tends to be intensive, with a high output per acre.

External Convertibility. A currency with non-resident convertibility, freely convertible between foreign holders but with limited convertibility for the people of the issuing country.

External Debt. Debt owing by one country to another. Of the British National Debt of £52,000 million in 1975 only £7,137 million was external, the remainder being owed to people or institutions in Great Britain. External debt is more serious than internal because the payments of interest and repayment of the capital sum form debit items in the balance of payments.

External Deficit. An alternative term for a deficit in a country's balance of payments (*q.v.*).

External Diseconomies. Economies of scale lead to the expansion of a firm, but eventually diseconomies occur causing a rise in average cost and so limiting the firm's expansion. If more workers are required as the firm expands it may have to employ less efficient workers.

External Economies. Economies of large-scale production which can be enjoyed only by an industry as a whole through its localisation and not by a single firm as is the case with internal economies. *See* Localisation of Industry.

External Surplus. An alternative term for a credit balance in a country's balance of payments (*q.v.*).

Extra Cost. An alternative term for marginal cost (*q.v.*).

Extractive Industry. Often known as primary production. Extractive or primary industries are those concerned with all types of farming, agricultural, pastoral, and lumbering, all kinds of mining and quarrying, and fishing. Primary production includes the oldest occupations and provides Man with food and with the raw materials required for manufacturing industry.

Extra-Marginal. When an individual has achieved an equilibrium distribution of his resources, an extra unit of any one of the commodities he has bought would yield too little satisfaction to make it worth buying. Such a unit is said to be extra-marginal.

Extra-mural Courses. Most British universities have extra-mural departments which organise classes, usually in the evening, for adults who wish to improve their education.

Ex-warehouse. A quotation of the price of a commodity excluding all delivery charges; the price, in fact, to be paid if the purchaser collected the goods himself from the warehouse where they are stored at the time.

F

F.a.a. Abbreviation of Free of All Average. *See* Average.

Fabian Society. An association established in London in 1884. It takes its name from Quintus Fabius Maximus, the Roman consul who earned the nickname of Cunctator (Delayer) in Rome's struggle against Hannibal. The policy of the members of the Fabian Society is to promote socialism by gradual and democratic means (its symbol is a tortoise), the early members of the society including G. B. Shaw, the Webbs, and H. G. Wells.

Face Value. An alternative term for the nominal value of stocks and shares. A stock may have a face value of £100 and yet be quoted on the stock exchange at only £74. The term 'face value' is also used in connection with coins, the face value of which is generally greater than the value of the metal in the coins.

Factor. 1. An alternative name for a wholesaler in some trades as, for example, boots and shoes.

2. A firm which takes over trade credit from others, acting as a sort of debt collector. *See* Factoring Company.

Factor Cost. (i) In the modern usage of the term this is the price of a commodity paid by the consumer, less any tax or duty included in its price. Thus, an article priced at £44 including £4 payment for V.A.T. has a factor cost of £40, that being the amount paid to the factors of production that have taken part in its manufacture and distribution, the remaining £4 being an indirect tax payment to the State. The National Income, reckoned as the value of the total volume of production, is calculated at factor cost, since otherwise its total real value for one year could not be compared with the previous year, as a change in indirect taxation would falsely affect the amount of the total.

(ii) Lord Keynes, however, used the term, factor cost, to mean the cost of factors of production to a piece of manufacturing, less the cost of the raw materials, which he termed user cost. Since, however, all costs of production are ultimately payments to factors of production, the present use of the term is to be preferred.

Factories and Workshops Act (1893). This Act related to dangerous trades, the Home Secretary being given power to issue special regulations from time to time for trades scheduled as dangerous. *See* Factory Acts.

Factoring Company. A firm which will take over the collection of trade debts on behalf of others, thereby enabling them to obtain insurance against bad debts. The procedure is for the factoring company to buy up its clients' invoices and then itself claim payment of them. A firm employing a factoring company will thus have more capital at its disposal, an important consideration in a time of credit restriction. Factoring has been expanded in Great Britain since 1960 and has extended to foreign trade transactions. Among the leading firms engaged in this kind of business are International Factors (a joint enterprise of the First National Bank of Boston and Hill Samuel & Co.), Heller and Hambros, Shield (Rothschilds). In each one of these a merchant bank is concerned. *See* Financial Intermediaries.

Factor Markets. The markets for factors of production. At any given period there is a certain demand for factors of production and a certain supply available. Thus, we have the two market forces of supply and demand, and in conditions of perfect competition these two factors would determine the prices of the various factors. Even in actual conditions where competition is imperfect the influence of supply and demand cannot be neglected. It is possible to conceive of a single factor market for each factor, though in fact there are really separate factor markets for each specific type of a factor as also for the non-specific type of that factor. Otherwise, there would be single prices for labour, land, and capital, irrespective of type. Clearly, the separate markets, for example for the factor, labour, are related to one another, an increase in demand for labour in one labour market leading to an increase in the supply of labour in that market if the price of labour in that market has risen, though the more specific the labour the more difficult it will be for other labour to enter it. It is possible too to think in terms of a single wide market for all factors, since the general level of economic activity will have some influence on the demand for all factors in relation to their supply. Thus, in a trade depression the prices of all factors will tend to be depressed, just as in a period of over-full employment and inflation there will be a tendency for all their prices to be high. The fact that there are separate, though connected, markets for different kinds of labour is the main reason for differences of wages in different occupations.

Factors Act (1889). An Act which defines a bill of title as any document used in the ordinary course of business which gives the possessor of it the ownership of the goods to which it refers, such as a bill of lading, dock or warehouse warrant, etc.

Factors of Production. The resources required for production. The early economists recognised only three factors of production (alternatively called agents of production or inputs)—land, labour, and capital. Land comprises all the natural resources, labour was human effort, and capital consists of such things as industrial plant, machinery, tools, etc. For even the most primitive forms of production all three factors were required. Towards the end of the nineteenth century a fourth factor was added—the entrepreneur. Marshall thought that organisation was sometimes sufficiently important to be regarded as a factor of production, and though most economists now recognise the entrepreneur as a separate factor, there are some who consider it to be merely a special kind of labour, and some of these would speak of two factors—the human factor (labour and the entrepreneur) and the non-human factor (land and capital). In the interests of clear thinking there is much to be said for a more precise separation of the factors, since there are important differences between land and capital as also between labour and the entrepreneur. Those who argue against the entrepreneur being considered a separate factor from labour assert that a certain amount of organising is required of all labour, the only difference between labour and the entrepreneur being the extent of the organisation undertaken. Those who support the idea of a separate entrepreneurial factor point out that the main difference between labour and the entrepreneur is not merely that the entrepreneur spends most of his time in organising whereas most labour spends only a tiny fraction of its time in this way, but that the whole character of the organisation is different: labour organises its own work, but the entrepreneur organises the work of others, and is also responsible for making vital decisions of policy regarding the method of production to be employed and the amount of a commodity to be produced. Another important point is that to the entrepreneur the other factors of production are simply productive resources at his disposal, and to a certain extent a degree of substitution between them is possible, whereas none of these other three factors can be substituted at all for the entrepreneur.

An alternative method of classifying the resources of production—land, labour, and capital—is to consider them as specific or non-specific. The great advantage of this method is that it emphasises the similarity of these three resources, and distinguishes them from the entrepreneur. Specific factors are of a specialised nature and can generally be used only for a particular kind of employment, whereas the non-specific factors are more easily transferred from one occupation to another. In favour of this classification it can be said that it is often easier to substitute one kind of labour for one kind of capital than it is to substitute one kind of labour for another kind of labour or one kind of capital for another kind of capital, the entrepreneur deciding whether such substitution should take place.

Factory. 1. A place where manufacture is carried on.

2. A trading post.

Factory Acts. A series of Acts passed to improve working conditions in factories. The evils of the early factories were inherited from the domestic system. Also there was the transfer of pauper children to the early factories as 'poor-law apprentices'. There was some improvement in factory conditions in 1802, in 1819, and again in 1831, but the first Act of importance to the new factory workers was the Act of 1833. This prohibited the employment of children under the age of nine; forbade night work, except in the lace industry, to those under eighteen; and limited the working day to 12 hours and the working week to 69 hours to all under the age of eighteen. The Act of 1849 reduced the working day to 9 hours and the working week to 48 hours for children under the age of thirteen except those working in silk mills, but the most outstanding feature of this Act was the appointment for the first time of State Inspectors to ensure that the Factory Acts were carried out. Two earlier Acts affected women, the Act of 1842 prohibiting women and children from working underground in mines, and the Act of 1844 prohibiting the employment of women on night work. The working day for women was limited to 12 hours. The effect of these Acts, none of which specifically applied to men, was automatically to improve conditions for them also, since most factories were unable to function unless all workers were employed at the same time. In 1847 came the 'Ten Hours Bill'. After 1850 there came a succession of Factory Acts applying to particular industries, though even as late as 1870 there were many occupations where the workers were still unprotected. Then in 1878 came a Consolidating Act, and in 1891 the Factory and Workshops Act which gave the Home Secretary power to issue special regulations for trades scheduled as dangerous.

In 1937 all existing factory legislation was repealed and new regulations framed, general principles being laid down to be followed in all kinds of factories and workshops, covering such matters as health (the amount of space per worker, ventilation, cleanliness, temperature inside the building, lighting), the safety of the workers (fencing of machinery), and the welfare of the employees (the provision of drinking and washing facilities). In 1946 the administration of the Factory Acts was transferred from the Home Office to the Ministry of Labour, factory inspectors being employed to ensure that all factories and workshops maintain the required standards. The administration of the Factory Acts has since been passed to the Department of Employment. An Act of 1959 made minor amendments to the Act of 1937. The most recent in a long line of Factory Acts was the Health and Safety at Work, etc., Act (1974) (*q.v.*), perhaps the most sweeping in its reforms of any Factory Act since 1833. It makes any

Factory Cost. This comprises Prime Costs (q.v.) and Oncost (q.v.).

Factory Inspectorate Division. The section of the Department of Employment concerned with the inspection of factories to ensure that the provisions of the Factory Acts (q.v.) are carried out. For this purpose the department employs factory inspectors of various grades under the Chief Inspector of Factories who visit and inspect factories to ensure that the Factory Acts are carried out.

Factory System. Working in factories succeeded the domestic system where the workers did their work at home, either themselves visiting a merchant to obtain their raw materials or being visited by merchants who supplied them with raw materials and took from them the commodities they had made. The use of larger machines and the introduction of power—at first water power, later steam—made it necessary to put up large buildings to house the machinery and provide the power. To do this required capital and in many cases the earliest manufacturers were men who had previously been merchants and possessed the necessary capital. The factory system led to greater specialisation of production, the growth of towns, and an expansion of distribution of the products, and so required also the development of improved means of communication. The factory system developed more quickly in some industries than others, the cotton industry being among the first to become a factory industry. The woollen industry changed over to the factory system at a much later date, possibly because it was a much older industry than cotton and was already well entrenched as a domestic industry when the changes of the industrial revolution began to take place, whereas cotton was a new industry. In both the woollen and cotton industries spinning became a factory industry before weaving. Many hand loom weavers were still at work in 1840. One of the last modern industries to change over to the factory system was the boot and shoe industry which remained a domestic industry until the end of the nineteenth century and in some cases even later. Though there were many disadvantages to the workers in the early days of the factory system—long hours of work often in unhealthy conditions—some of the workers had had to put up with even worse conditions when they worked at home, which was often little more than a small factory in which it was necessary for them both to live and sleep. Gradually as a result of the Factory Acts conditions in the factories improved. The factory made large-scale production possible and eventually led to a rise in the standard of living of the factory workers, many of whom had been exceptionally poor under the domestic system. Though the overseers in the early factories were often hard taskmasters the independent home worker was—often indeed had to be—a hard taskmaster both to himself and to his family since he had to do a considerable amount of work and put in long hours in order often to eke out a bare subsistence.

Faculty of Actuaries. Scottish association of actuaries, similar to the English Institute of Actuaries of London.

Faculty of Advocates. A body which in Scotland conducts examinations for those who wish to qualify for admission to the Scottish Bar.

Faculty Theory of Taxation. An alternative term for the 'Ability-to-pay' theory of taxation (q.v.), according to which everyone should be taxed according to his ability to pay. It is not easy, however, to measure with accuracy and fairness the ability to pay of people even in superficially similar circumstances.

Fællesbank. A bank which acts as central banker to the Danish savings banks in addition to its own ordinary banking business. The Fellesbank performs a similar function in Norway.

Fair. A market, usually large, held at longer intervals than ordinary markets. In England in the Middle Ages when travelling was difficult and for many people impossible, fairs were held annually in the more important towns, and they were often combined with local holidays. In those days fairs were the only means by which goods from distant places could reach consumers. Some fairs specialised but generally a wide variety of goods was sold, people having to wait until the next fair was held to buy many things. The Industrial Revolution led to the development of larger towns and the factory system made it necessary for more people to have to rely on shops for things which previously they had made for themselves. The range of commodities also increased and for both these reasons there came a great expansion of retailing, and with it a decline of fairs, which survived mainly as amusements for holidays. The term, fair (or trade fair), is still used of large national or international exhibitions, which may be held annually or at much longer intervals. One of the best known of modern fairs is that of Leipzig which has a continuous history of over 800 years. Other important modern fairs are held at Milan, Frankfurt-am-Main, Brussels, Paris, Utrecht. In Great Britain there is the British Industries Fair. *See also* Exhibitions.

Fair Competition. *See* Fair Trade Practices.

Fair Prices. There is a popular idea that the price of a commodity should be fair, but to whom? to consumers or producers? It is very difficult to define the meaning of fair in this connection. If a service is deliberately run at a loss, it is clearly to the advantage of everyone making use of the service, but those who do not use it are having to subsidise those who do. The free working of the price mechanism, with sufficient restrictions on it as are in the interest of the whole community, has even so its disadvantages, but these are outweighed by the advantages where the State watches the interests of the community as a whole. It has been suggested that if the State intervenes in the market it should be to make a price as near as possible to the long-run normal price in a perfect market. In wartime price control sets a maximum to try to make prices fair to consumers; guaranteed prices aim at making some prices fair to farmers, though in this case, consumers may have to pay more, either directly or through higher taxation. *See also* Just Price.

Fair Trade Practices. In some countries, as for example the United States, codes have been laid down to define what are considered to be the fair trade practices for particular industries.

Fair Trading Act (1973). An Act to give greater protection to consumers, it established a Consumer Protection Advisory Committee appointed by the Government. It also set up the Office of Fair Trading with a Director-General of Fair Trading at its head. This office took over the functions of the Registrar of Restrictive Trading Agreements. It is independent of the Government. *See* Consumer Protection.

Fair Wear and Tear. A term used to cover the normal depreciation over a period of some form of property, repairs necessitated as a result of this not being covered by insurance.

Fallacy. Much of economic theory has been evolved by logical deduction, but one of the dangers of this method is that the argument may contain a flaw and so give rise to a fallacy. The economist, therefore, must always be on his guard against this type of error. One of the commonest fallacies is the 'Non sequitur' —because one event follows another it does not mean the second is the result of the first. Another common error is to assume that what is true of a part of an aggregate is true also of the whole, but what is good for the individual is not necessarily good for the community as a whole, as for example saving during a period of trade depression. Though the demand for the product of an individual producer may be elastic the demand for the commodity as a whole may be inelastic. *See also* Economic Paradoxes.

Fall-back Pay. Also known as Attendance Money, it is the payment to dock workers under the Dock Labour Scheme, introduced in 1947, the dock worker being entitled to 'fall-back pay' if he failed to obtain work.

Fallow Field. The practice of periodically leaving a field uncultivated in order to give it a rest period and so restore its fertility. In medieval England, when the three-field system was operated, it was usual to leave each field fallow in turn once every three years. The improvements in farming methods of the eighteenth century made it possible to abandon the practice and 'rest' a field from grain production and yet at the same time use it for growing root crops.

Family Allowances. Payments made to reduce somewhat the burden of bringing up a family since wages rarely take account of the size of the worker's family. For a long time this has been a recognised practice in the Armed Forces. The term is more particularly applied in Great Britain to the Family Allowances granted under the Act of 1946 in respect of every child except the first, there being no test of income, though the allowances are regarded as income for income tax purposes. The allowances are paid to the mother at post offices. Family Allowances are administered by the Department of Health and Social Security. They are not on a large enough scale in Great Britain to have much effect on family size. In France, where family allowances were introduced in 1939, they double the average wages of a skilled worker with a family of three children, and in that country their purpose was definitely to check a decline in population. In April 1977 family allowances and income tax allowances on children were replaced by Child Benefit. *See also* Family Income Supplement.

Family Budget. The way in which a family distributes its expenditure on such things as food, clothing, rent and rates, drink and tobacco, household goods, entertainment, etc. Surveys of family budgets of people within a defined range of incomes form the basis for the weighting of the Index of Retail Prices.

Family Income Supplement (F.I.S.). A payment made since 1972 to make up the income of a family, depending on the number of children, to an amount regarded as a basic minimum where the family income falls below this sum. The scheme is administered by the Department of Health and Social Security. *See* Negative Income Tax.

Family Reform Act (1969). An Act which reduced the age of a legal 'infant' from 21 to 18 years as recommended by the Latey Committee (1967).

Family Size, Average. In estimating future changes in the population of a country, the average family size is an important factor. This and the Net Reproduction Rate (*q.v.*) are probably of much greater importance than the birth-rate, which is calculated per thousand of the population. For a long period down to 1880 there was little change in the birth-rate, which was high, but in earlier times the death-rate was so high that only a small proportion of the children born survived. After 1880, although the death-rate continued to fall, the average family size began to decline, and in many countries, including Great Britain, reached its lowest (apart from war periods) in the early and mid-1920s. Since 1945 there has been a tendency for the average family size to increase in all countries, including the more economically advanced countries such as the United States and the countries of Western Europe. It is interesting to note that there is some relationship between the occupation of the father and the average family size, the families of miners and agricultural labourers being considerably larger than the families of professional workers.

Famine. When means of communication and modes of transport were poor districts were more isolated from one another and the failure of one or more crops often caused a famine. With improvements in communication famine has become rarer, though it can still occur to peoples who suffer crop failures and who are too poor to buy food from elsewhere. The Food and Agricultural Organisation (F.A.O.) of the United Nations has made great efforts to improve output in the poorer countries, and nowadays the more advanced countries of the world would come to the assistance of any country suffering from famine. Even so the danger of famine still remains in India and some other parts of the world.

F.A.O. Abbreviation of Food and Agricultural Organisation (q.v.), a department of the United Nations Organisation.

F.a.q. Abbreviation of Fair Average Quality, a term used on commodity markets when goods are bought and sold without being previously inspected.

Farm Co-operatives. Co-operative marketing of farm produce had its origin in Denmark. In the United States there are farm co-operatives for the sale of the products of a large number of small producers. The Agricultural Marketing Boards for potatoes, milk, hops, established under the Agriculture Act of 1931, provide examples of a sort of co-operative marketing.

Farmers' Clubs. These clubs have two aims: (i) to provide a means by which men in similar occupations can exchange ideas; (ii) to provide social intercourse for people who often work in somewhat isolated conditions.

Farming of Taxes. A method of tax collection whereby in return for a fixed sum paid to the State the tax-gatherer has the privilege of collecting taxes from the people and retaining what he collects.

Farm Prices. Under the Agriculture Act (1947) (q.v.) farmers are guaranteed minimum prices for their products.

Farm Price Supports. A term used in the United States for the arrangement whereby farmers producing certain commodities are guaranteed prices, the Government purchasing at this price any surplus left unsold in the ordinary markets. The effect of the policy has been to reduce the demand for some commodities which consumers considered to be too highly priced and also to encourage farmers to expand production. Disposing of the farm surpluses resulting from this policy provides the Federal Government of the United States with a difficult problem.

Farm Subsidies. More correctly known as Agricultural Support Subsidies, these are grants made to British farmers for the purchase of fertilisers, lime, for ploughing up grassland, for field drainage, for the rearing of hill sheep and cattle, for a great variety of improvements to farms and farm land. These items together account for about a third of the total subsidy, the remainder being in the form of price supports for cereals, fatstock (cattle, sheep, pigs), wool and potatoes. The aim is to increase both the total output of these commodities and their quality, as proposed in the Agriculture Act (1947) (q.v.).

Farm Surpluses. A problem of the Federal Government of the United States resulting from its policy of Farm Price Supports (q.v.).

Farriers. One of the 82 Guilds or Livery Companies of the City of London whose existence dates back to the medieval gilds.

Farrow's Bank, Ltd. Established as a private bank by Thomas Farrow in 1904, it became a joint-stock bank three years later. It had deposits of about £4 million when payment was suspended in December 1920, the bank being wound up in 1921. This is the only recent example of the failure of a commercial bank in England.

Farthing. From Old English *feorda* meaning a fourth. Originally it was a silver coin weighing one quarter of the weight of the silver penny, first introduced by Edward I in 1279. In earlier times it had been the custom to cut pennies into halves and quarters for smaller payments. During 1542–69 half-farthings were intermittently in circulation and were revived for a short period during the reign of Queen Victoria. The declining value of money gradually led to farthings falling into disuse, though there was a revival during the Second World War when price control and the rationing of some commodities in very small quantities required the payment of a farthing. No farthings have been issued since 1956 and they ceased to be legal tender in 1960.

F.a.s. Abbreviation of Free Alongside Ship (*q.v.*).

Fascism. A form of political system in which every economic consideration is subjected to one criterion—not whether it is likely to increase the people's standard of living, as may be the case under either capitalism or communism, but whether it adds to the military strength and prestige of the country. Fascism was superficially capitalist, since it arose to check the spread of communism, but although private ownership of capital was permitted, it was controlled by extensive Government regulations. Politically and economically its main feature is extreme nationalism, and so self-sufficiency was the goal. In Italy, where a fascist state was established by Mussolini in 1921, and given a corporative character, each main industry was under the control of a corporation which was responsible for production in that industry. Strikes and lock-outs were both declared illegal. A degree of efficiency in the economic sphere was achieved in Italy under fascism not previously found in that country. The German Nazi regime was similar in some ways, though perhaps more militarist in its aims. In both countries the first emphasis was on the production of armaments, and the result of this was a lower standard of living for the people at large, exemplified in the much-quoted summing-up of Nazi economic policy as a choice between 'guns and butter', the State having chosen the former.

Fashion. An important influence on charges of demand. From the point of view of producers it presents them with a greater difficulty in anticipating the demand for certain products for, although some changes in fashion can be expected at certain times, as for example with women's clothing, other changes are quite unpredictable and quite arbitrary, and might better be described as passing or temporary fads. Taste, on the other hand, is likely to change only slowly, and so changes of taste present fewer difficulties to producers than do changes of fashion.

'Fate.' A banking term used with regard to the honouring of cheques. To be informed of the 'fate' of a cheque means to be informed of the state of the drawer's account, that is whether there are sufficient funds to meet it.

Fatigue Allowance. In working out the time standard for a job (as for some bonus systems of wage payment) an allowance is made for some loss of speed and efficiency in the later hours of the day.

Favourable. A term used in connection with the Balance of Payments and the Balance of Trade to indicate an excess of receipts from abroad over payments to other countries. *See* Balance of Payments.

F.B.A. Designatory initials of a Fellow of the British Association (*q.v.*).

F.C.A. Designatory initials of a Fellow of the Institute of Chartered

Accountants. *See* Chartered Accountant.

F.C.C.A. Designatory initials of a Fellow of the Association of Certified Accountants. *See* Certified Accountant.

F.C.C.S. Designatory initials of a Fellow of the Corporation of Secretaries (*q.v.*).

F.C.I. Abbreviation of Finance Corporation for Industry (*q.v.*).

F.C.I.A. Abbreviation of Foreign Credit Insurance Association, a U.S. body comprising more than seventy insurance companies, which provides insurance for American exporters against all commercial risks, political risks being covered by the U.S. Import–Export Bank (*q.v.*).

F.C.I.I. Designatory initials of a Fellow of the Chartered Insurance Institute.

F.C.I.S. Designatory initials of a Fellow of the Institute of Chartered Secretaries and Administrators (*q.v.*).

F.C.M.A. Designatory initials of a Fellow of the Institute of Cost and Management Accountants.

Fco. Abbreviation of Franco (*q.v.*).

F.E.B.A. (London). Abbreviation of Foreign Exchange Brokers Association of London (*q.v.*).

Federal Advisory Council. A body representing the twelve Federal Reserve Districts which offers advice to the Board of the Federal Reserve System (*q.v.*).

Federal Deposit Insurance Corporation. A public institution established in 1933 by the Government of the United States to undertake the insurance, at first up to a maximum of $5,000 but later raised to $10,000, of bank deposits of commercial banks, the insurance of such deposits being made compulsory for all American commercial banks which are members of the Federal Reserve System, but optional for other banks in the country. The Act was passed at the most serious banking crises in history when over 7,000 banks had been compelled to close their doors to check a run on them. The aim of the Act, therefore, was to prevent a run on a bank, especially by smaller investors, in time of crises and rumours of crisis.

Federal Reserve Bank. Central banking in the United States is in the hands of the Federal Reserve System, but because of the size and varied conditions of the country, for central banking purposes the United States has been divided into twelve Federal Reserve Districts, each with its own Federal Reserve Bank, the districts varying enormously in size on account of the wide differences in the economic importance of the various states. The monetary policy of the twelve Federal Reserve Banks is co-ordinated through the Federal Reserve system, with its various Advisory Boards, and so, although bank rate may not always be exactly the same in every district at the same time, nevertheless, the decentralisation of central banking in the United States is more apparent than real. Until 1935 Federal Reserve Banks each issued their own bank-notes. The member banks of the Federal Reserve System maintain reserves with the Federal Reserve Bank of their district. *See* Federal Reserve System.

Federal Reserve City. One of the twelve cities in which the Federal Reserve Banks of the United States are situated—New York, Philadelphia, San Francisco, Chicago, Boston, St. Louis, Cleveland, Minneapolis, Kansas City, Richmond, Dallas, and Atlanta.

Federal Reserve Open Market Committee. One of the two main committees which advise the Board of Governors of the Federal Reserve System of the United States.

Federal Reserve System. The central banking system of the United States. Although attempts were made in 1811 and 1836 to establish a national bank in the United States, that country had no central bank until the passing of the Federal Reserve Act of 1913. On account of the vast area of the country, and the greater difficulties of travelling at the time when the Federal Reserve System was established, the country was divided into twelve Federal Reserve Districts, each with its own Federal Reserve Bank, their activities being co-ordinated through the Federal Reserve Board in Washington. With the increasing importance of economic and monetary policy the Federal Reserve System has become more and more centralised. At its head is the Board of Governors, which is advised by the Federal Advisory Council and the Federal Open Market Committee, the latter directing the open market operations of the System. The Board then advises the Federal Reserve Banks, and exercises general supervision over them. The Federal Reserve Banks in their turn hold the reserves of the member banks (that is, the commercial banks which are members of the Federal Reserve System), supply them with currency if necessary and act to them as lenders by re-discounting bills. The Board determines the reserve requirement of the commercial banks, which since 1936 has been variable in the United States. The Board too really determines discount rates (corresponding to the English Bank rate), though the Federal Reserve Banks do not always have the same discount rate. The Federal Reserve System, in collaboration with the Government, determines monetary policy and, aided by the Federal Reserve Banks, carries it out.

Federation of British Industries. A voluntary association of manufacturers and other producers. It was founded in 1916 and received a royal charter in 1924. Its aim is to assist the development of British industry both at home and abroad. At its headquarters its experts collect information on all subjects relevant to the interests of British manufacturers. In 1965 it merged with the British Employers' Confederation and the National Union of Manufacturers to form the Confederation of British Industry (*q.v.*).

Federation of Wholesale Organisations. An Association representing the larger wholesalers of Great Britain, it watches all matters which might affect their interests.

Fee Simple. A freehold estate.

Fen. A fractional unit of the currency of China, 100 fen being equal to one renminbi or yuan.

Ferries. *See* Car Ferries; Train Ferry.

Fertility of Land. This, according to Ricardo, was the cause of differences in the economic rent of different plots of land. *See* Rent.

Fertility Rate. One of the most useful aids to population projection, it is the number of births per thousand women of child-bearing age (that is between the ages of 15 and 45). It is much more useful for assessing possible population trends than the crude birth-rate. Age-specific fertility rates also are sometimes calculated showing the number of births per thousand women of selected ages.

F.F.I. Abbreviation of Finance for Industry (*q.v.*).

F.H.A. Abbreviation of Finance Houses Association (*q.v.*).

F.I.A. Designatory initials of a Fellow of the Institute of Actuaries. *See* Actuary.

F.I.A.C. Designatory initials of a Fellow of the Institute of Company Accountants.

Fiat Money. Anything intended to serve as a medium of exchange, that is, money, because it has been declared by the State to be legal tender. Even so, it will not serve as money unless it is generally acceptable.

F.I.B. Designatory initials of a Fellow of the Institute of Bankers. *See* Institute of Bankers.

Fidelity Guarantee. A branch of insurance, whereby an employer can insure himself against loss resulting from the dishonesty of employees who have to handle large sums.

Fiduciary Issue. An issue of bank-notes not backed by gold, but by Government securities. At the time of the passing of the Bank Charter Act of 1844 the Bank of England had a fiduciary issue of £14 million and at that time there were many other note-issuing banks. Under this Act the Bank of England was permitted to increase its fiduciary issue by two-thirds of the amount of the lapsed issue of any other bank, no new bank being allowed to issue notes, and any bank amalgamating with another or operating a London branch office also having to cease issuing notes. During the latter half of the nineteenth century there were many bank amalgamations, and as a result of the lapsed issues the Bank of England's fiduciary issue had increased to £19 million by 1913. By 1921 the Bank of England was the only bank in England with the right to issue bank-notes, but during the First World War the Treasury itself had begun to issue notes in denominations of £1 and 10s. (£0·50) to replace the gold coins that were withdrawn, these notes being entirely fiduciary in character. In 1928 the Bank of England, which for a long time had not issued notes of a lower denomination than £5, took over the Treasury issue, and since then all paper money in England has been issued by the Bank of England. The Scottish and Northern Irish banks retain limited rights of note issue. Between the two World Wars the fiduciary issue varied between £200 million and £275 million, more than half the total issue of Bank of England notes still being backed by gold until 1939, when nearly the whole of the gold of the Bank of England except for a mere £354,000, was transferred to the Treasury's Exchange Equalisation Account. Since 1939, therefore, the note issue in this country has been almost entirely fiduciary. In 1939 it totalled approximately £600 million, but during the Second World War it increased to £1,400 million. Since 1945 it has increased to over £5,850 million. Under the Currency and Bank Notes Act of 1928 changes in the size of the fiduciary issue require the assent of Parliament, but this has now become a mere formality, and temporary increases take place in the fiduciary issue every Christmas and again in the summer when there is an increased demand for cash.

A general increase in the fiduciary issue may be an indication of inflation, since higher prices require the use of more cash, but an increase in the fiduciary issue is not a cause, but a result of inflation, generally a consequence of an increase in the volume of bank deposits. An expanding economy, even if it were possible without some degree of inflation, would probably require an increase in the note issue, although an increase in the general use of cheques for the payment of wages might make a smaller note issue serve the needs of the people, since it might also lead to more payments by cheque.

Field Staff. Those employees whose work takes them away from a firm's premises, as for example, insurance agents, commercial travellers.

Field Test. After the plant for a certain piece of production has been set up and production is ready to start it is given a preliminary run known as a 'Field Test' to test the efficacy of the assembly.

F.I.F.O. Abbreviation of 'first in, first out' (*q.v.*).

Fifty New Pence. Introduced in 1969 this coin replaced the ten shilling note. With the decline in the value of money and their increasing use, ten shilling notes were soon worn out. Not since the withdrawal of the gold half sovereign in 1915 has a coin of this value circulated in the United Kingdom. A distinctive feature of the coin is its heptagonal shape—a new departure in British coinage.

Fil. A fractional unit of the currencies of Iraq, Jordan, Bahrain and Kuwait.

Filler. A unit of the currency of Hungary, 100 fillers being equal in value to one forint.

F.I.M.T.A. Designatory initials of a Fellow of the Institute of Municipal Treasurers and Accountants now known as C.I.P.F.A. (*q.v.*).

Final Products. An alternative name for consumers' goods, the ultimate aim of all production is to produce consumers' goods.

Final Utility. An alternative term for Marginal Utility (*q.v.*), used by Alfred Marshall and Stanley Jevons.

Finance. A business must be supplied with finance at the moment it requires it. Where there is a regular inflow of receipts from sales and a regular outflow of payments for the expenses of operation no serious problem arises, but in many cases a considerable time must elapse between expenditure being incurred and the receipt of income. It is the purpose of financial institutions to assist in the financing of business during this interval. Business firms look to the capital market and the commercial banks to assist them. In the case of the State the revenue comes in mainly in the fourth quarter of the financial year, so recourse has to be had to Treasury bills to finance expenditure during the earlier part of the financial year.

Finance Act. The Act of Parliament which embodies the Chancellor of the Exchequer's budget proposals as accepted by Parliament, although tax changes announced in the Budget take effect almost immediately. The Finance Act relates to budget changes, permission to raise the total revenue being embodied in an Appropriation Act (*q.v.*). At the committee stage many of the proposals are hotly debated, and it often takes Parliament some time to complete this work but it must become law before 1st August.

Finance and Development. Quarterly publication of the I.M.F. and I.B. (*qq.v.*). It contains articles, generally written by officials of these institutions, on international economic and financial problems of current interest.

Finance Bill. 1. A bill of exchange drawn as a means of borrowing and not to finance a trade transaction. Such bills nowadays are most frequently used by Governments, the British Government borrowing regularly by means of Treasury bills.

2. A bill put before Parliament by the Government of the day concerning the raising of finance. The budget statement each year becomes a finance bill when under discussion and debate in the House of Commons, and after being passed becomes the Finance Act (*q.v.*) of the year.

Finance Company. *See* Finance House.

Finance Corporation for Industry Ltd. (F.C.I.). Established in 1945 along with the Industrial and Commercial Finance Corporation Ltd. for the purpose of lending to industry for longer periods than the commercial banks were prepared to do, that is, to provide medium-term capital for industry, as recommended by the Macmillan Committee in 1931. The Finance Corporation for Industry restricted its loans to amounts in excess of £200,000, the Industrial and Commercial Finance Corporation lending amounts between £5,000 and £200,000. In 1973 it merged with the I.C.F.C. to form Finance for Industry (F.F.I.) (*q.v.*).

Finance for Industry (F.F.I.). A holding company formed in 1973 to take over the Finance Corporation for Industry (F.C.I.) (*q.v.*) and the Industrial and Commercial Finance Corporation (I.C.F.C.) (*q.v.*). It continues to operate through these two finance institutions. The capital was provided by the Bank of England and the commercial banks. A new function of the F.F.I. was to provide capital to enable the State to assist private industry.

Finance House. An institution primarily concerned with the financing of hire purchase transactions. Some retailers finance their own hire purchase business, but since this requires them to have a large amount of capital tied up in debts owing to the firm, the bulk of hire purchase finance is now in the hands of institutions, more than 60% of the finance for hire purchase coming from this source. Ten of the larger Finance Houses are now controlled by the English commercial banks. Finance Houses obtain their funds partly by accepting deposits at fairly high rates of interest or by borrowing from the banks. At the time of the Radcliffe Committee's Report (1959) there were seventeen large Finance Houses, of which only seven were independent of the commercial banks. In addition there are eighteen smaller firms in this line of business. In 1972 certain finance houses were allowed to become banks, United Dominions Trust and Mercantile Credit *inter alia* taking advantage of this privilege.

Finance Houses Association. A body which represents the Finance Houses of Great Britain and includes in its membership all the larger institutions including those in which the commercial banks have an interest. The aim of the association is to watch the interests of Finance Houses especially in relation to changes in Government monetary policy which might affect them.

Finance Markets. There are a number of finance markets in Great Britain: (i) the money market; (ii) the discount market; (iii) the capital market; (iv) the securities market or stock exchange; and (v) the foreign exchange market. Each of these is considered under its appropriate heading (*qq.v.*).

Financial Intermediaries. A term that can be taken to include all financial institutions engaged in some form of borrowing and lending. In this wide sense it would include the commercial banks, but it is more usual to restrict the term institutions other than the commercial banks—savings banks, building societies, hire purchase finance companies, insurance companies, pension funds, investment trusts, and factoring companies. The Radcliffe Report (1959) noted the growing importance of these financial intermediaries which by acting as alternative sources of finance to the commercial banks tended to render less effective any restrictions on credit imposed on the banks by the monetary authorities.

Financial Times. A daily newspaper, established in 1888, devoted mainly, though not exclusively, to stock exchange and business matters.

Financial Times **All-Share Index.** An index of stock exchange prices based on 150 shares.

Financial Times **Industrial Ordinary Share Index.** An index of stock exchange prices based on 30 'blue chip' industrial shares. *See also* F.T./Actuaries Index.

Financial Year. The period of twelve months covered for fiscal purposes by the Budget estimates, running in Great Britain from 6th April of one year to 5th April of the next. The financial year of a business firm can run from any date, though many allow it to coincide with the calendar year.

Financier. A term widely applied to persons having to do with finance, such as bankers, company promoters, issuing houses, discount houses, etc. In a more restricted form it may refer to a firm which supplies finance for some particular transaction.

Financing of Foreign Trade. There are four main instruments by which payments in connection with foreign trade can be made: (i) the foreign bill of exchange; (ii) the documentary credit; (iii) the bank draft; (iv) the telegraphic transfer. Each of these is explained under the appropriate heading.

Financing of Industry. Industry obtains its finance from the capital market. The capital of the smallest firm may have to come entirely from the private savings of the sole proprietor himself, or he may be able to add to this by borrowing from relatives or friends. Only after he has established himself will other sources of finance become available to him. A small partnership or small private company may start in the same sort of way, the only difference being that the capital is provided by a greater number of people. In Great Britain many firms obtain some, if not all, their circulating capital by borrowing from the commercial banks, a large proportion of bank advances being devoted to this purpose. A firm may also increase its circulating capital by buying on credit from its suppliers, and wholesalers assist many small retailers in this way. For fixed capital the smallest firms may have to rely again on the savings of their members, but the provision of fixed capital to industry is the main business of the capital market. In Great Britain it is only rarely that the commercial banks help industry in this way, although in France there are several specialist investment banks which exist primarily to provide certain industries with fixed capital, as, for example, the French Agricultural Bank (*q.v.*), the Bank of Building and Public Works, etc. In a serious emergency, like the Great Depression of 1929–35, the Bank of England gave assistance to a number of very large firms, the failure of which might in the circumstances have been catastrophic.

The typical business unit of the present day in Great Britain is the public limited company, and this has made it possible for projects requiring huge amounts of capital to obtain from the capital market the capital they require, by the public issue of shares, mainly ordinary shares, but sometimes supplemented by the issue of preference shares, or direct borrowing by an issue of debentures. The issue of such shares in units of as little as one shilling up to £1 or more, has made it possible for small investors to help to provide capital for large firms, though nowadays it is the big institutional investors (who themselves collect the savings of small investors) that take up most of the shares in public limited companies—insurance companies, investment companies, and unit investment trusts, to which have been added in recent years some private operators of pension funds. The existence of the stock exchange for the transfer of shares has made small investors willing to purchase shares in public limited companies. Many large businesses finance expansion partly or wholly out of undistributed profits, which is in effect financing expansion out of their own savings in similar fashion to the sole proprietor who expands his business in this way.

The Finance Houses obtain finance by borrowing from the commercial banks and by accepting deposits from the general public. Building Societies too accept deposits from the general public to provide themselves with funds to finance the buying, and sometimes building, of houses. Since the banks prefer to lend for relatively short periods and the capital market provides permanent capital, the Macmillan Committee as long ago as 1931 stressed the need for the establishment of some new institutions for the provision of medium-term capital, but it was not until 1945 that this recommendation was carried out when the Industrial and Commercial Finance Corporation Ltd. and the Finance Corporation for Industry Ltd. were established, their capital being provided by the Bank of England, the English and Scottish Commercial banks, insurance companies, and investment trusts. The two corporations have subsequently been merged to form Finance for Industry.

Fineness. A term used of monetary metals to indicate the amount of precious metal contained in coin or bullion. Thus, the British gold sovereign was described as 11/12 fine, that is, it contained eleven parts of pure gold to one part of base metal, gold being too soft a metal to be used alone for coinage purposes, though some of the earliest gold coins issued in England were made of gold as pure as refining at the time would permit.

Fine Rate. An alternative term for prime rate (*q.v.*).

Fine Trade Bill. A term used in connection with the Bank of England's eligibility rule when acting as 'lender of last resort'. The Bank of England will only re-discount or accept as collateral security bills of exchange accepted by a bank (a bank bill) or by a well-known business whose credit-worthiness stands high in the Bank's estimation.

Fire Insurance. Fire was probably the first risk to be insured against, the first company undertaking this type of business being established in 1680 in London. The early insurance companies operated their own fire brigades in order to try to minimise their losses. Some very old companies are still in existence, e.g. the Sun, founded in 1710. See Insurance.

Firm. A business unit formed for the purpose of carrying on some kind of economic activity. It can take many forms, the simplest being that of the sole proprietor. Other types of firm under free enterprise are the partnership, the private limited company, and the public limited company. Public enterprise is mainly in the hands of public corporations or is directly undertaken by the State (as was the Post Office until 1962) or by Local Authorities.

Firm, Expansion of. See Large-scale Production.

First-class Mail. Mail on which a higher rate of postage is paid and which has priority over second-class mail.

First Cost. An alternative term for Prime Costs (q.v.).

First Fruits. A feudal tax on inheritance, whereby the profit of an office during the first year it was held was payable to the king or, in the case of an ecclesiastical office before the breach with Rome, to the Pope. See Annates.

'First in, First out' (F.I.F.O.). An accountancy system where assets are valued at the price at which each was acquired. See also 'Last in, First out.'

First Lord of the Treasury. An office always held by the Prime Minister, and held by him before the office of Prime Minister was officially recognised. See Treasury.

First National City Bank of New York (Citibank). Founded in 1812, it was in 1977 the second largest commercial bank in the United States and the world. Its head office is in New York. It has over one hundred foreign branches including two in London. It has an interest in Hill, Samuel & Co. Ltd., the London merchant bankers and in National and Grindlays Bank Ltd.

First National Finance Co. Ltd. Formerly known as the Birmingham Wagon Co. Ltd., it is a merchant bank and finance company. See also Wagon Finance Corporation.

First of Exchange. When a Bill of Exchange is used as a means of payment in foreign trade three copies are required, these being known respectively as the First, Second, and Third of Exchange.

F.I.S. Abbreviation of Family Income Supplement (q.v.).

Fiscal Drag. An increase in the burden of taxation without any change in tax rates, brought about by inflation.

Fiscal Policy. The use of taxation through the budget as an adjunct to monetary policy. See Budget, Monetary Policy.

Fiscal Year. A term used in the United States for the period covered by the Budget. The American Fiscal Year starts on 1st July and ends on 30th June of the following year. See also Financial Year.

Fisher Act. The Education Act of 1918. See Education Acts.

Fisher Equation. An alternative term for the Equation of Exchange (q.v.), it attempts to illustrate the Quantity Theory of Money, which had excited some degree of interest since the sixteenth century, but which was greatly improved by the American economist Irving Fisher in the twentieth-century by the introduction of two new variables—the velocity of circulation and the output of goods and services.

Fisheries Department. A division of the Ministry of Agriculture, Fisheries and Food.

Fishery Limits. See Territorial Waters.

Fishmongers' Company. One of the more important of the 82 Guilds or Livery Companies of the City of London, whose existence dates back to the days of the medieval gilds.

Five-pound Note. The large Bank of England five-pound notes, printed on white paper, were replaced in 1957 by a note of more convenient size. In 1963 they were still further reduced in size. During 1946–64 the five-pound note was the highest denomination issued by the Bank of England.

Five Towns Surveys. Sample social surveys of the conditions of the working classes, to try to discover the prevalence of poverty, undertaken in 1912–14 and again in 1923–24, the five towns selected for this purpose being Reading, Northampton, Warrington, Bolton, and Stanley. Earlier surveys had been undertaken in a small district of London by Booth in 1888, in Manchester and Salford in 1899, and by Rowntree in York in 1901 and 1936. *See* Poverty.

Five Year Plans. The name applied particularly to the two pre-1945 plans conceived by Russia to develop the country's industries. The first Five Year Plan was formulated in 1928 and aimed at producing heavy capital and developing the under-developed mineral resources of the country. It was, therefore, principally devoted to the manufacture of capital goods, industrial plant, power-stations, factory buildings, etc. The second Five Year Plan of 1933 was also mainly of a capital-producing character, the aim on this occasion being to increase the country's supply of lighter forms of capital. Both plans, therefore, aimed at expanding the country's productive capacity. War broke out before the next stage, which was to be an expansion of the production of consumer's goods, could be undertaken. After 1945 much of the country's resources had to be devoted to rebuilding industrial plant that had been destroyed or damaged during the war, and also to an expansion of the production of armaments. Although a seven-year plan was launched in 1959 there was a return to the idea of the five year plan for 1966–70. Though the term has been mostly employed by the U.S.S.R. plans of similar length have been adopted also by other countries, especially under-developed nations.

Fixed Assets. In the balance sheet of a firm the fixed assets include such items as factory property or other industrial premises, land and any other buildings the firm may own. Ordinarily over the years the value of the fixed assets will have to be written down to allow for depreciation, but in a period of inflation the money value of some fixed assets may actually increase. Their purpose is to assist production or distribution; they are not for re-sale. *Cf.* Floating Asset.

Fixed Capital. The assets of a firm which are of a fairly durable character, such as the premises, fixtures, and fittings in the case of a retailer, or the factory buildings and equipment in the case of a manufacturing firm. Since, however, even durable goods in time wear out or become out-of-date and have to be replaced, an allowance for their depreciation must be made each year.

Fixed Charge. When a farmer borrows from a bank he may offer as security for a loan a 'charge' on his agricultural assets, including livestock. In the case of a fixed charge, the property to serve as security is specified in the agreement with the bank. *See also* Floating Charge.

Fixed Costs. The costs of a firm which do not vary with every change of output. For example once a firm has built a factory and installed the necessary machinery the fixed costs remain the same whether the firm is working at full or less than full capacity. In either case the same amount will have to be paid in rent or rates. Depreciation will be a fixed cost, and so will interest payments on existing loans. The cost of administration will vary little over a wide range of output and so in the short period is regarded as a fixed cost, but if a firm finds its business declining and output remains below full capacity for a long time it will then reduce its administrative costs. Indeed, the distinction between fixed and variable costs (costs that vary directly with output) is largely a period distinction. As pointed out, administrative costs become a variable cost even in what might be termed the medium period; the remainder of the fixed costs—usually known as supplementary costs—become variable in the long period. In some forms of production fixed costs form a high percentage of total cost, as for example, in the running of a railway, whereas in other firms the fixed costs form only a small proportion of total cost, as in the operation of a road haulage firm or omnibus company. This has an important effect on marginal cost, which will drop very steeply as output increases where there are heavy fixed costs, so that, for example, the cost of running an extra train is relatively small, whereas marginal cost falls only very slowly, if at all, where the fixed costs are small or negligible.

Fixed Debentures. A type of mortgage debenture secured by a specified asset.

Fixed Exchange Rates. Where the rate of exchange between two or more currencies does not vary, or at least varies only within narrow limits, as on the gold standard, in contrast to fluctuating exchange rates which vary according to supply and demand in the foreign exchange market.

Fixed Prices. For most consumers' goods the custom of the fixed or rather specified price has replaced the older custom of haggling over price, although haggling still persists in some branches of retail trade, more especially in the sale of antiques and second-hand articles, as also on some of the organised produce exchanges where business is carried on by private treaty.

Fixed Production Coefficient. A term used to describe a condition where two factors of production must always be employed in the same proportion, the Elasticity of Substitution between such factors then being zero.

Fixed Trust. A unit investment trust where the managers are compelled to limit their investments to a fixed list of securities, usually in such cases a relatively small number as compared with the number of investments of a flexible trust. This type of unit investment trust was more common in the early days of such trusts in Great Britain before the Second World War. *See* Unit Trust.

Fixtures and Fittings. One of the fixed assets of a business. In the case of a business these are usually the property of the tenant where premises are rented, but in the case of a householder they are the property of the landlord, and remain so even if the tenant has improved or installed them, although it is customary in such cases for the tenant to come to an agreement with the landlord with regard to the possibility of his sharing the cost.

Fl. Abbreviation of the Dutch florin or guilder (*q.v.*).

F.L.A. Abbreviation of Fellow of the Library Association (*q.v.*).

Flags of Convenience. The registration of shipping under the flags of countries to which they do not really belong in order to avoid heavy taxation. Countries which have offered such 'flags of convenience' include Liberia, Panama, Honduras, and Lebanon. As a result Liberia, with over 17 million gross tonnage, ranks third in the world for merchant shipping.

Flat Rate (or **Yield**). If the present price of 4% stock dated 1985-95 is quoted on the Stock Exchange at 80, then an outlay of £80 will yield interest of £4 per annum, giving a flat rate yield of 5%, which ignores the capital gain of £20 spread over the period to the date of redemption, which would give a gross yield of well over 5%.

Fleck Report (1955). A report on the organisation of the National Coal Board, it provided a survey of the industry. Its main recommendation was that there should be a functional board. Thus, there are now members with specific responsibility for production, marketing, finance, industrial relations, and a scientific member.

Fletchers' Company. One of the 82 Guilds or Livery Companies of the City of London whose existence dates back to the Middle Ages. Like the other livery companies its members are entitled to wear a distinctive dress.

Flexibility of Prices. A feature of perfect competition and the perfect market, changes in the condition of supply or demand affecting the equilibrium price of a commodity. Under modern conditions of imperfect competition in its various forms there is a tendency for prices to become less flexible, advertising wars between competitors often replacing price competition.

Flexible Bond. An alternative term for a Managed Bond (q.v.).

Flexible Exchange Rates. A system of foreign exchange rates where the rate of exchange is permitted to fluctuate within an agreed range, as distinct from free exchange rates where rates are completely free to fluctuate. *See* Adjustable Peg, Crawling Peg, Freely Fluctuating Exchange Rates, Wider Band.

Flexible Trust. A unit investment trust where the managers are empowered by the trust deed to vary, usually within prescribed limits, the securities held by the trust. This enables the managers of the trust to use their investment skill to reduce or sell completely their holdings in companies whose prospects they do not favour and re-invest the proceeds in more promising companies. The unit holders usually informed at each distribution of dividends of the constitution of the trust's investments at that particular time, and they will then be able to see what changes have been made since the previous distribution. *See* Unit Trusts.

Flight from Cash. A tendency to avoid cash transactions and revert to barter, a feature of hyperinflation (q.v.).

Flight from the Pound. Similar to a Flight of Capital (q.v.) where the currency concerned is the pound sterling. In the case of Great Britain it is likely to be more serious than it would be for some other countries, since this country is an important world financial centre and holds much short-term as well as long-term foreign investment. Great Britain also being a great trading nation, a very large number of foreign banks hold sterling balances here to facilitate payments arising out of foreign trade. A flight from the pound, on rumours of an impending financial crisis, would have a serious effect on the country's Balance of Payments. Heavy withdrawals in time of crisis only make the situation worse for the country concerned.

Flight of Capital. When, on account of unsettled economic conditions in a country, especially if the Government is in financial difficulties, or in an extreme case fear of devaluation or serious depreciation of the currency, large numbers of those who have investments in that country will probably wish to transfer them elsewhere. If this occurred on a large scale it would be known as a flight of capital. The effect, of course, is only to increase the difficulties of the country from which the 'flight' takes place.

Floating Asset. Sometimes known as a current asset, it is held for only a short time and easily converted into cash. *Cf.* Fixed Assets.

Floating Capital. An alternative term for working capital (q.v.). *See also* Floating Asset.

Floating Charge. A farmer who wishes to borrow from a bank may offer as security for a loan what is known as a charge on his agricultural assets, including his stock. In the case of a floating charge it may include the whole of the agricultural assets of the farmer, including any stock born after the agreement with the bank, or it may refer only to items specified in the agreement.

Floating Debentures. A type of

mortgage debenture secured by the assets of the firm generally, as distinct from Fixed Debentures which are secured by a particular asset.

Floating Debt. That part of the National Debt which consists of short-term borrowing by the Government. There are 'Ways and Means Advances' from the Bank of England but the British floating debt nowadays consists almost entirely of Treasury bills. Last century it was considered to be a sound principle of public finance that the floating debt was mainly to finance expenditure in advance of income from taxes, since expenditure is more evenly spread throughout the year, whereas income tends to be concentrated in the fourth quarter of the Financial Year. Debt in excess of what was required for this purpose, it was thought, should be funded. The effect of the two World Wars has been to increase the floating debt, which for the period since 1945 has been greatly in excess of the amount required for current expenditure.

Floating Policy. A term used in marine insurance for a policy that provides specified general insurance without actually naming the ships of the shipping company to which it refers. Such a policy might cover any ships of a shipping company used for certain specified voyages as, for example, Liverpool to New York, though before each sailing the name of the ship and the value of its cargo would have to be declared to the insurers or underwriters. The policy expires when total insurance has been effected to the amount originally agreed upon.

Floating Pound. Sterling being allowed to fluctuate freely on the foreign exchange market in response to supply and demand, as in 1919–25, 1931–32 and since 1972. Floating exchange rates, although possessing some advantages, have the serious drawback that they are not good for international trade. *See* Flexible Exchange Rates; Exchange Rates and Freely Fluctuating Exchange Rates.

Floating Rate. An alternative term, used particularly since 1970, for a Flexible or Freely Fluctuating Rate of Exchange. *See* Freely Fluctuating Exchange Rates.

Floor. *See* Stock Exchange.

Florin. This coin was so called because it was the same weight as the Florentine florin, for a time being known as a Florence. It was first issued in England in 1343 by Edward III, made of gold and worth £0·30. There were half and quarter florins of proportionate value. When the florin was revived in 1849 it was as an experimental step towards decimalisation and it was given a value of one-tenth of £1 which it retained until 1971. For a brief period (1887–90) double florins also were minted. On the decimalisation of the currency in 1971 the florin was replaced by a coin of the same size and of equal value with the denomination of Ten New Pence. The Dutch guilder is also alternatively known as a florin, its value now being greater than that of its British namesake.

Flotsam and Jetsam. Goods lost at sea as a result of a ship foundering or on account of being jettisoned and washed ashore, flotsam being goods that float on the surface of the water. If unclaimed within a year all such goods revert to the Crown. *See* Jettison.

Flow Production. An alternative term for mass production. It occurs where there is a large output of a commodity which passes or 'flows' through a series of machines one after the other, each being responsible only for a very small process, division of labour being carried to a high degree.

Flows. With reference to the inflow and outflow of gold, *see* Foreign Exchange; Gold Standard.

Fluctuations, Cyclical. The ups and downs of business activity, employment and prices. *See* Trade Cycle; Full Employment.

Fluidity of Labour. An alternative term for Mobility of Labour. *See* Mobility.

F.o.b. Abbreviation of Free on Board (*q.v.*).

F.O.C. Abbreviation of Free of Charge.

'Follow the Leader' Price Policy. *See* Price Leadership.

Food and Agricultural Organisation (F.A.O.). A department of the United Nations Organisation, with headquarters in Rome, which devotes its activities to problems of food production throughout the world to meet the needs of an expanding population and to deal with the problem of the large number of underfed peoples. Research is conducted in attempts to improve the output of food in different climatic and geological conditions, and efforts are made to educate economically backward peoples in the use of more up-to-date methods of production.

Food Investigation Organisation. One of the research stations of the Department of Scientific and Industrial Research (*q.v.*).

Food, Ministry of. A Government department established in both World Wars primarily to administer the rationing of foodstuffs, but in the Second World War also to undertake bulk buying from abroad, the highly organised produce exchanges in Great Britain being mostly closed down as normal trading was impossible. In 1955 it was merged with the Ministry of Agriculture and Fisheries as the Ministry of Agriculture, Fisheries, and Food (*q.v.*).

Food Rationing. Operated by the Ministry of Food and introduced in Great Britain during both World Wars, in the First War mainly for basic foodstuffs, but in the Second War for a much wider range of foodstuffs, including many that it had been thought previously impossible to ration. For things like butter, sugar, etc., the system operated by allotting coupons to each individual, one for each week, entitling him to a certain quantity of a commodity, payment of course also being required. For many things this system was unsuitable, as with many tinned goods of which there were insufficient supplies to allow one tin per person. To overcome this difficulty a 'points' system was introduced, whereby a certain number of points (which could be varied to suit changes in supply) had to be given for such things. This system allowed a certain element of choice and in addition things in plentiful supply could be marked at a small number of points, some people preferring to obtain a larger quantity of such things than a small quantity of something for which a large number of points had to be surrendered. *See also* Rationing.

Foodstuffs, Distribution of. In the case of some foodstuffs sale is direct from the producers to the consumers, as with dairy farmers whose farms lie on the outskirts of towns. Some farmers still take butter to local markets. In the case of some agricultural commodities like potatoes where production is in the hands of a very large number of small producers it is customary for merchants to buy in bulk from them (often taking the whole crop) and arrange for their sale at large wholesale markets, from which they often pass through the hands of a more local wholesaler before reaching the retailer. In the case of perishable foodstuffs like fresh fruit and fish special arrangements have to be made for their speedy despatch to the wholesale markets. Where food has to be processed and packed in cartons, tins, or jars its distribution is similar to that of manufactured goods, either through wholesalers or often in the case of branded products direct from the processor to the retailer. Foodstuffs from abroad are received by import merchants who arrange for their sale at highly organised markets, the buyers usually being large wholesalers or distributors. Tea, sugar, coffee and many other imported foodstuffs are dealt with in this way.

Food, Taxes on. Such taxes tend to be regressive in that they fall more heavily on large than on small families. *See* Taxation.

Football Pools. Although there is a tax on the whole pool, individual winnings, however large, are not subject to tax.

F.o.r. Abbreviation of Free on Rail (*q.v.*).

'Forced Frugality.' A term used by Bentham for what is now known as Forced Saving (*q.v.*).

Forced Loan. A loan compulsorily levied by the ruler of a State on certain classes of the community, especially at one time on the Jews, no interest usually being paid on such loans. In England the best known forced loans were those levied by the Tudor and Stuart monarchs, to which there was very strong opposition, especially in the time of Charles I. It was often difficult, if not impossible, to secure repayment of forced loans. During the Second World War a portion of the very high rate of Income Tax levied at that time was regarded as a post-war credit, that is, as a compulsory loan to be repaid after the war. These were really forced loans and no interest was paid on those outstanding until 1961, after which date $2\frac{1}{2}\%$ was paid. *See* Post-war Credits.

Forced Saving. If the term, saving, is defined as reduced expenditure on consumers' goods in order to make possible the production of capital goods, then any action which reduces consumers' expenditure can be regarded as saving. Thus, forced saving occurs in a period of rising prices—during a mild inflation—if unaccompanied by a corresponding rise in personal incomes.

Forecasting. Since a great deal of production takes place in anticipation of demand, forecasting the future level of business activity, sales and production, etc., is an essential function of business management. *See* Anticipation; Expectations; Market Research.

Foreclose. If property has been mortgaged as security for a loan which the borrower finds himself unable to repay, the lender may foreclose on the mortgage, that is, sell the security and indemnify himself out of the proceeds to the extent of the amount owing to him, but the right to foreclose requires the sanction of the appropriate court.

Foreign Banks. Many foreign and Commonwealth banks have branches in Great Britain. In the financing of foreign trade, especially where documentary credits, bank drafts, or telegraphic transfers are employed, it is essential to have branches or agents abroad. A foreign branch is to be preferred where the amount of business justifies it. Where there is insufficient business to make this worthwhile a foreign bank will act as agent. The number of American banks with branches in London increased very considerably during the 1960s mainly because of the development of the Eurodollar market (*q.v.*).

Foreign Banks and Affiliates Association. A body representing foreign banks which have branches in Great Britain or banks to which they are affiliated.

Foreign Bill of Exchange. A bill of exchange used for making a pay-

---

$400

Thames Wharf,
London,
10th February, 197–.

Ninety days after sight of this FIRST of Exchange (second and third of the same tenor and date being unpaid) pay to my order the sum of Four Hundred dollars, value received.

To R. S. Hoover,
  Thirty-second street,   J. W. Hinton.
  New York.

ment arising out of foreign trade. It is very similar in many respects to the inland bill of exchange (*q.v.*). It is drawn by the creditor, accepted by the debtor and, unless payable at sight, it allows the debtor a period of credit (usually three months), and at the same time enables the creditor to receive payment at once if it can be discounted. The ordinary foreign bill of exchange is much less used than formerly in the making of payments between merchants in different countries, but it is still required in connection with the documentary credit. The foreign bill of exchange, unlike the inland bill, is drawn in a set of three, known respectively as the First, Second, and Third of Exchange, the First of Exchange usually taking the form shown on p. 206. The period for which a foreign bill is drawn runs from the date of its acceptance.

Foreign Currency Unit. *See* Monetary Unit.

Foreign Exchange. The system whereby one currency is exchanged for (or converted into) another, though sometimes the term is used as if it were synonymous with foreign currency itself. There are three main types of foreign exchange system: (i) the gold standard in its various forms; (ii) freely fluctuating exchange rates; and (iii) the several varieties of exchange control. Each of these is described under its appropriate heading. The fact that each country has its own monetary system is one of the principal complications of international trade and balances of payments. Barter has many obvious drawbacks but under that system exchange between merchants of different nationalities was as simple as between people of the same nationality. When commodity money, such as cattle, came into use it was a type of money generally acceptable to people of different nationalities. The precious metals were even more generally acceptable and even after they had been turned into coins the metals could be weighed and payments between different peoples were still relatively easy. In fact, gold and silver coins of many different issuing authorities often circulated in many countries. It was when money reached its final stage of being merely paper that complications of exchange between merchants of different nations really became complicated. So long as the paper was convertible on demand into gold the difficulties were less serious, but with the introduction and use of inconvertible paper money the real difficulties of foreign exchange began. *See* Gold Standard; Freely Fluctuating Exchange Rates; Exchange Control.

Foreign Exchange Broker. A broker who operates on the foreign exchange market. He may be acting on behalf of a bank or other financial institution or the Government of a State.

Foreign Exchange Brokers Association (F.E.B.A.). A company established in 1964 by the nine foreign exchange brokers of the city of London to deal in Eurodollars with continental countries.

Foreign Exchange Market. A market in which foreign currencies are exchanged for one another. If it is a free market it means that there are no restrictions on such exchanges. Since 1932 there has been intervention in the foreign exchange markets by the Exchange Equalisation Accounts of Governments.

Foreign Investments. When foreign investment is undertaken it is equivalent to expenditure on imports, in that it gives rise to a payment abroad in the Balance of Payments on Capital Account. In general, therefore, foreign investment should be undertaken only when a country has a favourable Balance of Payments on Current Account. Once such investment has been undertaken it yields income from abroad and thus can become an important invisible item in the current Balance of Payments. During the nineteenth century Great Britain used surpluses in its Balance of Payments on Current Account to build up its foreign investment, as a result of which it was able to have a regular deficit in its Balance of Trade, financed by invisible credit items of which income from investment abroad was an important one. The First World War weakened Great Britain's position somewhat in this respect, but the Second World War was very much more serious in its effects, since many foreign investments had to be sold in the early years of the war. After 1945, therefore, great efforts were made to increase Great Britain's visible exports to make up for the loss of income from foreign investment once again. By 1960 income from foreign investment had again become an important invisible item in the British Balance of Payments (*q.v.*).

Foreign Trade. Trade between nations. This can be bi-lateral, as when one country agrees to exchange a stated quantity of one commodity in exchange for a certain amount of another (a barter transaction) or where two countries attempt to balance their trade with one another; or it may be multi-lateral where each nation buys and sells with whatever other country it wishes. Multi-lateral trade results in a greater volume of trade being carried on than where trade is governed by a series of bi-lateral agreements. One of the great complications of foreign trade is that each country has its own independent currency system. *See* Balance of Payments; International Trade. For details of the procedure in foreign trade, *see* Export Trade, Financing of Foreign Trade; Import Trade.

Foreign Transactions Advisory Committee. A body, established in the 1930s, to watch over British investments abroad. It was superseded in 1939 by the Capital Issues Committee (*q.v.*).

Foreign Travel. Expenditure on foreign travel, whether for business or tourist purposes, is an invisible item in a country's balance of payments, expenditure of its own nationals abroad being a debit item and the expenditure of foreigners in one's own country being a credit item. For many countries, catering for foreign visitors has become a major industry on account of its favourable effect on the balance of payments. In recent years foreign tourists have been attracted in increasing numbers to Great Britain, especially American visitors, so that, whereas it was formerly a debit item for this country, it is now self-balancing.

Foremanship. This may be based on a functional relationship, in which case a group of men are in the charge of an expert at a particular job, or if there is line organisation the man in charge of the group receives his instructions from above.

Forestalling. A term used by Adam Smith for cornering the market in a commodity in order to re-sell it at a much higher price. The purchase of goods from a merchant before reaching the market in order to resell at a higher price was frowned upon and, when possible, prohibited in the Middle Ages, as being against the prevalent idea of a 'just price'.

Forestry Commission. A State body, established in 1919, its purpose being the preservation of the British forests by undertaking planting and regulating the felling of trees.

Forex. An association of foreign exchange dealers.

Forfeited Shares. When shares are not fully paid-up and the company calls for the outstanding amount, the shareholder may be unable to pay the amount asked of him, and if so his shares can be declared forfeit.

Forged Transfer Acts (1891 and 1892). A forged share transfer does not affect the rights of the share holder concerned, a company being compelled to compensate such a person out of its funds for any loss he may have suffered in this way.

Forgery. Altering the writing on a document or imitating the writing of some other person on a document with intent to defraud. Forgery with regard to cheques may refer either to the signature or to an alteration of the amount for which the cheque was drawn.

Forint. The standard unit of currency in Hungary, introduced after the great inflation following the Second World War, when it replaced the pengo. It is divisible into 100 fillers.

Formation of a Company. There are three main stages in the formation of a company: (i) the drawing up of the Memorandum of Association (*q.v.*) which must be signed by seven people in the case of a public company and two in the case of a private company, each of whom agrees to take up at least one share in the company. The Memorandum indicates the name of the company, the address of its registered office, its objects (*see* Objects Clause), whether its liability is limited, and the amount of its share capital; (ii) the framing of the Articles of Association which concern the internal working of the company; (iii) a Declaration that all the legal requirements under the Companies Acts have been carried out. In the case of a new insurance company the sanction of the Department of Trade is also required. Not until these formalities have been completed is it eligible to receive a Certificate of Incorporation from the Registrar of Companies and a certificate to commence business.

Fort Knox. Situated in Kentucky, it is the official place of storage for the gold reserves of the United States.

Forward Exchange. A means of hedging against fluctuations in the rate of exchange between different currencies. It is very similar to a 'futures' market for commodities. In addition to a 'spot' rate of exchange for current exchange transactions, there are also rates for dealings at some future date—one month, two months, or three months ahead. A forward market enables a dealer to hedge against exchange rate fluctuations, which hamper and increase the risks and uncertainties of foreign trade.

Forward Exchange Market. That section of the foreign exchange market which deals in forward exchange. (*q.v.*).

Forwarding Agent. A firm which specialises in the collection of goods from the premises of the sender and passes them on to the main carrier who is to take them to their destination.

Forward Integration. This occurs when a firm amalgamates with a business which markets its products.

Forward Marketing. Making a bargain for the purchase of goods to be delivered at a specified future date at a price agreed at the moment. Contracts for future delivery led to the development of 'futures' as a means of hedging or insuring against serious fluctuations in price, as is often the case with raw materials and other primary products. *See* Futures.

'Foul.' When applied to a Bill of Lading it means that some of the goods to which it applies are not in perfect condition. Very often a contract in foreign trade stipulates for a 'clean' Bill of Lading.

Founders' Shares. These shares are so called because they are usually taken up by the promoters or founders of a company, often in lieu of purchase money. Where such shares exist the ordinary shares usually then carry a fixed rate of dividend, the founders' shares taking the residue of the distributed profit.

Four Field System. *See* Norfolk Course.

Fourpenny Piece. A former British silver coin, in earlier times known as a Groat (*q.v.*).

Fox, Fowler & Company. The last small English bank to lose its privilege of being able to issue banknotes. This occurred when it amalgamated with Lloyds Bank Ltd. in 1921.

F.P.A. Abbreviation of Free of Particular Average (*q.v.*).

Fr. Abbreviation of franc(s) (*q.v.*).

Fractional Banking. A banking system where it is customary or legally compulsory to maintain a definite ratio between total deposits and cash. *See* Cash Ratio; Liquidity Rules Bank.

Fragile. Fragile articles sent by post must be properly packed and the parcel marked conspicuously 'Fragile, with care'.

Franc. The standard unit of the currency of a number of countries including France, the former French territories overseas, Belgium, Switzerland, Luxembourg, Monaco, Liechtenstein. The franc is divided into 100 centimes, though the great depreciation in the value of the franc in some countries as a result of the two World Wars led to the disappearance of the centime in those countries. A new franc was introduced in France in 1960 equal to 100 of the francs previously in circulation, and this resulted in the reintroduction of the centime into the French currency. Before 1914 the franc had the same value in all the West European countries in which it circulated, and among the members of the Latin Currency Union— France, Belgium, Switzerland, Luxembourg, and Italy (where the lira at that time also had the same value) —the currencies were interchangeable, but at the present day there are wide differences in the value of francs of the various countries that use them. The franc is a fractional unit of the Moroccan currency, the dirham being subdivided into 100 francs.

Franco. A term used in foreign trade transactions, it is a price quotation which includes not only the cost of the commodity but also insurance, freight, and all delivery charges to the importer's warehouse.

Franked Income. A term used of a company which derives income from the profits of another company which have been subjected already to corporation tax. Such income is said to be 'franked' and so is not liable to corporation tax a second time.

Frankfurt-am-Main. The financial centre of the Federal Republic of West Germany.

Franking Machine. To firms with a large amount of correspondence the Post Office will provide franking machines to save time affixing stamps to letters. In addition to indicating the amount of postage paid the machine also can be made to print the name of the firm or advertisement matter. The machine registers the total amount of the postage, and can be set by an official of the Post Office to cover a certain amount, after which the machine locks itself and cannot be used again until it has been reset. Payment has to be made in advance. The Post Office itself is prepared to frank batches of letters if the amount involved exceeds a certain amount.

Franking of Letters. The right to send up to ten letters per day free of charge was permitted to Members of Parliament during the period 1764-1840, when the privilege was withdrawn. The term is now used of franking machines (*q.v.*) supplied by the Post Office, but these machines are simply to facilitate the stamping of letters and postage has to be prepaid.

Franks Reports. 1. **(1964).** Recommended the establishment of Business Schools at London and Manchester universities.

2. **(1965).** Set up to inquire into the remuneration of higher civil servants, this Committee based its findings on the 'principle of comparability' (*q.v.*), that is, the remuneration of people in comparable occupations outside the civil service.

Frauds, Statute of (1677). This states that no guarantor can be compelled by law to fulfil his obligations unless his responsibility is clearly set down in a written document. This Act made many contracts enforceable if there was evidence in writing, the Law Reform (Enforcement of Contracts) Act of 1954 greatly reducing this number.

Fraudulent Preference. A payment made by a debtor to one of a number of his creditors within three months of his going bankrupt is regarded as fraudulent and becomes void.

F.R.Econ.S. Abbreviation of Fellow of the Royal Economic Society.

Free Alongside Ship (f.a.s.). A term used in foreign trade. As a price quotation it includes carriage of the goods only as far as the ship by which they are to be carried.

Free Banker. A member of a banking school of thought which believes that bankers should be less exacting in their standards for collateral security against loans and overdrafts.

Free Capital. A term sometimes used of capital in the form of money, since its owner is free to turn it into any form of real capital that suits his purpose.

Free Coinage. This occurs when the law compels the Mint to accept unlimited quantities of metal for coinage. This was the case with the Royal Mint for gold of the correct degree of fineness when Great Britain was on the gold standard.

Free Competition. Theoretically an environment in which production and distribution take place without any form of interference from the State, with free play for the forces of supply and demand and the working of the price mechanism. *See* Perfect Competition; Perfect Market.

Free Docks. An exporter's price quotation which includes the cost of the goods, but transport charges only as far as the docks from which the goods are to be shipped.

Freedom of Choice. The basis of capitalism and free enterprise, producers tending to produce what consumers as a whole desire. Freedom of choice of the individual is mainly limited by the size of his income. All Governments, however, limit freedom of choice by prohibiting or restricting the production and sale of certain things which are generally regarded as harmful, physically or morally, and still further by reducing consumers' income by progressive taxation in order to set free resources for the production of things or the supply of services which the Government thinks desirable for the community as a whole. It is argued too that the effect of competitive advertising is to restrict consumers' freedom of choice.

Free Economy. In its extreme form, a type of economic system where there is no interference by the State in production and distribution, that is, where the composite demand of all consumers determines what entrepreneurs shall produce, in contrast to the State-planned system where the Government decides on the allocation of factors of production among different industries and so determines what shall be produced. In actual conditions the State in all countries is responsible for some forms of production of both goods and services, and in recent times there has been a tendency for States to accept more and more responsibility in this matter. In many countries, including Great Britain, the system is described as a 'middle way', since part of the economy is under Government control and part left to free enterprise.

Free Enterprise. An economic system in which individuals are free, singly or collectively, to own capital and undertake economic activity within the framework of social legislation designed to protect the interests of the individual. In its extreme form it is the direct opposite of the State-Planned economy. Most capitalist systems now take what is called the 'middle way', that is, some State planning occurs even though most economic activity may still be left to free enterprise, though increasingly restricted by legal regulations. *See also* Free Economy.

Free Goods. 1. A term sometimes used in economics to indicate 'gifts of nature' or things in unlimited supply and which, therefore, have no market price determined by the forces of supply and demand. It is almost impossible to give examples of such 'goods' though sometimes the air we breathe is quoted as an example. In fact, free goods, if any exist, do not enter into the subject matter of economics at all.

2. A term used in foreign trade for imported goods that are free of customs duty. *See* Entry for Free Goods.

Freehold. Land held in fee simple, and real property and estates where the owner is not subject to charges to a higher landlord, in contrast to leasehold property where the owner, for example, of a house has to pay an annual rent for the land which is owned by some other person.

Free List. A list of goods that can be imported without payment of duty.

Freely Fluctuating Exchange Rates. A system of exchange rates where the value of one currency in terms of another is free to fluctuate. In this case, the rate of exchange is determined in the foreign exchange market by the demand for a currency in relation to the supply available in the market. Since there is a separate foreign exchange market in every important country there could be different rates of exchange between the same currencies in each market were it not for the fact that all such markets nowadays are connected by telephone and that money can be telegraphically transferred from one centre to another, so that if a discrepancy in the rate of exchange between two currencies did appear speculators would immediately undertake arbitrage, that is, purchase currency in the centre where it was cheaper and sell it in the centre where it was dearer, and such action would be profitable and therefore continue until the value of the currency was the same in all centres. A change in the value of a currency in one market, therefore, immediately brings about a similar change in all markets, that is, there is almost a perfect world market for foreign currency.

As a country increases its imports its demand for foreign currency increases; as it increases its exports it increases its supply of foreign currency. So, in the last resort, the rate of exchange under this system of foreign exchange depends on the relation between a country's imports and exports. To expand imports will cause its currency to depreciate in terms of others; to expand its exports will cause its currency to appreciate in terms of others. When its currency depreciates all foreign imports become dearer but its own exports become cheaper to foreign buyers. When its currency appreciates all foreign imports become cheaper but its exports become dearer to foreign merchants. The effect of this is to bring the country's balance of payments into balance. The advantage of free exchange therefore is that a country never has to worry about a loss of gold nor about balancing its payments, as appreciation (in the case of an excess of exports) or depreciation (in the case of an excess of imports) will always restore equilibrium. It will, of course, be concerned if its currency seriously depreciates in terms of others.

The great advantage claimed for free exchange rates is that it enables a country to pursue an independent monetary policy to suit the economic situation of the time, whereas the gold standard forces a deflationary policy on a country whenever it is losing gold, even though at the time an inflationary policy to stimulate economic activity may be more appropriate to the situation. Deflation is unpopular because it tends to increase unemployment and check economic activity. A country with free exchange rates need never deflate, but continued depreciation of its currency might easily lead to a severe inflation and perhaps even a runaway inflation, the dangers of which are greater on this system. A weak government, for example, may be afraid to risk unpopularity by taking the stern measures necessary to balance its budget, with the result that the currency will depreciate further, since the rate of exchange prevailing in the market is subject to many outside influences of both an economic and political nature. Exchange control systems all aim at giving stability of exchange rate without the drawbacks of the gold standard, but these systems have their own drawbacks. One of the greatest drawbacks to free exchange rates is that fluctuating rates of exchange, even though forward exchange rates are quoted (q.v.), are an unsettling influence on international trade. The gold standard gives stable exchange rates, but debars a country from adopting an independent monetary policy; free exchange rates have the advantage of allowing a country to adopt an independent monetary policy, but have the drawback of hindering and thereby reducing foreign trade. To combine the advantages of both systems and avoid the drawbacks of both systems was the aim of the International Monetary Fund, set up under the Bretton Woods Agreement, under which exchange rates are fixed at least in the short period, though provisions exist in the constitution of the Fund for modification of rates if circumstances are such as to require it.

From 1951 sterling was permitted a small degree of fluctuation on the foreign exchange market, until 1967 between $2·78 and $2·82 to the £, and 1967–71 between $2·38 and $2·42 to the £, though several times there were suggestions that the pound sterling should be set free and allowed to fluctuate (the modern term, a floating rate, being given to this), but the I.M.F. came down strongly in favour of fixed rates of exchange whenever countries have temporarily allowed rates to float, for example, West Germany and the Netherlands in 1971 and the U.K. in 1972. The I.M.F. considered fluctuating rates to have a bad effect on international trade. In recent years flexible exchange rates have again been favoured. The reason for this has been the difficulties which some countries (especially Great Britain) have experienced in maintaining equilibrium in their balances of payments, with the consequent necessity to deflate, thereby checking economic growth.

Free Market. 1. In an economic sense a market where the price of a commodity is determined by the free play of the forces of supply and demand, the market price then being the equilibrium price. The term is often used on the Foreign Exchange Market.

2. A stock exchange term used of a stock or share which is fairly easily obtainable by buyers in reasonably large amounts if required.

Free of Particular Average. A term used in marine insurance. A Particular Average loss is a partial loss, as for example, if in rough seas water penetrated into the hold of a ship and damaged the cargo. A policy of insurance covering particular average would permit a claim to be made to cover this partial loss, but if the policy was Free of Particular Average, the insurers would be free from such liability.

Free of Stamp (F.O.S.). A term used of securities that can be dealt in free of stamp duty. Being newly issued securities, dealings take place in the allotment letters that have been issued.

Free of Tax. A term used of an interest or dividend payment where the income tax is not deducted at source. On most Government stocks income tax at the standard rate is deducted by the Bank of England, the holder thus having to pay no further income tax at the basic rate on the amount he receives. There are several Government stocks, however, where tax is not deducted at source, for example, $3\frac{1}{2}\%$ War Stock, and in these cases the holder receives the gross amount of interest, and has then, if his income is large enough, to pay the tax himself. All Government stocks on the National Savings Stock Register (as distinct from the Bank of England Register) are paid 'free of income tax'. Where tax is deducted at source and the holder of the stock is not liable to the standard rate of tax he can reclaim the amount due to him from the Inland Revenue. Obviously, a person not liable to tax finds it more convenient to invest in stocks 'free of income tax'. In the case of building society interest, however, the society pays an agreed lump sum to cover tax on the interest it pays to its depositors and shareholders, and so those who have building society accounts and who are not liable to income tax cannot reclaim a refund from the Inland Revenue.

Free on Board (f.o.b.). Prices quoted on these terms include carriage only from the suppliers' premises as far as the port from which the goods are to be despatched, the remainder of the cost of carriage having to be borne by the purchaser of the goods.

Free on Rail (f.o.r.). Prices quoted on these terms include carriage only from the supplier's premises to the railway station from which the goods are to be despatched, the buyer having to pay the railway charges.

Free Port. A port which allows free entry to goods which are to be re-exported (entrepôt trade). This avoids the repayment of Customs Drawbacks as occurs in those ports where customs duty is charged on the entry of all goods irrespective of their ultimate destination. *See also* Free Zone.

Freepost. A means whereby the sender of a letter can charge the postage on it to the receiver.

Free Reserves. An American term for reserves held in excess of legal requirements. *See* Excess Reserves.

Free Trade. A condition of international trade where nations do not impose customs duties or other taxes on the imports of goods from other countries. The theory of International Trade (*q.v.*) shows that trade for the world as a whole will be at its greatest if it is not subject to restriction by tariffs, quotas, etc. Nevertheless, there has never been a period when trade between nations has been entirely free. Perhaps the world came nearest to free trade in the 1860s, largely due to the influence of Napoleon III of France, although as great trading nations both Great Britain and Holland clung to free trade longer than other nations, Great Britain abandoning it only in 1932. The desire to establish industries of their own, the aim of self-sufficiency, and the political influence of the growth of nationalism all contributed to the decline of free trade. It is significant, however, that both free trade and the volume of world trade reached their lowest ebb this century during the Great Depression of 1929-35. It was a desire to expand world trade, which is to the benefit of all taking part in it, that led to a reaction in favour of free trade after the Second World War. The efforts of G.A.T.T. (*q.v.*) have been directed towards a general reduction in tariffs and its efforts have met with some degree of success. The formation of regions with the eventual aim of becoming areas of free trade is another post-1945 move in the direction of freer trade.

Free Trade Area. A group of countries which have decided to impose no duties of any kind on imports from other members of the group. Immediately after the Second World War Belgium, the Netherlands, and Luxembourg decided to form a single customs union which came to be known as Benelux. The European Economic Community (E.E.C.), better known as the European Common Market (*q.v.*), is aiming at this objective by easy stages, as also is the European Free Trade Association (*q.v.*).

Freeze. 1. When used of wages it means that wages are to be held at their existing level for a certain period of time irrespective of any increase in prices during that time. *See* Wage Freeze.

2. The term is also used to indicate that an asset cannot be claimed by its owner either for a stated period of time or indefinitely. The Blocked Accounts which formed part of the pre-1939 German system of exchange control were frozen since their foreign owners were unable to draw on them freely. During the Second World War, Great Britain

was compelled to import on credit and the balances due to the suppliers were 'frozen' during the war and for some time afterwards.

Free Zone (or **Free Trade Zone**). An area near a seaport or airport in which firms can import goods duty free if they are to be re-exported or used in the manufacture of goods for export. There is a free zone of this kind in the neighbourhood of Shannon Airport in the Republic of Ireland.

Freight Integration Council. Established under the Transport Act (1968), its members include *ex-officio* the chairmen of British Rail and the National Freight Corporation. Its function is to assist the Minister of Transport in an advisory capacity in promoting the integration of all forms of internal transport of freight.

Freightliner. Also known as a liner train, it is a freight train operating on a fast regular service. *See* Beeching Plan.

Freightliner Company. A subsidiary of the National Freight Corporation (*q.v.*).

Freight Note. A document used in foreign trade, it is issued by the shipping company and gives details of the charge for the freight for a particular cargo for a specified journey.

French Agricultural Bank. A French investment bank or *banque d'affaires* which specialises in providing credit for farmers, although it also undertakes a certain amount of ordinary banking business.

Frequency Distribution. A method of tabulating facts relating to some topic. In economics one of the most interesting and most useful of frequency distributions is a table showing the number of people in the various age groups. This showed, for example, that in 1963, that in the United Kingdom there were more people in the 10–14 age group than in any other five-year age group, with another large number in the 35–39 age group. From the age-group 50–54 the numbers in each five-year age group naturally fall rapidly. Such frequency distributions can be represented graphically. *See* Population Pyramid.

Frictional Unemployment. Unemployment due to economic frictions, such as changes of demand or supply, the invention of new machines, the introduction of automation. If all factors were perfectly mobile these economic frictions would lead to very little unemployment. Frictional unemployment is generally of short duration unless it occurs during a period when there is also mass unemployment. *See* Unemployment.

Friendly Societies. Associations formed voluntarily for the purpose of rendering mutual assistance to members. Originally they comprised small groups of people who were all well acquainted with one another and who contributed regularly to a common fund from which payments could be made to members who required help on account of sickness or to widows and children of deceased members, or to cover funeral expenses. Some small societies of this kind existed as long ago as the seventeenth century, but during the early years of the Agrarian and Industrial Revolutions, when there was little provision against hardships caused by economic frictions, their numbers multiplied. Since, however, members were expected to pay a regular subscription the very poor who could not afford to make such payments had to rely on the Poor Law.

There are five main types of friendly society: (i) Affiliated Orders (*q.v.*) which are large federations with local lodges; (ii) Accumulating Societies (*q.v.*) which are more centralised and provide a wider range of benefits; (iii) Dividing Societies (*q.v.*) which are local and independent, and periodically divide their surplus funds among their members; (iv) Deposit Societies (*q.v.*) which combine insurance benefits with savings; (v) Burial Societies (*q.v.*) which exist primarily to provide funds to cover funeral expenses, which at one time were large in relation to income.

Many trade unions began as friendly societies and some still provide a measure of social insurance for their members. The National Insurance Act of 1911 employed 'approved' friendly societies as agents, but the Act of 1948 greatly curtailed their activities and usefulness. Although many of the smaller friendly societies decided to cease their activities, some of the larger ones have actually in recent years increased both their membership and total funds.

Fringe Benefits. In recent wage agreements there has been a tendency in Great Britain and some other countries, especially the United States, to supplement the agreed monetary payment with other benefits, known as fringe benefits. Under this heading come such things as holidays with pay, sick leave, medical attention, subsidised canteens where cheap meals can be obtained, luncheon vouchers, compensation for redundancy, removal expenses, expense accounts, pensions, or the provision of a car. In some occupations it has always been customary for employees to receive some payment in kind in addition to their money wages. For example, many workers are provided with uniform, others receive board and lodgings, some are provided with houses or are supplied free with gas or electricity. Coal-miners have always been allowed a quantity of concessionary coal and transport workers travel free to and from work and often receive other travel concessions. Married women may be allowed time for shopping. Most firms allow their employees to purchase limited quantities of the goods they make or deal in at reduced prices. In comparing wages in different occupations payments in kind and any fringe benefits must obviously be taken into account since they have a monetary value and reduce the expenditure of the recipients. Since fringe benefits are tax-free they are worth more—considerably more for those who pay high rates of income tax—than their monetary equivalent, and this is one of the main reasons for the great increase in such benefits in recent times. An economic objection to fringe benefits is that they tend to increase immobility of labour.

F.R.S.A. Designatory initials of a Fellow of the Royal Society of Arts.

F.S.S. Designatory initials of a Fellow of the Statistical Society.

F.S.S.U. Abbreviation of Federated Superannuation System for Universities.

F.T./Actuaries Index. An index of stock exchange prices compiled by the *Financial Times* (*q.v.*) in association with the Institute of Actuaries of London and the Faculty of Actuaries of Edinburgh. At present the base date is April 1962. This index covers a much wider field than the *Financial Times* industrial ordinary share index.

F.T.I.I. Designatory initials of a Fellow of the Institute of Taxation.

Fuel Research Station. One of the research stations of the Department of Scientific and Industrial Research (*q.v.*).

Fuji Bank. The largest commercial bank of Japan.

Full-cost Pricing. It is impossible in practice to calculate precisely the demand curve for a product. In spite of the development of market research, a firm can only estimate the effect a reduction of price is likely to have on the sales of its product. In practice a given output (perhaps the same as the previous year) is taken and the cost per unit of output is worked out on that basis, since there is no single cost of production for a commodity unrelated to the quantity of output. This calculation, with the mark-up for the entrepreneur, gives the price at which the product is to be offered for sale. The theory of perfect competition shows that in such conditions price is equal to marginal cost, but clearly, where fixed costs are high, this would make it impossible for a firm to make a profit. In practice, therefore, full-price costing is the rule.

Full Employment. There has never been general agreement as to the meaning of this term. Lord Beveridge defined it as a condition where there are 'more jobs than men', but in the light of experience since the Second World War many economists would describe this as a condition of over-full employment. In a dynamic economy, where there are changes in both demand and supply, the development of more efficient capital and an expanding national income creating new wants, it is impossible for everyone who wishes to work to be employed all the time. In such conditions some short-term temporary unemployment is unavoidable and indeed, economic progress would be impossible without it. Perhaps the best definition of full employment is that unemployment is at a minimum and the number of unemployed is no greater than the number of vacancies. With full employment there should be no mass unemployment, where nearly all industries are suffering at the same time from a deficiency of demand, and in addition measures should be taken to check unemployment due to economic frictions such as changes of demand and technical progress. Lord Beveridge laid down three conditions for the maintenance of full employment: (i) Demand must be adequate, and so if private investment falls short of the amount necessary to provide full employment, the State should undertake public investment to make up the deficiency, and if necessary the budget should be deliberately unbalanced in order to increase the volume of purchasing power in the hands of consumers; (ii) Location of industry must be controlled to give greater variety of industry, especially to those areas where industries are highly localised; (iii) Organised mobility of labour, he thought, was necessary so that men could move from declining to expanding industries more easily. The concentration of industry in London and south-east England has led to some modification of this view, and there is now greater support for the idea that new industries should be encouraged to set up in areas where the basic industry is declining; (iv) The trade unions must adopt a responsible attitude to the new conditions if full employment is to be permanently maintained without serious inflation.

Only since the publication of the White Paper on Employment Policy in 1944 has the British Government accepted responsibility for the maintenance of full employment and the ideas of Lord Keynes accepted in preference to the doctrine of the classical economists that supply creates its own demand. Lord Beveridge described this White Paper as 'epoch making'. From 1945 to 1970 the problem was mainly one of over-full employment and inflation, the only real efforts to maintain full employment in the face of declining demand occurring in 1958–59, when Government measures quickly restored the situation, and during 1962–63. On the other hand, measures taken in 1971, when unemployment reached its highest level for over 25 years, were slow to take effect. Although a high level of employment continued to be maintained in the southern part of the country and in the Midlands, some of the older industrial areas of highly localised industry—mainly heavy industry—had a high level of unemployment by modern standards. The problem of regional unemployment has become a serious one, and greater variety of industry is not easy to achieve. Nevertheless, a high degree of success has been achieved in south Lancashire where the cotton industry has shrunk to a very considerable extent without excessive unemployment on account of the success of the policy of attracting new industries, though this has not prevented a high level of unemployment persisting on Merseyside.

The greatest danger of full employment is that it leads to persistent inflation, and efforts to check inflation, on account of labour not being perfectly mobile, tend both to increase unemployment and to check economic expansion. The inflationary conditions that arise in these circumstances are largely due to the persistent demands for wage increases that are not matched by equal increases in productivity, and the fact that wage increases are more easily obtained in times of full or over-full employment because employers too are willing to grant such increases when they believe they can be passed on in the form of higher prices to consumers, so that the inflationary wages-prices spiral is stimulated. Over-full employment also shows itself in shortages of labour, so that the average standard of efficiency tends to decline as less efficient labour is employed. Apart from a number of minor recessions it can be considered that full employment was fairly successfully maintained in Great Britain down to the 1970s, except for brief periods when anti-inflationary policies required the adoption by the Government of deflationary measures. The most serious lapse from full employment was during 1974–77, when serious unemployment affected most of the leading industrial countries of the world.

Fully-paid Shares. Shares where their value has been paid up in full either on their issue or at some later date, as distinct from shares which are only partly paid up, the company in such a case being able to call for the balance if it wishes to increase its capital. The advantage of fully-paid shares is that no further calls can be made on the holder. It is rarer now than formerly for shares not to be fully-paid up.

Fulton Report (1968). The report of the committee on the civil service under the chairmanship of Lord Fulton. It recommended *inter alia*: (i) the creation of a new ministry to be known as the Civil Service Department; (ii) the abolition of 'classes' within the civil service; (iii) the establishment of a Civil Service College for the training of civil servants.

Functional Relationship. 1. This occurs when a definite relationship exists between two variables, as for example, between the price of a commodity and the quantity of it demanded in the market, or the relationship between its price and the quantity supplied. Between Income and Consumption the functional relationship is known as the Propensity to Consume, the higher the income the greater the propensity to consume.

2. The organisation of a business according to the functions performed by the employees, as an alternative to a Line Relationship (*q.v.*). If organisation is entirely based on function all men engaged in one operation are under the direct control of a supervisor in the same trade as themselves. In actual conditions organisation is rarely purely functional since it leads to too many cross-relationships between departments. A combination of Line and Function is the more usual type of organisation.

Functions of Money. Money came into use as a medium of exchange to obviate the clumsiness and inconvenience of barter transactions. Most of the functions of money really derive from its use as a medium of exchange. It also serves as a unit of account, that is, as a calculating medium and as a means of assigning prices to commodities and services. Money generalises purchasing power, since it can be used in payment for any kind of goods offered for sale, as distinct from ration cards, which were applicable often to single commodities only. Money also serves as a store of value and as a standard for deferred payments, but in both these cases the usefulness of money to fulfil these functions depends on its retaining a fairly stable value. Money which is declining in value soon ceases to fulfil these functions, as is apparent in any severe or runaway inflation. Money enables the price mechanism to operate, and money also has a dynamic function in a modern economy. Control over the supply of money and its regulation is one of the means by which a Government, having accepted responsibility for the maintenance of a high level of economic activity and full employment, attempts to carry out its undertaking.

Fundamental Disequilibrium. A fundamental disequilibrium occurs in a country's balance of payments when the official rate of exchange of that country's currency does not correctly value it in terms of other currencies. In a period of inflation, for example, the internal value of a currency may fall although the official external rate remains as before. If inflation to the same extent has not taken place in other countries, such a currency would be overvalued externally and the result would be a tendency for imports to rise (imported goods appearing to be cheaper) and for exports to fall (exported goods becoming dearer to other countries). The result would be an unfavourable balance of payments which would persist until the internal and external values of the currency were brought into line. This could be done by raising the internal value of the currency by a policy of deflation which might have serious repercussions on the level of business activity and employment. Alternatively the external value of the currency could be reduced by devaluation. It was thought, for example, both in 1949 and 1967, that sterling was over-valued in terms of the dollar and therefore, that British difficulties with the balance of payments were of a 'fundamental' kind, that is, due to the exchange rate overvaluing sterling externally, and it was for this reason that sterling was devalued. On account of the bad effects on international trade of competitive devaluation of currencies before 1939, the Bretton Woods Agreement include a clause declaring that devaluation of a currency should take place only when a country had a fundamental disequilibrium in its balance of payments.

Funded Debt. Originally this term was restricted to that part of the National Debt the interest on which was a charge on the Consolidated Fund and for which there was no redemption date. It is now more usual to regard as funded debt all Government securities which are marketable on the stock exchange. These include Consols, various issues of Savings Bonds, Conversions, Loans. The greater part of the British National Debt is now in this form.

Funding Loans. The name given to a number of Government stocks: 4% Funding Loan 1960–90; 5½% Funding Loan 1982–84; 3½% Funding Loan 1999–2004 and a number of others.

Funding Operations. 1. Either reducing the Floating Debt and replacing it by a Funded Stock for a definite or an indefinite period of years, or taking advantage of a time of low interest rates to repay stocks at the earliest date possible and replacing them by new stocks bearing a lower rate of interest.

2. The term is also used of Bank of England operations in Treasury bills and Government bonds with less than five years to run either to reduce or increase the liquidity of the economic system to suit what the monetary authorities consider to be the economic needs of the time. This is a relatively recent development of one form of debt management as an instrument of monetary policy.

3. The term is sometimes nowadays given a third meaning—when a company with a very large bank overdraft decides to repay it with money raised by an issue of debentures.

Funds, The. An alternative term for gilt edged, that is Government, stocks.

Funeral Expenses. One of the benefits under the National Insurance Scheme, a Death Grant being payable for funeral expenses. During the nineteenth century a number of Burial Societies (*q.v.*) were formed to provide insurance for small sums to cover funeral expenses.

Funeral Societies. An alternative name for Burial Societies (*q.v.*). *See also* Friendly Societies.

Furs as Money. Owing to a shortage of coin among the traders who did business with the Hudson's Bay Company furs for a time served as money. *See* Commodity Money.

Further Education. A term used of education in Great Britain for pupils who have left secondary schools. It may be full-time, leading to a professional or trade qualification, or in some cases to an external degree of the University of London, or it may be part-time. In the case of part-time attendance at institutions of further education most students still attend only during the evening, but an increasing number of employers permit their young employees to attend for a half-day or in some cases two half-days per week during ordinary working hours. Further education is provided by Polytechnics, the regional Colleges of Technology (or senior Technical Colleges), the other Technical Colleges, Colleges of Further Education, Technical Institutes and small Evening Institutes.

Futures. Essentially a means by which merchants or other large buyers hedge against price fluctuations of a commodity—usually a raw material—in which they deal. To be employed effectively it is necessary that the goods concerned should be capable of being accurately graded, so that dealings can take place without their actually having to be seen and examined at the time. Futures can be applied to a number of commodities—such as cereals, sugar, coffee, cocoa, rubber, wool—but futures have been most highly developed in the case of raw cotton. Originally, a futures contract was simply a contract for the delivery of a specified quantity of a certain grade of cotton at an agreed price at a named future date, the price for immediate delivery being known as the 'spot' price. This in time led to the buying of 'futures' so that in the meantime if the spot price varied from the price at which the futures were bought the one would offset the other, a gain on the futures offsetting the higher spot price, or vice versa. The result of such action is a steadying of prices for the buyers, who are in effect by this means insuring against price fluctuations, which are more frequent and wider in extent for raw materials than for manufactured goods.

Fwd. Abbreviation of Forward, as in Carriage Forward (*q.v.*) and Brought Forward. *See also* B/f.

G

G.A.B. Abbreviation of General Arrangements to borrow (*q.v.*).

Gabelle. A tax on salt imposed in France before the French Revolution.

Gaitskell Report (1958). The report of a Commission, of which the Rt. Hon. H. T. N. Gaitskell was chairman, set up by the Co-operative Union to make a survey of co-operative production, wholesaling, and retailing. Its recommendations included some administrative reforms, the amalgamation of smaller retail societies, and various measures to increase efficiency and put both wholesaling and retailing on a more modern basis.

Galloping Inflation. An alternative term for Hyperinflation (*q.v.*). *See also* Inflation (3).

Gambling. Some nineteenth-century writers on economics made much of the notion that gambling involves economic loss, the marginal utility of £1 lost always being greater than the marginal utility of £1 gained. *See* Diminishing Marginal Utility, Law of.

Gantt System. A system of wage payment named after H. L. Gantt, an American, who first introduced it. Known as a task-bonus system it offered the employee a very large bonus if a specified piece of work was accomplished within a certain time, but the task set was a very severe one —usually double that of an average worker—no bonus being paid if the worker just failed to achieve his target. Consequently, the system tended to defeat its objective, the severity of the task deterring many workers from attempting to achieve it.

Garnishee Order. A Court order on behalf of a creditor attaching funds held by a third person who owes money to the debtor and warning the third person, known as the garnishee, not to make any payment to the debtor until directed to do so by the Court.

Gas Consultative Councils. Bodies set up to watch over the interests of consumers. For each regional Gas Board there is a Consultative Council, half the members representing municipal corporations, and the other members representing the interests of commerce, industry, and general consumers.

Gas Council. A body set up under the Act of 1949 which nationalised the gas production industry. It was suceeded by the British Gas Corporation (*q.v.*) in 1971.

Gas Stocks. Stocks issued by the Gas Council to provide compensation to the previous owners of gas undertakings or to finance expansion and development.

G.A.T.T. Abbreviation of General Agreement on Tariffs and Trade (*q.v.*).

G.C.E. Abbreviation of General Certificate of Education (*q.v.*).

G.D.P. Abbreviation of Gross Domestic Product (*q.v.*).

Gearing. A term applied to the capital of a limited company to indicate the proportion between the various types of shares and debentures that it has issued. The gearing is said to be high if the prior charges on the issued debentures and preference shares absorb a large proportion of the earnings of the company before anything is available for the ordinary shareholders. The gearing is said to be low if the prior charges are low.

Geddes Reports. 1. Appointed in 1922, it recommended drastic cuts in Government expenditure (the 'Geddes Axe').

2. Appointed in 1963 to review the system of licensing road haulage vehicles—A, B, C, licences—and to report on the effects of this system. It recommended the abolition of the

licensing system for road haulage in order to restore competition in this field. *See* A Licence, etc.

3. The report, published 1966, of a committee appointed to inquire into British shipbuilding. It recommended a rationalisation of the industry by a reduction in the number of shipyards from 17 to 5 and in the number of marine engine builders from 18 to 4. It suggested too that the number of trade unions representing employees in the industry should be reduced from 15 to 5. These reforms, it was thought, could result in output being doubled.

General Agreement on Tariffs and Trade (G.A.T.T.). An international body established in 1947 with the aim of reducing tariffs, as an aid to increasing the volume of international trade. It was not originally intended to be a permanent institution, although in fact it became one. (*See* International Trade Organisation.) During 1947–62 five international conferences were held —three at Geneva and one each at Torquay and Annecy. These conferences have achieved a much greater measure of success than the trade conferences of the period between the two World Wars, as it is more generally realised than ever before that high tariffs restrict the volume of world trade. The greatest tariff reductions, however, were achieved in what was known as the 'Kennedy Round' (*q.v.*), agreed in 1967 and so called because it was initiated by the U.S. President. The headquarters of G.A.T.T. are at Geneva.

General Arrangements to Borrow (G.A.B.). The arrangements by which the Group of Ten (*q.v.*) agreed to supplement the resources of the International Monetary Fund.

General Average. A term used in marine insurance. In the case of a mishap at sea there may be either total loss or partial loss. In this connection the term 'average' is used to mean loss, there being General Average and Particular Average, the latter referring to partial loss. General Average applies to such cases as the following: (i) If in a storm or other emergency some of a ship's cargo has to be jettisoned the loss will be partly borne by the owners of the cargo and partly by the shipowners, since the loss was incurred to try to save the ship; (ii) If a ship has suffered severe damage and has to be towed into port, the expense incurred will not fall entirely on the shipowners but also to some extent on the owners of the cargo, since it was also in their interests that the ship should not become a total loss. The York–Antwerp Rules (*q.v.*) were framed to regulate the apportionment of General Average. In the case of Particular Average (*q.v.*) the partial loss is borne entirely by either the shipowners or the owners of the cargo. In all cases of partial loss the extent of the damage has to be assessed by an independent official.

General Certificate of Education (G.C.E.). A certificate instituted in 1951 for pupils in England attending secondary schools or technical colleges. There are three levels of examination: Ordinary ('O'), Advanced ('A'), and Scholarship ('S'). Admission to English universities depends mainly on a candidate's performance at G.C.E. examinations. In 1976 it was decided to combine the G.C.E. and the C.S.E. (*q.v.*) in the near future in a unified examination for the Certificate of Education.

General Clearing. The main section of the London Bankers' Clearing House (*q.v.*) that deals with all cheques other than those dealt with by the Town Clearing (*q.v.*).

General Crossing. A cheque crossing where no bank is named. *Cf.* Special Crossing.

General Equilibrium. *See* Particular and General Equilibrium.

General Grant. *See* Block Grant.

General Index of Retail Prices. *See* Index of Retail Prices; General.

General Partner. Formerly known as an Ordinary Partner, he is entitled to take a full share in the management of the business.

General Sales Tax. *See* Sales Tax.

General Strike. A strike in which all trade unions take part at the same time, thereby completely dislocating the economic life of a country. The only General Strike to take place in Great Britain was that of 1926, called in support of a strike of coalminers. It lasted only ten days, most people being opposed to the attempt to coerce the Government, which organised emergency food distribution, transport, etc., and even published its own newspaper, the *British Gazette*. The Act outlawing general strikes was repealed in 1947.

General Union. A type of trade union—an alternative name for an Industrial Union (*q.v.*).

Geneva Conference (1947). The foundation meeting of G.A.T.T. (*q.v.*).

Genoa Conference (1922). A monetary conference called to consider monetary difficulties arising from the First World War, its main recommendation was that every country should have a central bank to control its currency arrangements.

Geographical Mobility. The ease with which a factor of production, especially labour, can be transferred from one place to another. *See* Mobility.

Geometric Mean. The nth root of n items multiplied together, n being the number of items taken into consideration. For example, the geometric mean of 4, 6, 72 would be $\sqrt[3]{4 \times 6 \times 72} = 12$, whereas the arithmetic mean would be 27.3. Its advantage over the arithmetic mean is that it is less influenced by a single extreme item. The geometric mean is therefore, preferred in the construction of index numbers.

Geometric Progression. A series of numbers increasing by the same multiple, *e.g* 2, 4, 8, 16. . . . *See* Malthusian Theory of Population.

George Noble. An English gold coin first issued in 1526, it was worth one third of £1. *See* Noble.

Gerrard & National Discount Co. Ltd. One of the larger discount houses of the City of London, it was formed in 1970 by a merger of Gerrard & Reid Ltd. and the National Discount Co. Ltd.

Gibson Paradox. The view that over a longish period the level of prices and the level of interest rates move in the same direction. Keynes showed this to be true in the period 1791–1939, but the period 1939–46 was remarkable for the fact that prices and interest rates moved in opposite directions.

Giffen Goods. The demand for some commodities gives rise to exceptional demand curves where over a portion of the curve a rise in price shows a greater and not a smaller quantity demanded. Goods of this type are known as Inferior Goods or Giffen Goods after Sir R. Giffen (1837–1910) who was first to point out this case of exceptional demand. Cheap necessary foodstuffs form one of the best examples. Most people vary their demand for such things as bread and potatoes vary little over a very wide range of prices, but in the case of the very poor it may be that at a low price they may be able to afford a certain amount of these cheaper foodstuffs together with a little of the more expensive foods. A rise, however, in the price of the cheaper foods compels them to curtail their expenditure not on the cheaper foods but on the more expensive ones, and in fact make good the deficiency by purchasing more of the cheaper foods in spite of the fact that they have increased in price, as this is the only way by which they can obtain the same amount of food as before without increasing their outlay on food.

'Gift of Nature.' One of the characteristics peculiar to land according to the classical economists. *See* Land.

Gift Tokens. The National Savings movement has arranged with the Post Office for the sale of gift tokens for £1, £3, and £5, which can be offered as presents.

Gifts *Inter Vivos*. Such gifts are now covered by Capital Transfer Tax (*q.v.*).

Gilbert's Act (1782). An Act which

encouraged parishes to form unions for Poor Law purposes with Guardians to supervise relief of the poor. The aged, the infirm, and pauper children could be accommodated in workhouses, but work had to be found for the able-bodied poor.

Gild (or **Guild**). An association established during the Middle Ages to protect the interest of members of the same craft and to ensure that new members reached a certain standard of competence before being admitted as full members. Thus, a period of apprenticeship had to be served, and a satisfactory piece of workmanship produced, known as a 'masterpiece', before an apprentice could become a journeyman and qualify to become master on his own account. The early gilds too had a religious side and put on religious pageants and plays. They also took an important part in the government of medieval towns. Most of the livery companies of London had their origin in the medieval gilds. The feature of that gild was that apprentices, journeymen, and masters were all members of the same body. In the smaller towns of an earlier period the gild merchant included members of all the crafts of the town, but as the towns grew larger each craft tended to form a separate gild. The gilds framed regulations aimed at securing equality for all members and at maintaining a certain standard of workmanship. With the expansion of industry and commerce the gilds began to decline, as they were unsuited to large-scale industry.

Gild Merchant. An association of the craftsmen of all trades in towns in the early Middle Ages. As the towns grew the gild merchant split into separate craft gilds. *See* Gild.

Gilt-edged. Stock exchange securities which carry a minimum of risk, that is, as regards the regular payment of the interest on the due dates, and the redemption of the stock (unless undated) at the time stated. The term is usually restricted to British Government stocks, though sometimes also applied to loans of British Local Authorities and some Commonwealth Governments.

Giro. *See* National Giro.

G.L.C. Abbreviation of Greater London Council which in 1965 replaced the L.C.C., Middlesex and a large number of smaller local authorities in Greater London.

G.m.b.H. Abbreviation of Gesellschaft mit beschränker Haftung, the German company with limited liability.

G.N.P. Abbreviation of Gross National Product (*q.v.*). *See also* National Income.

'Go-go.' A term used of a unit trust where the aim is to maximise growth. Generally only a small portfolio of shares is held and the managers are more active on the stock exchange than is usual with unit trusts.

'Going Concern.' A business that is in full working order so that the buyer will be expected to pay a sum for goodwill (*q.v.*), the amount depending on the prosperity of the business and whether its profits have been increasing or declining.

Gold and Silver (Export Control) Act (1920). During the First World War the import and export of gold had been controlled, and this Act gave statutory form to these wartime measures. Until Great Britain returned to the gold standard in 1925 gold from Empire countries all passed through the London gold market, whatever its ultimate destination.

Gold Bullion. As held by central banks and gold dealers gold bullion takes the form of gold bars, each weighing 400 ounces.

Gold Bullion Standard. A form of the gold standard as adopted by Great Britain in 1925. There was no gold coinage, the currency being exchangeable only in large quantities for gold bars of 400 ounces, each worth approximately £1,560. Apart from this, the gold bullion standard has all the features of the full gold standard, both its advantages and disadvantages, but it has the additional advantage that it economises the use of gold, gold not being required to back the internal note issue.

Gold Certificate. A type of paper money issued in the United States during 1865-1933, the paper being fully backed by gold.

Gold Clause. A country which had frequently devalued its currency often found it difficult to borrow in the capital market unless the loan contained a 'gold clause', which offered lenders repayment in terms of the gold equivalent of the currency at the time of the loan. Thus, if by the date of redemption the currency had fallen to only half its value in terms of gold repayment would require double the amount of currency borrowed.

Gold Coins. The first gold coin to be issued in England was the gold penny of fine gold of 1257. Then came the gold florin of 1343 worth £0·30, the noble of 1344 worth one third of £1, the ryal or royal of 1465 worth at first £0·50 and later £0·60, the angel worth one third of £1 when first issued in 1465 and gradually raised in value to £0·58 by 1661, the sovereign or double ryal of 1489 which varied in value between £1 and £1·50, the crown of 1526 worth £0·25, the unite of 1604 worth £1, the guinea of 1663 which varied in value between £1 and £1·30, and finally a revival in 1816 of the sovereign worth £1. In addition to the coins mentioned above there were fractions of most of them, halves and sometimes quarters, and also multiples of some, doubles, trebles, and fives. In the early centuries few gold coins were minted owing partly to the scarcity of gold, and partly to the fact that gold coins were too valuable for most people in times when prices and wages were very low. In early days gold coins were mainly used by merchants.

Gold Discoveries. During the period when gold was the principal monetary metal, and especially when most of the important commercial countries were on the gold standard, the discovery of new sources of supply of gold had important repercussions on the value of money. The new discoveries of gold in the sixteenth century led to an increase in the quantity of money, and was one of a number of reasons for the rise in prices in Western Europe at that time. During the nineteenth century important new gold discoveries were made about 1849 and again about 1896. The nineteenth century too was a period during which there was an explosion of all kinds of production, both raw materials and manufactured goods, but production did not expand at an even pace. When the output of gold was expanding faster than the output of other goods there was a general tendency for prices to rise; when the output of gold lagged behind the production of other goods there was a tendency for prices to fall. The relation between the production of gold and the production of other goods during the period when Great Britain was on the gold standard accounts for the medium term movement of prices that took place during the nineteenth century. Thus, between 1820 and 1849 there was a tendency for prices to fall, between 1849 and 1874 for prices to rise, and between 1874 and 1896 again for prices to fall with a further rise in prices after 1896. The new discoveries of gold in Australia, California, and Russia helped to raise prices after 1849 and again after 1896. By 1874 the rate of production of other goods overtook the increase in the output of gold and so helped to cause a fall in prices, which the discovery of gold in South Africa and the Klondyke in 1896 checked. *See* Price Movements (ii).

'Golden Handshake.' Compensation given by a firm to an executive for loss of office. Only the first £5,000 of any such payment is now not liable to tax.

Gold Exchange Standard. A form of the gold standard, first adopted in the mid-1920s by the Scandinavian countries. On this standard there is neither a gold currency in circulation nor gold reserves held for external purposes, the external reserves being mainly held in securities of countries on the gold standard at the time. This type of standard gives the maximum economy in the use of gold, but it has a serious disadvantage both for the country that adopts it and also for the 'parent' country, the currency of which it uses for its reserves. If the 'parent' country devalues its currency without warning or leaves the gold standard, the value of the reserves might fall considerably overnight. On this account a close watch has to be kept on the economic situation of the 'parent' country, and at the least sign of weakness there, the securities will be exchanged for gold, thereby increasing the economic difficulties of the 'parent' country. In recent years both the pound and the dollar have suffered at times from being reserve currencies.

Gold Fixing. Determining the price of gold on the London Gold Market (*q.v.*).

Gold Market. *See* London Gold Market.

Gold Points. Sometimes known as Specie Points, these indicate the extent of the variation of a currency on the gold standard from the par rate of exchange, the amount depending on the cost of insurance and the transport of gold between the countries concerned. If the rate of exchange were to vary outside these limits it would become cheaper to export or import gold as the case might be.

Gold Pool. Formed in 1961 by eight leading countries to support the gold market against temporary heavy demands. Fear of a devaluation of the U.S. dollar led in March 1968 to an exceptionally heavy demand for gold. At a meeting in Washington, D.C., a two-tier system was agreed upon, whereby there should be a market for gold open only to Central Banks in which the price of gold was to be fixed, and a free market in which the price would be determined by the market forces of supply and demand. The gold pool, therefore, was no longer required.

Gold Reserve Act (1934). An Act of the American Federal Government which devalued the dollar for purely competitive reasons, and also authorised the establishment of an Exchange Stabilisation Fund (similar to the British Exchange Equalisation Account) in order to intervene in the foreign exchange market to influence the price of the U.S. dollar in terms of other currencies. Soon afterwards the Tripartite Agreement between Great Britain, France, and the United States (1936) was signed.

Gold Reserves. On the gold standard a reserve has to be maintained for two purposes: (i) as a backing for the note issue; (ii) for making foreign payments when the country has an adverse balance of payments. In Great Britain the gold reserve was the responsibility of the Bank of England throughout the period that Great Britain was on the gold standard. When the Exchange Equalisation Account of the Treasury was set up in 1932 this also acquired gold, and so the function of holding the gold reserve came to be shared between the Bank of England and the Treasury, until 1939 when almost the entire stock of gold held by the Bank of England was transferred to the Treasury. When the Bank of England held the reserve its amount could always be found from a study of the Weekly Return of the Bank of England. For some time after 1939 the Treasury did not publish the amount of its gold reserve. After the Second World War U.S. dollars were regarded as being as good as gold and when the amount of the reserves came to be published they were known as the Gold and Dollar Reserves until January 1959 when sterling and a number of other currencies became convertible, and since then the British reserves have been known as the Gold and Convertible Currency Reserves. A favourable over-all balance of payments increases the reserves, just as an adverse balance of payments reduces them. The amount of the reserves is now published monthly. In general the reserves have been regarded as inadequate since 1945 and so the Government has tended to watch them closely, any serious reduction being viewed with great alarm and great efforts being made to expand them. Consequently an adverse balance of payments is treated as a serious situation, and has tended to cause the Government sometimes to adopt policies to rectify it which have tended to check the economic growth of the country.

Goldsmiths. Workers and dealers in gold, many of the London goldsmiths adopted banking as a sideline to their main business, and many of them finally hived off the banking side of their business as separate purely banking undertakings. Their earliest banking function was dealing in foreign exchange, but they soon began to accept deposits on account of the facilities they possessed for storing valuables which most merchants lacked. Later they became lenders, and later still it was their receipts which became the first bank-notes.

Goldsmiths' Company. One of the twelve more important of the Guilds or Livery Companies of the City of London whose existence dates back to the gilds of medieval times, being incorporated in 1327. The Goldsmiths rank fifth in civic precedence among the guilds. The company still exercises its hall-marking function. The earliest bankers in England were all London goldsmiths and members of the Goldsmiths' Company.

Gold Standard. On the full gold standard the monetary unit consists of a fixed weight of gold at a definite fineness; the price of gold, therefore, in terms of the national currency is fixed; and there is complete freedom to buy or sell gold, to import it or export it. From the thirteenth century England had both silver and gold coins. Until the early eighteenth century this country could be said to be on a silver standard, but early in the eighteenth century without any deliberate act Great Britain went over to a gold standard, largely because of the increasing importance of gold coins as the commerce of the country expanded. The Napoleonic Wars caused the temporary abandonment of the gold standard, and cash payments were not resumed until 1821. When Great Britain has been on the gold standard, the Bank of England has been legally compelled to buy and sell gold at fixed prices per standard ounce, that is, gold eleven-twelfths fine. Changes in the supply of gold or in the demand for it, therefore, could have no effect on its value in terms of the national currency, and so a change in the price of gold could be seen only indirectly through changes in the prices of other goods. Thus, the great gold discoveries of 1849 and 1896 left the price of gold unchanged but caused a general rise in prices of other things. On the gold standard the rate of exchange was determined by the amount of pure gold in the standard unit of each country's currency, this being known as the mint par of exchange. The maximum variation in the rate of exchange between two currencies on the gold standard was between the gold or specie points, determined by the cost of transport and insurance of gold during transport between the two countries concerned. Thus, an important feature of the gold standard was the stable rate of exchange, which was good for international trade.

The gold standard had really two functions: internally it was the basis of the currency, and externally it regulated the rate of exchange between all countries that maintained the standard. The two functions were, however, closely interlinked. On the full gold standard gold coins were in circulation and bank-notes were exchangeable on demand for gold of equivalent value, so that a gold reserve had to be maintained to meet this demand. Though the Bank Charter Act of 1844 permitted a small fiduciary issue, the rest of the note issue had to be fully backed by gold. Another important feature of the gold standard, therefore, is that the amount of cash in the country is limited by the amount of gold held in reserve by the central bank, and since there must be a cash basis for credit creation, the volume of bank deposits too is directly related to the amount of the gold reserve. The gold reserves are also required to cover a deficit in the balance of payments, and the reserves would be increased by a credit balance on international account. Thus a loss of gold arising from an adverse balance of payments, by reducing the gold reserve, actually reduced the quantity of cash and compelled the Bank of England to adopt a policy of credit contraction in order to reduce the total deposits of the commercial banks. In opposite circumstances an inflow of gold resulting from a favourable balance of payments increased the quantity of money in the country and led to an expansionist credit policy to increase the volume of bank deposits.

Thus, the internal and the external functions of the gold standard reacted on one another. It used to be said that the gold standard was automatic or self-regulating in that it set in motion a train of events which 'automatically' corrected an adverse balance of payments or alternatively restored equilibrium when there was a favourable balance of payments. Thus, an outflow of gold, by reducing the internal supply of money, caused a fall in internal prices, including wages, thereby reducing the demand for imports which remained at the previous price, and also stimulating exports because these were now cheaper to foreign merchants, this process continuing until the deficit in the balance of payments was wiped out and the equilibrium restored. In the reverse circumstances of a favourable balance of payments, there would be a rise in the internal quantity of money which would cause a rise in prices and wages, stimulate demand, including the demand for imports, but check exports since these would then be dearer to foreign merchants, and again this process would go on until equilibrium restored. This, at least, is the theory of the working of the gold standard. It depended, however, on all countries keeping to the two 'rules': (i) to adopt a policy of deflation when gold was flowing out, and (ii) to adopt a policy of inflation (in this case a controlled inflation) when gold was flowing in. The Report of the Cunliffe Committee (1918) described the working of the gold standard in this way, but few people nowadays believe that even in the nineteenth century the gold standard ever worked as smoothly, effectively, and automatically as the members of that Committee apparently believed.

The gold standard possessed a number of advantages: (i) a stable rate of exchange; (ii) so long as the 'rules' are rigidly obeyed there can be no 'runaway' inflation, since the expansion of the quantity of money depends on the acquiring of more gold; (iii) the balance of payments automatically rights itself.

On the other hand, there were serious disadvantages to the gold standard: (i) internal purchasing power can be increased only by acquiring more gold and not to meet the needs of an expanding economy; (ii) the main drawback is the linking of the internal and external functions of the gold standard, which made internal monetary policy depend on whether gold was flowing into the country or out. Thus, it might happen that an internal policy of deflation might have to be adopted even though there was a trade depression, simply because of an outflow of gold, or an internal inflationary policy might have to be adopted, even though a country was already suffering from inflation, merely because gold was flowing in; (iii) it is nowadays regarded as wasteful to have to maintain a gold reserve as a backing for the note issue.

In the years following the First World War, during which the gold standard was suspended, it was felt that most of the world's international monetary difficulties were caused by the suspension of the gold standard, its restoration being regarded as a necessary pre-requisite to recovery. As a result there came a general return to the gold standard, Great Britain returning to gold in 1925. The British restored gold standard was, however, a gold bullion standard (*q.v.*). Some other countries, including those of Scandinavia, adopted yet another form of the gold standard, known as the Gold Exchange standard (*q.v.*).

Breakdown of Gold Standard. There were many causes of the breakdown of the gold standard in the early 1930s: (i) The unwillingness of countries to obey the 'rules', especially an unwillingness to deflate sufficiently when gold was flowing out, together with the fact that in most cases the amount of deflation required was much greater than it had ever been on the pre-1914 gold standard. Great Britain carried out a severe bout of deflation during 1931, even though unemployment was already serious and the effect was to increase it, but even so it was insufficient to enable this country to remain on the gold standard. In the mid-1920s the United States, on the other hand, was suffering from inflation but an inflow of gold by the rules of the gold standard required even further inflation. It was the continuance and repetition of this sort of situation that eventually led the United States to 'sterilise' the inflow of gold, that is, not allowing it to affect the internal monetary system. (ii) Short-term capital movements were on a much greater scale than ever before, and these were mainly of a speculative nature, so that capital was often withdrawn from a country just when such action would increase its difficulties. The existence of the gold exchange standard increased the likelihood of such capital movements. (iii) One of the most important causes of Great Britain's difficulties was the fact that this country returned to the gold standard in 1925 at the pre-1914 parity with the U.S. dollar, the price of gold being fixed in sterling at the pre-1914 level. This grossly overvalued sterling, which had suffered as a result of the war, whereas the war had strengthened the dollar in relation to most other currencies. To maintain this high value of sterling required an impossible degree of deflation to raise the internal value of the currency to the external value given to it. There were other immediate causes of the breakdown of the gold standard in the 1930s.

Gold Tranche. That part of the subscription of a member of the I.M.F. which formerly had to be paid in gold. During 1977–80 this gold is to be returned to members.

Good. This term is used of any commodity or service for which there is a demand, irrespective of whether it is in any sense 'good' or 'bad'. *See* Economic Good.

Goodwill. In assessing the value of a business, usually when the business is to be sold, the price asked for it may be increased by an amount known as 'goodwill' to cover the value of the business built up in the past, this depending on its prosperity, the rate of profit, whether profits over recent years have been increasing or declining, etc. Goodwill is an intangible asset and a well-managed company will wish to write down the item in as short a time as possible.

Gosbank. The principal bank of the U.S.S.R., it claims to be the largest bank in the world (but *see* Bank of America). Although it has over 5,000 branches it is more like a central bank than a commercial bank, being the specialised agency of the Soviet Government, its primary function being to watch over the progress of economic plans. Like other central banks it holds the country's reserves of bullion and currency.

'Go Slow' Tactics. An alternative to the strike in an industrial dispute

Gosplan. Abbreviation for the State Planning Commission of the U.S.S.R., it is responsible for working out the plan of production for each year, the distribution of factors of production among different employments, and also for longer-term planning, for example, five-year plans.

Gourde. The standard unit of the currency of Haiti, though the U.S. dollar is also in use in that country. The gourde is sub-divided into 100 centimes.

Governed Economy. An alternative term for the 'middle way' type of economy. *See* Mixed Economy.

Government Actuary. A State official employed to work out actuarial calculations whenever required by the Government, as for example, contributions to State-operated pension schemes, such as those of teachers, etc.

Government Annuities. Until 1962 Government annuities from £1 to £300 could be purchased through any bank. Their issue was withdrawn as demand for them had declined, mainly because better terms could be obtained from insurance companies and friendly societies.

Government Broker. The broker who acts on the stock exchange on behalf of the Government to buy or sell Government stocks in order to influence their price and, therefore, the prevailing rate of interest on such stocks. Officially, he is broker to the National Debt Commissioners.

Government Ordinary Expenditure and Revenue. As shown in the budget, it is mainly current as distinct from capital, expenditure, and revenue. *See* Budget.

Government Securities. Funded stocks and Treasury bills.

Government Stocks. Usually known as gilt-edged, these are the funded loans of the British Government, being known under various names, such as Consols, Treasury Stocks, Exchequer Stock, Funding Loan, etc.

Government Training Centres. These were set up under the Industrial Training Act (1964) to train labour for skilled work and to retrain labour that has become redundant in declining industries for other work.

Grace, Days of. *See* Days of Grace.

Grading. Some imported raw materials and foodstuffs can be graded with a high degree of accuracy so that it is not necessary for the commodity itself to be present when a deal takes place. This is the case with raw cotton and wheat. The effect is that dealings tend to take place by private treaty, whereas when the commodity cannot be very accurately graded its quality has to be tested by prospective buyers at the time of purchase and it is then usually sold by auction. Also where commodities can be easily graded dealings in futures (*q.v.*) can take place.

Graduated Pension Scheme. The National Insurance Act (1959) brought into operation, from April 1961, a new graduated pension scheme, contributions and retirement pensions being graduated, within certain limits, according to earnings. Where private pension schemes were in operation the operators (but not individuals) were able to contract out of the new scheme on behalf of all members of the scheme. An improved scheme was introduced in 1969, contributions to which began in 1972. Further improvements were made in 1975.

Grand National Consolidated Trades Union. The earliest large trade union, its formation in 1834 being encouraged by Robert Owen. Membership was open to all workers, whatever their trade, and its membership at one period totalled over a million, but opposition at the time to trade unions caused its decline.

Grants-in-aid. Grants made by the Government to local authorities to supplement their revenue from the levying of rates. *See* Block Grant; Rate Deficiency Grants.

Gratuity. Sometimes known as a Lump Sum, it is an amount payable under some pension schemes at the time when the pension is due to commence. It is not liable to income tax. *See also* 'Golden Handshake'.

Great Depression. The period of low economic activity and very high unemployment which characterised the greater part of the period between the two World Wars, and more particularly the years 1929–35, when it became world-wide. In the primary producing countries its feature was very low prices, in the manufacturing countries very high unemployment, highest in the United States, followed by Germany and then Great Britain. The trade cycle had been a feature of economic life in the nineteenth century and down to 1914, but the periods of depression had been short and soon followed by equally short booms. The Great Depression did not, however, affect all industries and districts to the same extent. In Great Britain it was the period of the expansion of the motor car industry and many light industries in south-east England. In the midlands and south-east England unemployment was much less severe than the national average, and there was some drift of population to these parts from those more severely affected. The areas of highest unemployment were those in which the old-established heavy industries were situated—County Durham, South Wales, South Lancashire, West Cumberland, and Clydeside. In the worst parts of these so-called depressed areas unemployment was exceptionally high. At first Governments did very little, apart from the payment of unemployment benefit and public assistance, as most economists still believed that demand creates its own supply, and therefore it was expected that the situation would right itself in time. In the United States Roosevelt introduced his 'New Deal' policy, and towards the end of the period most Governments attempted some relief, though without a great deal of success. Relief eventually came with rearmament and the outbreak of war, though it took some years of war before unemployment disappeared in Great Britain. It was to try to prevent the recurrence of a depression that many Governments after the Second World War accepted responsibility for the maintenance of full employment.

Great Exhibition (1851). *See* Exhibition.

Great Western Railway. Former British Railway, nationalised in 1947, its oldest line was the one from London to Bristol, opened in 1841. Until 1892 it operated on a wider gauge than the standard 4 ft 8½ in, but to facilitate through running it had to fall into line with the other railways.

Greenbacks. An American fiduciary note issue, first issued by the U.S. Treasury in 1862.

Green Belt. An area on the periphery of a conurbation scheduled to be left in its existing conditions, and not to be built upon or developed in any other way without special permission of the Ministry of Housing and Local Government (under the Department of the Environment), which took over the function of the former Ministry of Town and Country Planning.

Green Label Service. A number of countries agree to permit articles liable to customs duty to be sent by post. In such cases a special green label must be attached to the letter or packet. The service applies between the United Kingdom and the Channel Islands and the Irish Republic.

Green Paper. An official paper issued by the Government, setting out in general terms proposed legislation with relevant background information. It is intended to be for discussion only. *Cf.* White Paper; Blue Book.

Greenwood Act (1930). A Housing Act, Mr. A. Greenwood being Minister of Health at the time, it regulated the housing subsidies in order to make it possible to rehouse slum dwellers at rents within their means.

Gresham's Law. A statement generally attributed to Gresham, finance minister of Elizabeth I, that 'bad money drives out good', people always tending to hoard good money and spend bad money when the two forms of money are in circulation at the same time.

Grey Area. A popular term for an Intermediate Area (*q.v.*).

Groat. An English silver coin, worth fourpence, first struck in 1279, although not regularly issued until 1351, when half groats also were issued. It was revived in 1838 as the fourpenny piece but was withdrawn from circulation in 1901. It remains in use nowadays only in the form of Maundy Money (*q.v.*).

Grocers' Company. One of the twelve more important of the 82 Guilds or Livery Companies of the City of London, and ranking second in order of civic precedence. Its existence dates back to the gilds of the Middle Ages, although it did not receive its final charter until 1428, by which time the power of the gilds had considerably declined.

Grocers' Institute. A body which concerns itself with matters of interest to grocers, it encourages the education and training of grocers by organising examinations which lead up to the M.G.I. (Member of the Grocers' Institute) qualification. It also awards the higher qualification of F.G.I. (Fellow of the Grocers' Institute).

Groschen. A unit of the Austrian currency, 100 groschen being equal to one schilling.

Grossbanken. The 'Big Three' German commercial banks—the Deutsche Bank, the Dresdener Bank, and the Commerzbank.

Gross Domestic Product. The money value of all the goods and services produced within a country but excluding net income from abroad. The Gross National Product (*q.v.*) includes net income from abroad.

Gross Fixed Investment. The addition during a period of time—usually a year—to a country's stock of fixed capital without making any allowance for the depreciation of existing fixed capital. *See also* Net Investment.

Gross Income. A person's total income from all sources before deduction of tax.

Grossing up. Increasing the amount of interest for income tax purposes where it has been paid free of basic tax, as with interest paid by building societies.

Gross Interest. The amount of interest receivable on an investment before payment of tax.

Gross National Product. This is the money value of all the goods and services produced in the country during one year at factor cost, *i.e.* excluding indirect taxes such as V.A.T.:

It comprises goods and services produced by:
    Agriculture, forestry, and fishing
    Manufacture, mining, building, public utilities
    Transport, distribution
    Insurance, banking, finance
    Dwelling-houses
    Services provided by local authorities
    Domestic services to households
    Net income from abroad
    Other services
    Stock appreciation

A deduction for capital consumption gives National Income (*q.v.*).

Gross Profit. Total profit before expenses have been deducted. On a single article the gross profit is the difference between the seller's buying price and his selling price, no account being taken of the expenses he has had to incur in order to effect the sale. Gross profit in this case is often known as the mark-up. To calculate the gross profit of a business for a trading period of (say) six months it is necessary to draw up a Trading Account. A specimen Trading Account for the period July 1st to December 31st for a firm is shown on p. 233. In order to draw up a Trading Account it is necessary to

Trading Account

		£			£
July 1	To opening stock	600	Dec. 31	By sales (*less* returns)	9,800
Dec. 31	To purchases (*less* returns)	6,700		,, closing stock	500
	,, balance (being gross profit)	3,000			
		10,300			10,300

take stock at the beginning and end of the period under review. *See also* Net Profit.

Gross Yield. The rate of return on a security before payment of tax. Where there is no date of redemption it is a flat yield, for example $2\frac{1}{2}\%$ Consols, purchased at £50, give a gross flat yield of 5%. On the other hand a stock bearing nominal interest of 3% and purchased at £80 and dated 1980–85 would give a gross yield to the latest date of $3\frac{3}{4}\%+$ a capital gain of £20 spread over the years from the date of purchase to the date of redemption, the gross yield being over 5%.

Ground Rent. An annual payment for a specified number of years—99 or even 999—paid in the case of leasehold property to the owner of the land.

Groupement. A term used of a group of seven banks in Geneva which act together in connection with international accounts.

Group Insurance. Members of many professional and other organisations can obtain better terms of insurance—particularly life assurance—as a group than as individuals. There are two reasons for this: (i) reduction of the cost of administration; (ii) the expectation of life of certain groups of people is much higher than the general average.

Group of Companies. A number of companies associated together, usually as a result of amalgamation or take-overs, a majority of the shares of the larger ones being in the hands of a holding company, many of the smaller companies being under the control in a similar way to the larger, so that in effect all are under one control. In some cases the shareholding arrangements are very complicated by cross-holdings between companies.

Group of Ten. A group of ten countries which agreed to lend if required to the I.M.F. to increase its lending resources. The following are the ten countries concerned: the United States, the United Kingdom, West Germany, France, Italy, Japan, Canada, the Netherlands, Belgium and Sweden. The original agreement was for four years but it has been extended indefinitely. Amounts lent to the I.M.F. are repayable in five years—or earlier if the lending country finds itself with a deficit in its balance of payments. The Group of Ten has extended its original functions and co-operated with the Bank for International Settlements (*q.v.*) in giving assistance to the U.K. in the sterling crises of 1964–65, 1967–68 and 1975–76. The Group was responsible for the new currency parities agreed in 1971. *See* Basle Arrangements.

Group Trading. A method by which wholesalers and independent retailers, more particularly in the grocery trade, attempt to compete on more equal terms with multiple shops and some department stores. A wholesale concern attaches to it a group of independent retailers who agree to make bulk purchases of different commodities from time to time at lower prices. This then enables the retailer to cut the prices of his goods, often sold in slightly larger quantities than consumers have been used to purchasing. Price cutting of branded goods began after the passing of the Restrictive Trade

Practices Act (1956) and increased after the Resale Prices Act (1964) (*qq.v.*) was passed.

Growth. *See* Economic Growth.

Growth Stock. A stock or share which can be expected to appreciate in value in the future, the policy of the directors of the company being to plough back each year a considerable portion of the profits for the purposes of expansion. Because of their 'growth' possibilities such shares tend to have a rather high price on the stock exchange and a rather low current rate of yield, and are bought mainly for long-term investment.

Growth Zone. A term used since 1963 for districts of particular promise for industrial development.

Guarani. The standard unit of the currency of Paraguay, it is divided into 100 centimes.

Guarantee. 1. An undertaking given by a manufacturer regarding the quality of a product. *See* Warranty.

2. Under the Companies Act the liability of a company may be limited by guarantee and it may be formed with no capital, the members being liable. The liability of some professional organisations is limited in this way.

Guaranteed Prices. The prices of farm products guaranteed to British farmers by the Government under the Agriculture Act (1947). When the actual market prices of these products are below the guaranteed prices the Government makes up the difference by 'Deficiency Payments' (*q.v.*).

Guaranteed Stocks. Stocks issued either as compensation to the previous owners of nationalised industries or issued by the nationalised industries themselves in order to increase their capital, in either case guaranteed by the British Government, and therefore ranking as gilt-edged stock. Guaranteed stocks include the various Gas, Electricity, and Transport Stocks.

Guaranteed Wage. A system whereby employees are guaranteed a minimum payment per week. It aims to overcome the evils of casual employment of labour and was introduced after the Second World War for dockers.

Guarantor. Though a bank may be unwilling to grant a loan to one person it may do so if a second person stands guarantor for him, that is, undertakes to repay the loan if the borrower fails to do so.

Guardian Royal Exchange Assurance Co. Ltd. Formed in 1968 by a merger of the Guardian Assurance Co. Ltd. (founded 1821) and the Royal Exchange Assurance Co. Ltd. (founded 1720) and many smaller companies. The Royal Exchange Assurance Co. Ltd. shared with the London Assurance Co. Ltd. the distinction of being the oldest assurance company in the United Kingdom.

Guardians of the Poor. Persons appointed under the Poor Law Amendment Act (1834) to administer the Poor Law in each union (area). At first they were appointed by the Justices of the Peace, but later they were elected. Boards of Guardians were abolished in 1929 and their duties transferred to public assistance committees of local authorities.

Guild. *See* Gild.

Guilder. The standard unit of the currency of the Netherlands, alternatively known as a Florin. It is divided into 100 cents.

Guild Socialism. A form of socialism whose supporters believe that different forms of production should be organised in associations somewhat similar to the medieval gilds and managed by the members of the trade concerned, the local gilds to be federated into a national association.

Guillebaud Report. 1. **(1956).** This report reviewed the prospective cost of the Health Service. Although it was found that during the previous five years the net cost of the service had risen by 16%, this was no more than 3% if the general decline in the value of money was taken into account. The Committee was of the opinion that during the ensuing years the Health Service would cost about 8% more (unless further increased by a fall in the value of money), partly due to the expected increase in population and partly to the increasing number of old people. The Committee recommended an annual expenditure of £30 million on hospitals during seven years 1958–65.

2. **(1960).** The report of a committee which inquired into the rates of pay of railway workers. It accepted the 'principle of comparability' (*q.v.*), that is, that railway workers should be paid wages similar to those in comparable occupations.

Guinea. A coin first issued in Great Britain in 1663, most of the gold coins issued before that date having ceased to be issued on account of the appreciation of gold in terms of silver. The coin derives its name from the fact that the first guineas were made from gold imported from the Guinea Coast of West Africa by the African Company. It was made of gold 11/12 fine like the later sovereign and at first was worth £1. By 1696 its value had been raised to £1·30 but it was reduced to £1·07½ in 1669 and to £1·05 in 1717, the value by which it is best known. Five-guinea pieces, two-guinea pieces, half guineas, and quarter guineas, of proportionate value, were also issued. In 1797, during the Napoleonic War, gold coins were withdrawn from circulation, but when cash payments were resumed in 1821 after the war it was superseded by the sovereign worth £1, as being a more convenient denomination. The guinea, however, was retained in England as a means of pricing some goods and professions fees until the decimalisation of the currency in 1971, after which no further prices were to be quoted in guineas.

G.U.S. Abbreviation of Great Universal Stores Ltd., a holding company controlling a number of multiple shop organisations.

H

Haberdashers' Company. One of the twelve more important of the 82 Guilds or Livery Companies of the City of London, ranking eighth in order of civic precedence. Its existence dates back to the gilds of the Middle Ages, although it did not receive its charter until 1448.

Habit. One of the influences on demand which results in consumers continuing to buy the same quantity of a commodity as before in spite of a change of price, simply because they have acquired a habit of buying it. A good deal of ordinary personal expenditure is incurred too from habit, though a steep rise in price will generally reduce consumption. Smoking is largely a matter of habit, and successive increases in taxation have done little to check the consumption of tobacco, although in this case there is also the effect of its being a mild drug.

Hackney Carriage. Legally any vehicle which plies for hire, and so the term includes not only taxi-cabs, but all public service vehicles using the roads.

Haggling. Bargaining over prices as an alternative to fixed prices for commodities. Most consumers' goods have prices attached to them by the sellers nowadays, although some goods—antiques and second-hand goods—may be subject to haggling over price before being sold.

Half-crown. An English coin, first issued in 1526 as a gold coin worth one eighth of £1, and then as a silver coin in 1552, but later consisting of an alloy of cupro-nickel. The half-crown was demonetised and withdrawn from circulation in January 1970.

Half Farthing. These coins circulated intermittently between 1542 and 1569 and were revived for a short period in the reign of Queen Victoria.

Half Guinea. An English gold coin, issued between 1663 and 1797. *See* Guinea.

Halfpenny. The penny of sterling silver is the oldest English coin and dates back to the eighth century. For a long time it was permissible to cut pennies into halves or quarters for small payments. The first silver halfpenny coins were issued about the year 900 but did not circulate for long. They were revived in 1279 by Edward I. After the debasement of the coinage in the time of Henry VIII silver halfpennies ceased to be minted, and when the halfpenny reappeared it was made of copper, and later bronze. The halfpenny was demonetised and withdrawn from circulation in August 1969. The decimalised halfpenny was issued in 1971.

Half Sovereign. The ryal or royal was the ancestor of the half sovereign. Gold half sovereigns, under that name, were first issued in 1544, though generally still referred to as ryals. Between 1663 and 1797 it was replaced by the half guinea, but when cash payments were resumed in 1821 after the Napoleonic Wars the half sovereign, a gold coin, returned to circulation. Along with the sovereign it was finally withdrawn from circulation in 1915.

Half-time System. The practice of children working for part of the day and attending school for the other part. This system was first introduced by the Factory Act of 1833 which made attendance at school for two hours per day compulsory for all children between 9 and 13 years of age who were employed in factories. In some parts of the country the half-time system persisted, though only for older children, down to the early years of the twentieth century. It was abolished by the Education Act of 1918.

Halifax Building Society. Founded in 1853, it is the largest building society in Great Britain, being formed by the amalgamation of the Halifax Permanent and the Halifax Equitable Building Societies. It is one of the few British building societies with branches (as distinct from agencies) throughout the country. Its only serious rival for size is the Abbey National, which is more than double the size of the third largest society, the Nationwide Building Society. *See* Building Society.

Hallmarks. Stamps on gold or silver articles to indicate that they have been tested and conform to the requirements of purity. They were first instituted in the reign of Edward I, and Assay Offices, each with its own distinctive stamp, were set up to carry out the testing. The number of such offices has been reduced to four, those still functioning being at London (Goldsmith's Hall), Sheffield, Birmingham, and Edinburgh.

Halsbury Committee. A committee set up in 1961 'to advise on the most convenient and practical form which a decimal coinage might take' in Great Britain, to advise on the changeover and to estimate the probable cost. The Committee published its report in 1963, four of the six members favouring the retention of the present £1 divided into 100 cents together with a half-cent coin, the other two members preferring a new unit equal to 10s. in value divided into 100 cents. *See also* Decimal Coinage.

Halsey System. A bonus system of wage payment whereby the worker can earn a bonus equal to half the hourly rate for time saved on a piece of work to which a standard time has been given.

Hambros Bank Ltd. A merchant bank established in 1839 with head office in London, it also undertakes ordinary banking business. It controls Laidlow & Co. of New York and it has subsidiaries in San Francisco and Milan.

Hammered. This occurs when an announcement is made at the London Stock Exchange that a member has defaulted. The term takes its name from the fact that officials hammered for silence before making the announcement. Since 1970 the new London Stock Exchange has used a bell.

Handicapped Persons. Under the Disabled Persons (Employment) Act (1944) the Ministry of Labour (now Department of Employment) maintains a register of disabled persons, arranges courses of training, and employs some of them in its own factories run by Remploy Ltd.

Hang Seng. Index of the Hong Kong stock exchange. Started in 1964 by the Hang Seng Bank (hence its name), but taken over in 1969 by the Hong Kong stock exchange.

Hanseatic League. A medieval trading association of German cities which also for a time wielded political influence in the areas of western Europe with which they traded. The earliest members of the league were Hamburg and Lübeck, with Cologne, Brunswick and Danzig joining later. The League maintained agencies or 'factories' in London, Bruges, Bergen, and Novgorod. At its greatest extent the League included over eighty cities.

Harbour Dues. Payments made by shipowners for the use of port installations by their ships.

Hard Currency. A term used of a currency which is in short supply in relation to the demand for it by other countries. The term was applied particularly to the U.S. dollar in the years following the Second World War when there was a huge demand for the exports of the United States at a time when many countries found it difficult to produce and export their own goods, on account of the ruinous effect of the war on their internal economies.

Harmony of Interests. Some writers on economics, following the notion of Adam Smith's *Invisible Hand*, formerly thought that economic forces always brought about a community or harmony of interests between the individual and society as a whole.

Harvest Theory of the Trade Cycle. The theory put forward by Jevons that the trade cycle had its origin in harvest fluctuations, sometimes known as the 'Sun-spot' theory because fluctuations in harvests were thought by some people to be related to sun spots. In modern conditions agriculture is of much less importance than manufacturing. *See* Trade Cycle, Causes of.

'Hat Money.' An alternative colloquial term for Primage (*q.v.*).

Havana Charter. A document drawn up by the conference held at Havana in 1947–48 with the aim of establishing an International Trade Organisation. Though this idea was not fully accepted, it led to the establishment of G.A.T.T. (the General Agreement on Tariffs and Trade) (*q.v.*).

Hawker. An itinerant salesman, the distinction between a hawker and a pedlar being that the hawker carries his goods on a vehicle whereas the pedlar carries his wares on his back. With the exception of a few commodities like fish and coal, a hawker must first obtain a licence before he can carry on his trade.

Hawthorne Experiment. An experiment carried out by the Western Electric Co. at Chicago 1929–32, it showed that many employees worked harder and were more likely to give of their best when they felt themselves to belong to a small group or team, the other members of which they came to know personally.

Health and Morals of Apprentices Act (1802). The first Factory Act to be passed in Great Britain, it limited to twelve the hours of work of apprentices working in cotton and woollen mills.

Health and Safety at Work etc. Act (1974). This Act makes any breach of the new safety and health regulations a *criminal* offence.

Health and Social Security, Department of. A Government department created in 1968 by the merging of the Ministry of Health and the Ministry of Social Security, its political head is the Secretary for Social Services. The department is responsible for the administration of the National Health Service and the welfare services of local authorities in England and Wales. Supplementary benefits and war pensions also come within its scope. Separate divisions of the department concern themselves with the hospital service, medical, dental, pharmaceutical and nursing services.

Health Insurance. *See* National Health Service; National Insurance.

Health, Ministry of. Created in 1919 to be responsible for matters relating not only to health but also to housing and local government. Its housing and local government functions were transferred in 1951 to a Ministry of Housing and Local Government (later absorbed into the Department of the Environment), as the establishment of the National Health Service had given it much additional work. Since 1951, therefore, it has been almost entirely concerned with health, medical, and hospital services. In 1968 it was combined with the Ministry of Social Security to form the Department of Health and Social Security. *See* Health and Social Security, Department of.

Health Service. *See* National Health Service.

Hearth Money. A tax imposed during the seventeenth century on houses, according to the number of hearths each possessed, at the rate of 2*s*. per hearth, the aim being to impose a larger tax on the larger house. *See also* Houses, Taxation of.

Hedging. Action taken to mitigate fluctuations in prices. The best examples are markets in futures, where a gain on futures may offset a loss incurred by a change of price, or vice versa. An investor can hedge against inflation by purchasing equities, instead of putting all his money in gilt-edged stocks, since, other things being equal, a general fall in the value of money will be offset by a rise in the money value of equities (ordinary shares).

Heller. A sub-unit of the currency of Czechoslovakia, 100 heller being equal to one koruna.

Hemp. A commodity which served as money for a time in the British colonies of North America.

Herbert Committee. A Committee appointed to inquire into the Electricity Supply Industry, 1956. It recommended that the central authority should cease to be responsible for the generation and transmission of electricity, these functions to be left to a new body known as the Central Electricity Generating Board. This became law in 1958.

Hereditaments. A legal term denoting property which must be bequeathed to the heir to an estate unless disposed of by will or during the lifetime of the previous owner.

Her Majesty's Stationery Office. Official institution, established 1786, to be responsible for all Government publications—White Papers, Blue Books, Reports, etc. Retail business is also undertaken, and in addition to the London offices, there are branch retail departments at Manchester, Edinburgh, Cardiff, Birmingham, Bristol, and Belfast.

Heyworth Committee (1965). A Committee that proposed the setting up of a Social Science Research Council.

'Hidden Hand.' An alternative phrase to Adam Smith's *Invisible Hand*, it implied that in general—though not always—whatever the individual did in the economic sphere for his own advantage set in motion forces ('the Hidden Hand') which made such action also to the advantage of the community as a whole.

Hidden Price Increase. This occurs when the price of the commodity or service remains unchanged but the quality of the commodity or service is reduced.

Hidden Reserve. If the assets of a firm have been deliberately undervalued, perhaps because their value has increased, the difference between their value as shown in the firm's balance sheet and their real value provides the firm with a 'hidden reserve', of which most shareholders will be unaware. The Companies Act (1948) stated that a company's balance sheet should show its true financial position. Only banks and insurance companies were to be permitted not to make a full disclosure of their position. Following the passing of the Companies Act (1967) efforts were made to bring these into line with other companies.

Hidden Tax. A term sometimes used of indirect taxes which are included in the prices of commodities without the amount being shown separately, as for example, in the case of cigarettes and whisky.

Hidden Unemployment. Alternative term for Disguised Unemployment (*q.v.*).

Higgling. *See* Haggling.

High Coupon. An investment yielding a high rate of interest.

Higher National Certificate and Diploma in Business Studies. *See* National Certificate in Business Education.

'Highs and Lows.' This phrase refers to the columns on the stock exchange page of a newspaper, especially papers like the *Financial Times* and *The Economist*, showing the highest and lowest prices for each stock and share over a stated period.

High Wages, Economy of. The theory that higher wages are advantageous to employers since they increase the efficiency of the workers. This will be the case if the higher wages increase the physical well-being of the workers. In underdeveloped countries low wages are often associated with a low level of efficiency. There is no doubt that to increase the wages of workers who are being paid little more than a bare subsistence wage will increase their efficiency, though it may take a little time for this to take effect.

Highway. A general term covering not only roads but footpaths and bridle paths. In early days the maintenance of highways was the responsibility of the people in the areas through which they passed, each male adult having to give so many days' work per year, this later being commuted to a money payment. The idea survived for a long time and during the nineteenth century the local authorities became responsible for the maintenance of the roads within their areas. During the eighteenth and early nineteenth centuries turnpike trusts (*q.v.*) were established to improve and maintain stretches of road by the levying of tolls on vehicles passing along them. The expansion of the railways and the decline of road traffic eventually caused the turnpike trusts to be wound up. The gradual return of traffic to the roads with the development of the motor vehicle presented a serious problem to the mainly rural counties through which main roads passed carrying traffic between places outside the county. The classification of roads as 'A' and 'B' roads had alleviated the problem to some extent, the State bearing half the cost of the 'A' roads and a smaller proportion of the cost of 'B' roads, only unclassified roads being wholly maintained by the local authorities. This classification of roads also led to the numbering of roads to assist travellers. In 1936, however, the Trunk Roads Act declared that certain main roads, used mainly by through traffic, should be designated trunk roads and be maintained entirely by the State. The most modern development has been the construction of special motorways. During 1935-39 Germany built roads of this type, mainly for military purposes, most of the ordinary German roads being very poor. Since 1960 Great Britain has followed the example of Germany, Italy, and some other countries in embarking on a programme of motorway building. In some countries tolls are charged on such roads. *See* Motorways; Road Transport.

Highway Authority. For all roads except trunk roads (*q.v.*) the county councils are the Highway Authorities. The Ministry of Transport is responsible for trunk roads.

Highways Act (1959). A consolidating Act, it brought together all matters dealt with by the Trunk Roads Acts of 1936 and 1946 and earlier legislation affecting highways. *See* Highways Authority; Trunk Roads.

Hilary Scott Report (1973). The report of a committee appointed to consider the law relating to unit-linked assurance. It commented favourably on the standards adopted by companies offering these plans, although it recommended a number of additional legal safeguards.

Hill, Samuel & Co. Ltd. A London merchant bank, established in 1831, it has interests in Australia, New York, South, West, and Central Africa. A portion of its shares is held by the First National City Bank of New York. It also has an interest in International Factors, a factoring company.

Hinterland. Originally a geographical term for the area behind a port on which its trade mainly depends. The term has been extended to mean a Shopping Hinterland, the area from which a city that is an important shopping centre draws its customers. *See* Shopping Hinterland.

Hire Purchase. The features of hire purchase are that usually a deposit has to be paid and the rest of the purchase price is spread over a period—six months, two years, or sometimes even longer, the article being regarded as the property of the seller until the final payment has been made. The purchase of relatively expensive goods has always been difficult for people who find it hard to save up the purchase price in advance, and it was to overcome this difficulty that hire purchase was introduced, first in the United States and later in Great Britain. At first hire purchase transactions were limited to relatively expensive durable goods, the sale of which could be greatly expanded by this method of sale. As a result it has spread to the sale of a wide range of articles, including less durable things like clothing. In the early days of hire purchase the more unscrupulous salesmen often took advantage of customers to persuade them to buy more than they could afford, with the result that many failed to keep up with their payments and the seller was able to reclaim the goods. In Great Britain the first Act to protect those who wish to buy in this way was passed in 1938. This stated that the cash price of all goods should be clearly shown, so that the customer if he wishes can calculate how much more he will have to pay if he buys on hire purchase. The Act further laid it down that if the customer had paid more than one-third of the total amount due the retailer could reclaim the article only if he first obtained an order of the court to do so. This Act applied only to goods up to a maximum value of £100, but following the fall in the value of money an Act of 1954 raised the amount to £300, the idea being that it was only the poorer people who required to be protected. An Act of 1964 raised the limit to £2,000, and introduced a three days' 'cooling-off' period.

At first, the financing of hire purchase transactions was undertaken by the retailers concerned, and some of the larger firms continue to do so. In other cases retailers may borrow from the commercial banks, but nowadays most hire purchase is financed by specialist finance companies, which raise the finance partly by themselves borrowing from commercial banks and partly by accepting deposits from the general public and offering a high rate of interest to attract such deposits. All the large English commercial banks have controlling interests in finance companies.

The variations in the terms under which hire purchase can be undertaken has in recent years become an important adjunct to monetary policy. When the British monetary authorities wish to curtail demand hire purchase regulations are stiffened by increasing the minimum deposit and reducing the period of repayment, and in some branches of retail trade this has proved a very effective method of checking demand. If it is desired to expand demand to combat unemployment hire purchase regulations are relaxed, the initial deposit reduced and the length of the period of repayment increased, and again in some branches of retail trade this has often had the desired effect. Thus, hire purchase became one of a variety of instruments used to implement monetary policy, alongside fiscal policy and the traditional instrument, bank rate. However, the Crowther Report (1971) recommended that hire purchase should be free from controls over the initial payment and the length of period for repayment. *See* Consumer Credit Act.

Historical School. A school of economic thought developed by those economists who wished to replace the deductive method of the Classical School by observations from past history.

Hives Committee. *See* National Council for Academic Awards.

H.M.S.O. Abbreviation of Her Majesty's Stationery Office (*q.v.*).

H.N.C. Abbreviation of Higher National Certificate. *See* National Certificate in Business Studies.

H.N.D. Abbreviation of Higher National Diploma. *See* National Certificates and Diplomas in Business Studies.

Hoarding. As used by Lord Keynes, this term refers to liquidity preference, interest being a reward for not hoarding. It means the mere accumulation of money as distinct from saving. In the case of hoarding, the money, temporarily at least, passes out of the economic system, whereas saving is a pre-requisite to real capital investment and so promotes production and employment. *See* Liquidity Preference.

Holder in Due Course. A person who takes a bill of exchange before it is due for payment, for value received, and in good faith that there

Holding Company. A purely financial concern which uses its capital to acquire controlling interests in other firms, sometimes as little as just over 50%, but often very much more than this, and sometimes obtaining the entire issue of ordinary shares. It is the modern method of bringing a number of firms under one control. A great advantage of this type of organisation is that the constituent firms—members of the 'group'—can retain their original names and the goodwill that goes with them. A serious drawback to the holding company, however, is that it makes possible what is known as pyramiding. At the top is the holding company which has a controlling interest in a number of companies, each one of which may have its own subsidiaries, and even some of these may have further subsidiaries. The total capital of all the companies under the control of the holding company may be many times greater than that of the holding company itself, and complete control of the whole group can be obtained by a person holding just over 50% of the shares of the holding company. Such control is made even easier where only a limited number of shares in a company carry voting rights, for this makes it possible for a person with only a small holding to have complete control over a company with total capital many times greater than the amount he holds. The holding company has become the principal type of organisation for large concerns in both Great Britain and the United States.

Holidays with Pay. Since 1938 most workers have been entitled to a certain number of days of holiday with pay, the length of such holidays tending to increase as the years go by. The effect of the Act was to increase the number of *insured* workers enjoying holidays with pay from 4 million to 15 million. Holidays with pay and the shorter working week are indirect methods of increasing the wage rate.

Home-grown Cereals Authority. A body set up under the Cereals Marketing Act (1965) to assist the marketing of wheat, barley, and oats grown in the United Kingdom.

Home Office. A government department of which the political head is the Secretary of State for Home Affairs. Its functions are of a varied kind, though from time to time as the work has expanded new ministries have been created to take over some of them. Perhaps its primary function nowadays is the maintenance of law and order. Therefore, it has control of the police, the treatment of offenders against the law, naturalisation of aliens, and indeed all internal matters not specifically assigned to other ministries.

Home Ownership. The number of people in Great Britain who 'own' their homes has increased enormously during the past fifty years. This has been made possible by the expansion of Building Societies, which accept deposits and use these funds to lend to people who wish to buy their homes, the method being to mortgage the property to the society for a stated number of years, during which the amount owing is usually paid off in equal instalments. The amount of the loan may be as much as 90% (occasionally even more), and repayment may be spread over twenty-five or even thirty years, though obviously the longer the period of the loan the greater the total amount of interest that will have to be paid.

Home Safe. A locked money box, issued by some banks, which retain the keys, to encourage small savers by preventing easy access to their savings while they keep them at home.

Homestead Act (1862). An Act passed by the Government of the United States, it gave every citizen over the age of 21 the right to 160 acres of land free of charge provided that he cultivated it himself for at least five years.

Home Trade. The branch of commerce comprising wholesaling and retailing (*qq.v.*).

Homework. The practice of supplying raw materials to workers who then produce the finished article at home, their payment depending on the amount of work done. The practice was prevalent in England under the Domestic System (*q.v.*), especially in the woollen industry of the West Riding of Yorkshire, merchants supplying cottage workers with raw wool and collecting from them the finished cloth. In England, the last large-scale industry to be carried on in this way was the boot and shoe industry, which became a factory industry only in the early years of the twentieth century.

Homogeneous Commodity. One of the assumptions of perfect competition (*q.v.*) and the perfect market is that all units of a commodity are identical with one another. For the condition of perfect oligopoly (*q.v.*) this assumption is also made.

Homogeneous Factor. A factor of production every unit of which is identical with every other unit.

Hong Kong and Shanghai Banking Corporation. A Far Eastern Bank with its head office in Hong Kong but with an office in London, it controls the Mercantile Bank and the British Bank of the Middle East (both with head offices in London) and the Hong Kong and Shanghai Banking Corporation of California. It also has an interest in the Roy West Banking Corporation. It has over 200 branches.

Honorarium. A voluntary payment of a fee for a service which the payee would not himself demand.

Honour. To meet an obligation when it is due, as with a bill of exchange or cheque.

Hoover Moratorium. A plan agreed upon in 1931 at the suggestion of President Hoover of the United States that for a period of one year all payments between the Allies of the First World War, arising out of that war, and all reparations payments by the powers defeated in that war, should be suspended.

Hops Marketing Board. One of the Marketing Boards established in 1931 under the Agriculture Act. Only farmers who were permitted by the Board were allowed to grow hops, each being allotted a quota. *See* Marketing Boards.

Horizontal Amalgamation. An amalgamation of firms at the same stage of production as, for example, a group of firms all engaged in dyeing or in cotton spinning.

Horizontal Integration. With reference to the structure of an industry it is the tendency for firms to specialise in single processes instead of undertaking the entire production of the commodity from start to finish. The worsted section of the West Riding wool textile industry consists mainly, but not entirely, of firms which specialise in this way. Horizontal integration, therefore, occurs where there is regional division of labour.

Horizontal Mobility. A change of occupation where no change occurs —or is thought to occur—in the status of the worker. *Cf.* Vertical Mobility.

Horticultural Society, Royal. A society to promote the study and practice of horticulture founded in 1805 and incorporated in 1809.

'Hot Money.' Short-term capital movements from one country to another seeking either a higher rate of interest or, more often, safety of capital irrespective of the rate of interest. Such capital movements can have a very disturbing effect on a country's balance of payments on capital account and, therefore, on its reserves.

Houblon-Norman Awards. Fellowships and grants to aid research into the working of industry and finance in Great Britain and elsewhere awarded by the Trustees of the Houblon-Norman Fund.

Hours of Work. In the early days of the Factory System employees had to work very long hours, mainly because it had been customary for those employed on the land and for those who worked at home under the domestic system to work long hours. However, long hours in a factory are more onerous than in either of the earlier cases. Gradually the Factory Acts have reduced the number of hours of work. During the past twenty years trade unions in most countries, especially in the United States and Great Britain, have aimed at reducing the length of the working week and increasing the amount of paid holidays. The extension of automation should make possible a further reduction in hours, though its main effect is more likely to be a release of labour to meet the increasing demand for service occupations.

House Duty. A tax imposed in 1778 on inhabited houses. *See* Houses, Taxation of.

Housekeeping Money. If a husband gives his wife a certain sum each week as housekeeping money, half of any amount not spent is legally the property of the husband, and could be reclaimed in a court of law, but if the husband makes his wife an allowance, out of which she has to pay for the housekeeping, any balance after meeting this expenditure remains her property.

Houses, Taxation of. In the seventeenth century there was the Hearth Tax, each inhabited house being taxed according to the number of hearths. This was replaced by the Windows Tax, houses being taxed according to the number of their windows, the tax rising from 4s. for those with under ten windows to 8s. for those with over twenty. The Windows Tax was modified in 1775, so that every house was taxed at 3s. together with 2d. for those with not more than seven windows, rising to 2s. for those with twenty-five or more. Adam Smith described the Windows Tax as inequitable—although he regarded taxation of houses generally as equitable—since an expensive house in London might have fewer windows than a fairly cheap house in the country. Local Rates (*q.v.*) are a method of taxing houses and other property approximately according to their annual rent which is supposed to determine their rateable value. There are many objections to basing local taxation on the rateable value of houses, for although by and large it does bear some relation to the income of the owner or occupier, it is not related closely enough to ability to pay. On the other hand it has the advantage of being a locally based tax. Until 1963 owner-occupiers also had to pay income tax (Schedule A) on the notional income (*q.v.*) derived from their property.

Housing Acts. Housing problems in Great Britain date back to the Industrial Revolution and the rapid growth of ill-planned industrial towns. The first Act relating to housing was passed in 1851, giving local authorities power to build housing suitable for artisans. The Public Health Act of 1875 made it compulsory to provide drainage and sanitation. A number of Commissions were held to inquire into housing during the latter part of the nineteenth century, and culminated in the Act of 1890 which consolidated previous legislation on the subject. It made possible the clearance of slum areas by giving local authorities powers for the compulsory purchase of land. They were also permitted to build houses. The Act of 1909 was the first of many Acts relating to town planning. The Acts passed immediately after the First World War were to encourage the building of houses that could be let at low rents, and to do this subsidies were granted both to local authorities and to private builders of small houses. These Acts included the Addison Act of 1919, the Neville Chamberlain Act of 1923, the Wheatley Act of 1924, and the Greenwood Act of 1930 (*qq.v.*), the last-named being mainly concerned with slum clearance. After the Second World War further Housing Acts were passed relating to subsidised house building and slum clearance, with other Acts relating to town planning. An Act of 1949 empowered local authorities to provide new houses for *all* sections of the community. The Housing Act of 1957 consolidated all previous legislation on the subject, with sections relating to compulsory purchase of land, slum clearance, overcrowding, the building of new houses, etc. The Housing Act of 1961 imposed additional duties on landlords to maintain dwellings with leases of less than seven years.

Housing and Local Government. From 1919 to 1951 housing and local government was the concern of the Ministry of Health. In 1970 it became a division of the Department of the Environment (*q.v.*). *See also* Housing Acts.

Housing Boom. Often the forerunner of recovery from a trade depression, a housing boom is more likely to occur when interest rates are low. Because of the great variety of materials employed a housing boom stimulates a great variety of industries. Recovery from the Great Depression of 1929–35 began with a housing boom.

Housing Corporation. *See* Housing Societies.

Housing Finance Act (1972). *See* Rent, 3.

Housing Societies. Philanthropic bodies which built houses and charged rents only sufficient to cover the cost of maintenance. A number of these societies came into existence during 1850–1900. The idea was revived in the Housing Act (1961). The Housing Corporation was set up in 1964 to promote the growth of housing societies.

Housing Subsidies. Grants to Local Authorities and to private builders to enable them to build houses at a lower cost than the ordinary conditions of the time would allow. For example, high interest rates tend to check house building, especially the building of small houses to rent. It was to encourage the building of such houses that State subsidies were granted to house building after both World Wars. *See* Housing Acts.

H. P. Abbreviation of Hire Purchase (*q.v.*).

Hudson's Bay Company. A British trading company chartered in the reign of Charles II, the trade of the company being mainly in furs. The company was reorganised in 1863 and it still continues its activities.

Human Capital. Sometimes used as an alternative term for the factor of production, labour.

Human Relations in Industry. Since the contact between workers in modern industry is very considerable the 'human relations' problem has become an important one for the management of a firm. Workers must be treated as individual human beings, and not merely as units of the factor of production, labour, if the best use is to be made of them. Thus attention must be paid to all personal relationships that affect the worker and his work. Hence the increasing importance of the Personnel Officer and his staff, but other things for which the general management is more directly responsible, such as the environment in which employees have to work, etc., have to be taken into account as well. The advantage to the firm is seen in increased output.

Hunt Report (1969). The main recommendation was that in addition to Development Areas a number of other districts should be designated as Intermediate Areas (*q.v.*).

Husband's Responsibility for Wife's Expenditure. In the past a wife was regarded as the agent of her husband and thus could make purchases for which her husband had to pay. However, the Matrimonial Proceedings and Property Act 1970 abolished this procedure.

Hyperemployment. An alternative term for Over-full Employment, that is, a condition where the demand for labour greatly exceeds the available supply—a feature of inflation.

Hyperinflation. An alternative term for a 'runaway' or 'galloping' inflation, where so great an increase takes place in the amount of money in circulation that eventually it becomes almost worthless and a new currency has to be instituted. When statesmen speak of the 'danger of inflation' it means that they are afraid that a persistent inflation may get out of control and develop into a hyperinflation. In a hyperinflation all those people whose savings are in monetary form—bank deposits, Government securities, etc.—find that they cease to have any value. Consequently in the early stages of a hyperinflation there is an increasing desire to exchange money for real goods, and this only causes the inflation to proceed even more rapidly than before. In all cases of hyperinflation the value of the currency concerned has depreciated to a much greater extent than was warranted simply by the increase in the quantity of money. In the later stages of a hyperinflation, therefore, the increase in the velocity of circulation becomes more important than the increase in the quantity of money. Hyperinflations occurred in Germany, Austria, and Russia after the First World War, and in Hungary, Romania, Greece, and China after the Second World War, and, more recently, in several countries in South America.

Hypermarket. A particularly large supermarket, generally defined as one with more than 2,500 square metres of selling space. It is of American origin. Hypermarkets are usually located well away from town centres and provide extensive parking facilities for customers' cars. In Europe hypermarkets are most widely established in West Germany, France and Belgium. As yet there are very few retail establishments in the United Kingdom that can fairly be described as hypermarkets.

Hypothecation, Letter of. This often accompanies a documentary bill (*q.v.*) authorising the selling of the goods in the foreign centre for the best price obtainable if payment or acceptance of the bill is refused.

Hypothesis in Economics. A set of facts regarded for the purpose of argument as true and from which inferences can be drawn. In economics, Marshall declared, all assumptions on which an argument or deduction was based should be distinctly stressed, this being more necessary in economics than in other sciences because so much of the subject-matter is based on experience within the knowledge of many non-economists.

I

I.A.T.A. Abbreviation of International Air Transport Association (*q.v.*).

I.B. (or **I.B.R.D.**). Abbreviation of International Bank for Reconstruction and Development, often known as the World Bank (*q.v.*).

I.B. 1. Abbreviation of the insurance term Industrial Business (*q.v.*).
2. Abbreviation of Institute of Bankers.

I.B.A. Abbreviation of (i) Industrial Bankers' Association (*q.v.*), and (ii) Independent Broadcasting Authority.

I.B.M. Abbreviation of International Business Machines.

I.B.P. Abbreviation of International Biological Programme.

I.B.R.D. Abbreviation of International Bank for Reconstruction and Development (*q.v.*).

I.C.A. Abbreviation of International Co-operative Alliance (*q.v.*).

I.C.A.E.W. Abbreviation of Institute of Chartered Accountants of England and Wales. *See* Chartered Accountant.

I.C.A.O. Abbreviation of International Civil Aviation Organization (*q.v.*).

I.C.A.S. Abbreviation of Institute of Chartered Accountants of Scotland. *See* Chartered Accountant.

I.C.F.C. Abbreviation of Industrial and Commercial Finance Corporation (*q.v.*).

I.C.F.T.U. Abbreviation of International Confederation of Free Trade Unions (*q.v.*).

I.C.I. Abbreviation of Imperial Chemical Industries Ltd. (*q.v.*).

I.C.L. Abbreviation of International Computers Ltd.

I.C.M. Abbreviation of the Institute of Commercial Management.

I.C.M.A. Abbreviation of Institute of Cost and Management Accountants.

I.D.A. Abbreviation of International Development Association (*q.v.*).

I.D.A.C. Abbreviation of Import Duties Advisory Committee (*q.v.*).

I.E.A. Abbreviation of Institute of Economic Affairs (*q.v.*).

I.F.C. Abbreviation of International Finance Corporation (*q.v.*).

I.H.A. Abbreviation of Issuing Houses Association (*q.v.*).

Illth. A term used by Ruskin for goods of a useless or harmful kind produced because of a demand for them in contrast to wealth which to Ruskin comprised goods which added something to people's well-being. *See* Social Net Product.

I.L.O. Abbreviation of International Labour Organisation (*q.v.*).

I.M.F. Abbreviation of International Monetary Fund (*q.v.*).

Immature Creditor Nation. A country which has developed its resources sufficiently to have a favourable balance of trade, and having paid off debts incurred during its period of development is able to begin investing its trade surplus abroad.

Immature Debtor Nation. A country with resources not fully developed which is borrowing from abroad in order to develop them more quickly but which in the meantime has an adverse balance of payments, with probably an adverse balance of trade in the early stages of its development.

Immediate Annuity. *See* Annuity.

Immigrant Remittances. An adverse invisible item in a country's balance of payments as, for example, money sent back to relatives in Ireland by Irish immigrants to the United States, or by Italian workers in Switzerland to relatives in Italy, or by West Indian or Pakistani immigrants to Great Britain to their people at home.

Immigration. As a result of immigration many countries have received an influx of workers who have often provided a valuable addition to the labour force of the country receiving them. Thus, in the thirteenth century England received numbers of highly skilled Flemish weavers who had much to do with the development of woollen manufacturing in this country. In more recent times many highly qualified Jews, mainly German or Austrian, sought refuge in other countries which were glad to have them. During the nineteenth century the United States received large numbers of people from Great Britain and Ireland and later from other parts of Europe. Immigrants have often been attracted by the better economic conditions of the countries receiving them as compared with conditions in their former homes, but often too their reasons for seeking new homes have been religious or political persecution. Since 1938 Great Britain has received from Europe many people seeking political asylum, whereas people have come to this country from the West Indies and Pakistan mainly for economic reasons. Switzerland has received so many immigrants in recent years that 10% of its labour force now consists of foreign workers. In times of inflation and over-full employment when the demand for labour exceeds the supply immigrants are especially welcomed. Immigration in Great Britain comes under the jurisdiction of the Home Office. Immigration into the United Kingdom was restricted by the Immigration Act (1971).

Immobility. A term applied to factors of production which cannot easily be moved either (i) from one location to another, or (ii) from one type of employment to another. *See* Mobility.

I.M.O. Abbreviation of International Money Order (*q.v.*).

Impact Effect. A term used of the immediate effect of a change in Demand when Supply cannot immediately respond to the new situation. Thus, an increase in Demand, when Supply is fixed in the short run, may raise price in the short run to a higher lever than it will be when a new equilibrium has been established. Consider the follower diagram:

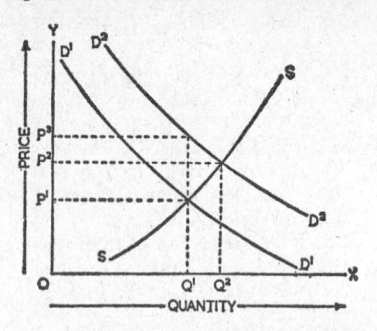

Before the change in demand occurred the equilibrium price was OP^1 at which the quantity supplied and demanded was OQ^1. The Impact Effect of an increase in demand from D^1 to D^2 is to raise price to OP^3, but after supply has readjusted itself to the new situation a new equilibrium will be established at price OP^2, at which the quantity OQ^2 will be both supplied and demanded.

Imperfect Competition. The general environment in which production and distribution take place under actual conditions at the present time. It lies between the two extremes of perfect competition and monopoly (*qq.v.*). In ordinary speech, however, the term monopoly is generally used to mean a condition of very imperfect competition. Theories of perfect competition and monopoly are relatively easy to develop owing to the ease of definition of both these conditions, but imperfect competition exists in a great variety of forms, ranging from near-monopoly at one extreme to nearly perfect competition at the other. Until thirty years ago economists thought that economic forces always tended towards an equilibrium of perfect competition, with monopoly as a rare and exceptional condition, so that before that time imperfect competition received scant, if any, attention at all. The publication of Joan Robinson's *Economics of Imperfect Competition* in England, and

Chamberlin's *Theory of Monopolistic Competition* about the same time in the United States, marked the beginning of the development of a study of economic theory in the environment of imperfect competition, that is, in conditions nearer to those of actual life. Sellers often combine together, or the expansion of an industry may be restricted by economic influences such as the fact of a large amount of capital being required or artificially by branding or patent rights. In consequence, competition has become imperfect, and these conditions are now the rule.

The great difficulty in formulating a theory of imperfect competition is that it takes many forms, so that only a few well-defined types can be closely studied. In conditions of perfect competition two conditions must be fulfilled: (i) there must be a large number of producers, each of whom produces so small a proportion of the total output of the commodity that he cannot seriously affect the total supply by restricting output; and (ii) the commodity must be homogeneous, so that buyers have no special preference for the product of any one producer. Under imperfect competition one or both of these conditions will be unfulfilled. Thus in one variety of imperfect competition there is a large number of producers but differentiation of product, this condition being known as monopolistic competition. In other types of imperfect competition there will be only a few producers and this gives rise to oligopoly, or duopoly if there are only two producers. Then there are two types of oligopoly, perfect where the commodity is homogeneous, and imperfect where there is differentiation of the product. *See* Duopoly; Imperfect Market; Monopolistic Competition; Oligopoly.

Imperfect Market. A market where the following conditions required for a perfect market are not completely fulfilled: (i) The commodity is homogeneous; (ii) There is a large number of both buyers and sellers; (iii) Buyers and sellers are in close touch with one another; (iv) There must be no favourable treatment of some buyers or discrimination against others; (v) The commodity must be transferable. Where these conditions are not fulfilled the market will be to some degree imperfect. Only a few markets come near to perfection, such as the stock exchange or a free market in foreign exchange. Wholesale markets are more nearly perfect than retail markets, the latter being notoriously imperfect. In retail markets it is impossible for all buyers to be in close touch with all sellers, since consumers are unwilling to waste time comparing the prices charged by all the sellers of a commodity even in the same town, and they often prefer one shop to another. Nor do they regard all brands of a commodity as homogeneous. The market in houses is imperfect because although the ownership is transferable, the commodity cannot be moved. *See* Imperfect Competition.

Imperfect Oligopoly. This occurs when the production of a commodity is in the hands of only a few producers, their products being differentiated in some way such as by branding. The extent of the differentiation may be quite small, and may be mainly due to the advertising campaigns conducted by the rival producers, each of whom attempts to make consumers believe that his brand is superior to all others. Thus, imperfect oligopoly often leads to 'cut-throat' competition, in the form of price wars or advertising wars.

Imperial Preference. A term used of the policy of granting a preferential tariff to countries of the British Empire. The idea was put forward in 1903 by Joseph Chamberlain, then Colonial Secretary, but his party was heavily defeated at the general election of 1906. Although the McKenna Duties of 1919 reduced the tariff on certain goods from the Empire, and the Empire Marketing Board was set up in 1926 to stimulate demand in Great Britain for Empire products, imperial preference could not be fully put into effect until Great Britain abandoned its free trade policy in 1932. At the Ottawa Conference, held later that year, the principle, on a reciprocal basis, was accepted. As a result trade between Great Britain and the Commonwealth expanded at a time when world trade generally was contracting. At the present day trade with other countries of both Great Britain and other members of the Commonwealth is expanding.

Impersonal Accounts. A bookkeeping term for a ledger account such as cash account or capital account in contrast to personal accounts.

Import Commission Agent. A person employed to obtain supplies, especially of commodities such as dairy produce, from abroad for an importer, such agents being paid on a commission basis. *See also* Commission Agent.

Import Deposit. A method of restricting imports first employed by the U.K. in 1968. This method was chosen because the U.K. has agreements with G.A.T.T. not to increase import duties. *See also* Import Restrictions; Import Surcharge.

Import Duties. Taxes imposed on goods entering a country, the purpose being either to increase the State's revenue or to protect home producers of the commodity by making the imported article dearer. Contrast Excise Duties, which are imposed on home-produced goods. *See* Customs Duties; Excise Duties.

Import Duties Act (1932). This Act, which imposed duties on a wide range of imports, marked Great Britain's departure from free trade.

Import Duties Advisory Committee. A body set up under the Import Duties Act (1932) to recommend to the Treasury any further import duties in addition to those imposed by the Act. In 1939 the Board of Trade took over its functions.

Import Entitlement Accounts. Under some systems of exchange control, exporters are credited with a certain percentage of the foreign currency they have earned, this amount being placed to their credit in Import Entitlement Accounts, from which payment can be made for imports.

Importer. A merchant to whom goods from abroad are consigned, either in response to direct orders or on consignment. In the latter case the importer will generally have to arrange to warehouse and then sell the goods for the best price obtainable, generally in the case of British imports on one of the organised produce exchanges, which are to be found in London or some other port. It will, too, be his responsibility to see that all necessary legal formalities are carried out at the port of entry.

Import-Export Bank. A U.S. institution established in 1961 to provide credit insurance for American exporters, it also provides cover against political risks. Its functions are somewhat similar to those of the Export Credits Guarantee Department of the British Department of Trade.

Import Licence. Under some systems of foreign exchange control merchants are only permitted foreign currency to pay for imports sanctioned by the monetary authorities. In such cases licences have to be obtained before goods can be imported. Similarly, where imports of certain goods are subject to quota restrictions, such goods can be imported only by merchants who have obtained the necessary import licences.

Import Procedure. Generally imports from abroad are landed only at approved places. On entering a port certain formalities must be observed: (i) The Master must 'report' the arrival of his ship; (ii) He must supply information regarding his cargo—marks and numbers of packages, with particulars of any damaged goods, this information being entered on the Dock Landing

Account; (iii) The cargo must be unloaded by the Port Authority's employees; (iv) Customs formalities must be complied with, the appropriate forms being completed—Entry for Free Goods, Entry for Home Use, or Entry for Warehousing (*qq.v.*). Before the arrival of the goods the importer should be in possession of an Advice of Shipment and a copy of the bill of lading, to which should be attached a certificate of insurance, a *pro forma* invoice, and probably a bill of exchange. No goods can be removed without the presentation of these documents.

Import Quotas. An alternative to the tariff as a means of restricting imports. The amount of a commodity to be imported during a period is first determined, and then licences are issued to the supplying countries assigning a quota to each. The practice has been condemned by G.A.T.T. (*q.v.*).

Import Restrictions. Imports from abroad can be restricted by (i) tariffs, (ii) import quotas, (iii) restriction of foreign exchange of importers, (iv) direct prohibition. Other devices include import deposits and the import surcharge. The aim may be to protect home producers or to try to correct an adverse balance of payments, or to prohibit goods considered to be harmful to health or morals. Restriction of imports on a large scale, however, generally also leads to a fall in exports, since it reduces other countries' earnings of foreign currency. Since 1945 efforts have been made to reduce all trade barriers which have the effect of reducing the volume of international trade. The I.M.F. attempted to remove monetary obstacles to trade expansion and G.A.T.T. tried to get rid of tariffs, while the E.E.C. and E.F.T.A. sought to create areas of free trade.

Import Specie Point. One of the extreme points of variation in exchange rates on the gold standard—the point at which it becomes cheaper to import gold than to deal in foreign currency in the foreign exchange market. *See* Specie Points.

Import Surcharge. A tax on imports, as a temporary device to check imports in order to reduce a balance of payments deficit.

Import Trade. Goods are imported either in response to direct orders or on consignment. In the second case they are consigned by a foreign exporter to an importer who then sells them for the best price he can. In the case of Great Britain food and raw materials are generally imported on consignment, and manufactured goods more generally, but not always, in response to direct orders.

Imprest Account. A sum provided by a firm to cover cash expenditure as, for example, for petty cash payments, and periodically brought up to the same amount.

Imputation System. A method by which double taxation of distributed profits can be eliminated. *See* Corporation Tax.

Inbond. An association of international bond dealers.

Inc. Abbreviation of Incorporated, a term attached to the names of firms in the United States to indicate limited liability (as Ltd. in the United Kingdom), such firms being known as corporations (*q.v.*).

Incentives. 1. With reference to wages, a system of wage payment which offers an inducement in the form of a bonus to encourage workers to maintain a high level of output. Opportunity of promotion is another type of incentive that can be offered to the workers. *See* Premium Bonus; Task Bonus.

2. With reference to the taxation of wages and profits, it means a tax system designed to encourage an expansion of output.

Incentive Shares. Shares issued to high executives by some companies, usually on advantageous terms, for example, at a discount, and sometimes convertible at a later date into ordinary shares.

Incidence of Taxation. The incidence of a tax is on the person who actually pays it. In the case of Income Tax it clearly falls on the person earning the income. In the case of indirect taxes, however, the incidence may be on the buyer or the seller or it may be divided in any proportion between them, depending on the elasticity of demand for the commodity on which the tax has been imposed. If the demand for a commodity is perfectly inelastic the price will rise by the full amount of the tax, and so its incidence will be entirely on the buyer. If demand is fairly inelastic the tax will fall mainly on the buyer. If, however, the demand for the commodity is perfectly elastic the seller will have to reduce his price by the full amount of the tax, so that its incidence will be entirely on the seller. If demand is fairly elastic the tax will fall more heavily on the buyer than on the seller. Compare the diagrams A, B, and C: S^1 is the supply curve and OP^1 the price before the tax was imposed; and S^2 the supply curve and OP^2 the price after its imposition. In case A, where demand is perfectly inelastic, the tax falls entirely on the buyer; in case B, where demand is moderately elastic, the tax falls partly on the buyer and partly on the seller, but rather more heavily on the seller; in case C, where demand is perfectly elastic, the tax falls entirely on the seller. Similarly, the incidence of national insurance contributions may be entirely on either the employer or the employee or divided between them according to the elasticity of demand for labour.

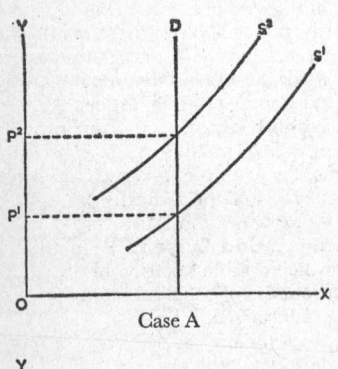

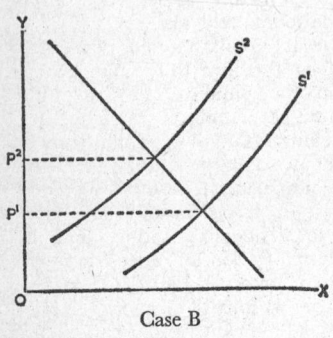

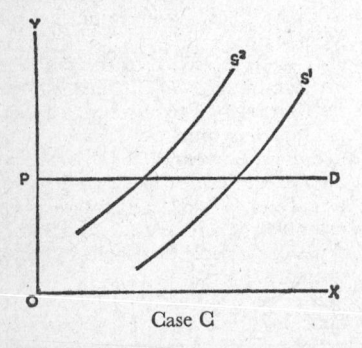

Incipient Inflation. An alternative term for Suppressed Inflation (q.v.).

Income Bond. See Insurance Bond.

Income Determination. The total income of a country is dependent on the amount of real capital investment in that country, the amount of investment depending on a number of factors such as saving, consumption, the rate of interest, marginal efficiency of capital, expectations of entrepreneurs, as shown by the diagram on p. 252. See also National Income.

Income Effect. One of the two effects of a change in the price of a commodity, the other being a Substitution Effect. A fall in the price of a commodity makes it possible for a consumer to buy the same quantity as before for a smaller outlay, the money so saved being available for some other purpose. One effect of such a price change, therefore, is similar in its effect to a rise in income.

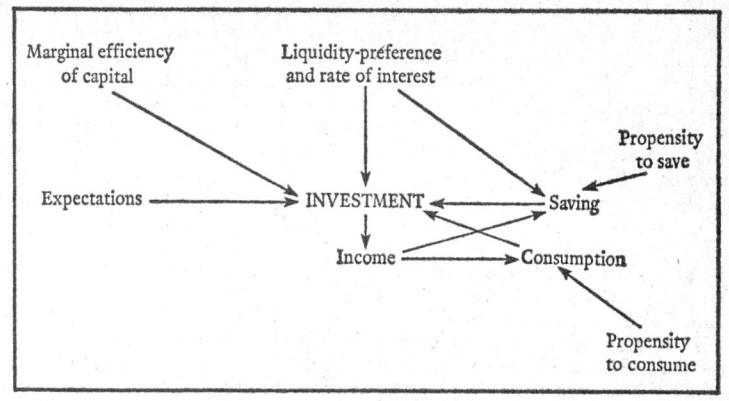

```
Marginal efficiency      Liquidity-preference
   of capital            and rate of interest

                                                          Propensity
                                                           to save
Expectations ─────────▶ INVESTMENT ◀──────── Saving
                             │
                          Income ──────────▶ Consumption
                                                          Propensity
                                                          to consume
```

Income Elasticity of Demand. One of the determinants of elasticity of demand, the other being Elasticity of Substitution (*q.v.*). Income Elasticity of Demand for a commodity shows the extent to which a consumer's demand for that good changes as a result of a change in his income. If Income Elasticity of Demand for a commodity is low it means that there will be little change in a consumer's demand for that commodity if he experiences an increase or decrease in his income, as for most people might be the case with bread. For some commodities Income Elasticity of Demand may be high, perhaps in the case of motor cars, so that demand will change considerably following a change of income.

Income, Inequality of. *See* Inequality of Income.

Income, Real. Income in terms of the goods and services it will buy.

Income, Re-distribution of. *See* Re-distribution of Income.

Income, Sources of. Income is derived from two sources: (i) The performance of personal services, that is, undertaking some kind of work; (ii) The ownership of factors of production like land and capital—that is, some kind of property—used to assist production. The diagram below shows the different sources of income.

Incomes Policy. The failure of efforts to check the inflationary spiral (*q.v.*) led to suggestions that the Government should persuade the trade unions to agree to an Incomes Policy, whereby increases in wages should be related to increases in the real national income, to prevent wage increases having an inflationary effect. The policy has generally found little favour with the trade unions, who have tended to regard it merely as an attempt to restrict their efforts to secure wage increases for their members. *See also* Prices and Income Policy.

Income Tax. A tax on all types of income—rent, wages, interest, and

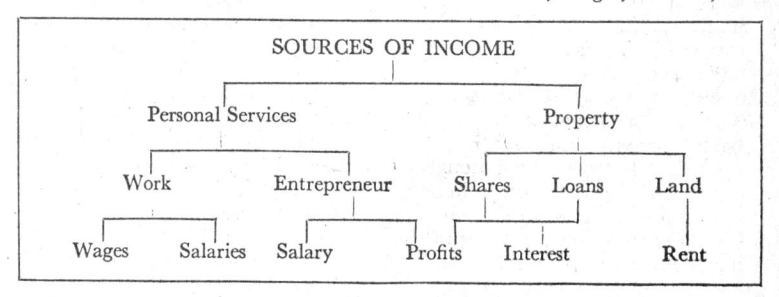

```
                        SOURCES OF INCOME
                               │
              ┌────────────────┴────────────────┐
         Personal Services                  Property
              │                                │
         ┌────┴─────┐              ┌───────────┼───────────┐
       Work    Entrepreneur      Shares      Loans        Land
         │           │             │           │            │
      ┌──┴───┐     Salary      Profits     Interest        Rent
    Wages  Salaries
```

profit. First imposed in 1799 by William Pitt as a temporary measure during the Napoleonic Wars, at a rate of 10% on gross income, though no tax was payable on incomes below £60 a year and there was a graduated scale for incomes between £60 and £200. It was repealed in 1815 but revived by Peel in 1842. Both Peel and later Gladstone expected the tax to be temporary. During the nineteenth century the rate varied between £0·03 and £0·06. During the First World War is reached £0·30 and during the Second World War £0·50. Since then it has varied between £0·30 and £0·83. For some time the British Income Tax has been steeply progressive. Taxpayers are granted tax free allowances according to their circumstances—whether they are single or married, the number of their dependants. On higher incomes higher rates of tax are imposed. In addition there is a surcharge of 10% to 15% on the higher levels of investment income, thereby giving a maximum tax rate in 1976–77 of 98%. *See* Direct Taxation; Layfield Committee.

Incomes Structure. The relation between incomes in different occupations.

Income, Types of. Factors of production are paid for their services to production and receive rent, wages, interest and profit, but it is an over-simplification to regard rent as the income accruing to land, wages to labour, interest to capital, and profit to the entrepreneur, since a factor often receives more than one type of income. Thus, there are often elements of rent in wages and in profit. Nor is it always easy to distinguish between interest and profit.

Income Velocity of Circulation. The rate of change in the total of bank deposits and other liquid assets in relation to the national income. Thus, a fall in the volume of liquid assets relative to the national income would indicate a rise in the income velocity of circulation.

Inconvertible Bank-notes. Bank-notes which cannot be exchanged for gold of equivalent value. Before 1914 Bank of England notes were individually convertible for gold on demand (except for a few years during the Napoleonic Wars); between 1925 and 1931 they were convertible for gold only in large quantities—sufficient to exchange for gold bars, each weighing 400 ounces. Since 1931 Bank of England notes have been inconvertible. At first paper money was generally acceptable only if it was known that it could be exchanged on demand for gold. It was only gradually that people became accustomed to inconvertible paper money.

Incorporated Insurance Broker. A member of the Corporation of Insurance Brokers (*q.v.*).

Increasing Marginal Cost. This occurs when the cost of each additional unit of a firm's output is greater than the marginal cost of the previous one. Consider the following table:

Cost of Revenue Schedule with Increasing Marginal Cost

Units of output	Total cost (£)	Average cost (£)	Marginal cost (£)
10	100	10	—
11	112	10·2	12
12	127	10·6	15
13	145	11·1	18
14	167	11·9	22

Both Marginal Cost and Average Cost are increasing.

Increasing Population, Effects of. For a long time it has been thought that the advantages of an increasing population greatly outweighed the disadvantages of a declining population. Nevertheless, there are some quite serious drawbacks to an expanding population. In a country such as Great Britain the greater the population the greater the amount of food that has to be imported. The greater population means that there is a larger labour supply and an expansion of production can be expected, but this means that a greater quantity of raw materials must be imported. Thus, there will be a large increase in imports, and unless there is an equal increase in exports—which is not at all certain—the country's difficulties with its balance of payments will be aggravated. There will be an increased demand for houses and schools and greater demands on the social services. It will too become more difficult to retain 'green belts' on the fringe of large cities and problems of traffic congestion will be aggravated. *See also* Declining Population, Effects of; Population Problem.

Increasing Returns. Generally associated with the scale of production, and so more correctly described as Increasing Returns to Scale, since they arise as a result of economies of large-scale production, in contrast to Diminishing Returns which are generally associated with changes in the proportions in which the factors of production are combined. Strictly, there are two pairs of laws, one pair relating to scale and the other pair to proportions. *See* Returns, Laws of.

Indefinitely Dated Stocks. Stocks due for redemption at an unstated time after a specified date. Thus $3\frac{1}{2}\%$ War Loan is due for redemption at any time the Government chooses after 1952, and as long as the Government is unable to borrow so cheaply it is likely to remain unredeemed. Other indefinitely dated stocks include 4% Consols, $3\frac{1}{2}\%$ Conversion Stock, 3% Treasury Stock and $2\frac{1}{2}\%$ Treasury Stock.

Indent. A term used in foreign trade of orders from abroad, more particularly when such orders are placed with agents or exporters. An indent may be (i) open, in which case the agent receiving the order can obtain the goods from whomsoever he pleases; or (ii) closed, in which case the foreign buyer specifies the manufacturer from whom the goods are to be purchased.

Indenture. An instrument or deed, so called because originally the document was cut or indented so that the parties retained pieces which would exactly fit together.

Independent Broadcasting Authority. A public corporation established in 1954 as the Independent Television Authority, to provide an alternative television service to that of the B.B.C., and so break its monopoly. Its revenue comes mainly from advertising. It became the I.B.A. in 1972 when a network of local radio stations was set up under contract to the authority.

Indexation. A system of relating income, especially from investment, to the retail price index in a time of inflation in order to offset the fall in the value of money. It was first employed in South America where a number of countries in recent times have suffered inflation at a persistently high rate. The earliest attempts at indexation in the United Kingdom took the form of cost-of-living bonuses during the two World Wars. Attempts too have been made to keep State pensions, especially the National Insurance retirement pension, closely in line with rising prices. The first indexation of investment income, although only on a very limited scale, occurred in 1975 when Retirement Savings Certificates, up to a maximum holding of £500, were made available to people of retirement age only, together with an indexed S.A.Y.E. scheme open to all. In both cases the interest is determined by changes in the General Index of Retail Prices. Until 1977 indexation had not been applied to taxation which becomes heavier as the value of money falls. In 1977, however, it was recommended that personal allowances for income tax should be related to the price index.

Index of Industrial Production. An index compiled to measure changes in the volume of production, based in most cases on physical output but in a few cases on value where measurement of physical output is not possible. Separate indices are compiled for each main industry. Industries are weighted according to what is regarded as their importance, *e.g.* mining and quarrying 72 (out of 1,000), manufacturing 748, gas, electricity and water 54, etc. With 1958 as base year the index was given number 100 for that year.

Index of Retail Prices, General. In the U.K. two index numbers to measure the purchasing power of the £ are calculated: (i) the General Index of Retail Prices (R.P.I.) compiled by the Department of Employment to measure monthly changes; and (ii) the Consumer Price Index (C.P.I.) compiled by the Central Statistical Office to measure annual changes.

Index numbers of wholesale prices were first calculated during the nineteenth century, but the first index number of retail prices did not come into use until 1914. Owing to the smaller number of markets and the greater degree of perfection that exists in wholesaling there is greater uniformity of prices over the country as a whole, whereas much wider variations occur in retail prices in different parts of the country or even in the same town, retail markets for most commodities being very imperfect. This was for long regarded as an insurmountable difficulty in the construction of an index number of retail prices. However, a so-called Cost-of-living Index, based on the expenditure of 'working-class' families, was introduced in 1914, with that year as its base. To obtain the 'weights' for the various items of expenditure a survey had been taken in 1907, and this index was probably representative of about 60% of the people at that time. It showed that on average 60% of expenditure of people in the group considered went on food, a further 36% on rent, rates, fuel and light, clothing, and footwear, leaving only 4% of expenditure for all other things. By the 1930s it was realised that the weighting of this index was out-of-date on account of the rise in the standard of living that had taken place since 1907, and a new survey was undertaken during 1937–38 of the expenditure of families with annual incomes of under £250 a year. The outbreak of war in 1939 caused the introduction of the new index to be postponed until more settled conditions. An interim index was, however, introduced in 1947, based on the weighting resulting from the 1937–38 survey; but the weighting for this index really being out-of-date even at the time of its introduction, a new index with up-to-date weighting was compiled with 1952 as its base year. The weighting was again revised for the 1956 index, which was based on the expenditure of

Commodity groups	1914 index	1947 index	1952 index	1956 index	1962 index	1974 index
	%	%	%	%	%	%
I. Food	60	34·8	39·9	35·0	31·9	23·2
II. Alcoholic drink	—	21·7	16·8	7·1	6·4	8·2
III. Tobacco	—			8·0	7·9	4·6
IV. Housing	16	8·8	7·2	8·7	10·2	10·8
V. Fuel and light	8	6·5	6·6	5·5	6·2	5·3
VI. Durable household goods	—	7·1	6·2	6·6	6·4	7·0
VII. Clothing and footwear	12	9·7	9·8	10·6	9·8	8·9
VIII. Transport and vehicles	—	—	—	6·8	9·2	14·9
IX. Miscellaneous	4	3·5	4·4	5·9	6·4	7·1
X. Services	—	7·9	9·1	5·8	5·6	5·2
XI. Meals away from home	—	—	—	—	—	4·8
	100	100	100	100	100	100

people with incomes up to £1,000 a year. A further revision of the weighting of the index took January 1962 as its base. Since then the weights have been revised annually. The table on p. 256 shows the weights adopted at various dates for different groups of commodities and services. An index number of retail prices can be applicable only to the group of people whose expenditure is similar to that of the weighting of the various commodities and services. The lower the general standard of living the more homogeneous the group and the less the difference between the expenditure of one family and another. For this reason the 1914 index was more representative than the more recent ones, for the higher the standard of living the greater are the differences between people's expenditure. Periodic revision of a retail price index is necessary to take account of changes in the standard of living, changes in taste, changes in the composition of the population, etc. Thus, index numbers of retail prices can be used to compare prices only at dates not too far apart. Though index numbers are the best available means of measuring changes in the value of money they have serious limitations.

Indication, Letter of. A document supplied by a bank to a customer to whom it has issued a Letter of Credit (*q.v.*). It bears a copy of his signature as a safeguard for the paying bank.

Indifference Curves. A method of analysing consumers' demand. Since all goods are scarce relative to the demand for them everyone has to make a choice between alternatives. For the construction of Indifference Curves it is assumed that there are only two commodities available to the consumer, and a curve is drawn to show all the possible combinations of the two commodities that yield exactly the same amount of satisfaction to the consumer concerned, so that he is indifferent as to which of these combinations he has.

To the right of the first curve a second curve can be drawn, again showing a series of combinations of the two commodities yielding the consumer the same amount of satisfaction, but all yielding a greater amount of satisfaction than any position on the first curve. A whole series of Indifference Curves can then be drawn as follows:

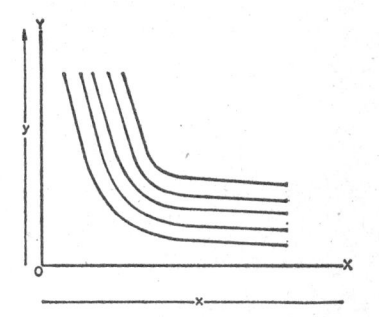

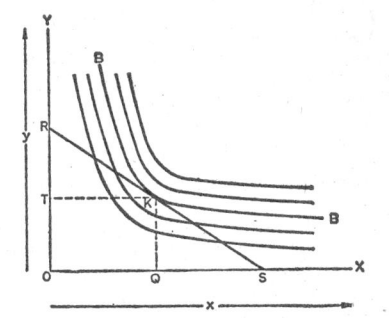

To obtain the greatest possible amount of satisfaction the consumer can select any point on the curve farthest to the right. His actual choice will depend on the amount of money he has to spend and the prices of the two commodities. On the diagram below the line *RS* represents all the choices open to the consumer. If he purchases *OR* of commodity *y* he will have no money left to purchase any of commodity *x*; if he purchases *OS* of commodity *x* he will have to go completely without commodity *y*. His actual preference will lie between these two extremes but at some point on the line RS. He will obtain the maximum satisfaction from the expenditure of his limited resources if he selects a point on RS which is also on the farthest Indifference Curve to the right, that is, curve B in the diagram. Thus, if he is able to make a perfectly rational choice he will purchase OT of commodity y and OQ of commodity x. Indifference Curves are thus a useful device to represent choice between two alternatives.

Indirect Arbitrage. Dealings in foreign exchange when more than one centre is involved. It is also known as Compound Arbitrage. *See* Arbitrage.

Indirect Parity. The rate of exchange between two currencies, calculated in terms of a third currency. It is also known as the Cross Rate ($q.v.$).

Indirect Production. In early days each individual had to produce everything for himself. The introduction of specialisation vastly increased total output, but necessitated exchange. A person who specialises in the production of one thing and is paid for his labour can then use the money he has earned to purchase the things he himself wants and which he would have spent his time making for himself if he had not specialised. In this way specialisation and exchange results in indirect production.

Indirect Taxes. Taxes on goods or services, sometimes therefore being known as outlay taxes, as distinct from taxes on income. It is argued that, on grounds of equity, indirect taxes tend to be regressive and should be abandoned and replaced by higher income taxes which can be made progressive in character. In the days when indirect taxes were imposed mainly on foodstuffs in common consumption this appeared to be a strong argument against them, since they resulted in poor people with large families paying more in tax than richer people with small families. Nowadays, however, the net of indirect taxation has been more widely spread and since many are *ad valorem* taxes, they no longer tend to fall so heavily on the poor, though not so precisely related to income as income taxes. Owing to the large revenue required by modern states income taxes would have to be very high if indirect taxes were to be dispensed with, and high income taxes have the drawback that they act as a disincentive and so might check the expansion of the real national income and economic growth.

Individualist School. The belief that individuals acting in their own interests at the same time act for the good of others. In the economic sphere this was the view of Adam Smith.

Indivisibility. Since some units of capital are large and cannot be employed fractionally a greater proportion of capital may have to be employed to produce a certain output than is actually required. The concept of Indivisibility is important in connection with Increasing Returns to Scale, since an expansion of production may not require more capital but merely that existing capital be used more fully. Similarly, fractions of a man cannot be employed and so the optimum proportion between the factors of production cannot always be precisely maintained.

Indoor Relief. Assistance under the Poor Laws given to the poor in workhouses as distinct from Outdoor Relief which was given to them in their own homes.

Indorsement. *See* Endorsement.

Inductive Method. One of the methods of studying economics. When this method is employed a mass of data relative to the problem to be studied must first be collected, these facts being collated and then used as a basis for generalisations. The inductive method is sometimes employed to check the findings of economic theory, developed by the deductive method ($q.v.$).

Industrial Accidents. *See* Industrial Injury.

Industrial Action. A comprehensive term covering strikes, 'working to rule', bans on overtime, etc. adopted by a trade union to support its demands.

Industrial and Commercial Finance Corporation Ltd. An institution established in 1945 along with the Finance Corporation for Industry (*q.v.*) for the provision of medium term capital for industry, as recommended as long ago as 1931 by the Macmillan Committee. The purpose of the Corporation was to provide loans of between £5,000 and £200,000 for periods intermediate between the short-term bank advance and the permanent share. For loans in excess of £200,000 there had to be recourse to the Finance Corporation for Industry. In 1973 it merged with the F.C.I. to become Finance for Industry (F.F.I.), (*q.v.*).

Industrial and Provident Societies Acts. The Act of 1852 gave Co-operative Societies similar protection to that enjoyed by friendly societies. The Act of 1862 provided limited liability for members of Co-operative Societies and permitted some of the profits to be devoted to 'education'. The Industrial and Provident Societies Act of 1929, defined the conditions under which a society can be registered as an industrial and provident society, these conditions now being similar to those for friendly societies.

Industrial Assurance. *See* Industrial Business.

Industrial Bankers. A title adopted by the smaller finance houses, their main business, like that of the large finance houses, being the financing of hire purchase transactions, but whereas the finance houses obtain their funds mainly by accepting deposits from commercial and industrial concerns, the eleven industrial bankers receive deposits chiefly from private individuals whose savings they try to attract by the offer of higher rates of interest on deposits than the commercial banks pay. From 1972 finance houses in certain conditions became entitled to turn themselves into banks. *See* Finance Houses.

Industrial Bankers' Association. A body which represents the eleven smaller finance houses.

Industrial Business (I.B.). The branch of life assurance where the policies are generally for small amounts, the premiums being collected weekly by the company's agents, in contrast to Ordinary Business (O.B.), where premiums are usually paid annually or quarterly. The leading assurance undertakings for industrial business are the Prudential, Pearl, Liverpool Victoria, Royal London, Refuge, and the Co-operative companies.

Industrial Court. A special type of court, established in 1919, to consider industrial disputes when both the employers' association and the trade union concerned agree to submit the case to arbitration.

Industrial Democracy. An economic system in which the workers have a share in the management of industry. *See* Bullock Report.

Industrial Designs Rules. These rules were first drawn up in 1949 in order to give a more precise meaning to the term, industrial design, for the purposes of the Registered Designs Act of that year. The rules were revised in 1955.

Industrial Development Certificate. A document issued by the Board of Trade permitting the industrial development of sites in excess of 1,000 sq. ft. in London, South-east England, and the Midlands, or in excess of 5,000 sq. ft. in the remainder of the country. Its purpose was to enable the Government to influence location of industry.

Industrial Disputes Tribunal. An institution for the consideration of industrial disputes, it was established in 1951 as an alternative to the Industrial Court.

Industrial Economics. A term for economic analysis as applied to industry. This branch of applied economics assumed greater impor-

Industrial Estates. Also known as Trading Estates, they were established under the Acts of 1934 and 1937 as a means of attracting new industrial development to the Special Areas (*q.v.*). On these estates factory buildings were provided on very favourable terms.

Industrial Estates Management Corporations. Set up by an Act of 1960 to take over the management of the property of the former Development Area trading estates, the capital of the corporation being obtained from the Board of Trade.

Industrial Fluctuations. *See* Trade Cycle.

Industrial Injury. A small additional contribution under the National Insurance scheme covers insurance against injury sustained at work. The National Insurance (Industrial Injuries) Act (1946) made it compulsory for all employees to make this contribution whether they were members of the full scheme or not, and irrespective of the number of hours per week worked.

Industrial Injury Benefit. Compensation payable under the National Insurance (Industrial Injuries) Act (1946) for injury sustained at work.

Industrial Organisation and Development Act (1947). An Act setting up Development Councils, one for each industry, to consider methods of increasing industrial efficiency.

Industrial Production Index. *See* Index of Industrial Production.

Industrial Psychology. The study of man in relation to his work, covering such matters as suitability for different types of employment, the effect on efficiency of his working environment, human relationships in industry, etc. *See also* Ergonomics.

Industrial Relations. Relations between employers' associations and trade unions. Machinery has been set up to deal with industrial disputes in order to reduce the possibility of strikes. At the Department of Employment there is an Industrial Relations Department which concerns itself with the settlement of industrial disputes.

Industrial Relations Act (1971). An Act aimed at improving industrial relations. Trade unions were to retain their privileges for strikes called within the rules of the unions, but in other cases they became liable to damages. Other reforms included greater use of the secret ballot, the introduction of a 'cooling off' period of 60 days, and the abolition of the closed shop unless specifically agreed. Breaches of the Act and practices designated as unfair could be brought before a National Industrial Relations Court. There was strong opposition to the Act from the trade unions. On a change of government in 1974 the Act was repealed, thus restoring the trade unions to the position they held in 1971. It was replaced by the Trade Union and Labour Relations Act (1974) (*q.v.*).

Industrial Reorganisation Corporation (I.R.C.). A public corporation, established in 1966, to assist the rationalisation of those sections of British industry where there are too many small firms and where in consequence productivity was low. It was wound up in 1971.

Industrial Revolution. A term used of the period covering the latter half of the eighteenth and early years of the nineteenth century (although precise dates cannot be assigned to it, it is generally regarded as the period bet ween 1780 and 1820) when a series of inventions affecting the production of power and in the textile and iron and steel industries and transport resulted in a complete change in the character of production in Great Britain. The factory system replaced the domestic system and power-driven machinery superseded hand labour, and since the factories and workshops had to be built near to the coalfields, their new source of power, new towns grew up round them of a type not previously known.

Since the coalfields were situated in the Midlands, the North of England, South Wales, and the Lowlands of Scotland, there was not only a drift of population from the country to the new towns but also from the South of England to the Midlands and the North. The improvements in transport occurred side by side with the industrial developments, which both made them necessary and were accelerated as a result of them.

Industrial Training Board. Set up under the Industrial Training Act (1964), one for each main industry, to improve the training of apprentices. Representatives of industry, educational bodies, and Government departments sit on each board.

Industrial Transference Board. A public body established in 1928 to promote greater mobility of labour by assisting workers to move from areas of unemployment to work in other areas. Since 1945 official policy has been mainly directed towards trying to persuade new industries to set up in areas of higher than average unemployment.

Industrial Union. A trade union representing all grades and types of worker in a particular industry, though many skilled workers prefer to remain members of small craft unions. In industrial unions unskilled workers vastly outnumber the skilled. Whereas some craft unions have fewer than 500 members, the largest of the powerful industrial unions has more than a million members. The large industrial unions have come into existence as a result of the amalgamation of numbers of smaller unions—over fifty in the case of the Transport and General Workers Union.

Industrial Welfare. The conditions under which people work—health, their suitability for particular jobs, factory conditions, housing, travelling to work, social amenities for workers, etc.

Industry. It is difficult to give a satisfactory definition of an industry. An industry has been defined as a group of firms competing against one another, but in a monopoly or a nationalised industry the firm and the industry are one and the same. A firm too may make several products, each belonging to a different industry. Even to define an industry as one branch of production making a single product as, for example, shipbuilding, is not always very satisfactory since there is often overlapping.

Industry Act (1975). This Act set up the National Enterprise Board (*q.v.*) to enable the State to acquire an interest in private industry.

Industry, Department of. Established as a separate department in 1974, it is responsible for general industrial policy, including industrial aspects of regional policy and planning. The Post Office and the British Steel Corporation fall within its scope, as does industrial research.

Inelastic Demand. Where a considerable rise or fall in the price of a commodity has little effect on the quantity demanded. Demand tends to be inelastic when there are no close substitutes for a commodity, or in the case of necessaries of life, or when demand is based on habit, or when expenditure on the commodity concerned forms only a small proportion of a person's total expenditure. The higher a person's income the more inelastic tends to be his demand for an increasing range of commodities and services.

Inelastic Supply. Where a rise in the price of a commodity on the market fails to call forth an increase in output. If supply is perfectly inelastic it will remain unchanged however great the change in the price of the commodity. In the short run many things are fixed in supply on account of the difficulty of increasing their supply quickly. Time is an important influence on elasticity or inelasticity of supply; the longer the period under consideration the more elastic the supply tends to be.

Inequality of Incomes. This is mainly due to differences in the amount of income from the ownership of property, mostly inherited, and to a lesser degree the result of differences in earned income. Inequality of incomes has been much reduced by (i) steeply progressive death duties imposed on inherited wealth, and (ii) steeply progressive income tax from employment and the still heavier tax on income derived from investment.

Inertia Selling. Delivering goods that have not been ordered and offering them on approval for a specified period on the expiry of which it is assumed that the receiver has decided to purchase them. This leads to goods being purchased simply because it is too much trouble to return them to the sender.

Infant. Formerly, according to English law, a person under the age of twenty-one. It is of legal importance because the law often applies less severely to such persons. The capacity of an infant to make a contract is limited, but in general contracts for necessaries and for the infant's own benefit are binding on him. The Family Reform Act (1969) reduced the age of legal majority from 21 to 18 years. The term *infant* was in this Act replaced by *minor*.

Infant Industry Argument. An industry that has been newly established. It is said that if such an industry has to face foreign competition during its early stages it will never be able to establish itself permanently. This would apply more particularly to an industry enjoying increasing returns to scale. Such an industry should, it is argued, be protected until it is firmly established. This is probably one of the few really sound arguments in favour of protection but, as is frequently pointed out, infant industries appear never to grow up, reasons constantly being put forward for the continuance of protection.

Infant Mortality. At one time very high, the fall in the infant mortality rate was one of the main causes of the fall in the death-rate and, therefore, of the increase in population during the nineteenth century, while during the early twentieth century it did something to offset the decline in the birth-rate.

Inferior Goods. Also known as Giffen Goods (*q.v.*).

Inflation. There are three senses in which this term is used:

1. *Inflation on the Gold Standard* where a moderate and controlled expansion of bank credit is encouraged by the central bank whenever there is an inflow of gold. The extent of an inflation in these circumstances is rigidly controlled since it is dependent on the amount of gold the country concerned has acquired.

2. *Persistent (or Creeping) Inflation*, is a condition where the volume of purchasing power is persistently running ahead of the output of goods and services available to consumers and producers, with the result that there is a persistent tendency for prices and wages to rise, that is, for the value of money to fall. This type of inflationary situation can arise either because of an undue stimulation of demand as a result of an increase in the volume of purchasing power, or because of a curtailment of the production of consumers' goods, both these causes encouraging inflation in wartime, but in any case once full employment has been achieved any further expansion of demand will stimulate inflation. When the main influence on the inflationary spiral is demand outrunning supply it is sometimes described as a 'demand inflation', but when the main influence is rising wages—a condition likely to be associated with the maintenance of full employment —it is described as a 'cost inflation'. Since 1939 all countries have experienced varying degree of persistent inflation.

3. *Hyperinflation* (alternatively known as a 'galloping' or 'runaway' inflation) occurs when a persistent inflation gets out of control and the value of money declines rapidly to a tiny fraction of its former value and eventually to almost nothing, so that a new currency unit has to be adopt-

ed. Inflations of this kind occurred after both world wars—in Germany, Austria, Poland, and Russia during 1920–23 and in Hungary, Rumania, Greece, and China after the Second World War and, more recently, in several countries in South America. *See also* Value of Money.

Inflation Accounting. A system of accounting that attempts to allow for the effects of inflation by valuing assets at their current value instead of at cost. *See* Sandilands Report.

Inflationary Gap. A term used of that part of Government expenditure which is not covered by taxation or borrowing from the general public, and which is covered by borrowing from banks or other financial institutions, or by the Government itself creating money. Borrowing from the general public is not inflationary because when an individual lends he must forgo an equivalent amount of purchasing power for a period, whereas borrowing from banks leads to the creation of an equivalent amount of purchasing power. Instead of borrowing from banks some Governments might instead cover the inflationary gap by themselves issuing new paper money to cover this expenditure.

Inflationary Spiral. A term used of a persistent inflation in which a rise in prices causes demands to be made for higher wages, the granting of which increases the costs of producers who then again put up their prices, and so increases in prices through increases in wages induce further increases in prices, which in such circumstances become increasingly difficult to check.

Informative Advertising. Advertising serves two main purposes: (i) To try to persuade customers to buy one manufacturer's brand of a commodity in preference to a similar brand made by another manufacturer; (ii) To bring information to people's notice. The former type of advertising, known as competitive advertising, is regarded as one of the principal wastes of imperfect competition and would not be found in conditions of perfect competition. This kind of advertising tends to make goods dearer to consumers. Informative advertising is regarded in a different light, and since its aim is simply to supply information it is considered to be useful, but it is often very difficult to distinguish between the two. *See* Advertising.

Inheritance Taxes. Taxes on inherited wealth. A true Inheritance Tax varies, however, like the former British legacy duty (*q.v.*), with the nearness of relationship of the inheritor to the deceased, such a tax falling less heavily on a surviving spouse than on the children, and less heavily on the children than on more distant relatives. Inherited wealth is regarded as a suitable object of taxation, but there are different possible methods of calculating it—according to the total value of the estate (as with Capital Transfer Tax at present), or according to the wealth and income of the inheritor, or according to the nearness of the relationship of the inheritor to the deceased. Inheritance Taxes are imposed partly for the sake of the revenue derived from them by the State, but also with the aim of reducing inequality of income, since inherited wealth is one of the principal causes of inequality of income.

Initial Allowance. An amount a business is allowed to deduct in respect of the cost of a new capital asset in addition to the usual deduction for depreciation when calculating its profit, before its profit is assessable to tax. Initial allowances reduce the amount of tax payable in the first year, but over the life of the capital asset, the total tax payable is the same. In this way it differs from an Investment Allowance which, in addition to giving greater relief of tax in the first year, also reduces the total tax paid over the whole period. Both Initial and Investment Allowances were introduced in order to stimulate capital investment. From January 1966 investment allowances were replaced by investment grants, larger allowances being available to firms in Development Districts. In 1970 investment allowances replaced investment grants.

Injunction. An order by a court of law restraining a person from acting in a specified way. The result of infringement of an injunction is contempt of court.

Inland Bill of Exchange. *See* Bill of Exchange.

Inland Revenue, Board of. The body set up in 1849 to be responsible for the collection of revenue from income taxes, death duties, and stamp duty. Since 1908 excise duties have been the responsibility of the department of Customs and Excise.

Inland Waterways. Canals and navigable or canalised rivers come under this heading. Carriage by inland waterway is still used for some commodities owing to its cheapness compared with other means of transport. Canals linking rivers are most used, such as the Trent & Mersey, the Forth & Clyde. Birmingham is linked by canal to the rivers Trent, Thames, Severn, and Mersey. In France all the main rivers are linked together by canals. Through traffic on British canals is hindered by differences of gauge—depth, width, size of locks. Ship Canals in many parts of the world make inland ports into seaports, as for example, the Manchester Ship Canal and the St. Lawrence Seaway, or provide links between seas separated by narrow isthmuses, as for example the Suez and Panama Canals. In Great Britain, 2,500 miles of navigable waterway were nationalised as British Waterways by the Transport Act of 1947. *See also* British Waterways Board.

Inner Reserve. An alternative term to Hidden Reserve (*q.v.*). It occurs when the balance sheet of a firm undervalues one or more of its assets.

Innovations. A term sometimes used as an alternative to 'inventions' (*q.v.*). It is better to restrict the term to its use in connection with imperfect competition. In order to obtain some degree of monopoly power producers differentiate their products by branding, and then advertise this slight differentiation. Similarly, there is always apparently some demand for new 'gadgets', the monopoly element being secured in this case by patent. The first producer in the field can often make a considerable monopoly profit. After a time demand may fall off if the article does not fulfil expectations, but if it proves to be useful the expansion of demand will bring new producers into the field with somewhat similar products which just avoid infringing the patent rights of the first producer, and prices will fall as a result of the increased competition, and as a result monopoly profit may disappear.

In Place of Strife. A White Paper issued in 1969 outlining the Government's plans for trade union reform.

Inputs. A term sometimes used for the amounts of the various factors of production (*q.v.*) employed by a producer.

Inscribed Stock. A type of stock where no certificate is issued. Instead a register of stockholders is kept showing how much each holds, their names thus being inscribed or registered. It is also known as Registered Stock.

Insolvency. A business or individual becomes insolvent when liabilities (except to the owners of the business) exceed the total value of the assets.

Instability of Demand. In the case of some commodities, for example many foodstuffs and household goods, there is a fairly steady and regular demand, whereas for other goods demand is liable to severe fluctuations. Heavy industry, that is, capital producing industry, is particularly liable to fluctuations, and this is generally true of all forms of derived demand, as the Acceleration Principle shows. The demand for a country's exports too is liable to wide fluctuation.

Instalment Credit. An American term for hire purchase finance. *See* Hire Purchase.

Instalment Trading. A method of buying and selling whereby the customer pays for what he has bought by equal instalments, weekly or monthly, spread over a period, the goods usually being obtained when the first payment is made. This system differs from hire purchase in that the goods immediately become the property of the purchaser, whereas under the hire purchase system the goods are regarded as the property of the seller until the final payment has been made. The increased popularity of hire purchase has almost ousted the instalment system, though it has been retained in cases where services are concerned since these are impossible to reclaim, as for example in the case of air fares, which some airlines permit to be paid by instalments.

Institute of Bankers. An institution, founded in 1879, to further interest in matters connected with banking. During the year a number of lectures on banking subjects are given at the Institute's headquarters in London, and the branches of the Institute in different parts of the country arrange meetings, lectures, and discussions on topics of interest to those engaged in banking. The Institute holds examinations. The Institute also publishes a journal. There are three grades of membership—A.I.B., M.I.B., and F.I.B. (*qq.v.*).

Institute of Chartered Secretaries and Administrators. A professional body offering membership to those who have passed its qualifying examinations. Members, who include Associates (A.C.I.S.) and Fellows (F.C.I.S.), are described as chartered secretaries. Subjects in which candidates are examined include economics, accounting, general principles of law, company law, and secretarial practice. In 1971 it took over the Corporation of Secretaries.

Institute of Economic Affairs. An educational trust established in 1957 to make more widespread a knowledge of basic economic principles, especially those affecting market analysis. Authors are invited to contribute papers, and these are then published.

Institutional Investors. A term used of insurance companies, pension funds, investment trusts, unit trusts, which invest in all kinds of stock exchange securities, and banks, which generally restrict their investments to Government stocks. Institutional investors hold 50% of all negotiable securities.

Instrument. A term applied to many documents. *See* Negotiable Instrument.

Instrumental Capital or **Auxiliary Capital.** These terms were used by Alfred Marshall to cover all goods that aid labour in production—machinery, raw materials, means of transport, etc. Such goods would nowadays be described as capital goods or producers' goods, or simply as capital. Marshall regarded consumer's goods as Consumption Capital.

Instrumental Industries. An alternative term for capital producing industries, capital being instrumental to the production of other goods.

Instruments of Monetary Policy. The traditional instruments of monetary policy, employed before 1945, were bank rate and open-market operations, although bank rate had remained unchanged at 2% since 1932, except for a few weeks after the outbreak of war in 1939. During the period of the gold standard the Bank of England had regarded bank rate as its principal instrument of monetary policy, although later most economists were of the opinion that it was only through open-market operations that bank rate was made effective. It was the belief that bank rate was an ineffective instrument of policy that led to its falling into disuse after 1932. Before 1939 it had been suggested that fiscal policy through the budget should take the place of monetary policy, at that time an expansionary budget, preferably in deficit, being suggested as a means of stimulating demand and employment.

When, however, fiscal policy came to be adopted it was in the inflationary conditions of the post-war period, and to meet these circumstances it was thought that a large budget surplus was required to reduce purchasing power in the hands of consumers in order to check excessive demand. During the war and for many years afterwards physical controls, in the form of rationing of consumers' goods and some producers' goods and capital investment, were employed. Failure to check inflation led to a demand for the revival of bank rate, but when this was done in 1951 it was accompanied by a new instrument of policy—the Treasury directive, which was used on a number of occasions during the ensuing years. At first the directive was 'qualitative', that is, banks were requested to restrict their loans to purposes in the 'national interest', but later it was 'quantitative' in character, the banks being requested to reduce their total volume of lending.

Other modern instruments of monetary policy that have been tried include the variation of hire purchase regulations and indirect taxes either to check or encourage an expansion of demand. The most recent instrument of policy that has been employed is that of Special Deposits, the Bank of England being empowered to request these from the commercial banks in order to reduce their cash basis and thereby check their lending, the repayment of these deposits having the reverse effect of making possible an expansion of bank lending. This device is less clumsy than the old-fashioned type of open-market operations, and places less strain on the banks than the Treasury directive. The use of a number of instruments of monetary policy in combination with one another is known as the 'package deal'.

Insulation. An alternative term for Sterilisation of Gold (*q.v.*), it means the offsetting of the inflow or outflow of gold so that these movements do not affect the internal volume of credit as they would on the gold standard.

Insurable Interest. A condition of insurance is that the insured must suffer an equivalent loss before he is entitled to compensation by insurance, that is, he must have an 'insurable interest' in whatever risk he insures against.

Insurance. In return for the payment of a premium an insurer or underwriter agrees to compensate the insured in the event of his suffering a specified loss. A great variety of risks can nowadays be covered by insurance. The main principle underlying insurance is 'the pooling of risk', a large number of people contributing to a fund out of which compensation can be paid to those experiencing a particular type of loss. From past experience the probability of many risks can be calculated with great accuracy. Some of the commoner risks which it is usual for businessmen and private individuals to insure against are the destruction of property or stock by fire, losses arising from burglary or other causes, goods in transit, motor vehicles, and 'third-party' claims arising out of accidents. Marine insurance forms a separate branch of insurance on account of the many special factors involved.

Life assurance (*q.v.*) is in a different category from other types of insurance since, sooner or later, the risk is certain to occur, whereas in other cases the contingency insured against may never occur. For this reason a distinction is often made between insurance (where there is no certainty) and assurance (where certainty exists, the only uncertainty being the time of occurrence). In addition to those enumerated many other risks can be insured against. In Great Britain insurance business is conducted by insurance or assurance companies and by underwriters who are members of Lloyd's. Insurance against sickness, unemployment, and old age is undertaken by the State in many countries nowadays. *See also* Financial Intermediaries; National Insurance.

Insurance Bond. A form of personal

investment including a measure of life assurance obtained by a single lump sum payment. Bonds are usually for fixed periods—5, 10 or 15 years. In some cases the investor can make regular withdrawals, such bonds usually being described as income bonds. *See also* Managed Bond.

Insurance Broker. An independent agent who puts clients seeking insurance in touch with insurers who undertake that type of business. He can advise clients which insurers can offer them the most favourable terms.

Insurance Policy. A document setting out the exact terms and conditions of an insurance transaction—the precise risk covered, the period of cover, and any exceptions there may be.

Intangible Assets. Items in the balance sheet of a business such as Goodwill or Patent Rights.

Integration. A term used either of the structure of an industry or of an amalgamation of firms. Thus, an industry is horizontally integrated if there is a general tendency for firms in that industry to specialise in single processes, as in the worsted section of the West Riding of Yorkshire wool textile industry. An amalgamation of firms at the same stage of production would be an example of horizontal integration. If the structure of an industry is such that most firms carry through the production of a commodity from the raw material stage to the finished product, this would be an example of vertical integration, as also would be an amalgamation of firms at different stages of production in the same industry.

Intensive Cultivation. This occurs when the output per acre is very high as a result of the employment of large amounts of labour and capital with relatively small amounts of land. Intensive cultivation is found in densely populated countries like Belgium, Holland, and Great Britain where land is particularly scarce in relation to other factors of production.

Interbank. A U.S. credit card organisation, formed by 3,000 banks, their credit card being known as Master Charge (*q.v.*). *See* Credit Card.

Interest. A payment by a borrower for the use of a sum of money for a period of time, it is one of the four types of income, the others being rent, wages, and profit. In ancient and medieval times the receiving of interest was condemned as usury whether the rate of interest was high or low. The payment of interest, however, is a payment for a service rendered by one person to another person or institution. The change in the attitude to the receiving of interest has come with a change in the character of the borrowers. In early times borrowers were poor people, who had generally suffered some misfortune which in those days could not be insured against, and the lenders were people who were well-to-do. Nowadays borrowing is mostly undertaken by businessmen, who have to be regarded as creditworthy if they are to obtain loans, and who hope to employ the money borrowed in such a way as to yield them more profit than the interest they have to pay on the loan.

Three elements can be distinguished in interest: (i) payment for the risk involved in making the loan; (ii) payment for the trouble involved; (iii) pure interest, that is a payment for the use of the money. At any particular time there is a prevailing rate of interest, which many regard as a price determined like other prices in markets, by the demand to borrow in relation to the supply of loanable funds. This is pure interest. Differences in the rate of interest on different loans made at the same period of time must, therefore, be due to differences in the risk or trouble involved. Thus, the rate of interest charged by a moneylender on an unsecured loan will be higher than the rate charged by a bank to one of its customers who can offer satisfactory collateral security. Similarly, the Government has generally to offer a higher rate of interest on a long-term than on a short-term loan.

A number of theories have been put forward to explain the rate of interest. Mention has already been made of the supply-and-demand analysis which explains the rate of interest as a price determined by the demand for and the supply of loans. Generally, the higher the rate or price the greater the supply of loans that will be forthcoming, although a good deal of saving is independent of the rate of interest. Time-preference theories, including that of Böhm-Bawark, stress the idea that most people prefer to have a smaller sum of money at the present moment rather than a larger sum at a future date, so that interest arises because one person may prefer to have £500 now than a larger sum at some time in the future, (say) £575 in three years' time, whereas another person may prefer the larger sum in three years' time to the smaller sum at the present moment. The rate of interest has also been explained in terms of the productivity of capital. If the expected return on a new item of capital costing £1,000 is expected by the entrepreneur to yield him an extra profit of £60, then he will be unwilling to borrow in order to obtain this capital at a higher rate than 6%. Thus, the rate of interest affects the rate of real capital accumulation, for at a high rate of interest only enterprises likely to yield a high rate of profit will be undertaken. Then there is the monetary theory of the rate of interest, according to which interest is a payment for willingness to forgo liquidity, so that the rate of interest depends on liquidity-preference at the time. If liquidity-preference is strong it will require a high rate of interest to tempt people to forgo it.

Thus, some theories attempt to explain the rate of interest in real terms and others in monetary terms. It may be that the rate of interest is partly determined by real and partly by monetary forces.

Interest Equalisation Tax (1963). A U.S. tax on purchases of foreign securities by U.S. residents to check the outflow of capital.

Interest Warrant. A draft for the payment of interest due on Government stocks, debentures, and other fixed interest securities. It can be crossed like a cheque.

Interim Budget. An additional budget presented part way through the financial year, as occurred in 1931, and on several occasions between 1947 and 1964, when it was considered that a change in economic conditions since the previous budget required an increase of taxation. Interim budgets have rarely been introduced for the purpose of reducing taxation, though this occurred in 1971. Since 1973 interim budgets have been introduced more frequently, sometimes twice in one year.

Interim Dividend. In order to permit shareholders to receive their dividends in two instalments many companies pay an interim dividend during the course of the year, the balance being paid as a final dividend after the end of the company's year when the company's financial position is fully known.

Interlocking Directorates. This occurs when a number of persons are members of the boards of several companies. These are ostensibly competing against one another, and in consequence they can pursue a common policy, their association being less obvious than outright amalgamation or the creation of a holding company. In some of the states of the United States where branch banking is not permitted this local restriction has in principle been circumvented by a number of banks having interlocking directorates.

Intermediary. An alternative term for a middleman, agent, or broker.

Intermediate Area. An area with more than average unemployment but yet not serious enough for it to be declared a Development Area, but nevertheless requiring some

State assistance. It is also known as a Grey Area.

Intermediate Goods. A term sometimes used to describe partly-finished goods.

Internal Debt. That part of a country's national debt owed by the State to its own people or institutions within its own borders. *See* National Debt.

Internal Economies of Scale. Economies which a single firm can enjoy by expanding its output, as distinct from external economies which an industry alone can obtain. *See* Economies of Scale.

International Air Transport Association (I.A.T.A.). A body which represents the leading airlines of the world.

International Bank for Reconstruction and Development (I.B. or I.B.R.D.). A bank established under the Bretton Woods Agreement of 1944 at the same time as the International Monetary Fund. It is popularly known as the World Bank. The purpose of the I.M.F. was to assist countries experiencing temporary difficulties with their balances of payment, the purpose of the I.B. being to give countries in need of it a greater measure of assistance than the I.M.F. could provide, such as loans to cover reconstruction or capital development, the full name of the bank being the International Bank for Reconstruction and Development. Its capital was subscribed by members of the I.M.F. on a quota basis. Loans were to be made to governments or to companies or corporations only if there was a government guarantee for the loan.

International Banking Services. A bank consortium formed in 1968 by Barclays Bank, Lloyds Bank, the Australia and New Zealand Bank, the National Bank of New Zealand, and BOLSA (now Lloyds International).

International Chamber of Commerce. An international body established in Paris in 1920 for the exchange of ideas on commercial matters of international importance.

International Civil Aviation Organisation (I.C.A.O.). A body which concerns itself with problems that affect civil aviation such as safety, traffic control, etc. Its headquarters are in Montreal. *Cf.* I.A.T.A.

International Coffee Council. A body representing the main coffee-producing countries of the world which have agreed to regulate their production and sale of coffee. *See* Commodity Control Schemes.

International Commercial Bank. A banking consortium formed in 1967 by the National Westminster Bank, the Commerzbank, the Hong Kong and Shanghai Banking Corporation, the Irving Trust Company, and the First National City Bank of Chicago, to enable these banks to deal more easily in foreign exchange and other international monetary business.

International Confederation of Free Trade Unions. (I.C.F.T.U.). An international institution representative of trade unions in non-communist countries, its headquarters being in Brussels. The American A.F.L./C.I.O. withdrew its membership in 1969. *See also* World Federation of Trade Unions.

International Co-operative Alliance (I.C.A.). Founded in 1895 with headquarters in London, an international congress is held every three years. The Alliance keeps members informed of co-operative happenings in other countries. It also concerns itself with international Co-operative policy.

International Currency. No international body has ever issued currency that could be used by all nations in international transactions. The original proposals put forward at Bretton Woods when the establishment of the International Monetary Fund was under discussion included suggestions for an international unit of account, Lord Keynes suggesting the name 'bancor' and the Americans the name 'unitas', but these were not intended to serve as international currencies. In the nineteenth century sterling, along with gold, came nearest to being an international currency, Great Britain at that time being the outstanding trading nation of the world. At the present day the U.S. dollar and sterling share this function, many countries holding their reserves in one or other of these currencies. For this reason they are often known as reserve currencies. Though there are advantages to the countries concerned there is also the serious drawback to the 'parent' countries that any balance of payments crisis will be aggravated since loss of confidence in a currency will lead to heavy withdrawals of it at such times, as has been the experience of Great Britain on a number of occasions since 1951.

International Development Association (I.D.A.). An international body established in 1960 to promote the economic development of underdeveloped areas of the world and thus to supplement the activities of the International Bank.

International Economics. The branch of economics dealing with international trade in theory and practice and cognate problems such as foreign exchange, the balance of payments, etc.

International Factors. A factoring company (*q.v.*).

International Finance Corporation (I.F.C.). An international institution, established in 1956 to supplement the activities of the International Bank, by providing assistance for private enterprise in underdeveloped countries.

International Financial News Survey. A weekly publication of the International Monetary Fund, it gives particulars of the Fund's dealings, and quotes comment from newspapers and journals, published all over the world, on financial matters of current interest in those countries.

International Labour Organisation (I.L.O.). A body established by the League of Nations after the First World War, but also including the United States as a member although that country was never a member of the League. After the establishment of the United Nations the I.L.O. became associated with that body. Its function is to consider problems affecting the employment of labour, its aims being to improve labour standards and living conditions. Its headquarters are at Geneva, and it also has an office in London.

International Monetary Fund (I.M.F.). An international institution established under the Bretton Woods Agreement of 1944. The members of the I.M.F. had first to announce the parity of their currencies, theoretically in terms of gold, actually in terms of U.S. dollars, after which there were to be restrictions on changes of parity, although a change in value of up to 10% could be made merely by announcing this fact to the I.M.F. For a change greater than 10% permission had to be given by the I.M.F., a decision having to be given within seventy-two hours when the desired change was less than 20%. One of the aims was to stimulate multilateral trade, and it was expected that all currencies would be made convertible after a short transition period. It was hoped that the stability of exchange rates associated with the gold standard would be achieved but with greater flexibility than that standard provided. The I.M.F. created a Pool from the contributions of members, the amount of each country's contribution depending on the quota assigned to it, 75% of the contributions being in its own currency and the remainder being either in gold or partly in gold and partly in U.S. dollars. Thus, Great Britain was given a quota of $1,300 million, the United States of $2,750 million, France of $450 million, and so on. The purpose of the Pool was to enable a country with a temporary deficit in its balance of payments to obtain from the I.M.F. foreign currency in exchange for its own up to a maximum of 25% of its quota in any one year, but if at any time the I.M.F. has a supply of a member's currency equal to double its quota foreign currency can be obtained from the Fund by the country concerned only in exchange for gold. In 1959 the quotas of members were increased. Thus, the purpose of the Fund is only to assist countries with temporary difficulties with their balances of payments, such countries being given a period in which to put their affairs in order. In 1968 the I.M.F. agreed to issue S.D.R.s (Special Drawing Rights) (*q.v.*) to supplement members' reserves. Gold had been the corner stone of the international monetary system inaugurated at Bretton Woods, but the introduction in 1972 of floating exchange rates greatly reduced the role of gold in international dealings, and it ceased to be the standard of valuation for members' currencies. The I.M.F., therefore, decided to sell most of its holding of gold. The I.M.F. publishes quarterly, with the I.B., *Finance and Development*.

International Money Order (I.M.O.). A means, provided by post offices, of transferring relatively small sums of money from one country to another. Barclays Bank Ltd. also issues I.M.O.s.

International Payments. When international trade ceased to be carried on by barter, payments between nations were made in some form of commodity money which was acceptable to the sellers, the precious metals soon proving to be most useful for this purpose. The introduction of different national coinages did not seriously hamper international dealings, for such coins could be weighed and treated as bullion. There has never been an international currency, although both sterling and gold came very near to this in the heyday of the gold standard in the latter part of the nineteenth century. Since 1945 gold has again served as an international standard. It was proposed at the Bretton Woods Conference of 1944 that there should be an international monetary unit but it was intended merely to be a unit of account and not to circulate, but the suggestion was not adopted. Few international payments, however, are made in cash. For a long time the foreign bill of exchange was the principal international means of payment, but it has been largely superseded by the documentary credit, the bank draft, and the telegraphic transfer (*qq.v.*).

International Postal Reply Coupons. A means by which the postage on the reply to a letter sent abroad can be prepaid. In Great Britain these coupons can be purchased at the larger post offices and when received abroad they can be exchanged for stamps to cover postage on a letter back to the country of issue.

International Postal Union. *See* Universal Postal Union.

International Settlements, Bank for. *See* Bank for International Settlements.

International Telecommunications Union (I.T.U.). Founded in 1865 as the International Telegraphic Union, it is concerned with the international regulation of telegraph, telephone, and radio services.

International Trade. The earliest trade between countries occurred when they were able to supply one another with goods which they were unable to produce for themselves. International trade would not have reached its present volume if trade between countries had been limited in this way. Countries nowadays import many things which they could produce themselves, in the same way that individuals purchase many things they could make for themselves. Division of labour and specialisation, followed by exchange, result in a greater output of everything, and the same applies to international trade also. The principle underlying international trade is that a country should specialise in the production of those things for which it has the greatest advantage over others. The result of such specialisation will be a larger total world output of these things than if every country tries to be as nearly self-sufficient as possible. The theory of international trade is, therefore, based on the Principle of Comparative Cost (*q.v.*). In the same way that division of labour and specialisation within a country make necessary a greater amount of distribution, so greater division of labour in the international field necessitates an expansion of international trade. Nevertheless, in spite of the advantages accruing to international specialisation as shown by the theory of international trade, and in spite of the great efforts made by G.A.T.T. to reduce tariffs and other hindrances to international trade, restrictions on international trade are still widespread. However, a number of attempts have been made to develop wider regional areas of free trade, such as the European Common Market, and the European Free Trade Area. *See also* Balance of Payments; European Common Market; Protection.

International Trade Organisation (I.T.O.). A proposed international institution, not yet established, which it was expected would supersede G.A.T.T. (*q.v.*).

International Westminster Bank. A subsidiary of the National Westminster Bank, it was formerly known as the Westminster Foreign Bank.

Intervention. A form of exchange control (*q.v.*) in which a department of the State intervenes on the foreign exchange market to buy or sell its own or foreign currencies with the aim of influencing the rate of exchange between its own and other currencies. Great Britain was the first country to adopt this system in 1932 when it set up the Exchange Equalisation Account as a department of the Treasury with the Bank of England as its agent. France soon afterwards adopted a similar policy, as did many other countries, including the United States, which named its account the Exchange Stabilisation Fund. The aim has generally been to keep exchange rates stable, though at first the aim of the British Treasury was to try to offset the effects of speculative capital movements. After the Second World War when the International Monetary Fund began to operate it was expected that exchange rates, once decided upon, would not fluctuate, but a number of countries, including Great Britain, intervene on the foreign exchange markets to restrict fluctuations to definite narrow limits.

Intervention Price. A device employed in the farming policy of the European Economic Community. *See* Target Price.

Intestacy. The estate of a deceased person who has not made a will and therefore dies intestate is distributed according to the procedure laid down in the Administration of Estates Act (1925) and the Intestates' Estate Act (1952). The general principle is that the surviving spouse must be protected, and then the children. Only where there is no surviving spouse and no children are other specified relatives entitled to share in the estate. If there is none of these then the estate goes to the Crown (Escheat).

Intra-city Concentration. A term used to describe a banking development in those states of the U.S.A. which permit a bank to have branches only within the boundaries of the city in which its head office is situated, the extent of such intra-city concentration depending, therefore, on the size of the city.

Intrinsic Value. The popular idea that a commodity as, for example, a precious metal, has an innate, objective value apart from its price. Economists regard value as subjective, depending on the demand of consumers in relation to the available supply. According to this view, therefore, there is no such thing as intrinsic value.

Introduction. With reference to an issue of shares, *see* New Issue Market (ii).

Inventions, Economic Effects of. From the time of the Luddites, who thought the answer to the problem was to smash up the new machinery, workers have generally been suspicious of the effect of new inventions on their employment. Most new inventions are labour-saving, and so the immediate effect of their introduction has been to cause unemployment. Since, however, the employment of more and better capital is the principal method by which the national income can be increased, the long-run effect of the use of new inventions has been eventually to raise the general standard of living. The ultimate effect, therefore, of new inventions has been to increase productivity and so make possible a rise in wages, and the resulting expansion of demand, added to the demand for the new machines themselves, will increase the total demand for labour in industry generally, so that unemployment caused by the introduction of the machines is really structural unemployment of temporary duration and due more to lack of mobility of labour than to the inventions themselves. In times of rapid technological progress such unemployment, however, can be serious in the short-run if inventions follow one another so rapidly that those thrown out of work by one invention have not been absorbed into other forms of employment before further unemployment is caused by the next invention. *See also* Innovations.

Inventory. A term of American origin, and more frequently used in the United States than in Great Britain, for the quantity of stock (or its value) held by a business. Thus, Inventory Appreciation is an alternative term for Stock Appreciation and similarly Inventory Control is the equivalent to Stock Control.

Inventory Revaluation. A term now used in the British White Paper on National Income and Expenditure. If during a period the value of stocks and work-in-progress rise gross profit will increase, but for national income purposes it is usual in the calculation of the Gross National Product to make an adjustment for any such increase (or fall) in the value of 'inventories'.

Inverted Take-over. A colloquial term for a take-over where a smaller company takes over a larger, the smaller company being probably more go-ahead and expanding whereas the larger most likely has been making losses and is declining. The purpose of such a take-over is generally to enable the smaller company to obtain a stock exchange quotation, which the larger company possesses, without having to apply to the Stock Exchange. To take over a company which has been making a loss also means that this loss can be offset for tax purposes against the profits of the more prosperous company.

Investment. This term has two related meanings: (i) In economic theory it is generally taken to mean the actual production of real capital goods. Thus, the construction of a new motorway or the erection of new factory buildings are examples of real capital investment; (ii) As a financial term it refers to the purchase of stock exchange securities or Government securities issued through the Post Office, or the deposit of money in building societies, banks, or other financial institutions, with the aim either of securing an income or the refund of a greater sum at some future date.

Investment Advisers. Experts on monetary investment employed by insurance companies and investment trusts to advise on the investment of their funds.

Investment Allowances. *See* Initial Allowance.

Investment Bank. A bank that provides long-term fixed capital for industry, generally by taking up shares in limited companies. During the nineteenth century both German and French banks undertook this kind of business, but British banks did not care for it on account of the fluctuations in the value of shares. Investment banking declined between the two World Wars, but it was revived in France after 1945 when a number of specialist credit institutions were set up by the State to give assistance to particular industries, these banks in France being known as *Banques d'Affaires*, although they also undertake some ordinary banking business. Banks of this type in France include the Bank for Building and Public Works, Sugar and Commercial Credit, the Bank of Food and Colonial Products, the French Agricultural Bank, the Cotton Bank, etc. The International Bank (or World Bank), set up under the Bretton Woods scheme, was for the purpose of assisting real capital investment. In 1958 the European Economic Community established the European Investment Bank.

Investment Bonds. These may take the form of Insurance Bonds or Managed Bonds (*qq.v.*).

Investment Club. An association of small investors interested in investment in stock exchange securities, who pool their resources in order to make regular investment. Advice on the formation and running of such clubs is supplied by the National Association of Investment Clubs.

Investment (Control & Guarantees) Act (1946). This Act made permanent the regulations for the control of investment introduced during the Second World War. In 1939 a Capital Issues Committee had been set up to which application had to be made before a new issue of shares could be made. The purpose of the Committee was to ensure that new capital was raised only for those purposes regarded as being in the 'public interest'.

Investment Counsellor. A person or firm who, for a fee, undertakes to manage an individual's investments.

Investment Department. See Special Investment Department.

Investment Dollars. For investment abroad dollars can be purchased only in a special market, the premium payable for the purchase of such dollars depending on their supply in relation to demand for them in that market. *See also* Dollar Premium; Property Dollars.

Investment Income. For tax purposes formerly known as Unearned Income (*q.v.*).

Investment Multiplier. *See* Multiplier.

Investment Portfolio. A list of the investments of an individual or institution such as an investment trust. The character of the portfolio will depend on the aim of the investor—whether his purpose is to secure a high income or capital growth—but in either case the feature of an investment portfolio is that there should be as wide a spread of risk as possible.

Investments, Foreign. An important 'invisible' item in the Balance of Payments. *See* Invisibles.

Investment Surcharge. An additional tax on investment income. When first imposed in 1973–74 the rate was 15% on investment income in excess of £2,000.

Investment Trusts. There are two kinds of investment trust, though their aim is similar, namely, to give the investor of small or moderate means the opportunity of spreading his investment over a range of securities, perhaps a hundred or more.

1. The *investment trust company*, like other companies, issues shares which can be bought or sold on the stock exchange, the capital so raised being used for the purchase of shares in other companies or other securities. Of Scottish origin, the first investment trusts of this type were established in the eighteenth century.

2. In the case of the *unit investment trust*, however, a company manages the trust, and the managers issue units, generally at any time to suit individual investors or by block issues, the managers also undertaking to re-purchase units at any time. The investors in this type of trust are thus merely holders of units, the prices of which vary from day to day with variations in the stock exchange prices of the underlying securities, but such unit holders are not shareholders in the company operating the trust. Some investment trusts re-

strict their investments to particular fields, such as banking, insurance, mining, consumers' goods, or have a particular aim—high yield or capital growth. A trust may be fixed, the managers then not being permitted to vary the trust's investments, or flexible in which case the managers have power to vary the trust's investment portfolio according to their views on investment possibilities. Unit investment trusts were first established in the 1930s, though they did not become popular until the 1950s. They expanded very greatly in the 1960s. *See also* Financial Intermediaries.

Invisible Balance. The balance of payments and receipts for what are known as 'invisible' items in a country's balance of payments. Invisible items are services and comprise shipping, banking, insurance and other financial services, income from investments abroad, Government expenditure abroad, immigrants' remittances, payments for travel. In the case of Great Britain an adverse visible balance has for a long time been covered in most years by a favourable invisible balance.

Invisible Exports and Imports. *See* Invisible Balance; Invisibles.

'Invisible Hand.' A term used by Adam Smith to explain his concept that though each individual in his economic affairs acts in his own interest such actions are guided by a sort of 'invisible hand' which ensures that they are also to the advantage of the community as a whole.

'Invisibles.' Payments and receipts in the Balance of Payments arising from services, as distinct from Visible items which comprise payments and receipts from the import and export of goods. *See* Invisible Balance.

Invoice. A document used in business giving a complete summary of a transaction involving the sale of goods. For example, an invoice received by a retailer who has made a purchase from a wholesaler will show a list of the goods bought, each being briefly described and its catalogue number quoted, the quantity of each purchased, their prices, the charge for packing, the means of transport to be employed for the delivery of the goods, the terms of delivery and the terms of payment. An invoice is not always regarded as a demand for payment, this usually following later. In such a case it is simply as a record of a particular transaction.

Involuntary Saving. An alternative term for Forced Saving (*q.v.*).

Involuntary Unemployment. This occurs when an individual is out of work through no fault or wish of his own, the term 'voluntary unemployment', referring to an individual who prefers not to work even though suitable work is available for him. *See* Unemployment.

I.O.U. An acknowledgement of a debt made in writing. The name of the document is an abbreviation of the opening phrase—'I owe you'. It is not a negotiable instrument but merely evidence of a debt.

I.P.C. Abbreviation of International Publishing Corporation, a holding company which controls Daily Mirror Newspapers, Fleetway Publications, International Printers, Odhams, George Newnes, Iliffe, National Trade Press, Paul Hamlyn, and over a hundred other companies mainly concerned with the publication of newspapers, magazines, and other periodicals. In addition it has an interest in Associated Television and British Relay Wireless and Television.

I.R.C. Abbreviation of Industrial Re-organisation Corporation (*q.v.*).

I.R.I. Abbreviation of Istituto per la Ricostruzione Industriale, a State-owned Italian holding company set up to acquire shares (in some cases upwards of 100%) in Italian commercial banks, the Alitalia airline, motorways, steel, shipbuilding, the Alfa-Romeo motor manufacturing firm, and several hundred other industrial enterprises.

Iron and Steel Board. A body set up in 1953 under Ministry of Power by the Act which denationalised the iron and steel industry, its first task being to sell back to private ownership the part of the industry which had been nationalised in 1950. On the re-nationalisation of the iron and steel industry in 1967 it was superseded by the British Steel Corporation.

Iron and Steel Corporation. A holding company set up under the Act of 1950 which nationalised the iron and steel industry, it was established to take over the shares of 96 undertakings, together with all their subsidiaries. It had one shareholder only—the State. It was short-lived, being superseded on the denationalisation of the industry in 1953 by the Iron and Steel Board (*q.v.*), this in its turn giving way to the British Steel Corporation (*q.v.*) in 1967 when the industry was re-nationalised.

Iron and Steel Exchange. One of the highly organised London commodity markets.

'Iron Law' of Wages. Also known as the Subsistence Theory of Wages, according to which wages tend to keep down to subsistence level since, it is asserted, if wages rise above this level it will inevitably lead to an increase in population, as a result of which wages will fall again to subsistence level. This theory was put forward by the French school of economists known as Physiocrats, and it was probably supported by conditions in France at that time, but recent history provides little support for it. The term 'subsistence' too is very ambiguous, for a rising standard of living tends to raise the standard it connotes.

Ironmongers' Company. One of the twelve more important of the Guilds or Livery Companies of the City of London whose existence dates back to the gilds of the Middle Ages. The company ranks tenth in order of civic precedence among the guilds of London. It was active in the thirteenth century, when it was known as the Ferroners' Gild, though it did not receive its charter until 1463.

Irrationality. Consumers in practice often behave irrationally—making a purchase on the spur of the moment or from force of habit without considering where the commodity stands on their scales of preference, or assuming that because one article is of higher price than another it means that it is of correspondingly better quality. In spite of this fact economists find it necessary to assume that people in their economic dealings always behave perfectly rationally, since otherwise it would be impossible to formulate a theory of consumers' demand. *See* Assumptions.

Irredeemable. Stocks which have no date of redemption, $2\frac{1}{2}\%$ Consols being the best known. A number of other Government securities are redeemable only if the Government so wishes after a stated date, for example, $3\frac{1}{2}\%$ War Stock after 1952. If it wishes the Government can regard these as irredeemable and the assumption that this is so affects the prices of these stocks on the stock exchange. *See also* Indefinitely Dated Stocks.

Irredeemable Debentures. These are debentures for which no undertaking regarding their redemption was given at the time of their issue. Such debentures would be redeemable only on non-payment of interest or on the company's being wound up.

Irregular Employment. This was one of the main causes of poverty in the nineteenth century. Since 1945 great efforts have been made to reduce the extent of casual labour, as for example among dock workers.

Irrevocable Credit. An alternative term for a Confirmed Credit (*q.v.*).

Iso-outlay Curves. Lines on a diagram joining all combinations of factors of production of equal outlay to the entrepreneur.

Iso-product Curves. Lines on a diagram joining all combinations of factors of production which yield equal products.

Isoquants. An alternative term for Iso-product Curves (*q.v.*).

Issue. A term used of (i) a bank's issue of banknotes or (ii) of a limited company's or corporation's issue of shares or stock.

Issue by Tender. The issue of a stock for which a minimum price is usually stated but for which applicants have to tender by stating the price at which they are prepared to buy. For example, the Greater London Council made such an issue in 1966, the first tender issue by a local authority since 1905.

Issued Capital. The actual amount of capital issued by a company and allotted in shares to investors. It may be the same or less than the Authorised Capital.

Issue Department. One of the two departments into which the work of the Bank of England was divided by the Bank Charter Act (1844), the other being the Banking Department. The Issue Department is solely concerned with the issue of Bank of England notes, and its balance sheet is shown separately in the Weekly Return, published every Wednesday. From this can be seen the total issue, the value of the notes in circulation and the reserve of notes held in the Banking Department, and also the extent to which the note issue is backed by Government securities (the fiduciary issue) or gold. *See* Bank Return.

Issuing House. A financial undertaking which specialises in making public issues of shares on behalf of public limited companies, the issuing house generally taking up the entire issue or a large part of it (thereby enabling the company to obtain its capital immediately) and then offering the shares publicly at a slightly higher price. In the case of a very large issue an issuing house will distribute portions of the issue among other firms willing to act as sub-underwriters.

Issuing Houses Association (I.H.A.). A body representing issuing houses, it has fifty-seven members.

I.T.A. Abbreviation of Independent Television Authority (*q.v.*).

Itinerant Salesman. Hawkers, pedlars, or other door-to-door salesmen. The term may perhaps be extended to include any retailer with no permanent place of business, and so can include street sellers ('barrow-boys'), market stall-holders, and the modern mobile shops.

I.T.O. Abbreviation of International Trade Organisation (*q.v.*).

I.T.U. Abbreviation of International Telecommunications Union (*q.v.*).

J

Jack Committee (1961). Appointed to inquire into rural bus services, it reported that 98 route miles were withdrawn in 1960. It estimated that the decline in rural bus traffic began about 1952, the decline being at an average rate of $3\frac{1}{2}\%$ per annum since that date. It found that the decline was due to two factors: the increased use of the private car and the falling off in evening traffic.

J.A.L. Abbreviation of Japanese Airlines.

Jenkins Report (1962). A report, on company law, its recommendations *inter alia* included (i) that no company should be exempt from disclosing its reserves, and (ii) that a holder of 10% or more of the ordinary shares of a company should have to disclose this fact. Most of the recommendations of the Jenkins Committee were embodied in the Companies Act (1967). *See* Company Law.

Jeon. A sub-unit of the currency of both North and South Korea, 100 jeon being equal in value to a won.

Jetsam. *See* Flotsam and Jetsam.

Jettison. In a storm or other circumstance of danger it may be necessary to lighten a ship by deliberately throwing overboard, that is, jettisoning, a part or the whole of the cargo. Such acts give rise to General Average (*q.v.*).

Job Analysis. The analysis of a piece of work to discover what qualities a worker should possess if he is to carry it out efficiently.

Jobber. A member of the London Stock Exchange. The jobbers are the actual dealers in securities but transact business only with brokers who act on behalf of investors. Jobbers specialise in particular groups of shares—gilt-edged, mining shares, oil, food, drapery, and stores, etc. When asked to quote a price for a stock or share in which he deals, a jobber will give two prices, the higher being his selling price and the lower his buying price, without knowing at the time whether the broker is seeking to buy or to sell. In recent years the number of firms of jobbers on the London Stock Exchange has declined, though their size has increased.

Jobber's Turn. The difference between the two prices quoted by a jobber for a stock or share, the higher being his selling price and the lower his buying price at that particular time.

Jobbing Backwards. The practice of stressing the past progress of the company or trust as an inducement to new investors, as in a prospectus relating to an issue of additional shares or an additional 'block' issue by a unit investment trust.

Job Card. *See* Operation Job Card.

Job Evaluation. The calculation, usually by a points system, of the qualifications required for the various jobs in a factory or workshop, in order to assist the management in selecting the most suitable men for particular jobs.

John Buchanan Fund. A fund of £48,000 established in 1932 for the reduction of the National Debt. *See* National Fund.

Joint Account. An account at a bank in the names of two persons (most frequently husband and wife), on which either is permitted to draw —by cheque in the case of a current account.

Joint Annuity. *See* Joint Pension.

Joint Consultation. Discussion between the management of a business and the workers in works committees or councils on matters of general interest to both—safety regulations, overtime arrangements, works rules, absenteeism—but not matters appertaining to trade unions such as wage rates. The aim is to

Joint Demand. When two commodities are complementary to one another they may be jointly demanded, as for example, bread and butter, tea and sugar, etc. A change in the demand for one commodity will, therefore, bring about a similar change in demand for the other. It is very unlikely that conditions of supply will be exactly the same for both commodities, and so the changes in price resulting from the change in demand will not be the same for both commodities, the more inelastic the supply the greater the change of price. Consider the following diagram:

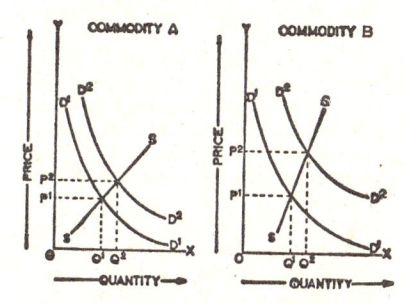

[Diagram: two price-quantity graphs for Commodity A and Commodity B, each showing demand curves D^1, D^2 and supply curve S, with prices P^1, P^2 and quantities Q^1, Q^2.]

This diagram shows a similar increase in demand for each of two commodities, A and B, which are in joint demand, in both cases the quantity demanded increasing in the same proportion from OQ^1 to OQ^2. The price of A rises only a little, from OP^1 to OP^2, but the price of B rises very considerably on account of the supply of B being more inelastic than the supply of A. Generally, however, the proportion between two commodities in joint demand can be varied, at least to some extent.

Joint Industrial Council. A permanent body set up in an industry for the purpose of settling industrial disputes. They are sometimes known as Whitley Councils, because their establishment was recommended in 1916 by the Whitley Committee for all industries where no such machinery already existed.

secure the co-operation of the workers and to avoid discontent.

Joint Pension (or **Annuity**). A pension or annuity payable throughout the lifetime of a husband and wife (or two other persons not so related) and until the death of the survivor.

Joint Production Councils. Meetings of representatives of the management and workers in an undertaking, set up during the Second World War, to discuss matters concerning production with a view to increasing output and efficiency.

Joint Products. *See* Joint Demand; Joint Supply.

Joint-stock Bank. A term formerly used to distinguish banks which were public limited companies from private banks which were partnerships. For over a hundred years the Bank of England was the only joint-stock bank in England, though the Bank of Scotland had no such monopoly of joint-stock banking in Scotland. Bank failures were fewer in Scotland than in England and after the banking crisis of 1825–26, during which no joint-stock bank failed although eighty English banks had to close, this was regarded as proof of the greater strength of joint-stock banks. An Act of 1826 permitted the establishment of joint-stock banks in England, but with unlimited liability and only so long as they were outside a radius of 65 miles from London, the Bank of England retaining its monopoly of joint-stock banking in this part of the country until 1833. Private banks tended to be local, but joint-stock banks soon expanded by opening branches. Between 1840 and 1890 the number of private banks fell from 321 to 155, and by the later date there were over a hundred joint-stock banks, the largest ten of which had no fewer than 949 branches. By amalgamation the number of English joint-stock banks has been greatly reduced. Although it has no longer any special significance, the term, *joint-stock bank*, is till used by many bankers, though generally writers on banking now prefer the term *commercial bank*.

Joint-stock (or **Limited**) **Company.** This type of business unit developed out of the partnership for undertakings requiring a large amount of capital. The feature of the joint-stock company is the division of the capital into shares of small denomination so that investors can invest small or large sums as they please, the profit being distributed in proportion to the number of shares held. The earliest joint-stock enterprises were trading companies, such as the British East India Company, established in 1600. In 1720, after the crisis known as the South Sea Bubble, when large numbers of people subscribed for shares in bogus companies, the first Act to control the establishment of joint-stock companies was passed. From that date there were to be two types of joint-stock company: (i) the Chartered Company, incorporated by Royal Charter, and (ii) the Statutory Company, established by Act of Parliament. The early British railway companies were all statutory companies. Following the Industrial Revolution the number and size of industrial enterprises increased to such an extent that another method of incorporation had to be employed. An Act of 1825 permitted the establishment of a joint-stock company by registration, a Registrar of Companies being appointed to ensure that all the required legal formalities were carried out. The application after 1862 of limited liability to all companies—both public and private—led to a great increase in the number of joint-stock companies, and this type of business enterprise can be regarded as the typical business unit of today. The Companies Act of 1948 refers throughout to the joint-stock company simply as the limited company. *See also* Close Company; Private Company; Public Company.

Joint Supply. When commodities are in joint supply a change in the supply of one brings about at the same time a similar change in the supply of the other. Examples of joint supply include wool and mutton, beef and hides, petrols and heavier oils, gas and coke, etc. In such cases a change in the demand for one commodity will affect the price of the other through the change in its supply. Consider the following diagram:

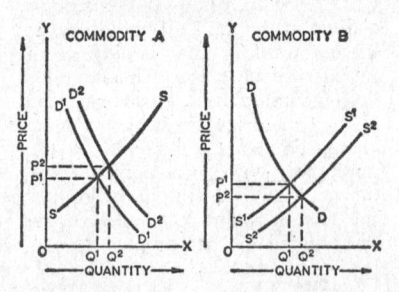

The increased demand for A raises its price from OP^1 to OP^2 and increases its supply from OQ^1 to OQ^2. The supply of B also increases from OQ^1 to OQ^2 but since there is no change in the demand for it, its price falls from OP^1 to OP^2. It is rare for the proportions between the joint products not to be able to be varied, though the extent to which this can be done may not always be very great. For example, Australian sheep are reared mainly for their wool, New Zealand sheep mainly for meat.

Jonathan's Coffee House. A place where stockbrokers used to meet to do business in the eighteenth century before the opening of the London Stock Exchange.

Journal. Theoretically a book in which entries are made daily. In book-keeping the journal is now only used to a limited extent in Great Britain, being generally restricted to items outside the scope of other books.

Journeyman. A skilled worker recognised as such because of his having served the required period of apprenticeship to his trade, and so entitled to the full rate of pay. Under the medieval gild system an apprentice qualified as a journeyman if the gild found his 'masterpiece' or test work satisfactory. He might continue in the employment of the master under whom he had served his apprenticeship in order to gain further experience before setting up on his own as a master.

Judgment. A decision of a court of law.

Judgment Summons. When a debtor who has been ordered to pay fails to do so, he will receive a judgment summons, after which failure to pay will lead to the debtor being sent to prison.

Junior Chambers of Commerce. Bodies established for the benefit of younger business executives, many of whom fail to become members of Chambers of Commerce before middle age. They discuss matters of current commercial importance, promote exhibitions, undertake inquiries and publish reports. They are affiliated to the association of British Junior Chambers of Commerce. *See* Chambers of Commerce.

Junta. A term used by the Webbs for the group of people who influenced trade union ideas and policy in England in the mid-nineteenth century.

Just Price. In the Middle Ages it was believed that there was a 'just price' for everything—labour service as well as goods. Customary prices were regarded as 'just' prices. It was considered to be equally wrong for sellers to put up their prices in times of scarcity as for buyers to beat down prices when there was a glut of a commodity.

K

Kaffirs. A stock exchange term for South African gold-mining shares.

Kartell. The German form of Cartel (*q.v.*).

Kas-associate. A Dutch bank which, in addition to its ordinary banking business, acts as a clearing house for transactions in securities.

Keelage. Dues paid by a ship on entering and staying in a British port.

Kennedy Round. A term used of an all-round reduction of tariffs made by members of G.A.T.T. (*q.v.*) and agreed upon in 1967, so called because the negotiations were undertaken at the suggestion of the U.S. President who had been impressed by the tariff reductions achieved by the E.E.C. and E.F.T.A. (*qq.v.*). The Kennedy Round tariff reductions were the greatest accomplished by G.A.T.T.

Kerb Market. A street market, generally relating to the carrying on of stock exchange transactions in the street after the exchange has closed.

Key Industry. An industry which is of importance to other industries and a country's entire economy. Anything which affects a key industry will have repercussions also on other industries.

Keynes Plan. An international currency scheme, mainly the work of Lord Keynes, put forward by the British Treasury immediately before the Bretton Woods Conference of 1944. It aimed at increasing multilateral trade through stable exchange rates and freely convertible currencies. It envisaged the setting up of an international institution such as the International Monetary Fund and the introduction of an international unit of account, Lord Keynes suggesting the name Bancor for this. Under the Keynes Plan the I.M.F. would have had power to grant overdrafts like a commercial bank. The Bretton Woods Scheme (*q.v.*) was a compromise between the Keynes and American Plans.

Key Worker. A highly skilled worker whose work is of vital importance to other workers in the factory or workshop in which he is employed. In the period after 1945 when a number of firms transferred their activities to Development Areas or opened new branches there they were only permitted to transfer key workers to these places, the aim being to provide work for people already living in those areas.

Kind, Payment in. Payment in goods—or, possibly, services—instead of in money wages. Some people even today still receive part-payment in kind as, for example, board and lodging for many domestic workers, the provision of uniform for many workers, an allowance of coal for coal miners, a certain amount of free travel for many transport workers, etc. In comparing wages in different occupations it is necessary to take these 'free' benefits into account. *See* Truck System.

Kip. The standard unit of the currency of Laos.

Kite. 1. The mark adopted by the British Standards Institution to indicate its approval of a commodity.

2. A colloquial term for an Accommodation Bill (*q.v.*).

Kleinwort Benson Ltd. A firm of merchant bankers in the City of London, established in 1792. It has branches in New York, Brussels, and Geneva.

K.L.M. Koninklijke Luchvaart Maatschappij—Royal Dutch Airlines, the principle airline of the Netherlands.

Knights of Labour. An American labour movement, founded 1869, it was the first attempt in the United States to organise labour on a national basis. It declined in 1886 with the rise of the more conservative American Federation of Labor.

Kobe. The financial centre of Japan.

Kobo. Sub-unit of the currency of Nigeria, it is worth one-hundredth of a Naira.

Kopek (or Copek). A fractional unit of the Russian currency, it is worth one hundredth of a rouble.

Koruna. The standard unit of the currency of Czechoslovakia, it is sub-divided into 100 heller.

Kr. Abbreviation of krona, krone, or kronor in the currencies of Denmark, Norway, Sweden, and Iceland.

Krona. The standard unit of the currencies of Sweden and Iceland, the Swedish krona being subdivided into 100 öre and the Icelandic krona into 100 aurar. *See* Crown.

Krone (pl. Kronor). The standard unit of the currency of Denmark and Norway, in both cases being subdivided into 100 öre. *See* Crown.

Krugerrand. A South African coin containing one ounce of 22 carat gold, minted since 1967. It became popular as a hedge against inflation after April 1973 when United Kingdom citizens were again permitted to hold gold coins.

Kulak. A rich Russian peasant who had a share of the land of his commune as well as land of his own.

Kurus. A sub-unit of the currency of Turkey, 100 kuras being equal to one lira.

Kwacha. The standard unit of the currency of Zambia, it is sub-divided into 100 ngwee. It is also the standard unit of the currency of Malawi, being equal in value in that country to 100 tambala.

Kyat. The standard unit of the currency of Burma, it is subdivided into 100 pyas.

L

Labour. One of the factors of production—human effort that contributes towards production, except that of the entrepreneur, though some people do not recognise the entrepreneur as a separate factor of production and so regard the entrepreneur merely as a special kind of labour. (For a summary of the argument for regarding the entrepreneur as a separate factor of production, *see* Entrepreneur.) Labour is, therefore, generally considered by economists to include all forms of labour, manual or otherwise, with the exception of organisation and management. As a factor of production labour is economically similar to the other factors, land and capital, in that it is one of a number of productive resources at the disposal of entrepreneurs, though differing from land and capital in being human. A measure of substitution is possible between these three factors: for example, more capital and less labour may be employed, or more labour and less land.

Labour, Division of. *See* Division of Labour.

Labour Economics. The branch of economics that deals with problems that affect labour—efficiency, redundancy, wages, etc.

Labourers, Statute of (1351). The Black Death (1349) brought about a shortage of labour, as a result of which many wage-earners began to demand higher wages. Parliament passed this law to try to check the rise in wages. It laid down that all labourers should receive the same wages (including any payments in kind) as they had received before the Black Death. At the same time Parliament attempted to keep commodity prices steady.

Labour Exchange. Former name of Employment Exchange (*q.v.*).

Labour Exchange Bank. A term used of some early nineteenth-century schemes for replacing money as a medium of exchange by notes representing the amount of labour put into the manufacture of goods. *See* 'Labour Notes' *and also* Labour Theory of Value.

Labour Exchange Act (1909). The Act which established labour exchanges. Later their name was changed to Employment Exchanges (*q.v.*).

Labour Force. *See* Labour, Supply of.

Labour Intensive. A form of production requiring a high proportion of labour in relation to the other factors of production employed. *Cf.* Capital Intensive.

Labour Legislation. Acts of Parliament relating to working conditions, trade unions, etc. *See* Factory Acts; Trade Union.

Labour, Marginal Productivity of. The addition to the total production of a firm resulting from the employment of one more unit of labour. *See* Marginal Productivity Theory.

Labour Market. The environment in which wages are determined. Since there is a supply of labour and a demand for labour, there exist the two main conditions required for a market, in which the price of labour (wages) is determined, as are prices in other markets. Labour, however, is not homogeneous, for in addition to non-specific labour, there are many different kinds of specific labour, and therefore as many separate markets for labour, though these are not completely independent of one another. Hence wages vary between different occupations.

Labour, Ministry of. Former name of the Department of Employment, it was set up as an independent department in 1916 and changed its name in 1970.

'Labour Notes.' In 1820 Robert Owen suggested that people should be paid in labour notes for goods they had produced according to the amount of work done and that these notes should then be used as money for making purchases of consumers' goods. His suggestion had its origin in the Labour Theory of Value (*q.v.*) which Adam Smith had favoured.

Labour-saving Invention. The type of invention which makes it possible to use less labour in production, in contrast to capital-saving invention as a result of which less capital will be required.

Labour, Supply of. This may be taken to mean the total number of men, women, and children of working age in a country, or it may be regarded as the supply of labour service, which can be varied either by a change in the size of the labour force or by a change in the number of hours worked. Thus the supply of labour depends in the first place on the population of the country concerned, the average age of leaving school, the age of retirement, the extent to which women—especially married women—go out to work, and the average number of hours worked per year.

Labour Theory of Value. The view that the value of a commodity depends on the amount of labour required to produce it. Adam Smith said that it was 'natural' that an article that required two days to make should be double the price of an article that could be made in half that time. It is, however, very difficult to measure the amount of labour that has gone into the production of a commodity. Labour is not all of equal quality, and labour may be misdirected. To support his political opinions Karl Marx accepted the Labour Theory of Value, overcoming one criticism by defining labour as 'socially necessary labour', in order to assert that the worker was entitled to the entire fruit of his labour.

Labour Turnover. The rate at which workers change from one firm to another. In times of full or over-full employment the rate of labour turnover tends to be high, with a consequent falling off in efficiency.

Labour Union. An American term for a Trade Union.

L.A.F.T.A. Abbreviation of Latin American Free Trade Association. *See* Regional Trade.

Laissez-faire. The doctrine that State interference in industry and commerce should be kept to a minimum. Adam Smith advocated this policy as an alternative to the trade restrictions of the mercantilism of his day. Adam Smith's views had great influence in England until the second half of the nineteenth century.

Lancashire Cotton Corporation Ltd. A combine of cotton-spinning firms formed during the Great Depression of the 1930s to buy up other firms in the industry in order to reduce total capacity and costs of production by closing down the less efficient firms and concentrating production at the more efficient.

Land. One of the factors of production, land comprises all kinds of natural resources—the natural fertility of the soil, mineral wealth, climate, etc.—as distinct from capital which has to be produced. Early economists classified the factors of production into rigidly defined groups. Ricardo considered land to be fundamentally different from the other factors of production in three ways: (i) Land was a 'gift of nature', that is, it owed nothing to man's efforts as it did capital; (ii) Land, unlike the other factors, is strictly limited in supply; (iii) Production in industries primarily dependent on land was peculiarly subject to the Law of Diminishing Returns. Against Ricardo it is argued that: (i) Though land is not man-made it is of no economic importance unless labour is applied to it; (ii) It is not strictly true to say that the supply of land is absolutely fixed since coast erosion decreases the supply and reclamation from the sea, as in the Netherlands, increases the supply, though only to a relatively small extent. The quality of land too can be improved by irrigation or drainage or the use of fertilisers; (iii) The Law of Diminishing Returns is of general application to all forms of production and applicable to manufacturing as well as to agriculture and mining whenever the factors of production are not combined in the optimum proportions. The main characteristic of land is its use as a site where some form of economic activity can be carried on.

Land Bank. Alternatively known as an Agricultural Bank, its function is to lend to farmers either for the purchase of land or for its development. There are banks of this kind in the United States and some Commonwealth countries but not in Great Britain.

Land Certificate. A document giving particulars of a piece of land that has been registered with the Land Registry. Any future transfer of ownership of the land requires the production and endorsement of this certificate.

Land Commission. Established in 1967, it had powers to acquire and dispose of land and to collect a betterment levy whenever the development of land was realised by sale or development. It was abolished in 1971.

Land Commissioners. Before the establishment of the Board (later Ministry) of Agriculture in 1889, the land commissioners were officials appointed to administer certain Acts of Parliament relating to land, such as the Tithe Act (1836) and the Settled Land Act (1882).

Landeszentralbanken. *See* Deutsche Bundesbank.

Landlord. An owner of property—houses, shops, industrial premises—which he permits others to use in return for a payment of rent.

Landlord and Tenant. The branch of English law dealing with the relations between a landlord who owns a property and the person to whom he has let or leased it, mainly covered in various property Acts, the Landlord and Tenant Acts, Housing Acts and the Rent Acts of 1957 and 1968.

Landlord's Property Tax. A term often applied to Income Tax Schedule A, under which until 1964 owner-occupiers were taxed on the notional income they were assumed to derive from their property.

L. & N.E.R. The London and North Eastern Railway, one of the four British railway groups formed under the Act of 1921, it became part of British Railways in 1947.

Land Registry. In England and Wales titles to the ownership of land may be registered at the Land Registry. This enables a change of ownership of land to be effected more simply and more expeditiously, and therefore more cheaply, than is the case with unregistered land.

Lands Improvement Company. This undertaking makes loans, which are secured by terminable rents, to cover the cost of agricultural improvements.

Land-value Tax. Henry George and others advocated the taxation of increases in land values, since the owners of such land have done nothing to increase its value. Since economic rent is unearned, to tax it, even up to its full extent, can have no adverse economic effect. The main difficulty is to distinguish the portion of payment for the use of land that is a payment for this service and the portion that is pure economic rent. An attempt was made during 1945–50 to 'nationalise' land values, individual owners only to be entitled to its 'use value'. The large amount of work involved and the huge sum required to be paid as compensation to existing owners, particularly during an inflationary period, led to a very considerable modification of the scheme. A further attempt was made in 1967 when the Land Commission (*q.v.*) was set up, but this effort too was short-lived.

Large Numbers, Law of. The principle of insurance that if a sufficiently large number is involved only a certain proportion, calcu-

Large-scale Production. One of the main features of industrial development during the past hundred years has been the increase in the scale of production. Before then it was unusual for a firm to employ more than a few men. The development of the limited company as the typical business unit made possible undertakings with huge amounts of capital, subscribed by tens of thousands of shareholders. There are now upwards of a hundred companies in Great Britain each of which employs over 5,000 workers, though 99% of all firms in this country employ less than 2,000 workers. Businesses have increased in size partly as a result of natural expansion and partly by amalgamation. There have been three main motives for expansion: (i) To reduce the average cost of each unit of output as a result of internal economies of scale; (ii) To secure some degree of monopoly profit; and (iii) To produce a variety of products as a safeguard against a fall in demand for one of them. An extension of division of labour requires an expansion of distribution, and this in its turn depends on improved means of transport. An expansion of production requires an expansion of the market, and this has been achieved partly by: (i) the fall in the prices of many commodities resulting from economies of scale, and (ii) the rise in the standard of living during the past hundred years. *See also* Economies of Scale.

Disadvantages of Large-scale Production. (i) The larger the firm the more bureaucratic its organisation tends to be; (ii) The larger the output the greater is the loss from an error of judgment; (iii) There is a slower response to changes in the case of the large firm, partly because decisions cannot be taken as quickly as with the sole proprietor, and partly because of the greater cost of making changes where re-tooling is involved; (iv) The salaried manager is often said to be motivated less by self-interest than the sole proprietor with a resulting loss of efficiency.

Limits to Large-scale Production. (i) The extent of the market; (ii) The extent to which variety is preferred to standardisation, as for example with clothing; (iii) After a time average cost per unit of output will rise as a result of the increasing complexity of the organisation of the very large firm; (iv) Increasing cost of factors of production resulting from an increased demand for them.

Large-scale Retail Trade. There are several forms of large-scale retail trade—department stores, multiple shops, consumers' co-operative societies (*qq.v.*). *See also* Hypermarket, Supermarket.

Last Days. The number of days agreed upon by the owners and charterers for the loading or unloading of ships.

'Last in, First out.' Often abbreviated to L.I.F.O., this is a method of costing adopted by firms which carry many items of stock of the same kind bought at different times and at different prices as shown in the books. Under the more common F.I.F.O. ('First in, first out') system it is assumed that whenever an item is sold it was the first to be purchased, whereas under the L.I.F.O. system it is assumed to have been purchased last. In a time of rising prices the F.I.F.O. method will give a larger profit than L.I.F.O., the position being reversed when prices are falling. *See also* Base Stock Method.

'Last in, Last out.' A method of costing stock bought at different times. *Cf.* 'Last in, first out,' and 'First in, first out.'

Lateral Integration. This occurs when a firm branches out or absorbs other businesses engaged in producing commodities related in some way to its own main products, as occurs in the chemical industry with its great variety of modern products.

Latey Committee (1967). Appointed by the Lord Chancellor under the chairmanship of Mr Justice

Latey, this committee favoured lowering the age of legal majority from 21 to 18. The Family Reform Act (1969) carried out this reform.

Latin Monetary Union. An agreement made in 1865 between France, Belgium, Switzerland, and Italy, with Greece and some other countries joining later, to make the metal content of the standard units of their currencies of equal value so that these coins became interchangeable. The aim was to control the amount of silver coined each year. The agreement lapsed in 1914.

Laurel. An alternative name for the unite, a gold coin, minted in 1619, and worth £1.

Lausanne Conference (1932). A meeting held at Lausanne to consider the problem of inter-Allied debts arising out of the First World War. Most of the creditor countries had to accept some degree of repudiation.

Law. Common law was originally based on custom and was so called because it was common to the whole country and not one locality. It is unwritten law. The other great branch of unwritten law, known as equity, covered certain matters which were outside the scope of common law and until the passing of the Judicature Act of 1873 and 1875 it was administered in a separate court from the courts of common law. A third important branch of English law is case law, built up on previous judicial decisions, based on the principle that what has been decided in a previous case is binding on similar future cases. Finally, there is statutory law expressed in Acts of Parliament.

Law, Economic. *See* Economic Law. For particular laws see under specific name, for example, for Law of Diminishing Returns *see* Diminishing Returns, Law of.

Law Merchant. The forerunner of English mercantile law, it was that branch of law that had to do with commercial transactions and which before it was merged in common law was administered by special mercantile courts. It was based on the customs prevalent among traders.

Law Reform (Contributory Negligence) Act (1945). Previous to the passing of this Act a person who had suffered an accident for which he himself was partly to blame, that is, where there had been contributory negligence, was completely debarred from claiming damages. The effect of this Act was to make such claims possible, the damages being reduced in proportion to the extent of the contributory negligence.

Law Society. Professional association of solicitors in Great Britain, it was established in 1825. The society conducts examinations for intending solicitors.

Layfield Committee (1976). Recommended that Local Authorities be allowed to raise a local income tax to supplement rates.

Lay-off Pay. The American term for Redundancy Payment (*q.v.*).

Lazard Brothers & Co. Ltd. A merchant bank in the City of London, it was established in 1877. It is one of three closely linked firms of similar name, the others being in New York and Paris.

L/C. Abbreviation of Letter of Credit (*q.v.*).

L.C.C. 1. Abbreviation of London County Council, replaced by G.L.C. in 1965.

2. Abbreviation of Lancashire Cotton Corporation (*q.v.*).

3. Abbreviation of London Chamber of Commerce.

Lead. The syndicate which first puts its name on the slip presented by the placing broker who wishes to secure insurance cover from Lloyd's underwriters for a particular risk. The large syndicates are experts in their own particular fields, and once the placing broker has placed one of these as a lead for a substantial percentage of the total risk the smaller syndicates will more readily take up smaller portions of the risk.

'Leads and Lags.' With reference to international payments and their effect on the balance of payments this term refers to the hastening or delaying of payment, in order to take advantage of expectations of changes in the rate of exchange. Such actions can have serious effect in the short-run on the balance of payments, as occurred immediately before the devaluation of sterling both in 1949 and 1967.

Lease. A contract giving possession of a property for a specified period of time—one year, several years, or a very long period. Such contracts are most common when the property is situated in city centres and, therefore, likely to appreciate in value more quickly than elsewhere. In London leases since the late eighteenth century have been for the relatively short period of 99 years, though nowadays leases for 999 years are more common elsewhere. By an Act of 1967 a leaseholder has the option of extending his lease for a further 50 years at a revised rent.

Leaving Certificate. A document required by an employee before he could change his job during the First World War. *See also* Essential Work Orders.

Ledger. A book-keeping term, it is the book to which are posted all entries made in books of original entry. A large firm will keep the Ledger in several parts, as for example, Purchases Ledger, Sales Ledger, etc.

Legacy. A bequest by will of a specified article or a sum of money.

Legacy Duty. A tax on inheritance, the amount depending on nearness of relationship to the deceased, first levied in 1796. In 1949 it was merged with Estate Duty, popularly known as Death Duty. Capital Transfer Tax replaced Estate Duty in 1974.

Legal and General Assurance Co. Ltd. Established in 1836, it is the second largest British insurance company.

Legal Tender. A form of payment which by law a creditor is compelled to accept in settlement of a debt. Thus, in England and Wales Bank of England notes are legal tender up to any amount. The legal tender limits for coins are: 20p for bronze new pence, £5 for cupro-nickel, and £10 for 50p coins.

Leipzig Fair. With a continuous history of over 800 years this is one of the best known fairs in Europe. *See* Exhibitions; Fairs.

Leisure. As opposed to the desire for income in order to be able to satisfy more wants, the desire for leisure acts as a disincentive to work. Since for most people the law of diminishing marginal utility applies to income, leisure becomes increasingly desirable after a certain level of income has been reached. The effect of a progressive system of taxation is to make leisure preferable to income at an earlier stage.

Lek. The standard unit of the currency of Albania, it is subdivided into 100 qintar.

Lempira. The standard unit of the currency of the Republic of Honduras, it is subdivided into 100 centavos.

'Lender of Last Resort.' An essential function of a central bank is that it should be willing to lend—on its own terms, of course—when the commercial banks are unwilling to do so. Only since 1866 has the Bank of England on its own initiative acted as lender of last resort. Only the discount houses are entitled to this privilege. They can do so either by rediscounting first class bills at bank rate or by borrowing from the Bank of England at a rate—usually $\frac{1}{2}\%$—above bank rate, depositing bills as collateral security for the loan. The Bank of England charges a higher rate than the market rate in order to discourage such borrowing.

Lend-Lease. Under an Act of 1941 the United States gave assistance to Great Britain and its allies during the Second World War by supplying them with all kinds of goods that might, directly or indirectly, aid their war effort, such goods being regarded as lent or leased and not given, though most of these goods were expendable. In return these countries had to provide reciprocal assistance to the United States which received in return about 12½% of the amount it had supplied.

Leone. The standard unit of the currency of Sierra Leone, it is subdivided into 100 cents.

Lepta. A unit of the currency of Greece, worth one-hundredth of a drachma.

Lessor. The owner of a property who allows someone else (the lessee) the use of it for a stated period of time.

Letter Cards. Obtainable at post offices, pre-stamped, they offer the sender the privacy of a letter.

Letter of Allotment. An applicant for a new issue of stock or shares who is successful, or an investor who has taken up a 'rights' issue offered to him, will receive a Letter of Allotment showing how much stock he is to receive. For a short time after their issue such documents can be dealt in, usually free of stamp duty.

Letter of Credit. A document authorising a bank to pay the bearer a specified sum of money, it provides a useful means of settlement for a foreign trade transaction, the purchaser establishing a credit in favour of his creditor at a bank. Payment by means of a Letter of Credit involves action between two banks, one in the importer's country and one in the exporter's country, and has an advantage over a foreign bill of exchange, the acceptor of which may be unknown in the exporter's country. A Confirmed Letter of Credit is one that has been confirmed by the paying bank. An Unconfirmed or Revocable Letter of Credit can be cancelled at any time.

Letter of Hypothecation. *See* Hypothecation, Letter of.

Letter of Indication. *See* Indication, Letter of.

Letter of Renunciation. *See* Renunciation, Letter of.

Letters of Administration. When a deceased person has not made a will, or if he has failed to appoint an executor of his will, his estate cannot be administered on his death until Letters of Administration have been granted.

Leu. The standard unit of the currency of Romania, it is subdivided into 100 bani.

Lev. The standard unit of the currency of Bulgaria, it is subdivided into 100 stotinki.

Levant Company. A monopolistic trading company established originally in 1581 as the Turkey Company to carry on trade with the Near East. It took the name of the Levant Company in 1592, and carried on business until 1825.

Level of Living. An American term for standard of living.

Levy, Capital. *See* Capital Levy.

Liabilities of a Bank. The main liability of a bank is for the deposits of its customers, these forming 99% of its total liabilities. Other liabilities include the capital of its shareholders, reserve funds, acceptances, the last item being self-balancing with the liability of customers for acceptances on the assets side of the balance sheet. The only bank liability of economic importance is deposits, on current and deposit account, since bank deposits can be drawn upon by cheque and so form purchasing powers.

Liabilities of a Company. Among other things the Balance Sheet of a company shows that it is liable to its shareholders for (i) the capital they have subscribed, (ii) the reserves of the company, (iii) sundry creditors, (iv) bank loan (if any), (v) interest on loan capital (debentures) (if any), (vi) dividend on preference shares (if any), (vii) dividend on ordinary shares, etc. The balance which equalises the liabilities and the assets of the company will be the undistributed profit for the year concerned.

L.I.B.O.R. Abbreviation of London Interbank Offered Rate, that is, the rate of interest in the interbank market.

Library Association. Professional association of librarians and employees in libraries. Founded in 1877, it was incorporated in 1898. The association conducts examinations and its membership comprises associates (A.L.A.) and fellows (F.L.A.).

Licence. A legal permit to do something, as for example to sell alcoholic liquor, to drive or run a motor vehicle, to own a dog, to engage in business as a hawker, or to sell postage stamps. When imports are regulated by quotas licences are issued to exporters showing the amounts allotted to them. When rationing of raw materials was in force many things could be obtained by producers only under licence.

Licensed Dealer. A person licensed under the Prevention of Fraud (Investments) Act, to do business in stocks and shares on his own account, more generally known as an Outside Broker (*q.v.*).

Lien. The right to retain possession of the property of another until certain legitimate demands, such as payment of debt, are satisfied. Thus, a banker has a lien on collateral security until the loan is repaid. An hotelier has a lien on a guest's luggage in the case of non-payment of an hotel bill.

Life Assurance. One of the main branches of insurance, some companies specialising in it. It is of more recent origin than some other branches of insurance, such as fire, though two British life assurance companies have been in existence since 1720—the Royal Exchange and the London. There are two main types of life policy: (i) Endowment, where the assurance is for a specified number of years or until the attainment of a certain age, the sum assured being paid either on the death of the assured or at the agreed time; (ii) Whole life assurance, where the payment of premiums must continue until the death of the assured, this nowadays being much less common than endowment assurance. Policies are issued 'with profits' or 'without profits', an annual bonus, depending on the profits of the company, being added in the former case to the sum assured. In order to give some protection against a fall in the value of money the sum assured can be linked to the value of units in a unit investment trust. *See also* Industrial Business; Ordinary Business.

Life Style. The standard of living to which a section of the community has become accustomed—an important influence on Consumer Behaviour (*q.v.*).

L.I.F.O. Abbreviation of 'Last in, first out' (*q.v.*).

Lighterage. The charge for the carriage of goods in a lighter.

L.I.L.O. Abbreviation of 'Last in, last out' (*q.v.*).

Limit. A stock exchange term, it denotes the maximum price an investor authorises his broker to pay for a purchase of a stock or the minimum he is prepared to accept in the case of a sale.

Limitation Act (1939). *See* Statute of Limitations.

Limited by Guarantee. Under the Companies Act the liability of a company may be limited by guarantee. The liability of some professional associations is limited in this way.

Limited Company. The modern name for Joint-stock Company (*q.v.*).

Limited Letter of Credit. A Circular Letter of Credit payable only in the towns listed on it. The issuing bank can then inform its agents or correspondents in these towns and supply them with copies of the signature of the payee, who will not then require a Letter of Indication as would otherwise be necessary.

Limited Liability. The liability of shareholders in a company, public or private, is limited to the amount they have paid for fully paid-up shares, or to the amount outstanding on shares purchased which were not fully paid up. The granting of limited liability to companies has been one of the most important factors in the development of the company as a business unit since, without it, cautious people would have been unwilling to invest in such undertakings. Chartered and statutory companies were first permitted limited liability by the Act of 1720, but the Act of 1825 which recognised a third type of company, the registered company, withdrew the privilege of limited liability from companies. An Act of 1825, however, restored limited liability, but only to companies (other than banks) with shares of a nominal value of £10 or over. An Act of 1862 extended limited liability to all companies, banks having obtained the privilege in 1858.

Limited Partnership. Under the Limited Partnerships Act (1907) the liability of a limited partner is restricted to the amount of capital he has invested in the business, whereas the general partners are fully liable for the debts of the firm. A limited partner, though he cannot withdraw his capital without the consent of the other partners, is not allowed to take a share in the management of the business. He is, however, permitted to have access to the books and he can offer advice to the general partners. Limited partnerships must be registered with the Registrar of Public Companies. In all limited partnerships there must be at least one general partner with unlimited liability. In other respects a limited partnership is similar to an ordinary or general partnership. It is not a popular type of business unit, the small close limited company being preferred, since it gives all shareholders limited liability.

Limping Standard. A term applied to the gold standard during the period 1925-31 when it did not work as effectively as before 1914 because many countries did not keep to the 'rules', namely, to inflate when gold was coming in and to deflate when gold was being exported. The term is also sometimes applied to a gold standard under which silver was not completely demonetised as in France and Germany in the nineteenth century.

'Lien and Functional' Organisation. *See* 'Line' Relationship.

'Line and Staff' Organisation. *See* 'Line' Relationship.

Line of Credit. A sum of money on which the debtor can draw but only to obtain goods on credit from his creditor. The American Loan to Great Britain of December 1945 was in effect a line of credit since it could be drawn upon only to obtain goods from the United States.

Liner. Passenger or cargo vessel plying over a regular route according to an advertised time-table. The term can also be applied to a freight train working a regular time schedule.

'Line' Relationship. In any large industrial organisation delegation of duties is essential. The term 'line' is used to indicate the 'line of authority', as with different ranks in the armed forces, where the line of authority is clear. Similarly, in a workshop there might be the works manager, foremen, chargehands, and workmen. Between many employees of a firm there will be a functional relationship, as for example, between the Sales Manager and the Chief Buyer or Purchasing Officer. In practice the line and functional relationships are likely to be combined. A staff relationship exists between an assistant to the Managing Director and the various Heads of Departments, and some firms are therefore organised on a 'Line and Staff' basis.

Liner Train. An alternative name for freightliner (*q.v.*).

Liquid Assets. Assets either in the form of money or in a form that can easily be turned into money. The liquid assets of a bank are cash ('coin, notes, and balances at the Bank of England'), 'money at call or short notice', and 'bills discounted'. *See* Liquidity Rules, Bank.

Liquidated Damages. The amount stated in a contract as compensation to be paid for non-fulfilment of the agreement.

Liquidation. The act of terminating or 'winding-up' of a company, usually because of its insolvency. Liquidation may be *compulsory* as a result of a Court order or *voluntary* following a resolution of the shareholders.

Liquid Capital. Capital in the form of money.

Liquidity, Control of. According to the Radcliffe Report monetary policy influences total demand by altering the liquidity of financial institutions and others, and liquidity can be influenced through changes in the structure of interest rates rather than through changes in the supply of money.

Liquidity, Excess. *See* Excess Liquidity.

Liquidity, International. The gold standard was abandoned in the domestic sphere because it was felt that the expansion of an economy should not be limited by a country's stock of gold. The Bretton Woods Scheme of 1944, however, retained gold in the international sphere although, with the credit facilities provided under the I.M.F., it allowed more latitude than the former gold standard. Since, however, there must always be a close connection between the internal and external monetary situations an adverse balance of payments, with the consequent reduction in a country's gold reserves, is likely to check internal expansion. On several occasions since 1945 suggestions have been made that the price of gold should be raised. During the negotiations at Bretton Woods Lord Keynes had proposed a system that would have provided for an expansion of credit for international dealings similar to that provided internally by banking systems. Since 1945 there has been a great expansion in international credit facilities. The main source is the I.M.F. (*q.v.*) which provides: (i) Drawing rights as laid down in its constitution; (ii) A borrowing scheme by the Group of Ten (*q.v.*); (iii) Standby Agreements (*q.v.*) under which member countries negotiate immediate drawing rights in advance of need; (iv) Special Drawing Rights (*q.v.*) which the I.M.F. began to issue in 1971.

Greater international liquidity is required on account of the need for the volume of international means of payment to keep pace with the expanding volume and monetary value of international trade. Means of payment have been related to gold and the world output of this metal has increased at only a fraction of the rate at which foreign trade has expanded. For a long time the gap in international liquidity was made good by the use of sterling as a reserve currency. In recent years the U.S. dollar has shared this role with sterling. In the mid-1960s both these currencies came under pressure and led to demands for other means of international payment. Hence the decision of the I.M.F. to issue S.D.R.s.

Liquidity Preference. The extent to which investors—individuals and institutions—prefer to keep their assets liquid, that is, in the form of money, rather than in some form of investment. This concept is important to Keynes's theory of money and the rate of interest. To Lord Keynes interest was the reward for parting with liquidity. In his theory of money he defined the demand for money as the demand to hold money as distinct from investing it. Thus, an increase in the demand for money is the same as an increase in liquidity preference. A certain amount of money must be held to cover current transactions together with a little more as a reserve against unforeseen contingencies. Money held in excess of what is required for these purposes is held at a certain cost, namely, a loss of interest. If securities can be purchased at a low price then the yield on such securities will be high. Thus, if it is expected that the prices of securities are likely to fall in the future (that is, for the rate of yield to rise) it will be advantageous to delay acquiring them, so that as a result liquidity preference will be strong. If, on the other hand, the prices of securities are expected to rise in the future it will be better to purchase them without delay, so that in this case liquidity preference would be weak.

Liquidity Rules, Bank. Bankers have always been concerned for the liquidity of their assets on the one hand and their desire to increase their lending on the other. Advances to customers form the least liquid of bank assets and the greater the extent of a bank's lending the greater the likelihood of demands for cash. It was this that led bankers to maintain a definite ratio between their deposits and the amount of cash held. Thus it became the first liquidity rule of British banks at one time to maintain a cash ratio of 10%, this being reduced in 1946 to 8%. The other liquid assets of a bank, in addition to cash, are money at call or short notice (short-term lending to the money market) and bills discounted. Before 1939 it had become the second liquidity rule of British banks to keep these three liquid assets taken together at 30% of total deposits, the remaining 70% of their assets comprising investments and advances to customers. The Second World War upset what had come to be regarded as the recognised structure of the balance sheet of the English commercial banks, mainly on account of the huge size of Treasury Deposit Receipts, introduced during the war as a means of Government borrowing. The disappearance of this item from the banks' balance sheet during the post-war period helped to bring back the structure of the banks' balance sheet nearer to its pre-war pattern, though the introduction of Special Deposits again temporarily affected it. The banks developed these two liquidity rules in their own interests, especially the cash ratio, but it appears from the Radcliffe Report that the Bank of England would also insist on the maintenance of the second liquidity rule that the more liquid assets should be kept now at not less than 28% of total deposits, this rule being regarded as more important than the cash ratio, since if the cash ratio falls it can be restored fairly quickly at the expense of money at call or short notice, whereas a fall in the 28% ratio requires a bank to restrict credit. Until 1963 a ratio of 30% was maintained. In 1971 the Bank of England introduced a new liquidity rule: commercial banks should maintain a ratio of 12½% between their combined cash, money at call, Treasury bills, a portion of their commercial bills and Government stocks within one year of maturity and their total assets.

Lira (pl. Lire). The standard unit of the currency of Italy. Formerly it was divided into 100 centesimi, but the depreciation of the lira during the past sixty years has reduced it to less than one-fortieth of its former value, and so a smaller monetary unit is no longer required. The lira is also the standard monetary unit of Turkey being subdivided into 100 kurus.

List. A term used in connection with the piece-rate system of wage payment in the cotton and wool textile industries, the aim being to adjust piece-rates on the introduction of new machinery in order to keep earnings fairly uniform and to allow a firm to gain a reduction in its costs, thereby encouraging firms to introduce improved machinery. Different systems of adjustment were in force in different areas, these being known as Lists—for example, the Oldham List.

Listed Stocks. Stocks or shares dealt in on the stock exchange.

List Price. As with the catalogue price, when quoted by wholesalers to retailers, these prices are subject to trade discount, the list price often being the retailer's selling price.

Lit. Abbreviation of Italian lira or lire.

'Little Neddies.' An acronymic term used of the regional development councils, set up under the N.E.D.C. (q.v.).

Liverpool Corn Trade Association. A body which undertakes the grading of wheat so that it can be sold by grade by private treaty on organised markets (corn exchanges).

Liverpool Cotton Association. A body which includes members who are engaged in every branch of the cotton industry. One of its principal activities is the grading of raw cotton imported from abroad so that cotton can be sold by grade.

Liverpool Cotton Exchange. The principal organised market in England for the buying and selling of raw cotton. The method of sale is by private treaty since the cotton can be graded, the Liverpool Cotton Association undertaking this task.

Livery Company. The London guilds are often known by this name on account of their right to wear distinctive dress. *See* Gild.

Living on Capital. *See* Capital Consumption.

Livre. Pre-Revolutionary French coin (pound) equal in value to 20 sous.

Lloyd Jacob Report (1949). A report on Resale Price Maintenance (*q.v.*). It was estimated by the Committee that at that time 30% of goods sold to consumers were subject to resale price maintenance. It was recommended that resale price maintenance should be permitted, and also that an individual manufacturer should have the right to cut off supplies to a retailer who sold his products for less than the manufacturer's price, but that it should be made illegal for concerted action to be taken by a group of manufacturers against a retailer who had cut the fixed price. *See* Restrictive Trade Practices Act (1956).

Lloyd's. An association of London underwriters, incorporated in 1871, so called from Edward Lloyd, the proprietor of a seventeenth-century coffee house, where underwriters at that time met to do business. The underwriters are organised in syndicates who undertake fractions of the risks brought to them by brokers acting on behalf of shippers. Members bear risks with unlimited liability. Lloyd's is best known as a centre for marine insurance, but all kinds of insurance are accepted, and in fact at the present day marine insurance comprises less than half the total business undertaken. Since 1871 Lloyd's has been a corporation established by Act of Parliament. Until 1968 membership was restricted to citizens of the Commonwealth.

Lloyds and Scottish Finance Ltd. A finance house with head office in Edinburgh, it is jointly owned by Lloyds Bank and the National Commercial Banking Group of Scotland. It is a member of the Finance Houses Association.

Lloyds Bank. One of the 'Big Four' English commercial Banks. Established in Birmingham in 1765 as a private bank, it became a joint-stock bank in 1865. Since then it has expanded by a series of amalgamations. It has over 2,100 branches throughout England and Wales and through the National Commercial Banking Group it operates in Scotland. It also has an interest in the Lloyds International Bank. It is also associated with the Yorkshire Bank, the National and Grindlays Bank, the National Bank of New Zealand, the Bank of West Africa and Intercontinental Banking Services. It also has a hire purchase subsidiary (Lloyds & Scottish Finance) and in 1966 it established a unit trust.

Lloyds Bank Review. A quarterly publication of Lloyds Bank Ltd., it contains authoritative articles on matters of current economic and monetary interest.

Lloyd's Bonds. Introduced by J. H. Lloyd to enable a statutory company to borrow in excess of the amount permitted to it by law, they were issued mainly by British railway companies.

Lloyds International Bank. A merger in 1971 of Lloyds Bank Europe, with branches throughout Europe and BOLSA (the Bank of London and South America), with branches throughout the world.

Lloyd's List. A publication of Lloyd's which gives shipping news to those engaged in marine insurance.

Lloyd's News. A publication of Edward Lloyd, the seventeenth-century coffee house proprietor, giving information on shipping movements for the benefit of his customers. *See* Lloyd's.

Lloyd's Register of Shipping. A society mainly concerned with the classification of ships, those with the highest standard of efficiency being placed in Class A1. A classified list of British and foreign ships—Lloyd's Register Book—is revised annually.

L.M. & S.R. The London, Midland, and Scottish Railway Company, the largest of the four British railway groups formed under the Act of 1921, it became part of British Railways in 1947. Most of the English and north Welsh lines of the L.M.S. form the London Midland Region of B.R., the Scottish lines being transferred to the Scottish Region of B.R.

Loan. The borrowing of a sum of money at an agreed rate of interest, usually for a specified period of time by a Government, an institution, a business firm, or an individual. Governments borrow on long-term by the issue of stocks to the capital market or on short-term by the issue of Treasury bills to the money market. The larger local authorities and sometimes public corporations also make issues on the capital market. Local authorities supplement these issues by mortgage loans for short periods made directly with borrowers. Public companies often issue loan stocks or debentures and also borrow from commercial banks. Individuals can obtain loans from commercial banks, or, for the purchase of houses, from building societies. Both individuals and business firms borrow for specific purposes from hire purchase finance companies.

Loanable Funds Theory. The theory that the rate of interest is a price and, like other prices, determined by the forces of supply and demand in a market: the supply of loanable funds in relation to the demand to borrow.

Loan Account. Borrowing from a bank can be either by overdraft or by loan account. In the case of the overdraft the customer is permitted to draw cheques up to an agreed amounting in excess of the amount at the time standing to his credit in his current account, interest being paid only on the amount by which the account is overdrawn. In the case of a loan account, however, the customer's current account is credited by the full amount of the loan and at the same time a loan account is opened for him for this amount, on the whole of which he has to pay interest for the period of the loan. *See also* Personal Loan.

Loan Market. *See* Capital Market; Money Market.

Loan Society. A society established under the Loan Societies Acts of 1840 and 1863 for the purpose of making loans to people with small incomes, the rules of the society to be approved by the Registrar of Friendly Societies, and no loan to exceed £15.

Loan Stock. An alternative name for Debentures (*q.v.*).

L.O.B. Abbreviation of Location of Offices Bureau (*q.v.*).

Local Employment Act (1960). This Act empowered the Government to assist any part of the country where the level of unemployment was persistently in excess of 4%, in the same way as the districts scheduled as Development Areas under the Distribution of Industries Act (1945) had been helped. Such areas were to be designated Development Districts. *See* Planned Location of Industry.

Local Government Act (1929). This Act transferred the administration of the Poor Law from the Boards of Guardians and the Unions of parishes, many of which were heavily in debt to Local Authorities. It also exempted agriculture from local rates and derated industrial premises.

Local Government Board. A former Government Department, its functions were taken over by the Ministry of Health in 1918.

Localisation of Industry. The concentration of a particular industry mainly in one area, as occurred with many industries in Great Britain during the nineteenth and early twentieth centuries. Thus, the cotton industry came to be established in south Lancashire, the woollen industry in the West Riding of Yorkshire, the manufacture of cutlery in

Sheffield, the manufacture of pottery in north Staffordshire, tin-plate manufacture at Swansea, and shipbuilding in a number of places where coal and iron were usually to be found close to the sea. The reasons for such localisation of industry were mainly economic. In addition to the fact that production could generally be carried on at lowest cost in these areas, further economies, known as external economies, could be enjoyed when a large number of firms in the same industry were located in close proximity to one another. This made regional division of labour possible, with specialisations of processes between firms, and a consequent increase in output at lower average cost, as in other forms of division of labour. Other advantages of localisation of industry were the establishment in the same locality of industries subsidiary to the main industry, the development of a pool of the appropriate kind of skilled labour, and the rise of organised markets and special financial facilities for the industry. There is, however, one serious drawback to localisation of industry: it makes a district too dependent on the prosperity or otherwise of the basic industry. If the main industry declines or suffers a setback in a trade depression the whole area is affected and unemployment concentrated into it. This disadvantage of localisation was seen during the Great Depression of 1929-35 when a number of distressed areas developed rates of unemployment very much in excess of the national average. It was this that led to suggestions that industries should be more widely distributed since, even if full employment is successfully and permanently maintained, the decline of a highly localised industry could create a pocket of serious structural unemployment. It was for this reason that Lord Beveridge's policy of full employment laid down as one of its three conditions: Planned Location of Industry (*q.v.*). *See also* Location of Industry.

Local Loans. The larger local authorities generally, if the Government permits them, go into the capital market to raise loans at the current rate of interest. These authorities also borrow for specified periods of time by mortgage loans, the lender being able to choose the period at the time he makes the loan. The smaller local authorities borrow from the Treasury, usually at a lower rate of interest than is current in the markets. For some years after 1945 all local authorities were compelled to borrow from the State, the Government then obtaining funds by borrowing in the capital market. Since Government borrowing adds to total purchasing power it tends to be inflationary, whereas borrowing from the capital market reduces the purchasing power of the lenders by an equivalent amount. It was, thus, to check inflation that the larger local authorities were forced into the capital market. *See* Public Works Loan Board.

Local Taxation. *See* Rates.

Location of Industry. Industries tend to be located in those places where the costs of production are lowest at the time of their establishment. In days when transport was difficult most people in inland areas had to rely on their own efforts to satisfy their wants, unless they lived near to navigable rivers. The introduction of power-driven machinery led to the establishment of industries near the source of power, of necessity at first when water-power was used, and to reduce costs of production when steam-power was employed, since coal increased rapidly in price the greater the distance it had to be carried from the mines. During the nineteenth century, therefore, nearness to coalfields became the principal locating influence on the siting of new industries, especially for heavy industry. Next in importance came nearness to raw materials—iron ore for the iron and steel industry, clay for the making of pottery, etc. Other factors which helped to determine what industry might be attracted to a particular coalfield included soft water in the case of the textile industries and the moist climate also for the cotton industry. Between the two World Wars, the development of new forms of power, such as electricity and oil, and further developments in transport, together with the fact that the newer industries were 'light' in character (coal forming a smaller part of their total costs), reduced the locating influence of coal and increased the importance of nearness to centres of population as markets for their products, which were mainly consumers' goods. After 1945 the British Government embarked on a policy of Planned Location of Industry (*q.v.*) and during a period of mainly full employment nearness to a labour supply became of greater importance as a locating factor for new industry, so that many light industries were set up in small towns in rural areas, with the result that industry in Great Britain became more widely distributed than at any time during the preceding two hundred years. *See also* Localisation of Industry; Planned Location of Industry.

Location of Offices Bureau (L.O.B.). An official body established in 1963 to offer advice and to encourage firms to transfer their offices from Central London to the suburbs or to other parts of the country. From August 1977 the prime function is to promote better distribution of office employment throughout the U.K. Information is available to further this aim. Their terms of reference enable the L.O.B. to attract international concerns to the location of office employment in the U.K. and to give attention to the promotion of office employment in the inner urban areas.

Lock-out. This occurs when employers refuse to employ their workers unless they agree to accept the employers' terms. A strike may take place when workers demand higher rates of pay; a lock-out is most likely to occur if employers decide to reduce the rate of pay.

'Lock-up.' A stock exchange term, used of securities which are regarded as worth buying as a long-term investment, their market price not being expected to rise for some time.

Loco Price. A commercial term which when used in foreign trade in a price quotation means the local price, that is, the price at the warehouse of the exporter. Therefore, an importer buying on these terms will himself have to pay carriage to the docks at the port of export, all dock dues, charges for freight and insurance between the two ports, and the cost of delivery from the docks at the port of arrival.

Lombank. A finance house, it is an associate of Lombard Banking. It is a member of the Finance Houses Association.

Lombards, The. A group of Italian bankers and merchants from Lombardy in north Italy who established themselves in London during the fourteenth to seventeenth centuries. They were the first bankers to operate in England.

Lombard Street. A term almost synonymous in London for the Money Market, since most of the discount houses and head offices of the English commercial banks are in or near this street.

Lomé Agreement. A trade agreement, signed in February 1975, between the E.E.C. and the forty-six A.C.P. (*q.v.*) countries.

London Assurance Co. Ltd. Established in 1720, the year in which the Royal Exchange Assurance Co. Ltd. also was founded, it shares with that company the distinction of being the oldest life insurance company in the United Kingdom. It also does accident, fire, and motor insurance business.

London Bankers' Clearing House. An institution established by London banks for the clearing of cheques. Representatives of each of the six member commercial banks (*see* London Clearing Banks) and the Bank of England meet one another to exchange and clear cheques paid into their banks and drawn on other banks. So far as is possible indebtedness between banks is offset and the final settlements are made by cheques drawn on the Bank of England, where each of the clearing banks maintains an account. Since the total amount drawn on a bank is closely related to its credit policy the commercial banks must all keep in line in this respect, for if one of them expanded credit to a greater extent than the rest it would have a persistent debit balance at the Clearing House together with a persistent fall in its credit balance at the Bank of England and, therefore, since this balance at the Bank of England is regarded as cash, a fall in its cash ratio.

London Chamber of Commerce. The London Chamber was not established until 1881, over a hundred years after the establishment of the Glasgow Chamber of Commerce, the oldest in Great Britain. It has over 9,000 members, representing all branches of commerce—home and foreign trade, transport, banking, and insurance, etc. Like other such bodies the London Chamber of Commerce collects information on all matters of interest to its members and watches legislation that may affect their interests. In addition the London Chamber of Commerce acts as an examining body in a wide range of commercial subjects.

London Clearing Banks. The six banks that are members of the London Bankers' Clearing House—the 'Big Four' (the Midland, Barclays, Lloyds, the National Westminster) together with Williams & Glyn's and Coutts & Co. In addition to their own business, these banks also act as agents for others that are not members of the London Bankers' Clearing House.

London Commercial Salesrooms. *See* London Commodity Exchange.

London Commodity Exchange. An organised market located at Plantation House, Mincing Lane, London. It deals in tea, coffee, cocoa, spices, and other commodities imported from tropical and semi-tropical regions, including rubber. Until 1941 rubber was bought and sold at the London Rubber Exchange and the other commodities at the London Commercial Salesrooms, but in 1945 these two markets amalgamated to form the London Commodity Exchange. In 1973 the markets for cocoa, coffee, sugar, wool and vegetable oils moved to new premises in the Corn Exchange in Mark Lane. *See* Organised Markets.

London Discount Houses Association. An association of discount houses in the London money and discount markets. Each Friday when Treasury bills are offered to the market the London Discount Houses Association makes a syndicated tender. It is understood that at this price the discount houses will together take up whatever amount of Treasury bills may be offered to them.

London Discount Market. *See* Discount Market.

London 'Dummy' Dollars. *See* 'Dummy' Dollars, London, *and also* English Equivalent.

London Economic Conference. Also known as the World Economic Conference, it was held in London in 1933 to consider ways of increasing world trade which during the world trade depression had shrunk to small proportions. The economic policies of many countries—higher tariffs and increasingly restrictive exchange control regulations—had tended still further to reduce the volume of international trade. Nevertheless, countries were unwilling to make concessions to liberalise trade, and the conference failed to achieve its objectives.

London Gazette. An official British Government publication. In addition to official announcements, such as orders in council, State appointments, etc., it lists dissolutions of partnerships, notices of proceedings in bankruptcy, etc.

London Gold Market. Gold dealings take place each morning at the premises of N. M. Rothschild in

London. The traditional 'gold-fixing' is carried out by representatives of four firms of bullion dealers. Rothschild's are represented both as refiners of gold and as agents of the Bank of England, through which gold reaches the market from South Africa. Since 1968 there has also been an afternoon fixing and prices have been fixed in U.S. dollars. The gold market is much wider than this and a greater quantity of gold is dealt in at free market prices outside Rothschild's premises.

London Match-girls' Strike (1888). This strike was mainly noteworthy because it was the first successful strike of unskilled low-paid workers, its success being largely due to Annie Besant, who roused public sympathy for the girls.

London Metal Exchange. An organised market for copper, tin, lead, zinc, and silver. It also deals in Silver Futures.

London Money Market. *See* Discount Market; Money Market.

London Multinational Bank. A bank consortium formed in London in 1970, it comprises Barings, the U.S. Chemical Bank, Crédit Suisse and the Northern Trust.

London Passenger Transport Board. A public corporation established in 1933 to take over, co-ordinate, and operate passenger transport in the London area, previously operated by independent concerns— the main line railways, underground railways, motor bus, tramway, and trolley bus companies. Under the Transport Act of 1947 a separate executive was set up to take over the services of the former London Passenger Transport Board. In 1963 the London Transport Executive became the London Transport Board (*q.v.*).

London Rubber Exchange. *See* London Commodity Exchange.

London School of Economics and Political Science. A constituent college of the University of London, it was established in 1895 primarily for the study of the social sciences— economics, politics, law, sociology, etc.

London Silver Market. Dealings in silver conducted at the premises of Mocatta & Goldsmidt. The minimum deal is 5,000 ounces. *See* London Metal Exchange.

London Stock Exchange. *See* Stock Exchange.

London Transport Board. One of the boards set up under the Transport Act of 1963 to take over the functions and property of the British Transport Commission, one of these being the London Transport Board, which is to be responsible for the work previously delegated to the London Transport Executive. By the Transport Act (1968) the responsibility for London Transport was handed over to the G.L.C. The capital debt of the London Transport Board was written off, but future losses, if any, were to be borne by the G.L.C.

London Wool Exchange. An organised market in London for the sale of raw wool, mostly imported. Since wool is a commodity that cannot easily be graded prospective buyers must be allowed to sample the wool before the sale takes place. The importer is responsible for warehousing the wool on its arrival, after which he issues a catalogue listing the lots for sale. Buying brokers acting on behalf of wool textile firms or specialist buyers employed by these firms visit the warehouse and make their own estimates of the wool offered for sale as a guide to their bidding at the auction that follows. There is also a wool market in Bradford as well as in Melbourne and other wool-producing countries. *See* Organised Markets.

Long Draft. Alternative name for a foreign bill of exchange (*q.v.*).

Long-end of the Market. That part of the Market in gilt-edged securities dealing with long-dated stocks. *See* Stock Exchange.

Long Period and Short Period. A distinction first made by Marshall in connection with a change in demand. In the short run the supply of a commodity may be fixed since it often takes time for supply to adjust itself to a change of demand. Thus, in the short term an increase in demand may result in a steep rise in price from OP^1 to OP^2 with no change in the quantity, OQ^1, supplied:

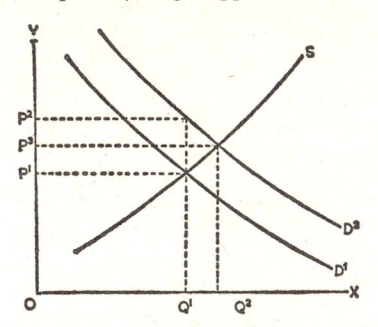

After a time, supply adjusts itself to the new situation (without any change in the condition of supply) and a new equilibrium price of OP^3 will be established at which the quantity supplied will be OQ^2. In the case of some commodities, especially manufactured goods, an expansion of production may result in economies of scale, so that conditions of supply eventually change and the final result may be a lower price, OP^4, than the original price, OP^1, with a considerable increase in output from OQ^1 to OQ^3:

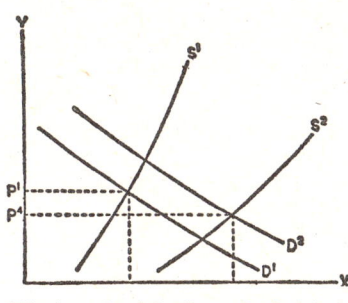

The length of the Long Period is the time taken by a firm to vary the amount of the factors of production that it employs.

Long Rate. The rate of interest charged by a bank for discounting a foreign bill of exchange with the period to run to maturity common to the market.

Long Run. *See* Long Period and Short Period.

Long-term Loans. Some Government stocks are issued for an indefinite period of time or even in perpetuity. Old 2½% Consols have no longer a date of redemption. Other stocks are due for redemption at an unstated time 'after' a certain date. Of this type is 3½% War Loan (after 1952), many holders of which expected the loan to be repaid in 1952. Similarly, there are 4% Consols (after 1957), 3½% Conversion Stock (after 1961), and 3% Treasury Stock (after 1966). Only if the rate of interest at which the Government is able to borrow falls below the rate on these indefinitely dated stocks are they likely to be repaid. Thus 2½% Treasury Stock (after April 1975) will most probably eventually take its place alongside 2½% Consols as an irredeemable stock.

Lords Commissioners of H.M. Treasury. This Board of Commissioners has seven members—the Prime Minister (who is also First Lord of the Treasury), the Chancellor of the Exchequer, and five junior Lords. The Chancellor of the Exchequer is responsible for policy.

Loriners' Company. One of the 82 guilds or livery companies of the City of London whose existence dates back to the time of the medieval gilds.

Loss Leader. It is a practice, more common in the United States than Great Britain, of many department stores to run one department deliberately at a loss by offering goods for sale in that department at a very low price in order to attract customers into the store, since it is hoped that, once inside, they will also make purchases in other departments. The Resale Prices Act (1964) made this practice illegal in the United Kingdom.

Lot. A method of deciding which stocks shall be redeemed each year, e.g. Victory Bonds.

L.O.T. The State airline of Poland.

Louis. A former French coin worth 20 francs.

L.P.T.B. Abbreviation of London Passenger Transport Board (*q.v.*).

£.s.d. Abbreviation used for British currency until its decimalisation in 1971—pounds, shillings, pence. *See also* Coinage, British.

L.S.E. Abbreviation of London School of Economics, one of the constituent colleges of the University of London.

L.T.B. Abbreviation of London Transport Board (*q.v.*).

Ltd. Abbreviation for Limited, used as part of the name of a limited company, most of which by law must include this word. *See* Limited Liability.

L.T.E. Abbreviation of London Transport Executive.

Luddites. The name given to groups of workers who during 1811–16 went about smashing up new machinery, the introduction of which they blamed for their distress. The name is taken from Ned Ludd, a boy of weak mind who in a fit of temper had broken a machine in Leicester some years earlier.

Lufthansa. The airline of West Germany.

Lump Sum. Some contributory pension schemes include the payment of a lump sum on retirement in addition to a pension, the amount of both depending on (i) the length of the period during which contributions have been made and (ii) average salary during the last few years of employment.

Luncheon Vouchers. Purchased by employers and given to their employees—mainly clerical workers—to enable them to have lunch at specified restaurants or cafés without paying for it. They are equivalent to additional tax-free income, as is the case with free uniform in some occupations or concessionary coal to miners.

Luxury Taxes. Luxuries have often been regarded as suitable objects of taxation from the social point of view and when Purchase Taxes were introduced in Great Britain very high rates were imposed on jewellery and lower rates on clothing. Since, however, demand in general for luxuries tends to be more elastic than for necessaries the total revenue from luxury taxes tends to be relatively small.

L.V. Abbreviation of Luncheon Voucher (*q.v.*).

Lzb. Abbreviation of the West German Landeszentralbanken. *See* Deutsche Bundesbanke.

M

M. Abbreviation of Mark der Deutschen Demokratische Republik, the standard unit of the currency of East Germany. It is subdivided into 100 pfennig. *Cf.* DM.

M1; M3. Symbols used to indicate the money supply. M1 represents the narrow version of money, comprising the total value of bank-notes and coin in circulation together with sterling bank deposits on current account. M3 represents a broader version of the money supply comprising, in addition to M1, interest-bearing deposit accounts (including non-sterling deposits held by U.K. residents) and certificates of deposit (other than those held by banks). The symbol M2 is no longer in use.

McKenna Duties. Import duties imposed in 1915 on motor-cars, musical instruments, and cinema films by Mr. R. McKenna, the Chancellor of the Exchequer at the time. The aim of the duties was to cut down unnecessary imports in wartime, but later they were retained for the protection of home industry, and thus became the first serious lapse of Great Britain from its policy of free trade.

McKinley Tariff. The tariff introduced by the United States in 1890 after a presidential election won on a policy of developing the home market, achieving self-sufficiency, and protecting American labour against low wages elsewhere. The duties on a few commodities were actually lowered, but on most imports the duty was increased. The tariff contained a 'reciprocity' clause, whereby the U.S. Government could offer concessions to other countries in return for concessions to the United States.

Macmillan Committee on Finance and Industry (1931). The Report of this Committee, published in 1931, condemned, among other things, the practice of 'window-dressing' (*q.v.*) by the English commercial banks and recommended the establishment of some institution to provide medium term lending to industry. It considered that London had too large a volume of short term liabilities. It considered too the effects of Great Britain's return to the gold standard in 1925 at pre-1914 parity. If favoured Great Britain's staying on the gold standard. The Committee regarded bank rate as a delicate instrument which affected the internal situation through its influence on long-term rates of interest. It suggested that the rate of interest on the National Debt should be reduced. Two of its recommendations were eventually adopted. 'Window-dressing' came to an end in 1946 and the Finance Corporation for Industry and the Industrial and Commercial Finance Corporation (*qq.v.*) were established in 1945.

'Macmillan Gap.' The lack of provision of medium term capital for industry to which reference is made in the Macmillan Report. It was to remedy this state of affairs that the Finance Corporation for Industry and the Industrial and Commercial Finance Corporation were established in 1945.

Macroeconomics. That branch of economics which considers the relationship between large aggregates such as the volume of employment, the total amount of saving and investment, the national income, etc.

Magnified Demand. *See* Acceleration Principle.

M.A.I.B.L. Abbreviation of Midland and International Banks Ltd. (*q.v.*).

Mail Order Business. Buying and selling by post. Some firms specialise in this type of business; others, like department stores, undertake it in addition to ordinary retailing. Catalogues or price lists are issued and sometimes order forms are printed in newspapers or other journals. The purchaser sends his order by post, enclosing payment or a deposit where hire purchase terms are offered, or the goods may be despatched C.O.D. During recent years there has been a huge increase in mail business in Great Britain.

Majority, Age of. In the United Kingdom the age of majority was reduced from 21 to 18 years by the Family Reform Act (1969).

Malthusian League. A society formed by Annie Besant and Charles Bradlaugh for spreading knowledge of birth control, so-called because Malthus had predicted that if population continued to expand it would lead to a fall in the standard of living. *See* Malthusian Theory of Population.

Malthusian Theory of Population. The theory put forward by the Rev. T. R. Malthus in 1798 in his *Essay on the Principle of Population*. He said that population increased in geometric progression whereas the output of food increased only in arithmetic progression, so that unless the checks of earlier years—famine, war, pestilence—were replaced by moral restraint a decline in the standard of living would follow. So far as Great Britain was concerned the events of the nineteenth century appeared to prove Malthus to have been wrong, since between 1800 and 1900 Great Britain's population increased by eight times simultaneously with an enormous rise in the standard of living, even though food output had declined. This had been achieved by the opening up of new lands—the United States, Australia, etc.—and the tremendous industrial development of Great Britain. The world population problem of the second half of the twentieth century appears to justify to some extent the fears of Malthus, though he exaggerated the difference between the rate of expansion of population and of means of subsistence.

Managed Bonds. A form of investment, usually obtained by a single lump sum payment, the bonds running for fixed periods. The investment is generally spread over (i) equities, (ii) property, and (iii) fixed interest securities, the managers varying the proportions to suit the conditions of the time. Regular withdrawals can be made as with Income Bonds.

Managed Currency. A currency is said to be 'managed' if the Government of the country concerned intervenes in some way to influence the prevailing rate of exchange. Exchange management can take the form of the most extreme type of exchange control or, as in the case of Great Britain, France, and the United States in the 1930s, the setting up of Exchange Equalisation Accounts. *See* Exchange Control; Exchange Intervention; Exchange Restriction.

Management. The carrying out of the functions of the entrepreneur (*q.v.*). Though it is recognised that to a certain extent managers are 'born and not made' there is no doubt that the efficiency of managers can be greatly increased through education in Management Studies—economic aspects of industry, legal aspects, the nature of management, psychological aspects, financial accounting, budgetary control, etc. The importance of education for management was first recognised in the United States and only belatedly in Great Britain. Courses in Management Studies are offered by the Universities of London, Manchester and Bradford, most polytechnics and many Colleges of Technology, and senior Technical Colleges. *See* British Institute of Management.

Management Accounting. The Institute of Chartered Accountants of England and Wales, the Chartered Accountants of Scotland and Ireland, the Institute of Cost and Works Accountants, and the Association of Certified and Corporate Accountants have combined to provide an advanced qualification in management accounting which requires the passing of an examination, the writing of a thesis and several years' experience of this grade of work.

Managerial Revolution. A term used by the American writer, J. Burnham, in his book of that name, for his forecast that, with the expansion in size of the business unit, world affairs will eventually be in the hands of a few powerful managers.

Managing Director. A director of a limited company appointed to take charge of the day-to-day management of the firm, he is quite often a large shareholder, often possessing a sufficient number of shares to give him a controlling interest.

Manchester Royal Exchange. For a long time an important organised market for the buying and selling of cotton. On account of the contraction of the cotton industry and the consequent fall in its membership the exchange had to close in 1968.

Manchester School. A group of economists and political thinkers who, following the teachings of Adam Smith, supported free trade and *laissez-faire* principles, opposing State interference in industry and commerce.

Manchester Ship Canal. Built towards the end of the nineteenth century to accommodate ocean-going ships, and opened in 1894, it made Manchester one of the leading British ports. The canal is 36 miles long.

Mandate. As used in banking it is an authority given in writing for another person, a specimen of whose signature is attached, to draw on a person's account.

Mandats. Issued to serve as money during the French Revolution, Mandats were somewhat similar to Assignats (*q.v.*), and like them they rapidly depreciated in value.

Manifest. A form to be completed by the captain of a ship, it gives particulars of the ship, its cargo, and destination. Before the ship leaves port it must be left with the customs officer.

Manorial System. The medieval system of village organisation under which most of the land belonged to the lord of the manor (who might be the king, a noble, or a cleric), who retained a portion, known as the Lord's demesne, for his own use. The Lord's demesne was worked by the villeins for a certain number of days per week, with extra time at harvest in return for a share in the narrow strips in each of the three main fields, one of which in turn was kept fallow. In addition there was some common land on which animals could be grazed. In the early fourteenth century some villeins obtained the right to receive wages from the lord of the manor for their work on his demesne, and they had then to pay rent for the land they worked for their own use. The commutation of land service for money payments was greatly accelerated by the shortage of labour caused by the Black Death.

Manpower. The amount of labour, both male and female, available in a country at a particular time.

Manpower Economics, Office of. *See* Office of Manpower Economics.

Mansholt Plan. An E.E.C. scheme for the unification of the prices of cereals. It was adopted in December 1964.

Manufactured Goods, Distribution of. Many manufactured goods reach the retailer by what is still regarded as the normal route, that is, by way of the wholesaler. Many branded goods, however, go direct from the manufacturer to the retailer, as do some expensive goods where the rate of turnover is slow. Large-scale retailers such as department stores and multiple shops buy direct from the manufacturer on account of their large turnover, though a multiple shop organisation will then have to distribute the goods to its many branches. Some manufacturers sell direct to consumers by opening their own retail shops, as is the case with boots and shoes, or by setting up mail order departments.

Manufacturer's Agent. A seller who acts on behalf of a manufacturer, more especially in the export trade. Sometimes he accepts responsibility for any credit risk.

Manufactures Royales. Industrial concerns outside the control of the gilds set up in France during the late eighteenth century. Colbert was responsible for this policy which helped to expand French industry.

Manufacturing. The second great division of production and so sometimes known as secondary production. Manufacturing industries turn primary products into manufactured goods.

Margin. The marginal unit of anything is the last to be added or the first to be taken away from a supply. Marginal considerations concern the smallest possible increase or decrease in one's stock of a commodity. The marginal unit of something is the smallest additional amount the consumer considers to be worth buying. The marginal concept can be applied to satisfaction (utility) or psychological influences such as the propensity to consume. *See* Marginal Cost; Marginal Firm; Marginal Product; Marginal Utility, etc.

Marginal Benefit. *See* Fringe Benefit.

Marginal Buyer. A buyer who is just prepared to pay the present price for a commodity or service and who will drop out of the market if the price is increased.

Marginal Cost. The extra cost of increasing output by one more unit. Thus if it costs £110 to produce 50 units of a commodity and £112 to produce 51 units, marginal cost is £2. If marginal cost is falling production will be under conditions of increasing returns, whereas if marginal cost is increasing production will be subject to diminishing returns.

Marginal Demand Price. A term used by Alfred Marshall for the price a person is willing to pay to obtain an additional increment of a commodity. Since the more one has of a thing the lower its marginal utility, so too the marginal demand price diminishes as one's supply increases.

Marginal Disutility of Labour. The loss of satisfaction associated with having to perform an additional small amount of work.

Marginal Dose. The term 'dose' was used by James Mill and Alfred Marshall for amounts of labour and capital applied to land. Thus, the marginal dose would be the smallest possible amount that could be added.

Marginal Efficiency of Capital. *See* Capital, Marginal Efficiency of.

Marginal Firm. An undertaking which only just finds it worth while to continue in a business. A rise in average cost or a fall in average revenue would result in its falling out of production. In conditions of perfect competition for such a firm price = marginal cost = marginal revenue = average revenue = average cost.

Marginal Income. The last increment to be added to one's income as for example, payment for overtime. The concept is important in connection with a progressive income tax, for such a tax falls most heavily on marginal income, thereby exaggerating its disincentive effect.

Marginal Land. 1. Land at the margin of cultivation, that is, land that is just worth cultivating at the present cost of doing so and the present prices of commodities that could be grown on it. Clearly, therefore, marginal land is not land of a definite quality or degree of fertility, for a change in costs or the prices of the products of land will raise or lower the quality of marginal land.

2. Land which is the first to cease being used for a particular purpose is marginal land in the economic sense, irrespective of its fertility. The first land to be withdrawn from agriculture will rarely be the least fertile land and it may indeed be the most fertile, since it depends on which land is open to alternative use, a point neglected by Ricardo in his theory of rent.

Marginal Producer. *See* Marginal Firm.

Marginal Product. The extra output resulting from the employment of one more unit of land, labour, or capital.

Marginal Productivity Theory.
The marginal productivity of a factor of production is the addition to output resulting from the employment of an extra unit of a factor—land, labour, or capital. According to the marginal productivity theory no factor in conditions of perfect competition can expect to receive in payment for its services a sum greater than the value of its marginal product, that is, its marginal revenue productivity. Thus, if the employment of an additional man results in an addition of £10 to a firm's total net revenue, the entrepreneur, it is said, will not pay that man more than £10, since to do so will result in his making less net profit than before, According to this theory, therefore, a higher payment can be made to a factor only if its marginal revenue productivity is increased. This can be brought about in either of two ways: (i) by increasing the efficiency of the factor, or (ii) by employing a smaller amount of the factor.

Marginal Propensity to Consume.
A term used by Lord Keynes for the effect of a change in total income on the keenness of people to purchase consumers' goods.

Marginal Propensity to Save. A term used by Lord Keynes for the effect of a change in total income on the extent to which people and institutions are willing to save.

Marginal Purchase. A purchase which a person thinks it is just worth his while to make.

Marginal Rate of Substitution.
The rate at which an individual will exchange successive units of one commodity for another. If at the beginning he has a small amount of Commodity A and a large amount of Commodity B, then he will probably be willing to offer a large amount of B for an extra unit of A. As his supply of A increases he will offer successively smaller amounts of B for additional units of A. This concept is the basis of Indifference Curves (*q.v.*) and the modern theory of Demand.

Marginal Relief. In connection with Income Tax it refers to tax reliefs which occur at certain levels of income. For example, a taxpayer over 65 years of age has an allowance of two-ninths on unearned income provided his total income does not exceed a specified amount. Where his income only slightly exceeds this amount he receives marginal relief. Similarly with the tax on old people with small incomes there is marginal relief when the total income slightly exceeds the ordinary limit.

Marginal Return. An alternative term for Marginal Product (*q.v.*).

Marginal Revenue. The extra revenue obtained from the sale of one more unit of output. Under perfect competition marginal revenue = price, since in these conditions it is assumed that the demand for the product of any single firm is perfectly elastic. Under imperfect competition and monopoly marginal revenue falls as output increases, since to sell a larger quantity of a commodity necessitates a reduction in price.

Marginal Revenue-product. The money value of the marginal product (*q.v.*).

Marginal Significance. Alternative term, used by P. Wicksteed in his *Commonsense of Political Economy*, for Marginal Utility (*q.v.*).

Marginal Unit. *See* Margin.

Marginal Utility. The extra amount of satisfaction to be obtained from having an additional small increment of a commodity. It is marginal utility which determines an individual's demand for a thing and not its total utility. The greater one's supply of a commodity the smaller its marginal utility. *See* Diminishing Marginal Utility, Law of.

Marginal Utility of Income. The larger a person's income the less satisfaction he derives from a small addition to it. This principle is the basis of a progressive system of taxation, the loss of satisfaction resulting from taxation being less for a rich than for a poorer person.

Maria Theresa Dollar. A coin circulating in North Africa. Although not legal tender it is generally acceptable and circulates freely. The coins are all dated 1780, even though minted in London and other places during the nineteenth and twentieth centuries.

Marine Insurance. The branch of insurance relating to ships and their cargoes, it is perhaps the oldest kind of insurance. This type of business is undertaken by Lloyd's underwriters and also by marine insurance companies. Policies can be taken out to cover (i) the ship and (ii) the cargo, and they can be arranged to give cover either for a specified period of time or a particular voyage. There may be either total loss—Actual Total Loss or Constructive Total Loss (*qq.v.*)—or partial loss. If some or all of the cargo has to be jettisoned in order to ensure the safety of the ship the loss is averaged between the shipowners and the owners of the cargo (General Average, *q.v.*). Particular average occurs if there is damage to part of the ship or its cargo, the partial loss in this case being borne entirely by the shipowners or the owners of the cargo. Responsibility, for example, for a collision would lie entirely with the shipowners. A marine policy taken out 'free of particular average' gives cover only against total loss and general average, but a policy 'with particular average' gives full cover against all risks at sea.

Marine Insurance Broker. An agent employed by a shipper who wishing to insure his ship or cargo approaches underwriters at Lloyd's in order to obtain the cover required.

Mark. Originally a measure of weight (8 ounces approx.), mainly used for gold and silver, it was widely used in Western Europe during the 11th to 14th centuries. Its value in England in the 12th century was 160 pence. It became the standard unit of the currency of Germany, until 1923, when it was replaced by the Reichsmark, this in turn being superseded after the Second World War by the Deutsche Mark in West Germany and the Ostmark in East Germany, though in both countries the simple term, Mark, is still widely used. It is subdivided into 100 pfennig.

Marked Cheque. A cheque can be marked at the request of the drawer by the bank on which it is drawn as 'good for payment', the required amount being retained in the drawer's account to meet it. The practice is not favoured by bankers, who prefer a banker's draft to be used instead.

Market. The function of a market is to enable an exchange of goods or services to take place, a means by which buyers and sellers are brought into contact with one another. It may denote a particular place where commodities are bought and sold as with the open-air markets held in market towns or the highly organised markets such as that for cotton at Liverpool or for wool and many other commodities in London. In a wider sense, however, a market can signify any area in which buyers and sellers are in contact with one another and this area may in fact comprise the whole world. Prices in a free market are determined by the combined actions of buyers and sellers. *See* Imperfect Market; Market Price; Perfect Market.

Marketable Securities. Those dealt in on the stock exchange. *Cf.* Non-marketable Securities.

Market Behaviour, Theory of. The determination of price in a market by the forces of supply and demand—the higher the price the smaller the quantity that will be demanded but the greater the quantity that will be supplied; the lower the price the greater the quantity that will be demanded but the smaller the quantity that will be supplied; with equilibrium in the market at a price which equates supply and demand. *See* Price Determination.

Market Forces. The forces in a market that determine the price of a commodity or service namely Demand and Supply (*qq.v.*).

Marketing. The business of distributing a product, either from its place of production or from the port at which it was imported, to the people—consumers or producers—who want it. *See* Market Research.

Marketing Boards. The agricultural Marketing Acts, 1931–33, permitted the setting up of a marketing board for any agricultural commodity where the producers of most of the output so wished, the minority producers then being compelled to join the scheme, so that a cartel with a central selling agency could then be established. Although limitation of output was not the aim in every case, all producers are required to have a licence from the appropriate board, which thus had power to restrict entry, the aim being to organise production and distribution and to control prices. Marketing boards have been established for hops, milk, potatoes, and a number of other agricultural products.

Marketing Name. Shares in U.S. and Canadian companies are often registered in the name of a broker or financial undertaking. This simplifies transfers of ownership and also saves the cost of the transfer fee.

Market Overt. Goods purchased in good faith in a recognised public market, that is, in an 'open market', give the buyer a good title to them even though they may be stolen goods.

Market Price. The short-run equilibrium price determined in a market at a particular time by the forces of supply and demand ruling in the market at that time. *See* Equilibrium (i).

Market Rate of Interest. The actual rate of interest ruling in the market in the short run charged by the banks. This is unlikely to be exactly the same as the Natural Rate which equates the demand for loans with the supply of loanable funds. *See* Natural Rate of Interest.

Market Research. The study of consumer demand by a firm in order to assist it in expanding its output and the marketing of its product.

Market Schedule. The demand of all possible buyers in a market over a range of prices, based on the combined demand schedules of the individuals concerned. *See* Demand Schedule.

Markets, Law of. Formulated by J. B. Say, and often known as Say's Law of Markets, it asserts that supply always creates its own demand. This view was generally accepted by the classical economists and it was not seriously questioned until the Great Depression of 1929–35, when Keynes showed that it did not apply under modern conditions of production and distribution.

Market Town. A town which has the right to hold a market—usually in the open air—on one or more days each week. The right to hold a market was at one time granted by royal charter to lords of manors, monasteries and later to municipal corporations. Since 1858, however, Acts of Parliament have given local authorities the right to hold markets.

Markings. The number and prices of recorded transactions on the Stock Exchange, published in the Stock Exchange Official List and reproduced in some daily newspapers. Since the 'marking' of bargains is not compulsory the List does not provide a complete record.

Markka. The standard unit of the currency of Finland, it is subdivided into 100 penniä (or pennies).

Mark System. The early Teutonic organisation of farming. A small part of the land—the 'home mark'—was where the people lived, each family having a permanent share of it. Another portion of the land was common to all. The largest area was divided into three main fields and, as under the English medieval manorial system, sub-divided into strips for division among the families in the village, each field being left fallow every third year.

Mark-up. The amount a seller adds to his buying price to determine his selling price. Thus, it is the same as the gross profit on an article. It is usually expressed as a percentage of the buying price.

Marriage Age. An important influence on the growth of population. Where early marriage is the custom the length of time of a generation is reduced and population tends to increase more rapidly. Since 1945 the marriage age in Great Britain has fallen for both men and women, and this has been an important factor in checking the possibility of a future decline in the population of this country.

Marshall Aid. Assistance provided by the United States under the Marshall Plan (*q.v.*).

Marshall Plan. A scheme named after the U.S. Secretary of State, to provide assistance to countries, mainly in Europe, the economies of which had been so seriously affected by the Second World War that their recovery was likely to be slow. A condition of the Washington Loan (*q.v.*), was that Great Britain should make sterling freely convertible by July 1947. The failure of Great Britain to maintain the convertibility of sterling for more than a few weeks opened the eyes of the Americans to the serious economic situation of Great Britain and many other countries, including West Germany and Italy. Altogether under the Marshall Plan Great Britain received goods to the value of nearly £1,500 million. To administer the plan the E.C.A. (European Co-operation Administration) was set up in the United States and the O.E.E.C. (Organisation for European Economic Co-operation) in Europe. The plan operated for three years. At the time of its inception the motive was economic, political considerations coming later. It was followed by Defence Aid to help the re-armament of Western Europe. The plan speeded up the recovery of Western Europe and though this was undoubtedly also to the advantage of the United States, there is no previous example in history of assistance by one country to others on so generous a scale.

Mass Production. The manufacture of a standardised commodity on a large scale with a consequent reduction in average cost and the price of the commodity. Mass production is achieved by carrying division of labour to great lengths and by introducing the greatest possible amount of mechanisation. *See* Large-scale Production.

Mass Unemployment. This occurs in a general slump when there are large numbers of workers in nearly all industries unemployed. Its cause is a general deficiency of demand. It is the most serious kind of unemployment against which plans for full employment are mainly directed. *See* Unemployment.

Master and Servant. *See* Employer and Employee.

Master Charge. A U.S. credit card. *See* Credit Card; Interbank.

Master of the Mint. The controller of the Royal Mint. This post is now always held by the Chancellor of the Exchequer, the Royal Mint being a Government department.

Match-girls' Strike (1888). *See* London Match-girls' Strike.

Material Goods. Alfred Marshall classified goods that satisfy human wants as Material and Non-Material. Material Goods comprised all useful, material things, including under this heading not only agricultural products, manufactured goods, etc., but also shares in companies and such things as access to good scenery.

Materialism. The view that in all their actions men are inspired only by economic motives, it was the basis of Karl Marx's concept of history.

Mate's Receipt. A document used when goods are loaded on to a ship by lighter. It is exchanged afterwards for a Bill of Lading.

Mathematical Treatment of Economics. By the use of mathematical symbols and geometrical diagrams some principles of economics can be tersely expressed and more clearly illustrated. Though a knowledge of mathematics is often very useful it is by no means essential. To many people it would appear that some mathematical economists have gone too far in their application of mathematics to economics.

Mature Creditor Nation. A country with a well-developed internal economy which has extensive investments abroad so that it is possible for it regularly to have a debit balance in its balance of trade, usually offset by a credit balance in its invisible items, as is still the case with Great Britain.

Mature Debtor Nation. A country which has borrowed from abroad in the past in order to speed up its economic development and reached the stage when its balance of trade yields a sufficient credit balance to offset the payments of interest it has to make to its creditors.

Mature Economy. *See* Mature Creditor Nation.

Maturity. 1. The date when a stock is due for repayment or when some instruments such as a bill of exchange falls due for payment.

2. During the Great Depression of 1929–35 the theory was put forward in both Great Britain and France that as an economy reaches maturity it tends to lead to stagnation as the urge to economic growth declines. The economic history of the United States, France, West Germany, and other countries during the past twenty years clearly disproves this theory.

Maundy Money. Coins specially minted for distribution to the poor by the King or Queen on the Thursday before Easter, replacing gifts in kind. These are now the only silver British coins and they are issued in four denominations—1p, 2p, 3p, and 4p. First issued in the time of Charles II, the custom for a time fell into abeyance but was revived in 1838.

Maximum Social Advantage. A principle of taxation suggested by Lord Dalton. According to this principle the test of a tax which transfers income from one group of people to another is whether such a transfer increases the economic and social welfare of the community as a whole.

May Report (1931). The Report of the Committee on National Expenditure which forecast a large deficit in the budget. It recommended that Government expenditure, including unemployment pay, should be reduced and taxation increased.

M.Com. Abbreviation of Master of Commerce, a higher degree awarded by some British universities for advanced work or research in some branch of Commerce.

Meade Report (1978). A Report on the structure and reform of direct taxation. It recommended that the basis for personal taxation should be expenditure rather than income.

Mean. *See* Arithmetic Mean; Geometric Mean.

Means of Production. An alternative term for the factors of production (*q.v.*), though sometimes restricted to land and capital.

Means Test. During 1929–35 many workers were unemployed for long periods and so exhausted their entitlement to unemployment benefit. After 1931 further assistance depended on whether they or their families had any other income, this being known as a means test. There are means tests at the present time for many benefits depend on one's income, *e.g.* social security payments, family income supplements.

Measure of Value, Money as a. One of the functions generally attributed to money is that of serving as a measure of value, though it is better termed 'money as a unit of account', since in the theory of economics value is regarded as being incapable of being measured. Nevertheless, in practice people often regard prices as at least an indication, if not a precise measure, of relative values. *See* Functions of Money; Unit of Account.

Mechanics' Institutes. Founded originally for the education of artisans, the movement had its origin in Scotland in the eighteenth century, though the first institution as such was the London Mechanics' Insti-

tute, founded in 1823. Some of them were the forerunners of technical colleges.

Mechanisation. The employment in production of a large amount of machinery in relation to labour. The mechanisation of industry began with the Industrial Revolution and has continued at an increasing pace ever since. It is out of mechanisation that automation (*q.v.*) has developed.

Median. The item halfway in a series of numbers, as for examples in a table of individual incomes, it is a more useful concept in general than the arithmetic average.

Mediation. A method of settling industrial disputes, the mediator bringing the two sides together and assisting them to come to a compromise agreement.

Medibank. The National Health Service of Australia.

Medium of Exchange. This is one of the principal functions of money. Anything which serves as a medium of exchange, not being wanted for its own sake and used to overcome the difficulties of barter and facilitate exchange, can be regarded as money. *See* Money.

Medium-term Credit. The Macmillan Committee (1931) had recommended that provision should be made for medium-term credit for industrial borrowers since for many purposes the period for which commercial banks were prepared to lend was too short. This recommendation was not acted upon, however, until 1945 when the Finance Corporation for Industry (F.C.I.) and the Industrial and Commercial Finance Corporation (I.C.F.C.) (*qq.v.*) were established. During the 1960s a number of international institutions were established in Europe for the purpose of granting medium-term credit for periods of from three to eight years, such as the Banque Européenne de Crédit à Moyen Terme, the Compagnie Internationale de Crédit à Moyen Terme, the Banque Internationale de Commerce, and the Société Financière Européenne. As with the two British institutions the shares in these new organisations are mainly held by banks—British, European, and American. These international institutions obtain their funds by borrowing in the Eurodollar Market.

Megalopolis. A city of Ancient Greece formed from 38 villages. (Greek *mega* = great; *polis* = city); it is now used, mainly in the United States, as an alternative term for Conurbation (*q.v.*).

Méline Tariff. Imposed by France in 1892, it marked the abandonment of free trade by France.

Member Banks. An American term for those commercial banks in the United States that are members of the Federal Reserve System. All the National Banks and a large number of State Banks are member banks.

Memorandum of Association. One of the documents that has to be drawn up when a new company is formed, it gives the title of the company (including 'Ltd.'), particulars of the types of business to be undertaken, the amount of its authorised capital, the address of the registered office, particulars of the shares into which capital is to be divided, and a statement that its liability is limited.

Mercantile Credit Co. Ltd. A finance house in which the Westminster Bank Ltd. and Barclays Bank Ltd. have interests. It is a member of the Finance House Association. In 1972 it became a merchant bank. Since 1975 it has been under the control of Barclays Bank.

Mercantile Law. That part of the common law, supplemented by judicial decisions and statutory law, having to do with commercial transactions—the law of contract, agency, sale of goods, etc.

Mercantilism. The economic belief, prevalent in the seventeenth and early eighteenth centuries, that it was to the advantage of a nation always to strive for an excess of exports over imports, the balance being received in silver or gold.

Mercers' Company. One of the 82

Guilds or Livery Companies of the City of London whose existence dates back to the Middle Ages, when their trade was mainly in the more expensive fabrics, it ranks first in civic precedence of all the guilds. It received its first charter in 1393, but a Mercers' Guild existed in the twelfth century.

Merchandise Marks. Markings on packages, especially goods entering into foreign trade, to enable them to be distinguished and used for reference purposes on trade documents.

Merchandise Marks Act (1887). This Act laid down that all foreign manufactured goods imported into Great Britain should be marked with the name of the country of origin. It also made illegal the use by foreign firms of British trade marks.

Merchant. A person who assists the distribution of a commodity, usually at some stage between its place of production and the manufacturer or retailer who requires it, the term in the latter connection often being synonymous with wholesaler (*q.v.*). Some retailers also are often described as merchants. *See also* Middleman.

Merchant Adventurers. The name of several trading companies founded in the thirteenth century, those of London, York, and Bristol being the best known, which worked together though retaining their independence and established trading depots in Antwerp, Emden, Hamburg, and other places. They were mainly concerned with the export of woollen cloth. Though they lost their monopoly in 1689 they survived until the early nineteenth century.

Merchant Banks. Sometimes known as Accepting Houses, these banks owe their name to the fact that in most cases the banking and financial sides of their business originally developed as a sideline to their trading activities. As merchants they tended to specialise in trade with particular parts of the world, and as a result they came to possess unrivalled knowledge of the financial standing of merchants in those areas. This became the basis for their acceptance business—accepting bills of exchange, on payment of a fee, drawn on merchants in the area with which they were familiar. The growth of their acceptance business led them to hive off their financial business from their ordinary trading activities. With the development of London as the financial and commercial centre of the world many foreign merchant bankers found it convenient to transfer their headquarters to London—hence the number of merchant banks in England with foreign names. In addition to their acceptance business they also began to undertake some ordinary banking business. The decline in the use of bills of exchange has so reduced the business of merchant bankers that they have been compelled to seek new outlets and expand their ordinary banking business.

Merchant Gild. *See* Gild Merchant.

Merchant Navy. All the ships of a country engaged in commerce, as distinct in the case of the United Kingdom from the warships of the Royal Navy. *See* Merchant Shipping.

Merchant Shipping. The expansion of air freight traffic has resulted in a contraction of the merchant fleets of the leading shipping nations. The leading merchant fleets of the world are (1975): 1. Liberia, 2. Japan, 3. Great Britain, 4. Norway, 5. Greece, 6. Russia, 7. U.S.A. The high position of Liberia is due to that country's flag being used as a Flag of Convenience (*q.v.*).

Merchant Shipping Act (1876). The Act of 1876 compelled all ships to be marked with a load-line, generally known as the Plimsoll Line, and made it an offence to send a ship to sea if it was unseaworthy.

Merchant Taylors' Company. One of the principal Guilds or Livery Companies of the City of London whose existence dates back to the gilds of medieval times. The members of the company in the Middle Ages enjoyed a monopoly of tailoring, but not since the seventeenth century have they concerned themselves with this trade. Since then their interests have been in charity and education.

Merger. An amalgamation of two or more firms to form one new company, the shareholders of the two firms receiving shares in the new company in an agreed proportion in exchange for shares in the old companies. *See also* Amalgamation; Takeover Bid.

Merit Rating. *See* Employee Rating.

Mersey Docks and Harbour Board. A body established by Parliament in 1857 to take control of the Mersey ports of Liverpool and Birkenhead.

Messina Powers. The six countries which met at Messina in 1955 to consider the establishment of the E.E.C. (*q.v.*).

Metallic Currency. *See* Coinage.

Metamarketing. The critical study of marketing as a branch of applied economics.

Metayage. *See* Metayer System.

Metayer System. A system of land tenure, prevalent in some parts of southern Europe until recent times, under which the landlord provided the buildings, some farm implements and livestock, the tenant cultivating the land.

Metrication. The metric system as applied to weights and measures. In 1967 it was proposed that Great Britain should adopt this system.

Metroliners. A term used of the very speedy commuter trains that operate between New York and Washington D.C.

Metrology. The science that has to do with systems of weights and measures, including monetary units.

M.G.I. Abbreviation of Member of the Grocers' Institute (*q.v.*), a qualification obtained by examination.

M.I.B. Designatory initials of a Member of the Institute of Bankers (*q.v.*).

Microeconomics. The branch of economics which is concerned with individual firms, their output and costs, the production and pricings of single commodities, wages of individuals, etc., as distinct from macroeconomics, which is concerned with aggregates—production, consumption, income of a community as a whole.

Middleman. Any wholesaler, merchant, broker, or agent who has to do with the distribution of goods between their place of production and the manufacturer (in the case of raw materials) or the retailer (in the case of foodstuffs and manufactured goods). The more complicated the distribution or the greater the degree of specialisation of function the greater will be the number of middlemen required. Thus, one wholesaler may suffice between the manufacturer and the retailer of manufactured goods like hardware. On the other hand several middlemen may be required in the distribution of home-produced foodstuffs on account of the large number of small producers and the wide consumption of the commodities. An even greater number of middlemen will be required in the case of imported foodstuffs and raw materials because of the greater number of stages in their distribution and the greater need of specialists—exporters, importers, selling brokers, buying brokers, etc. It is a popular idea that there are too many middlemen engaged in distribution, but there is no compulsion on the retailer or manufacturer to deal with middlemen, and presumably they do so because it is to their advantage. If a middleman is performing a useful and necessary function his presence in the chain of distribution is clearly justified. Only if a middleman is doing nothing to assist distribution can he be said to be unnecessary and in such a situation he is not likely to survive for long. When a manufacturer claims to be cutting out the wholesaler—and sometimes also the retailer—it will be found that he is in fact doing the work of these people in addition to his own, thereby incurring additional costs and not necessarily reducing the cost of distribution.

Middle Price. The price midway

between the offer and the bid prices for stock exchange securities and unit trusts, it is the price taken into account for purposes of the Capital Gains Tax (1965).

Middle Way. *See* Mixed Economy.

Midland and International Banks Ltd. (M.A.I.B.L.). A bank established in 1964 jointly by the Midland Bank, the Standard Bank, the Commercial Bank of Australia, and the Toronto-Dominion Bank for the purpose of undertaking international financial transactions.

Midland Bank. One of the 'Big Four' English commercial banks founded in 1836 and originally known as the Birmingham and Midland Bank. By expansion and amalgamation it has become one of the largest banks in England, with over 2,400 branches. It does business in Scotland through its subsidiary, the Clydesdale Bank and in Ireland through its subsidiary the Northern Bank. It has interests in the Midland and International Banks Ltd. and the Standard Bank Ltd. (*qq.v.*), the Banque Européenne de Crédit à Moyen Terme, the European-American Banking Corporation. It wholly owns the Forward Trust Ltd., a hire purchase finance house which specialises in financing the purchase of industrial plant. Other subsidiaries are the Midland Bank Finance Corporation, the Clydesdale Bank Corporation, and the Midland Bank Executor and Trustee Co. Ltd. In 1972 it became the principal member of a consortium that purchased Thos. Cook & Son (*q.v.*) from the Government.

Midland Bank Review. The quarterly journal of the Midland Bank Ltd., it contains articles on topics of current economic and monetary interest.

M.I.Ex. Designatory initials of a Member of the Institute of Export (*q.v.*).

Migration. *See* Emigration; Immigration.

Mil. The sub-unit of the currency of Cyprus, the pound being sub-divided into 1,000 mils.

Milan. The financial and commercial centre of Italy.

Milk Act (1934). This Act enabled needy school-children in Great Britain to receive one third of a pint of milk per day free, other children to pay a halfpenny per day. In 1971 an Act restricted the provision of free milk to school-children.

Milled Edge. The more valuable gold and silver coins were given a milled edge in order to check coin clipping.

Minimum Lending Rate. The minimum rate at which the Bank of England will discount eligible bills, until 1972 known as Bank Rate (*q.v.*).

Minimum Sacrifice. A principle of taxation, based on the Law of Diminishing Marginal Utility as applied to money. To carry out this principle in practice would require exceptionally heavy taxation of all incomes above a certain level and relief from taxation for those with incomes below this level. The main argument against such a tax system is the harmful effect it would have on economic progress on account of its disincentive effect.

Minimum Wage. For long it was the aim of many workers' organisations to secure a legal minimum wage for all their members as a guarantee of a minimum standard of living. In some industries in Great Britain, the United States, and other countries trade unions by negotiation with employers have secured minimum wage agreements.

Minor. Since 1969 a person under the age of 18. *See* Infant.

M.Inst.T. Designatory initials of a Member of the Institute of Transport (*q.v.*).

Mint. An institution set up to make coins from metal. In early days there were often several mints, privately owned and operated, but it soon came to be regarded as the sole prerogative of the State to produce coins. *See* Royal Mint.

Mintage. A charge made by a Mint for turning metal of the required degree of fineness into coins.

Mint Par of Exchange. The rate of exchange between two currencies as determined by the relative amounts of pure metal in the standard unit of each currency. Thus, on the full gold standard as operated before the First World War the gold sovereign contained the same amount of gold as a German 20 mark piece. The mint par of exchange, therefore, was £1 sterling = 20 German marks.

Mint Ratio. The ratio between the value of the two metals where a bimetallic currency system is in operation.

Minutes. A record of the proceedings of a meeting.

M.I.O.M. Designatory initials of a Member of the Institute of Office Management. *See* Office Management.

Misdirected Demand. This is demand which stimulates production and a demand for labour in areas of high employment and does little to stimulate production in areas of low employment. An example of misdirected demand would be an increase in the demand for motor cars at a time when there was full employment in the motor car industry and heavy unemployment in (say) the cotton industry.

Mistake. In a contract only mistakes of fact concerning a vital matter will invalidate it and not mistakes of law, since everyone is presumed to know the law.

M.I.T. Abbreviation of Massachusetts Institute of Technology, Boston, the leading technological university of the United States.

Mite. An old Jewish coin, the lowest in value at the time, as mentioned in St. Mark xii, 42. It was a popular term for the half-farthing minted in England in the nineteenth century.

Mitsui Bank. One of the leading commercial banks of Japan and the oldest, being founded in 1683, that is, eleven years before the Bank of England. Its head office is in Tokyo.

Mixed Economy. A term used to describe an economic system, such as that of Great Britain, where some planning of production is undertaken by the State, directly or through its nationalised industries, and some is left to private enterprise.

Mixed Income. An income which comprises two or more types, such as that of an independent retailer, who may regard the whole of his net income as profit whereas in fact it consists partly of wages, partly of interest on his capital, and only partly of profit.

'Mixer.' A colloquial term for a share with a relatively high yield, acquired by an investor to raise the average yield of his total investments.

M.O. Abbreviation of Money Order (*q.v.*).

Mobile Shop. A motor van arranged as a shop which customers can enter, it may be operated by an independent trader or by a retailer to supplement his ordinary business. The number of these 'shops' has increased, especially in country districts but also in the suburbs of large towns.

Mobility. The ease with which a factor of production can be transferred from one occupation to another. This often also involves geographical mobility, that is movement from one place to another. Though land clearly cannot be moved, it can be used for alternative purposes. Many kinds of capital can easily be moved though they may not be mobile in the sense of being able to be used for a purpose other than that for which they were originally intended. Some large units of capital would be too expensive to move. Occupational mobility depends on the degree of specificity of a factor. In the case of labour only those who have been specially trained are able to undertake highly skilled work and specific labour, therefore, tends to lack occupational mobility. Unskilled labour is more easily transferred from one occupation to another. Although human beings are capable of moving from one place to another many people are disinclined to move to other areas to work, preferring to stay in districts where they have been brought up, where they have friends and relations or other ties, or because of the cost of removal. Large numbers of people, however, have at various times migrated from one country to another under economic, religious, or political compulsion. Nevertheless, labour is not nearly so mobile as might be expected. Mobility of factors of production is of great economic importance. If labour was perfectly mobile there would be no unemployment due to technological progress or change of demand. Structural unemployment is due to lack of mobility of labour. Since economic progress is largely the result of technological developments and since too it is often accompanied by changes in demand, it is necessary to increase mobility of labour in order to reduce structural unemployment. The present policy is for the Government to encourage new industries to set up in areas of declining industry, and labour made redundant in one industry must be retained for alternative employment.

Mocatto & Goldsmidt. City of London dealers in silver meet at the premises of this firm. *See* London Silver Market.

Mode. The item which occurs most frequently in a group of numbers. It is thus more typical of a group than either the arithmetic mean or the median (*qq.v.*).

Model. A term used of a theoretical environment assumed by an economist who wishes to work out the implications of a theory in precisely known conditions.

Moiety. A half—a term mostly used in connection with the payment of rates or taxes when paid in two instalments.

Molony Report. This report recommended the establishment of a Consumer Council (*q.v.*) and a variety of measures for the protection of consumers and the abolition of the £300 limit as imposed by the Act of 1954 for the protection of customers making hire purchase transactions. The limit was raised to £2,000 in 1964.

Monday Men. A term sometimes used in connection with the manorial system of Bordars (*q.v.*) who were given this name because they worked on the land of the lord of the manor only one day per week.

Monetary Correction. Alternative term for Indexation (*q.v.*).

Monetary Economy. An economic system in which exchange is facilitated by the use of money, as distinct from a barter system, where no money is employed. The use of money makes it possible to carry specialisation and division of labour to the fullest extent, thereby increasing total output and the real national income. Money, however, creates its own problems on account of its dynamic function (*q.v.*).

Monetary Policy. On the gold standard monetary policy was primarily related to the protection of the central bank's gold reserves. Thus, when an adverse balance of payments led to an outflow of gold, bank rate was raised and open-market operations undertaken to reduce the cash basis of the commercial banks' credit policy and thereby bring about a reduction in the total quantity of money in the country. With gold flowing in the opposite policy would be pursued. In a complex economic system, in which saving and investment are carried out by different groups of people, money takes on a dynamic function in addition to serving as a medium of exchange. It becomes capable of influencing the size of the national income, the level of employment, the demand for both consumers' goods and producers' goods and therefore the volume of both saving and investment.

Since 1945 the aims of monetary policy in Great Britain have been (i) to try to maintain full employment, neither more nor less; (ii) to keep inflation in check; and (iii) to rectify an adverse balance of payments. Therefore, when there has been less than full employment the aim has been to stimulate demand and production and through that the demand for labour; when there has been overfull employment and in consequence an inflationary situation the aim has been to check demand and to try to keep prices fairly stable. One of the greatest difficulties in deciding what form of monetary policy to adopt is that the external situation—an adverse balance of payments—may require a restrictive policy which is not always appropriate to the internal situation. Other aims also often conflict. Thus, it is regarded as very desirable to expand the real national income in order to raise the standard of living and this may be checked by an anti-inflationary policy intended to keep the value of money reasonably stable. In the strict sense of the term monetary policy is carried out by monetary means—the traditional instruments of policy, namely bank rate (since 1972 the Bank of England's minimum lending rate) and open-market operations.

The wider aims of monetary policy in recent times led to experimentation with several new instruments of policy—the Treasury directive, Special Deposits, the Regulator (*q.v.*), and the variation of hire-purchase regulations, perhaps the most important new development has been the supplementing of monetary policy by fiscal policy through the budget, that is, increasing or reducing taxation to stimulate or check consumers' demand. *See* Instruments of Monetary Policy.

Monetary Reform. After a country has suffered a hyperinflation a new currency unit has to be introduced, usually worth a very small specified fraction of the former unit as, for example, when the forint replaced the pengo in Hungary after the Second World War. This is regarded as monetary or currency reform. The term might be applied too to the introduction of a new currency unit when the former unit has depreciated as a result of inflation as, for example, the issue of the New Franc in France in 1960 to replace the old franc, the new franc being given the value of 100 old francs. Another type of monetary reform occurs when an entirely new decimal currency is introduced, as in Australia in 1966.

Monetary School. A term used in the United States of those economists who believe that the purpose of control of bank credit should be to promote stability of business activity.

Monetary System. The internal and external monetary arrangements of a country. Internally, it covers the standard monetary unit and its divisions, whether bank notes are convertible or not, legal tender, and token coinage. Externally it refers to the foreign exchange standard in use—the gold standard in some form, freely fluctuating exchange rates, some type of exchange control or the Bretton Woods Scheme or some modification of it.

Monetary Union. An arrangement between a number of countries to maintain an agreed exchange rate between their currencies, as with the Latin Monetary Union and the Scandinavian Monetary Union (*qq.v.*).

Monetary Unit. The standard unit of a country's currency. On the gold standard and under the Bretton Woods Scheme the monetary unit consists of a definite weight of gold of a specified fineness, though when most countries were fixing the parities of their currencies as agreed at Bretton Woods they did so in relation to the U.S. dollar. Before gold became the main monetary metal the monetary unit was given a parity in terms of silver. On the gold standard the pound sterling consisted of 123·274 grains of gold, eleven-twelfths fine.

The following are the standard units of the principal countries of the world. Further details will be found under the name of the monetary unit.

Afghanistan	Afghani
Albania	Lek
Algeria	Dinar

Country	Currency
Argentina	Peso
Australia	Dollar
Austria	Schilling
Bahamas	Dollar
Bangladesh	Taka
Belgium	Franc
Bermuda	Dollar
Bolivia	Peso
Botswana	Pula
Brazil	Cruzeiro
Bulgaria	Lev
Burma	Kyat
Canada	Dollar
Chile	Peso
China	Yuan or Renmimbi
Colombia	Peso
Costa Rica	Colon
Cuba	Peso
Cyprus	Pound
Czechoslovakia	Koruna
Denmark	Krone
Dominican Republic	Peso
Ecuador	Sucre
Egypt	Pound
El Salvador	Colon
Ethiopia	Dollar
Fiji	Dollar
Finland	Markka
France	Franc
Gambia	Dalasi
Germany, East	Mark
Germany, West	Deutsche Mark
Ghana	Cedi
Gibraltar	Pound
Greece	Drachma
Guatemala	Quetzal
Guyana	Dollar
Haiti	Gourde
Honduras	Lempira
Hong Kong	Dollar
Hungary	Forint
Iceland	Krona
India	Rupee
Indonesia	Rupiah
Iran	Rial
Iraq	Dinar
Ireland, Republic of	Pound
Israel	Pound
Italy	Lira
Jamaica	Dollar
Japan	Yen
Jordan	Dinar
Kenya	Shilling
Korea	Won
Kuwait	Dinar
Lebanon	Pound
Liberia	Dollar
Libya	Dinar
Luxembourg	Franc
Malawi	Kwacha
Malaysia	Dollar
Malta	Pound
Mexico	Peso
Morocco	Dirham
Netherlands	Guilder (or Florin)
New Zealand	Dollar
Nicaragua	Cordoba
Nigeria	Naira
Norway	Krone
Pakistan	Rupee
Panama	Balboa
Paraguay	Guarani
Peru	Sol
Philippines	Peso
Poland	Zloty
Portugal	Escudo
Rhodesia	Dollar
Rumania	Leu
Saudi Arabia	Riyal
Singapore	Dollar
South Africa	Rand
Spain	Peseta
Sri Lanka	Rupee
Sudan	Pound
Sweden	Krona
Switzerland	Franc
Syria	Pound
Tanzania	Shilling
Thailand	Baht
Tunisia	Dinar
Turkey	Lira
Uganda	Shilling
United Kingdom	Pound
United States	Dollar
Uruguay	Peso
U.S.S.R.	Rouble
Venezuela	Bolivar
Vietnam	Dong
West Indies	Dollar
Yugoslavia	Dinar
Zambia	Kwacha

Money. Something which serves as a medium of exchange. Anything which is generally acceptable can serve this purpose. Before money came into use exchange took place by means of barter, that is, goods were exchanged for goods. It was to overcome the disadvantages of barter that a medium of exchange came to be employed. At first the medium of exchange had to be something in common use that was considered to be valuable for its own sake, either for use or ornament, and therefore was generally acceptable. At different periods of time and in different parts of the world many different commodities have served as money —cattle, sheep, furs, leather, fish, tobacco, tea, salt, cowrie shells, etc. To serve effectively as money a commodity should be fairly durable, easily divisible, and portable. None of the above-mentioned commodities possessed all these qualities, and in time they were superseded by the precious metals, silver and later gold, the amount of metal at first being weighed out whenever a payment had to be made. The next stage was the cutting of the metal into pieces of definite weight and so coins came in to use, but whenever debasement was suspected merchants again had recourse to weighing the coins as metal. At first coins were expected to be worth their full face value as metal, but later token coins of limited value as legal tender were issued. Paper money first came into use in the form of receipts given by goldsmiths in exchange for deposits of coin. The London goldsmiths became bankers, and their receipts became bank-notes. Such notes for a long time were acceptable only if they were convertible, that is, exchangeable on demand for coins of the same value. It was not until the twentieth century that people became willing to accept inconvertible paper money, for it is not necessary for the medium of exchange that serves as money to be valuable in itself, though it must, of course, be generally acceptable. So long as people are confident that they can make purchases with it they will themselves be prepared to accept it in payment. For it to continue to serve as money inconvertible paper money must retain people's confidence in it. In many countries at the present day the bank deposit, transferable by cheque, has become the most important kind of money. It is the bank deposit and not the cheque itself that is money. The quantity of this type of money depends on the monetary policy being pursued in the country concerned. *See* Functions of Money; Monetary Policy; Value of Money.

Money at Call and Short Notice. One of the more liquid assets of an English commercial bank, it represents the lending of the bank to the London money market—discount houses and bill brokers, the term of these loans varying from call money, where no notice is required, to fourteen days. The item is very important to British banking practice. Instead of borrowing from the Bank of England when short of cash English banks call in some of their loans to the money market and thereby compel the discount houses to borrow from the Bank of England, which lends to them in its capacity as 'lender of last resort'.

Money Capital. This is capital in the form of money as distinct from real capital (machinery, factory buildings, etc.).

Money Changers. Merchants who specialised in changing money before banks existed. The rate of exchange between different issues of coins depended on the amount of precious metal contained in them.

Money, Demand for. *See* Demand for Money.

Money, Functions of. *See* Functions of Money.

'Money Illusion.' A term first used by the American economist, Irving Fisher, for failure to realise that the value of a unit of a currency is liable to vary in value in terms of what it will buy. Though many people still regard a pound as a pound, wider experience than ever before of changes in the value of money since 1939 has greatly reduced the number of people who suffer the 'money illusion'.

Money in Circulation. The amount of money held by individuals and institutions other than the Bank of England. 'Notes in Circulation' forms one of the liabilities of the Issue Department of the Bank of England, the other being the reserve of notes held in the Banking Department. Notes and coin are put into circulation through the commercial banks in exchange for Bankers' Deposits, the coins being purchased at their face value from the Royal Mint. The amount of money in circulation generally reaches its peak in August, with a secondary peak in December. The increased demand for cash at these times is met by an increase in the fiduciary issue. During the past 25 years the note circulation has increased each year. The amount of money in circulation is closely related to, and dependent on, the volume of bank deposits.

Moneylender. An Act of 1900 made it necessary for a person to be registered before he could carry on the business of moneylender. An Act of 1927 attempted to protect people who borrowed from moneylenders by making illegal the charging of compound interest on loans or a rate of interest in excess of 48%. This Act also made it necessary for moneylenders to take out a licence annually. These Acts do not apply to banks. Further restrictions were imposed on moneylenders by the Consumer Credit Act (1974) (*q.v.*).

Moneyless Economy. An economic system which dispenses with the use of money. For a short period after the Revolution (1917) the Russians experimented with such a system.

Money Letter. Forerunner of the Money Order (*q.v.*), it was first issued in 1792 by a group of Post Office clerks, but after 1838 by the Post Office itself. The Money Letters were introduced to enable money to be transferred safely from one place to another on account of the danger from highwaymen when money was sent by mail coach.

Money Market. The market for very short-term loans—borrowing at call or short notice from the commercial banks by discount houses, with the Bank of England as lender of last resort. *See* Discount Market.

Money Order. A means of payment provided by the Post Office for people wishing to transmit sums of money abroad. There is no longer an inland money order service other than the telegraphic money order.

Money Supply. Generally taken to mean the total value of bank deposits, on both current account and deposit account, of the commercial banks together with the total amount of cash in bank-notes and coin. Other means of payment are regarded as substitutes for money, or 'near-money'. The aim of monetary policy is to vary the money supply. Some writers take the view that inflation is mainly the result of an excessive increase in the money supply.

'Money Trust.' A term used in the United States to express dislike of the concentration of banking into large units. Fear of a 'money trust' has been responsible for many states in that country completely prohibiting branch banking. In consequence the United States, in sharp contrast to Great Britain, has the huge number of over 4,000 independent commercial banks.

Money, Value of. *See* Value of Money.

'Money Veil.' Too much attention to the monetary aspects of economic problems tends to hide—or cover with a veil—the real economic forces that are at work. Thus, in a period of full employment it is not the monetary cost of a proposed Government project that is of most importance, but its real cost, that is, the fact that it will require labour and other factors of production to be transferred from their present employment to work on it.

Money Wages. Wages in terms of money as distinct from real wages (wages in terms of what they will buy). To have any meaning money wages must be considered along with the general level of prices, since a rise in money wages may be offset by a steeper rise in prices. In an inflationary period money wages sometimes tend to lag behind price rises, so that real wages tend to fall, whereas in a deflationary period prices usually fall more rapidly than money wages, with the result that real wages tend to increase.

Monometallism. A monetary system based on a single metal, silver or gold, as distinct from bi-metallism (*q.v.*) which attempts to base a currency on two metals.

Monopolies and Mergers Act (1965). This Act empowers the then Board of Trade, now the Department of Trade, to look into any proposed merger that is likely to lead to monopoly power (defined as in the Monopolies Act of 1948 as production of 30% of total output of a commodity) or if the value of the assets to be taken over exceed £5 million. The Board of Trade first used this power to prevent a merger of Smith's Potato Crisps with the Imperial Tobacco Co. Ltd., which would have given the latter 75% of the total output of potato crisps. The Department can refer any case to the Monopolies Commission. The Monopolies and Mergers Act (1965) charged the Commission to look into proposed mergers referred to it and to decide whether such mergers were in the public interest. In all matters brought to its notice the Commission only has the power to report its findings, and it is then for the minister concerned to take what action he considers appropriate.

Monopolies and Mergers Commission. Established by the British Government in 1948 as the Monopolies Commission, this body was given powers to inquire into any industry in which one firm, or a combination of firms, produced 30% (reduced to 20% in 1973) or more of the total output of a commodity. The Commission has issued reports on the production of over twenty commodities in addition to reporting on restrictive practices. Since 'monopolists' today are reluctant to take full advantage of their power for fear of attracting unwelcome attention to their activities few of the Commission's reports were very condemnatory, but even when certain undesirable monopolistic practices were uncovered the Commission only had power to report its findings to the Government. It was to make more positive action against monopolies possible that the Restrictive Trade Practices Act (*q.v.*) was passed in 1956.

Monopolistic Competition. One of the forms of imperfect competition, it occurs when there is a large number of producers but differentiation of their products or services, so that the product of one firm is not regarded as a perfect substitute for that of another. An example of monopolistic competition is to be found in the retail trade. Ease of entry results in excess capacity and differentiation takes the form of difference of location (each shop being more conveniently situated for some people), the general attitude and behaviour of the shopkeeper, and the extent of the service provided.

Monopoly. In the strictest sense of the term a monopoly occurs when there is only one producer of a commodity for which there is no substitute. This condition is sometimes termed absolute monopoly. It is rare for there to be only a single producer of a commodity and even rarer for there to be no substitute for it. For example, all beverages are to a greater or less degree substitutes for one another, since they are required for the same purpose. Since, too, people only have limited amounts of money to spend, dissimilar things, such as house decoration as against a holiday, compete against one another. Absolute monopoly, therefore, like perfect competition, does not occur in real life. Actual conditions vary between the two extremes of near-monopoly and nearly perfect competition and these conditions have been termed imperfect competition (*q.v.*). Unfortunately, the term, monopoly, is widely used to mean near-monopoly or very imperfect competition, the word being used in this sense not only in ordinary speech but also by politicians and some economists. It thus becomes possible to speak of degrees of monopoly—a high degree of monopoly in the case of the Coffee Institute of Brazil, a small degree of monopoly in the case of a manufacturer of branded goods, where no other producer is allowed to use the same trade name. Although neither absolute monopoly nor perfect competition actually exist economists find it useful to study each of these extremes since the theoretical conditions necessary for each are clear and simple and they provide a basis for the more difficult study of the many different varieties of imperfect competition. *See* Monopolies and Mergers Act (1965); Monopolies Commission; Monopoly Output; Monopoly Power, Control of.

Advantages of Monopoly. It is sometimes claimed that production can be more efficiently carried on when in the hands of a monopolist by making possible rationalisation of an industry to cut out excess capacity, elimination of wasteful competition, especially the wastes of imperfect competition, and greater standardisation to secure economies of scale.

Disadvantages of Monopoly. Exploitation of the consumer is the great disadvantage of monopoly. Prices are almost certain to be higher and output lower than under perfect competition, nor is the assortment of goods produced that which consumers as a whole would have preferred. Lack of competition too may reduce somewhat the incentive towards greater efficiency.

Monopoly, Degrees of. In the strict sense of the term a monopoly occurs only when the entire output of a commodity for which there is no substitute is in the hands of a single firm. The term, monopoly, is however generally taken to mean a very imperfect form of competition, and since there are degrees of imperfection it has become common to speak of degrees of monopoly, even though this term appears to be self-contradictory.

Monopoly Output. It is assumed that the aim of the absolute monopolist, like that of any other entrepreneur, is to maximise his profit. Even though an absolute monopolist will have complete control over supply he has not complete control over demand, though he may attempt to influence it through advertising. He must, therefore, take account of the fact that more of a commodity can be sold at a low than at a high price. He can, therefore, either fix his price, in which case consumers' demand will decide the quantity he can sell, or he can decide on his output and let consumers' demand decide the price he will charge. The greater the degree of elasticity of demand for the commodity the less the power of the monopolist. As with all other producers, irrespective of whether competition is perfect or imperfect, the monopolist will produce at an output at which his marginal revenue is just equal to his marginal cost, since at this output his profit will be at its maximum. Under perfect competition the further conditions are fulfilled that average cost is equal to average revenue and that price is equal to marginal cost. Under monopoly, however, average revenue is greater than average cost and marginal cost, so that in addition to normal profit, which is regarded as a cost, the monopolist obtains an additional profit, known by various names— surplus profit, monopoly profit or

Units of output	Average revenue (price per unit) £	Total revenue £	Marginal revenue £	Average cost £	Total cost £	Marginal cost £	Surplus profit £
70	8·75	612·50	—	6·17	432·50	—	180·00
80	8·50	680·00	6·75	5·33	457·50	2·50	222·50
90	8·25	742·50	6·25	5·42	492·50	3·50	250·00
100	8·00	800·00	5·75	5·50	550·00	5·75	250·00
110	7·75	852·50	5·25	5·67	620·00	7·00	232·50
120	7·50	900·00	4·75	5·92	710·00	9·00	190·00

net revenue. Consider the table on p. 323. This table shows that the monopolist will not expand his output beyond 100 units, since after that point his total profit begins to fall.

Monopoly Power, Bases of. The following are some of the conditions which give rise to some degree of monopoly power: (i) When one firm, or a group of firms in combination, controls a large proportion of the supply; (ii) Where highly specific plant is in use, new entrants being discouraged by the high cost of entry; (iii) Where duplication of the service would be wasteful, as in the case of public utilities; (iv) The branding of goods, each producer then attempting to show that his brand is different from others; (v) Patent rights, which give the owner the exclusive right to a new machine or process for a period; (vi) Copyright, which similarly protects publishers of books and manufacturers of gramophone records; (vii) Local monopolies where costs of transport are heavy so that more distant producers find it difficult to compete; (viii) Tariffs can be used to protect a monopolist in the home market from foreign competition; and (ix) Restrictions limit entry to many occupations, these taking the form of qualifying examinations, insistence on a long period of apprenticeship, or limitation of the number of articled clerks or apprentices.

Monopoly Power, Control of. A number of methods have been employed to try to prevent the exploitation of consumers by producers who possess some degree of monopoly power: (i) Legal action against monopolies has taken the form in the United States of outlawing monopoly, while in Great Britain a Monopolies and Restrictive Practices Commission (*q.v.*) was set up in 1948 and under the Restrictive Trade Practices Act of 1956 (*q.v.*) Restrictive Practices Courts were established; (ii) Legal controls were imposed in Great Britain in cases where monopolies had to be permitted, as in the case of railways and public utilities, the controls generally taking the form of restrictions on charges; (iii) Giving the operation of public monopolies to local authorities which might be expected to operate them in the interests of the people living in their areas; (iv) State operation of monopolies—transport, fuel and power, etc.—these to be operated in the 'public interest'; (v) Taxation of monopolies has been suggested in order to encourage them to expand their output, but no practicable plan has been put forward.

Monopsony. This occurs when there is only one buyer of a commodity or service. The only buyer in Great Britain of the specific labour of railway workers, such as engine drivers and signalmen, is British Rail. Similarly, the National Coal Board is the only employer of coal-miners.

Montagu (Samuel) & Co. Ltd. A London merchant bank. It has an office in Paris and an affiliate in Zürich.

Monthly Account. A method of paying monthly instead of paying each individual transaction as it arises.

Monthly Digest of Statistics. A monthly publication of H.M. Stationery Office giving the latest statistics, with earlier statistics for comparison, on population, production, trade, banking, wages, prices, etc.

Moodies Services Ltd. A firm which supplies statistical information regarding public limited companies to enable investors to assess their prospects. Information, summarised on a 'card', is made available to stockbrokers and other subscribers.

'Moral Suasion.' Used as an adjunct to monetary policy when the monetary authorities make strong recommendations to the banks regarding their lending policy. *See* Treasury Directive.

Moratorium. The granting by one government to a debtor government of an extended period of time in which to repay a loan or to pay the interest on such a loan. The term was also used in 1933 of the permission granted to the U.S. Government to American banks to delay meeting their obligations for a period.

Morgan Grenfell & Co. A London merchant bank.

Mortality Rate. *See* Death-rate.

Mortgage. A deed showing that money has been borrowed with land or property as collateral security. Building societies assist people to buy houses by lending a portion of the purchase money, the property being mortgaged to the society until the loan, with interest, has been repaid. The borrower is known as the mortgagor and the lender as the mortgagee.

Mortgage Bank. An alternative name for a Building Society (*q.v.*)—not used in Great Britain.

Mortgage Debentures. These are debentures that are issued on the security of the company's assets.

Mortmain. Common law was opposed to land falling into the 'dead hand' of a corporation, since in feudal times the Crown and lords of manors received payment on the transfer of ownership of land. The idea has survived down to modern times, so that special provision has had to be made for corporations to hold land. The Companies Act (1948), however, exempted statutory companies from this disability.

Moscow Narodny Bank. A Russian bank established in London in 1919, it took the sub-title of 'Bank for East–West Trade' in 1959. In their dealings with the West, other banks in Eastern Europe operate through the Moscow Narodny.

'Most Favoured Nation' Clause. Commercial treaties between nations often contain this type of clause, each party agreeing to extend to the other any more favourable treatment offered in the future to any other nation.

Motivational Research. Inquiry into the reasons why people buy a commodity, generally as a preliminary to developing an improved public appreciation of it in order to stimulate sales.

Motor Show. Usually held in October, its aim is to put on view the latest models of motor cars and their accessories for the benefit of trade buyers (home and foreign) and the general public.

Motorways. Roads specially built for and restricted to motor vehicles, they usually have dual carriageways, but their main features are the small number of junctions, crossroads being carried by bridges over or under the main road. The earliest roads of this kind were built in the 1930s in Italy (*autostrade*) and Germany (*autobahnen*), the German roads being mainly intended for military purposes. Since 1950 many other countries have built motorways—the United States, Great Britain, France, Belgium, Holland, Austria, Switzerland, Yugoslavia, with short stretches in Sweden, Czechoslovakia, and a number of other countries. In Great Britain an extensive system of motorways is under construction. In the United States a number of motorways have been constructed by private enterprise and on these a toll is charged. Tolls are also levied on the Italian autostrade and the French autoroutes.

M.Sc. (Econ.). Abbreviation of Master of Science, a higher degree in the Faculty of Economics, awarded by the University of London and some other universities.

Multilateral Trade. This occurs when countries are perfectly free to trade with one another, thus enabling international division of labour to be carried out to the fullest extent. As a result the total combined output of all countries is at its maximum, and after exchange has taken place all countries are able to enjoy a greater amount of everything than they would if trade was hampered by tariffs, bilateral trade agreements, exchange control, etc. When bilateral trade agreements are in force each country must balance its imports and exports individually with every other country and these will have to be balanced at the level of the country which wishes to import the smaller amount. The advantage of multilateral trade over bilateral trade can best be shown diagrammatically. In the following diagram arrows indicate the direction of each country's exports, a minus sign indicating the country of origin and a plus sign the importing country, the figures representing units of exports or imports:

(a) Multilateral Trade			(b) Bilateral Trade		
Country A	Country B	Country C	Country A	Country B	Country C
+40 ←────────	−40		+40 ←────────	−40	
−60 →→ +60			−40 →→ +40		
	−100 →→ +100	−80		−80 →→ +80	−80
	+80 ←────────			+80 ←────────	
−50	─────→ +50		−50	────→ +50	
+70 ←────────		−70	+50 ←────────		−50
+110 −110	+140 −140	+150 −150	+90 −90	+120 −120	+130 −130

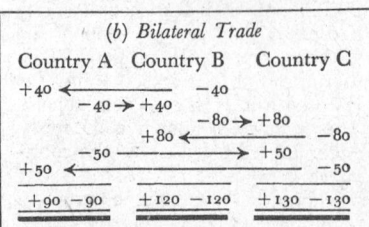

This shows that if bilateral trade replaces multilateral trade all three countries will import less and export less. Since 1945 great efforts have been made to bring about multilateral trade, which requires free convertibility of currencies and the abolition of tariffs and other restrictions.

Multinational Companies. Very large international companies with production units in several countries, *e.g.* Ford, Shell. The turnover of some of these companies is huge—greater than the national income of countries such as the Netherlands or Switzerland. Since the introduction of floating exchange rates in 1972 company treasurers have begun to exchange currencies in order to obtain the most favourable rates. This practice can have serious consequences if there is a run on a currency.

Multiple Equilibrium. This occurs when there is more than one position of equilibrium in a given situation. For example, a monopolist's marginal revenue may equal his marginal cost at an output of 550 units of production per day and also at 750 units of output per day, equilibrium therefore occurring at both these points on his output curve, thereby giving multiple equilibrium.

Multiple Exchange Rates. When a restrictive system of exchange control is in operation it becomes possible for a Government to have different exchange rates according to the purpose for which the currency is required. The simplest form of multiple exchange rates occurs when a country introduces a special tourist rate in order to encourage foreign tourists. Germany in the 1930s was the first country to have multiple exchange rates, a favourable rate being granted to importers of commodities useful for preparation for war and less favourable rates for other importers. The practice was condemned in 1944 by the Bretton Woods Conference, but since 1945 a number of countries, including Spain, Chile, and Argentina, have employed multiple exchange rates.

Multiples. An alternative term for multiple shop organisations. *See* Multiple Shops.

Multiple Shops. Sometimes known by the American term 'chain stores' these are groups of shops in the same branch of retail trade under the same management. In most large towns there are to be found groups of shops under one control from the main shop, but these cannot really be regarded as multiple shops, the direction of which is from headquarters comprising offices and warehouse. Large multiple shop organisations have hundreds of branches—a few have over a thousand—and they often cover the whole country. They are found in a variety of branches of retail trade such as boots and shoes, furniture, grocery, chemists, ready-made clothing, etc. There are three main types: (i) Shops opened by manufacturers for the sale only of their own products; (ii) Large-scale retailers who buy direct from manufacturers; and (iii) The 'bazaar' type of shop which sells a variety of goods at moderate prices —the former 'fixed-price' stores.

Multiple Shops Federation. An association representing multiple shops, it gave evidence to the Radcliffe Committee.

Multiple Taxation. This occurs when the same basis of taxation is used by two or more tax authorities on the same person. In the United States, for example, income taxes may be levied by the Federal Government, the state government and perhaps the city authority. If, as has been suggested, local rates in Great Britain were based on the incomes of ratepayers, there would be a dual income tax in this country.

Multiple Voting Shares. A company may issue two sets of ordinary shares with different voting rights, with perhaps one vote per share for one kind of shares and one vote per 20 shares for the other, or one set of shares carrying a vote and another set of shares (often known as 'A' shares) being non-voting shares. This device is sometimes employed when a small limited company wishes to expand and issues new shares to the general public with little or no voting rights in order to permit control of the business to remain in the hands of the few people who controlled it when it was small.

Multiplier. The effect on total employment or on total consumption of a certain amount of real capital investment. Thus, investment in the form of a new series of motorways may give direct employment to 1,000 men, but the provision of materials for the motorway may give employment to a further 1,200 men, while the additional demand generated by the increased earnings may create additional employment for another 800 men. Thus, as a result of investment employing 1,000 men an eventual total of 3,000 men are found new employment, that is, three times the orginal number, so that in this case the Multiplier is 3. Contrast the Multiplier with the Acceleration Principle (*q.v.*).

Multi-product Firm. A firm making a variety of products partly to achieve economies in marketing and partly to even out fluctuations in the demand for some of the products.

Municipal Enterprise. Business activity undertaken by municipal authorities. One of their earliest activities was the letting of stalls or sites in the town's market place. Modern business activities of local authorities date from the mid-nineteenth century when they obtained the right to build public baths and wash-houses. Before the end of that century many local authorities owned and operated water-works, gasworks, electricity undertakings, and provided local transport by tramways. Many ports own harbours, quays, and piers. Other activities include ownership of airports, civic restaurants, public libraries, the provision of entertainments (especially seaside resorts). Birmingham is the only local authority that runs a savings bank, and Hull the only one to operate a telephone service. One view is that municipal enterprise is particularly suitable for the operation of local activities that are wasteful unless run as monopolies, consumers then being free from the risk of exploitation. In some forms of municipal enterprise—for example, public libraries—no attempt is made to run them on a commercial basis. In the case of their gas and electricity undertakings most local authorities used to make profits which were devoted to relief of rates. This was also true at one time of local passenger transport services, but the increase in the number of private motor cars and other vehicles has greatly reduced the number of passengers using municipal transport, with the result that there are demands in some quarters for these services to be maintained and run at a loss 'as a service'. Another view is that municipally operated services should 'break even', that is, they should make neither profit nor loss.

Municipal Treasurers and Accountants, Institute of. A professional body, now no longer in existence, the members of which were employed in the Treasurer's department of a local authority or by the Gas Corporation, Electricity Council or Hospitals. *See* C.I.P.F.A. and *also* Chartered Accountant.

Muscovy Company. Founded in 1553, originally for the purpose of seeking a north-east passage to the Far East. When this project proved not to be feasible, it devoted its activities to trade with Russia, for which purpose it established a warehouse at Archangel. Its period of prosperity lasted for barely a century.

Mutilated Bank Notes. If only slightly mutilated and if more than half the note remains notes can be changed at banks or post offices. If seriously mutilated application must be made, either through a bank or direct to the Bank of England which then considers each case on its merits. In some countries only a partial payment is made for mutilated notes, depending on how much of the note remains, but the Bank of England meets all claims it recognises in full.

Mutual Aid. Two main motives inspired the formation of voluntary societies for the provision of social services, one being mutual aid, that is, the desire of a group of people in similar circumstances to help one another to provide some security against misfortune which might overtake any one of them. The friendly societies, as their name implies, were of this type. The Registrar of Friendly Societies has the oversight of a great variety of mutual aid societies. The establishment of the second group of voluntary societies has been the result of philanthropic societies, these being under the supervision of the Charity Commissioners. In the case of the philanthropic societies the more fortunate help the less fortunate. In the mutual aid organisations the funds come from the members' contributions, but the philanthropic organisations depend mainly on donations and endowments. There are several hundred philanthropic societies in Great Britain in spite of the expansion of national insurance and national assistance.

Mutual Funds. The American term for unit trusts (*q.v.*).

N

N.A.F.T.A. Abbreviation of New Zealand and Australia Free Trade Area.

Nails. Used as money according to Adam Smith, in some parts of Scotland as recently as the eighteenth century. *See* Commodity Money.

Naira. The standard unit of the currency of Nigeria, it is subdivided into 100 Kobo.

Naked Debenture. An alternative term for Simple Debenture (*q.v.*).

N.A.L.G.O. Abbreviation of National and Local Government Officers' Association, the body representing the interests of employees of local authorities and public corporations.

Name Day. A stock exchange term, it is the day when the names of buyers are transmitted to the sellers of securities.

'Names.' A term used by Lloyd's underwriters for sleeping partners in their syndicates who leave the actual business to the head of the syndicate. Nevertheless, a 'name' must be a person of financial standing and be able to show that he is worth at least £75,000.

Napoleon. A former French gold coin, similar to the Louis, worth 20 francs. Double Napoleons also were issued.

Narrow Market. A term used more particularly of stock exchange securities of which there is only a small supply available in the market.

National and Commercial Banking Group. Formed in 1969, it comprises the Commercial Bank of Scotland (founded 1810) (which is affiliated to Lloyds Bank with which it jointly owns Lloyds and Scottish Finance Ltd., a finance house), the Royal Bank of Scotland and Williams & Glyn's.

National and Grindlays Bank. One of the smaller commercial banks which are members of the London Bankers' Clearing House. Its head office is in London. It has branches in Europe, the Middle East, Asia and Africa. The First National City Bank of New York has an interest in it. It has 147 branches.

National Arbitration Tribunal. A body set up in 1940 during the Second World War to settle trade disputes, arbitration being made compulsory since strikes could not be allowed to hinder the war effort. It operated only until 1951.

National Assistance. The present system of national assistance was introduced by the Act of 1948, its aim being the relief of poverty and distress of people not eligible for benefit under the national insurance scheme or whose benefit under that scheme is insufficient to provide the minimum standard of living now regarded as necessary. Much, though not all, assistance goes to old people who have little income other than retirement pensions. Unlike national insurance, the cost of which is met mainly from contributions, the cost of national assistance is borne entirely by the State. The National Assistance Board was abolished in 1966, its functions being taken over first by the Ministry of Social Security (known until then as the Ministry of Pensions and National Insurance), and in 1968 by the Department of Health and Social Security.

National Association of Investment Clubs. An association to which local investment clubs are affiliated and from which they can obtain advice.

National Bank. A type of American commercial bank established by Federal charter as distinct from States banks which are established by State charter. All the National Banks but only about one-fifth of the State Banks are members of the U.S. Federal Reserve System.

National Bank of Australasia.
With its head office in Melbourne, it is the second largest of the Australian trading banks. It has over 970 branches.

National Bank of Belgium. *See* Banque Nationale de Belgique.

National Board for Prices and Incomes (N.B.P.I.). A body set up by the Department of Economic Affairs in 1965 to enable the Government to carry out its 'incomes policy', that is, to relate increases in wages to increases in productivity and to prevent what it regards as unreasonable price increases. The Board had to be given notice of intended claims for wage increases or increases in prices, and it had to decide how far these should be allowed. It ceased to function in 1971. *See* Prices and Incomes Policy.

National Bus Company. Formed under the Transport Act (1968) to control and operate the road passenger services taken over from the Transport Holding Company and the British Electric Traction Co. Ltd. It co-operates with the Passenger Transport Authorities in areas where they have been established. At the time of the formation of the National Bus Co. there were 22,000 buses in 45 operating units.

National Capital. The money value of all the real capital of a country at a particular time.

National Carriers Ltd. (N.C.L.). A division of the National Freight Corporation (*q.v.*). Over 7,000 vehicles are operated from 104 depots.

National Certificates and Diplomas in Business Education. These Certificates and Diplomas are awarded by Colleges of Commerce, Technical Colleges and Colleges of Technology under the auspices of the Business Education Council (BEC) set up by the Department of Education and Science. From 1978 courses are being offered at three main levels: (1) the General Award (Certificate); (2) the National Award (Certificate and Diploma); and (3) the Higher National Award (Certificate and Diploma). This scheme replaced the former Ordinary and Higher National Certificates in Commerce. The aim is to provide a series of vocational courses for students who have embarked (or are about to do so) on careers in industry, commerce or public administration. Part-time courses of two years' duration lead to the two diplomas. Some subjects of study (termed 'modules') are compulsory for all students. A wide range of optional subjects is available to suit the needs of students in the various occupations within the field covered by the courses. *See also* Business Education Council (BEC).

National Coal Board (N.C.B.). A body set up by the Coal Mines Nationalisation Act (1946) to take control of some 1,500 coal mines in England, Wales, and Scotland from 1st January 1947. The aim of the Board was to develop the industry efficiently and provide coal in such quantities and at such prices as 'to further the public interest'. For administrative purposes Great Britain was divided into eight coal-producing regions. *See* Fleck Report (1955).

National Council of Credit. An American body to which U.S. banks have to apply if they wish to carry on any form of banking not allotted to them under the banking laws.

National Debt. This is the debt owed by a Government to people and institutions within its own borders (internal debt) and/or to foreign creditors (external debt). The British National Debt as we know it came into existence in 1694 when the Bank of England was founded for the purpose of lending to the Government of the day. Despite Great Britain's borrowing from the United States (the Washington Loan) and from Canada immediately after the Second World War and the foreign debts incurred during 1964–67, the British National Debt is still 90% internal in character. The history of the British National Debt is very nearly a history of the wars in which Great Britain has been engaged during the past 270 years as the following table indicates:

Amount of Debt

£ million

1694	1·2	
1714	49	After wars of William III and Marlborough
1785	244	After War of American Independence
1815	858	After Napoleonic War
1919	7,800	After First World War
1945	23,000	After Second World War
1975	51,000	

In general the National Debt has been slightly reduced between wars, but since 1945 it has increased more rapidly then ever before in peacetime. The figure of £51,000 million for 1975 excludes the Guaranteed Stocks issued as compensation to the previous owners on the nationalisation of certain industries—coal, railways, gas, electricity, etc. Although these Guaranteed Stocks—British Transport Stocks, British Gas Stocks, British Electricity Stocks, etc.—are clearly debts they are of the type known as reproductive, that is they are covered by real assets of the same value at the time of their creation. The National Debt proper is, therefore, deadweight debt, that is, unsupported by any real assets. A part of the National Debt is in the form of National Savings Certificates, Defence Bonds, National Development Bonds, and Premium Savings Bonds, all issued through the Post Office, and since they are intended for small savers holdings of them have always been limited. The remainder of the National Debt is either 'floating' or 'funded' debt. The floating debt is mainly in the form of three-months Treasury Bills. In addition there is a small amount borrowed directly from the Bank of England by Ways and Means Advances. The funded debt, formerly restricted to undated stocks, now comprises a variety of Government Stocks, with varying periods to run to maturity, from irredeemables like old 2½% Consols, those which can be regarded as irredeemable if the Government so wishes, like 3½% War Loan (after 1952) to dated stocks, some long-term like 5½% Treasury Stock (2008–12), some medium-term like 6% Exchequer Stock (1970) and 3% Savings Bonds (1965–75), and some short-term within a year or two of maturity. These stocks are held by individuals, commercial banks, insurance companies, and other institutions, including Government departments.

The management of the National Debt has become to the Government an important instrument of monetary policy, the Government broker intervening in the market either to buy or to sell Government Stocks with the purpose of influencing the prevailing rate of interest. The Radcliffe Committee actually regarded the National Debt as indispensable to monetary policy. In any case there is no likelihood of a return to the nineteenth-century policy of reducing the National Debt through a sinking fund. Between 1815 and 1853 the National Debt fell from £858 million to £771 million, and between 1856 and 1899 from £831 million to £635 million. As recently as 1914 the National Debt was only £656 million.

National Debt, Burden of. The extent to which the National Debt is a burden on the community depends on whether it is an internal or external debt. It is the external debt which is the more serious burden since its repayment and the payment of interest involves a payment to another country and it therefore affects the balance of payments. On the other hand, the payment of interest on the internal debt merely requires transfer payments to be made from one group of people to another (those receiving most usually being those who pay most in taxes) and so the community as a whole is no poorer. The greater, however, the National Debt the greater the amount of taxation required to provide the interest on it, and this may check expenditure on more desirable objectives. In a period of inflation the burden of the National Debt tends to fall with the decline in the value of money. In terms of what money would buy the British National Debt in 1975 was little more than half of the debt in 1945 in spite of its increase during those years of £28,000 million.

National Debt Commissioners. The official body which collects the deposits of the Post Office Savings Bank and the Trustee Savings Banks and invests them in Government securities. The Commissioners are responsible for debt management and purchase both short-term investments like Treasury bills (which they obtain 'on tap') and long-term securities, subscribing to new Government issues (some of which are made directly to the Commissioners) or making purchases from the Issue Department of the Bank of England.

National Debt Reduction Funds. *See* National Fund.

National Defence Contribution (N.D.C.). A tax on business profits imposed in 1937 to help towards the cost of re-armament.

National Development Bonds. A Government security first issued in 1964 to replace Defence Bonds. In 1968 they were superseded by British Savings Bonds (*q.v.*).

National Diploma in Business Studies. *See* National Certificates and Diplomas in Business Studies.

National Discount Company. A London discount house which merged in 1970 with Gerrard & Reid Ltd. to form the Gerrard & National Discount Co.

National Dividend. An older term for National Income (*q.v.*).

National Dock Labour Board. A body set up under an Act of 1946 to administer the scheme for ending casual labour (*q.v.*) at the docks.

National Economic Development Council. Often referred to as 'Neddy', it is a body set up by the Government in 1962 to undertake some degree of economic planning with the aim of increasing the rate of economic growth in Great Britain. It has four main functions: (i) To advise the Treasury; (ii) To discuss what obstacles have hindered Great Britain's economic growth in recent years; (iii) To seek means of stabilising industrial incomes; (iv) To make the general public more fully aware of the importance of the development and application of new ideas to industry. It has an Incomes Review Division and a Prices Review Division. Its sub-committees are known as Economic Development committees (*q.v.*) or 'Little Neddies'. *See also* National Plan.

National Enterprise Board. Set up under the Industry Act (1975) to acquire on behalf of the State interests in companies in the private sector.

National Farmers Union. An organisation representing British farmers.

National Film Corporation. A specialist financial institution established after the Second World War to provide medium term capital for the film producing industry.

National Finance. *See* Budget.

National Freight Corporation. Formed under the Transport Act (1968) to take over the road haulage and shipping assets of the Transport Holding Company and the freightliner assets and cartage vehicles of the British Railways Board, and to operate road haulage and freightliner services. The N.F.C. is responsible for the movement of goods originating by road while British Rail retains commercial responsibility for the movement of goods originating by rail.

National Fund. A Fund established in 1927 by an anonymous gift of £500,000, other gifts being made later, for the purpose of eventually redeeming the National Debt. Additions and interest had increased the Fund to over £3 million by 1964.

The huge increase in the National Debt after 1939 made the prospect of redemption extremely remote. Other similar Funds are the Elsie Mackay Fund (£1·6 million) established in 1929, and the John Buchanan Fund (£48,000) established in 1932.

National Giro. A giro banking system was established in Great Britain by the Post Office in 1968. The feature of a giro service is that all accounts are kept at one centre—the National Giro Centre at Bootle, Lancashire. To open a giro account an initial minimum deposit of £20 is required. Debts between account holders can be settled by transfers from one account to another or in the case of non-account holders by giro cheques. No interest is paid on giro accounts and charges are made for cash withdrawals. Since 1975 the National Giro has provided a full banking service, including overdrafts, standing orders, transfers to foreign giro systems, and the issue of travellers' cheques and foreign currency. It is associated with Mercantile Credit for personal loans repayable over two years in monthly instalments.

National Health Service. It covers medical, dental, optical, pharmaceutical and hospital treatment and is available to all, irrespective of whether they contribute to national insurance. It is mainly financed by the State, only a small fraction of the national insurance contributions being assigned to it. Since 1968 it has been administered by the Department of Health and Social Security.

National Income. There are two ways of looking at the national income of a country. It can be regarded either as the money value of the total volume of production of goods and services or the total of all incomes derived from economic activity during a specified period, generally one year, after allowance has been made for capital consumption. Calculation of the national income by either method should give the same total since the amount paid for any commodity comprises a collection of payments to the factors of production concerned with its production and distribution, all such payments becoming income to the owners of the factors of production receiving them. Thus, 'national income' and 'volume of production' are really alternative terms for the same thing. To measure the heterogeneous mass of goods comprised in the volume of production, money is the most convenient unit of measurement although a far from satisfactory one since, unlike other units of measurement, its own value is also liable to change. Thus, the British National Income more than doubled in money value between 1955 and 1971, but much of this increase was the result of rising prices. If there had been no change in prices the increase would have been 34%. Detailed information regarding the British National Income is given in a Blue Book on *National Income and Expenditure* published by Her Majesty's Stationery Office in September of each year for the previous calendar year, with preliminary estimates in a White Paper in the preceding April. The Blue Book contains a recalculation of the National Income for recent years in terms of prices ruling in a selected base year, thereby enabling comparison to be made between the latest year and previous years in *real* terms. A third method of calculating the national income is to add together the total expenditure of the community and total saving during the year.

Calculations of the British National Income in increasing detail have been made by the British Government since 1941. The State has shown concern for economic progress, on which a people's standard of living depends, only in quite recent time, though economists, from the time of Marshall, have considered the size of the real national income as the best measure of a country's economic progress. The size of the national income is the main determinant of the standard of living of a people, the second being the manner of its distribution.

The size of the national income depends on a number of factors including: (i) A country's stock of the factors of production—the entrepreneur, land, labour, and capital—and their quality, its natural resources, the skill of its labour, the extent and quality of its real capital, and the amount of entrepreneurial ability; (ii) The state of technical knowledge in the country; and (iii) Political stability, for economic progress is bound to be slow in a country subject to frequent political upheavals.

Reference has already been made to one difficulty in measuring the national income, namely the fact that the value of money itself is liable to variation. Other difficulties include: (i) Information is incomplete, some income not being recorded, as for example when a person does a job in his spare time for a friend or neighbour; (ii) Care must be taken not to count the same article twice, for example, both the raw material and the finished product must not be counted as this would result in the raw material being counted twice; (iii) Since only goods and services for which payment is made are included all services which people do for themselves are excluded, so that the more people do for themselves the smaller will be the national income; (iv) Government expenditure is devoted partly to the provision of services to the community as a whole and partly to the payment of pensions and interest on the National Debt. The former clearly increases the national income but the latter are merely transfers of income from one group of people to another; (v) Since the purpose is to calculate the *net* national income an allowance must be made for depreciation, a certain proportion of total output being for the replacement of obsolete or wornout capital goods; (vi) Housing includes not only the income of landlords but also the 'notional' income of owner-occupiers of dwellings; (vii) Allowance has to be made for net income from abroad; (viii) Gains in business profit due to the appreciation in value of stocks or work-in-progress are not included in the national income, an allowance for this being made under the heading of 'inventory revaluation'.

National Incomes Commission. A body, often referred to as 'Nicky', set up in Great Britain in 1962 by the Chancellor of the Exchequer in an attempt to pursue an Incomes Policy, that is, to relate as far as possible increases in money incomes to the rate of increase of the real national income. The policy found little favour with the trade unions, which viewed its activities with suspicion from the start, believing its purpose merely to be to check the efforts of the unions to raise the wages of their members. It was superseded in 1965 by the National Board for Prices and Incomes (*q.v.*).

National Industrial Relations Court. A body set up under the Industrial Relations Act (1971) to consider cases of unfair industrial practices brought to its notice. It was replaced in 1975 by the Employment Appeals Tribunal (*q.v.*).

National Institute of Economic and Social Research. A body established in 1938 to undertake economic research into the behaviour of the British economy and on special projects. It is financed by the Treasury and British business firms.

National Insurance. The first country to adopt a scheme of national insurance was Germany and, though the benefits were small, the German system became the model for later schemes in other countries. In Great Britain national insurance dates from the National Insurance Act of 1911, although non-contributory pensions of £0·25 per week had been awarded in 1908 to people of limited means on reaching seventy years of age. The Act of

1911 (Lloyd George being Chancellor of the Exchequer at the time) provided insurance against sickness, and gradually the scheme was expanded to include retirement pensions at 65, insurance against unemployment, and widow's pensions. A fund from which benefits were to be paid was set up, and contributions were to be paid by employers, employees, and the State, the scheme to be based on the insurance principle of the 'pooling of risk' and therefore was to be self-supporting. Employers were made responsible for their employees' contributions, which were deducted from wages. Most salaried workers were at first excluded from the scheme but in 1937 those with annual incomes of less than £400 a year were permitted to become voluntary contributors for a limited range of benefits, including widows', orphans', and old-age pensions, but excluding sickness and unemployment benefits.

The present scheme of national insurance in Great Britain was established by the Act of 1946, which set up a Ministry of Pensions and National Insurance (known since 1966 as the Ministry of Social Security) with offices throughout the country to operate it from July 1948. In his *Report on Social Insurance* Lord Beveridge had outlined a comprehensive scheme of social insurance covering the entire population with more extensive and higher rates of benefit, but also with higher contributions in order to retain the insurance principle of relating benefits to contributions. The scheme actually introduced in 1946 provided more generous benefits than the contributions justified, and with successive increases, especially in retirement pensions, it has tended to become more a scheme of social security than of national insurance. The principal benefits under the present scheme include: (i) Retirement pensions; (ii) Unemployment benefit; (iii) Sickness benefit, that is, payment while the insured person is unable to work, medical attention being provided by the National Health Service, the cost of which falls almost entirely on the State; (iv) Maternity grants; and (v) Funeral grants; and (vi) Industrial injuries. Family allowances were provided under a different Act. When regarded as necessary retirement pensions are supplemented by National Assistance. In 1961 an additional graduated pension scheme was introduced with pensions of up to half average earnings. Since 1968 it has been administered by the Department of Health and Social Security.

National Insurance Advisory Committee. A body set up in 1947 to advise the minister on matters arising from the National Insurance Act (1946).

National Insurance (Industrial Injuries) Act (1946). Under this Act the State accepts responsibility for providing compensation to people who have been injured at work, an extra contribution by both employer and employee being added to the weekly national insurance payment. It replaced the former Workmen's Compensation Acts.

Nationalisation. Bringing ownership and management of an industry under the control of the State. Nationalisation of the 'means of production, distribution, and exchange' had for long been socialist policy and the policy of the British Labour Party from its foundation. Therefore, when the Labour Party won an electoral majority in 1945 it embarked on a wide scheme of nationalisation, the only important commercial undertakings previously operated in Great Britain by the State being the Post Office and airways, though in many European countries railways had been operated by the State for some time. The Bank of England was nationalised in 1946 and this was followed in 1947 by the nationalisation of the coal industry, in 1948 by inland transport and electricity, and in 1949 by the gas industry. The iron and steel industry was nationalised in 1951, denationalised shortly afterwards, and renationalised in 1967. Road transport was denationalised in 1951, but British Road Services continued to operate more than half the total of road haulage vehicles. A new scheme for passenger road transport was introduced by the Transport Act (1968) (*q.v.*). Previous owners of nationalised industries usually received compensation in fixed interest Government-guaranteed stocks. Most nationalised industries were given monopolies in their own particular lines, but some, such as coal, electricity, and gas, compete against one another. Some people believe that nationalised industries exist to provide services and, therefore, should not necessarily be run at a profit, while others believe that the aim should be to 'break even', that is, they should just cover their costs. *See* Price Policy of Nationalised Industries.

National Plan. Published in September 1965, it covered the period 1965–70, its aims being (i) to achieve a more rapid rate of economic growth, than had been accomplished previously; (ii) to bring the balance of payments into balance after the large deficit in 1963–64; (iii) to increase industrial efficiency to make up for an expected deficiency of labour by 1970. It outlined the investment required in different industries, the growth rate for each, and the consequent changes in the labour forces of each. It stressed the necessity for greater mobility of labour, both occupationally and geographically, to meet the needs of the changing pattern of industry. The severe credit restrictions of 1966–67 made it impossible to achieve the rate of economic growth envisaged and so the plan had to be abandoned. *See also* Planned Economy.

National Ports Council. A body responsible for the development of British ports. The Rochdale Report recommended that there should be co-ordinated development of the ports.

National Product. An alternative term for National Income (*q.v.*).

National Research Development Corporation. A body established in 1948 to assist the development of inventions in order to give British industry the opportunity of benefiting from the work of British inventors.

National Savings. A term covering National Savings Certificates, British Savings Bonds, Premium Bonds, the National Savings Bank and the Trustee Savings Banks, that is, the means provided for small savers to lend to the State. *See* Page Report.

National Savings Bank. Until 1969 known as the Post Office Savings Bank. It is the largest savings bank in Great Britain, operating at all large post offices and many small ones. It was established in 1861. Interest is paid on deposits, the money being paid over to the National Debt Commissioners. *See* Trustee Savings Banks.

National Savings Certificates. Originally issued in 1916, as 'War Savings Certificates' during the First World War, they are a means by which the Government encourages small savers, the interest being free of tax. They are issued in small denominations, which over the years have varied between £0·75 (15*s*.) and £1.00 each. Interest accrues in the form of an addition to the value of the certificate, those of the first issue becoming worth £1 after five years, though later issues have all carried a lower rate of interest. There has been a number of issues, the terms of issue being varied to keep in line with changes in the prevailing rate of interest. They can be bought at post offices, banks, and national savings centres. They are the most popular of Government non-marketable securities, the interest on them not being subject to income tax, but only a limited number can be held by any one person. In 1975 an indexed certificate, known as a Retirement Certificate (*q.v.*) was made available to people of retirement age. The amount now outstanding, exclusive of accrued interest, is over £2,000 million.

National Savings, Department for. Formerly known as the Post Office Savings Department.

National Savings Gift Tokens. Issued by the Post Office in denominations of £1, £3, and £5. The recipient can exchange them for National Savings Certificates, British Savings Bonds, Premium Bonds, or they can be used to make deposits in a trustee savings bank.

National Savings Group. *See* National Savings Movement.

National Savings Movement. The aim of the movement is to encourage saving. It has established National Savings Groups throughout the country, these being affiliated to the National Savings Committee, to enable small savers to purchase by instalments National Savings Certificates, British Savings Bonds, and Premium Bonds, or alternatively the savings can be deposited in the Post Office Savings Bank or a trustee savings bank.

National Savings Stamps. To encourage small savers National Savings Stamps were issued by the Post Office, but were discontinued in 1976.

National Savings Stock Register. Until 1969 known as the Post Office Register, it lists all stocks that can be purchased through the Post Office. The main advantage of such stocks is that the interest is paid without deduction of income tax. A list of these stocks is given in the *Post Office Guide*, the list being liable to variation.

National Shipbuilders' Security. A company formed by shipbuilders in 1930 primarily for the purpose of reducing capacity in the industry, as did the Lancashire Cotton Corporation and Woolcombers Ltd. in the cotton and wool textile industries respectively, by purchasing and closing down some firms. Finance was obtained partly from the Bankers' Development Corporation and partly by a levy on all sales of ships by members. During 1930–35 shipbuilding capacity in Great Britain was reduced by 40%.

National Trust. A voluntary body, it was founded in 1895 to care for historic houses and scenic areas of land which have been bequeathed to it or which it has purchased.

National Union of Manufacturers. A somewhat similar body to the Federation of British Industries with which it amalgamated in 1963 to form the Confederation of British Industry (*q.v.*).

National Wealth. The total money value of goods and property of all kinds in a country at a particular time. Not only will the value of all real capital be taken into account, but also all personal possessions. Any calculation must be little more than a very rough estimate since the value of some things cannot even be estimated. In such a calculation only the value of real assets must be included and money, unless in the form of metal coins, must also be excluded, as must all paper titles—Government stocks, share certificates, etc.—some of these merely representing Government debt or simply claims to wealth. Little attention is paid nowadays to calculations of national wealth since national income is regarded as a more reliable indicator of the economic welfare of a people, though the national capital—a country's stock of real capital—is an important influence on the size of the national income.

National Westminster Bank. One of the English 'Big Four' members of the London Bankers' Clearing House, it was formed in 1968 by the amalgamation of the National Provincial Bank (established 1833) and the Westminster Bank. It controls Coutts & Co., the Isle of Man Bank, the Ulster Bank, and the Roy West Banking Corporation, and it also has interest in the Yorkshire Bank, the National & Grindlays, the Standard Bank, and the International Commercial Bank. It has interests in hire-purchase finance through its wholly-owned subsidiary, the North Central Finance Co. and the Mercantile Credit Co., in unit trusts and in credit card business through the Diners' Club. In 1977 it was the twentieth largest bank in the world.

National Westminster Bank Review. First issued in November 1968 as successor to the former *National Provincial Bank Review* and the *Westminster Bank Review* after the merger of the two banks concerned. It contains articles on matters of current economic and financial interest.

National Workshops. These were established in Paris during the revolution of 1848 by Emile Thomas, as a result of the influence of Louis Blanc, author of *The Right to Work*. Owing to the economic dislocation caused by the revolution little work was available, either in the workshops or elsewhere, and large numbers of unemployed flocked to them. When the new republican government abolished them bitter fighting occurred in the streets of Paris.

'Nation of Shopkeepers.' Napoleon's contemptuous reference to the British nation.

Nationwide Building Society. The name adopted in 1970 by the Co-operative Permanent Building Society. It is the third largest building society in the U.K.

N.A.T.S.O.P.A. Abbreviation of National Association of Operative Printers Graphical and Media Personnel.

Natural Economy. An alternative term for a barter or non-monetary economy in which goods are exchanged for goods.

Natural Increase. The increase in population resulting from the difference between the crude birth-rate and the crude death-rate.

Natural Monopoly. Some monopolies arise either because the climate and soil of a region restrict the production of a commodity to that area, or because a large part of the total output of a mineral may be found in one region. For example, the production of jute is restricted to the Ganges delta and little nickel is mined outside Canada.

Natural Order. The doctrine of the Physiocrats and their followers that everyone is entitled to the greatest possible degree of freedom, that being the 'natural order' of things, and therefore State interference with the individual should be kept to a minimum.

Natural Rate of Interest. The equilibrium rate of interest which equates the demand for loans with the supply of loanable funds. At any given time the actual or market rate of interest charged by banks to borrowers may be above or below the natural rate. Wicksell used this concept of the natural rate of interest to explain periodic over-creation of credit by banks, an excessive demand to borrow from the banks occurring if the market rate is below the natural rate with a tendency for an over-expansion of credit to follow. If, on the other hand, the market rate is higher than the natural rate credit expansion will be checked, a check to production will occur and unemployment will increase.

Natural Wastage. The decline in the amount of labour in a particular occupation resulting from retirement, death, and voluntary transference to other forms of employment. Together with new entrants (*q.v.*) it helps to bring about a redistribution of labour between different occupations without causing economic friction and structural unemployment, but it is slow to take effect.

Nave Paise. The fractional unit of the currency of India, one rupee being worth 100 nave paise.

Navigation Acts. The Mercantilists thought that a nation should always strive to achieve a favourable balance of payments and as part of their policy supported the development of shipping, both naval and mercantile. The earliest Navigation Act, passed in 1381, declared that all British imports and exports should be carried in British ships unless these were not available. A whole series of Navigation Acts followed, and in the seventeenth century led to the wars with the Dutch. The Navigation Acts were not repealed until 1849.

N.C.B. Abbreviation of National Coal Board (*q.v.*).

N.C.L. Abbreviation of National Carriers Ltd. (*q.v.*).

N.D.C. 1. Abbreviation of National Defence Contribution (*q.v.*).
2. Abbreviation of National Debt Commissioners (*q.v.*).

'Near' Money. A term sometimes used of something which, though it cannot technically be regarded as money, nevertheless performs some of the functions of money. Thus, a bill of exchange can be considered as 'near' money. Some people might also regard bank deposits as 'near' money, but since bank deposits subject to withdrawal and transfer by cheque have become in some countries the principal means of payment and the main type of purchasing power they are probably best regarded as the final stage in the development of money.

N.E.D.C. Abbreviation of National Economic Development Council (*q.v.*), often referred to acronymically as 'Neddy'.

Nederlandsche Bank. The central bank of the Netherlands, it was founded in 1814. Its head office is in Amsterdam, but it has branches in all the main cities as well as agencies in many smaller places. Since 1948 it has been the sole bank of issue in the Netherlands. Since that date, it has concentrated on central banking activities, leaving ordinary banking business to the commercial banks.

N.E.D.O. Abbreviation of National Economic Development Office.

Negative Income Tax. An American term for a concept better known in Great Britain as Reverse Income Tax (*q.v.*). It is a scheme whereby the State makes payments to people with incomes below a certain level as a means of ensuring that no one falls below the poverty line. It is the basis of the Tax Credit System (*q.v.*). *See also* Family Income Supplement.

Negligence. The legal definition of negligence is failure to do something which a reasonable man would be expected to do, that is, breach of a duty to take care. Before anyone can bring an action for the tort of negligence he must have suffered damage as a result of it.

Negotiable Instrument. A document possessing certain qualities and entitling the holder to a specified sum of money. This right can be transferred, usually by endorsement, to another party, as for example with bills of exchange, cheques, dividend warrants, etc.

Negotiation Credit. An authority given by a shipper to his bank to purchase bills of exchange on his buyer overseas.

Neo-classical School. Alternative name sometimes applied to the Cambridge School (*q.v.*).

Neo-Malthusianism. Limitation of family size by birth control. Malthus suggested 'moral restraint', by which he meant postponing marriage until a family could be afforded.

Net Book Agreement. An agreement between publishers and booksellers that books marked at a net price should not be sold below that price, an example in effect of resale price maintenance. However, the Restrictive Trade Practices Court in 1963 decided that this practice was not contrary to the public interest, and it was thus permitted to continue.

Net Earnings of Management. An alternative term used by Alfred Marshall for Pure Profit (*q.v.*).

Netherlands Trading Bank (Nederlandsche Handel-Maatschappij). The largest commercial bank of the Netherlands, it has very considerable overseas business.

Net Income. The income of a business after the expenses of running the business have been deducted. In the case of individual income it is the amount received after payment of income tax.

Net Interest. An alternative term

used by Alfred Marshall for Pure Interest (*q.v.*).

Net Investment. The amount of investment during a period after allowance has been made for the depreciation of existing capital.

Net National Product. A term used in connection with calculations of the national income, it is the money value of the total volume of production (that is, the gross national product) after allowance has been made for depreciation. *See* National Income.

Net Price. A price not subject to a discount.

Net Profit. In order to calculate net profit a Profit and Loss Account must be drawn up, showing on the credit side the gross profit, brought forward from the Trading Account, and on the debit side the various expenses that have been incurred during the period under review, such as rent, rates, taxes, wages, insurance, interest on loans (if any), advertising, light and heat, depreciation. Gross Profit less these expenses gives Net Profit.

Net Rate of Tax. This is the amount that an investor who does not pay the full rate of income tax can reclaim from the Inland Revenue in the case of dividends taxed at source. In the case of overseas investments or investment trusts with some overseas investment the net rate of tax used to be less than the standard rate. Since April 1966, however, the net rate in the case of unit trusts has been the same as the standard or basic rate.

Net Reproduction Rate. This forms a better guide to population trends than the crude birth and death rates. It takes account only of the number of female children per family. If the average number of girls per family is one, then the net reproduction rate = 1; if each family averages two girls, then the net reproduction rate = 2. For a population just to maintain itself, there must therefore be a net reproduction rate = 1. If the rate exceeds 1 the population will increase, but if the rate is less than 1 it will decline.

Net Saving. Total saving less allowances for depreciation and stock appreciation.

Net Working Capital. The excess of current assets over the current liabilities of a firm.

Net Worth. The excess of assets over liabilities as shown by a firm's balance sheet, that is, the capital owned by a business.

Neutralisation. With reference to the effect of an inflow of gold on the supply of money, *See* Sterilisation of Gold.

Neutral Money. Money performing the passive functions of serving as a medium of exchange and unit of account, but having no dynamic functions which affect the economy.

Neutral Rate of Interest. A term used by Lord Keynes of the equilibrium rate of interest which equates investment to actual savings when no 'forced saving' is taking place.

New Deal. A term used of the policy of President F. D. Roosevelt of the United States, more particularly during his first term of office, 1932–36. This policy aimed at stimulating recovery from the Great Depression and comprised an extensive programme of Government investment, a scheme for increasing farmers' incomes by reducing output in order to raise the prices of farm products, and social legislation, including unemployment pay and old-age pensions.

New Entrants. The simplest way, though a slow one, by which labour is redistributed among different occupations is through new entrants, who will tend to go in greater numbers into expanding industries, 'natural wastage' being allowed to reduce the amount of labour in declining industries.

New Issue Market. That part of the capital market which deals with new public issues of stocks and shares. There are various methods by which a new issue of shares can be placed; (i) A private placing, the shares being entirely taken up by a finance company or by a group of financial institutions such as insurance companies or investment trust companies; (ii) A stock exchange introduction, the company concerned applying to the stock exchange for a quotation for its shares; (iii) A stock exchange placing, when a stock exchange introduction is accompanied by an arrangement with a number of insurance companies and investment trust companies which undertake to purchase the shares to be issued, or an issuing house may agree to take the entire issue and then re-sell to the market; (iv) A public issue, for which the Companies Act requires a prospectus to be issued, the usual method being for an issuing house to underwrite the issue, though most likely it will arrange for a number of sub-underwriters to cover part of it, or a public issue may take the form of an offer for sale by an issuing house or some other financial institution which has previously purchased the shares from the company; (v) A 'rights' issue to existing shareholders in cases where the shares are already dealt in on the stock exchange, such issues generally being on favourable terms, so that even if they do not wish to keep them shareholders will accept their quota of shares and then re-sell them at a profit.

New Model Unions. Generally restricting their membership to skilled workers, these unions were established during the 1850s and 1860s. They combined the functions of trade unions and friendly societies and in general favoured co-operation with employers, though retaining the strike as a weapon of last resort.

New Penny. The fractional unit of the British decimal coinage system, 100 New Pence being equal to £1. It is equal in value to 2·4 old pence. *See* Decimal Coinage.

New Towns. The New Towns Act (1946) proposed the establishment of a number of new towns to check the growth of London and other large conurbations. The sites chosen were close to existing small places from which they took their names, a Development Corporation being set up for each town, and early development being financed by loans from the Treasury. Eight of the new towns are within a short distance of London, just too far to prevent their becoming merely 'dormitory' towns, the intention being that the people living in the new towns should also work there. Towns built to check the expansion of London are Crawley to the south, Bracknell to the west, Stevenage, Welwyn, Hatfield, and Hemel Hempstead to the north and north-west, and Harlow and Basildon to the east. The aim is to expand all these places until their populations reach 50,000 to 80,000 or, in the case of Basildon, 106,000. Progress was slow at first but by 1965 most of the first group of towns had reached the size originally planned for them. Other places being developed as new towns are Newton Aycliffe, Washington and Peterlee in County Durham, Killingworth in Northumberland, Corby in the East Midlands, Redditch in the West Midlands, Skelmersdale and Runcorn in Lancashire, Dawley in Shropshire, Cwmbran in South Wales, and Glenrothes, Cumbernauld, East Kilbride, and Livingston (West Lothian), and Irvine (Ayrshire) in Scotland. The population aimed at for these places is 80,000 to 100,000. More ambitious schemes have been put forward for what might be termed New Cities one to the south of Preston (Lancashire), its name not yet decided, with a population target of 400,000, a town near Milton Keynes (Bucks) with a population of 250,000, Dawley (Shropshire), and Craigavon (Northern Ireland) with a population of 150,000. Dawley has been merged with Oakengates and Wellington to form a new town of 220,000, known as Telford. Planned expansion of Northampton, Daventry, Peterborough, and Ipswich is going forward.

New Towns, Commission for. A body set up in 1961 under the New Towns Act (1959) to take over the assets and liabilities of the Development Corporations of the New Towns when they reach the first stage of their development. The Commission has taken over from the Development Corporations of Crawley, Hemel Hempstead, Hatfield, and Welwyn Garden City.

New Unionism. Previous to 1889 membership of trade unions had been mainly restricted to unskilled workers, the new unions developed during 1889-1900 including unskilled as well as skilled workers. These new unions became the great industrial unions whereas the craft unions of skilled workers had usually been small. As a result trade union membership greatly increased.

N.F.C. Abbreviation of National Freight Corporation (*q.v.*).

N.F.U. Abbreviation of National Farmers' Union (*q.v.*).

Ngwee. A sub-unit of the currency of Zambia, 100 ngwee being equal in value to one kwacha.

N.H.S. Abbreviation of National Health Service (*q.v.*).

N.I.C. Abbreviation of National Incomes Commission (*q.v.*), often referred to as 'Nicky.'

Nickel. A colloquial American term for a five-cent piece.

'Nicky.' A popular term for the former National Incomes Commission (*q.v.*).

Night Safe. In the outside wall of a bank providing this service there is a metal door which can be opened from the outside by customers with keys to the lock. Money to be deposited is placed in a locked wallet, put on a shelf inside the night safe, and when the door is closed it is tipped down into the bank's strong room. Night safes make it possible for shop-keepers to deposit their takings at a bank after it has closed.

'Ninepence for Fourpence.' A phrase used by Lloyd George when Chancellor of the Exchequer to popularise his National Insurance scheme established by the Act of 1911. He failed to appreciate, however, that in certain circumstances the incidence of the levy on the employer as well as that on the employee might fall entirely on the employee, whereas at other times the incidence of both contributions might be on the employer. *Cf.* Incidence of Taxation.

N.I.T. Abbreviation of Negative Income Tax (*q.v.*).

N.N.P. Abbreviation of Net National Product (*q.v.*).

Noble. An English gold coin, first issued by Edward III in 1344, then worth £0·33, with half and quarter nobles of proportionate value. In 1464 the value of the noble was increased to £0·43 but in 1526 a George noble of the original value was again minted, half-George nobles also being issued. In the reign of Elizabeth I Double George Nobles were issued.

Nominal Accounts. A book-keeping term for accounts such as Cash, Sales, and Purchases, as distinct from the personal accounts of customers.

Nominal Capital. *See* Authorised Capital.

Nominal Price. In the case of stock exchange securities this is the price attached to the stocks and shares and in the case of redeemable Government stocks the price at which they will be redeemed. The stock exchange prices of stocks and shares at a particular time often vary considerably from their nominal prices. Thus if £100 of $2\frac{1}{2}$% Consols stands at £50, the nominal price is £100.

Nominal Wages. Wages in terms of money as distinct from real wages (wages in terms of the goods and services they will buy). Sometimes the term is taken to mean that part of wages paid in money when there is an additional payment in kind such as board and lodging, uniform, free meals, free transport, etc.

Nominee. An agent who acts on behalf of a principal, as sometimes occurs in the purchase of shares when the purchaser does not wish to disclose his identity.

Non-assented Stock. Stock held by an investor who has not agreed to some changes suggested by the body issuing it.

Non-contributory Pensions. *See* Old Age Pension.

Non-durable Consumers' Goods. Most consumers' goods are quickly consumed, for example, food, tobacco, newspapers, etc., such goods being known as non-durable consumers' goods to distinguish them from durable consumers' goods like furniture, motor cars, etc.

Non-employed. For purposes of national insurance a person who is not engaged in any form of paid employment but who is compelled to contribute to the scheme. The rate of contribution is higher than that for an employee but less than that for a self-employed person. Those in this category are not entitled to all benefits under national insurance.

Non-marketable Securities. That part of the National Debt not dealt in on the stock exchange, it forms nearly 30% of the total. About half of the total of non-marketable debt is in the form of National Savings Securities—National Savings Certificates, British Savings Bonds, and Premium Bonds. Since they are not subject to income tax the amounts that can be held are limited. All can be purchased at post offices or banks in small denominations since their purpose is to encourage small savings, and they can be redeemed at short notice. Another form of non-marketable debt is provided by tax reserve certificates, which are issued both to individuals and business firms, where taxes are paid in January and July and not in weekly or monthly instalments, as under the P.A.Y.E. system. Interest is payable on them, tax free, but only if they are used for the payment of income tax, surtax, or profits tax. Other non-marketable debt occurs where official funds are in terminable or perpetual annuities (*qq.v.*). Finally, there is the debt owing to foreign governments, which forms about 7% of the total National Debt, about half of this being owed to the United States. Also under this heading there is debt to the International Monetary Fund.

Non-material Goods. A term used by Alfred Marshall. *See* Material Goods.

Non-monetary Advantages and Disadvantages. These influences affect the wages paid in some occupations through their effect on the supply of labour. Thus, some work is more congenial and in certain occupations there is greater security. These are non-monetary advantages. In other occupations the work may be dangerous or unhealthy, or the hours of work may be inconvenient These are non-monetary disadvantages. In general, the greater the non-monetary advantages of an occupation, the more labour it is likely to attract and the lower are likely to be the wages. Much disagreeable work, however, requires little skill, so that often the supply of labour available is large in relation to the demand for it, with the result that it is poorly paid in spite of its non-monetary disadvantages. Only in times of over-full employment does it usually become necessary to offer higher wages to attract labour to unskilled occupations with non-monetary disadvantages.

Non-participating Employments. Those occupations with their own private pension schemes the members of which are excluded from the National Insurance graduated pension scheme.

Non-resident Convertibility. In January 1959 sterling was given non-resident convertibility, that is, sterling became freely convertible to foreign holders, though restrictions were still retained for British residents in order to control the export of capital from Great Britain for investment abroad.

Non Sequitur. Latin for 'it does not follow'. Also known as *non propter hoc*, this is one of the commonest fallacies met with in the social sciences. It occurs when a writer or speaker implies that one thing is the consequence of another merely because the first preceded it in time.

Both conditions, however, may be true though independent of one another.

Non-specific Factors of Production. Those factors of production which can easily be transferred to alternative forms of employment.

Non-voting Shares. Some public companies issue two sets of ordinary shares, one set being distinguished as 'A' shares, and voting rights may be restricted to holders of one set of shares—generally the smaller issue—the purpose being to keep the control of the company in the hands of a small group of people, probably those who controlled the firm before it became a public company. It is clearly undesirable for the majority of ordinary shareholders to be deprived of voting rights in this way.

No-par-value Shares. Shares which have been given no nominal value (which is of little importance) and only have the value currently determined on the stock exchange.

Nordic Council. A body established in 1952 by the Scandinavian countries—Norway, Sweden, Denmark, and Iceland—to develop co-operation between them on economic and other matters through a number of standing committees.

'No Rent' Land. According to Ricardo this was land that was just worth cultivating, the value of the excess yield of a more fertile piece of land over the field of 'no rent land' being the rent of the more fertile land.

Norfolk Course. One of the farming developments of the Agrarian Revolution (*q.v.*) was the elimination of the fallow field, root crops or clover being alternated with corn to give a four-year system of crop rotation. It was first attempted in Norfolk by Lord ('Turnip') Townshend.

Norges Bank. The central bank of Norway. Its head office is in Oslo and it has 20 branches. It is the sole bank of issue in Norway.

Normal Price. The long-run equilibrium price of a commodity with supply adjusted to demand, as distinct from market price, the short-run equilibrium price. *See* Equilibrium(i).

Normal Profit. The amount of profit required to keep an entrepreneur in a particular line of production. It thus acts as a regulator of the distribution of factors of production among different employments. When most firms in an industry are earning more than normal profit other firms will be attracted into that industry; if firms are earning less than normal profit the industry will tend to contract. Normal profit varies between different industries according to the risk involved. Normal profit can be regarded as the minimum payment that an entrepreneur is prepared to accept, and as such it forms one of the costs of production. In considering the profit of a monopolist, normal profit is always taken to be a cost, the monopolist's profit being in excess of normal profit. In conditions of equilibrium in perfect competition the entrepreneur would earn normal profit, neither more nor less. Normal profit is a useful but highly theoretical concept for the economist, although in practice it could not be precisely calculated.

Normal Value. A term sometimes taken to mean the 'labour' value of a commodity as opposed to its 'scarcity' value. *See* Labour Theory of Value; Value.

North Central Finance Ltd. A finance house with its head office in Rotherham, it is wholly owned by the National Westminster Bank Ltd. It is a member of the Finance Houses Association.

Northern Counties Technical Examinations Council. A body with headquarters in Newcastle upon Tyne which organises examinations in commercial and technical subjects for part-time students at evening institutes and technical colleges.

Northern Stock Exchange. Formed in 1965 by a merger of the stock exchanges of Manchester, Liverpool, Leeds, Sheffield, Newcastle upon Tyne, Bradford, Huddersfield, Halifax and Oldham. In 1973 a unified stock exchange was set up for the whole country with branches or 'floors' in the old centres.

Norwich Union Assurance Co. Ltd. Established in 1797 as a fire insurance office, it is one of eight insurance companies formed before 1800. It first began to undertake life assurance in 1808. It is now one of the larger insurance companies in Great Britain.

Nostro Account. (Nostro = Italian for *our*.) These are accounts conducted by London banks with banks abroad. *Cf.* Vostro Account.

Notarial Act of Honour. When a bill of exchange has been protested another person, who wishes to protect the credit and good name of the party on whom it is drawn, may pay it, such a payment having to be attested by a notary public and known as a notarial act of honour.

Notary Public. An official who is empowered to attest documents by attaching his seal on them. When in the case of a dishonoured bill of exchange it has to be 'noted' and 'protested' attestation by a notary public is required.

Note Issue. *See* Bank-note; Fiduciary Issue.

Notice. The period which an employer must allow to elapse after he has informed an employee that he wishes to dispose with his services. According to law the period of notice must be 'reasonable', that is, it must be what is customary in the trade or occupation concerned. An employee who has committed a serious misdemeanour, such as being found guilty of embezzlement, can be dismissed without notice, but in other cases the employee could sue his employer for wrongful dismissal if proper notice had not been given. To avoid such a possibility an employer may give an employee wages for the required period in lieu of notice. The Contract of Employment Act (1963) related the period of notice to the length of time a worker has been employed by a firm. Further modifications, with the purpose of giving employees greater security of employment against 'wrongful dismissal' were made by the Contracts of Employment Act (1972) and the Trade Union and Labour Relations Act (1974) (*q.v.*).

Noting a Bill. With reference to the dishonour of a bill of exchange, it is the first step towards the protest (*q.v.*) of the bill.

Notional Income. Income which an investment is assumed to yield to its owner, although actually he receives nothing, as for example, from owner-occupancy of a house. Until 1963 this notional income was taxable under Schedule 'A'.

'Not Negotiable.' These words on a cheque or postal order act as a safeguard in case it is stolen, since it gives the holder of it no better right to it than the previous holder.

Novation. The discharge of a contract in consideration of another person undertaking a similar obligation in a new contract.

N.P. Abbreviation of Notary Public (*q.v.*).

N.U.B.E. Abbreviation of National Union of Bank Employees.

N.U.G.M.W. Abbreviation of National Union of General and Municipal Workers, one of the large industrial unions.

N.U.M. Abbreviation of National Union of Mineworkers.

Numeraire. A term sometimes used of the function of money as a measure of value.

Numismatics. The study and collection of coins. *See* Coinage.

N.U.R. Abbreviation of National Union of Railwaymen, an industrial union, skilled groups of railway workers having their own smaller unions.

N.U.T. Abbreviation of National Union of Teachers.

N.V. Abbreviation of Naamloze Vennootschan, the Dutch equivalent of Ltd. Co.

O

O.B. Abbreviation of Ordinary Business (*q.v.*), a term used in life assurance.

Objects Clause. The clause in the Memorandum of Association of a company which indicates the field of activity in which the company proposes to operate. Nowadays the 'objects clause' is often very widely drawn as a company may wish to diversify its range of products to meet possible changes of demand.

Obsolescence. One of the reasons for scrapping capital goods is that they become out of date and require to be replaced by more efficient and more up-to-date capital. This may often necessitate scrapping machinery which is still in good running order. In calculating the *net* national product allowance must be made for production to replace obsolete or obsolescent machinery as well as worn out machinery.

Occupational Disease (or **Hazard**). The risk of accident or illness associated with a particular type of work, as in coal mining, iron smelting, building, painting, etc. Wages tend to be higher in dangerous occupations as fear of risk tends to reduce the supply of labour. *See* Non-monetary Advantages and Disadvantages; Wages.

Occupational Mobility. The ease with which a factor of production, especially labour, can be transferred from one occupation to another. *See* Mobility.

Occupations, Classification of. Paid occupations fall into four main categories: (i) Primary or extractive occupations which include all kinds of farming, mining, quarrying, and fishing, the products being raw materials and food; (ii) Manufacturing or secondary production, in which the raw materials produced in primary production are turned into finished goods; (iii) Commercial services, which are concerned with the movement, storage, and distribution of goods and so include transport, all kinds of trade—wholesale and retail, import and export—together with banking, insurance, and advertising; (iv) Direct and personal services of all kinds other than those concerned with the production and distribution of goods, and including doctors, dentists, teachers, clergy, lawyers, police, members of the armed forces, entertainers, authors, musicians, professional sportsmen, domestic servants, hotel workers, and many others. Service occupations are sometimes classed as tertiary occupations. The greater the extent to which division of labour is carried the greater will be the number of people in Group (iii). The more economically advanced the country the greater will be the number of people in Group (iv). Thus, the introduction of new methods of production—mechanisation, automation—tends to reduce the proportion of a nation's labour force in Groups (i) and (ii).

Octroi. An internal tariff system between the different regions of a country, such as existed at one time in France.

Oddfellows. A term formerly applied to all members of friendly societies (*q.v.*) but now restricted to those societies including the name in their titles.

Odd Lot. With reference to stock exchange securities it signifies a smaller number of shares than the amount usually dealt in.

O.E.C.D. Abbreviation of Organisation for Economic Co-operation and Development (*q.v.*).

O.E.E.C. Abbreviation of Organisation for European Economic Co-operation (*q.v.*).

O.F.C. Abbreviation of Overseas Food Corporation (*q.v.*).

Offer. Before a contract can exist an offer must be made and accepted. An offer, which must be clearly and definitely made, may be made to a particular person or to anyone who cares to accept it, and the person making the offer may make it conditional if he so wishes. Goods displayed for sale, however, are not regarded as being on offer, but only placed there to invite prospective purchasers to make offers for them. *See* Contract.

Offer for Sale. One of the methods by which a new issue of shares is made, an issuing house having bought the share issue from the company in order to re-sell to investors. *See* New Issue Market.

Offer Price. With reference to stocks and shares, the price at which an investor can buy a security at a particular time. The managers of unit investment trusts quote two prices, the 'offer price' at which investors can buy units and the 'bid price' at which investors can re-sell to the managers.

Office Management. The study and practice of organising an office in the most effective way.

Office Management, Institute of. A body the members of which are engaged in office work involving management responsibilities. It concerns itself with the study of problems of office management. There are Associate Members and Ordinary Members (M.I.O.M.). Membership can be obtained by passing the examination for the Institute's Diploma in Office Management.

Office of Manpower Economics. Established in 1970, it provides a secretariat for three pay review bodies where collective bargaining is not appropriate: (i) the armed forces, (ii) doctors and dentists, (iii) higher public services.

Official List. Published by the Stock Exchange every business day, it gives the prices of securities ruling on that day and the number of 'markings' that have been reported.

Official Rate. When exchange rates are controlled this is the rate assigned to a currency by a country's monetary authorities and, therefore, the rate at which they are prepared to deal. In the foreign exchange market, however, a different rate may prevail unless the authorities by their intervention are able to influence the market rate by buying or selling their currency in the market in order to bring the two rates into line.

Official Receiver. An official of the Department of Trade who, in case of the bankruptcy takes over the property of the bankrupt. The Official Receiver or some other person may then be appointed to act as liquidator.

Offshore Funds. Investment Trusts or companies established in places such as Bermuda, the Bahamas, the Channel Islands, where taxation is low or where other economic advantages are available.

Old-age Pensions. The Act of 1908 offered non-contributory pensions to old people of 70 years of age whose incomes were below a certain amount. The award of a pension under the Old Age Pensions Act (1908) depended solely on the financial circumstances of the beneficiary and not on the payment of contributions. *See* Retirement Pension.

Old Colonial System. Under this system a nation's colonies were economically subordinated to the home country. Until the eighteenth century this was the general attitude of European countries to their colonies and in some cases to an even later date. The British attitude to colonies changed after the American War of Independence (1775–83) and the loss of the American colonies, the idea gradually developing that colonies were to be governed by Great Britain only until they were deemed to be capable of governing themselves.

Oldham List. An adjustment to the piece rate system of wage payment in the cotton-spinning industry whereby allowance is made for the quality of the yarn and the age of the machinery, both of which affect the amount of yarn spun in a period of time. *See* List.

'Old Unionism.' The old, generally small, craft unions which limited membership to men skilled in a particular craft and whose policy was to restrict numbers in order to keep up their rate of pay. The expansion of the factory system with the demand for semi-skilled workers weakened many of the old craft unions.

'O' Licence. The operator's licence ('O') was introduced by the Transport Act (1968) to replace the former 'A' and 'B' licences.

Oligopoly. A form of imperfect competition where there are only a few producers in contrast to perfect competition where there is a large number of producers. Two forms of oligopoly can be distinguished—perfect oligopoly where the commodity is homogeneous and imperfect oligopoly where some degree of differentiation exists between the products of different firms. In conditions of perfect competition price is outside the control of an individual producer, but a feature of oligopoly is that the price policy of a firm is influenced by that of its rivals. Under perfect oligopoly consumers have no preference for the product of one firm as compared with another, the commodity being homogeneous, so that a price cut by one will lead to similar price cuts by the other producers, price leadership generally being with the largest firm. Under imperfect oligopoly the effect of differentiation—even if nothing more than a brand name—is to make one product not a perfect substitute for another. In these conditions competition tends to be very keen, that is, of the type described as cut-throat competition, and this may take the form of a price-cutting war, but since any advantage to be obtained from price-cutting will go only to the first firm to do it, an advertising war may be preferred. *See* Imperfect Oligopoly; Perfect Oligopoly.

Ombudsman. A popular term of Swedish origin for the Parliamentary Commissioner for Administration (*q.v.*).

O.M.E. Abbreviation of Office of Manpower Economics (*q.v.*).

O.N.C. Abbreviation of Ordinary National Certificate. *See* National Certificate in Business Studies.

Oncost. An alternative term for Overhead Costs or Fixed Costs (*q.v.*).

O.N.D. Abbreviation of Ordinary National Diploma. *See* National Certificates and Diplomas in Business Studies.

One-man Business. A type of business where one man is responsible for providing the capital, bears the entire risk, and receives the entire profit. He may, of course, employ a large number of employees. *See* Sole Proprietor.

'One-man' Company. A private company with only two shareholders, one of whom holds most of the shares, the other shareholder being merely his nominee.

One-off. A term used of the production of an article to suit the individual requirements of a particular customer.

Onerous Rates. A term used by Alfred Marshall, who considered local rates to be of two types, those that yielded a benefit to the ratepayers, as when the money was spent on street lighting, drainage, etc.; and those levied for the purpose, such as to pay interest on a loan, which yield no compensating benefit. The former he regarded as Beneficial Rates and the latter as Onerous Rates.

O.P.E.C. Abbreviation of Organisation of Petroleum Exporting Countries (*q.v.*).

Open Account. A method of doing business in foreign trade when the buyer is a customer of the seller of long standing, the seller sending the relevant shipping documents to the buyer, who thus obtains complete control over the goods.

Open Cheque. An uncrossed cheque, and therefore one which can be cashed at the branch of the bank on which it has been drawn. It is often

OPEN COVER wrongly taken to mean Blank Cheque (*q.v.*).

Open Cover. *See* Open Policy.

Open-end Trust. An American term for a unit investment trust the managers of which are permitted to vary the underlying investments.

Open-field System. Under the manorial system of agriculture there were, in addition to the lords' demesne, three (in earlier times, two) large fields divided into strips, each villager cultivating a number of strips in the various fields. On one field wheat was usually grown, on the second field barley or oats, the third being left fallow. *See* Manorial System.

Open Indent. An order from abroad to a merchant in this country with freedom to purchase the goods from any manufacturer he pleases, as distinct from the Closed Indent which names the manufacturer from whom the goods are to be obtained.

Open Market. A market in which there are no restrictions on buyers and sellers, and where prices are determined by supply and demand.

Open-market Operations. This is one of the two traditional instruments of monetary policy of the Bank of England, the other being bank rate. It refers to the sale or purchase by the Bank of England—through its broker—of Government stocks on the open market, that is, on the stock exchange. Since the other parties to these transactions will be customers of the commercial banks (except for a very small number who are customers of the Bank of England itself) these transactions will affect the level of deposits of the commercial banks. Thus, if the Bank of England were to buy £10 million of securities (Government stock) on the market it would pay the sellers by cheques drawn on itself, and most of these sellers would pay their cheques into their own accounts at the various commercial banks. At the Clearing House, since all these cheques have been drawn on the Bank of England, settlement will result in the total balances of the commercial banks at the Bank of England increasing by approximately £10 million. The commercial banks regard their balances at the Bank of England as cash—justifiably so since the Bank of England will permit their withdrawal in cash. An increase in the cash held by a commercial bank will raise its cash ratio above the customary rate, and so make it willing to increase its lending, thereby increasing its deposits and total purchasing power. Open-market operations will, therefore, increase the quantity of money, just as a sale of securities by the Bank of England will lead to a reduction in the quantity of money.

Down to the outbreak of the Second World War open-market operations and bank rate were the only two instruments of monetary policy available to the British monetary authorities. The Bank of England always regarded bank rate as its primary instrument of policy, open-market operations being undertaken only, so it was said, to make bank rate effective. Between the two World Wars many economists thought that bank rate was an ineffective instrument and results attributed to bank rate had in effect been due to open-market operations. Since 1951 the British monetary authorities have made use of other means of influencing the credit policy of the commercial banks. In recent times open-market operations have often been employed to influence the interest rates on Government stocks, purchases by the Bank of England pushing up the prices of stocks and thereby reducing their rate of yield, and sales of stocks having the reverse effect. *See* Instruments of Monetary Policy.

Open Policy. Also known as a Floating Policy, it is a policy of marine insurance providing cover for a period of time to a stated maximum amount without the voyage having to be specified in the policy, though each consignment of goods must be declared to the insurers on its despatch. *See also* Floating Policy.

Open Price Agreement. A number of firms in an industry may agree to inform one another of proposed price changes or, without a formal agreement, they may accept the price leadership of one of their number, probably (though not always) the largest firm, the aim being to avoid the necessity of reporting the agreement to the Restrictive Practices Court. Price leadership is a feature of oligopoly.

Open Shop. A term used of a firm which employs people irrespective of whether they are members of a trade union or not, as distinct from a Closed Shop.

Open System. An economic system which is considered in relation to happenings in other countries which may influence things in the country under discussion, in contrast to a closed system when it is assumed that happenings in a country are quite independent of happenings elsewhere.

Open Union. A trade union that opens its membership to all types of workers, *e.g.* the Transport and General Workers Union. *See also* Closed Union.

Operator's Licence. *See* 'O' Licence.

Operating Costs. An alternative term for Variable Cost (*q.v.*).

Operational Research. In business problems, the consideration and evaluation of all possible alternatives in order to find the best solution by balancing and reconciling conflicting aims.

Operation Job Card. In a workshop job cards are used for each operation. When completed these show the time that has been spent on each particular job.

Opic. Abbreviation of Overseas Private Investment Corporation (*q.v.*).

Opinion Research. *See* Market Research.

Opportunity Cost. People cannot satisfy all their wants since all things are in limited supply and, therefore, they must choose between one thing and another, so that the satisfaction of one want involves doing without something else. In the same way, since the supply of factors of production is limited, the production of one thing may involve not producing something else. The real or opportunity-cost of anything is the alternative that has been forgone. If a person has to choose between buying a camera and an encyclopaedia, the real cost of the camera, if that is his choice, is the encyclopaedia which he has to do without. The real cost of a rearmament programme is the mass of other goods that might have been produced if the factors of production has been otherwise employed.

Opportunity Line. Also known as a Consumption Line (*q.v.*). *See also* Indifference Curves.

Optical Service. A branch of the National Health Service (*q.v.*).

Optimum. A term used to mean the best of something from the economic point of view. Thus economists speak of the optimum population (*q.v.*) of a country or the optimum firm (*q.v.*). One might also refer to the optimum combination of factors of production, etc.

Optimum Firm. A firm which has reached its most efficient size, at which its costs of production per unit of output will be at a minimum, so that it has no motive either to expand or reduce its scale of production. Thus, as a firm expands towards the optimum size it will enjoy increasing returns to scale, but if it goes beyond the optimum diminishing returns will set in. Though it is easy to envisage the optimum firm as a theoretical concept, it would be difficult in practice to decide whether or not a particular firm had actually reached or gone beyond the optimum size. Not only is the optimum likely to vary between different industries but it also is likely to vary in the same industry at different periods of time. Then, too, it has been suggested that at any given time there may be more than one optimum, a lower and a higher, expansion from one to the other being difficult because at intermediate sizes the firm would fall below the optimum. The optimum size may change as a result of changing conditions, such as the development of new techniques or changes in the relative prices and efficiency of factors of production. When economic progress is being made and such changes are taking place firms may be tending to expand towards the optimum but never reaching it. Only under static conditions and perfect competition might firms be expected to reach optimum size. One of the great difficulties a firm has to face when it is striving to reach the optimum is the probability that the different divisions of the firm—finance, administration, production, marketing, etc.—will not all reach their individual optimum at the same output. For example, the optimum administrative division for a firm may be greater or less than the optimum technical unit, since in some industries the optimum technical unit is often extremely large, whereas in other industries it may be relatively small. Similarly, the optimum marketing unit may not suit either the optimum technical or the optimum administrative division. In such cases some sort of compromise will be necessary in order to reconcile the different optima.

Optimum Population. That population which provides a labour force which, when combined with the other factors of production, yields the maximum output per worker. Thus, a large population does not necessarily make a country overpopulated unless it is too large to make the most efficient use of its supplies of the other factors. A country, therefore, is over-populated only if its population exceeds the optimum. Similarly, a country will be under-populated only if its population falls below the optimum, its population then being too small to make the best use of its other factors.

Option. The right, in return for a fee, to buy or sell some kind of property—real estate or stock exchange securities—during a specified period if one so wishes. Stock exchange options are of three kinds: put, call, or double ($qq.v.$).

Opulent Society. An alternative term for Affluent Society ($q.v.$).

O/R. Abbreviation of Owner's Risk ($q.v.$).

Order Cheque. A cheque made payable to a person or firm 'or Order', the significance of the words 'or Order' being that the payee must endorse it unless he pays it into his own banking account. Previous to the passing of the Cheques Act (1957) only 'Bearer' cheques did not require to be endorsed, but since then an 'Order' cheque requires to be endorsed only if the payee is to receive cash for it (this being necessary even if the cheque is drawn by the payee himself and made payable to 'Self') or if he intends to transfer it to someone else.

Orders of Goods. A term used by A. Marshall, in his classification of goods as (i) consumers' or consumption goods, and (ii) producers' or production or instrumental or intermediate goods.

Ordinary Business (O.B.). The branch of life assurance business where the premiums are paid at longer intervals—monthly, quarterly or annually—than is the case with Industrial Business (I.B.), for which payments are made weekly.

Ordinary Department. Deposits in the Ordinary Department of a Savings Bank receive interest at the lowest rate paid by such banks, but such deposits can be withdrawn either on demand or at short notice. The first £25 of interest on these deposits is free of income tax. The Savings Banks pay higher rates of interest on deposits in their Investment Departments and on Term Deposits ($qq.v.$).

Ordinary Partnership. Older term for a General Partnership. *See* General Partner.

Ordinary Shares. Often known as equities, these shares receive the residue of the distributed profit after commitments on preference shares and any other shares carrying priority have been met. Thus dividends on ordinary shares vary with the profitability of the business. Holders of ordinary shares are the owners of the business and usually have voting rights proportionate to their holdings.

Ore. A unit of the currencies of Denmark, Norway, and Sweden, 100 ore being equal in value to one krone or krona.

Organisation. First recognised as a factor of production by Alfred Marshall. Previously only the three factors land, labour, and capital were regarded as factors of production. It is now more generally known as the Entrepreneur (*q.v.*).

Organisation Chart. A diagrammatic representation of the 'line' and 'functional' relationships (*qq.v.*) in a firm.

Organisation for Economic Co-operation and Development (O.E.C.D.). An organisation set up in 1959 with a membership of twenty countries, including the United States, Canada, Great Britain. It superseded the O.E.E.C. in 1961. The aim of the organisation was to increase the national incomes of the members by 50% during the period 1960–70.

Organisation for European Economic Co-operation (O.E.E.C.). A body established in 1948 in connection with 'Marshall Aid', the scheme being administered in the United States by the European Co-operation Administration (E.C.A.) and in Europe by the O.E.E.C. In addition the O.E.E.C. aimed at stimulating economic co-operation between the European members, to encourage intra-European trade and so help Europe to help itself. It was superseded in 1961 by the Organisation for Economic Co-operation and Development (*q.v.*).

Organisation for Trade Co-operation (O.T.C.). A body which it was expected would replace G.A.T.T. (*q.v.*).

Organisation of Petroleum Exporting Countries (O.P.E.C.). A body established in 1960 representing the main oil exporting countries to enable them to adopt a uniform policy towards the oil importing countries.

Organised Markets. Markets held in premises where all the principal buyers and sellers can meet and where business is transacted according to a prescribed set of rules, sometimes only members being admitted. They are large-scale wholesale markets and often deal mainly in imported commodities. Since buyers and sellers are in close touch with one another in these markets there is a tendency towards perfection. (*See* Perfect Market.) An organised market is most likely to develop when (i) the commodity is fairly durable, (ii) large consignments are dealt in, (iii) the price of the commodity is liable to wide fluctuation. If the commodity can be fairly accurately graded this will be an advantage, but if not facilities must be provided for sampling the commodity. When grading is possible business will generally be by private treaty, but when sampling is necessary sale is usually by auction. Organised markets or produce exchanges have been established for cotton, wool, tea, coffee, wheat, rubber, timber, tin, copper, and many other commodities, most of the British organised commodity markets being situated near the port of London. Some others are to be found in other ports. Organised financial markets include the stock exchange and the foreign exchange market.

Orientation. A term used in personnel management for the function of introducing a new employee to his job—acquainting him with the work of the firm and with his position in the firm, informing him exactly what he has to do, and introducing him and showing him his relationship to other members of the department in which he is to work.

Orient Express. A train service

formerly operating between Paris, Strasbourg, Vienna, Budapest, Bucharest, Istanbul and Athens. *See also* Direct Orient Express; Simplon Express.

Origin. The point after which the Law of Diminishing Marginal Utility begins to operate. A certain minimum amount of any commodity is required before effective use can be made of it. Only when further amounts in excess of this minimum are obtained does this law begin to operate. *See* Diminishing Marginal Utility, Law of.

Original Entry. A book-keeping term for subsidiary books, such as the Purchases Book, Sales Book and Journal, in which entries are made before being posted to the Ledger.

Original Goods. A term sometimes used of goods regarded as 'gifts of nature', such as land, mineral deposits, etc., which Man has not had to produce, as distinct from produced goods such as manufactured goods. So-called 'gifts of nature', however, are of no economic importance until factors of production have been applied to them. *See* Land.

Original Producers. A term sometimes used of the owners of 'original goods' (*q.v.*) who, in return for a payment, permit someone else to use them. It is also sometimes used of the worker who offers his labour in return for a wage.

Orion Termbank. A banking consortium comprising the National Westminster Bank, the Royal Bank of Canada, the Chase Manhattan Bank, the Westdeutsche Landesbank and the Girozentrale.

Osborne Judgment. In 1909, a member of a trade union having objected to a portion of his subscription being used for political purposes, it was decided that a trade union was not legally entitled to use its funds in this way. The Trade Union Act of 1913 (*q.v.*) rescinded this judgment. *See also* Taff Vale Case.

Oslo Convention (1930). An agreement between the three Scandinavian countries (Denmark, Norway, and Sweden) and the three countries later known as Benelux (the Netherlands, Belgium, and Luxembourg) for a mutual reduction of tariffs.

O.T.C. Abbreviation of Overseas Trading Corporation (*q.v.*).

Other Deposits. One of the liabilities shown in the Weekly Return for the Banking Department of the Bank of England, it is subdivided into (i) Bankers' deposits (the deposits of the London Clearing Banks) and (ii) Other Accounts (the balances of Commonwealth and foreign banks and of the ordinary customers of the Bank of England).

Other Securities. An asset of the Banking Department of the Bank of England, it is subdivided into (i) Discounts and Advances (*q.v.*) and (ii) Securities. In either case the asset consists of securities purchased on the stock exchange, or in the discount market, the former item arising on the initiative of discount houses which wish to borrow from the Bank of England, and the latter being securities obtained by the Bank on its own initiative.

Ottawa Agreement (1932). In 1932 Great Britain abandoned its traditional policy of free trade and shortly afterwards at Ottawa concluded an agreement with the Dominions which introduced imperial preference on a wide scale, the effect of which was greatly to increase the Commonwealth countries' share of British trade.

Outdoor Relief. Assistance under the Poor Laws to poor people living in their own homes as distinct from the provision of Indoor Relief to the poor in workhouses.

Outer Seven. The original members of the European Free Trade Area (*q.v.*), so-called because of their geographical situation in relation to the original members of the European Economic Community, 'The Six'.

Outlay. Total expenditure on currently produced consumer goods and services, on producers' goods and on public services, that is, on consumption and real capital investment, private and public. On total outlay on these three things Lord Beveridge showed that the level of employment depended. If total outlay is inadequate to give full employment then the State should increase public outlay to make good the deficiency.

Outlay Taxes. An alternative, and probably preferable, term for indirect taxes, that is, taxes that are paid only when the taxpayer purchases particular goods or services. Purchase taxes and duties on tobacco, petrol, etc., are obviously outlay taxes. *See* Indirect Taxes.

Out-of-date Cheque. *See* Stale Cheque.

Output. It is one of the assumptions of economics that every producer will aim at producing that output that will yield him maximum profit. No producer, therefore, will expand his output beyond the point where marginal revenue is equal to marginal cost, since to do so would increase his total cost by a greater amount than his total revenue. This is equally true under conditions of perfect or imperfect competition or monopoly.

Outright Rate of Exchange. A forward rate of exchange where account has been taken of the forward premium or discount instead, as is more usual, of quoting simply the amount of the forward premium or discount.

Outside Broker. A colloquial term for a member of the Association of Stock and Share Dealers. He buys in fairly large amounts through members of the stock exchange and then re-sells in smaller amounts to investors. Unlike individual members of the stock exchange he can solicit business by the issue of circulars.

Outside Tenders. At the weekly tender for Treasury bills the London discount houses make a syndicated tender. Outside tenders come from foreign and Commonwealth banks.

Outturn. A term used in the budget statement to show the actual return from taxes imposed in the previous budget in relation to the budget estimate.

Over-capitalisation. An undertaking can be said to be over-capitalised when the value of its real assets is less than its issued capital. This may be the result of failure to make a sufficient allowance for depreciation or of a rise in the value of money in a deflationary period or of having paid an excessive price on acquiring some of the assets, as many British railways did for their land.

Overcrowding. The Report of 1936 decided this not only according to the average number of rooms per person in dwelling houses (1·36 in 1951), but also in relation to the size of the rooms and the sex composition of families. According to the Report about $3\frac{1}{3}\%$ of working-class families were living in overcrowded conditions.

Overdraft. One of the methods of borrowing from a bank, the borrower being given permission by his banker to draw cheques for an agreed sum (the amount of the overdraft) for a specified period of time in excess of the amount standing to the credit of his account, interest being calculated on a daily basis only on the amount by which the account is overdrawn.

Overend, Gurney & Co. A London discount house which went down in the great financial crisis of 1866, a crisis mainly noteworthy because the Bank of England accepted its duty as a central bank to act as 'lender of last resort'. From that time onwards, this was regarded as an essential function of a central bank.

Over-full Employment. If full employment (*q.v.*) is defined as a condition where no more people are unemployed than the number of vacant jobs, any unemployment thus being entirely of a structural kind, then there will be over-full employment if there are more vacancies than unemployed, the result being a shortage of labour in many industries. Over-full employment is, therefore, a characteristic of an inflationary situation, since with demand tending to run ahead of supply, there tends also to be a greater total demand for labour than the available supply.

Overheads (or **Overhead Costs**). *See* Fixed Costs; Supplementary Costs.

Overheated Economy. An alternative term for an inflationary situation.

Over-investment. Some writers believe that in the later stages of a trade boom the production of capital goods tends to become excessive in relation to the demand for the consumers' goods which the capital goods are to help to produce. It is thought then that the boom will collapse before much of the new investment has been completed. A similar situation is likely to arise in the early stages of a runaway inflation. In all cases over-investment is the result of an over-optimistic view of the economic situation, that is, when expectations of the future have been too high, so that disappointment is bound to follow.

Overlap Area. A term used in the Royal Commission's report on Equal Pay (1946) for work on which either men or women could be employed.

Overnight Telegram. A telegram despatched for delivery by post next day. Such telegrams, which can be despatched up to midnight the previous day, are sent at half the rate charged on ordinary telegrams.

Overpopulation. A country with a population in excess of the optimum population (*q.v.*).

Over-saving. The theory that over-saving may result in under-consumption. J. A. Hobson believed this was the cause of the downswing of the trade cycle. The main cause of over-saving, he believed, was inequality of income, since as one's income increases so does both one's ability and propensity to save. In his day it was generally believed that thrift was a virtue to be commended at all times. At the present day saving is encouraged only in inflationary periods and discouraged when demand has to be stimulated to restore full employment.

Overseas Food Corporation. A body established along with the Colonial Development Corporation in 1946 to assist the development of Commonwealth territories.

Overseas Investment. A country with a credit balance in its balance of payments can use it for investment abroad, the interest or dividends on such investment becoming a useful 'invisible' export afterwards. *See* Balance of Payments.

Overseas Private Investment Corporation (Opic). A U.S. Government agency which insures American companies against the risk of expropriation abroad.

Overseas Review. A publication of Barclays Bank Ltd. giving much useful information for British exporters regarding overseas countries in which the bank or its subsidiary, Barclays Bank (D.C.O.) Ltd., is represented.

Overseas Trading Corporation. A privileged status for tax purposes granted to a British trading company (as distinct from a financial undertaking such as a bank, insurance company, etc.) which carries on its entire business abroad.

Overtime. Additional time worked in excess of the number of hours laid down as the normal working week for an industry. When a time-rate system of wage payment is in operation overtime is paid at a higher rate than the standard rate—'time and a half' or 'time and a quarter'. Many workers support claims for a shorter working week, not because of a wish for more leisure, but in order to enable more overtime to be worked and a higher rate of pay to be obtained. During periods of over-full employment when the demand for labour exceeds the supply workers often prefer to work for a firm that can offer them overtime.

Own As You Earn. A share-owning scheme introduced in 1973. It offers all full-time employees of companies operating the scheme the opportunity to acquire shares in their company on favourable terms.

Ownership. At law this is the legal

relationship which gives a person the right to a piece of property as distinct from possession which means having the actual use of the property. Thus, a person may own a thing and yet, in return for a fee, allow someone else to have possession or use of it. *See also* Bailment.

Ownership and Management. In a business organised as that of a Sole Proprietor, one and the same person owns and manages it, and in the case of the partnership the general partners are both owners and managers. One of the main features of the large public company, however, is the separation of ownership and management. In this type of business ownership may be vested in a large number of shareholders, most of whom have little interest in the business other than to know how much dividend is to be paid, and most of whom never even attend a shareholders' meeting. Management policy is determined by a board of directors, who may or may not be large shareholders, one or more of whom may be appointed managing directors, or a general manager may be appointed by the board.

Ownership of Wealth. It is said that the ownership of wealth determines the character of an economic system. Under private enterprise most wealth is owned by individuals, only a minimum being collectively owned. Even under a communist system people would be permitted some personal possessions, but capital goods would all be owned by the State. In Great Britain and many other countries today there is a mixed system in which some capital is publicly owned and some privately owned.

Owner's Risk (O/R). A condition for the carriage of goods where the sender undertakes to bear the risk of loss or damage. Goods are sent at Owner's Risk when the sender wishes to effect their insurance during transit through an insurer of his own choice. *Cf.* Carrier's Risk.

P

Package Deal. A term used in the Radcliffe Report of the practice developed since 1951 of combining the traditional instrument of monetary policy, bank rate, with newer instruments of policy, such as the budget surplus or deficit, variations of purchase tax rates, variation of hire-purchase regulations, the Treasury directive, or Special Deposits. Used singly these instruments may prove ineffective but employed together they may fulfil the purpose the monetary authorities have in mind. *See* Instruments of Monetary Policy.

Packaging. The tremendous increase in the packaging of commodities, previously sold by measure, has resulted in a vast increase in the range of widely advertised branded goods, thereby extending imperfect competition over a wider field.

Packman. An itinerant trader who used to travel round the country with packhorses to carry his wares, visiting especially the remoter districts.

Page Report (1973). The report of a committee, under the chairmanship of Sir Harry Page, set up to inquire into national savings. Its main recommendations were: (i) the voluntary savings movement should be ended and all existing saving schemes (except Premium Bonds) should be wound up; (ii) the Trustee Savings Banks should be hived off from the State and provide a wider range of banking services; (iii) a new five-year security should be introduced and possibly an index-linked bond. The committee stressed that there should be a 'safe and remunerative investment' available to very small savers, but suitable forms of saving were already in existence for other people. As a result (i) the trustee savings banks in 1974 were allowed to expand their services by being permitted to grant loans; and (ii) in 1975 two index-linked securities were issued—Retirement Certificates (*q.v.*) and an indexed S.A.Y.E. scheme. *See* National Savings.

Paid-up Capital. The actual amount of capital that shareholders have subscribed. It may be less than the authorised capital (*q.v.*).

Paid-up Shares. Shares are fully paid-up when the full amount has been paid. Most shares have to be fully paid for on their being issued. Sometimes shares are only partly paid-up (a practice less common nowadays than formerly), the company being able to call for the balance to be paid whenever it requires this additional capital.

Paisa. A unit of the currency of Pakistan, its value being one-hundredth of a rupee.

Panama Canal. Fifty miles long and connecting the Pacific Ocean with the Caribbean Sea and Atlantic Ocean, it was built by the Government of the United States and opened in 1914. It shortens routes from the eastern ports of the United States to the western ports of South America, the Far East and Australia, and also provides an alternative route between Great Britain and New Zealand.

Pan-American Airlines. One of the American airlines engaged in international traffic.

P. & O. Abbreviation of Peninsular and Oriental Steam Navigation Co. Ltd., now associated with the Orient Line.

Panel. A term used in the National Insurance Act (1911), doctors in the scheme having lists of 'panels' of patients.

'Paper bid.' An offer of its own shares by a company making a takeover offer.

Paper Money. *See* Bank-note.

Paper Profit. An increase in the value of an investment which is still retained. Such a paper profit will

become a realised profit only if the investment is sold.

Paper Titles. Documents entitling their owners to some real wealth or to money, as for example, share certificates, Government bonds, bills of exchange, etc.

Par. The face or nominal value of stocks and shares. Most Government stocks, for example, are redeemable at a stated date at par, that is, at their face value. If a stock is below par its price is less than its face value; if it is above par its price will be above its face value. In the case of shares the par value is of little importance, and in some countries the issue of shares of 'no par value' is permitted.

Para. A sub-unit of the currency of Yugoslavia, introduced in 1966. One hundred para equal in value one dinar.

Paradox of Value. *See* Value in Exchange and Value in Use.

Parallel Rate of Exchange. Alternative term for Unofficial Rate where two rates of exchange for a currency are in operation.

Parcel of Bills. A number of bills of exchange put together by a bank because they have the same due date, and also in order to have approximately the same amount falling due each day. This is only necessary with trade bills, since Treasury bills are issued in round sums dated for any day of the following week the purchaser desires.

Parent Company. A holding company or an operating company which has control over a number of others, known as its subsidiaries.

Pareto's Law. After a comparative study of the distribution of income in a number of countries Pareto came to the conclusion that there is a tendency for income to be similarly distributed in all countries whatever might be their political systems or their systems of taxation. This theory does not seem to be supported by recent experience.

Pari Passu. With reference to a new issue of shares it means that the new shares will rank equally for dividend with an existing similar issue.

'Paris Club.' A popular term for the Group of Ten (*q.v.*).

Parliamentary Commissioner for Administration. An official appointed by the State to act as a kind of watchdog over citizens' rights and liberties, with no power to investigate cases of alleged unjust action by administrative departments. He can investigate complaints against the executive and report, but he cannot himself instigate criminal proceedings. In 1966 the British Government decided to appoint such an official, popularly known as an Ombudsman.

Par Rate of Exchange. When the International Monetary Fund was established member countries had to decide within a certain time the values of their currencies in terms of gold. In practice members adopted par values for their currencies in relation to the U.S. dollar which had a gold value of 0·888671 grammes of fine gold. Thus, at first the par rate of exchange for sterling was $4.03 to £1.

Parsimony. Adam Şmith regarded parsimony as the basis of the accumulation of capital and wealth both for the individual and the State. *See* Saving.

Partial Equilibrium. An alternative term for Particular Equilibrium. *See* Particular and General Equilibrium.

Partial Loss. In marine insurance partial loss or damage to a ship or its cargo gives rise to Particular Average (*q.v.*).

Participating Preference Shares. In addition to receiving a fixed dividend the holders of these shares are entitled to an additional amount or bonus if the dividend on the ordinary shares exceeds a specified amount.

Particular and General Equilibrium. A state of equilibrium exists when there is no inducement for a condition to change. At the equilibrium price, for example, the quantity of a commodity supplied is exactly equal to the quantity demanded, and while these conditions exist there will be no tendency for the price to change. If the study of prices is taken for a single commodity in isolation the equilibrium price will be an example of Particular (or Partial) Equilibrium, as distinct from General Equilibrium which takes account of the effect of a price change of one commodity on the prices of other commodities. *See also* Equilibrium.

Particular Average. A term used in marine insurance, it occurs when the cargo or ship suffers partial loss or damage. *See also* General Average.

Partnership. A form of business organisation in which two or more persons up to a maximum of twenty (except in the case of solicitors, accountants, and stockholders) join together to undertake some form of business activity. In an Ordinary or General Partnership all the partners share the responsibility of running the business, though their shares of the profits will usually be proportionate to the amount of capital each has invested in the firm. The partnership has many of the advantages and disadvantages of the Sole Proprietor but it possesses greater continuity of existence. In a Limited Partnership the liability of a limited partner is restricted to the amount of capital he has invested in the business. All ordinary partners are responsible up to the full value of their personal estates, for the debts and obligations of the firm, the actions of all such partners being binding on the undertaking. A limited partner, however, is not permitted to take any share in the management of the firm. *See also* Limited Partnership.

Partnership Acts. Two Acts provide the legal basis of partnerships: (i) The Act of 1890 which defines general partnerships; and (ii) The Act of 1907 which permitted the formation of limited partnerships. *See* Partnership.

Partnership, Deed of. *See* Deed of Partnership.

Part III Accommodation. The provision of Old People's Homes under Part III of the National Assistance Act (1948).

Pass. With reference to dividends it means to omit payment.

Pass Book. A book, supplied to customers by a bank, in which entries are made of all deposits and withdrawals. Pass books are now only used by savings banks and for savings or deposit accounts of commercial banks. To enable machine bookkeeping methods to be employed loose-leaf statements are used for current accounts, customers being provided with folders in which the statement can be filed.

Passenger Transport Authorities. Set up under the Transport Act (1968) to integrate local short-distance passenger services within the main conurbations, five being initially designated—Greater Manchester, Merseyside, Tyneside, West Yorkshire, and the West Midlands. (London has had a similar sort of transport authority since 1933.) The Minister of Transport has powers to establish Transport Authorities for other regions. The members of the authorities will be drawn mainly from the localities concerned, but the Ministry of Transport will also be represented.

Passive. An alternative term for an unfavourable or debit Balance of Payments (*q.v.*).

Pastoral Finance Companies. Australian institutions which provide sheep farmers with loans for longer periods than those for which banks are willing to lend.

Patent Office. The State department which deals with all matters relating to patents—granting patents and their registrations, trade marks and their registration, copyright, etc.

Patent Rights. The granting by the Crown of the exclusive right to a new machine or process for a period of sixteen years with the possibility of renewal for a further five or ten years. The possession of patent rights gives the owner some degree of monopoly power and so is one of the causes of competition being imperfect.

Paternalism. A term used of the assistance given in the nineteenth century by the Governments of France and Germany to the industrial development of their countries in contrast to Great Britain where the State gave no such assistance.

Pauper. A poor person in need of assistance; a person assisted under the Poor Laws, more especially one living in a workhouse.

Pauper Children. The children of paupers. The Poor Law of 1601 said that such children should be apprenticed to trades. In the early nineteenth century labour for the new factories was often obtained by taking pauper children from the workhouses to live in or near the factories where they had to work very long hours.

Pawnbroker. A person who lends with some article pledged as security by the borrower, who may redeem his pledged property on his repaying the loan within a period of just over six months. Otherwise the pawnbroker, who is also a dealer in second-hand goods, can sell the property. To do business as a pawnbroker it is necessary to obtain a licence from the Inland Revenue.

Payback. A method of calculating the expected profitability of an item of capital investment by measuring the time it will take it to produce a cash income equal to the capital cost of the investment. *See also* Rate of Return.

Pay Day. An alternative stock exchange term for Account Day (*q.v.*).

P.A.Y.E. Abbreviation of Pay As You Earn, a system of paying income tax where the tax payable is deducted from current earnings, weekly or monthly, employers being made responsible for the collection of tax under Schedule E. When P.A.Y.E. was first introduced in 1943 the amount of tax depended on earnings during the previous financial year, the amount being deducted in equal instalments, but in 1945 deductions were made dependent on earnings during the current financial year. To give employees some degree of privacy with regard to their private affairs each is given a code number dependent on his personal allowances. Employers receive Tax Tables showing the amount to be deducted.

Payee. The person or persons to be paid. The payee in the case of a cheque is the person or persons to whom the cheque is made payable.

Paying-in Slip. A document to be completed when making a deposit at a bank, showing how much has been deposited in different kinds of cash and in cheques.

Paymaster-General. The political head of the Government department responsible for payments to members of the armed forces and the civil service, etc. His departmental duties are negligible.

Payment by Results. Systems of wage payment where the amount of the wage depends on the amount of work done as, for example, piece rates and premium bonus systems.

Payment in Due Course. Payment of a bill of exchange at maturity.

Payment in Kind. Payment in goods or services instead of money wages. This practice was made illegal by the Truck Acts (*q.v.*). Money payments, however, are often supplemented by payments in kind, such as the provision of uniform or board and lodging, some free transport for transport workers or the concessionary coal allowance of coalminers. *See* Fringe Benefits.

Payment, Means of. In Great Britain means of payment are provided by: (i) The State—coins; (ii) The State through the State-owned Bank of England—bank-notes; (iii) The Commercial Banks—personal cheques, bank drafts, travellers' cheques, telegraphic transfers, postal transfers; (iv) The Post Office—money orders, postal orders, stamps, (v) Businessmen themselves—bills of exchange. In some countries the postal giro (*q.v.*) is used and in others the promissory note (*q.v.*).

Payments Agreement. The effect of the German system of exchange control during the 1930s was to strangle European trade with Germany and reduce what remained almost to barter. Some countries made bilateral agreements with Germany known as Clearing Agreements (q.v.). Great Britain made Payments Agreements with Germany, this being really an improved type of Clearing Agreement as it enabled traders to use normal credit facilities to finance the transaction.

Payment, Terms of. Goods may be purchased on any of the following terms: (i) Cash with order; (ii) C.O.D. (cash on delivery); (iii) Prompt cash (payment within a few days); (iv) Monthly account; (v) Hire-purchase terms; (vi) Credit terms.

Pay Pause. A period during which there should be no further wage increases, as proposed by the British Government in 1961 after wages had been increasing more rapidly than production. *See also* Prices and Incomes Policy; Wage Freeze.

Payroll Tax. A tax on business undertakings according to the number of people employed. In a time of over-full employment and shortage of labour a payroll tax might check firms from retaining more labour than they really require. *See* Selective Employment Tax.

P/e. Abbreviation of price/earnings ratio (q.v.).

Peabody Trust. One of the best known of a number of housing trusts established in the 1850s and 1860s to build houses or flats, the rents on which were devoted solely to maintenance and repairs.

'Peaceful Picketing.' The right of a trade union which has called a strike to dissuade employees from working. The unions obtained this right by the Trade Union Act of 1875. It was reaffirmed by the Trade Disputes Act (1906). The picketing of trade union militants in 1972 was far from 'peaceful'.

Pearson Report. The report of the Commission on Internal Development set up by the World Bank with Lester B. Pearson of Canada as chairman. The Commission, which was assisted by technical and economic advisers surveyed all aspects of aid to developing nations.

Pedlar. A door-to-door salesman who carries his stock-in-trade about with him. *See also* Hawker.

Peg. A term used in connection with foreign exchange when the monetary authorities of a country decide to maintain or 'peg' the rate of exchange of their currency at a fixed rate. The term is also sometimes used of the control of prices.

Pending. Older name of the penny (q.v.).

Pengo. The standard unit of the currency of Hungary before the great inflation in that country after the Second World War. As a result of the inflation the pengo became worthless and was replaced by the forint (q.v.).

Penny. Though some coins known as pennies or pendings were struck some years earlier the history of the penny really dates back to the year A.D. 760 when Offa, King of Mercia, had 240 pennies struck from a pound by weight of silver. The coins varied in weight but 240 of them were regarded as a pound. During the early twelfth century the penny was known as a sterling. For most of the period down to 1257, the penny was the only coin in circulation in England, though it was regularly cut into halves or quarters for smaller payments. In 1257 a gold coin worth 20 pence was struck. In 1797 copper pennies, each weighing one ounce, were issued. The bronze penny was not introduced until 1860. On the decimalisation of the currency in 1971 the penny was replaced by a new penny worth 2·4 old pence. The old penny was indicated by 'd' from the Latin *denarius*, but 'p' was chosen to represent the new penny.

Penny Banks. The name formerly given to many savings banks established in the second half of the nineteenth century because they were prepared to accept as little as a penny as a deposit. The name survived in the title of the Yorkshire

Penny Bank long after it had become a commercial bank, the word 'Penny' being dropped from the title only in May 1959.

Pension. Regular payment, usually on retirement, for the remainder of a person's life. Under the National Insurance scheme all contributors who have made the minimum number of contributions are entitled to retirement pensions, men at the age of 65 and women at 60. A number of occupations have their own pension schemes—the armed forces, civil service, local government services, teachers, banks, insurance companies, and an increasing number of businesses. Some of these 'private' schemes are non-contributory, but most now require employees to contribute 5% or 6% of their income, the employers also making a contribution.

Pension Funds. Some firms with private pension funds hand over their operation to insurance companies; others appoint their own investment advisors and manage them themselves. These Pension Funds have joined insurance companies and investment trusts as large operators on the stock exchange and in the capital market. *See also* Financial Intermediaries.

Pensions and National Insurance, Ministry of. Former name of the Department of Health and Social Security (*q.v.*).

P.E.P. Abbreviation of Political and Economic Planning.

Peppercorn Rent. A nominal sum paid as rent for a period.

P/E Ratio. Abbreviation of Price/Earnings Ratio (*q.v.*).

Per Contra. A self-balancing item in a balance sheet as, for example the item in a bank's balance sheet: 'Liabilities of Customers for Acceptances as *per contra*'.

Percy Committee. A Committee appointed by the British Government in 1944 to consider technical education in England and Wales. It recommended that advanced technological courses should be provided by a selected number of Technical Colleges, these to be known as Colleges of Advanced Technology.

Perfect Competition. A theoretical environment in which production is assumed to take place in order to make possible a more accurate study of influences on production when the disturbing effects of actual conditions are removed. The primary assumption of perfect competition is that there should be a large number of firms each of which produces only a small fraction of the total output of the commodity, the result being that no firm can influence the market price of the commodity by expanding or contracting its output, so that in perfect competition firms must take the price at which they are to sell as fixed. It is assumed that at this price every firm can sell as much as it cares to produce, for to expand its sales requires no reduction in price since its total output is assumed to be only a small fraction of total production. Thus, in conditions of perfect competition the demand for the product of an individual firm is perfectly elastic. A second assumption of perfect competition is that the commodity is perfectly homogeneous so that buyers have no motive for preferring the product of one firm to another, and therefore if a firm raised its price at all its sales would fall to zero. In perfect competition there would be no restraint on the entry of new firms to an industry. A very precise definition of perfect competition would also assume perfect mobility of factors of production and their complete divisibility and absence of all economic friction. It has been suggested that if perfect competition were given this higher degree of perfection the less perfect condition should be described as 'pure competition'.

Perfect Market. A theoretical condition assumed by economists as an environment in which prices are determined. For a market to be perfect the following conditions must be fulfilled: (i) The commodity in question must be homogeneous, so that buyers have no preference for the commodity of any particular seller; (ii) There must be a large number of buyers and sellers, so that no single buyer or seller deals in so large a quantity of the commodity that he can unduly influence the price prevailing in the market; (iii) Buyers and sellers must be in close contact with one another, though the telephone no longer makes it necessary for them to meet; (iv) There must be no preferential treatment of any buyer; (v) The commodity must be easily transferable from one person to another. The conditions in most actual markets are far from perfect, but some markets are more nearly perfect than others, the stock exchange, some highly organised commodity markets, and the foreign exchange market (in the absence of exchange control) being among the most nearly perfect of actual markets.

Perfect Monopoly. An alternative term for Absolute Monopoly (*q.v.*).

Perfect Oligopoly. A form of imperfect competition (*q.v.*) where the commodity is homogeneous and there are only a few producers. In these conditions only one price is possible in the market, so that a cut in price by one producer will cause other producers to follow suit. Price leadership generally—though not always—will be with the largest producer.

Performing Rights Society. An Association which collects fees on behalf of composers and music publishers from the public performance of music. The Society has arrangements with similar societies in other countries.

Period Analysis. A method of showing that Saving and Investment are equal only if the Investment of one period is compared with the Saving of the next. *See* Equality of Saving and Investment.

Perpetual Annuity. *See* Annuity.

Perpetuities and Accumulations Act (1964). Before the passing of this Act a testator could not postpone a bequest of any property for a period longer than 21 years following the death of any living person. By this Act he was given the alternative of a period of up to 80 years. The aim is to prevent over-large accumulations resulting from the investment of sums at compound interest for long periods of time.

Per Pro. Abbreviation of *per procurationem* (Latin), meaning for and on behalf of, used when one person signs a letter on behalf of another, having the authority to do so.

Persistent Inflation. *See* Inflation (2).

Personal Cheque Service. A limited banking service at a low cost, which is known in advance, for people who wish to make payments by cheque but who do not wish to take advantage of other services provided by banks. Many American banks provide such a service but British banks have not as yet entered this field.

Personal Loan. A loan made by a bank to a private individual to cover personal expenditure of a specified kind—an alternative to hire-purchase.

Personal Tax. The tax on personal income which combined income tax and surtax from 1973.

Personal Taxes. A distinction is sometimes made between personal taxes, such as income tax, and taxes on things, such as customs duties and purchase tax. This distinction is pointless since all taxes have ultimately to be paid by people. More important distinctions are between direct and indirect taxation or between income and outlay taxes.

Personalty. Property other than realty (*q.v.*).

Personal Wealth. This consists of personal belongings which give satisfaction to the owner, as distinct from Business Wealth (*q.v.*) and Social Wealth (*q.v.*).

Personnel Management, Institute of. An association whose members are engaged in the personnel function of management, its aim being to establish through training high standards of qualification and performance. The main grades of

Personnel Officer. A person employed by a firm to take charge of such matters as interviewing and selection of workers, the introduction of new workers to their jobs, the education and training of new employees, the application of wage agreements, health and welfare services, etc. The duties of personnel officers vary considerably between one firm and another.

Peseta. The standard unit of the currency of Spain, it is subdivided into 100 centimos.

Pesewa. A fractional unit of the currency of Ghana, 100 pesewa being equal in value to one cedi.

Peso. The standard unit of the currency of Mexico, Argentina, Chile, Uruguay, Colombia, Bolivia, Cuba, the Dominican Republic, and the Philippines. In all cases it is subdivided into 100 minor units, these being known as centesimos in Uruguay, as escudos in Chile and as centavos in the other seven countries.

Pestilence. One of the three causes —the others being war and famine— given by Malthus for the slow growth of population before his time.

Petty Cash. An allotment of money by a business from which small cash payments can be made. *See* Imprest Account.

Pfennig. The fractional unit of the currencies of both West and East Germany, there being 100 pfennig to the mark.

Phillips Committee (1954). On account of the increasing number of old people and the consequent increase in the cost of retirement pensions this Committee recommended that the retirement age for men should be raised from 65 to 68 and for women from 60 to 63.

Phillips Curve. A curve showing that a definite relationship exists between unemployment and the rate of change of money wages, so-called because Prof. A. W. Phillips first stressed this relationship.

Phœnix Assurance Co. Ltd. Founded in 1782 it is one of eight British insurance companies established before 1800.

Physical Controls. The direct control of production and consumption by the licensing of building and raw materials and the rationing of consumers' goods as occurred during both World Wars and for some years after the Second World War. Physical controls can be used as an alternative to monetary and fiscal policy and to supplement other instruments of control.

Physical Distribution. An alternative term for Commercial Distribution (*q.v.*).

Physical Mobility. With reference to factors of production, it is an alternative term for Geographical Mobility (*q.v.*).

Piastre. A currency unit of Lebanon, Egypt, Syria and the Sudan, its value in all cases being one-hundredth of a pound.

Picketing. *See* Peaceful Picketing.

Pickford. The oldest road haulage firm in Great Britain, having operated without a break from the days of the turnpike road trusts, it also acts as a travel agency. When road haulage was nationalised in 1947–48 it was not taken over by British Road services as were other road haulage firms, but was allowed to retain its name on account of the goodwill attached to it.

Piece Rates. A method of wage payment where the worker is paid according to the amount of work he has done. Piece rates can be applied only when the amount of work accomplished can be easily measured. Passers have to be employed to check the work in order to ensure that a minimum standard is maintained. The aim is to increase output by giving the worker an incentive to produce more.

Piecework. *See* Piece Rates.

Pie Powder (or **Piedpoudre**) **Court.** A court formerly set up in England at fairs and markets to settle disputes between buyers and sellers.

Pilgrim Trust Report. A survey of

unemployment and the circumstances of those who had been unemployed for long periods in six British towns in 1936.

Pilkington Reports. 1. (1960). The Report of a Royal Commission appointed to inquire into rates of remuneration of doctors and dentists, it stressed that their pay should be comparable to that of men and women with similar qualifications in other professions.

2. **(1962).** The report of a committee set up to inquire into broadcasting.

Pink Book. A Government publication, published by the Central Statistical Office, it is somewhat similar to a *Blue Book*. A Balance of Payments *Pink Book* is published annually.

Pink Button. A stock exchange term for a jobber's clerk.

Pipelines. A method of transporting oil or gas from their sources of supply to ports or from ports to inland refineries, the latter being a more recent development. The earliest pipelines were to carry oil from the oilfields of Iraq and Iran to ports on the Mediterranean coast to avoid the long voyage round Saudi Arabia and through the Suez Canal. More recently oil pipelines have been constructed from the Central Sahara to the Mediterranean coast, the South European pipeline from the south of France to Karlsruhe, the Rhine–Danube pipeline from Karlsruhe to Ingoldstadt and the Trans-Alpine pipeline from Trieste to Ingoldstadt with a possible extension to Vienna. Gas pipelines have been constructed from Groningen in the Netherlands to Cologne and the Ruhr. In Great Britain natural gas is distributed from the ports and gas fields of the North Sea by pipeline. Over 300,000 miles of pipeline are in use in the United States.

Pit. An American term for the floor of an organised produce exchange where business takes place.

P.K. Banken. Abbreviation of Postoch Kreditbanken, a Swedish bank. It is the largest bank in Scandinavia.

P.L.A. Abbreviation of Port of London Authority (*q.v.*).

Placing. With reference to an issue of shares. *See* New Issue Market, (i) and (iii).

Placing Broker. An insurance broker who approaches members of Lloyd's to seek syndicates willing to cover portions of a risk he is attempting to cover on behalf of a client.

Plagues. As a check to the growth of population, *see* Pestilence.

Planned Economy. Generally taken to mean a State-planned economy. In its most extreme form the State would be responsible entirely for production and distribution and, therefore, the allocation of factors of production, including labour, among different forms of employment in order to produce those quantities of goods and services which the State planning committee had decided upon. This committee, and not consumers' demand, would decide what should be produced and how much should be produced. In all countries nowadays there is an increasing amount of State planning of production, though in those having a 'mixed' economy consumers' demand determines production over a large part of the field. *See* National Plan.

Planned Location of Industry. A term first used by Lord Beveridge for a policy whereby the location of industry is planned to give each industrial area a variety of industry, large industries being dispersed and not localised. During the nineteenth century the basic industries became highly localised, largely because of their dependence on coal and therefore their need to be near the coalfields. The great disadvantage of localisation is that a change of demand affecting a localised industry may cause structural unemployment, on such a scale as to produce a pocket of mass unemployment even though there is full employment in the rest of the country. If the requisite measures are taken to maintain full employment the most serious type of unemployment becomes structural unemployment in localised industries. When industries are dispersed those who become unemployed as a result of a change of demand are more easily absorbed into other industries. The aim of planned location of industry in Great Britain has also been to check the industrial expansion in London and the South-East, which between the two World Wars attracted many new industries. As a first step towards planned location of industry in 1945 the Distribution of Industries Act was passed. Certain parts of the country were designated as Development Areas (*q.v.*), most of these having highly localised industries, and new firms or older firms opening new branches were encouraged to set up in these areas rather than elsewhere, a policy helped by control of investment through the Capital Issues Committee (*q.v.*) in the post-war period. The Local Employment Act of 1960 empowered the Government similarly to assist any part of the country where unemployment exceeded 4%. These areas were designated Development Districts. The Industrial Development Act (1966) made a further change. The Development Districts were absorbed in enlarged Development Areas. By this Act increased grants and investment allowances were to be given to firms setting up in these areas. Regional Employment Premiums too were to be paid to these firms according to the number of people they employed. More recently attention has also been paid to Intermediate or Grey Areas (*q.v.*). These are old industrial areas with declining industries and falling employment.

The most serious problem affecting location of industry in recent years has been the uneven distribution of unemployment in the country. The average rate of unemployment for the country as a whole has been greater than the rate for London and the South-east while the rate in North-east England, Scotland, and Wales has been considerably above the national average, with even higher rates in particular places. In spite of efforts to 'take work to the workers' the drift from the areas with higher than average unemployment to areas of low unemployment has continued. To deal with these problems Regional Economic Planning Councils have been established, the aim being to bring about a more balanced economic development of the country as a whole. In Greater London office development is being controlled, and some Government departments have been moved to other parts of the country. The building of New Towns (*q.v.*) was the method employed to check the further expansion of London and some other large conurbations. *See also* Localisation of Industry; Location of Industry; Regional Economic Planning Councils.

'Playing the Market.' A colloquial phrase for the activities of a speculator in stocks and shares.

Plimsoll Line. The load-line marked on ships to indicate the maximum extent to which they are permitted to be loaded, so called because of the work of Samuel Plimsoll (1824–98) for the greater safety of seamen.

Ploughing back Profits. Instead of distributing the whole of its profits a company can 'plough back' some of them to finance its expansion instead of raising further capital on the capital market.

Plowden Reports. 1. **(1965).** The report of an inquiry into the aircraft industry, it recommended that the Government being almost a monopsonist buyer (*see* Monopsony), should acquire a majority shareholding in firms responsible for the building of aircraft, such as the British Aircraft Corporation and the air-frame section of Hawker-Siddeley, but not firms making aero engines.

2. **(1967).** The report on primary education of a committee under the chairmanship of Lady Plowden.

Plutocracy. A state in which government is in the hands of the wealthy.

P.m.h. Abbreviation of Per Man Hour, a term used with reference to output.

P.O. 1. Abbreviation of Post Office (*q.v.*).

2. Abbreviation of Postal Order (*q.v.*).

Point Elasticity. The degree of elasticity at a point on a curve, as distinct from arc elasticity, the average degree of elasticity between two points. *See* Elasticity.

'Points' System. A method of rationing adopted during the Second World War for commodities, such as tinned goods, the supplies of which were not sufficient to allow one of each kind to each person or where people's tastes were likely to differ considerably. Each person was allocated a regular supply of 'points' and certain classes of foodstuffs were 'priced' in both points and money, these 'points prices' being varied according to the supply available and the demand for them, the 'money prices' remaining controlled. *See also* Food Rationing.

Policy. In insurance this is a document which sets out precisely the insurance cover provided.

Political Economy. The older name of Economics.

Poll Tax. Strictly a tax on a certain amount per head of the population. In practice, as was the case with the English medieval poll taxes, each village was assessed at a certain amount per head, that giving the total sum to be paid by the village, but the richer people generally paid more than the poorer people.

Polytechnic. A term formerly used of some technical colleges, especially in the London area, and selected in 1966 by the Department of Education and Science to be applied to a number (originally 30) of technical institutions designated as regional colleges of higher education, most of them previously being known as colleges of technology. In some towns the new institutions will be formed by grouping together several existing institutions where separate colleges of technology, commerce, and schools of art existed. The new polytechnics provide courses leading to degrees.

Pool. 1. A loose combination of business undertakings generally, like the price ring, to keep up the price of a commodity.

2. The reserve of member countries' currencies and gold held by the International Monetary Fund. Members' contributions are paid into the pool and they are then entitled to certain drawing rights (*q.v.*), that is, they can purchase specified amounts of foreign currency in exchange for their own.

3. During the Second World War the sale of branded petrols was not permitted in Great Britain, all petrol being pooled.

4. Football pools (*q.v.*).

Pooling of Risk. The basic principle of insurance is that a number of people who wish to cover themselves against a certain risk contribute to a pool out of which payments are made to those who actually suffer that particular risk. The amount of the contribution or premium depends on the probability of the risk.

Poor Law (1601). An Act which codified the existing Poor Laws. Each parish was to be responsible for its own poor, assistance to be given to the infirm and work found for the ablebodied, for the idle in workhouses or 'houses of correction'.

Poor Law Amendment Act (1834). An Act which grouped parishes in unions each with its elected Board of Guardians. Finance was to be provided by levying a Poor Rate. Outdoor relief was to be given only to the sick and infirm, the able-bodied being able to obtain relief only by entering workhouses. Thus the Speenhamland system (*q.v.*) of suplementing wages was brought to an end. The Act achieved its main object of reducing the cost of assisting the poor, but for some time, wages being low, it caused great hardship.

Poor Law Guardians. *See* Guardians of the Poor.

Poor Relief. *See* Poor Law (1601); Poor Law Amendment Act (1834); Public Assistance; National Assistance.

P.O.P. Abbreviation of Post Office Preferred with reference to the size of envelopes the Post Office proposes to carry at standard rates, those in excess of this size to be charged at higher rates.

Population Explosion. A term used of the rapid increase in population that has occurred since 1950 in Latin America, but especially in those parts of the world such as North America and Western Europe where it had been previously expected that the population was likely to decline.

Population Problem. Linked as it is with the problem of food production, it was one of Man's earliest economic problems. The first economist to give serious study to the population problem was the Rev. T. R. Malthus. His *Essay on the Principle of Population as it affects the Future Improvement of Society* was first published in 1798 and was revised five times. Malthus was struck by the fact that the population of Great Britain had begun to increase more rapidly than ever before and, relating this fact to the Law of Diminishing Returns, he thought it would be impossible to expand food production in the same proportion. He, therefore, forecast a fall in the standard of living in Great Britain before the end of the nineteenth century unless this increase in population was checked. Events appeared to prove that Malthus was wrong since by 1900 the people of Britain were enjoying a much higher standard of living than in his day, largely due to the development of new food producing areas in North and South America, Australia, and New Zealand.

As far as Great Britain and some other western countries were concerned the problem appeared to take a new form in the twentieth century—the possibility of the population beginning to decline. (This actually happened in France in 1937–39.) The persistent fall in the birth-rate and the reduction in the average size of family from 5·5 in 1850 to 2·2 in 1930 seemed to indicate the probability of an actual fall in the population of the U.K. during the latter half of the twentieth century. Since expectation of life was also increasing the problem seemed to be one of both a declining and ageing population. After 1943, however, the birth-rate in the U.K. gradually rose to 18·6 per thousand in 1965, falling to 13·3 in 1974. *See* Population Projection.

For the world as a whole the problem is that of a 'population explosion' with a danger of population outstripping food production, as was the case for some years after the Second World War, the problem being exaggerated by soil erosion and other short-sighted farming in some parts of the world. The seriousness of the problem was widely stressed and under the auspices of the Food and Agricultural Organisation of the United Nations a great deal of research has been undertaken and assistance given to under-developed countries. As a result food production has been expanded recently more rapidly than the growth of population in spite of the change of the trend of population in those countries which once feared a decline. Although large numbers of people in some parts of the world are still underfed by modern standards the dangers of world-overpopulation has been postponed. Recently a more optimistic view has been taken of the possibilities of increasing the world output of food. Even so it would seem that the problem feared by Malthus is likely to return. Although every improvement in food production puts off the day when food output per head begins to decline, it seems that a time must eventually come when food output for the world can no longer keep up with an expanding population. The papal encyclical of 1968 against the use of artificial means of birth control seemed likely to exacerbate the population problem in Catholic countries, especially in Latin America. *See also* Ageing Population; Declining Population; Increasing Population; Optimum Population.

Population Projection. A forecast of the population of a country or the world based on existing trends. If changes occur in the trend a new projection will yield a different result. In Great Britain a projection based on the trend of 1919–20 indicated a rapidly increasing population, but a projection made a few years later indicated that the population of this country might begin to decline after 1944; a projection made in 1935 postponed the date of decline to 1970, and a projection of 1947 gave the year 2000 as the likely date of decline. Projections made in the late 1950s created some doubt as to whether the population of Great Britain would begin to decline in the foreseeable future. Projections made in 1960 showed the possibility of the population of Great Britain increasing to over 70 million by the year 2000. By 1970 projections were being based on a slower rate of growth which gave 67 million as the likely population by 2000.

Population Pyramid. A triangular-shaped diagram showing the distribution of population between the different age groups. Starting at the top with the highest age groups the numbers are small, while the largest numbers are found in the lowest age groups at the bottom, though the sides of the triangle will not slope regularly upwards on account of recent changes in birth-rate trends.

Population, Royal Commission on (1949). The Report of this Royal Commission pointed out that the main influence on population trends was the average family size. Based on the trend at the time the Commission forecast a fall in the number of births during the next fifteen years, a forecast which has proved incorrect owing to a change of trend. *See* Population Projection.

Portfolio. A list of the securities held by an investor. A good portfolio will show a wide spread of investments in order to reduce the risk of loss.

Port of London Authority. Established in 1908, it was one of the earliest public corporations to be set up in Great Britain. Of its members eighteen are elected and ten appointed by the State. It is responsible for the control of all the docks comprising the Port of London.

Possession. Having actual physical control over a thing, in contrast to ownership, which means having a legal right to a thing.

Postage Stamps. A means by which small sums can be sent by post.

Postal Cheque. An alternative term for the means of payment provided by a Postal Giro System (*q.v.*).

Postal Giro. A means of making monetary transfers provided by post offices as an alternative to the postal order, money order, or registered letter. Many West European countries and Japan have operated postal giro systems for some time, the earliest being established in Austria in 1883. The French Service des Chèques Postaux is the largest giro system in the world. A giro banking service was introduced by the British Post Office in 1968. *See* National Giro Service.

Postal Order. A means of payment provided by the Post Office for sums from 10p in multiples of 2½p to £1 and then in multiples of £1 to £10. A postal order is useful for the transmission of small sums of money by post, especially to people who do not possess cheque books. They can be purchased without formality at post offices and, unless crossed, they can also be cashed at post offices.

Postal Transfer. *See* Postal Giro.

Postal Union Universal. *See* Universal Postal Union.

Postcode. A device to assist the mechanical sorting of mail, it follows the address, *e.g.* HD5 3XZ. First employed in a somewhat different form in Norwich, it was widely extended during 1968–69.

Postdate. To date a cheque (or document) for some time in the future, generally in the case of the cheque because the debtor does not expect to have the necessary funds to meet it until this later date.

Poste Restante. A service provided by the Post Office. Postal packets can be addressed to any post office to be called for, such packets being marked either *Poste Restante* or *To be called for.*

Postmaster-General. The political head of the Post Office until 1969 when the Post Office became a public corporation, headed by a chairman. *See* Posts and Telecommunications.

Post Office. Although postal services existed earlier the British Post Office dates from 1657 when an Act was passed establishing a single post office under the control of a Government official to be known as the Postmaster-General. Postage was heavy until 1840 when, as a result of the efforts of Rowland Hill, penny postage was introduced. When the Post Office became a public corporation in 1969 it continued to operate postal, telephone and telex services, the issue of postal orders and money orders, its agency services for the Department of Health and Social Security, and the national giro (*q.v.*). Responsibility for national savings was transferred to the Treasury and broadcasting to a new Ministry of Posts and Telecommunications now the Division of Posts and Telecommunications in the Department of Industry. Since 1970 it has acted as agent for the Nationwide (formerly Co-operative) Building Society for life assurance linked to building society investment.

Post Office Guide. An annual publication of the Post Office, with monthly revisions, it gives full details of postal regulations and of all services provided by the Post Office.

Post Office Reform. A pamphlet written by Rowland Hill advocating cheaper postage.

Post Office Register. Since 1969 known as the National Savings Stock Register (*q.v.*).

Post Office Savings Bank. Since 1969 known as the National Savings Bank (*q.v.*).

Posts and Telecommunications. Government department responsible since 1969 for the oversight of the Post Office. The Department has now been absorbed by the Department of Industry.

Post Town. A distributing centre for postal packets. The names of such places must be clearly shown in addresses on letters, etc., preferably being printed or typed in capital letters.

Post-war Credits. During the Second World War part of the payment of income tax—arising from the temporary reduction of certain allowances—was regarded as a compulsory loan, repayable after the war, taxpayers being given Post-War Credits for the years 1941-42 to 1945-46. Repayment was gradual, at first only men aged 65 and over and women aged 60 and over being repaid, but the age of repayment both for men and women has been reduced, first to 63 and 58 and then to 60 and 55 respectively. From 1958 interest at $2\frac{1}{2}\%$ per annum was paid on credits. All outstanding Post-War Credits were repaid in 1972.

Potato Famine. The disastrous failure of the Irish potato crop in 1845 coupled with the high price of bread caused great suffering in Ireland, and resulted in many deaths and large-scale emigration to the United States. It was also an important factor in determining Sir Robert Peel to repeal the Corn Laws in 1846 in order to make bread cheaper.

Potato Marketing Board. First established in 1936, it was allowed to lapse, but was re-established in 1954. Its functions are similar to those of the other Marketing Boards (*q.v.*).

Pound. Originally a pound by weight of silver, 240 silver pennies, first struck in the eighth century in Mercia, being equal to and known as a pound. However, until sovereigns were minted in the reign of Henry VII, the pound remained simply a unit of account. After being superseded by other coins the sovereign was revived on the resumption of cash payments in 1821, the guinea ceasing to be minted. Since that date the pound has been the standard unit of the currency of Great Britain. Many British territories and other countries with close trading or financial links with Great Britain also adopted the pound as the standard unit of their currencies. Thus, until they went over to the decimal system South Africa, Australia, and New Zealand all used the pound. Other countries to use the pound included many other British territories (but not Canada), the Republic of Ireland, Egypt, Lebanon, Israel, the Sudan, Syria, etc. Since decimalisation the pound has been subdivided into fractional units such as piastres in some Arab countries, agorots in Israel and mils in Cyprus. In the form *lira* it is used in Italy and Turkey.

Poundage. An additional charge as with postal orders and money orders, to cover the cost to the Post Office of dealing with them.

Pound Note. The first pound notes (together with two-pound notes) were issued in 1797 during the Napoleonic Wars, but in 1821 they were withdrawn and replaced by gold sovereigns. Between 1821 and 1914 no bank-notes were issued in England of a lower denomination than £5. On the outbreak of war in 1914 the Treasury began to issue notes to the value of £1 and £0·50 and continued to do so until 1928 when the issue was taken over by the Bank of England. *See* Bank-note; Convertibility.

Poverty. A person or a country is poor either because he or it possesses little wealth or because he or it has only a small income. The term is relative since what is regarded as poverty today would have been considered to be a state of modest comfort a century ago. If the real national income of a country is small that country will be poor, and a higher standard of living for its people can be achieved only by an increase in the total volume of production. Individuals may be poor because of the inequitable distribution of the national income or on account of the character of their work (seasonal unemployment, casual labour), their own character (unwillingness to do more than a minimum amount of work, personal misfortune), sickness or, in the case of old people, a fall in the value of money during an inflationary period. At one time unemployment was the main cause of poverty, whereas at the present day poverty is mainly to be found among old people. Poverty might be defined today as having insufficient income to provide what is now regarded as a minimum standard of living.

Power Forces. In the Bargaining Theory of wage determination one of the 'power forces' influencing wages is said to be the trade unions.

Power, Ministry of. Former Government department responsible for matters affecting the industries producing coal, gas, and electricity. These functions have been transferred to the Department of Industry.

Power of Attorney. The right of one person to act on behalf of another as embodied in a deed.

P.p. Abbreviation of *Per Pro* (*q.v.*).

Precautionary Motive. One of the three motives for holding money as distinguished by Lord Keynes. In addition to the money required for current transactions most people, for precautionary reasons, keep something in hand to meet unexpected contingencies. *See* Demand for Money.

Preference, Scale of. *See* Scale of Preferences.

Preference Shares. These shares rank for payment immediately after debentures (if issued), a fixed rate of dividend being payable on them before any sum is allotted to the ordinary shares of a company. Special types of preference share include Redeemable Preference Shares (*see* Redeemable Bonds), Cumulative Preference Shares (*q.v.*) and Participating Preference Shares (*q.v.*) Preference shareholders are not entitled to vote at ordinary meetings of the company.

Preferential Duty. An import duty favouring one group of suppliers against others. *See* Imperial Preference.

Premium. 1. A payment made in respect of assurance or insurance.

2. A payment made to a solicitor, accountant, etc., in return for his accepting an articled clerk—a practice that is rapidly dying out.

3. Securities are said to be 'at a premium' when they stand above par on the stock exchange. The term is also used of currency when above par on the foreign exchange market.

4. For 'dollar premium' *see* Investment Dollars; Property Dollars.

Premium Bonus System. A system of wage payment under which a bonus is added to the hourly rate of pay. Each piece of work has assigned to it a standard time, and the worker's bonus is based on the percentage of time saved. There are several varieties of premium bonus system,—Halsey, Rowan, Weir (*qq.v.*).

Premium Savings Bonds. First issued in 1956, these bonds carry no interest but a sum equal to what would have been the interest is expended on prizes ranging from £25 to £50,000 awarded to bonds bearing the numbers drawn. The prizes are free of tax.

Prevention of Fraud (Investments) Act (1939). An Act passed to protect investors against unscrupulous dealers or company promoters. For example, the Act made it necessary for dealers in stocks and shares to be licensed by the Board of Trade if they were not members of stock exchanges. It also made concealment of important facts about a company in a prospectus an offence.

Price. The amount of money that has to be paid for a commodity or service. *See* Equilibrium (i); Market Price; Price Determination.

Price Association. An alternative term for Price Ring (*q.v.*).

Price Changes. *See* Index of Retail Prices; Value of Money.

Price Commission. A body set up to control prices under the British Government's anti-inflationary policy, January 1973.

Price-Consumption Curve. A curve on a diagram showing how the consumption of a commodity changes when its price changes, consumers' incomes remaining unchanged. It illustrates, therefore, what is known as the price effect (*q.v.*).

Price Control. This may take the form of the State either fixing a maximum price in order to protect consumers against high prices or fixing a minimum price in order to protect producers against low prices. It is more usual to restrict the term 'price control' to the former and designate the latter as Price Support (*q.v.*). Price control is mostly associated with wartime when the difficulties of supply would otherwise lead to exceptionally large increases in prices. Price control was applied in many countries during both World Wars and was retained in Great Britain for many years after the end of the Second World War. This price control means controlling price at a level below the equilibrium, and at such a price the quantity of the commodity demanded will exceed the supply available. Some form of rationing would, therefore, be necessary, either officially and fairly by the State or unofficially and probably less equitably by retailers.

Price Determination. The study of prices is one of the main branches of economic theory. Some economists regard the study of price theory as the basis of all economics, H. J. Davenport in his *Economics of Enterprise* defining economics as 'the science that treats phenomena from the standpoint of price'. Since all goods are scarce relative to the demand for them, the basic problem of economics becomes the distribution of scarce goods among the large number of people wanting them. One method is for the State to do this by some form of rationing, another is to employ the price mechanism, the function of which is to equate supply and demand. At the equilibrium price the quantity of a commodity demanded and the quantity supplied are equal, so that there is neither a shortage (which would occur if demand exceeded supply) nor a surplus (which would only occur if supply exceeded demand). An increase or decrease in either supply or demand will affect the price of the commodity, a new equilibrium price eventually being established at which again the quantity demanded and the quantity supplied are equal. To understand the determination of price, therefore, requires a study of supply (*q.v.*) and demand (*q.v.*). A study is first undertaken of price determination in the theoretical conditions of perfect competition (*q.v.*) and monopoly (*q.v.*) and finally in the actual conditions of imperfect competition (*q.v.*). *See also* Market Price; Normal Price.

Price Differentiation. A consequence of imperfect competition, it arises from Product Differentiation (*q.v.*).

Price Discrimination. This means the charging of different prices to different groups of customers for a similar commodity or service. This is possible only when the production of the commodity or service is in the hands of a monopolist who is able to keep the markets separate from one another without incurring heavy costs in doing so. Such a policy is possible only if the elasticity of demand for the commodity is not the same in each market. Discriminatory prices are possible in the case of personal services which cannot be transferred from one person to another as, for example, medical service. The home and foreign markets can be separated by means of a tariff on imports, prices in such cases being higher in the home than in the foreign market. It is possible also to separate markets by time as in the case of new novels, a higher price being charged at first and a cheaper edition issued later. Other examples of price discrimination are provided by railway charges—the freight classification system, the issue of cheap passenger excursion tickets—and the tariff of the electricity undertakings which reduces the price per unit after a certain amount has been consumed.

Price/Earnings Ratio (P/e). The relationship between the stock exchange price of a share and the current earnings per share of the company concerned, usually after allowance has been made for Corporation Tax. The P/e is generally regarded as the best standard by which to judge the value of a share.

Price Effect. If prices change while money incomes remain unchanged consumers' distribution of expenditure will be subject to both a substitution effect (*q.v.*) and an income effect (*q.v.*), the combination of these being known as the price effect. Diagrammatically the price effect is illustrated by a Price-Consumption Curve (*q.v.*).

Price Fixing. An alternative term for: (i) Resale Price Maintenance; (ii) Price Control; (iii) Price Determination (*qq.v.*).

Price Freeze. *See* Freeze.

Price Leadership. When there are only a few producers of a commodity, as in conditions of perfect oligopoly, when all firms must charge the same price, one firm—generally but not always the largest—will usually take the lead in changing the price. *See* Perfect Oligopoly.

Price Level. This term is generally taken to mean the general level of prices at a particular time as compared with the general level of prices at some other time. Price changes for all commodities and services, however, do not keep in line, and the idea of a general price level is, therefore, erroneous. The Index of Retail Prices (*q.v.*) gives an indication of changes in the price level, but in its modern form it recognises the weakness of the concept of a general price level by also showing index numbers for sectional price levels for twelve separate groups of commodities and services.

Price Maintenance. *See* Resale Price Maintenance.

Price Mechanism. A system of price determination in which the equilibrium price equates supply and demand. *See* Price Determination.

Price Method. The American term for piece rates (*q.v.*) as a method of wage payment.

Price Movements. Three trends in price movements have been distinguished: (i) A long-period movement over the century during which there has been a general tendency for prices to rise, this tendency being most marked in the twentieth century; (ii) A medium-period movement of prices during the nineteenth century depending on the relative rates of expansion of industrial production and the monetary supply. When production was increasing more rapidly than the monetary supply, as during 1820–49 and 1874–96, prices were falling; when the monetary supply was increasing more rapidly than production, as during 1896–1914, prices were rising. In the nineteenth century the monetary supply was closely linked to the output of gold, and so new discoveries of gold, in 1849 in Australia, California, and Russia, and in 1896 in South Africa and the Klondyke, heralded in periods of rising prices; (iii) Also mainly associated with the nineteenth century is the short-term movement of prices of the trade cycle, one of the features of the downswing of the cycle being falling prices, with rising prices during the upswing. Both downswing and upswing were of an average duration of three to four years.

Price, Normal. *See* Normal Price.

Price Out of Market. A term generally used in connection with exports to foreign markets. If, as a result for example of wage increases, costs of production at home rise more than the costs of foreign competitors it is feared that sales to foreign markets may fall.

Price-output Policy. A firm will maximise its profits if it produces that output and sells at that price at which its marginal cost is equal to its marginal revenue.

Price Policy of Nationalised Industries. By their constitutions nationalised industries in Great Britain are to be operated 'in the public interest' but are expected to pay their way over a number of years. If an industry is deliberately operated at a loss on the ground that it is being run as a service there is no satisfactory test of its efficiency. Many economists believe that the aim should be 'to break even', that is, to make neither a profit nor a loss.

Price Ring. A group of firms in an industry loosely associated together to operate a common price policy.

Prices and Incomes Act (1965). An Act passed to support the Government's prices and incomes policy, the aim being to relate incomes to productivity. Notice had to be given of any proposed increase in prices or wages, and if considered necessary wage claims had then to go before the National Board for Prices and Incomes (*q.v.*). Part IV of the Act, inserted at the committee stage to support the Government's prices and incomes freeze for a minimum period of six months, imposed a penalty of £500 for any breach of this freeze either by employers or trade unions.

Prices and Incomes Policy. A term used since 1964 to describe Government policies to check inflation in Great Britain.

(i) *1964*. The aim was to relate wage increases to increases in productivity which had to be calculated for the economy as a whole. This then became the 'norm' for wage increases. A National Board for Prices and Incomes (*q.v.*) was established to administer the policy, and to which claims for higher wages or for permission to increase prices had to be referred. The devaluation of sterling in November 1967 made a policy of severe wage restraint essential if devaluation was to be successful in restoring equilibrium to the British balance of payments, and for the ensuing year the norm was declared to be nil. The task of carrying out the policy was given to the Department of Employment, but threats of strike action almost invariably enabled one trade union after another to obtain wage increases in excess of the norm. By late 1968 it was clear that the prices and incomes policy was going to be little more successful than previous attempts at wage restraint—the wage freeze of 1949–50 and the pay pause of 1961. In fact, wages and prices during 1969–71 increased more rapidly than ever before.

(ii) *1972.* After 1970 Government control of wages and prices was relaxed, but since this led to excessive increases in both wages and prices during 1971–72 a prices and incomes policy had again to be adopted. Two bodies were established—a Pay Board to control wages and a Prices Commission to control prices.

(iii) *1974.* Under the rather vague Social Contract between the Government and the T.U.C. wage increases were restricted in both 1975–76 and 1976–77. A measure of control too was exercised over prices.

Prices Current. A price list showing the prices ruling at a certain date. As a method of price quotation it is in wide use among dealers in raw materials.

Price Support. The U.S. Government's method of giving assistance to farmers. Prices are fixed well above the equilibrium level and so output cannot be completely disposed of on the market, the U.S. Government agreeing to purchase at the fixed prices any surpluses resulting from this policy. Compare the British system of Guaranteed Prices (*q.v.*) for some agricultural products.

Price System. An alternative term for Price Mechanism. *See* Price Determination.

Price Theory. One of the main branches of economics. *See* Price Determination.

Price War. Cut-throat competition by price-cutting as distinct from an advertising war. Since the gain of the firm which is first to cut prices is generally short-lived, all firms in the end suffering, the advertising war in recent times has generally been preferred to the price war.

Pricing Process. An alternative term for Price Mechanism. *See* Price Determination.

Priestley Report (1955). The report of a Royal Commission appointed to inquire into rates of pay in the civil service. The Commission favoured 'a fair comparison with comparable work'. *See* Comparability, Principle of.

Priestman System. A premium bonus system of wage payment first used by Priestman's of Hull in 1917 applicable to employees who work in groups, a group bonus being paid in addition to the ordinary time rate.

Primage. A payment made for care in loading or unloading a ship.

Primary Liquidity. A banking term used by the E.E.C. for assets that can be realised within one month. *Cf.* Secondary and Tertiary Liquidity.

Primary Production. This comprises all extractive occupations—farming, lumbering, fishing, mining, and quarrying, the products of which are foodstuffs and raw materials. *See* Occupations, Classification of.

Primary Risks. A banking term used by the E.E.C. for high-risk investments. *Cf.* Secondary and Tertiary Risks.

Prime Costs. The Variable Costs of an undertaking together with the cost of administration, that is, all costs that vary with output both in the short and long periods and which would not have to be incurred if, for example, the firm had to close down temporarily in a trade depression.

Prime Entry. 1. A term used in foreign trade as an alternative to Entry for Home Use (*q.v.*).

2. A book-keeping term. *See* Original Entry.

Prime Rate. An American term for Bank Rate (*q.v.*).

'Priming the Pump.' A popular term for State investment undertaken for the purpose of stimulating demand in order to reduce unemployment.

Principal. 1. The person on whose behalf an agent operates.

2. A sum of money, which has been invested, exclusive of the interest it has earned.

Principles. *See* under the title of the principle concerned, *e.g.* Comparative Cost, Principle of.

Principles of Economics. An alternative term for Economic Theory. *See* Economics.

Prior Charges. The amount a company has to pay on any debentures or preference shares before a dividend can be declared on its ordinary shares. *See* Gearing.

Private Banks. For a long time the Bank of England was the only joint-stock bank in England, all the others being private banks. The private banks were usually partnerships and generally small, at first being adjuncts to other businesses—goldsmiths in London, merchants or industrialists in the provinces. An Act of 1826 permitted the establishment of joint-stock banks outside a radius of 65 miles from London. In times of crisis the joint-stock banks proved themselves to be stronger than the private banks, the joint-stock banks becoming larger through expansion by opening new branches and by amalgamation. Some private banks had to close their doors, others amalgamated with the joint-stock banks, and a few turned themselves into joint-stock banks. In 1820 there were upwards of 800 private banks in England, but by 1913 the number had been reduced to 60. Although there were only 37 joint-stock banks in 1913, the average number of branches of these banks was 165, whereas the private banks averaged only 7 branches. During the past fifty years the private banks have been absorbèd by the large joint-stock banks.

Private Company. A type of business unit which permits all members to enjoy limited liability. There may be as few as two shareholders but the maximum number must not exceed fifty, not counting present and past employees of the firm. In the case of a private company a shareholder cannot dispose of his shares without the consent of the other shareholders, nor can an invitation be made to the general public for subscription to the shares. The exempt private company, which was exempt from making its accounts public, was abolished by the Companies Act (1967). This took away the main reason for the popularity of such companies. All companies have to be registered with the Registrar of Companies. *See* Close Company.

Private Enterprise. An economic system under which property of all kinds can be privately owned and in which individuals, alone or in association with one another, can own productive resources and undertake production. *See* Free Enterprise.

Private Net Product. A term first used by A. C. Pigou in his *Economics of Welfare*. The net national income is the value of goods and services produced during a period after allowance has been made for depreciation. Some forms of production, though adding to the national income, at the same time create a disservice, as for example the pollution of the atmosphere in many industrial areas. The social net product can, therefore, be defined as the private net product less the value of all disservices entailed in its production.

Private Placing. A finance company or issuing house may purchase at an agreed price the whole of a new issue of shares or debentures. The issuing house will then, in the case of a private placing, dispose of these shares or debentures privately to institutions such as insurance companies and investment trust companies. *See also* New Issue Market.

Private Property. A feature of private (or free) enterprise.

Private Sector. That part of the economy which is left to private enterprise.

Private Treaty. A method of sale where the price of the commodity is decided by bargaining between buyer and seller. This is the method of sale on organised produce exchanges, such as those for cotton and wheat, where the commodity can

P.R.O. Abbreviation of Public Relations Officer. *See* Public Relations.

Prodintorg. The Import–Export Corporation of the U.S.S.R.

Produce Broker. A buying or selling broker on a produce exchange.

Produce Exchange. An alternative term for an Organised Market (*q.v.*).

Producers' Co-operative Societies. In Great Britain producers' co-operative societies have had relatively little success as compared with consumers' co-operative societies, though some small ones still survive in Leicester and the Midlands, being members of the Co-operative Productive Federation Ltd. Producers' co-operatives, however, are a striking feature of dairy farming in Denmark.

Producers' Goods. Also known as capital goods, these are commodities desired not for their own sake but only to assist the production of other goods. Machinery, all kinds of capital equipment, factory buildings and workshops, raw materials, means of transport are all producers' goods. The term is used to distinguish these things from Consumers' Goods. (*q.v.*).

Product Contour. A line on a three-dimensional diagram representing equal products. *See* Contours.

Product Differentiation. One of the conditions of imperfect oligopoly, differentiation being by the use of brand names and by intensive advertising to stress that a particular product is superior to that of other producers.

Production. In economics production is taken to include the production of services as well as commodities, and even in the case of commodities production is basically the performing of services. Commodities are not actually created, production being concerned with changing the form of things—changing raw materials into finished articles, changing substances by chemical action, assembling many small parts to make something such as a watch or a motor-car, etc. Since the economist does not regard the process of production as complete until a commodity has reached the person who wishes to make use of it, production includes the commercial services of distribution—transport, wholesaling, retailing, etc.—and the holding of stocks of things until they are required. Direct services too are regarded as being produced. The total volume of production thus becomes the total of all goods and services produced during a period. The aim of production is to increase economic welfare, and the first essential for that is to increase production as much as is possible. A study of the economic problems of production—factors of production, division of labour, specialisation, economies of scale, location of industry—thus becomes one of the main branches of economics, and generally the first to be studied by the students of economics.

Production, Census of. Compiled at irregular intervals by the Department of Trade, to show the total output and value of all goods produced in the U.K. during a particular year, with details regarding costs of production and labour employed, together with analyses by industry and region.

Production Engineer. The executive of a firm in charge of the planning of production and control of the processes that have to be carried out, his function being to ensure that production is carried on as efficiently as possible.

Production, Factors of. *See* Factors of Production.

Production Goods. An alternative term for Producers' Goods (*q.v.*).

Productive Expenditure. State expenditure which will increase economic welfare in the future. This includes not only State investment on roads, etc., but also expenditure on education and the health service.

Productive Labour. A distinction

between productive and unproductive labour was made by Adam Smith, productive labour being that concerned with the production of goods, direct services being regarded by Smith as unproductive. All kinds of labour, however, are services, and nowadays production is taken to mean the production of both goods and services, and so the distinction is no longer valid.

Productive Potential. The rate at which an economy could grow during a period after taking into account the probable increase in its manpower, capital, and industrial efficiency.

Productivity. The amount of production in relation to the labour employed. Efforts are constantly being made to increase the productivity of labour by increasing its efficiency through education and training, by improving capital and by better organisation. *See also* Marginal Productivity Theory.

Productivity Bargaining. In return for higher wages employers in recent times have often tried to secure the agreement of the trade unions to the adoption of new methods of production or the employment of labour-saving machinery in order to increase productivity, and thereby make the payment of higher wages economically possible. At one time employers would have introduced new methods on their own initiative without consulting the unions, but the increasing power of the unions has made such action impossible. Trade unions, however, are often reluctant to make wage increases conditional on their giving up restrictive practices to which they have become traditionally accustomed. Productivity bargaining usually takes place at workshop level. *See* Restrictive Labour Practices.

Profit and Loss Account. A document used in book-keeping to show the calculation of net profit. Gross profit is shown together with all expenses that have been incurred during a period of trading, gross profit less expenses giving net profit.

Profiteer. A derogatory term applied to retailers and others who take advantage of shortages arising during periods of national emergency, especially time of war, to charge what are regarded as exorbitant prices. In both World Wars most countries introduced price control and some form of rationing to check profiteering, at least in the common necessaries of life.

Profit, Elements of. Three elements of profit can be distinguished: (i) Wages of management; (ii) Interest on capital; and (iii) Pure profit, the payment to the entrepreneur for undertaking the risks of production. Other factors of production receive contractual payments, that is, they know in advance what they are to receive for their services to production, whereas pure profit is a residual payment, namely, what is left of the producer's income after all other payments have been met. A certain level of profit is necessary if capital and the entrepreneur are to be retained in a certain line of production, and this has been called normal profit. Apart from this in perfect competition, if conditions were static, pure profit would tend to disappear since profit arises only under dynamic conditions. In such conditions there is uncertainty and uncertainty-bearing is the principal function of the entrepreneur, who is willing to bear uncertainty in the hope of profit. Differences in profit in different industries occur because the extent of uncertainty varies from one industry to another.

Profit, Gross. *See* Gross Profit.

Profit Margin. The amount of net profit accruing to a producer from the sale of his product. Profit margins may narrow if costs of production rise and if these cannot all be passed on to consumers. In times of rising prices profit margins tend to increase and in time of falling prices to fall.

Profit Motive. The assumption made by economists that the aim of the entrepreneur is always to maximise his profits. Though it is recognised that this is not true in all cases it would be impossible to build up a satisfactory theory of the firm without making this assumption.

Profit, Net. *See* Net Profit.

Profit, Normal. *See* Normal Profit.

Profits à Prendre. A right to use another person's land as, for example, to graze sheep on it.

Profit-sharing. A system of wage payment by which a firm attempts to give its employees a more direct interest in its prosperity, a portion of the profit being set aside for distribution among the employees in proportion to their wages or according to their length of service with the firm. The aim of profit-sharing schemes has been partly to give employees an incentive to increase their output and partly (perhaps mainly) to encourage good relations between management and labour. Many such schemes are still in operation, although their number tends to decline, the trade unions generally not being well disposed towards them.

Profits Taxes. Taxes on profits are generally condemned by theoretical economists on the ground that they check enterprise, being a penalty for success in business with no compensation for failure. In both World Wars Excess Profits Taxes were imposed and in these circumstances there is justification for such taxes, though an equitable assessment of what is 'excess' is really impossible. Somewhat similarly a tax on profits was imposed in 1937 in a time of re-armament, and known then as a National Defence Contribution. During 1945-65 varying rates of profits tax were levied, justifiable perhaps on the ground that since the Government has accepted responsibility for full employment, conditions favouring the earning of profit have been provided by the Government itself. Sometimes discrimination is made in favour of undistributed profits in order to encourage firms to 'plough back' profit into their businesses. In 1965 a Corporation Tax was introduced in the U.K. to replace profits tax and income tax on companies.

Pro-forma Invoice. A commercial document with four main uses: (i) A polite request for payment when a supplier is unwilling to allow his customer credit; (ii) With goods sent on approval, becoming an ordinary invoice if the goods are retained; (iii) When goods are sent to an agent to be sold; (iv) In foreign trade when goods are exported on consignment, informing the importer of the expected prices of the goods.

Progress Chaser. A person employed by a firm to keep track of work in progress through its various stages to ensure that production continues smoothly.

Progress, Economic. *See* Economic Progress.

Progressive Tax System. This is a tax system where the rate of taxation increases as income increases, so that a person with an income of £1,000 may pay £110 in income tax (that is, 11% of his income) whereas a person with an income of £5,000 may pay £1,350 in tax (27% of his income). Where great inequality of income exists a progressive system of taxation is regarded as being more equitable than a proportional system. British Income Tax and Capital Transfer Tax are both highly progressive.

Prohibition. Even under a capitalist system the State may prohibit the manufacture or sale of goods regarded as morally or physically harmful, thereby interfering with consumers' freedom of choice. For example, in Great Britain the sale of some dangerous drugs is forbidden as also is the sale of books of a pornographic character. For such prohibitions to be effective they must have the backing of the great body of the people. The most outstanding example of a prohibition is that to which the term is often restricted, namely the prohibition of the production and distribution of alcoholic drink in the United States during 1920-33. The law led to the illicit manufacture and sale of alcoholic drink on so large a scale that it had to be repealed.

Promissory note. A document stating that a person promises to pay another a specified sum at a certain date. Since it is a negotiable instrument it is very similar to a bill of exchange. Promissory notes are rarely used in business in Great Britain, although quite common in the United States.

Promoter. *See* Company Promoter.

Prompt Cash. Goods sold on these terms of payment must be paid for within a few days.

Propensity to Consume. One of the psychological influences on income determination (*q.v.*) put forward by Lord Keynes, it means the keenness of a person to buy consumers' goods. This and personal income are the important factors influencing total consumption.

Propensity to Save. One of the psychological influences on income determination (*q.v.*) put forward by Lord Keynes's theory, it means the keenness of a person to save. This and personal income are the main influences on the volume of personal saving.

Property. Legally there are two types of property: (i) Real property, that is, land and buildings; and (ii) Personal property, that is, all kinds of personal possessions. In economics the term 'property' is often used to mean anything yielding an income to the owner and so includes all kinds of investment, such as shares, Government stocks, Building Society balances, etc. Income is thus derived from wages (payment for labour service) or from the ownership of property, but the ownership of property yields income to the owner only when he permits someone else to have the use of it, as in the case of lending to the Government or other borrower or letting premises, payment being made in return for a service.

'Property Dollars.' Currency that must be obtained, with the Bank of England's permission, in the market for the purchase of property abroad. The premium payable for such dollars depends on their supply in relation to the demand for them at any particular time. In recent years they have been at a premium of between 32% and 40%. *See also* Investment Dollars.

Property Owners' Associations. Bodies which watch the interests of owners of property, especially the rating and taxing of property.

Property Tax. Property in the form of buildings has until recently been subject in Great Britain to taxation both by the State and Local Authorities. Schedule A of Income Tax included taxation of the owner of property according to the rateable value of the property. This tax was abolished from 1963–64. Local rates are assessed on the rateable value of property. Although the amount of real property owned was formerly a good indication of the relative wealth of different people this is no longer necessarily the case, and so rateable values are not as equitable a basis for local taxation as income.

Proportion. A Bank of England term for the relationship of notes and coin to the total assets of the Banking Department.

Proportional Tax System. A tax system where the rate of taxation is proportional to income. Under this system a man with £1,000 a year might pay £100 in tax while a man with £5,000 a year would pay £500. Though favoured by Adam Smith, a proportional system of taxation is nowadays regarded as being less equitable than a progressive system.

Proportions, Law of. If the proportion in which the factors of production are combined in the production of a commodity are varied so that they are moving away from the optimum—probably on account of the indivisibility of one or more factors—diminishing returns will set in. If the variation of proportions results in the proportion approaching the optimum increasing returns will occur. These two Laws of Proportions must not be confused with the Laws of Scale. *See* Returns, Laws of.

Proposal. A person wishing to take out any form of insurance, including life assurance, must complete a proposal form which requires him to answer a series of questions, so that it is in effect an application which the insurance company can accept or reject.

Proprietary Company (Pty). The term used in Australia and the Republic of South Africa of a private company (*q.v.*).

Prospectus. A public company about to make a public issue of shares will produce a prospectus which must comply with the requirements of the Companies Act and of the Stock Exchange. It gives particulars of the company's past history, its present position, and its prospects. Copies are made available to interested prospective investors.

Protection. The imposition of duties on imports in order to 'protect' home producers of these commodities by making foreign produced goods dearer. The Theory of International Trade, based on the Principle of Comparative Costs and international division of labour, shows that total world output will be at a maximum when there are no restrictions on international trade. Nevertheless this is a policy which countries generally have been reluctant to put into practice. The nineteenth-century period of 'free trade' gave way to one of protection, though Great Britain did not forsake free trade completely until 1932. After the Second World War there was a strong desire to reduce tariffs as it was recognised that the excessively high tariffs of the 1930s had caused a severe shrinkage of world trade. Since 1945 the efforts of G.A.T.T. (*q.v.*) have resulted in some tariff reductions, and this period has also seen the establishment of the European Common Market and the European Free Trade Area, both associations aiming at creating regional areas of free trade. Some arguments in favour of protection are as follows: (i) Governments are not influenced solely by economic considerations—the desire for self-sufficiency may be mainly political; (ii) The 'infant industries argument' that new industries need to be protected until they have become firmly established, this probably being the soundest economic argument in favour of protection, but once imposed protective duties are difficult to remove; (iii) To protect a country's standard of living against competition from countries with a low standard of living and where wages are low. This is a superficially attractive argument but quite contrary to the Principle of Comparative Cost; (iv) For protection against 'dumping' (*q.v.*).

Protection of Depositors Act (1963). In order to protect deposits that had been made with Finance Companies the Act compelled all such companies to deposit copies of their balance sheets with the Registrar of Companies and the Board (now the Department) of Trade.

Protective Duty. A customs duty levied on imports for the purpose of 'protecting' home producers. *See* Protection.

Protest. In the case of a bill of exchange where payment has been refused the first step towards dishonouring it is a protest signed by a notary public. *See* Dishonour.

Prox. Abbreviation of *proximo* (next), used of dates in order to avoid using the name of the next month. Formerly it was general commercial practice but it is rapidly dying out as it is just as easy and less likely to cause error to use the name of the next month or an abbreviation of it.

Proxy. If the Articles of Association so provide a shareholder in a public company has the right to nominate another person, who need not necessarily be a shareholder, to attend and vote on his behalf at shareholders' meetings.

Prudential Assurance Co. Established in 1848, it is the largest insurance company in the United Kingdom, undertaking accident, fire, life, and motor insurance. It also has the largest volume of industrial assurance.

Psychological Influences. The expectations of business men can influence the level and trend of business. Thus, in the nineteenth century when the fluctuations of the trade cycle were well known and recognised, a trade depression might come to an end on account of business men becoming more optimistic of the future and expecting a boom to follow a depression, as had happened in the past, and therefore acting accordingly. Similarly, in a boom they might become more cautious, expecting a depression to follow, and in consequence perhaps postponing the renewal of capital equipment, thereby helping to bring on a depression. No one, however, would attempt to explain the trade cycle solely in terms of psychological influences, but in his theory of income determination Keynes attached great importance to psychological influences such as expectations, the propensity to consume and the propensity to save (*qq.v.*).

P.T.A. Abbreviation of Passenger Transport Authority (*q.v.*).

Pty. Abbreviation of Proprietary. *See* Proprietary Company.

Public Assistance. On the abolition of Boards of Guardians in 1929 their duties were taken over by Public Assistance Committees of County Councils and County Boroughs, the function of which was to give assistance to people who were unemployed and who were not entitled to benefit under the National Insurance Act or had exhausted their benefit under that Act. After 1931 this depended on a means test. *See also* National Assistance; Unemployment Assistance Board.

Public Company. The most important type of business unit of the present day, it must have a minimum of seven shareholders but no maximum is fixed, and since it can make public issues of shares it can raise the large amounts of capital required for production on a large scale. The shares of a public company can be bought and sold on the stock exchange. Its balance sheet must be made public and must be a 'fair and true record' of the business. All companies have to be registered with the Registrar of Companies. *See also* Close Company; Private Company.

Public Corporation. A type of business organisation developed in Great Britain for State-owned activities. Early examples of public corporations were the Port of London Authority, the British Broadcasting Corporation, British European Airways and British Overseas Airways Corporation. During the years 1946–51, when a number of industries were nationalised, new public corporations were established, such as the National Coal Board, the Transport Commission, the Gas Council, and the Central Electricity Generating Board.

Public Debts. These comprise the National Debt, the debts of local government authorities and the debts of public corporations. Public debts comprise: (i) Reproductive debt where the debt is balanced by real assets for the purchase of which the debt was incurred, as is the case with the debts of the public corporations; (ii) Deadweight debt which is not covered by any real asset, as with the National Debt, most of which comes from the financing of past wars. *See* National Debt.

Public Deposits. One of the liabilities of the Banking Department of the Bank of England, it is the balance standing to the credit of the Government.

Public Enterprise. Economic activity undertaken by the State or local authorities. In Great Britain the Post Office has long been operated by the State and during 1946–51 a number of industries—coal, transport, gas, electricity—were nationalised and brought under State control. Most local authorities undertake some economic activity, such as the operation of passenger transport services (most large towns), a savings bank (Birmingham), entertainments (many seaside resorts), etc. At one time many local authorities had gas and electricity undertakings.

Public Expenditure. The amount spent by the State on defence, education, and other social services, interest on the National Debt, capital investment (directly or by nationalised industries), etc. *See* Budget.

Public Interest. A term used in several Nationalisation Acts. It was declared that an industry after nationalisation was to be operated in 'the public interest', a phrase to which no precise meaning can be attached.

Public Investment. *See* Public Works.

Public Issue. An issue of shares offered publicly to investors, as distinct from a Private Placing (*q.v.*).

Publicity. *See* Advertising.

Public Lending Right. The right of authors and their publishers to receive fees when their books are lent out by libraries. The Scandinavian countries were the first to introduce schemes for this purpose. In 1971 the British Government accepted the idea in principle.

Public Ownership. State ownership of property—industrial capital and social capital.

Public Relations. An officer or department of an undertaking or association whose duty it is to ensure that the public is given the most favourable impression of the undertaking's aims and policy.

Public Revenue. The total income to the State from taxes, etc. *See* Budget.

Public Sector. That part of the economy in which the State acts as entrepreneur.

Public Trustee. An official appointed by the State to act as executor or trustee to anyone wishing to make use of his services. He will also act as investment adviser. The fees charged are reasonable. The office of Public Trustee was established in 1908 before banks had begun to undertake this kind of work. Owing to declining business the Public Trustee's office was closed in 1972, but re-instated in 1974.

Public Utilities. Such services as local passenger transport, gas, and electricity undertakings.

Public Welfare. *See* Economic Welfare.

Public Works. Investment undertaken by the State, particularly when private investment is insufficient to maintain full employment. It has been suggested that the Government should compile a list of desirable public works to be undertaken whenever there is a fall away from full employment. *See also* Relief Work.

Public Works Loan Board. A Government body set up to make loans to local authorities, especially smaller authorities which might find it difficult to raise loans on the capital market. For a period after 1945 all local authorities were compelled to borrow from the Public Works Loan Board, the Government often lending to them at a lower rate of interest than that at which it could itself borrow. Then as a check to inflation the larger authorities were again forced into the open market.

Pudding Lane Salesrooms. One of the organised produce exchanges of London, it deals in imported fruits.

Purchase Day Book. *See* Bought Day Book.

Purchase Taxes. These are *ad valorem* taxes on specified commodities, the tax being a percentage of the wholesale price. First imposed in Great Britain in 1940 during the Second World War in order to check consumption of goods in short supply, they were retained as a source of revenue, but later they came to be regarded as an instrument of monetary policy, being increased in a period of inflation and over-full employment to check demand and reduced in a period of unemployment in order to stimulate demand. To increase the taxes in a time of inflation increased prices, however, pushed up the Retail Prices Index and stimulated demands for wage increases. Purchase taxes also had directional effects, that is, only the industries producing goods subject to these

Purchasing Officer. A person employed by a firm to take charge of the buying of the raw materials the firm requires. A Purchasing Officer has to study the market and decide when and how much to buy.

Purchasing Power Guarantees. An alternative term for Indexation (*q.v.*).

Purchasing Power Parity. A theory that attempts to explain the determination of the rates of exchange between currencies when exchange rates are free to fluctuate in terms of the relative purchasing power of the currencies in their home countries. Thus, if £1 will buy in England the same assortment of goods as 13 francs will buy in France, then according to this theory the rate of exchange between these two currencies will be £1 = 13 French francs. The theory was put forward by Cassel during the years following the First World War when a system of free exchange rates was in operation. Though it contains an element of truth the theory is open to three main objections: (i) People in different countries consume different assortments of goods; (ii) A change in the demand for an imported commodity will affect the rate of exchange and, as a result, the prices of all imports from whatever country they may come, but the prices of home-produced goods will be unchanged; (iii) Political and other influences affect rates of exchange—the fall of a Government, an economic crisis, etc. In fact, rates of exchange, being the price of one currency in terms of others, are determined like other prices in free markets by the forces of supply and demand. *See* Free Exchange Rates.

Pure Competition. *See* Perfect Competition.

Pure Economics. An alternative term for Economic Theory. *See* Economics.

Pure Interest. *See* Interest.

Pure Profit. *See* Profit, Elements of.

Purveyors, Statute of (1352). An Act of Parliament which made it illegal for the weight of English coins to be further reduced. The Act was effective in checking a reduction in the weight of coins until 1411.

Put Option. The purchase of the right to sell certain shares at an agreed price, usually in three months' time. *See* Option.

Putting-out System. A method of production where the manufacturer or merchant supplies the raw material to people who do the processing in their own homes. *See* Domestic System.

Pya. A fractional unit of the currency of Burma, 100 pyas being equal to one kyat.

Pyramiding. Having control of a group of companies with a large amount of capital through the possession of only a small fraction of the total capital involved. This becomes possible by having a controlling interest in a Holding Company which controls a number of companies, some of which also have their subsidiaries. *See* Holding Company.

Pyx, Trial of the. First held in the reign of Henry III, and afterwards at irregular intervals these trials are now held annually, and carried out by the Assay Office of Goldsmiths' Hall, to test the quality—weight and fineness—of coins issued by the Mint.

Q

Qantas. The Australian airline, the name being formed by the initials of the original company, formed in 1922—Queensland and Northern Territory Aerial Services Ltd.

Qindarka. A unit of currency of Albania, being in value one-hundredth of a lek, the standard unit.

Qualified Acceptance. With reference to a bill of exchange, it is an acceptance which varies the bill in some way as, for example, by the insertion of a condition.

Qualitative Credit Restriction. A Treasury directive which aims at restricting bank lending to purposes regarded as being in the national interest. *See* Treasury Directive.

Quality Control. During the production of a commodity the first to be produced will be closely inspected and there will be further periodic checks at irregular intervals to ensure that the desired quality of the product is being maintained.

Quantitative Credit Restriction. A Treasury directive which aims at reducing total bank lending irrespective of the purposes for which the money is required. *See* Treasury Directive.

Quantitative Economics. An alternative term for Macroeconomics (*q.v.*).

Quantity Equation. An alternative term for Equation of Exchange (*q.v.*).

Quantity of Money. *See* Money Supply.

Quantity Rebate. A reduction of price on the purchase of a large quantity of a commodity.

Quantity Theory of Money. This is one of the oldest theories of economics. It was the steep rise in prices coupled with the large increase in the quantity of money during the seventeenth century that led to the belief that there was some connection between them. In its earliest and crudest form the Quantity Theory stated that an increase in the quantity of money would bring about a proportionate increase in prices. When it came to be realised that this was not true the theory became discredited. It was, however, revived by Irving Fisher in the 1920s in a refined form, two new variables being introduced, namely the volume of production and the velocity of circulation. In its refined form the Quantity Theory is represented by the equation of exchange as follows:

$$MV = PT$$

The symbol M represents the quantity of money—the total of bank deposits, bank-notes and coin; V represents the velocity of circulation, that is, the average number of times each unit of money is employed during a period; T stands for the total of all transactions that take place for money and so is related to the volume of production; and finally P is the general price level. This equation shows that the general price level can be influenced not only by changes in the quantity of money but also by changes in the velocity of circulation and changes in the volume of production, and also that a change in M or V can be offset by a contrary change in T.

From the time of its revival the Quantity Theory of Money has been severely criticised: (i) It has been said that it is really not a theory at all but simply a way of showing that the four variables, M, V, T, and P are related to one another; (ii) It is said to be a truism because MV must always equal PT since they are merely different ways of looking at the same things; (iii) It is pointed out that the four variables M, V, T, P are not independent of one another, a change in one inducing changes in the others; (iv) There is really no general price level, it is said, but rather a series of section price levels, as the Index of Retail Prices recognises; (v) It is claimed that the theory only attempts to explain changes in the value of money but not how the value of money is in the first place determined; (vi) It is further pointed out that the theory is too much concerned with the supply of money and ignores the demand for money; (vii) It has been said that it is totally inadequate as a theory of money since it takes no account at all of the rate of interest.

It is generally admitted, however, that the Quantity Theory comes into its own in a period of severe inflation, when a large increase in the quantity of money occurs and to an even greater extent in a hyperinflation, when the great increase in the velocity of circulation cannot possibly be offset by a corresponding expansion of production, with the result that prices rise steeply. Only a minority of economists believe the Quantity Theory to be of more general application than that, the Supply and Demand Theory of Lord Keynes being preferred. *See also* Demand for Money.

Quarter Coins. The early silver pennies were of so high a value at the time in terms of goods that it was necessary to cut them into halves or quarters for smaller payments, the coins being marked in quarters to make it easier to do this.

Quarter Days. These are March 25th (Lady Day), June 24th, September 29th (Michaelmas Day), and December 25th, the days on which certain rents fall due.

Quarterly Bulletin. A publication of the Bank of England since December 1960, giving financial and other economic statistics together with articles on topics of current economic interest.

Quarterly Journal of Economics. The journal of the Department of Economics of the University of Harvard.

Quasi-Rent. This term was first used by A. Marshall to describe rent accruing to any factor of production other than land, but it is not usual nowadays to differentiate between rent received by land and rent received by other factors, and so the term is really no longer required. Nevertheless, since land is more likely to be permanently in fixed supply than other factors, rent to land is more likely to persist, whereas in the long run as the supply of other factors receiving rent increases the rent will tend eventually to disappear. The fact that quasi-rents tend to be temporary is sometimes regarded as justification for the retention of the term. *See* Rent.

Queen's Award for Industry. An award made annually since 1966 on April 6th, the Queen's birthday, it is open to all sections of industry, including agriculture. It is awarded to firms (i) which have made a significant expansion of exports; (ii) which have broken into a difficult market; or (iii) have made outstanding progress in some application of advanced technology. Firms which have won the award can display a specially dated emblem for five years and replicas of this can be used on the firms notepaper, packaging, and on the goods themselves.

Questionnaire. A document used in a survey as, for example, in consumer research, comprising a series of questions aimed at eliciting certain required information.

Quetzal. The standard unit of the currency of Guatemala, it is subdivided into 100 centavos.

Quick Assets. Liquid or fairly liquid assets, that is, they can easily be turned into cash.

Quit Rent. A rent formerly paid to a lord in lieu of a service.

Quorum. The minimum number of people who must be present before a meeting is permitted to proceed with its business as, for example, at a directors' meeting or a general meeting of a limited company, the number being laid down in its Articles of Association.

Quot. Abbreviation of Quotation (*q.v.*).

Quotas. 1. With reference to international trade, quotas have been used as an alternative to tariffs as a means of restricting imports. A country may allot quotas to its suppliers, these fixing the maximum amount of a commodity that can be imported during a period, and licences then being issued to the supplying countries.

2. Under international commodity control or restriction schemes quotas are assigned to the various producing countries in order to restrict output. Similarly, under President Roosevelt's New Deal Policy, American farmers producing certain commodities were allotted quotas showing the maximum amount of that commodity they were allowed to produce and which they must not exceed, the Government's aim being to raise prices by restricting output.

3. Under the constitution of the International Monetary Fund each member was given a quota. This, in the first place, determined the amount of the member's contribution to the I.M.F.'s pool. The quota also determines the extent of a member's drawing rights on the Fund, a member being entitled to obtain from the Fund in any one year up to 25% of its quota. The quotas of some of the members, as originally agreed, were as follows:

	$million
United States	2,750
United Kingdom	1,300
France	450
India	400
Canada	300
Holland	275
Belgium	225
Australia	200
Brazil	150
etc.	

Most of the quotas of members of the I.M.F. were increased in 1959, 1966 and 1970.

Quotas, Import. *See* Import Quotas.

Quotation. 1. A statement of a price. A purchaser may ask his supplier for a quotation for a particular order. When such a quotation is given it applies only to that particular transaction.

2. A company may apply to the Stock Exchange for a quotation in order that its shares may be dealt in there.

Quotations Committee. A committee appointed by the London stock exchange to consider applications from companies desiring a stock exchange quotation.

Quoted Company. A company whose shares are quoted on the stock exchange. *See* Public Company.

Qursh. A unit of the currency of Saudi Arabia, 20 qursh being equal to one riyal.

Q.v. *Quod vide* = which see (cross reference).

R

Race Relations Acts. The Act of 1965 restricted the number of immigrants permitted to enter Great Britain each year to 7,500. The Act of 1976 replaced the Race Relations Board by a new Commission for Racial Equality, the aim being to eliminate racial discrimination.

Race Suicide. A term used of the early 1920s when the steep fall in the birth-rate in many western countries led to estimates of an impending decline in the population of these countries. *See* Population Projection.

Rack Rent. A rent equal to the full annual value of a property.

Radcliffe Report (1959). The Report of the Committee on the Working of the Monetary System appointed in 1957 under the chairmanship of Lord Radcliffe, it gives an account of the working of the British monetary and financial system, with chapters on Government and private finance, the work of the Bank of England, the management of the National Debt, international aspects of the monetary system and the objectives and instruments of monetary policy. The Committee considered the 'package deal', that is, the use at the same time of a variety of monetary instruments as likely to be more effective in monetary policy than any single instrument of policy alone. It also considered the general liquidity of the financial system to be of greater importance than the quantity of money. *See* Monetary Policy, 'Package Deal'.

Radiotelegram. A means of communicating with ships at sea. Radiotelegrams can be handed in at any post office where telegraph business is undertaken.

Railex. A service provided by the Post Office, whereby an unregistered letter or postal packet is taken by special messenger from the place of acceptance to a railway station to be despatched by the next train, another special messenger collecting it from the destination station and delivering it. This service is available only at a limited number of post offices and railway stations.

Railway and Canal Commission. Set up in 1873 under the Regulation of Railways Act, this Commission became permanent in 1888, its purpose being to consider a great many matters affecting railways and canals, such as railway amalgamations, proposals of railways to buy up canals, the running of canals owned by railways, etc.

Railway Charges. Railway freight rates used to be based on the principle of 'charging what the traffic will bear'. Goods were arranged in twenty-one categories, those in Class I being charged at the lowest rate and those in Class XXI at the highest rate, thus providing an example of discriminating monopoly. The Transport Act of 1953 put the railways on the same footing with regard to their charges as other forms of transport.

Railway Clearing House. An institution established in 1842 to settle indebtedness between railway companies resulting from the issue of through tickets for passengers and freight covering journeys over more than one company's lines.

Railway Mania. The period of great speculation in railway construction, 1843–47, associated with George Hudson.

Railways. Excluding tramways built for the carriage of coal the first important steam-hauled railway was the Stockton and Darlington, opened in 1825, this being followed in 1830 by the Liverpool and Manchester Railway. The earliest lines were short inter-city connections, but by amalgamation of lines and extensions the British railway system developed. To encourage competition Parliament sanctioned the construction of an unnecessary number of lines. As each new line was opened a coach route was closed and soon long-distance traffic both for goods and passengers, had forsaken the roads for the railways. In spite of many amalgamations there were still over a hundred independent railway companies in Great Britain at the outbreak of the First World War in 1914. During that war (as also during the Second World War) the Government took over the operation of the railways. An Act of 1921 (operative 1923) compulsorily amalgamated the railways into four groups—L.M. & S.R., L. & N.E.R., G.W.R., and S.R. (qq.v.). Though the grouping was on a regional basis a considerable degree of competition was deliberately retained. With a route mileage of 20,000 British railways reached their maximum extent. The return to the roads came with the development of the petrol engine and since the early 1930s road transport, public and private has continued to expand, with a consequent shrinkage of the railways which have been compelled to close many stations and many lines. In 1947 the British railways were nationalised as British Rail (q.v.).

The opening up of some countries like the United States and Russia was largely due to the railways which were built out into undeveloped regions. However, as in Great Britain, railway systems have been severely reduced in the United States and many countries of Europe.

Railways Act (1921). Under this Act 121 railways in Great Britain and Northern Ireland were organised in four groups for greater efficiency of operation, the arrangement of groups being such as to retain some competition between them. The amalgamations took effect in 1923, the four groups taking the names of the London, Midland & Scottish Railway, the London & North Eastern Railway, the Southern Railway, and the Great Western Railway, the last named being the only one to retain its former name.

Ramsbury Building Society. The oldest building society in Great Britain with assets exceeding £500,000, it was established in 1840 at Ramsbury, Wiltshire.

Rand. The standard unit of the currency of South Africa since the decimalisation of its currency. It is subdivided into 100 cents.

Rateable Value. See Rates.

Rate Deficiency Grant. An additional payment by the Government to local authorities where the rates are above the national average, formerly known as an Exchequer Equalisation Grant (q.v.). The basis of comparison is the product of a penny rate in relation to population.

Rate of Exchange. The value of one currency in terms of another. See Foreign Exchange.

Rate of Interest. See Interest.

Rate of Return. A method of calculating the expected profitability of an item of capital investment based on the ratio of its expected profit to its capital cost. See also Payback.

Rates. The revenue of local authorities which is supplemented by Government grants. The assessment is on property-owners, each house, shop, factory, etc., being given a rateable value. The valuation of property is now undertaken by the Department of Inland Revenue, but at one time each local authority assessed the property in its own area. The rateable value is related to the rent which it is considered the property would yield, rates being paid in proportion to the rateable value. For example, if a rate of 15s. (£0·75) in the £ is imposed, the owner of property with a rateable value of £80 will have to pay £60. At one time rates were levied mainly for local purposes—local roads, street lighting, parks, etc., but nowadays less than 25% of local revenue is devoted to such purposes, the remainder having to be used on the administration of services on behalf of the State. The Government contributes a general 'block grant' to each local authority and there are also rate deficiency grants (*q.v.*) payable to the poorer local authorities. Nevertheless, local taxation based on the rateable value of the property tends to be regressive since it does not bear a very close relation to each ratepayer's ability to pay. However, as a tax for local government purposes, rates have the advantage of being locally based. *See* Layfield Committee.

Rates Rebate. A reduction in the amount to be paid in rates by people with low incomes. *See* Rating Act (1966).

Rate Support Grant. A grant made by the central government to British local authorities, it sometimes indicates an area of priority, *e.g.* pollution, slum clearance, etc.

Rating Act (1966). The aim of this Act was to reduce the amount payable in rates by people with low incomes in relation to the size of their families. In all cases the first £7 10*s*. (£7·50) is payable, but above that there is a rebate of two-thirds of the amount up to a stated maximum depending on the size of the ratepayer's family. Most of the cost of this concession is borne by the Exchequer, the remainder by the local authority.

Rating and Valuation Act (1961). An Act which brought to an end the de-rating (*q.v.*) of industrial premises and revised the current value of such property.

Rational Behaviour. One of the assumptions of economic theory. *See* Assumptions.

Rationalisation. A term used especially in the 1930s of schemes for reorganising industries where there was excess capacity due to a fall in the demand for the product or where the economics of large-scale production were so great that it was economically advisable to concentrate production at a smaller number of plants. *See* Lancashire Cotton Corporation.

Rationing. A system of distribution employed mainly in time of war to restrict the quantities of goods that consumers are permitted to purchase. It was first employed in Great Britain during the First World War for many foodstuffs. During the Second World War it applied to a wider range of foodstuffs and also to clothing, petrol, furniture. Rationing occurred in peacetime in 1947 when bread was rationed for a time and in 1956–57 during the Suez crisis in the case of petrol. The usual method of rationing is by coupons which are valid only during the period indicated on them, or by a 'points' system (*q.v.*). Unofficial rationing may be undertaken by retailers when goods are in short supply, goods often being kept out of sight, 'under the counter' (*q.v.*) for regular customers. *See also* Food Rationing.

Rationing by Price. A term sometimes used—more often in a derogatory sense—of the ordinary method of distribution through the working of the Price Mechanism (*q.v.*).

Raw Materials. These are primary products such as minerals, the skins or fleeces of animals, some products of the soil (cotton, flax, timber, etc.), all of which form the basis of manufacturing in industry.

R.C. Abbreviation of Royal Commission (*q.v.*).

R/D. Abbreviation of Refer to Drawer (*q.v.*).

R.D.A. Abbreviation of Retail Distributors Association.

Real. 1. A legal concept that has reference to property (realty)—real property (*q.v.*) as distinct from personal property.

2. In economics it refers to actual things, causes, etc., as distinct from monetary. *See* Real Terms.

3. A former Spanish coin with a value of a quarter of a peseta, it is still in circulation in some states of Latin America.

Real Causes of the Trade Cycle. *See* Trade Cycle, Causes of.

Real Cost. Also known as Opportunity Cost, the real cost of a good is the alternative that has to be forgone, since factors of production can only be set to one form of employment at one time. If factors are employed to build houses fewer factors are available for other purposes. The real cost of the houses, therefore, is whatever these factors of production might otherwise have produced.

Real Estate. Freehold land together with any permanent buildings erected on it.

Real Income. Money income in terms of the goods and services that it will buy. *See* Real Wages.

Real Investment. The actual production of a new piece of capital—a machine, a workshop, a motorway, etc.—as distinct from monetary investment such as the purchase of shares, Government stock, etc.

Realised Profit. When the value of an investment appreciates and becomes worth more than it cost it is said to yield a paper profit but if it is sold at this higher price the gain becomes a realised profit.

Real Property. In addition to the distinction between Choses in Possession and Choses in Action English law (unlike other legal systems) also distinguishes between Real and Personal Property. The feature of Real Property is that it can be recovered if the owner has been dispossessed. Freehold land is Real Property but a leasehold is regarded as Personal Property.

Real Terms. The study of an economic problem when all the monetary aspects have been removed. *See also* Real Cost.

Realty. Real property (*q.v.*).

Real Wages. Wages in terms of the goods and services the money wages will buy. Thus real wages may be falling, even though money or nominal wages are rising, if prices are rising more rapidly than wages, or real wages may rise while money wages are falling.

Rebate. A reduction of the price of a commodity allowed for some reason —for example, the purchase of a large quantity.

Rebecca Riots. Attacks on the property of Turnpike Trusts in South Wales in 1843, the name being taken from the title of a book *Rebecca and Her Daughter*. The rioters had many grievances but their main one was the high rate of toll charged by the Turnpike Trusts. As a result the Government replaced the trusts in South Wales by County Road Boards.

Receipt. An acknowledgment in writing of something—usually a payment—that has been received. Under the Cheques Act of 1957 a cheque is accepted as proof of payment and unless requested, a receipt need not be given. Stamp duty on receipts and cheques was abolished in February 1971. Receipts should be retained for six years.

Receiving Order. A Court order made after a bankruptcy petition has been received and the management of the debtor's property has been transferred to the Official Receiver.

Recession. A temporary falling off in business activity, this term being employed in both Great Britain and the United States to describe the temporary lapses from full employment that have occurred since 1945.

Reciprocity. In international trade it occurs when one country makes tariff concessions to another in return for similar concessions.

Reclamation. The bringing of land into cultivation that was previously unfit for production as, for example, by draining schemes (the English fens, the Zuider Zee, etc.) or by irrigation schemes, as in many desert regions. In this way the supply of land, which is very limited, can be slightly increased.

Recoinage. The issue of new coins of a different—in practice, generally less—weight and fineness from the previous issue following upon a debasement of the coinage or a general depreciation of the value of money. Recoinage occurred in England at intervals of forty years or so between the twelfth and eighteenth centuries, no fewer than four recoinages taking place during the sixteenth century. The fall in the value of money and the rise in the price of silver made it necessary to reduce the silver content of the British 'silver' coinage, until eventually a cupro-nickel alloy replaced silver altogether.

Reconciliation Statement, Bank. In order to enable a firm to check its cash book against its bank balance allowance must be made for cheques which have been drawn but not yet cleared and cheques received but not yet paid into a bank.

Reconstruction of a Company. The reorganisation of a limited company may be undertaken for any one of a number of reasons: (i) for the purpose of effecting a redistribution of the capital among the different classes of shareholders, (ii) to enable a bonus issue of shares to be made, (iii) to increase the capital of the company, or (iv) to give effect to amalgamation with another firm.

Recorded Delivery. A service provided for a small fee by the Post Office to enable the sender to have proof of delivery. A receipt of posting is given and the recipient has to sign a receipt on the delivery of the letter or packet.

Redeemable Bonds (or Stock). Government Bonds, Debentures, or Preference Shares which are repayable at par at a certain date or at some time between two stated dates.

Redemption Dates. The dates between which a stock is redeemable at par. For example, 5% Treasury Stock 1986–89 is redeemable at any time convenient to the Government between 1986 and 1989.

Redemption Yield. The yield of a stock, redeemable at par at some future date, calculated on its present purchase price and taking into account not only the rate of interest but also the difference between its present price and its par price. A stock of a nominal value of £100 with a nominal rate of interest of 3% may stand at present at £80, giving a rate of yield of $3\frac{3}{4}$% if the stock is irredeemable, but if the stock is redeemable at par in twenty years' time this means that its capital value will also increase at an average rate of £1 per annum, giving a total redemption yield of nearly 5%.

Redeployment of Labour. The redistribution of labour among different occupations to meet changing conditions affecting the demand for labour. For example, between 1950 and 1965 the number of people employed in Great Britain in agriculture, mining, and textiles fell respectively by 675,000, 227,000, and 237,000, while the number employed on engineering increased by 789,000.

Re-discount. To discount a bill of exchange which has previously been discounted as when the discount houses in the London Money Market, unable to borrow from the commercial banks, are compelled to rediscount at the Bank of England some of the bills they are holding and which they have previously themselves discounted on behalf of the drawers.

Redistribution of Income. In many countries today one purpose of taxation is to reduce inequality of income. To achieve this purpose taxation must be progressive, as in Great Britain today. Redistribution of income is further assisted by the provision of services financed out of taxation, which are more likely to benefit people in the lower income groups.

Redundancy. The reduction in the amount of labour required by a firm or industry as a result either of a contraction of the industry due to a fall in the demand for its product or of the introduction of new methods of production, such as automation, requiring the employment of less labour. Both have been serious causes of unemployment since the early days of the factory system, but the speed and extent of modern economic progress have made redundancy a much graver problem. To alleviate unemployment resulting from redundancy it is necessary to retrain labour for other kinds of work.

Redundancy Insurance. Compensation provided by a firm to employees who have become redundant. *See* Redundancy.

Redundancy Payment. Compensation paid by a firm to an employee whose services are no longer required by that firm on account of the introduction of automation or labour-saving machinery or because of a change of demand. It is also known as Severance Pay. *See* Redundancy Payments Act (1965).

Redundancy Payments Act (1965). An Act which made compensation payable to employees dismissed on account of redundancy. The cost is borne partly by employers and partly by the State. Employers have to pay a certain amount per week for each employee but the State bears 70% of the cost. The benefits depend on age and length of service, with £1,200 as the maximum after 20 years' service.

Re-exports. Goods imported by a country which is conveniently situated as a distribution centre from which the goods can be re-exported to other countries, such trade being also known as entrepôt trade. London, Rotterdam, and Singapore are all important for their entrepôt trade.

Ref. Abbreviation of Reference.

Referee (or Reference). An applicant for a post may be asked to give the names of persons who can vouch for his character and qualifications.

Referee in Case of Need. A phrase sometimes inserted on a bill of exchange, followed by the name of a person or company, to whom the holder of the bill can resort if it is dishonoured. After acceptance the referee in case of need becomes an Acceptor for Honour. *See* Acceptance of Honour.

References. Before a supplier will allow credit to a customer he will probably ask for references. These may be (i) trade references (*q.v.*)—the names of other firms with which the customer has previously dealt, or (ii) a banker's reference (*q.v.*)—the name of the customer's banker. *See also* Referee.

Refer to Drawer. A bank may return a cheque to the payee if the cheque has not been drawn correctly (for example, the amount in words and figures may differ) or if the drawer has insufficient funds in his account to meet it. In the latter case the cheque is said to be dishonoured.

Reflation. The easing of credit restrictions to encourage an expansion of production, it is the milder sort of inflation that accompanies the upward swing of a trade cycle.

Refugee Capital. Also known as 'hot money', such capital is liable to be moved at short notice from one centre to another, the owners seeking safety rather than the best return on their investments. Short-term capital movements of this kind have a disturbing effect on the balances of payment of the countries concerned, such capital being liable to be withdrawn just when a country is having difficulty with its balance of payments, its difficulties thereby being aggravated.

Regd. Abbreviation of Registered.

Regional (or Territorial) Division of Labour. Alternative terms for Localisation of Industry (*q.v.*).

Regional Economic Planning Boards. Set up by the Department of Economic Affairs to assist regional development as outlined in the National Plan for 1965–70. The function of each regional board was to produce draft plans for the region. These plans were then to be considered by the appropriate Regional Planning Council (*q.v.*). *See also* Economic Planning Regions.

Regional Economic Planning Councils. Set up in 1965 by the Department of Economic Affairs, their functions were: (i) to assist in the formulation of regional plans; (ii) to advise on the steps necessary to carry out these plans; (iii) to advise on regional implications of national economic policies. *See also* Economic Planning Regions; Regional Economic Planning Boards.

Regional Employment Premium. Introduced in 1967 under the Select Employment Payments Act to assist firms in Development Areas. Firms in these areas are to receive for at least seven years a certain amount for each man, woman, boy or girl they employ.

Regional Trade. A group of countries, usually contiguous to one another, which agree to pursue a common trade policy. The European Common Market and the European Free Trade Association (*qq.v.*) are examples of areas of regional trade.

Registered Capital. An alternative term for Authorised Capital (*q.v.*).

Registered Office. Every company is required to have a registered office to which communications to it can be addressed.

Registered Stock. Also known as Inscribed Stock (*q.v.*).

Registrar of Companies. The Government official responsible for the registration of public and private companies and limited partnerships.

Registrar of Restrictive Trade Practices. Under the Restrictive Trade Practices Act of 1956 all agreements between producers or distributors have to be registered with a Registrar. These agreements are then to be investigated by Restrictive Practices Courts which have to decide whether they are in the public interest, and if not, the Courts have power to dissolve them.

Registration. 1. Formerly on payment of a fee letters and parcels could be registered with the Post Office. In 1972 a new service, Compensation Fee Parcels (*q.v.*), replaced the registration of parcels. Registration of letters was, however, retained.

2. Registration of a Company. *See* Formation of a Company.

Registration Fee. A charge made by a company for the registration of shares in the name of a new shareholder.

Registration of Business Names Act (1916). Under this Act all businesses carried on under a name other than that of the proprietor or partners must be registered and the true names of the partners must appear on the firm's notepaper, commercial documents, etc., with their nationality if they are not British.

Regressive Supply Curve. An exceptional supply curve where over a part of its length a rise in price calls forth a smaller, instead of a larger, supply as, for example, when a rise in wages results in an increase in absenteeism, thereby in effect reducing the supply of labour.

Regressive Tax. A tax which falls more heavily on people with low incomes than on those with high incomes. Some indirect taxes, especially those imposed on foodstuffs, tend to be regressive, consumption of some commodities depending more on the size of the family than on income. Most countries today have progressive systems of taxation, but since the total revenue required by a modern state is so great it cannot all be provided from direct or income taxes. However, all indirect taxes, especially if on an *ad valorem* basis, are not regressive, many expensive articles that are taxed being beyond the means of people in the lower income groups.

Regulator. A modern instrument of monetary policy, the term is applied to the power of the Chancellor of the Exchequer to vary the rates of indirect taxes between budgets to meet the needs of a changing economic situation. It was used in 1975 to change the rate of V.A.T.

Reichsbank. The central bank of Germany until 1945. The central bank of West Germany is now known as the Deutsche Bundesbank (*q.v.*).

Reichsmark. The standard unit of the German currency for a period, replacing the mark after the great inflation of 1923–26, and being itself replaced by the Deutsche Mark in 1948.

Reisemark. The *travel* or *tourist* mark, issued during the 1930s by the German monetary authorities at a specially favourable rate to foreign tourists. Since 1945 many other countries—for example, Spain and Yugoslavia—have issued currency to tourists at favourable rates to encourage the tourist trade.

Relief Work. Work deliberately provided in order to reduce unemployment (often road-making) and to relieve distress in a period of heavy unemployment. This was the traditional method of helping the unemployed before national insurance.

Remedy. The amount of variation from the standard permitted to the Royal Mint.

Remploy Ltd. A company established by the Government to operate factories employing disabled men.

Remunerative Rates (or **Beneficial Rates**). Terms used by Alfred Marshall where the money obtained from rates is devoted to expenditure on lighting, street drainage, etc., a net benefit being conferred on the ratepayers in such cases, in contrast to Onerous Rates which yield no compensating benefit.

Rendu. An alternative term for Franco (*q.v.*).

Renminbi. An alternative term for Yuan (*q.v.*).

Rent. In ordinary speech rent is the payment for the use of someone else's property, generally land or buildings. In economics rent is given a more important connotation, and although early economists restricted its use to land, it is now used of any factor of production. Definitions of rent differ slightly, but all stress its main characteristics, namely that it is a surplus accruing to a factor of production, and could not be generally foreseen when the factor first entered that line of production. Rent can be considered to be any income received by a factor over the amount necessary to keep that factor in its present employment. Rent can also be defined in terms of its origin as the surplus accruing to any factor of production the supply of which cannot easily or quickly be increased, and arises on account of an increase in the demand for that factor.

Rent was formerly restricted to land because land is a factor some kinds of which are permanently fixed in supply as, for example, particular sites, the rise in site values being due to an increase in demand and inability to increase the supply. Following Marshall the term, 'quasi-rent' was formerly used of rents accruing to factors other than land. The principal difference between rent accruing to land and rents accruing to other factors is that rent of land tends to be more permanent whereas when rents are received by other factors their supply tends to increase and in the long run the rents, therefore, tend to disappear, so that such rents are likely to be only of temporary duration.

Rent often occurs in the case of highly specific labour, the supply of which can be increased only in the long run, if an increased demand for that type of labour occurs. The high earnings of some entertainers contain a large element of rent, as also do the earnings of exceptionally skilled surgeons, barristers, etc., the term, 'rent of ability' sometimes being applied in these cases. Similarly, large, expensive, highly specific capital may receive a rent as a result of an increase in the demand for it on account of the heavy cost of increasing its supply. The monopolist's profit is more of a rent than a true profit, though the 'scarcity' of the product is induced by the monopolist himself. An important point to remember in connection with rent is that the high price of a commodity or service is not due to the high rent the producer has to pay for a factor, but rather it is the high price the commodity or service will command that gives rise to the rent. *See also* Ricardian Theory of Rent.

Rent Acts. 1. **(1957).** This Act brought about some decontrol of rents (smaller houses remained controlled) but it did not fulfil the hopes of its sponsors in increasing the number of houses to rent, and some measure of rent control (*q.v.*) had to be restored.

2. **(1965).** This Act continued the control of the rents of $2\frac{3}{4}$ million houses and regulated the rents of a further 850,000. It set up local assessment committees to fix 'fair' rents. It also made it illegal for land-

lords to intimidate people with the intention of securing their eviction.

3. **(1972).** The Housing Finance Act (1972) laid down the principle that only those in need should pay less than a 'fair' rent, whether living in council houses or other property.

Rent Control. First instituted during the First World War as otherwise, with a temporary cessation of house building, rents would have risen to exorbitant levels. Rents were again controlled for the same reason during the Second World War. In both cases control was limited to houses up to a stated rateable value. The effect of rent control was to make it increasingly difficult for people to obtain houses to rent, as it was no longer profitable to build houses for this purpose, and the existing supply of such houses began to fall since, when they became vacant, landlords preferred to sell their houses rather than let them, as there was no control of the prices of houses for sale. Property let furnished was also outside control.

Rentenmark. A currency unit adopted in Germany in 1923 after hyperinflation had reduced the value of the mark almost to nothing. It was soon superseded by the Reichsmark (*q.v.*).

Rentes. French Government stocks.

Rentier Class. People who derive their incomes entirely or mainly from ownership of some type of property.

Rent of Ability. Rent accruing to highly skilled specific labour as a result of a high demand for it and the difficulty of increasing its supply owing to its uniqueness. *See* Rent.

Renunciation, Letter of. When a company makes an issue of shares on favourable terms to its present shareholders (a 'rights' issue) any shareholder is entitled to renounce the shares to which he is entitled.

R.E.P. Abbreviation of Regional Employment Premium (*q.v.*).

Reparations. An indemnity paid by a country that has been defeated in war to the victors, the amount often being based on an estimate of the cost of the war. During the First World War it had been said that Germany must pay for that war, but the cost was so stupendous that it was clearly impossible to make Germany pay the full cost. It was found too with the complex economies of the twentieth century that the disturbance to the economies of the countries receiving the reparations—whether paid in money or in goods—was so great that many people came to believe that it would have been better for the victors not to have demanded reparations at all, and this view was even more widely held after the Second World War, when few countries, except Russia, demanded reparations.

Repatriation. The selling of foreign investments and investing the money at home.

Replacement Cost Principle. The cost of replacing a piece of capital is of greater importance to a firm than the original cost of this capital, especially in a period of generally rising prices.

Reply Coupons. *See* International Postal Reply Coupons.

Representative Firm. As defined by Alfred Marshall, this is a firm that 'has had a fairly long life and fair success, which is managed with normal ability, and which has normal access' to both internal and external economies of production. Such a firm would be earning only normal profit.

Repressed Inflation. An alternative term for Suppressed Inflation (*q.v.*).

Reproductive Debt. That part of the National Debt covered by real assets, as distinct from Deadweight Debt (the compensation stocks issued by the nationalised industries).

Reproduction Rate. *See* Net Reproduction Rate.

Repudiation. Refusal of a country to acknowledge an obligation to another, more particularly debts incurred during a war (after the First World War many European countries repudiated their debts to the United States) or the debts of the previous régime overthrown by a Government that has come into power as a result of a revolution. (The Russian Communist Government repudiated foreign debts incurred by Czarist Governments.)

Resale Price Maintenance. Insistence by the manufacturer on a fixed price for his product. The practice was first introduced in the 1890s after agitation on its behalf by small retailers as a counter to price-cutting by large-scale retailers. It came to be the accepted practice with all branded goods. Though at first unwilling to introduce resale price maintenance manufacturers eventually came to insist on it, because of their desire to secure the maximum number of retail outlets. The Lloyd Jacob Committee (1949) condemned the practice. The Restrictive Trade Practices Act of 1956 made illegal concerted action by manufacturers in cutting off supplies to a retailer who had been selling the product of one of them at less than the fixed price, but this Act recognised the right of an individual manufacturer to do so. The Resale Prices Act of 1964 (*q.v.*) made resale price maintenance illegal from 1965 except where manufacturers could satisfy the Restrictive Practices Courts that it was in the public interest for it to be retained.

Resale Prices Act (1964). An Act abolishing resale price maintenance (*q.v.*). A producer is permitted to fix prices for his products only if the Restrictive Practices Courts permit him to do so. After the passing of this Act supplies to retailers could be cut off by manufacturers only if their products were being used as 'loss-leaders' (*q.v.*). The Act came into force in 1965. Though many manufacturers on the passing of the Act applied to the Restrictive Practices Court to retain price maintenance for their products most of these applications were withdrawn when it became clear that few applications were likely to be successful. In fact, very few applications to retain price maintenance were upheld—books being a noteworthy exception. By 1965, therefore, after being operated in some cases for over fifty years, resale price maintenance came to an end.

Research Institute for Consumers' Affairs (R.I.C.A.). A body which undertakes the testing of services in the interests of consumers, the first inquiry being into the services provided by estate agents. *See* Consumer Protection.

Reserve Bank of Australia. The central bank of Australia, formerly known as the Commonwealth Bank of Australia. It is now solely concerned with central banking business.

Reserve Bank of New Zealand. The central bank of New Zealand, founded in 1934. Its head office is in Wellington and it has branches in Auckland and Christchurch.

Reserve City. On account of the vast area of the United States and a banking system which permits only a limited amount of branch banking, correspondent banks are required for the clearing of cheques, balances being maintained at a number of Reserve Cities, to facilitate this. There are different legal reserve requirements for Country Banks and Reserve City Banks.

Reserve Currency. Foreign currency held by a country as part of its reserve and as a fund from which it can make international payments. A country on the gold exchange standard holds its reserves in a currency which is convertible for gold, such a currency being known as a reserve currency. In recent years both the pound sterling and the U.S. dollar have served as reserve currencies. *See* Gold Exchange Standard; International Currency.

Reserve Price. The price below which a seller is not prepared to sell. If the reserve price is not reached at an auction sale the goods will be withdrawn.

Reserve Ratio. *See* Cash Ratio.

Reserves. Instead of distributing its entire profits to its shareholders a company will place some to its reserves. A firm may maintain separate reserve funds for different purposes, such as a general reserve, depreciation reserve, etc. Many firms help to finance their expansion from reserves built up for this purpose. *See* Hidden Reserve.

Resettlement Transfer Scheme. A Government scheme to encourage the movement of labour from areas of unemployment to those where a shortage of labour exists. Lodging allowances are payable to the worker until he secures permanent accommodation, fares for the transport of his dependents, a grant towards the cost of household removal and towards legal fees if he is a house-owner.

Residual Payment. A payment received by the entrepreneur as the reward for his services to production after all contractual payments (*q.v.*) to the other factors of production have been met.

Residual Unemployment. People who, on account of physical or mental disability, are of so low a standard of efficiency that few employers can provide work they are capable of undertaking even in times when there is a serious shortage of labour. *See* Unemployment.

Residuary Legatee. The beneficiary under a will who is to receive the residue of the estate after provision has been made for all debts and other legacies.

Residuum. A term used by Alfred Marshal and others for the poorest stratum of a community.

Restraint of Trade. All agreements in restraint of trade, unless held by a court not to be unreasonable or against the public interest, are illegal. Common examples of restraint of trade are (i) where the seller of a business promises as a condition of sale that he will not set up in competition with the buyer, or (ii) where an employee, as a condition of his employment, has to promise not to set up in competition with his employer at any time in the future.

Restriction, Exchange. One of the principal methods of exchange control, under which the monetary authorities restrict the amount of foreign currency their own nationals are permitted to acquire, the aim being to maintain the exchange rate at a higher level than it would be in a free market. *See* Exchange Control.

Restriction of Imports. *See* Tariff, Quotas.

Restriction of Output. *See* Cartel; Commodity Control Schemes; Monopoly.

Restriction Schemes. *See* Commodity Control Schemes.

Restrictive Labour Practices. In an attempt to protect the interests of their members trade unions often insist that more men be employed on particular jobs than is necessary for efficient working as, for example, on the introduction of labour-saving machinery. Some over-manning, however, is the result of traditional practices such as the employment of craftsmen's mates. Deliberate time-wasting or 'working to rule' (*q.v.*) are other forms of restrictive labour practice.

Restrictive Practices Courts. Under the Restrictive Trade Practices Act (1956) agreements between producers or distributors were to be considered by five courts set up under the Act to determine whether such agreements were 'in the public interest'. These courts also have to decide whether to permit resale price maintenance to continue in the case of any manufacturer who appeals against its abolition under the Resale Prices Act of 1964.

Restrictive Trade Practices Act (1956). This Act made illegal concerted action by manufacturers against a retailer who had sold the product of any one of them at a lower price than that fixed by the manufacturer concerned, but the right of an individual manufacturer to insist on resale price maintenance was legally recognised for the first time. The Act also declared that all agreements between manufacturers or distributors should be registered and these investigated by Restrictive Practices Courts, of which five were to be established. Any agreement found to be contrary to the public interest was to be dissolved.

Retail Price Index. *See* Index of Retail Prices.

Retail Trade. Increased division of labour and an expanding range of consumers' goods has led to a great expansion of the retail trade which forms the final stage of distribution —the selling of goods to the people who actually wish to use them. The commonest retail outlet is the shop, of which there are over half a million in Great Britain. In addition there are street traders, pedlars, hawkers, market stall-holders, and the expanding mail-order business. Most shops are small, but an increasing proportion of retailing is in the hands of large-scale retailers—department stores, multiple shops and co-operative societies. A recent development has been the establishment of supermarkets and self-service stores. The main service of the retailer is to ensure that consumers are offered the things they want in the form and in the quantities in which they want them. He should therefore carry a varied stock. Hire purchase, financed either by retailers or finance companies, has brought about a large increase in the sale of the more expensive durable consumers' goods. Convenience of situation is also regarded as an important service of the retailer. The retail trade provides an example of mono-competition, differences in services and location causing differentiation between one retailer and another.

Retirement. An American term for repayment of public debt.

Retirement Certificate. An indexed national savings certificate available only to people of pensionable age. It was first issued in 1975. The interest is related to the General Index of Retail Prices. *See* Indexation.

Retirement Pensions. One of the benefits under the National Insurance scheme, men becoming entitled to a pension at 65, and women at 60 years of age. They replaced non-contributory Old Age Pensions. *See* Graduated Pension Scheme.

Returns, Laws of. There are two sets of laws of returns: (i) Increasing and diminishing returns resulting from variations in the proportions in which the factors of production are combined; (ii) Increasing and diminishing returns resulting from a change in the scale of production ('pure' returns to scale). If one or more factors remain fixed and increasing amounts of the other factor or factors are combined with the fixed factors, increasing returns will occur until the optimum proportion has been reached after which diminishing returns will set in. This is applicable to any form of production. Since it is often necessary to employ large, indivisible units of capital it is not always possible to combine factors in the optimum proportion. Assuming, however, the optimum proportion to have been reached, the scale of production can then be increased by increasing the amounts of the factors employed in this same proportion. Expansion of the scale of production may be accompanied by increasing returns to scale, though few economies of scale appear to be entirely independent of variation of the proportions in which factors are combined.

Returns to Scale. *See* Returns, Laws of.

Revaluation. The raising of the value of a currency in terms of others as occurred with the German and Dutch currencies in 1961.

Revenue. *See* Budget; Inland Revenue.

Reverse Income Tax. Also known as Negative Income Tax, it is a scheme whereby the State makes payments to people with incomes below a certain level as a means of ensuring that no one falls below the poverty line. It is the basis of the Tax Credit System (*q.v.*). *See also* Family Income Supplement.

Reverse Yield Gap. A condition that exists when the yield on equities is lower than on gilt-edged and other fixed interest securities. On account of the greater risk it was formerly usual for the yield on equities to be higher than the yield on gilt-edged stocks. Increased awareness of the effects of inflation has increased demand for equities and reduced the demand for fixed interest securities, and hence the reverse yield gap.

Reversionary Bonus. An addition to the value of an assurance policy 'with profits', made annually or triennially, the amount depending on the profits earned by the company or society in the preceding period.

Revocable Letter of Credit. *See* Letter of Credit.

Revolving Credit. A method of granting credit, it differs from a personal loan in that the borrower, as with an overdraft, need not take up the full amount. As repayment reduces the debt the borrower can increase the loan, if he wishes, up to the original amount. Repayments are usually made by regular monthly instalments.

Rial. The standard unit of the currency of Iran, it is sub-divided into 100 dinars.

R.I.C.A. Abbreviation of Research Institute for Consumers' Affairs (*q.v.*). *See also* Consumer Protection.

Ricardian Theory of Rent. Ricardo defined rent as 'that portion of the produce of the earth which is paid to the landlord for the use of the original and indestructible powers of the soil'. Thus Ricardo restricted rent to land. Rent he regarded as being due to differences in the fertility of different pieces of land. Land only just worth cultivating yielded no rent; the excess yield of more fertile land over this 'no rent' land was its rent. The theory could also be applied to land of equal natural fertility, some of which was cultivated more intensively than the rest, the excess yield on the more intensively cultivated land being its rent. The following are some of the main criticisms of Ricardo's theory: (i) He restricted rent to land; (ii) It is simply based on the natural variation of the fertility of different pieces of land; (iii) He took no account of the fact that there are competing uses for some land, and as a result it is not necessarily the least fertile land that will first go out of cultivation. *See* Rent.

Rice. Formerly used as money in Japan. *See* Commodity Money.

Richardson Committee (1964). A Committee appointed to consider the merits of Value Added Tax. It recommended that a tax of this type should not be imposed.

Richmond Commission (1882). A Royal Commission under the chairmanship of the Duke of Richmond set up to inquire into the causes of the depression in agriculture at that time. The Commission listed as the main causes bad harvests, heavy local rates, high rents, high railway rates, and foreign competition.

Riel. The standard unit of the currency of Kampuchea (Cambodia), it is subdivided into 100 sen.

Rights Issue. An issue by a company of new shares which are offered on favourable terms to the present shareholders of the company. Since the new issue increases the capital of the company it is often known as a capitalisation issue.

Rights Letter. A document entitling a shareholder to a number of shares in a new issue being made by the company. If the shareholder does not wish to acquire these additional shares the document can be sold on the stock exchange.

Rig the Market. Action by large speculators on the stock exchange aimed at temporarily offsetting the ordinary market forces and taking advantage of this situation to make a profit.

Ring. An association of firms at the same stage of production, formed for the purpose of keeping up prices.

Ring Money. Ornaments in the form of rings, bracelets, armlets, etc., made of gold or silver, which could be used either as money or for personal adornment.

Risk. Insurance provides cover against risks the probability of which can be mathematically calculated. Other risks associated with production, such as, for example, changes of demand, must be borne by the entrepreneur, this type of risk being better regarded as Uncertainty (*q.v.*).

Risk Capital. A term sometimes used of equities or ordinary shares, the dividend of which varies with the profits earned by the company.

Rival Commodities. A term used by Alfred Marshall of goods that are close substitutes for one another.

Rival Demands. An alternative term used by Alfred Marshall for Competitive Demand (*q.v.*).

Rival Supplies. An alternative term used by Alfred Marshall for Competitive Supply (*q.v.*).

Rivers. At one time rivers were the main form of inland transport and where deep enough for large ships are still so used. Rivers also, especially those with wide mouths, have always been serious obstacles to transport. In many cases ferries have to be used, but bridges and tunnels provide freer movement. In Great Britain the railways built long bridges across the wide estuaries of the Rivers Forth and Tay, and tunnels under the Thames, Mersey and Severn. Road bridges have been constructed over the Forth, Clyde, Tay, Severn, Tamar, and Humber, and road tunnels under the Thames, Mersey, Tyne and Clyde.

Riyal. The standard unit of the currency of Saudi Arabia, it is subdivided into 20 qursh.

RM. Abbreviation of Reichsmark (*q.v.*).

R.M. Abbreviation of Royal Mail.

Road & Rail Traffic Act (1933). The second of two acts passed to regulate road transport, the first being the Traffic Act of 1930 (*q.v.*) which related to passenger services. The Act of 1933 concerned road hauliers, who were divided into three classes: A—general hauliers, B—firms carrying their own goods but also having some general haulage business, and C—firms delivering only their own goods. The number of A and B licences was to be restricted, but C licences were to be available to all applicants entitled to them.

Road Fund. A fund into which the proceeds of the taxes on motor vehicles were paid between 1909 and 1937, the original aim being to provide for the cost of road improvements. Since 1937 the receipts from motor taxation have been regarded, like other taxes, as general Government revenue and not earmarked for any special purpose, and expenditure on roads is not related to the amount received from motor taxation.

Road Haulage Association. A body whose members are holders of 'O' licences for the carriage of goods by road. *See* Road and Rail Traffic Act (1933).

Road Licensing. *See* 'O' Licence; Road and Rail Traffic Act (1933); Road Traffic Act (1930); Transport Act (1968).

Road Research Laboratory. A division of the Department of Scientific and Industrial Research.

Road Safety Act (1967). In addition to the breathalyser test, this Act introduced annual tests for goods vehicles and laid down minimum standards for brakes, tyres, etc.

Road Traffic Act (1930). Under this Act the country was divided into 13 (later reduced to 11) traffic areas. All passenger transport services within the area must be licensed and their timetables and fares sanctioned by the Traffic Commissioners (*q.v.*).

Road Traffic Act (1972). This Act consolidates the law relating to road traffic.

Road Transport. The expansion of the railways during the latter half of the nineteenth century appeared at the time to have put an end to long-distance transport by road. In the 1890s, however, the railways found a competitor for suburban passenger traffic in the street tramways—horse-drawn, steam-driven or electrically operated—but it was not until an efficient petrol engine had been developed that there came a serious return to the roads. During 1919–39 expansion of road services for both passenger and goods was rapid, and this expansion continued at an even greater pace after 1945. Before the nationalisation of road haulage in 1947 there were over 20,000 operators with an average of fewer than three vehicles each. When road haulage was denationalised in 1953 many of the larger units (each comprising 150 vehicles) were retained, and some continued to be operated by British Road Services. In 1928 the railways had obtained power to operate road services, but they used these powers mainly to acquire a controlling interest in the large bus companies which had come into being as a result of both growth and amalgamation. Passenger and haulage services were regulated respectively by the Traffic Act of 1930 and the Road and Rail Act of 1933 (*qq.v.*). Recently the main competitors of the large public operators—road as well as railway—have been vehicles delivering a firm's own goods, and the private car. The Transport Act (1968) created the National Freight Corporation (*q.v.*) for road haulage and the National Bus Company (*q.v.*) for road passenger services. Road passenger transport in five of the larger conurbations—Manchester, Merseyside, the West Midlands, Tyneside, and West Yorkshire—was to be in the hands of Passenger Transport Authorities similar to the London Transport Board. Further P.T.A.s could be established as required.

Robbins Committee. A Committee set up by the Government to consider what further provision should be made for higher education. The Committee's report was published in 1963. It recommended that: (i) Places for students in higher education should be increased to 560,000 by 1980–81; (ii) Six new universities should be established immediately, and a further 22 should be planned; (iii) Colleges of Advanced Technology should be given university status with power to grant degrees; (iv) Ten universities should be formed from existing institutions.

Robeco. The largest investment trust in Europe, it is centred on Rotterdam.

Rochdale Pioneers. The name given to the twenty-eight weavers who in 1844 opened the first successful co-operative shop in Rochdale. *See* Consumers' Co-operative Societies.

Rochdale Report (1963). A report that recommended that there should be co-ordinated development of British ports.

Rolling Adjustment. A term sometimes used since Government accepted responsibility for full employment to describe a temporary falling off in business activity to indicate a milder condition than a depression or even a recession.

Rome, Treaty of (1957). The treaty which established the European Common Market (*q.v.*).

'Room.' The place at Lloyd's where the brokers meet the underwriters.

Roskill Report (1971). The report of a royal commission under the chairmanship of Lord Roskill, to consider the site for a third airport for London. Its recommendation of a site in Bucks was set aside in favour of Maplin.

Rotation of Crops. Growing different crops on a piece of land in different years in regular sequence. *See* Manorial System; Norfolk Course; Three Field System.

Rothschild (N. M.) & Sons. A firm of merchant bankers in London established in 1804 by Nathan M. Rothschild, one of the five sons of Mayer Amschel von Rothschild of Frankfurt-am-Main. During the first half of the 19th century the five branches of the family operated banks in Frankfurt, Vienna, London, Paris, and Naples. The only two to survive to the present day are the London firm and Rothschild Frères of Paris.

Rothschilds Intercontinental. A banking consortium formed in London in 1969, it comprises N. M.

Rothschild & Sons, Banque Rothschild, Banque Lambert, the National City Bank of Cleveland, the First City National Bank of Houston, Seattle First National City Bank, and two other banks.

Rouble. The standard unit of the currency of the U.S.S.R., it is subdivided into 100 kopeks (or copeks). *See also* Transferable Rouble.

'Roundabout' Method of Production. A more capitalistic method of production with more processes and greater division of labour, only possible when there is a large market for a commodity. An expansion of the market for a commodity may lead to production becoming more 'roundabout', just as a fall in demand for a commodity may result in its production becoming less roundabout.

Rowan System. A premium-bonus system of wage payment under which, in addition to the ordinary time-rate, the worker receives a bonus at half time-rate on the time saved on the standard time assigned to a piece of work.

Royal. An alternative name for the former English gold coin known as a ryal, and originally worth ten shillings.

Royal Agricultural Society. Founded in 1838 to encourage scientific research in agriculture, in order to increase output and reduce costs of production, and to disseminate this new knowledge among farmers. At the time of its foundation farming in Britain was depressed but, largely as a result of the Society's efforts, British farming in the third quarter of the nineteenth century enjoyed a period of prosperity.

Royal Bank of Canada. The largest Canadian commercial bank. It has over 1,350 branches.

Royal Bank of Scotland. The second oldest bank in Scotland, founded 1727, it is a member of the National and Commercial Banking Group (*q.v.*). In 1958 it acquired an interest in the British Wagon Co., a finance house. It was the first British bank to issue saving stamps.

Royal Commission. A body set up by the Government to take evidence and report on some aspect of social, economic, or political life, as for example on population, taxation, (*qq.v.*), etc. Some reports are better known under the names of the chairmen, as, for example, the Radcliffe Report, the Barlow Report (*qq.v.*), etc.

Royal Economic Society. A learned society established for furthering the study of economics, it publishes articles and reviews in the *Economic Journal*.

Royal Horticultural Society. *See* Horticultural Society, Royal.

Royal Mint. A Government department of which the Chancellor of the Exchequer is *ex-officio* the Master. It has a monopoly of the manufacture of coins in the United Kingdom, and it also makes coins for other countries. It buys metal in the market, and in Great Britain sells coins to the Bank of England at a considerable profit since these are all token coins. The commercial banks obtain coin as they require it from the Bank of England against withdrawals from the balances they maintain there. In 1968 it was transferred from London to Llantrisant near Cardiff.

Royal Niger Company. A chartered company founded as the National African Company in 1882, its name being changed in 1886, for the purpose of developing the area now known as Nigeria.

Royal Society of Arts. Founded in London in 1754 as the Royal Society for the Encouragement of Arts, Manufactures, and Commerce. The society organises lectures and has promoted exhibitions, but today it is probably best known as an examining body in commercial subjects.

Royalty. A payment made to an inventor, author, or composer for the use of a patented or copyright work or to a landowner for the extraction of minerals from beneath his land. *See* Copyright, Patent Rights.

R.P.I. Abbreviation of Retail Price Index. *See* Index of Retail Prices, General. *Cf.* C.P.I.

Rs. Abbreviation of Rupees (*q.v.*).

R.S.A. Abbreviation of Royal Society of Arts (*q.v.*).

R.T.E. Abbreviation of Radio Telefis Eireann, the national broadcasting organisation of the Republic of Ireland.

Rum. Used as money in the early days of the British West Indian colonies owing to a shortage of coins. *See* Commodity Money.

Runaway Inflation. An alternative term for Hyperinflation (*q.v.*).

Running Broker. A firm in the London Money Market which does not itself discount bills, merely acting as an agent on behalf of a bill broker.

Run on a Bank. Heavy withdrawals of cash by depositors of a bank who have lost confidence in it. No bank, however efficiently run, can withstand a run, and if faced with one would have to close its doors.

Rupee. The standard unit of the currencies of India, Pakistan, Sri Lanka and Mauritius, being subdivided in the case of India into 100 nave paise, in Pakistan into 100 paisa, and in Sri Lanka and Mauritius into 100 cents.

Rupiah. The standard unit of the currency of Indonesia, it is subdivided into 100 sen.

Rural Credit Bank. An institution which specialises in the provision of credit facilities for farmers, it is thus similar in function to an Agricultural Mortgage Corporation (*q.v.*).

R.V. Abbreviation of Rateable Value (*q.v.*).

Rx. Abbreviation of tens of Rupees (*q.v.*).

Ryal. An English gold coin, also known as a Royal, first issued in 1465 when it was worth 10s. In 1544 its value was 12s. The Double Ryal, issued by Henry VII in 1489 and worth 20s., came to be known as a sovereign. Half ryals and quarter ryals also were issued.

Ryder Report (1975). A report on British Leyland, the motor vehicle manufacturers, which recommended the re-organisation of the company's management and administration to make each division of the firm—goods vehicles, buses, motor cars—separate businesses.

S

S.A. Abbreviation of Société Anonyme, the French equivalent of Ltd. Co.

Sabena. The Belgian State Airline.

Sacrifice. With reference to taxation, the principle that a tax system should be so organised that the payment of taxes involves the minimum amount of sacrifice for all taxpayers. It is somewhat similar to the theory of basing taxation on the ability to pay. See Minimum Sacrifice.

S.a.e. Abbreviation of stamped addressed envelope.

Safe Custody. As a service for its customers, a commercial bank will allow them to store valuables—documents, etc.—in its strong room.

Safeguarding of Industry. Alternative term for Protection (q.v.).

Salary. Though there is no precise economic difference between wages and salary, both being payments for labour service of some kind, wages are paid by time-rates or piece-rates and in the case of time-rates according to the number of hours actually employed, whereas a salary is usually a rate per week or per month, not precisely related to the number of hours worked. Manual workers are paid wages, administrative workers salaries, wages being a variable cost whereas salaries are a fixed cost. See Wages.

Sale of Goods. Some of the main points from the acts relating to the sale of goods are: (i) In any contract for the sale of goods it is implied that the seller has a right to sell the goods in question; (ii) Goods must agree with either a sample or a description; (iii) There is an implied condition as to the quality of the goods. The Supply of Goods Act (1973) amended many clauses in the Act of 1893.

Sale or Return. A manufacturer or wholesaler may supply a retailer with goods which can be returned if they are not sold within a reasonable time, the retailer only paying for the goods he has sold. The term is often abbreviated to S.O.R.

Sales Department. The division of a manufacturing or wholesaling business concerned with the sale of the product. In a large firm the department will be under a sales manager, who will have control of an indoors office and administrative staff and an outdoor or field staff of travellers. Unless the firm is large enough to have a separate publicity department the sales department will undertake this work.

Sales Manager. An executive of a firm who is responsible for sales promotion.

Salesmanship. The art of persuading people to buy a particular commodity. If carried to extreme it becomes 'high pressure' salesmanship.

Sales Promotion. Efforts other than advertising (q.v.) to increase sales by creating or expanding the demand for a product. Means of sales promotion include displays, free samples, temporary reductions in price, offering trading stamps, etc.

Sales Tax. A tax levied on all retail sales, unlike Purchase Tax which is levied only on a selected group of commodities. Thus, variations in Sales Tax have not the directional effects (q.v.) of Purchase Tax (q.v.). See also Value-added Tax.

Salt. Used as money at one time in Abyssinia and Arabia. See Commodity Money.

Salters' Company. One of the more important of the 82 Guilds or Livery Companies of the City of London whose existence dates back to the gilds of the Middle Ages, and which ranks ninth in order of civic precedence. Although it is known to have been in existence in the early fourteenth century, it was not granted a charter until 1558.

Sample. Commodities, such as wool

and tea, which cannot be accurately graded, are sold by auction on produce exchanges. Before attending the auction to make their bids prospective buyers are given an opportunity to sample the various lots that are to be offered for sale.

Samuel Commission (1926). A Royal Commission under the chairmanship of Lord Samuel which reviewed the state of the coal-mining industry. It recommended: (i) That the subsidy paid to the industry for the purpose of keeping up miners' wages should cease; (ii) That royalties should no longer be paid to landowners under whose land coal was mined and that the State should compensate landowners for this loss of royalty; (iii) That pithead baths should be provided; and (iv) That coal-miners should have a seven and a half hours working day. The Commission was, however, opposed to the nationalisation of the industry. *See also* Sankey Commission.

Sanctions, Economic. The economic boycott of a nation by a group of countries such as the League of Nations or the United Nations as a protest against the policy that country is pursuing and in order to make it change its policy, as for example, against Italy in 1935 and against Rhodesia from 1966.

Sandilands Report (1975). The report of a committee set up to inquire into inflation accounting (*q.v.*).

Sandwich Courses. These are courses under which employees spend alternate periods of the year at an institution of higher education and in industry, leading to a degree or other qualification.

Sankey Commission (1919). Though this Commission recommended the nationalisation of coal-mines its recommendation was not acted upon until 1947.

S.A.S. Abbreviation of Scandinavian Air Services, an airline operated jointly by Denmark, Norway and Sweden.

Satang. A sub-unit of the currency of Thailand, 100 satang being equal in value to one baht.

Satiable Wants, Law of. An alternative term for the Law of Diminishing Marginal Utility.

S.a.v. Abbreviation of stock at valuation.

'Save as you Earn' (S.A.Y.E.). A scheme of contractual saving introduced in the 1969 budget for regular savings, the interest being free of both income tax and capital gains tax. An indexed S.A.Y.E. scheme was introduced in 1975, the interest payable at the end of the term (five or seven years at the investor's choice) being linked to the General Index of Retail Prices. *See* Contractual Saving and Indexation.

Saving. One of the determinants of income and employment, the total volume of saving depending on the size of income, the propensity to save and to a lesser extent on the rate of interest. Saving means a curtailment of consumption and its economic importance lies in its relationship to investment, that is, the production of real capital, saving being a necessary pre-requisite of investment.

Saving, Types of. Since saving reduces the demand for consumers' goods in order to enable factors of production to be employed on the production of capital goods, any course of action, therefore, which reduces consumption and assists the production of real capital can be regarded as saving. The following types of saving can, therefore, be distinguished: (i) Saving by individuals for their own personal reasons; (ii) Corporate saving by companies ploughing back profits into the business and so reducing the amount of profit distributed to shareholders. These two types of saving are both voluntary; (iii) Compulsory saving occurs when the State reduces consumption by deliberately increasing taxation for this purpose; (iv) Forced saving occurs in a mild inflation if this takes place without a general rise in incomes, since it will then bring about a reduction in the demand for consumers' goods.

Saving, Reasons for Personal. Though in general the higher the rate of interest the greater the amount of saving, many personal reasons for saving are independent of the rate of interest: (i) Since most people prefer to have a little money in reserve, some saving is to meet unforeseen contingencies; (ii) Many people save to make provision for some future purpose, such as for old age, education of children, or in the short term to enable them to purchase expensive goods. The expansion of State-provided social services in the one case and of hire-purchase in the other have somewhat reduced saving for these purposes; (iii) To accumulate wealth for the social status and power that it brings; (iv) The unplanned saving of the very rich. *See* Income Determination; Saving/Investment Theory.

Saving/Investment Theory. Saving and Investment (the actual production of capital goods) are unlikely to be equal because saving is undertaken by one group of people and investment by another, and yet equality of Saving and Investment are required because if Saving exceeds Investment there will be less than full employment and if Investment exceeds Saving an inflationary situation will arise. Keynes contended that the two things must always be equal, because the amount of Income generated by Investment would provide an equivalent amount of Saving. Keynes's demonstration of the equality of Saving and Investment is as follows. Taking National Income to be the total of all income derived from economic activity, personal income is either spent on consumers' goods or saved. Thus:

$$\text{National Income} = \text{Amount spent on Consumers' goods} + \text{Amount Saved}$$

that is: Income = Consumption + Saving
Therefore: Saving = Income − Consumption

Then taking national income in real terms as the total volume of production, which comprises consumers' goods and producers' goods (real capital or investment):

$$\text{National Income} = \text{Amount of Consumers' goods produced} + \text{Amount of Capital goods produced}$$

that is: Income = Consumption + Investment
Therefore: Investment = Income − Consumption

Since the Saving and Investment are each equal to Income − Consumption they must, therefore, be equal to one another, and so:

$$\text{Saving} = \text{Investment}$$

For a long time Keynes's view that Saving was always equal to Investment aroused great controversy. That this view is not necessarily incompatible with the older theory was shown by means of the period analysis (*q.v.*) of Sir Dennis Robertson and Prof. Ohlin of Sweden.

Savings Bank. *See* Trustee Savings Banks.

Savings Certificates. *See* National Savings Certificates.

S.A.Y.E. Abbreviation of Save As You Earn (*q.v.*).

Say's Law. *See* Markets, Law of.

Scale Effect. The effect on the size of a firm of a change in the demand for its product. Thus, an increase in demand may make possible an expansion of a firm to a size at which it will enjoy economies of scale, so that its average cost falls, and the increase in demand eventually leading to a fall in price instead of an increase in demand resulting in a rise in price, as would be the case if expansion of output was unaccompanied by economies of scale. A fall in demand will eventually result in a rise in price (and not a fall in price as might have been expected) if output is so reduced that economies of scale, previously enjoyed, are lost. Changes of output in the motor car industry provide good examples of the scale effect.

Scales of Preference. One of the assumptions of economic theory is that everyone always acts rationally. Faced, therefore, with a choice between two things, an individual will choose the one that will give him the greater amount of satisfaction. This implies that he has a scale of preference, a kind of list of his unsatisfied wants arranged in order of satisfaction. A commodity near the top of the list would give him more satisfaction than one lower down. Few people are consciously aware of having a scale of preferences, though most are aware that some wants are more pressing than others. For the purpose of economic theory, however, it is necessary to assume that everyone has a scale of preferences, since one person's scale will be quite different from another's. Each scale represents the preferences of an individual irrespective of ethical or moral considerations.

Scandinavian Monetary Union. Before 1914 some currencies were interchangeable over limited areas. For example, as a result of the formation of the Scandinavian Monetary Union, in 1873, the currencies of Norway, Sweden, and Denmark, all using the krone or krona as their standard unit, were indiscriminately acceptable in those countries. *See also* Latin Monetary Union.

Scarcity and Choice. In economics the term 'scarcity' simply means limited in supply. In this sense all things are scarce relative to people's desire for them. People's wants are many, but the resources, that is, factors of production, required for producing things to satisfy these wants are themselves limited in supply. It is, therefore, impossible to satisfy all the wants of everybody. Since, then, all things are scarce a choice has to be made as to how factors of production shall be employed, and consumers too must decide which of their wants are the most pressing. Scarcity and choice, therefore, are fundamental to economics. In a free economy what shall be produced is left to consumers' choice, producers attempting to meet consumers' demand. In a State planned economy the State decides what shall be produced and allocates the factors of production accordingly.

Scarcity Value. A term sometimes used of the high price of a commodity the supply of which is small and difficult or impossible to increase.

Scheduled Territories. The official name for countries that were members of the Sterling Area (*q.v.*).

Schedules. A term used of the different categories of Income Tax. For example, Schedule D applies to business profits, and Schedule E to people employed by others (P.A.Y.E.) (*q.v.*).

Schilling. The standard unit of the currency of Austria, it is equal in value to 100 groschen.

Schoolmen, The. A group of medieval philosophers of whom St. Thomas Aquinas was the leading member. Influenced by the writings of Aristotle they were opposed to 'usuary' by which they meant any payment of interest. They also believed that a 'fair price' should be asked for anything offered for sale. To try to obtain more than this price they regarded as unethical.

Schroder (J. Henry), Wagg & Co. An old-established firm of London merchant bankers. It was established in 1804.

Schuman Plan. A scheme from which the European Coal and Steel Community (*q.v.*) developed.

Schweizerische Bankerein. (The Swiss Banking Corporation.) With its head office in Basle it is the largest commercial bank in Switzerland. It has branches in London, New York, and San Francisco.

Schweizerische Kreditanstalt. (Swiss Credit Bank). One of the leading commercial banks of Switzerland, its head office being in Zurich. It has branches throughout Switzerland and in London and New York.

Schweizerische Nationalbank. The central bank of Switzerland, established in 1905. It has head offices at Berne and Zurich with branches in eight of the country's larger towns, together with over 500 agencies in smaller places. Since 1907 it has been the sole bank of issue in Switzerland.

Scientific and Industrial Research, Department of. Established by the British Government in 1916 to promote scientific research, particularly in subjects likely to affect trade and industry. There are fourteen main stations for different branches of the work—building research, chemical research, fuel research, etc. In 1964 most of its work was transferred to the Ministry of Technology and in 1970 to the Department of Trade and Industry, and in 1974 to the Department of Industry.

Scientific Management. The development of a set of principles of management based on a systematic study of the operations of production began with F. W. Taylor in the United States in the early years of the twentieth century. These principles were: (i) The various operations performed by employees should be scientifically studied; (ii) Workers should be employed on the kind of work for which they are best fitted; (iii) There should be co-operation between management and employees.

S.C.I.T. Abbreviation of Special Commissioners of Income Tax (*q.v.*).

Scott Report (1942). Recommended that planning powers should be used to prevent good agricultural land being taken for other purposes.

Scottish Agricultural Securities Corporation. *See* Agricultural Mortgage Corporation.

Scottish Trades Union Congress. A similar body to the T.U.C. (*q.v.*) with which it co-operates closely.

Scottish Transport Group. Set up under the Transport Act (1968) to co-ordinate passenger transport in Scotland. It took over some road and sea services previously operated by the Transport Holding Company.

Scrip Issue. A Bonus Share issue (*q.v.*).

Scriveners' Company. One of the smaller of the 82 Guilds or Livery Companies of the City of London whose existence dates back to the gilds of the Middle Ages. It existed in the fourteenth century, but did not receive a charter until 1616.

S.C.W.S. Abbreviation of Scottish Co-operative Wholesale Society. *See* Co-operative Wholesale Society.

S.D.R. Abbreviation of Special Drawing Right (*q.v.*).

S.E. Abbreviation of stock exchange.

Search Unemployment. An alternative term for structural employment (*q.v.*).

Seasonal Demand for Cash. Shortly before Christmas and again in summer there are heavy withdrawals of cash from the commercial banks to cover the heavy expenditure of consumers at these periods of the year. It has, therefore, become customary to make temporary increases in the fiduciary issue to meet the demand for cash at these times.

Seasonal Unemployment. In outdoor occupations bad weather may make it impossible for work to be carried on, and so there is usually an increase in unemployment, for example, in the building trades in winter. There is also some seasonal unemployment among people who are employed at holiday resorts during the summer months as there is little demand for their services during the rest of the year.

S.E.C. Abbreviation of Securities and Exchange Commission, a United States body (similar to the Council of the London Stock Exchange) which among other things decides whether a new share shall be given a stock exchange quotation.

Secondary Liquidity. A banking term used by the E.E.C. for assets that take between one month and two years to realise. *Cf.* Primary and Tertiary Liquidity.

Secondary Occupations. All occupations concerned with manufacturing. *See* Occupations, Classification of.

Secondary Risks. A banking term used by the E.E.C. for investments of average risk. *Cf.* Primary and Tertiary Risks.

Second-class Mail. Mail on which a lower rate of postage is paid. First-class mail has priority over second-class mail.

Sector. A division of the economy of a country. The economy can be divided into two main sectors, namely the public sector and the private sector, or into a number of smaller sectors. Thus, the public sector can be subdivided into Government, Local Authorities, and Public Corporations (nationalised industries), and the private sector into companies and persons.

Secular Trend. A long-period trend as distinct from cyclical fluctuations.

Secured Creditor. A creditor who holds a mortgage as security for a debt.

Secured Debenture. A debenture that forms a fixed charge on specified assets of a company. *See* Debentures.

Securities and Exchange Commission. The Wall Street Crash (1929) brought heavy losses to investors in stocks and shares throughout the United States. In 1933, therefore, the U.S. Government set up this body to supervise American stock markets, the aim being to stop unfair trading and the dissemination of false information, especially prior to a new issue of shares.

Securities Management Trust. A subsidiary of the Bank of England set up during the 1930s to assist industry during the Great Depression. Among firms receiving assistance were the Lancashire Cotton Corporation and Shipbuilders Security Ltd.

Securities Market. *See* Stock Exchange.

Security. 1. A general term for a stock exchange investment.

2. Collateral security against a bank loan. *See* Collateral Security.

Security Sterling. Investors outside the sterling area who sell British shares receive payment in blocked or security sterling.

Seigniorage. A charge made by a mint for turning bullion brought to it into coins. The Royal Mint never made any such charge for turning gold bullion into sovereigns when Great Britain had a gold coinage. The profit on the issue of a token coinage is also known as seigniorage. Although token coins are of less than their face value they are sold by the Mint to the Bank of England at their face value.

Selective Employment Tax (S.E.T.). A tax introduced in 1966, it is a variation of a Payroll Tax (*q.v.*), employers having to pay poll taxes on their employees. Its aim was partly to raise revenue and partly to encourage 'services' to employ fewer people so that a larger labour supply might be available for manufacturing industry since in the case of manufacturers (from 1967 only those in development areas), the full amount of tax together with a bonus per employee was returnable. The tax was criticised on the grounds that: (i) there was more hoarding of labour in manufacturing industry than in service occupations; (ii) in an advanced economy with a high general standard of living the proportion of people engaged in providing services increases. Value-added Tax replaced S.E.T. and Purchase Tax in 1973.

Self-employed. A person who is in business on his own account. For purposes of national insurance a person so classified must pay higher contributions than an employee or a non-employed person, but not as high as the combined contributions of employer and employee for those in paid employment. People in this category are not entitled to all the benefits of the national insurance scheme.

Self-interest. The classical economists believed that in his economic life the individual was motivated by self-interest though it was also believed that this coincided with the interest of the community as a whole.

Self-liquidating. This is said to be a

characteristic of bills of exchange drawn to finance the purchase of raw material by a manufacturer or of goods by a wholesaler, since the drawer of the bill eventually obtains the funds to meet it when it falls due from the sale of the same goods or goods made from the raw material.

Self-service. A type of shop where customers have to help themselves to the goods they wish to buy, the goods selected being checked and paid for on leaving the shop.

Self-sufficiency. To achieve self-sufficiency a country must make itself as far as possible independent of others by producing most of the things it wants itself. This was the aim of many of the new nations that came into existence in Europe after the break-up of the Hapsburg Empire following the First World War. There may be advantages in self-sufficiency in wartime but economically it is an unsound policy, being contrary to the Principle of Comparative Cost.

Seller's Market. A market in which at the moment demand exceeds supply, the tendency for prices to rise being to the advantage of sellers.

Selling Costs. Costs incurred to stimulate sales. Thus, advertising is the main selling cost. Competitive advertising is a consequence of imperfect competition. There would be no selling costs in conditions of perfect competition.

Sen. A fractional unit of the currency of Japan, 100 sen being equal in value to one yen, and of the currency of Kampuchea (Cambodia), where 100 sen are equal to one riel.

Seniority. Length of service with a firm, in some cases the basis for promotion.

Sequin. Former Venetian gold coin.

Serfdom. The system under which the villeins were bound to the lord of the manor, paying for the use of a small piece of land by working a certain number of days per year on the lord's demesne and also paying certain feudal dues. In England the manorial system began to break up towards the end of the fourteenth century as an increasing number of villeins were able to commute their labour services for money payments. On the continent of Europe serfdom lasted much longer. France abolished serfdom and the conquests of Napoleon hastened the end of serfdom in Germany west of the River Elbe where serfdom had been declining since the sixteenth century. East of the Elbe it had developed much later than in the west and so persisted to a later date. Serfdom was not abolished in Russia until 1863.

Serial Funding Loans. Stocks issued by the British Government for short periods of from one to three years.

Service Central des Risques. To reduce the risks associated with borrowing by individuals from more than one bank at a time, a common practice in France, the French National Credit Council set up this service, operated throughout France, except Paris, through the Bank of France, to provide lists of borrowers from banks, though not showing the amounts borrowed.

Service des Cheques Postaux. The French postal giro service. It is the largest postal giro system in the world.

Service Occupations. *See* Occupations, Classification of.

S.E.T. Abbreviation of Selective Employment Tax (*q.v.*).

Set of Bills. Foreign bills of exchange are drawn in triplicate, the three bills relating to the same transaction being known as a set.

Settlement. The period during which stock exchange transactions must be settled, it starts the day following the ending of the Account during which the deal was made and lasts until Account Day.

Settlement, Act of (1662). Each parish having been made responsible for its own poor, this Act gave the Justices of the Peace power to send new residents back to the parishes from which they had come.

Settlement (or Settling) Day. A stock exchange term, it is an alternative name for Account Day.

Severance Pay. An alternative term for Redundancy Payment (*q.v.*).

Sex Discrimination Act (1975). This Act made discrimination against either sex illegal. The scope of the Act was wide as it was not restricted to employment. *See* Equal Pay.

Share Certificate. A document, issued under the official seal of a company, showing ownership of share(s) in that company.

Share Pushing. A term applied to selling shares by high pressure salesmanship methods with glowing but unsubstantiated statements about the shares, in effect in order to dispose of them for higher prices than they are really worth. The publication of such statements is a criminal offence if they can be proved to be untrue and made with a deliberate intention to mislead investors.

Shares. The capital of a limited company is divided into shares which may be in units of £1 or more or of £0·50, £0·25, or of as little as £0·05. Shares are of two main types —ordinary shares and preference shares. Ordinary shares generally carry no fixed rate of dividend unless deferred ordinary shares are issued, but receive a dividend dependent on the amount of net profit earned by the company. Preference shares generally carry a fixed rate of dividend which is, however, payable before payment of the dividend on the ordinary shares. There are also other types of preference shares such as cumulative preference shares and participating preference shares (*qq.v.*) which give their holders additional privileges.

Shares of No Par Value. *See* No Par Value, Shares of.

Shekel. At first an ancient Jewish weight of about 224½ grains, later it became a coin of that weight (*Cf.* pound), and in size rather larger than the present British 10p coin. Half and quarter shekels also were minted.

Shell Company. A colloquial term for a Holding Company (*q.v.*).

Sherman Act (1890). An American anti-trust law which attempted to prevent the setting up of monopolies.

Shift. 1. With reference to employment it means employing relays during different periods of the day and night, a day shift and a night shift, or three shifts during the twenty-four hours. The aim is to spread the fixed costs of the firm over a greater output.

2. With reference to taxation it means the ability to pass on a tax to someone else. Some indirect taxes can be shifted from the seller to the buyer, but income tax cannot be shifted. *See* Incidence of Taxation.

Shilling. Originally used only as a unit of account, it was first issued as a silver coin in England by Henry VII in 1504, for a time being known as a Testoon. In the reign of Edward VI it became the first English coin to have its value marked on it. In 1947 silver was replaced by a cupronickel alloy. On the decimalisation of the currency it was replaced by a similar coin worth 5p (at least colloquially). It is possible that the term, *shilling*, may survive as the name of the new coin. The shilling, subdivided into 100 cents, is the standard unit of the currencies of Kenya, Uganda and Tanzania.

Shipbroker. An agent who arranges charter party contracts between shipowners and charterers. London shipbrokers are members of the Baltic Exchange.

Ship Canals. Canals capable of taking ocean-going ships, such as the Manchester Ship Canal (*q.v.*), the Suez Canal (*q.v.*), the Panama Canal (*q.v.*), Kiel Canal, Corinth Canal, and others.

Shipping. Ocean-going ships are mainly of two kinds: (i) tramp steamers which pick up cargo at any port and carry it where required, and (ii) cargo liners which ply over regular routes according to a pre-arranged time-table. Receipts from shipping are an important invisible item in the balance of payments, at one time giving Great Britain a considerable credit balance. In recent years Great Britain's net income from this source has greatly declined, partly on account of the increase in the number of ships under foreign flags and under 'flags of convenience', and partly because of the expansion of air transport for the carriage of both passengers and freight.

A considerable amount of Great Britain's internal trade is undertaken by ships which ply between the country's various ports. For example, coal is brought to London from the north-eastern ports and from South Wales to the South Coast by this means.

Shipping Advice Note. A document sent by an exporter to his shipping agent containing instructions for shipping the goods.

Shipping Conference. Agreements between shipping companies regarding fares and freight rates to reduce competition between them. Such agreements could only relate to liners.

Ship's Manifest. *See* Manifest.

Ship's Report. A document to be supplied by the Master of a ship on arrival at a British port. It gives particulars of the ship, crew, passengers (if any), and cargo.

Shop. 1. A retail outlet. *See* Retail Trade.
2. A workshop.

Shop Floor. A term used of the ordinary workers in a factory or workshop or of people who have had practical experience at this level.

Shopping Cheques. Also known as Trading Cheques, Vouchers or Club Cheques, they are issued by clothing clubs and similar organisations and can be 'spent' at a number of specified shops in the locality in which they are issued. Members generally repay the club in 20 or 21 weeks, usually paying £5·25 for each £5 cheque. The system provides an alternative to hire purchase.

Shopping Hinterland. The area from which a city which is an important shopping centre draws its customers. Improvements in means of transport and the development of mail-order business have helped to increase the extent of shopping hinterlands. The shopping hinterland of Manchester covers a wide area including most of South Lancashire, a large part of Cheshire, north Derbyshire, and the western part of the West Riding of Yorkshire, where it overlaps with the shopping hinterland of Leeds. Other cities with extensive shopping hinterlands include Birmingham, Bristol, Newcastle, and Edinburgh. With the development of mail-order business a shopping hinterland may include most of Great Britain.

Shops and Offices Act (1963). An Act aimed at improving working conditions for those employed in shops and offices, guaranteeing them a minimum amount of space and improved sanitary arrangements.

Shops (Early Closing) Act (1920–21). Under this Act a shop is not allowed to remain open until 9 p.m. except on one evening per week, and must close not later than 8 p.m. on other evenings.

Shop Steward. A representative of the trade union, elected by members, in a department or section of a firm. They have become more important in recent times with the increasing tendency for individual managements to make wage bargains with their workers, wage-bargaining at workshop or factory level tending to supplement national bargaining.

Short-end of the Market. That part of the market in gilt-edged securities dealing with short-dated stocks. *See* Stock Exchange.

Short Period. Alfred Marshall introduced the concept of the Long Period and Short Period into the study of changes of demand and changes of supply, the immediate effect of such changes in the short period being different from the ultimate effect in the long period. This is particularly the case where an increase in supply takes a considerable time to bring about. *See* Long Period and Short Period.

Shorts. Short-dated stocks, generally for periods of less than five years.

Short-term Capital Gains. The Finance Act of 1962 imposed a capital gains tax, at the standard rate of income tax, on capital gains on securities bought and sold within six months.

Short-term Rate of Interest. The rate of interest for loans for periods of up to three months. In general the short-term rate is lower than the long-term rate since the element of risk tends to increase the longer the period of the loan. However, if bank rate is very high the short-term rate may be higher than the long-term. The two rates of interest generally follow one another up and down, though not to the same extent, the short-term rate being liable to greater fluctuation. The short-term rate is regarded as the fundamental rate of interest, since it depends largely on liquidity-preference, the long-term rate being generally considered to be determined by it.

Short-time. Working fewer than the normal hours per week owing to a firm having insufficient work to keep its employees fully employed.

Shut-down Cost. An alternative term for Prime Cost (*q.v.*).

Sickness Benefit. One of the benefits under the British scheme of social security, it provides for payment to a person unable to follow his employment during sickness.

Sight Bill. A bill of exchange payable at sight. *See* Bill of Exchange.

Significance. A term used by Rev. P. Wicksteed as an alternative to Utility (*q.v.*).

Silver Certificate. A type of paper money still in circulation in the United States, each certificate representing a certain amount of silver.

Silver Market. *See* London Silver Market.

Simple Arbitrage. Also known as Direct Arbitrage, it refers to dealings in foreign exchange that are confined to one centre. *See* Arbitrage.

Simple Debenture. A term sometimes used of unsecured debentures to distinguish them from Mortgage Debentures (*q.v.*).

Simplon Express. The truncated service, formerly known as the Simplon Orient Express, now runs from Paris via the Simplon tunnel to Venice. It formerly ran as the Simplon Orient Express from Calais and Paris to Istanbul and Athens. Increased air traffic has reduced the demand for the long train journey.

Singer and Friedlander Ltd. A merchant bank with its head office in London and branches in Leeds, Birmingham, and Nottingham, it is a member of the C. T. Bowring Group. Its subsidiary, Singer and Friedlander Inc. is established in New York. It also has a branch in Zurich.

Single-tax System. At various times there have been suggestions that the State should raise its entire revenue from a single tax on income, since income taxes can be more equitably assessed on individuals than other taxes. To raise the enormous revenue required by modern governments such a tax would have to be extremely high and would therefore have a serious disincentive effect on the desire to work and as a result it would have an adverse effect on the size of the national income.

Single-use Goods. A term sometimes used of non-durable consumers' goods such as food and tobacco.

Sinking Fund. A fund established for the future redemption of a debt. It was formerly customary to build up a sinking fund by paying into it a certain sum each year from Government revenue for the eventual redemption of the National Debt. In the later years of the nineteenth century it was confidently expected that the National Debt would be completely redeemed early in the twentieth century. Two World Wars have scotched such ideas. On maturity a Government stock is nowadays usually repaid by issuing a new stock. On local authorities, however, the British Government imposes the condition that a debt incurred for some specific purpose must be repaid within a stated period of time.

Sit-down Strike. A strike in which the workers not only refuse to work but also refuse to leave the place where they are employed.

'Six' and 'Seven.' Originally the two free trade areas of Europe had six and seven members respectively—the European Common Market ('The Six') and the European Free Trade Association ('The Seven').

Sixpence. First issued as a silver coin in the reign of Edward VI. On the decimalisation of the currency it was retained for a time with a value of 2½p.

Skandinaviska Bank. The second largest of the 'Big Five' banks of Sweden.

Skinners' Company. One of the twelve more important companies of the Guilds or Livery Companies of the City of London with an existence that dates back to the medieval gilds. It ranks sixth and seventh in the order of civic precedence, the reason being that in the thirteenth century there were two companies. It has long since ceased to exercise its special rights with regard to the manufacture of furs, and like the other livery companies its activities are now restricted to charitable purposes.

Sleeping Partner. A member of a partnership who takes no active part in the management of the business, but is liable like the general partners for the debts of the firm. For example, a famous sportsman might lend his name to a sports outfitting business.

Sliding-scale. With reference to import duties a rate of tax that varies inversely with the price of the imported commodity. The Corn Laws, repealed in 1846, were of this type.

Slump. A period of high unemployment. During the 121 years from 1792 to 1913, during which the trade cycle was a pronounced characteristic of the economy, slumps and booms alternated with one another, the average interval between one slump and the next being about seven years, with a boom always sandwiched between them. These slumps were, therefore, of relatively short duration and also very much less severe than the Great Depression of 1929–35. Features of a slump are declining production, increasing unemployment and falling prices and wages. *See* Great Depression; Trade Cycle.

Small Firm, Survival of. Manufacturing has become increasingly a large-scale industry, but in retailing, though there is a tendency even here for large-scale operation to develop, large numbers of small firms still survive. There are several reasons for this: (i) Convenience of situation is important; (ii) The small retailer can give personal attention to his customers and cater for their particular tastes; (iii) He knows his customers personally and so, if he wishes, he can grant credit. In manufacturing the small firm is found: (i) Where the demand for the commodity is small; (ii) Where a large firm, in excess of the optimum size, puts out a process to a small firm. *See* Optimum Firm.

Smeed Report (1964). Recommended a system of charging motor vehicles for time spent in town centres and other traffic-congested areas.

Smithsonian Agreement (1971). The new rates of exchange agreed on the devaluation of the U.S. dollar in December 1971. The rate accepted for sterling was too high and had to be abandoned in June 1972. *See* Devaluation of U.S. Dollar.

'Snake in the Tunnel.' A term used of an exchange rate system for a group of countries (such as the E.E.C.) which maintain fixed rates with one another but permit these rates to fluctuate (or float) against other rates.

Social Accounting. A term sometimes used of that part of descriptive economics which relates to the production and distribution of the national income.

Social Capital. *See* Social Wealth.

Social Contract. An informal agreement made in 1974 between the Government and the T.U.C. to restrict wage increases for a period. *See* Prices and Incomes Policy.

Social Cost. The disadvantages suffered by the community from an enterprise, such as impurities from a chemical works, smoke from factory chimneys, or traffic congestion resulting from the excessive expansion of an urban area, etc. *See also* Social Net Product.

Social Credit. A scheme put forward in the early 1930s by Major Douglas, a Canadian engineer, based on the belief that in a modern economic system all costs incurred in production do not give rise to an equivalent amount of purchasing power, so that there is always a deficiency of purchasing power. Major Douglas proposed, therefore, that the State should make periodic monetary gifts to its people to remedy this deficiency, which he regarded as the cause of the Great Depression. The scheme is based on a fallacy, since all costs of production are received by some people and so do in fact become purchasing power. Keynes showed that underconsumption is due to insufficient investment.

Social Economics. That branch of applied economics which deals with problems such as population, unemployment, poverty, housing, national insurance.

Social Imbalance. A term used by Professor Galbraith to indicate the lack of balance between the output of privately produced goods and the supply of public services, the effect in the United States being 'private affluence amid public squalor'. *See* Affluent Society.

Social Insurance. *See* National Insurance.

Social Net Product. A term first used by Prof. Pigou, it comprises the net national income after a deduction has been made for any disservices arising in production, such as unhealthy conditions in industrial towns, wastes of imperfect competition (especially competitive advertising), possibly the manufacture and sale of intoxicants, and gambling activities.

Social Science Research Council. Set up on the recommendation of the Heyworth Committee, its first action was to establish a number of postgraduate studentships and fellowships in the social sciences.

Social Security. Provision by the State of assistance to people in need as a result of sickness, unemployment, or old age as suggested by Lord Beveridge. If such assistance is provided entirely out of taxation it can be regarded as a system of social security; if contributions towards the scheme are exacted from employers and employees it can be regarded as a system of national insurance. The British system of national insurance is a compromise between these two principles. *See* Beveridge Report.

Social Security, Department of. A Government department set up in 1966 to take over the functions of the Ministry of Pensions and National Insurance and the National Assistance Board. It has local offices in all large towns throughout the country. In 1968 it was amalgamated with the Ministry of Health to form the Department of Health and Social Security (*q.v.*).

Social Services. These can be defined as services which help people to lead fuller and more secure lives. Though some social services are provided by voluntary bodies, an increasing proportion of State expenditure during the past fifty years has been devoted to social services. These services include education, housing, health, national assistance, and the State's contribution to national insurance. *See* Health and Social Security, Department of.

Social Surveys. Inquiries into the standard of living, especially of the poorer sections of the community in certain towns, the first of these being that of Charles Booth—*The Life and Labour of the People of London*, carried out during 1891–1903. Seebohm Rowntree conducted a social survey of York in 1901, and social surveys have also been carried out for Merseyside, Sheffield, and the Potteries. *See also* Five Towns Surveys.

Social Wealth. Wealth which is owned collectively by the community as a whole. It includes all property owned by the State or local authorities—all public buildings, schools, libraries, and the assets of the nationalised industries.

Social Welfare. The extent to which social services are available to people. If their economic welfare is high because their real incomes are high they may make themselves responsible for their social welfare, but others may prefer to neglect their welfare and instead satisfy less necessary wants. So, even where economic welfare is high, some people believe it is necessary for the State to be responsible for social welfare in order to ensure that everyone has the benefit of it.

Société Financière. A bank consortium, established in 1967 with offices in Paris and Luxembourg. It comprises Barclays Bank, the Bank of America, Banque Nationale de Paris, Banca Nazionale di Lavoro and the Dresdner Bank.

Société Financière Franco-Britannique. A joint venture of the Banque Nationale de Paris and Kleinwort Benson Ltd., each taking a 50% share in the new undertaking. The head office is in Paris.

Société Générale. The second largest of the commercial banks of France, its full name being Société Générale pour favoriser le Développement du Commerce et de l'Industrie. It ranks tenth in the world.

Société Générale de Banque. The largest commercial bank in Belgium, it has over 600 branches. In 1965 it merged with the Société Belge de Banque and the Banque d'Anvers. It has an interest in the Banque Européenne de Crédit à Moyen Terme (*q.v.*).

Soft Currency. A currency in plentiful supply on the foreign exchange market as a result of the country concerned being inclined to import more than it exports.

Soil Conservation. A policy aimed at preventing further soil erosion. *See* Soil Erosion.

Soil Erosion. The loss of soil due to weathering in areas where natural grassland has been ploughed up in order to cultivate more profitable crops. As a result good stock-rearing districts of the United States have been turned into a great infertile dustbowl. Lack of concern for soil conservation increases the difficulty of expanding food supplies to meet the needs of an increasing world population. Governments now show more concern than formerly for soil conservation (*q.v.*).

Sol. The standard unit of the currency of Peru, it is divided into 100 centavos.

Sole Proprietor. Sometimes known as a 'one-man' business, it is a type of business unit where one person is solely responsible for providing the capital, for bearing the risk of the enterprise and for the management of the business. Among the advantages of this kind of business are: (i) The self-interest of the proprietor, which may make for greater efficiency; (ii) It is possible for the sole proprietor to keep in personal touch with all sides of the business; (iii) Decisions can be made and put into effect quickly. The disadvantages of this type of business include: (i) Too much depends on the ability of one man; (ii) Its capital is likely to be small and so expansion to the optimum size is not likely to be possible; (iii) The proprietor is personally liable for all the debts of the firm.

Sole Trader. An alternative term for Sole Proprietor (*q.v.*).

Solus. A method of retailing whereby selling points are permitted to sell the products of only one manufacturer or producer.

Somalo. The standard unit of the currency of Somalia, it is divided into 100 centesimi.

Sotheby's A London firm of auctioneers, dealing mainly in works of art. It has an affiliate in New York.

Sou. A pre-Revolutionary French coin, 20 sous being equal in value to one livre.

Source, Deducted at. Tax deducted from interest or dividends before their payment. This is the general practice in Great Britain for dividends and most Government stocks, but some Government stocks such as $3\frac{1}{2}\%$ War Stock and all stocks on the Post Office register are paid without deduction of tax. *See also* Withholding Tax.

South African Reserve Bank. The central bank of South Africa, its head office is at Pretoria.

Southern Railway. The smallest of the British railway groups formed under the Railways Act of 1921, it was an amalgamation of a number of previously independent railways, mainly the London & South Western, the London, Brighton & South Coast, and the South Eastern & Chatham Railways.

South Sea Bubble. Following the granting of special privileges to the South Sea Company, in return for which it agreed to take over the National Debt, high profits to the company were expected and a wave of extraordinary speculation followed. Many new companies were formed, some of which were openly fraudulent, and yet large numbers of people rushed to invest in them only to lose their money when soon afterwards the bubble burst.

Sovereign. An English gold coin worth £1 first issued by Henry VII in 1489. The existence of the ryal, worth £0·50 made the issue of half sovereigns unnecessary until 1544. Double sovereigns were also minted, and in the reign of Edward VI a triple sovereign was struck. In the seventeenth century the guinea replaced the sovereign. When cash payments were resumed after the Napoleonic Wars the sovereign was preferred to the guinea. Five pound and two pound pieces and half sovereigns were also minted. The sovereign ceased to circulate in Great Britain in 1915, but 'new' sovereigns were minted in 1968 and 1974. It is still used in some parts of the Middle East.

'Sovereignty of the Consumer.' If the price mechanism is allowed free play, the demand of consumers determines what shall be produced. If consumers' demand for a commodity declines, its price will fall and less of it will be produced; if consumers' demand for a commodity increases, its price will rise and producers will expand supply. Thus, the consumer is sovereign in the sense that he determines what shall be produced. Even a monopolist is subject to the sovereignty of the consumer since he can decide either how much to produce or the price of his product, but not both, since one or the other of these things depends on the demand curve.

S.p.a. Abbreviation of Societa per Azione, the Italian equivalent of Ltd. Co.

Special Areas. Areas of high unemployment named by the Acts of 1934 and 1937. *See* Location of Industry.

Special Buyer. The Bank of England's agent in the discount market.

Special Commissioners of Income Tax. A body concerned with matters associated with income tax, such as appeals against assessments, etc.

Special Contribution. A 'once for all' levy imposed by the Government on British industry in 1948. It was a sort of capital levy (*q.v.*).

Special Crossing. A precautionary measure to make a cheque safer as, for example, the following:

Southern Bank Ltd.
City Road, Guildford

A cheque so crossed can be paid only into the bank and branch named in the crossing. *See also* General Crossing.

Special Deposits. A device for assisting monetary policy introduced in 1960. In order to check an expansion of credit the Bank of England can call for Special Deposits from the commercial banks (a specified fraction of their total deposits—1% in 1960) in order to reduce their liquidity. Unlike ordinary Bankers' Deposits at the Bank of England Special Deposits are 'frozen' until released by the monetary authorities. As an instrument of monetary policy Special Deposits are to be preferred to the Treasury Directive which they replaced. Special Deposits are released when it is desired to encourage an expansion of bank credit, as occurred during 1962–63.

Special Drawing Rights (S.D.R.s). A device for increasing international liquidity, S.D.R.s are issued by the International Monetary Fund. They are not regarded in any way as borrowings from the Fund, but instead they supplement convertible currencies and so form part of each member's reserves. The I.M.F. makes annual distributions of S.D.R.s to its members in proportion to their quotas. S.D.R.s thus form a permanent addition to members' reserves whereas ordinary drawings do not. Since 1974 S.D.R.s have been based on the value of fixed amounts of sixteen currencies, weighted approximately according to their international importance. *See* International Monetary Fund.

Special Investment Department. A term used of deposits in Savings Banks (including the National Savings Bank since 1966) subject to one month's notice of withdrawal and in consequence carrying a higher rate of interest than deposits in the ordinary Department. Total combined deposits of an investor in the Special Investment Department and in Term Deposits (*q.v.*) must not exceed £3,000, but this is additional to the £5,000 he is permitted to have in the Ordinary Department. Before an account can be opened in the Special Investment Department an investor must have at least £50 in his Ordinary account.

Specialised Industries. A term sometimes used of industries operated by the State. *See* State Enterprise.

Specialist Broker. The equivalent on the New York stockmarket of the jobber on the London stock exchange.

Specie. Coin or bullion.

Specie Points. Also known as Gold Points, these are the extreme points of variation of the rate of exchange between two currencies on the gold standard. If the rate of exchange rises above the mint par of exchange together with the cost of transport and insurance it becomes cheaper to import gold; if the rate falls below the mint par of exchange less the cost of transport and insurance it becomes cheaper to export gold.

Specific Factors of Production. Factors suitable for highly specialised work, to which it would not be possible to apply other factors. The more specific the varieties of a factor the more difficult it is to substitute one for another and the more difficult it is to increase the supply of one of them, particularly in the short period. Examples of highly specific labour are all occupations for which a long period of training or special qualifications are required. Much capital is highly specific and so can be used only for the purpose for which it was originally intended. It is less easy to quote examples of specific land, since most land is open to alternative use, but the most important feature of land is its situation and sites are often highly specific.

Specificity, Degree of. The extent to which a factor of production is specific. The more specific a factor the more difficult it is to put it to some use other than that for which it was originally intended.

Specific Taxes. Taxes levied on a commodity according to the quantity purchased as, for example, the tax on petrol, as distinct from *ad valorem* taxes which are proportionate to the price of the commodity.

Speculative Motive. The most important of the three motives enunciated by Lord Keynes as influencing

Speedpost. An express postal delivery service, for which an additional fee is payable. It was introduced experimentally in 1975 between London and Brighton.

Speenhamland System. The supplementing of wages of agricultural workers by grants under the Poor Law of 1782, the wages of most of these workers being below 'subsistence level'. It was so called because these payments were first made at Speenhamland in Berkshire in 1795.

Spens Report. Three reports published in 1946-48 relating to the remuneration of doctors and dentists.

Spiral of Wages and Prices. *See* Inflationary Spiral.

Splitting. 1. With reference to shares in companies or units of unit investment trusts it means dividing the shares or units into units of smaller denomination in order to increase their marketability. If the £1 shares of a company stand at £3·60 on the stock exchange they would be less marketable than shares of a nominal value of £0·25 standing at £0·90. If the shares were split into four, both the total nominal value of the shares and their total market value would be unchanged. Small investors prefer small units and splitting occurs of investment trust units whenever the units have appreciated considerably in value. Thus, if units originally issued at £0·25 each appreciated to £0·80 the managers of the trust might split them into units of £0·40, each investor then having double the number of units, but their total value would be unchanged.

2. With reference to an issue of bonus shares or a 'rights' issue, splitting occurs if the shareholder decides to divide the offer with another person.

Spot Price. The price of a commodity for immediate delivery as distinct from its forward price for delivery at some date in the future.

Spread. With reference to an investment portfolio it means having one's investments in as wide a range of stocks and shares as possible. For the small investor the unit investment trust offers a spread of investment, often over more than a hundred different securities.

Squalor. 1. One of the four 'giant evils' listed by Lord Beveridge—the others being Want, Disease, and Ignorance—which he considered it should be the aim of social policy to eradicate.

2. A term used by J. K. Galbraith of public services ('public squalor'), more especially in the United States, in contrast to private affluence. *See* Affluent Society.

'Square Deal.' The slogan under which the four railways of Great Britain campaigned in 1938 for greater freedom in fixing their charges in competition with road haulage operators. A Transport Advisory Council recommended that most of these restrictions on railway charges should be removed.

'Square Mile,' The. A term sometimes used to denote the City (*q.v.*).

Squeeze. *See* Credit Squeeze.

S.R. Abbreviation of Southern Railway (*q.v.*). or Southern Region (of British Rail) (*q.v.*).

Staff Relationship. A management relationship. A staff relationship is said to exist between a personnel officer and the executives with whom he works.

Stag. A speculator who buys a large amount of a new issue of shares or stock if he thinks the price likely to rise above the offer price when dealings in it begin on the stock exchange, so that he hopes to be able to sell soon at a profit.

'Stagnation Thesis.' The belief that in advanced economies saving might be so great as to make the maintenance of full employment difficult. Few people now hold this view.

Stale Cheque. As defined by the Bills of Exchange Act (1882) a cheque is 'stale' if its date shows it to have been in circulation for 'an unreasonable time', the exact period of time never having been legally defined. Most banks regard as 'stale' cheques presented six months after date, such cheques being required to be confirmed by the drawer, though some banks take no action unless a cheque has been drawn twelve months.

Stallage. A charge for the use of a stall in an open-air market.

Stamp Duties. The stamping of certain documents as a source of revenue in Great Britain dates back to the seventeenth century. The range of these duties has been considerably reduced in recent years.

Stamped Money. A proposal of Silvio Gesell that, since there were no carrying costs (*q.v.*) for holding money whereas there was such a charge on the holder of stocks, money to retain its value should be stamped each month, stamps to be purchased at post offices.

Standard & Poor's Indices. An American Index Number of the prices of stock exchange securities. *See* Stock Exchange Indices.

Standard Bank. A British bank in which the Midland and the National Westminster Banks have an interest and which operates mainly in Africa. It controls the Standard Bank of South Africa and the Bank of West Africa. It also has an interest in the Midland and International Bank Ltd. and in the Irano-British Bank. In 1969 it amalgamated with the Chartered Bank to form the Standard Chartered Bank.

Standard Chartered Bank. One of the leading British overseas banks, it has over 1,400 branches. It was formed by the amalgamation of the Chartered Bank and the Standard Bank (*q.v.*).

Standard Coin. 1. The unit of a currency to which the value of other units is related. (For a list of monetary units *see* Units, Monetary.) Thus the franc is the standard unit of the Swiss currency and the centime has a value of one-hundredth of a franc.

2. A coin which is worth as metal its full face value.

Standardisation. If a commodity is to be produced on a large scale by mass production methods, to secure the greatest economies of scale it will have to be standardised, since the extent to which variety is required is a limiting factor on the scale of production. Variety of pattern is an important factor to be taken into account in the production of worsted cloth and so this industry comprises mainly small firms. In the motor car industry, although there is some differentiation of models, standardisation has been carried to great lengths in order to secure economies of scale, so this tends to be a large-scale industry. Standardisation is possible only if buyers are prepared to accept some restriction of choice. During the Second World War the British Government encouraged the production of standardised lines (known as 'utility') in order to simplify production.

Standard of Deferred Payments. One of the functions of money. Since money unlike many commodities can be stored it can be accumulated for making payments at some future time, though the longer the period of deferment the more likely will be the possibility that the value of money may fall.

Standard of Living. With reference to a person, family, or a body of people, it means the extent to which they can satisfy their wants. Thus if they can afford only the minimum amount of food, clothing, and shelter their standard of living is very low. If, on the other hand, they are able to enjoy a great variety of food, a good supply of good clothing, and live in a well-furnished house and in addition are able to satisfy a wide variety of other wants, then clearly such people are enjoying a high standard of living.

In the first place, the standard of living of a people depends on the size of the national income, and secondly on the manner of distribution of the national income. People in underdeveloped regions of the world are poor because the national income as an average per head is low; wide differences in the standard of living of people in the same country are the result of very unequal distribution of the national income. The higher standard of living of the more advanced economies is due to these countries having large stocks of up-to-date capital and well-trained labour, and the willingness of the people themselves to work for a higher standard of living. At the present day there is also less inequality of income in the more economically advanced countries than in many of the under-developed parts of the world. A great deal is being done to raise the standard of living in the less economically developed countries, since the accumulation of capital proceeds more rapidly the more a country has of it and this, therefore, otherwise tends to widen the gap between the developed and the under-developed nations.

Standard of Value. One of the functions of money is that it serves as a measure or standard of value or unit of account. Unlike other measures or standards, the value of money is itself liable to vary. Furthermore, it is accepted by economists that value cannot be measured Nevertheless, people take money-prices as approximate indications of the relative values of commodities. For making calculations as, for example, the total volume of production, or for comparing the relative cost of different methods of production, money is a useful unit of account.

Standard Rate. *See* Basic Rate.

Stand-by Agreement. An arrangement made by the I.M.F. whereby a member country can negotiate immediate drawing rights in advance of need.

Staple. Medieval export markets for the main products of a country. Staple towns included London, York, Calais, Bruges.

State Banks. American banks established under State (as distinct from Federal) laws. Not all state banks are members of the Federal Reserve System. The national banks, registered under Federal law, are all members of the Federal Reserve System.

State Enterprise. The operation of commercial or industrial undertakings by the State. For a long time the Post Office was the only commercial activity in Great Britain undertaken by the State, though there was considerable expansion of municipal enterprise during the first half of the twentieth century. State ownership of industrial undertakings in Great Britain really dates from 1946-50 during which period the coal mines, electricity, and gas undertakings and transport were nationalised.

State Lottery. A means by which the State raises revenue in some countries including France and Spain. State lotteries were run periodically in England between 1567 and 1826, when lotteries were made illegal. Since 1934 money has been raised for hospitals in the Irish Republic by the Irish Hospitals Sweepstake. An Act of 1954 regulated lotteries in Great Britain, only permitting those that are non-profit making and offer prizes of limited value. Premium Savings Bonds (*q.v.*), first issued in 1956, are not exactly like a lottery since, unlike lottery tickets which once bought cannot be redeemed, Premium Bonds can be redeemed whenever the holder wishes.

Statement. 1. A document sent out by a trader to customers who have monthly accounts with him, it summarises briefly all transactions, debit and credits for the previous month, showing the amount (if any) due for payment. The Statement will be despatched as soon as possible after the end of the month to which it applies, and a discount may be allowed if payment is made before a specified date.

2. The Bank Statement has replaced the pass book for current accounts. It lists all amounts withdrawn and all deposits and shows the balance, credit or debit, up to date.

State Planning. The planning of

production by the State. In a communist State the whole or the greater part of production is State-planned. Some degree of State planning is now regarded as essential even under a system of free enterprise. The N.E.D.C. (*q.v.*) was set up in Great Britain in 1962 to undertake some planning of production by the State. *See* Planned Economy.

Static Economics. The theoretical study of an economic situation in static or unchanging conditions, as distinct from dynamic economics which takes account of changes.

Stationary State. An alternative term for Static State. *See* Static Economics.

Statist, The. A journal (now defunct) which for a long time had compiled and published an index of wholesale prices.

Statistical Office, Central. *See* Central Statistical Office.

Statistician, The. The quarterly journal of the Institute of Statisticians.

Status Inquiry Agency. A business which will supply information to traders—especially wholesalers—regarding the credit-worthiness of firms with which they have not previously had dealings.

Statute of Limitation. This lays down the period of time within which action must be taken as, for example, for the recovery of a debt, the period in this case being six years after which the debt is said to be 'statute barred'. It is not necessary therefore, to keep receipts beyond this period of time.

Statutory Books. The books which under the Companies Act a limited company must keep include a Minute Book, a Register of Directors, and a Register of Members (shareholders).

Statutory Company. A company established by a specific Act of Parliament as was the case in Great Britain with the former railway companies.

Sterilisation of Gold. One of the rules of the gold standard was that an inflow of gold should lead to an expansion of the monetary supply, as a result of which prices were likely to rise. During the period of the restored gold standard (1925–31 for Great Britain) some countries, including the United States, did not keep to the rules. For example, gold flowing in was prevented from affecting the supply of money and prices, this process being known as 'sterilising gold'.

Sterling. The name given to British currency, and generally used of the pound sterling to distinguish it from the pound of some other currencies. It is thought to be derived from *sterling*, a coin with a star, the penny in the eleventh century bearing this design, and being known as a sterling. *See* Pound.

Sterling Area (or **Bloc**). This comprises those countries that linked their currencies to sterling. The history of the sterling area falls into three distinct periods:

1. *Before 1914.* It had its origin in the nineteenth century when the British Empire comprised a large number of territories economically dependent on Great Britain, which served as the monetary and banking centre for them and to which country they looked for capital for their development. Most of the banks in these territories had their head offices in London. Another factor making for the dominance of London was that Great Britain at that time was the most important country on the gold standard.

2. *Between the two World Wars.* After the First World War sterling ceased to be an international currency but the sterling area in a new form was revived after Great Britain left the gold standard in 1931, an increasing number of countries finding that to have their currencies linked to sterling gave them greater stability than was enjoyed by the countries which stayed on gold. During this period the sterling area not only included the Commonwealth (except Canada) and many European countries but also Argentina, Japan, and many others.

3. *Since 1945*. During the Second World War the sterling area shrank again, but after 1945 it expanded to include those countries, inside and outside the Commonwealth, which were prepared to pool their resources of U.S. dollars in the days when the U.S. dollar was a 'hard' currency, Great Britain acting as banker to the area.

The sterling area is a voluntary association with no constitution, and it was not legally defined until 1940. For purposes of exchange control the members came to be known as the 'scheduled territories'. Since 1947 meetings of Commonwealth finance ministers have been held periodically to discuss monetary matters, especially the protection of the area's reserves of gold and convertible currencies, and there is now a Sterling Area Liaison Committee. There has too been increased co-operation between the Bank of England and the central banks of member countries, but Great Britain's role is little more than that of leader and adviser to the area. Neither Canada nor strictly the Republic of South Africa is a member of the sterling area today.

During the 1960s the ties binding the members of the Sterling Area began to weaken. Recurrent sterling crises culminating in the devaluation of sterling in 1967 contributed to this. Many members began to diversify their reserves instead of maintaining them entirely in sterling, a movement that was still further encouraged by the losses many of them suffered when sterling was devalued. It was noteworthy too that when Great Britain devalued its currency in 1967 only a few other members of the sterling area did likewise. In 1968 Great Britain found it necessary to obtain a stand-by credit from the Group of Ten (*q.v.*) in case of heavy withdrawals of sterling balances. At the same time an exchange guarantee was given to overseas members of the sterling area to check serious withdrawals.

The decline in the importance of the sterling area, begun in the 1960s, continued in the 1970s. Entry to the E.E.C. reorientated Great Britain's economic outlook, and this country agreed in principle to an 'orderly rundown' in the sterling balances. The effect of this change of outlook may not seriously affect the position of sterling for some time though it may eventually do so. The most serious setback to the sterling area occurred in 1972 when it was decided to allow the pound 'to float', especially since this was accompanied by a decision to apply most exchange control restrictions to the overseas sterling area, with the exception of the Republic of Ireland, the Isle of Man, the Channel Islands, and Gibraltar. In effect this meant that the sterling area ceased to be a formal entity, as it was before 1945.

The future of both sterling and the sterling area is uncertain. The sterling area survived many changes in the past arising from the two World Wars and a world trade depression, and it may survive again, for sterling still retains some of its functions as an international currency. It seems fairly clear, however, that it is likely to play a much reduced role in the future. *See also* Sterling Balances.

Sterling Balances. 1. During the Second World War Great Britain was unable to export its products and so purchases from abroad (except from the United States with which country the 'lease-lend' system operated) had to be obtained on credit, the exporting country being credited in a Blocked Sterling Balance. *See* Blocked Accounts.

2. The countries that are members of the sterling area keep sterling balances in London. These are required to assist the making of payments arising out of international trade, and also for the working of the monetary arrangements of the sterling area. During the 1960s many members of the sterling area began to diversify their reserves by holding

other currencies in addition to sterling, such as U.S. dollars. The heavy losses to their reserves suffered by many of these countries on the devaluation of sterling in 1967 encouraged this tendency. Fear of possible further conversions of sterling balances led to the Basle agreements by which Great Britain's sterling liabilities were backed by a substantial credit. Sterling Area holders were given a dollar guarantee in return for their undertaking to hold a minimum proportion of their reserves in sterling. The devaluation of the U.S. dollar in 1971 upset this arrangement. On account of the effect on the British balance of payments of withdrawals of sterling balances, arrangements were made in 1976 and 1977 with the Bank of International Settlements and the Group of Ten central banks to protect Great Britain from the effect of such withdrawals.

Sterling Bloc. *See* Sterling Area.

Sterling Certificates of Deposit. A certificate which states that a specified sum has been deposited at the London office of the bank named on it and will be repaid at a certain date. If cash should be required before the certificate's maturity date it can be sold on the London discount market. Dollar certificates of deposit were first issued in London in 1966 by the London office of the First National City Bank of New York. By 1968 British banks had adopted this practice.

Sterling, Convertibility of. *See* Convertibility of Sterling.

Sterling Crises. Balance of payments crises caused by or aggravated by heavy withdrawals of short-term investments from London.

Sterling, Devaluation of. *See* Devaluation of Sterling.

Stg. Abbreviation of Sterling.

Stock Book. *See* Stock Control.

Stock Control. It is important for a business, such as that of a wholesaler or retailer, to stock the goods it sells in sufficient quantities to meet the demand for them without either running short of supplies or carrying more stock than its turnover warrants. A stock book will be kept in which amounts of new stock and goods sold are recorded, so that the amount in stock at any time can easily be ascertained.

Stock Exchange. A highly organised market for dealings in stocks and shares. Only members are admitted and business is transacted according to a prescribed set of rules. An investor who wishes to buy or sell securities must act through a broker. In addition to brokers there are also jobbers, each jobber dealing in a particular group of securities, such as 'gilt-edged', mining shares, industrials, etc. The broker, having received instructions from his client, approaches a jobber and asks his price. The jobber, without knowing whether the broker wishes to buy or sell, quotes two prices—his buying price and his selling price—the difference being the jobber's turn. The existence of stock exchanges means that it is generally possible to buy or sell securities at any time at the market price.

The first stock exchange in Great Britain was opened in London in 1773. Later a number of provincial stock exchanges were established in the more important commercial centres. In March 1973 the seven British stock exchanges and the Irish stock exchange in Dublin were amalgamated to form a unified stock exchange with a single set of rules, with branches or 'floors' in the old centres. Before 1973 only London brokers could deal direct with jobbers but since that date brokers on any of the eight 'floors' have been able to deal directly with the London jobbers. Security prices throughout the country tend to be approximately the same on any particular day. The London 'floor' with over 3,000 members is second only to New York in its volume of business.

Stock Exchange Gazette. A weekly paper devoted to stock exchange investment. It is not, however, the official organ of the Stock Exchange.

Stock Exchange Indices. Index numbers calculated for a number of share prices to show the movements of such prices. The best known of these indices include the *Financial Times* Industrial Ordinary Share Index, the *F.T.*-Actuaries Index, which takes account of the prices of 500 shares with April 1962 as its base, compiled by *The Financial Times* in association with the Institute of Actuaries of London and the Faculty of Actuaries of Edinburgh, the *Economist*-Extel Indicator (*q.v.*), calculated twice daily and supplied in Extel news service and published weekly in *The Economist*, and in the United States Standard & Poor's Indices (1941–43 = 100) based on 425 industrial shares, 50 utilities, and Government Bonds, and the Dow Jones Industrial Index.

Stock-in-trade. The type of goods applicable to a particular branch of trade.

Stockjobber. An alternative term for a jobber (*q.v.*) on the London Stock Exchange.

Stockpiling. The accumulation of stocks of strategic raw materials and feedstuffs on the expectation of war in the near future.

Stocks. One of the two main types of security dealt in on the stock exchange, the other being shares (*q.v.*). Stocks are usually quoted per £100 nominal value, but fractions may be bought or sold, whereas shares are not divisible. There are Government stocks, Corporation stocks, Debentures, etc.

Stocks, Fluctuations in. It has been suggested that a contributory cause of the trade cycle is the variation in the level of stocks held by merchants. When prices are falling they allow their stocks to run down by placing smaller orders with their suppliers, thereby checking production. When prices are rising they try to build up their stocks by placing larger orders with their suppliers and as a result production is stimulated. Fluctuations in stocks are sometimes related to the prevailing rate of interest, stocks being built up when interest rates are low and the cost of holding is, therefore, low. Stocks are run down when interest rates are high as this makes it more costly to hold stocks.

Stocktaking. A valuation of stock held by a firm, undertaken either once or twice each year, the information being required for the compilation of the Trading Account and the Balance Sheet. It is usual to value stock at cost price or market price whichever is the lower. *See* Inventory.

Stockton and Darlington Railway. The first important railway to be opened (1825) to provide transport for goods and passengers between towns. It became part of the North Eastern Railway and later of the London & North Eastern Railway, and it is now within the Eastern Region of British Railways.

Stock Transfer Act (1963). In order to speed up transfers of stocks and shares this Act made it no longer necessary for the seller's signature to the transfer to be witnessed and the buyer is not required to sign at all.

Stockturn. An alternative term for Turnover (*q.v.*).

Stock Watering. Overcapitalisation due to the issue of stock or shares to a greater value than the actual value of the assets.

'Stop-Go.' A term used of the alternating policies of credit expansion and contraction adopted during the 1950s and early 1960s. It arose from a desire to curb inflation and yet maintain full employment. As soon, therefore, as a disinflationary policy brought about an increase in unemployment the policy was reversed in order to restore full employment. The difficulty is to know exactly how much stimulus to give to the economy in order to maintain full employment exactly, neither more nor less.

Store of Value. One of the functions of money. In a monetary economy it is possible to defer one's satisfaction of a want to some time in the future or make provision for one's wants at a future date. During a period when the value of money is fairly stable money can be said to possess this quality, although stability in the value of money does not necessarily ensure that supplies of a particular thing will be available at the required time. Since 1913 there has been so severe a decline in the value of money that it can no longer be said that money provides a very satisfactory store of value. In Great Britain, for example, the purchasing power of money in 1973 was only 60% of what it had been in 1963 and only one-quarter of its value in 1939.

Stotinki. A sub-unit of the currency of Bulgaria, 100 stotinki being equal in value to one lev.

Strike. The combined voluntary withdrawal of their labour by employees. The strike has become the recognised 'weapon of last resort' of trade unions when negotiations with employers have broken down. Trade unions accumulate funds out of which they pay members when on strike. If the employees of a particular firm go on strike without the support of their trade union it is known as an 'unofficial' strike. When a trade union which is not concerned in a dispute calls a strike in support of another union whose members are on strike it is known as a 'sympathetic' strike. *See also* General Strike.

Structural Unemployment. At any time some industries are expanding while others are declining. If labour was perfectly mobile it would be possible to transfer redundant workers from declining to expanding industries. Since, however, labour is not perfectly mobile in either the occupational or geographical sense some unemployment results. This is described as structural unemployment because it is the result of a change in the structure of industry.

Subscribed Capital. An alternative term for Issued Capital (*q.v.*).

Subscription Shares. A form of investment popular with building societies. Investors are permitted to purchase shares by instalments on giving an undertaking to subscribe a fixed sum regularly. Building societies pay their highest rate of interest on these shares.

Subsidiary Company. A company controlled by another, the controlling company owning over 50% (sometimes 100%) of the ordinary shares of the subsidiary company.

Subsidies. A payment by the State to producers or distributors in order to reduce prices: (i) The oldest subsidies are those on exports in order to encourage their sale abroad. Subsidies to exports can be provided indirectly by deliberately running railways and other means of transport at a loss between the manufacturing centres and the ports. Subsidies, like tariffs, interfere with the free working of the Principle of Comparative Cost and so are not to the benefit of the world as a whole. (ii) Subsidies were paid during the Second World War on foodstuffs and some articles of clothing in an attempt to keep down the cost of living and so check demands for higher wages. (iii) Farm subsidies have been retained in order to encourage an expansion of the output of farm products. There are subsidies on animal feeding stuffs, a reduced tax on fuel oil and guaranteed prices. *See* Agriculture Act (1947).

Subsistence. A standard of living yielding no more than the bare necessaries of life, that is, the lowest standard compatible with existence.

Subsistence Theory of Wages. Also known as the 'Iron Law' of wages, it is the theory that wages cannot permanently rise above subsistence level. If wages temporarily rise above this level an increase in population, it is said, will inevitably follow, this increase in the supply of labour leading to a fall in wages. If, on the other hand, wages fall below subsistence fewer children will be born and malnutrition will bring about a rise in the death-rate, the reduction in the supply of labour then raising wages again to subsistence level. The theory is not accepted today, but it probably contained some element of truth in France in the eighteenth century when it was first put forward.

Substitutes. Non-members who work at Lloyd's of London.

Substitution. 1. With reference to Factors of Production, it is often possible up to a point to substitute a little of one factor for another as, for example, more capital can be employed and less labour, or more capital and less land, or more labour and less land. An entrepreneur, therefore, has some degree of choice as to the proportions in which he will employ factors of production, though one factor, however, can never be entirely substituted for another. Indeed, it is often easier to substitute a little of one factor for a little of another than it is to substitute one unit of a factor for another unit of the same factor.

2. With reference to Commodities. *See* Competitive Demand; Substitution, Marginal Rate of.

Substitution Effect. Price changes have two effects: (i) a substitution effect and (ii) an income effect. A rise in the price of one commodity may result in a decrease in the quantity demanded of it because another commodity is to some extent a substitute for it. This is the substitution effect. A rise in price is similar to a fall in income and so there will also be an income effect.

Substitution, Marginal Rate of. The rate at which over a range of prices a consumer substitutes one commodity for another. This concept is the basis of Indifference Curves and it is an attempt to explain Demand. *See* Substitution Effect.

Sub-underwriters. After an issuing house has agreed to underwrite the whole of a new issue of shares it may arrange for sub-underwriters to relieve it of an agreed fraction of its liability.

Succession Duties. Taxes on inheritance which vary inversely with nearness of relationship to the deceased.

Sucre. The stand unit of the currency of Ecuador, it is divided into 100 centavos.

Suez Canal. Built by a French company, it was opened in 1869 to link the Mediterranean and Red Seas and provide a shorter route from Europe to India and the Far East. It is 100 miles in length. In 1875 Disraeli purchased a controlling interest in the canal on behalf of the British Government. In 1956 it was nationalised and taken over by the Egyptian Government. It was closed between 1973 and 1976 as a result of the Arab–Israeli war.

Sugar Board. A body set up by the Government in 1956, it purchases sugar under the Commonwealth Sugar Agreement (*q.v.*) at agreed prices and then re-sells it to the trade at market prices.

Sugar Corporation. A State body responsible for production of sugar in Great Britain.

Sun Insurance Co. Ltd. Founded in 1710 it is the oldest British insurance company still in operation.

'Sun Spot Theory.' Arthur Jevons suggested that the cause of the trade cycle was to be found in harvest fluctuations induced by sun spots. There is no doubt that as a result of vagaries of the weather harvests fluctuate from one year to another, but no one today would attempt to explain the trade cycle entirely in terms of real causes. *See* Trade Cycle.

Superannuation Payment. A deduction from wages or salary towards a contributory pension scheme.

Supermarket. A large self-service shop selling a great variety of goods. Many shops of this kind are operated by multiple shop organisations and co-operative societies. The Supermarkets Association defines a supermarket as a shop with not less than 2,000 square feet of floor space.

Supertax. The original name of Surtax (*q.v.*) when first introduced.

Supplementary Costs. The costs of production of a firm can be classified as fixed and variable costs, the fixed costs being those which do not vary directly with output. Costs of administration are regarded as a fixed cost in the short period, but not in the long run. A further classification of costs is into prime costs, comprising the variable costs together with the administrative costs, and supplementary costs which, therefore, comprise the rest of the fixed costs.

Supplementary Pension. An addition to the Retirement Pension (q.v.) awarded to people in financial difficulties.

Supply. The second of the two forces—the other being demand—which influence the market price of a commodity or service. By supply is meant the amount that will come on to the market over a range of prices. The higher the price prevailing in the market the greater the quantity of a commodity that will be supplied. Thus, the supply curve (q.v.) generally slopes upwards from left to right. Only very rarely will it slope in the opposite direction and even then only for a very small part of its total length, such an exceptional supply curve being known as a regressive supply curve (q.v.). On the other hand, there are some commodities that are fixed in supply, so that whatever the price in the market no more can be offered for sale, the supply in this case being a vertical straight line at right angles to the base line. In the short run many things are in fixed supply, indeed all things where it takes time to increase supply. The amount of a commodity that will be supplied at a price depends on its cost of production, or, more precisely, its marginal cost. Thus, if the market price is low only those firms with low costs of production will continue to produce, but when the market price is high firms with higher costs will come into production. The higher price will also encourage low-cost firms to expand their output.

Supply and Demand, Laws of. (i) The lower the price of a commodity the greater will be the quantity demanded; (ii) The higher the price the greater will be the quantity supplied; (iii) At the equilibrium price the quantity demanded will be equal to the quantity supplied; (iv) An increase in demand will increase the price and the quantity supplied; (v) An increase in supply will reduce price but increase the quantity supplied.

Supply, Changes of. *See* Changes in Supply.

Supply Curve. A curve on a diagram showing the amounts of a commodity that will be supplied at each of a range of prices:

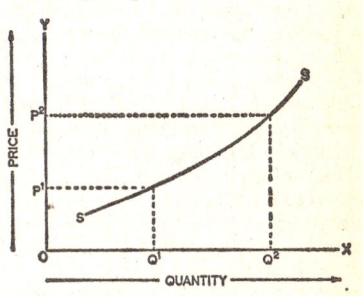

This curve shows that at the price OP^1 the quantity OQ^1 will be supplied and that at the higher price OP^2 the larger quantity OQ^2 will be supplied, thus illustrating the Second Law of Supply and Demand which states that the higher the price the greater the quantity which will be supplied. *See also* Regressive Supply Curve.

Supply, Elasticity of. *See* Elasticity of Supply.

Supply Price. The price at which a particular quantity of a commodity will be supplied.

Supply Schedule. A table showing the quantity of a commodity that will be supplied over a range of prices. The supply schedule for a commodity might be as follows:

Price per box	Quantity offered for sale per month (no. of boxes)
£15	500,000
£14	440,000
£13	390,000
£12	350,000
£11	310,000
£10	280,000
£9	250,000

The supply schedule provides the basis for the supply curve for a commodity.

Suppressed Inflation. In a time of inflation when demand is restricted by physical controls—rationing, licensing, price control—this merely suppresses inflation without getting rid of it, and by making the amount of purchasing power greater for goods and services not controlled pushes up their prices more than would otherwise have been the case. *See* Inflation.

Surcharge. An extra charge as, for example, (i) on investment income or (ii) on a postal packet on which insufficient postage has been paid. *See also* Import Surcharge.

Surety. A guarantor.

Surplus. 1. A surplus occurs in the market if the price is above the equilibrium price.

2. Rent is an unearned surplus accruing to a factor of production the supply of which is fixed (at least in the short period) when there is an increase in the demand for the services of that factor.

3. Monopoly profit is a surplus very much in the nature of a rent.

4. Profit is a surplus accruing to the entrepreneur after all other expenses of production have been met.

Surplus Capacity. An alternative term for Excess Capacity (*q.v.*).

Surplus Value. *See* Consumer's Surplus.

Surrender Value. The amount in cash an assurance company will repay to the holder of an endowment life assurance policy if he wishes to discontinue it at a date prior to that on which it is due to mature. The amount of the Surrender Value will depend on how much has already been paid in premiums and the length of time the policy still has to run.

Surtax. Known as supertax when first introduced in 1909, its name was changed in 1927. It was an additional steeply progressive income tax payable on higher incomes. Since 1973 it has been combined with income tax in a unified tax on personal incomes.

Suspense Account. A bookkeeping term for a ledger account to which entries may be posted temporarily.

Svenska Handelsbank. The largest commercial bank of Sweden.

Sveriges Riksbank. Founded in 1668, that is 26 years before the establishment of the Bank of England, it is now the central bank of Sweden. Unlike the other old-established central banks it has always been a State institution. Its head office is in Stockholm and it has branches in each of the 23 provincial capitals.

'Swap' Facilities. A service provided in recent years by the Bank for International Settlements (*q.v.*) at Basle for the central banks that are associated with it. When a central bank seeks the aid of other central banks the B.I.S. acts as intermediary. The 'swap' may be for gold, securities, dollars, or some other currency. In the first place the transfer is for three months.

Sweated Labour. Low paid workers who generally also have to work very long hours. A Report of a Committee of the House of Lords (1889) drew attention to this practice.

Swedish State Bank. *See* Sveriges Riksbank.

Swissair. The Swiss national airline.

Swiss Bank Corporation. *See* Schweizerische Bankverein.

Swiss Credit Bank. *See* Schweizerische Kreditbank.

Swiss National Bank. *See* Schweizerische Nationalbank.

Switching. Changing from one form of investment to another according to the conditions of the time, as for example, from gilt-edged to equities.

Symbiosis. A term used of the structure of a group of people organised for production. For example, each one of them may attempt to do as much as possible for himself, or a high degree of division of labour may be in vogue.

Symmetalism. A term used by Alfred Marshall of a monetary unit made of an alloy of gold and silver.

It was thought that this would reduce the effect on prices in general of changes in the price of the two monetary metals.

Synchropay. A system whereby wage increases in different industries all take place at the same time, the aim being to obviate competitive wage increases.

Syndicalism. An economic system under which each industry is operated to the sole advantage of the workers in it.

Syndicate. A group of people voluntarily working together. Lloyd's underwriters work in syndicates. Membership of each syndicate is shown on a slip of paper attached to all insurance policies issued by Lloyd's underwriters.

Syndicated Bid. The discount houses meet before bidding for Treasury bills each Friday in order to make a single, syndicated bid.

Syndicate Law (1884). A French law which gave legal recognition for the first time to trade unions and co-operative societies.

Systems Analysis. A method of evaluating costs in relation to benefit in activities where it is not possible to apply market analysis, *e.g.* public services. Having precisely defined a particular objective the problem is to organise the most economic method of achieving it. Cost/benefit analysis, operational research (*qq.v.*) and mathematical models are tools it employs. Critics of the system doubt whether these techniques, first employed in technological problems, can be applied to human affairs.

T

Tableau Économique. A diagram, published by the French economist, Quesnay, showing that agriculture was the source of all wealth which circulated through the other sections of the economy only to return to those engaged in agriculture.

Taff Vale Case. In 1900 the Taff Vale Railway successfully sued a trade union because some of its members had persuaded other members to break their contracts of employment. The Trade Disputes Act of 1906 (*q.v.*) gave trade unions immunity from such legal action.

Taft–Hartley Act (1947). A U.S. labour relations Act which gave the Federal Government power to delay the onset of a strike by 80 days. *See also* Wagner Act (1935).

Taka. The standard unit of the currency of Bangladesh. It is subdivided into 100 Paise.

Take-over Bid. An offer by one company for all or a large proportion of the shares of another company which it wishes to bring under its control. The offer will probably consist of a proportionate number of its own shares, together with a cash payment per share. The purpose of a take-over bid may be either to make possible large-scale production and so enjoy economies of scale or to obtain a larger share of the market.

Talent. An ancient Hebrew silver coin equal in value to 3,000 shekels (*q.v.*).

Talleyman. A door-to-door salesman, he usually carries with him samples of his wares or a catalogue, first taking orders and delivering the goods later. *See* Hawker.

Tally. From the eleventh to the seventeenth century when money was paid into the exchequer receipts were given in the form of wooden tallies, notched to show the amount paid, and split down the middle, the payer and the payee each keeping identical halves as proof of payment. Tallies were also given to people who lent money to the King, and Charles II made great use of tallies for this purpose. He also used tallies as a means of payment. They became negotiable, but on account of the difficulty of indorsing them they were eventually replaced by paper.

Talon. In addition to the interest coupons attached to bearer stock there is a slip, known as a talon, which is used to apply for further coupons when necessary.

Tambala. A sub-unit of the currency of Malawi, 100 tambala being equal in value to one kwacha.

Tap. Securities that are issued in unlimited quantities (though the amounts permitted to each individual may be restricted) and are available for purchase direct from the issuing authority at any time. The non-marketable Government securities for small savers—National Savings Certificates, Defence Bonds, Premium Bonds—are all of this type as also are tax reserve certificates. Marketable stocks which are issued on 'tap' include some funded stocks, which after issue can be bought and sold on the stock exchange, and some Treasury bills which are used for the temporary investment of Government funds, in the operations of the Exchange Equalisation Account, and by the Issue Department of the Bank of England. Tap Treasury bills are usually regarded as being non-marketable although some pass into the market as a result of the operations of the Issue Department of the Bank of England.

T.A.P. The Portuguese State Airline.

Tare. The weight of the packing case, container, etc., in which goods are packed for carriage, to be deducted from the gross weight to obtain the net weight of the goods.

Target Price. A device employed in the farming policy of the European Economic Community. For farming products the E.E.C. fixes prices (reviewed annually), which it is hoped that farmers might be able to obtain in the open market. Levies are then imposed on imports to raise their prices to the level of the target prices. At a specified price slightly below the target price, known as the 'intervention' price, institutional buying begins for the purpose of checking any further fall in the price on the market. To encourage production in particular areas higher regional target and intervention prices are sometimes set.

Tariff. The ranges of duties on imports. *See* Protection.

Tariff Company. An insurance company that agrees to a standard range of premiums or tariff.

Tariff Reform. A term used during 1903–6 of the policy advocated by Joseph Chamberlain, a Liberal Unionist, who wished to impose a protective tariff with preferential rates for British overseas territories. It was not until 1932 that this policy was adopted by the Ottawa Conference (*q.v.*). *See also* Imperial Preference.

Task Bonus System. A system of wage payment where a task is set, a bonus being paid if the task is completed by the worker within the standard time. In systems like the Gantt a very severe task is set and no bonus at all is paid to those who just fail. In the Emerson and other systems a more reasonable task is set and the amount of the bonus varies according to the time taken by the worker. *See also* Premium Bonus.

Taste, Change of. One of the causes of Changes in Demand (*q.v.*). *See also* Demand.

Taxable Capacity. The extent to which a people can be taxed. It is very difficult to decide what is the taxable capacity of a people, for it depends to a considerable extent on what the State does with the revenue from the taxes. The limit of taxable capacity might be considered to be the point beyond which the additional taxation would produce economically harmful results (such as a fall in the national income) that outweigh the gain from the services provided by the State from this additional taxation. Where the State uses taxes to provide services for the community it is really returning to taxpayers the money they have paid in taxes though, depending on his income, the gain to the taxpayer may be more or less than his loss of satisfaction resulting from the payment of taxes.

Taxable Income. The portion of a person's income that remains after his tax-free allowances—single or married allowance, children's allowances, etc.—have been deducted. *See* Income Tax.

Taxation. Compulsory payments by individuals and companies to the State. Local taxation imposed by local authorities is known as rates. (*See* Rates.) At one time Governments imposed taxes to raise revenue to cover the cost of administration, the maintenance of law and order at home and defence against external enemies. Taxes for these purposes can be regarded as contributions for the provision of services which can be more efficiently provided by the State than by individuals themselves. During the past eighty years State expenditure has been extended to a wide range of social services—education, housing, health, pensions, national assistance, family allowances, etc. More recently the Government has subsidised farming and other industries. Revenue too has to be raised to pay the interest on the national debt. In all these cases taxes are imposed to provide revenue to cover Government expenditure. In addition some taxation is for social or economic purposes. For example, surtax is imposed more for the purpose of reducing very large incomes, thereby reducing inequality of income, than for the revenue it yields. Since the budget came to be used as an ad-

Taxation, Direct. *See* Direct Taxation.

Taxation, Economic Effects of. Heavy direct taxation on income, especially if progressive, can have a serious disincentive effect on the wish to work, since it makes overtime appear to be very much more heavily taxed than the rest of one's income. Thus, taxation can be a deterrent to work. On the other hand indirect taxation—taxes on commodities—may actually increase the desire to work in order to earn the extra amount necessary to pay for things. Taxation too can act as a deterrent to saving, since it is equivalent to a reduction of income, though it may not always have this effect in the case of people saving for a particular purpose. Taxation of profits is regarded by some economists as taxation of enterprise and therefore likely to check the growth of the economy. Indirect taxation, imposed to check inflation, may have the opposite effect, the rise in prices resulting from the taxes stimulating the inflationary spiral and leading to demands for wage increases. Taxes on commodities, such as purchase taxes, can have directional effects by reducing demand for particular things and, therefore, their production, and so causing a diversion of economic resources from the production of the taxed goods to the production of other things.

Taxation, Incidence of. *See* Incidence of Taxation.

Taxation, Indirect. *See* Indirect Taxes.

Taxation, Institute of. A professional body whose members specialise in taxation or are professionally interested in the subject. There are two grades of members—Associates (A.T.I.I.) and Fellows (F.T.I.I.), admittance being based partly on qualifying examinations and partly on professional experience.

Taxation, Principles of. Adam Smith put forward four canons or principles of taxation: (i) The amounts payable by taxpayers should be equal, by which he meant proportional to income; (ii) The taxpayer should know for certain how much he had to pay; (iii) There should be convenience of payment; (iv) Taxes should not be imposed if their cost of collection was excessive. The proportional principle is not regarded today as the most equitable, since the payment of £30 by a person with £300 income per year is a heavier burden than the payment of £300 by a person with £3,000 a year. Under the progressive principle, which applies in most countries today, the amount of tax to be paid increases more than proportionately with income. Under this system each taxpayer can be granted a tax-free allowance depending on his individual circumstances, that is, whether he is single or married and the number of his dependants. Thus, if a tax system is progressive one person with £500 a year may pay only £1 in tax whereas a person with £5,000 a year might have to pay over £1,300.

Taxation, Royal Commission on (1953-1955). This Royal Commission was concerned with the taxation of profits and income and especially sought to discover what disincentive effects high marginal rates of taxation might have.

Tax Avoidance and Tax Evasion. It is important to distinguish between these two practices. Tax avoidance occurs when a taxpayer takes a perfectly legal course to keep down the amount he has to pay in taxes as, for example, by investing in National Savings Certificates or a building society instead of in Government stocks, or purchasing an annuity or taking out life assurance, etc. Tax evasion, on the other hand, is a criminal offence as it involves illegal means of reducing the tax payable by making false returns or by the deliberate omission from the return of some source of income. See Tax Havens.

Tax Credit. In the case of investment income it is equivalent to the basic rate of tax on the dividend to which it applies to be set against the income tax chargeable on a person's total income for that year.

Tax Credit Scheme. Also known as Negative Income Tax, it is a method of tax assessment in which tax credits, depending on the circumstances of the taxpayer, replace allowances and many social security benefits. Tax credits are deductible from tax due and where they exceed the tax due a payment will be received instead of a tax demand. A Green Paper outlining the scheme was issued in 1972.

Tax Havens. Countries which offer lower rates of tax generally in order to attract foreign funds. Tax havens include both developed and developing nations. Among others they include Bermuda, the Bahamas, Panama, Liberia, the Channel Islands and Switzerland.

Tax Mitigation. An alternative term for Tax Avoidance ($q.v.$).

Tax Planning. An alternative term for Tax Avoidance ($q.v.$).

Tax Reliefs. See Allowances.

Tax Reserve Certificates. Certificates formerly issued for the convenience of business firms and private individuals, mainly those assessed under schedule D, who were liable for large tax payments. Tax-free interest was paid on them, but only for a maximum of two years. They provided a useful means by which companies and others could keep a tax reserve until the tax was due for payment. The issue of these certificates ceased in 1973 but in 1975 they were replaced by a new type of certificate known as a Certificate of Tax Deposit ($q.v.$).

Tax Reserves. Since taxes on company profits are collected in arrears the amount has to be set aside for payment of tax.

Taylor System. A piece-rate method of wage payment where the rate increases as the worker speeds up his rate of working in contrast to the premium-bonus methods of payment under which the rate falls the more quickly the work is completed. It offers a greater incentive than straight piece-rates.

T.D.R. Abbreviation of Treasury Deposit Receipts ($q.v.$).

Tea. Used as money at one time in China. See Commodity Money.

Technical Education. See Education.

Technical (or Technological) Progress. The principle of influence on a country's Standard of Living ($q.v.$).

Technological Unemployment. In most cases the introduction of new machines results in some temporary unemployment. On occasions, therefore, this has led to opposition to the use of new machines and in extreme cases to the deliberate smashing of machinery. The long-run effect, however, of the introduction of new machinery is to expand production, increase the national income and raise the standard of living of the community as a whole. In time, therefore, the demand for labour is likely to increase, but since labour is not perfectly mobile the immediate effect is some structural unemployment. Even if full employment is successfully maintained there will from time to time be temporary structural unemployment due to technological progress which is to the long-run advantage of all. For this reason it is felt that more generous treatment than is available under the national insurance scheme should be provided for those who temporarily suffer from what ultimately is to the benefit of the whole community.

Technological University. A university which concentrates (though not exclusively) on technological studies. The best known is the Massachusetts Institute of Technology in the U.S.A. They are found in many countries. In Great Britain the Colleges of Advanced Technology, after being granted university status in 1965–67, in effect became technological universities, as also the new Universities of Bath and Loughborough.

Technology, Ministry of. A former Government department established in 1964 to be responsible for problems associated with technical progress and to assist technical advance. In 1970 it was merged with the then Department of Trade and Industry (*q.v.*).

Technostructure. An American term, used especially by J. K. Galbraith, author of *The Affluent Society* (*q.v.*), and Milton Friedman, of the Chicago School (*q.v.*), for the technical-managerial class. Prof. Galbraith believes these people dominate the economy through their control of large-scale production. Prof. Friedman refutes this view.

T.E.E. Abbreviation of Trans-Europe Express, a group of international express trains (first-class only plus a supplement) connecting the principal commercial centres of the E.E.C. countries, *e.g.* Milan–Lyons, Amsterdam–Geneva, etc. Their speed is maintained in spite of crossing national frontiers, as customs formalities are carried out on board. The scheme started in 1957 with 14 trains but by 1976 the number of T.E.E. trains operating daily had increased to 46.

Telegraphic Address. For a fee firms may register an abbreviated address with the Post Office in order to reduce the cost of telegrams to their clients.

Telegraphic Money Order. A means by which a sum of money can be expeditiously sent from one place to another. In addition to the cost of the money order the sender has to pay for the telegram. A message is telegraphed to the payee's post office, the payee having to give proof of his identity before being paid.

Telegraphic Transfer. The transfer by cable or telex of bank funds from one country to another as a means of making a payment in international trade.

Telephone Answering Services. There are several types of such services. During a subscriber's absence a line can be switched over to an agency which will take messages or pass on messages to callers. There are also machines which can record messages (for example, when an office or shop is closed) which can then be dealt with later.

Telex. A service provided by the Post Office. Instead of messages being sent verbally as by telephone, teleprinters are employed so that messages can be sent and received by day or by night, even after an office has closed. In Great Britain calls are made by dialling, each subscriber being assigned a Telex number.

Tender. 1. An offer made in response to an advertisement to undertake a piece of work or supply certain goods at a stated price.

2. An offer to purchase Treasury bills (*q.v.*).

3. Sometimes stocks are offered to tender. *See* Issue by Tender.

Ten Hours Bill. Popular term for Fielden's Factory Act of 1847 which made the ten-hour working day law for women. As a result men too had to be given a ten-hour working day.

Tennessee Valley Authority (T.V.A.). An American regional development scheme initiated in 1933 under President Roosevelt's 'New Deal' policy.

Ten-pound Note. The Bank of England ceased issuing notes of denominations greater than £5 in 1946. The ten-pound note, however, was revived in 1964, the considerable fall in the value of money since 1939 making necessary a note of higher denomination than £5. Like the new five-pound notes of 1959 and 1963 the new ten-pound note of 1964 was much smaller in size than the note issued previously.

Ten-shilling Note. After circulating for a period of 55 years ten-shilling notes were withdrawn in 1969 and replaced by coins of a value of Fifty New Pence (*q.v.*).

Tenth. A medieval tax, originally one tenth of the annual value of property, but the assessment made in 1332 came to be regarded as permanent.

Term Deposits. Deposits in a Savings Bank for which a long period of withdrawal is required; they carry the highest rate of interest paid by Savings Banks. The interest on such deposits is liable to income tax. *See also* Special Investment Department.

Terminable Annuity. An annuity payable for a fixed number of years. *See* Annuity.

Terminal Market. An alternative term for a Futures or Forward Market.

Terms of Delivery. *See* Delivery, Terms of.

Terms of Payment. *See* Payment, Terms of.

Terms of Trade. The relation between the prices of a country's exports and the prices of its imports, represented arithmetically by taking the export index as a percentage of the import index. Thus, in the base year if both the import and export price indices are taken as 100, the terms of trade index also will be 100. If, however, export prices fall relatively to import prices, the terms of trade index will fall below 100, the terms of trade then being said to be more favourable to the country concerned since it means that it can obtain more goods from abroad than before in exchange for a given quantity of exports. On the other hand, if the terms of trade are favourable to a country its customers will find it more difficult to obtain foreign currency to pay for imports and so exports may become more difficult to sell. When the terms of trade become unfavourable the terms of trade index will rise above 100.

Territorial Division of Labour. *See* Localisation of Industry.

Territorial Waters. The offshore sea area of a country with a seaboard over which it claims sovereignty and exclusive rights, for example, for fishing, prospecting for oil, etc. For a long time this area was regarded as stretching three miles out to sea from the land, but Iceland demanded recognition first of a 12-mile limit and later a 200-mile limit. The E.E.C. countries responded by introducing a 200-mile limit in 1977.

Tertiary Liquidity. A banking term used by the E.E.C. for assets that take two to four years to mobilise. *Cf.* Primary and Secondary Liquidity.

Tertiary Occupations. These include all kinds of services. *See* Occupations, Classifications of.

Tertiary Risks. A banking term used by the E.E.C. for low-risk investments. *Cf.* Primary and Secondary Risks.

Testoon. Original name of the shilling when first issued in 1405 by Henry VII.

Teviot Scale. The scale of salaries for teachers in Scotland.

Textile Council. A body, established in 1967, to represent the cotton and man-made fibres industries, it superseded the Cotton Board.

T.G.W.U. Abbreviation of Transport and General Workers' Union, the largest trade union in Great Britain.

Thaler. A silver coin, it was the standard unit of the German Monetary Union during 1857–73.

Theoretical Model. *See* Model.

'Think Tank'. Popular name for the Government's Policy Review Staff.

Third Party. An insurance term for some person other than the insured or the insurance company. Insurance against 'third-party' risks is compulsory in the U.K. for owners of motor vehicles. Thus, a cyclist as a third party might claim damages from a motorist with whom he has been involved in an accident.

Three Banks Group. A banking group comprising Williams and Glyn's Bank, the Scottish National and Commercial Group—the Commercial Bank of Scotland and the Royal Bank of Scotland.

Three Banks Review. Quarterly journal of the Three Banks Group (q.v.). It contains articles on matters of current economic and monetary interest.

Three-Field System. A feature of the medieval manorial system. Apart from the lord's demesne and the common grazing land, the rest of the land of the manor was divided into three large fields, each villein cultivating a few strips in each field. One of the three fields was usually given up to wheat, a second to barley or oats and the third was left fallow, rotation of crops being practised so that each field lay fallow every third year.

Threepenny Piece. Before decimalisation two coins circulated in Great Britain each worth threepence. The silver threepenny piece was first issued in 1552 by Edward VI. The twelve-sided threepenny piece of nickel brass was first issued during the 1930s. Until 1942 both types were issued. They were withdrawn in 1971 when the currency was decimalised.

Three-variable Analysis. The difficulty in constructing a diagram to show three variables is that it requires to be three-dimensional, though this can be overcome by the use of contours (q.v.).

Ticket Day. A stock exchange term, an alternative to Name Day (q.v.).

Tied Cottage. A house or cottage, owned by an employer who allows mainly an employee to rent it. At one time the facility was offered only to agricultural workers, but with the shortage of houses to rent after 1945 and often in many areas a shortage too of labour, many manufacturing firms bought houses for employees, including junior executives, as a means of attracting labour. A serious drawback to the practice is that it tends to make labour less mobile. The tied cottage became unpopular with workers and the imposition of legal restrictions led to a decline of the practice.

Tied House (or **Shop**). A retail outlet, controlled or owned by a manufacturer, and compelled to sell his products, either mainly or exclusively. Most public houses are tied to breweries which own them to ensure outlets for their own products.

Tight Money. An alternative term for dear money (q.v.).

Timber Exchange. One of the organised produce markets of London.

Time and Elasticity. 1. *With reference to Demand.* In the short period demand may be fairly inelastic. It may take time for all consumers to become aware of a change of price. It may be thought that price having fallen it may fall still further. It takes time for consumers to outgrow ingrained habits. In the case of durable goods it may be some time before it is necessary to renew them.

2. *With reference to Supply.* Time has a greater influence on elasticity of supply than on elasticity of demand. Often in the short period the supply of a commodity is fixed, that is, supply is perfectly inelastic. For many commodities it takes a considerable time to increase supply. It may be necessary to wait until the next harvest, perhaps a year ahead, or even longer in the case of some commodities, whisky, for example, taking seven years to mature.

Time and Motion Study. A study of the time taken by an employee and the way he carries out the work assigned to him to ascertain whether the work can be simplified, so that less time be taken over it as a means of increasing efficiency. *See also* Ergonomics.

Time Charter. The hire of a ship for a definite period of time as an alternative to hiring it for a particular voyage. *See* Charter Party.

Time Deposit. An American term for a bank deposit on deposit account.

Time-lags. Often a period of time must elapse before the effect of some action becomes apparent. For example, a change in bank rate may take time before it has any important effect; the multiplier effect of a new piece of investment may be subject to a time-lag; an increase in demand, accompanied by an increase in price, may not immediately bring about an increase in supply.

Time Preference. A theory of interest based on the idea that some people prefer to have money to spend at present and are prepared to pay for this privilege, while others, if paid interest for doing so, are prepared to postpone their spending to a future date.

Time Rate. A method of wage payment, the employee being paid according to the number of hours he has worked. Employees have to 'clock in' and 'clock out' so that a record can be kept of the number of hours worked.

***Times* Industrial Ordinary Share Index.** An index of stock exchange share prices, compiled by *The Times*, with 2 June 1964 as base (originally 2 June 1959) and published daily. In February 1977 it stood at 161·07. *See also* Financial Times Indices.

Time Wages. *See* Time Rate.

T.I.R. Abbreviation of Transports Internationaux Routiers. International road services.

Tithe. A tax of one-tenth of the value of the output of land levied for the benefit of the Church. An Act of 1836 commuted all tithes in England and Wales to money payments. An Act of 1936 transferred payment to the Crown (until 1996), the Church Commissioners being compensated by Government stock.

Tithe Redemption Annuities. *See* Tithe.

Title-deeds to Property. A type of security which a bank may accept as collateral against a loan. Title-deeds are not always an attractive form of collateral security, since in a trade depression the value of property, especially factory buildings, may sharply decline.

T.L. Abbreviation of Total Loss.

T.M.O. Abbreviation of Telegraphic Money Order (*q.v.*).

Tobacco. Used as money for a period in the sixteenth century in Virginia, owing to a shortage of coin. Cigarettes were used as money in Germany for a time immediately after the Second World War. *See* Commodity Money.

Token Coin. A coin with a face value greater than the value of the metal content of the coin. It was for this reason that token coins were made only limited legal tender. All coins in use in Great Britain today are of this kind.

Token Payment. An alternative term for Earnest Money (*q.v.*).

Tokens. Vouchers purchasable at one shop and valid for the purchase of goods at another shop. Book tokens were the first to be issued, followed by tokens for the purchase of gramophone records. Some shops issue vouchers that can be used only at the shops where they are issued.

Toll. A charge for travelling along a stretch of road or for using a tunnel, bridge, or ferry. The exaction of tolls from travellers had its origin with the turnpike trusts which raised some of their funds by this means for the maintenance of roads they had constructed or improved. With the decline of the turnpike system the cost of road maintenance fell to local authorities and the State, with the State taking an increasing share of the cost. There are still a few private roads and bridges subject to tolls. Most of the new bridges and tunnels constructed in Great Britain since 1945, are subject to toll, as are most ferries. In most countries the new motorways are free of toll except in France, Italy and the United States.

'Tolpuddle Martyrs.' The name applied to six Dorset farm labourers who in 1834 were sentenced to transportation for seven years for combining together in a union, membership of which included the taking of an oath. The men were pardoned after serving four years of their sentences.

Tommy-shop. A colloquial term used at the time for a truck-shop. *See* Truck System.

Tonnage. The capacity of ships is reckoned in 'tons', one ton for this purpose being 100 cubic feet. In the Royal Navy the tonnage of a ship is the weight of water displaced, which is equal to the gross weight of the ship.

'Top Hat' Pensions. Pensions for employees, usually in top management posts, where the premiums are paid by the employers.

Toronto-Dominion Bank. One of the leading commercial banks of Canada, it was formed in 1955 by a merger of the Toronto Bank and the Dominion Bank. It has over 750 branches.

Torrens Act (1869). This Act and the Cross Act of 1875 permitted local authorities to demolish slums.

Total Cost. The total sum of a firm's fixed and variable costs (*qq.v.*) in the production of a particular output.

Totalitarian State. A country in which economic activity—and generally other forms of political and social activity too—is controlled by the State, as in communist and fascist systems. *See* Communism, Fascism.

Total Revenue. The total receipts accruing to a firm from the entire sale of a particular output.

Tourism (and Travel). An *invisible* item of increasing importance in the balance of payments for many countries, such as Spain, Italy, Greece. For the United States it is a large debit, but for Great Britain it is now an almost self-balancing item. An Act of 1969 set up the British Tourist Authority with regional Tourist Boards (*q.v.*) for England, Scotland, Wales and Northern Ireland.

Tourist Boards. Bodies set up to assist the development of tourism in England, Wales, Scotland, and Northern Ireland. Financial assistance may be provided for tourist projects provided they are in development areas. Such projects must be designed to attract tourists from the U.K. but more especially from abroad.

Town and Country Planning Act (1947). An Act which made land development throughout the country subject to the control of local authorities and the State. It restricted industrial development and designated 'green belts' to separate industrial areas.

Town and Country Planning Act (1972). This Act consolidates earlier Acts and contains provisions affecting the liberty of an owner of land to develop and use it as he will. *See* Development Land Tax.

Town Clearing. The section of the London Bankers' Clearing House (*q.v.*) that deals with cheques drawn on and paid into branches of the Clearing Banks situated within the City of London.

Trade. Now generally taken to mean the buying and selling of goods, though formerly trade took place by barter (*q.v.*). It is one of the two main divisions of commerce, the other including aids to trade such as transport, banking, and insurance. Trade is usually classified as home (wholesale and retail) and foreign (import, export, and entrepôt). With increasing division of labour and specialisation the volume of trade has enormously increased. *See* Entrepôt Trade; Export Trade; Import Trade; International Trade; Retail Trade; Wholesale Trade.

Trade and Industry, Department of. A Government department formed in 1970 by merging the Board of Trade with the Ministry of Technology. Since 1974 there have been separate Departments of Trade and Industry. *See* Industry, Department of; Trade, Department of.

Trade Association. A body representing the interests of a branch of trade. Generally they represent all members of the trade, as does the Liverpool Cotton Association. Trade associations are mainly concerned to watch legislation which may affect their interests, but sometimes they become price rings, although price agreements would now be contrary to the Restrictive Trade Practices Act of 1956.

Trade Balance. *See* Balance of Trade.

Trade Barrier. Any hindrance to trade between nations that prevents the free working of the Principle of Comparative Cost. *See* Import Restrictions.

Trade Bill. A bill of exchange accepted by a trader or merchant. Some trade bills—'fine trade bills'—are held by banks, but since many traders are not sufficiently well known most trade bills are held until maturity by the traders who have received them or used as collateral security against bank loans.

Trade Bloc. A group of countries with close trading ties with one another. In some cases it may be an informal arrangement, but in others it may be brought about by a definite treaty. The sterling area is an example of the former and the E.E.C. of the latter.

Trade Boards Act (1909). An Act which fixed minimum wages for certain trades where wage rates were exceptionally low. *See* Wages Councils.

Trade Credit. Credit granted by one trader to another who has purchased goods from him. The trader who grants the credit has to forgo a sum of money for a period and so there is no addition to the total volume of purchasing power as is the case with bank credit. Nevertheless, trade credit is of monetary importance since it is likely to increase in a period when bank credit is being restricted.

Trade Cycle. The tendency of business activity to fluctuate regularly between boom and depression, a feature of the British and some other economies from the end of the eighteenth century to 1913. During the 121 years down to 1913 booms occurred at intervals of about seven or eight years and between each pair of booms there was a slump. Since 1913 the trade cycle has not clearly asserted itself, for the characteristic of the inter-War years was a prolonged deep depression, while since 1945 deliberate efforts have been made to make full employment a permanent feature of the economy of many countries. Nevertheless since 1945 there have been periodic recessions in the United States and the so-called 'Stop/Go' (*q.v.*) policy in Great Britain has also resulted in a series of mild recessions. During the downswing of the cycle there were falls in prices (including wages) and production and an increase in unemployment; during the upswing there was a rise in prices (including wages) and an expansion of production and a fall in unemployment. *See* Trade Cycle, Causes of.

Trade Cycle, Causes of. During the 1930s, the period of the Great Depression, many rival theories were put forward to explain the trade cycle. The truth probably is that the trade cycle had its origin in many causes—real, psychological, and monetary. (i) Some writers have stressed the real causes of the cycle, such as inherent fluctuations of industries producing capital goods on account of their durability and the fact that the demand for them is a derived demand. Any temporary increase in demand will upset the rhythm of production and cause a permanent kink in the graph of production. (*See* Acceleration Principle.) Another real cause is to be found in fluctuations in agricultural output (*see* Cobweb Theorem) and in the irregularity of economic progress itself. (ii) Some writers have tried to explain the origin of the trade cycle in psychological terms. Businessmen, it is said, are influenced alternately by waves of optimism and pessimism. After a slump has continued for a time they become convinced that better times are just round the corner. They decide to renew capital equipment while prices are low, and by this very action they set in motion the recovery they expect. Similarly, at the height of a boom they begin to think that it cannot last. They, therefore, postpone capital renewal or expansion and so help to start the downswing. (iii) Some writers think real and psychological causes of little importance and explain the trade cycle entirely in monetary terms. They stress changes in the quantity of money and say there is a tendency periodically for banks to over-expand credit so that this has to be followed by credit restriction. The effect of the rate of interest on holding stocks is regarded as another monetary cause, a high rate causing merchants to run down their stocks (and as a result curtailing production) and a low rate encouraging them to build up stocks and thereby stimulating production. Some writers stress too much saving and underconsumption and others point to over-investment. Lord Keynes put forward a Savings-Investment theory.

Trade, Department of. Established as a separate department in 1974, it is responsible for Great Britain's commercial relations with other countries. It helps to promote exports in various ways, including overseas trade fairs. Other concerns of the department include companies policy, an insolvency service, shipping and marine affairs, patents and copyright and an accident investigation branch.

Trade Descriptions Act (1968). An Act aimed at protecting consumers against false descriptions of goods. It prohibits misleading descriptions of goods or services.

Trade Discount. This may take the form of a rebate on the prices in a wholesaler's catalogue allowed to retailers. Prices are varied when necessary by altering the rate of trade discount instead of reprinting the whole catalogue. Sometimes trade discount is merely the difference between the retailer's buying price and his selling price, that is, his mark-up.

Trade Discrimination. See Discriminating Monopoly; Preferential Duty.

Trade Disputes Act (1906). An Act giving trade unions immunity from legal action by employers for breach of contract in the event of a strike. This was challenged in 1964 by a decision of the House of Lords.

Trade Disputes Act (1927). After the failure of the General Strike of 1926 this type of strike was made illegal and it became a criminal offence for anyone to incite another person to take part in such a strike. Another provision was that in future members of a trade union who wished to make a political contribution to their union had to 'contract in', whereas previously those who did not wish to do so had to 'contract out'. It was also made illegal for a public authority to make membership or non-membership of a trade union a condition of employment. This Act was repealed in 1946.

Trade Expansion Act. An Act passed in 1962 by the Congress of the United States. It gave the U.S. Government power to negotiate reciprocal tariffs on goods where exports from the United States and the European Common Market together account for 80% of world trade in those goods. Secondly, the U.S. Government was given power to negotiate with the European Common Market for reciprocal tariff concessions on all other goods. To protect American industry the U.S. Government was permitted to increase tariffs as a retaliatory measure against 'unreasonable' restrictions imposed by other countries on imports from the United States. Further, the U.S. Government was empowered to aid firms and workers who suffer from increased competition from abroad. Commodities of which the United States and the European Common Market together produce 80% of total world output include coal, most kinds of machinery, motor cars, tobacco. See also 'Kennedy Round'.

Trade Fair. See Fair.

Trade Gap. The amount by which the value of visible imports exceeds the value of visible exports. See Balance of Trade.

Trade, International. See International Trade.

Trade Journal. A publication such as the *Boot and Shoe Journal* devoted to a particular branch of retail and wholesale trade, containing articles on matters of interest to those in the trade and wholesalers' advertisements.

Trade Marks. Distinguishing marks attached to goods which have been registered under the Trade Marks

Acts and which then cannot be used by any other producer, thus giving the proprietor of the trade mark some degree of monopoly power. Registration in the first instance is for seven years but after that it is renewable. Trade marks and brand names are the basis of imperfect oligopoly (*q.v.*).

Trade Marks Registry. A department of the Patent Office responsible for the registration of trade marks.

Trade Protection Society. A body which supplies information regarding the credit-worthiness of firms. *See also* Status Inquiry Agency.

Trade Reference. A retailer seeking credit terms from a wholesaler may be asked for a trade reference, that is to say, to supply the name of some other wholesaler with whom he has dealt.

Traders' Credits. A system whereby a debtor can instruct his bank to pay a series of sums direct to the accounts of his creditors.

Trades Council. A body sometimes known as a Trades and Labour Council, found in the larger industrial towns representing the trade unions of that locality.

Trades Union Congress (T.U.C.). Established in 1868, it is a body to which most British trade unions are now affiliated. At national level it represents the trade unions *vis-à-vis* the Confederation of British Industry (C.B.I.) which represents employers. For example, the T.U.C. is represented on the N.E.D.C. At its annual conference member unions put forward for debate resolutions on policy and other matters affecting trade unions. A General Council is elected to watch over the interests of trade unions and to consider any disputes which may arise between unions.

Trade Tokens. A lack of small change in the seventeenth century led to shopkeepers and innkeepers issuing tokens, mainly in denominations of a halfpenny and a farthing. Since 1823 the issuing of such tokens has been illegal.

Trade Union. An association of workers in a particular craft or industry. It differs from the medieval gild in that its members comprise employees only, whereas the gild included both masters and journeymen. The conditions in the early factories made it necessary for the workers to act together, but the Combination Acts of 1799 and 1801 prohibited combinations formed for the purpose of improving wages. Repealed in 1824, these Acts were revived, though in a modified form in 1825. Until the Trade Unions Acts of 1871–76 members of a trade union continued to be liable to a charge of conspiracy. The early trade unions failed to gain much support because of their violence, but progress was more rapid after 1848. The early trade unions were generally small craft unions, but during the later years of the nineteenth century the 'New Unionism' widened the movement to include unskilled workers and paved the way for the large industrial unions of today. Before the introduction of national insurance many unions provided sick pay and some also unemployment pay for their members. The main function of a trade union is to enable workers to act together—the individual by himself being in a weak bargaining position—to negotiate with employers, that is, to make possible collective bargaining, the strike being their weapon of last resort to be used only after negotiations have broken down. The need for trade union reform led to the passing of the Industrial Relations Act (1971) (*q.v.*), later repealed and replaced by the Trade Union and Labour Relations Act (1974) (*q.v.*).

Trade Union Acts (1871–76). These Acts clarified the legal position of trade unions, gave them protection for their property, permitted 'peaceful picketing', and freed members from a charge of conspiracy.

Trade Union Act (1913). An Act giving trade unions the right to use their funds for political purposes, a right challenged in 1909 by the Osborne Judgment.

Trade Union and Labour Relations Act (1974). This Act repealed the Industrial Relations Act of 1971 (*q.v.*), and revised the law relating to trade unions, employers' associations, workers generally and their employers, including such matters as 'unfair dismissal' and the 'closed shop'. Whereas the aim of the 1971 Act was to check the growing power of the trade unions, the Trade Union and Labour Relations Act (1974) gave them even greater power than before 1971, for example legalising the 'closed shop' practice.

Trading Account. A document drawn up by a trader as a means of calculating his gross profit. It takes the following form:

Trading Account for the period July 1st to December 31st

			£				£
July 1	To opening stock	.	2,440	Dec. 31	By sales .	.	5,633
Dec. 31	,, purchases	.	2,706	,, 31	,, closing stock	.	2,120
,, 31	,, gross profit	.	2,607				
			7,753				7,753

Trading Banks. The commercial banks of Australia. The largest is the Commonwealth Trading Bank, closely followed by the Bank of New South Wales and the Australia and New Zealand Bank.

Trading Cheques. *See* Shopping Cheques.

Trading Estate. *See* Industrial Estates.

Trading Profit. An alternative term for Gross Profit (*q.v.*).

Trading Stamps. Stamps given by retailers to their customers in proportion to the value of their purchases and which can be exchanged for a great variety of goods. It is thus a kind of discount system. The stamps are bought from the stamp company at their face value of about 2½% of the retailer's turnover, the stamp company making its profit by buying its goods wholesale. Stamp trading is well established in the United States, covering about 80% of total retail trade. In Great Britain, although there had been some small-scale stamp or coupon trading for many years, stamp trading has increased considerably since 1963. Since 1965 it has been compulsory for stamps to have a money value. In most countries in the E.E.C. trading stamps are banned.

Trading Stamps Act (1964). An Act which regulated the issue of trading stamps and, among other things, laid down that the cash value of all trading stamps should be clearly shown, and from August 1965 all stamps were to be exchangeable for cash (usually at half their gift value).

Traffic Commissioners. Bodies set up under the Road Traffic Act (1930), one for each of the eleven areas into which the country was divided. Their duties were to license passenger transport services in their areas and to consider objections to applications to operate new services. By the transport Act of 1968 the functions of the Traffic Commissioners were taken over by Passenger Transport Authorities.

Traffic Department. The department of a department store responsible for the delivery of goods to customers.

Traffic in Towns. Official title of the Buchanan Report, 1963 (*q.v.*).

Train Ferry. The carrying of an entire train across a narrow stretch of water as between Dover and Dunkirk to give a through service between London and Paris. Train ferries are also operated between Germany and Denmark, between Denmark and Sweden, and between Germany and Sweden.

Tramp Steamers. Freight carriers which, unlike liners, do not ply regularly over a certain route, but instead pick up cargoes for almost any port and may journey from port to port for a long period before obtaining a return cargo to their home port.

Tramways. For city and suburban passenger transport in England, tramways were first tried out at Birkenhead in 1858. They were introduced in London in 1861. An Act of 1870 permitted the compulsory acquisition of tramways by local authorities. The first tramways were horse-drawn, later steam-powered and after 1891 electrically operated. At their peak there were over 2,600 miles of tramways in Great Britain, but as motor-buses increased in numbers in the 1930s tramways slowly declined, the small operators being the first to abandon them. London did not give up its trams until 1952. The last to run are those of Blackpool. In some towns they were replaced for a short period by trolley-buses.

Tranche. *See* Gold Tranche.

Transactions Motive. One of the three motives enumerated by Lord Keynes for the holding of money. Everyone requires to hold a certain amount of money to cover ordinary everyday expenditure. *See* Demand for Money; Liquidity-Preference.

Transferable Account. After the withdrawal of convertibility of sterling in 1947 convertibility was restored to sterling by easy stages. At one period there were three groups of countries, sterling being freely convertible within each group, but with only limited convertibility between the groups. One group comprised the sterling area (*q.v.*) and another the area of the American Account, the members of which were the United States, Canada, and some central American States. Other countries were members of the Transferable Account. Eventually almost the whole of the rest of the world came to be included in the area of the Transferable Account. Sterling in the Transferable Account was freely convertible between all members of the Account and also with members of the sterling area, but convertibility with members of the American Account was restricted. In January 1959 sterling was given convertibility to all people not resident in the United Kingdom. *See* Exchange Control.

Transferable Rouble. A device that facilitates trade settlements within the Soviet bloc. *See* Comecon.

Transfer Deed. An instrument by which the ownership of securities is transferred from one person to another.

Transfer Earnings. The amount a factor of production would receive in its next best employment, the difference between that and its current earnings being regarded as rent.

Transfer of Shares. A small charge is usually made by a public company for the registration of the transfer of shares bought on the stock exchange.

Transfer Payment. In calculating the national income, interest on Government stocks and old age pensions are not included since these are merely transfers from one group of people to another.

Transfer Stamp. Stamp duty imposed by the State on stock exchange transactions.

Transit Trade. An alternative term for Entrepôt Trade (*q.v.*).

Transport. One of the ancillaries of commerce. The tremendous improvements in means of transport that have taken place in the past two hundred years have had far-reaching economic effects. The expansion of railways in the great continental areas of North America and Europe opened up the interiors of those continents. The development of suburban transport and more recently the private car have brought about a sprawling expansion of the larger industrial areas. Improved means of transport were essential to greater division of labour and specialisation of production and made possible the mass production of many things. Speedier and larger aircraft are making possible an even greater degree of specialisation. Transport development and the improvement in means of communication generally have brought about a speedier diffusion of ideas and have also brought the economically advanced and the under-developed nations into closer contact with one another. *See* Air Transport; Canals; Railways; Road Transport; Shipping.

Transport Act (1953). An Act which (i) denationalised road haulage, (ii) removed the restrictions on railway charges imposed in 1845, thereby enabling the railways to compete on more equal terms with other means of transport.

Transport Act (1962). Under this Act the functions and property of the British Transport Commission were transferred to the following boards: the British Railways Board, the London Transport Board, the British Waterways Board, the British Transport Docks Board, and the Transport Holding Company. The British Railways Board was to set up regional boards, one for each of the six operational regions of British Railways.

Transport Act (1968). The aim of this Act was to reorganise public transport, promote the integration of road and rail transport and deal with the consequences of (*a*) a declining railway system, and (*b*) the expansion of private motoring. The British Railways Board, the British Transport Docks Board, and the British Waterways Board were brought directly under the Minister of Transport as also were the newly created National Freight Corporation, the National Bus Company, and the Scottish Transport Group. In the larger conurbations—Greater Manchester, Merseyside, the West Midlands and Tyneside—road passenger transport was entrusted to Passenger Transport Authorities, locally managed, and similarly the London Transport Board was transferred to the Greater London Council. To these two other 'metropolitan' areas were later added—West Yorkshire and South Yorkshire. The Transport Holding Company, set up under the Transport Act of 1962, was shorn of its transport operational activities—bus services, freight and shipping services—leaving it with the Thos. Cook travel agency (*q.v.*) and British Transport hotels. A new carrier licensing system was introduced for goods traffic, the 'O' Licence (*q.v.*). Within their areas the P.T.A.s took over the functions previously exercised by the Traffic Commissioners. The Act enabled freight in certain cases to be diverted from the roads to the railways and passenger traffic from private to public transport. In general transport services were expected to 'break even' financially except where unremunerative services could be shown to be socially necessary. Considerable financial assistance was given to reduce the operational costs of road passenger transport and of suburban rail services, grants made towards capital expenditure, and the debt of British Railways was written down.

Transport Commission. *See* British Transport Commission.

Transport Co-ordinating Council. A body set up in 1966 for London to deal with the growing problems of transport in the London area.

Transport, Institute of. A body established in 1919 and granted a Royal Charter in 1926, its aim is 'to promote, encourage, and co-ordinate the study and advancement of the science and art of transport in all its branches'. Admission as an Associate Member of the Institute (A.M.Inst.T.) is by examination.

Transport, Ministry of. For a time it was a division of the Department of the Environment, but has now been formed into a separate ministry once more. It is concerned with all matters relating to all forms of transport.

Transport Tribunal. A body established to take over some of the functions of the previous Railway Rates Tribunal and the Railway and Canal Commission.

Transport Users' Consultative Committee. A body which watches the interests of transport users. For example, it brings to the notice of the British Railways Board cases of hardship if a railway line or station is threatened with closure.

Travellers' Cheques. Issued by banks in denominations of £2, £5, £10, £20, and £50 to customers who have paid for them, travellers' cheques can be safely used for making payments where personal cheques would be unacceptable. For travellers to foreign countries they can be similarly used or exchanged for foreign currency. To prevent their misuse they have to be signed in the presence of the bank clerk who issues them and countersigned, when used as means of payment, so that the two signatures can be compared. Travellers' cheques were first issued by Thomas Cook & Son.

Treasury. The British Government department dating back over 200 years of which the Chancellor of the Exchequer (*q.v.*) is now the political head, although the Prime Minister is always First Lord of the Treasury. Its main concerns are national finance, economic, and monetary policy. In 1975 the work of the Treasury was re-organised into four main sectors: (i) the Chief Economic Adviser's Sector; (ii) the Overseas Finance Sector; (iii) the Domestic Economy Sector; and (iv) the Public Services Sector.

Treasury Bill. Created by an Act of 1877, largely on the suggestion of Walter Bagehot, they are a means of short-term (usually three months) borrowing by the Government. They were originally issued to cover expenditure in anticipation of revenue since revenue tends to be heavily concentrated in the fourth quarter of the financial year. During the twentieth century Treasury bills have become one of the usual methods of Government borrowing. The Treasury bill takes the following form:

Due 14 June 197-.

£10,000

TREASURY BILL
Per Acts 40 Vict. c 2 and 52 Vict. c 6.

London.

A

12,438

This Treasury Bill entitles..or order to payment of Ten Thousand Pounds at the Bank of England out of the Consolidated Fund of the United Kingdom on the 14th day of June 197-.

(Signed).................................
Secretary to the Treasury.

Treasury bills are offered for tender on Friday of each week, and they can be dated for any day of the following week. They are issued in denominations of £5,000, £10,000, £25,000, £50,000 and £100,000. Some Treasury bills are issued on 'tap' to Government departments.

Treasury Deposit Receipts. These represented compulsory borrowing by the Government from the commercial banks during the Second World War. They were first issued in July 1940 and carried interest of 1$\frac{1}{8}$%. In case of emergency a bank could cash them. By 1945 T.D.R.s had reached a total of over £1,800 million, but after that date they were gradually replaced by Treasury bills, and by 1962 they had disappeared from the commercial banks' balance sheets.

Treasury Directive. To supplement other instruments of monetary policy —bank rate, etc.—the Treasury in 1951 made a request to the commercial banks to restrict their lending to purposes clearly in the national interest. Thus the early directives were qualitative in character. When the monetary authorities found that credit was being insufficiently restricted a quantitative directive was issued to the banks asking them to cut down their lending, whatever the purpose for which it was required. The device of Special Deposits was introduced in 1960.

Treasury Notes. An alternative name for Currency Notes. They were issued in denominations of £1 and 10s. by the British Treasury during the First World War to replace the gold coinage. Treasury notes were taken over by the Bank of England in 1928 and replaced by Bank of England notes of the same amount in accordance with the recommendation of the Cunliffe Committee.

Treasury Special Account. The amounts of Marshall Aid given by the United States to Great Britain were credited to this account before being used for the reduction of debt.

Treasury Stock. The name of several British Government Stocks—$8\frac{1}{2}\%$ 1984–6, 5% 1986–89, 9% 1994, $8\frac{3}{4}\%$ 1997 and several others.

Treaty of Stockholm (1960). See Convention of Stockholm.

Trial Balance. In double-entry bookkeeping a means of checking arithmetical errors in writing up books of accounts (unless such errors cancel one another out). Debits and credits are extracted from the books and the totals of these should agree.

Trinity House. Founded in 1514 to assist shipping, it is now the body responsible for the maintenance of British lighthouses and is also the principal pilotage authority in the U.K.

Tripartite Agreement (1936). Having left the gold standard, Great Britain in 1932 established its Exchange Equalisation Account for intervention in the foreign exchange market. In 1936 both France and then the United States established similar accounts. In that year these three countries made the Tripartite Agreement, under which they each agreed to buy for gold any of their currency the other two might wish to sell, at previously agreed rates of exchange, which they undertook not to change without prior consultation of the other two parties to the agreement.

Triple Sovereign. See Sovereign.

Truck System. A practice common in the early days of the Industrial Revolution and the factory systems of compelling employees to purchase certain things from a shop owned by the employer, wages often being 'paid' in vouchers usable only in the employer's shop instead of in money. Very often inferior goods were supplied at high prices. On the other hand this meant that wages were spent on food and not on drink as often occurred, especially when wages were paid in public houses.

Trunk Roads. A number of roads were first designated as trunk roads by an Act of 1936. The maintenance of such roads, mainly used by 'through' rather than local traffic, was made the responsibility of the State through the Ministry of Transport.

Trust. 1. A sum of money or other property held by an individual, a group of persons, a bank or other institution on behalf of another person, group, or institution. The administrators of the trust are known as trustees.

2. A term of American origin for a very large amalgamation of firms, more particularly a vertically integrated combine like the American Iron and Steel Trust.

3. An investment trust company or a unit trust (*qq.v.*).

Trustee Investment Act (1961). An Act which enabled trustees to invest half the funds for which they were responsible in ordinary shares, either directly or through unit investment trusts. Previously their investments had been restricted to gilt-edged and Corporation stocks.

Trustee, Public. See Public Trustee.

Trustee Savings Banks (T.S.B.). Banks were specially established to encourage thrift among small savers by accepting small deposits. The first trustee savings bank was opened at Ruthwell near Dumfries in 1810. An Act of 1817 prohibited these banks from making a profit. Since 1844 trustee savings banks have been compelled to lend their funds to the National Debt Commissioners. In 1861 the Post Office Savings Bank (now the National Savings Bank) was established, and this is now the largest of all savings banks. Deposits in the Ordinary Department (*q.v.*)

of a Savings Bank carry a moderate rate of interest, but deposits in the Investment Department (*q.v.*) and Term Deposits (*q.v.*) carry higher rates. In recent times they have widened their activities. Since 1965 they have permitted their customers to have current accounts and use cheques. In 1967 they combined to set up their own unit trust. They also issue travellers' cheques and engage in foreign exchange business. In 1973 there were 73 separate trustee savings banks in the United Kingdom. Following the recommendations of the Page Report (*q.v.*) the number of trustee savings banks was greatly reduced and by 1975 the number had fallen to 20. The aim is to have 15 regional banks—10 in England, 4 in Scotland and one in Northern Ireland. See also National Savings Bank.

Trustee Securities. Securities declared by law to be suitable for the investment of money held in trust. At one time only Government stocks and a few other similar investments qualified as trustee securities, but since 1961 the equities of companies which fulfil certain conditions and unit investment trusts have qualified as 'wider range' trustee securities. See Trustee Investment Act (1961).

T.S.B. Abbreviation of Trustee Savings Bank (*q.v.*).

T.T. Abbreviation of Telegraphic Transfer (*q.v.*).

T.U. Abbreviation of Trade Union (*q.v.*).

T.U.C. Abbreviation of Trades Union Congress (*q.v.*).

T.U.C.C. Abbreviation of Transport Users' Consultative Committee (*q.v.*).

Tugrik. The standard unit of the currency of Mongolia.

Tunnage and Poundage. Import duties which were first levied in the Middle Ages, tunnage being a duty on imported wine and poundage a duty on other imports. It became customary for Parliament to grant the revenue from these taxes to the King for life.

Tunnels. A means by which barriers to communication—mountain ranges or wide rivers—have been surmounted. The Mont Cenis, Simplon, and St. Gotthard tunnels were constructed to enable railways to pierce the Alps. There are also railway tunnels beneath the Thames, Mersey, and Severn and many other rivers. Road tunnels have been constructed beneath the Thames (3), Mersey, Clyde, Tyne, Schelde, and Maas. A scheme to construct a tunnel under the English Channel from England to France was considered for many years, but has been shelved. Road tunnels under the Alps include the Grand St. Bernard (1964), the Mont Blanc (1965), and the San Bernardino (1971). A St. Gotthard road tunnel is to be opened shortly.

Turn. The difference between the price at which he is prepared to buy and that at which he is prepared to sell, quoted by a jobber on the London Stock Exchange when asked by a broker his price of a security.

Turnover. Total sales of a business during a particular period.

Turnover, Rate of. The number of times the value of the average stock of a business is sold during a period. If average stock is £500 and turnover £3,000, then the rate of turnover is 6. For expensive goods the rate of turnover is usually slow, but for commodities in regular consumption the rate of turnover is more rapid, and for perishable goods such as greengrocery most rapid of all.

Turnover Tax. A tax on the total sales of a business with whatever stage of production it is concerned. Contrast the Sales Tax which is levied only at the retail stage and Purchase Tax which is levied only at the wholesale stage. A Turnover Tax, therefore, is wider in its application and much heavier in its incidence than either of these other taxes. See also Purchase Tax; Sales Tax.

Turnpike Trust. A body which undertook to keep a specified section of road in repair in return for the right to levy tolls on those using it. Turnpikes were established by individual Acts of Parliament, the first being passed in 1663. Most turnpike trusts were established during the latter half of the 18th century. The turnpikes reached their zenith during the early 19th century but declined with the coming of the railways. Many turnpike trusts constructed new lines of road. Financially they were not successful and at their closure most of them were heavily in debt, but for the first time they made possible speedy travel. The term has recently been revived in the United States for modern motorways constructed by private enterprise and subject to tolls. *See also* Highways.

T.V.A. 1. Abbreviation of Tennessee Valley Authority (*q.v.*).
2. Abbreviation of *Taxe à la Valeur Ajoutee*, i.e. Value-added Tax (*q.v.*).

T.W.A. Abbreviation of Trans-World Airlines, one of the main American airlines operating on international routes. It also has a large amount of domestic business.

Twenty, Committee of. A committee of the I.M.F. set up in 1972 to consider reform of the Bretton Woods international monetary system.

Twenty-pound Note. Bank of England notes for £20 were withdrawn in 1946, though Scottish banks continued to issue them, but they began to be re-issued in 1970. The fall in the value of money has made it necessary to issue notes of higher denominations, the ten-pound note having been re-introduced in 1964.

T.W.I. Abbreviation of Training Within Industry. *See* Education.

Two-part Tariff. Differential charges for gas and electricity which may vary according to the amount consumed, the charge being lower after a certain amount has been consumed, or there may be a minimum fixed charge in addition to a charge varying with consumption, or there may be different charges according to the purpose of consumption as, for example, light and power or domestic and business. All these are examples of discriminating monopoly (*q.v.*), the markets being separated as indicated. Where fixed costs are heavy it is useful to be able to charge an initial supply at a higher rate.

Two-pound Note. This note has had only a brief history in England, being first issued in 1797 during the Napoleonic Wars and withdrawn in 1821 when it was replaced by the gold two-pound piece, though these coins were never issued in great quantity. The revival of the two-pound note has been suggested many times and, although notes of this value have been issued in Bermuda and some other British territories, the British monetary authorities have not been favourable to the idea.

Two-tier Systems. 1. A two-tier price system was operative for gold during 1968–73. *See* Gold Pool.
2. Differential charges for first-class and second-class mail were introduced by the Post Office in September 1968.
3. Interest rates. Most rates of interest used to rise or fall with bank rate, which often was raised mainly on account of the external situation and yet increase the cost of borrowing by the Government and from building societies. Since 1972, the commercial banks' base rate has been independent of the Bank of England's minimum lending rate.
4. Dual exchange rates as employed by France for a period in 1971.

U

U.C.A.T.T. Abbreviation of Union of Construction and Allied Trades and Technicians, an amalgamation of the bricklayers', painters' and woodworkers' unions.

U.D.E. Abbreviation of Union Douanière Equatoriale. *See* Equatorial Customs Union.

U.D.E.A.C. Abbreviation of Union Douanière et Economique d'Afrique Centrale. *See* Central African Customs and Economic Union.

U.D.T. Abbreviation of United Dominions Trust (*q.v.*).

Ulnage. A medieval tax on woollen cloth.

Ulster Bank Ltd. A bank of Northern Ireland established in 1836, now under the control of the National Westminster Bank Ltd.

Ultra-cheap Money Policy. A term used during 1945–48 when it was the aim of Dr. H. (later Lord) Dalton, Chancellor of the Exchequer, to keep the prevailing rate of interest at a very low level, bank rate being maintained, in spite of inflationary pressure, at $2\frac{1}{2}\%$. The failure of the issue of $2\frac{1}{2}\%$ Treasury Stock (redeemable after April 1975) marked the end of the period of ultra-cheap money.

Unauthorised Clerk. An employee of a stockbroker who is a member of the stock exchange and who, although permitted to assist his employer in the stock exchange, is not allowed to deal.

Unbalanced Budget. The budget is clearly unbalanced if estimated expenditure exceeds estimated revenue, but should only 'above-the-line' items be taken into account, or should 'below-the-line' items also be included? Many economists would consider the budget to be unbalanced only if there was a deficit above-the-line on the ground that the items below-the-line are mainly of a capital nature and generally there is a below-the-line deficit. Similarly, the budget can be regarded as balanced if there is a credit balance above-the-line, although in using fiscal policy as an adjunct to monetary policy the aim has sometimes been to have a substantial overall balance. It was during the Great Depression that it was first suggested that the budget should be used as an instrument of monetary policy and that in order to stimulate demand it should be deliberately unbalanced. At one time it was felt that the budget should balance each year, but it is now thought to be in order if the budget balances over a period of years.

Uncalled Capital. The balance on partly paid shares which a company can call on if it requires more capital.

Uncertainty. There are two categories of risk—one the probability of which can be calculated and which, therefore, can be insured against, and one the probability of which cannot be calculated so that it cannot be insured against. To the second type of risk the term, uncertainty, has been applied and this is the type of risk to be borne by the entrepreneur, for the bearing of uncertainty is his principal function.

Unconfirmed Letter of Credit. Also known as a Revocable Letter of Credit. *See* Letter of Credit.

U.N.C.T.A.D. Abbreviation of United Nations Conference on Trade and Development. It was called into being to consider how best to help developing nations.

Undercharge. To cover an undercharge a seller may send the buyer a debit note or a further invoice.

Under-consumption Theories of the Trade Cycle. These theories take several forms: (i) The belief that there is always insufficient purchasing power to buy all the goods and services that are produced, some purchasing power, according to the cruder versions of the theory, being somehow lost. The remedy, therefore, seemed to be for the State to make periodical distributions of money to the community in order to make up the deficiency. The suggestion that purchasing power is lost is a fallacy, since all costs of production become purchasing power to the people receiving these payments. (ii) The belief that there is too much saving and insufficient consumption. Once a depression has set in, too much saving will certainly aggravate the situation.

Under-developed Nations. See Developing Nations.

Underground Railways. Built to relieve traffic congestion in the streets of large cities, the first underground line was constructed in London. Other cities with underground railways include Glasgow, New York, San Francisco, Paris, Rome, Frankfurt, Madrid, Moscow, Athens.

Underpopulation. A country is underpopulated if it has insufficient labour to make the most efficient use of its land and capital, that is, if it is below the optimum. See Optimum Population.

Undertaker. A term used by Alfred Marshall as an alternative to 'entrepreneur'.

'Under the Counter.' Goods in short supply and not officially rationed have to be rationed by shopkeepers. In order to ensure supplies for regular customers they have to keep goods out of sight.

Undervaluation. With reference to foreign exchange, this occurs when a currency is given a lower value externally than internally, that is, a lower value than it would have in a free market. The effect of this is to make imports dearer and exports cheaper. Thus, the effect of undervaluation is to stimulate exports.

Under the Bretton Woods scheme in operation since the Second World War currencies tend to become undervalued in those countries suffering a smaller degree of inflation than others and so enjoying particularly favourable balances of payments. In such cases equilibrium can be restored to the international monetary system only by the revaluation of these currencies, as occurred with the West German Deutsche Mark and the Dutch guilder in 1961. See also Revaluation.

Underwriter. A person whose business it is to offer to cover or underwrite a portion of a risk, either in connection with insurance, especially marine insurance (see Lloyd's), or in connection with a new issue of shares by an issuing house (*q.v.*).

Undischarged Bankrupt. A bankrupt who has not secured his discharge is not allowed to obtain credit of £10 or more without informing his creditor of his position nor is he permitted to engage in trade under another name.

Unearned Income. 1. As formerly used by the Inland Revenue, it comprised income derived from investment. See Income Tax.

2. In economics unearned income comprises only pure economic rent and the surplus profit of the monopolist.

Unearned Increment. An increase in the value of land or other property as a result of increased demand and not due to any kind of improvement undertaken by the owner.

Unemployables. People who, on account of mental or physical disability, are unable to follow normal employment. They are no longer included in the numbers of the unemployed.

Unemployed Workmen Act (1905). An Act which gave local authorities power to organise schemes of public works for the unemployed and to establish Labour Exchanges, later to be known as Employment Exchanges (*q.v.*).

Unemployment. Several types of unemployment can be distinguished: (i) Mass unemployment is the most serious type since it is due to a general deficiency of demand and, therefore, affects nearly all industries at the same time, though the capital-producing industries are more seriously affected than others. It is sometimes known as cyclical unemployment as it was associated with the trade cycle. The Great Depression of 1929–35 provided the worst example of it, and in 1932, the worst year, Great Britain had over 20% of its insured workers unemployed. (ii) Structural unemployment, due to a change of demand, is an example of frictional unemployment, since the fall in demand for one thing is generally balanced by an increase in demand for something else, unemployment being mainly the result of lack of mobility of labour. (iii) Unemployment due to technological progress is another type of frictional unemployment. The immediate effect of the introduction of labour-saving machinery is to make some workers redundant, but in the long-run the demand for labour is likely to be increased. The new machinery itself has to be produced, and if average cost is reduced by the use of the new machinery the quantity demanded is likely to increase, and in time the higher standard of living will lead to a general increase in demand. In the short-run, however, there will be unemployment due to immobility of labour and also to the fact that any subsequent expansion of demand will take time to develop. (iv) Seasonal unemployment occurs in some kinds of work. Bad weather will cause a temporary suspension of work in building and other outdoor occupations. In some occupations there is a demand for labour only at certain periods of the year, as in potato-lifting and fruit gathering. In most seaside resorts demand for many kinds of labour is restricted to a few months of the year. (v) Residual unemployment covers unemployment due to all other causes, and includes those people regarded as unemployable on account of physical or mental disability. It is important to distinguish between different causes of unemployment if a policy of full employment is to be successfully pursued. Full employment policies aim principally to get rid of mass unemployment, but since economic progress requires the use of the most up-to-date machinery, and since too at any time some industries are declining while others are expanding, there is still likely to be frictional unemployment due to technological progress and changes of demand. *See* Full Employment.

Unemployment Assistance Board. A body set up under an Act of 1934 to adminster unemployment assistance for those whose entitlement under the National Insurance scheme had been exhausted. The Board had offices in various parts of the country. In 1940 its name was changed to Assistance Board and in 1966 its functions were taken over by the Department of Health and Social Security (*q.v.*).

Unemployment Benefit. One of the benefits under the National Insurance scheme. Before this scheme was introduced in 1911 some trade unions, mainly the smaller craft unions, offered their members unemployment benefit.

Unemployment Compensation. A term used in the United States for unemployment benefit.

Unemployment Rate. The percentage of insured workers who are unemployed at a particular date. This averaged 4·8% for the quarter-century before 1913, 14·2 during 1921–38, and less than 3% for the period between 1945 and the early 1970s. Regional and local rates often differ widely from the national average. For example, in 1937 when the average rate of unemployment for the United Kingdom was 10·4, the percentage for Wales was 24·3. Since 1945 the rate for many parts of the country has been below 2%, but in 1976 it reached over 9% for the country as a whole. Since 1955 it has been two to three times greater in Northern Ireland, Scotland, and north-east England than in the rest of the country.

U.N.E.S.C.O. Abbreviation of United Nations Educational, Scientific, and Cultural Organisation, a body set up by the United Nations to diffuse knowledge among nations and encourage collaboration through education, science, and culture.

Unfavourable Balance. A term used of a debit balance in the Balance of Payments or the Balance of Trade.

Unfunded Debt. Usually restricted to short-term Government debt. *See* Funded Debt.

Unigate Ltd. A holding company formed to take over United Dairies Ltd. and Cow and Gate Ltd. controlling upwards of 300 companies.

Unilever Ltd. A holding company controlling Lever Bros. Ltd., Macfisheries Ltd., Walls Ltd. and upwards of 200 other companies, making a variety of products.

Union. A group of parishes linked together for the purpose of carrying out the provisions of the Poor Law Amendment Act (1834) (*q.v.*).

Union Assurance Co. Ltd. Founded in 1714 it is the second oldest fire insurance company in Great Britain. *See* Fire Insurance.

Union Bank of Switzerland. The third largest commercial bank of Switzerland.

Union d'Assurance des Crédits Internationaux. *See* Berne Union.

Union Discount Company Ltd. One of the three large London discount houses.

Unitas. A term suggested during the discussions prior to the Bretton Woods Conference of 1944 by the American Treasury as a name for an international currency or unit of account. Lord Keynes suggested that the unit of account should be given the name 'bancor', but neither term was adopted.

Unit Assurance. The linking of life assurance to unit trusts (*q.v.*), the greater portion of the premium being used to purchase units in a specified trust, the monetary value of which is likely to increase if the value of money falls during the period of assurance, thereby providing a hedge against inflation.

Unit Banking. A banking system in which a bank is not permitted to open branches, as prevails in many states of the United States, in contrast to a branch banking system in which each bank has a large number of branches, as in Great Britain. Unit banks tend to be weaker in a crisis than branch banks. Thus, during the Great Depression of the 1930s there was a huge number of bank failures among the unit banks of the United States, but not a single British bank had to close its doors.

Unite. A British gold coin, worth £1, issued in 1604 after the union of England and Scotland.

United Airline. The largest American airline, its routes lie entirely within the United States.

United Dominions Trust. One of the two leading Finance Houses in Great Britain (the other being Mercantile Credit Ltd.), it is a subsidiary of Barclays Bank Ltd. In 1972 it became a commercial bank.

United Drapery Stores Ltd. A holding company controlling a number of multiple stores, including Alexandre Ltd., James Grant & Co. Ltd., Prices Tailors Ltd., John Collier Ltd. and about fifty other companies.

United International Bank. A banking composium formed in London in 1970, comprising Williams & Glyn, two North American and three European banks.

United Stock Exchange. *See* Stock Exchange.

Unit Elasticity. The elasticity of demand for a commodity is said to be equal to unity if a change of price brings about a proportionate change in the quantity of it demanded.

Unit of Account. One of the functions of money is to serve as a unit of account. By assigning money prices to goods one of the difficulties of barter is overcome. A unit of account is essential for purposes of calculation and money best serves this purpose, though it is not essential for the unit of account to be the same as the currency. In a period of severe inflation something other than the local currency may be used as the unit of account. Even if there were no money some unit of account would be required. For example, a unit of account would be required to calculate the relative cost of different methods of production or for comparisons of the national income between one year and another. For a long time the English shilling was only a unit of account, coins of that value not being minted until 1504. Instead of using an existing currency the accounts of the European Payments Union (*q.v.*) were kept in units of accounts, which had a gold value equal to that of the U.S. dollar.

Unit Trust. An investment trust which uses its funds to purchase a range of stock exchange securities and then offers units to investors, either on tap or in block offers, at the current offer price. The managers of the trust are prepared to purchase units at any time at the current bid price, which is a little lower than the offer price. Holders of units are not shareholders as they are in the case of an investment trust company (*q.v.*). Unit trusts have become very popular with small investors since the smallest investment in a unit trust may be spread over a hundred or more securities. Prices of units vary from a fraction of £1 to £2 or £3, but most unit trusts, prefer units of fairly small denominations. Of American origin, unit trusts were first introduced into Great Britain during the 1930s. Most of the English banks and some assurance companies are now associated with unit trusts. Many unit trusts now offer life assurance linked to unit trust investment.

Universal Bank. A bank that engages in all forms of banking activity—a feature of German commercial banking. Such banks undertake investment banking, including the holding of shares in public companies.

Universal Copyright Convention (1958). An international conference called to formulate a common policy towards copyright (*q.v.*).

Universal Postal Union. A body established in 1875 to regulate postal services between different countries, international congresses being held at intervals of five years. Almost all countries of the world are members.

University Entrance. *See* General Certificate of Education.

U.N.O. Abbreviation of United Nations Organisation.

Unofficial Strike. A strike which does not have the support of the trade union concerned.

Unpaid Services. These are not included in calculation of the national income. They include housewives' services, voluntary services of all kinds, and all services which people do for themselves or for one another.

Unproductive Expenditure. Adam Smith and his followers regarded private expenditure as productive and State expenditure as unproductive. This has long been regarded as a fallacy. Whether the State spends money better than private individuals depends on the purposes for which the money is spent.

Unproductive Labour. A term used by Adam Smith of the services of servants, members of the armed forces, churchmen, lawyers, physicians, musicians, men of letters, entertainers, etc., productive labour being that of those engaged in manufacture, etc. Even today there are people who regard those workers in a firm who do not actually handle the product as unproductive workers. The distinction is pointless, all labour being concerned with the provision of labour service and, therefore, productive, whether it has to do with goods or not. The more advanced a nation's economy the greater will be the number of people providing direct services.

Unrequited Exports. Exports for which no payment is made at the time, payment being made by the reduction of an outstanding debt arising from imports previously on credit. During the Second World War Great Britain, unable to produce goods for export at the time, purchased goods from many countries on credit, the amounts owing for these goods being placed in blocked accounts. When these blocked accounts were released the countries concerned were able to use them for the purchase of British exports, for which Great Britain was not entitled to receive any further payment. This added to Great Britain's difficulties with its balance of payments since imports of food and raw materials for current use had then to be paid for by additional exports.

U.N.R.R.A. Abbreviation of United Nations Relief and Rehabilitation Administration, an organisation established in 1943 to give relief after the Second World War.

Unsecured Creditor. A creditor whose claim is on the general assets of the debtor as distinct from a secured creditor whose claim rests on a specified asset of the debtor.

Unsecured Debentures or Loan Stock. A type of debenture (*q.v.*).

U.N.T.A.D. Abbreviation of United Nations Trade and Development Conference, established in 1964 to assist developing countries, particularly by raising the prices of primary product on which their economies are generally based.

Untested Prices. A stock exchange term used of prices assigned to stocks and shares by jobbers when business is too slight to affect prices.

Upswing. With reference to the trade cycle, the period of recovery from slump to boom.

Upward Mobility. A form of Vertical Mobility (*q.v.*).

Upward Phase. An alternative term for Upswing (*q.v.*).

Urgent Rate. An additional charge for dispatching telegraphic money orders more expenditiously to places abroad.

Urwick Report (1947). A report on education for management. As a result the British Institute of Management was established in 1947, and ten years later this body merged with the Institute of Industrial Administration. *See* British Institute of Management.

Usance. A term used in connection with bills of exchange with a period to run before becoming due for payment, in contrast to 'sight' bills which like cheques, are payable at sight.

U.S.E. Abbreviation of United Stock Exchange. *See* Stock Exchange.

User Cost. A term used by Lord Keynes for the cost of using machinery, in terms of depreciation and maintenance, in excess of the cost of leaving it idle.

Usury. A term now restricted to the charging of a very high rate of interest on a loan, but formerly used in connection with interest whether the rate charged was high or low. The medieval Church, following the law of Moses and the writings of Aristotle and other Greek philosophers, condemned the payment of interest on a loan as usury and unjust. The explanation of this attitude to the payment of interest is to be found in the different character of borrowers and lenders today and of earlier times. At one time borrowers were poor people or those who had suffered some misfortune in days before insurance cover was possible, and the lenders were of necessity wealthy persons. At the present day, however, the principal lenders are the commercial banks, and those who find it easiest to borrow are those whose financial position is basically sound. Only slowly did it come to be realised that, like any other payment, interest was a payment for a service. From the time of Henry VIII a succession of statutes was passed to regulate the rate of interest, but the Usury Laws, which interfered with the use of bank rate as an instrument of monetary policy, were not repealed until 1854. The rates of interest which pawnbrokers and moneylenders are permitted to charge, though relatively high, are still regulated. *See* Consumer Credit.

Usury Laws. Passed in the sixteenth century, these laws prohibited the charging of a rate of interest in England in excess of 5%. They were repealed in 1854, mainly to enable the Bank of England to develop the use of its bank rate as instrument of monetary policy, which on occasions might require a rate of interest in excess of 5%.

Uthwatt Report (1942). Recommended that the State should purchase development rights in land.

Util. Although utility cannot be measured this term is sometimes used for a unit of utility, more particularly to illustrate the Law of Diminishing Marginal Utility.

Utility. 1. The amount of satisfaction a person derives from some thing or service, without any reference to its usefulness. It has an important influence on demand, but it is not, however, total utility that influences demand but marginal utility and this declines the more a person possesses of a thing. *See* Diminishing Marginal Utility, Law of; Marginal Utility.

2. A term used during the Second World War of commodities—for example clothing, furniture—produced in a limited number of standardised lines in order to simplify production.

'Utmost Good Faith.' The insurance principles that all parties to an insurance contract must disclose all relevant particulars which might influence any party's willingness to make the contract. The principle also applies to some other contracts.

V

Valorisation Schemes. Government schemes to keep up the prices of some commodities, especially those for which the country concerned enjoys a very large share of the world market. The Government may pay producers to reduce their output (as occurred under the U.S. New Deal), or it may set up a State-owned monopolistic buying and selling agency and sell only a portion of total output, destroying the rest (as occurred with Brazilian coffee production), or where there are only a few producers (as with tin and rubber) they might make agreements to restrict supplies to the market.

Valuation. With reference to property, the rateable value (*q.v.*).

Value. The theory of value received great attention from early writers on economics, all of whom approached the problem from the supply side. In order to explain what he called the 'paradox of value', Adam Smith found it necessary to distinguish between 'value in use' (this depending on the amount of satisfaction to be obtained) and 'value in exchange' (this determining its price). Water, he pointed out had great value in use but little value in exchange, the reverse, he thought, being the case with diamonds. Value in exchange he considered to be determined by the relative amounts of labour required for the production of different things. According to Adam Smith, if one thing required twice as much labour to produce as another then it would be twice as valuable. This Labour Theory of Value was improved upon by J. S. Mill who put forward the Cost of Production Theory of Value, according to which value depends on the total cost of producing a thing, including not only the cost of labour but also the profit of the entrepreneur.

These early theories of value completely ignore the influence of demand. The development of the concept of diminishing marginal utility (*q.v.*)—approaching the problem this time from the demand side—resolved Adam Smith's 'paradox of value' which had its origin in a failure to recognise a distinction between *total* utility and *marginal* utility. Adam Smith and his followers regarded value as objective, whereas the marginal utility school considered value to be subjective, the one stressing the supply side and the other the demand side. Subjectively, value cannot be measured. All that a person can do is to arrange his wants in order of preference. However, if value is taken to mean the determination of price, it depends on the relation between demand (based on diminishing marginal utility) and supply (based on cost of production). In the short run demand is the more important influence: whatever a commodity may have cost to produce, once it has been produced the price it will fetch in the market depends on the demand for it. In the long run, however, costs of production must be covered or supply will be curtailed. *See* Demand; Equilibrium (i); Supply.

Value-added Tax (V.A.T.). A tax levied on the value of each of the processes carried out by a business. Thus, where an industry is horizontally integrated with firms specialising in single processes the tax would be based only on the work done by each firm and not, as in the case of a Turnover Tax (*q.v.*), on the full value of the product. In Great Britain Value-added Tax replaced Purchase Tax and Selective Employment Tax in 1973. Value-added Tax is more broadly based and falls less heavily on particular goods and services than Purchase Tax (*q.v.*).

Goods and services not liable to Value-added Tax may be zero-rated or exempt. When goods are zero-rated no tax is charged but a trader supplying such goods can reclaim tax on his inputs. When goods or services are exempt no tax on inputs can be reclaimed.

Value in Exchange and Value in Use. Terms used by Adam Smith in connection with what he regarded as the 'paradox of value'—the fact that the prices of diamonds and water appeared to vary inversely with their value. Value in exchange was the price of the commodity, and value in use depended on its importance. This difficulty arose because Smith approached the problem of value entirely from the supply size and ignored the influence of demand. *See* Value.

Value Judgment. An opinion as to what course of action should be taken, a matter of ethics rather than economics.

Value-linking. An alternative term for Indexation (*q.v.*).

Value of Money. By this term we mean what money will buy. If at one time a certain amount of money buys fewer things than at a previous time, it can be said that the value of money has fallen. Since money itself is used as a unit of account and as a means of measuring the 'value' of other things, its own value can be seen only through the price of other things. Changes in the value of money, therefore, are shown through changes in prices. Over the centuries there has been a general tendency for the value of money to fall. During the nineteenth century, when money in many countries was closely related to gold, the value of money varied with the relation between the output of gold from the mines and the production of other things. From the late eighteenth century down to 1913 there was a short-term variation in the value of money associated with the trade cycle. During the twentieth century the value of money throughout the world has fallen more rapidly than ever before as a result of two great wars and the inflationary tendencies since 1945. The extent of inflation in recent years has varied from country to country. During the ten years 1956–66, whereas the value of money declined at an average rate per year in the U.S.A. of only 1·8%, in Switzerland by 2·4%, and in Great Britain by 3%, the decline in France was 4·7%, and in Turkey 7·7%. During these years monetary depreciation was most severe in South America—an average per year of no less than 31% in Brazil, 24% in Argentina, and 20% in Chile.

Changes in the value of money are measured by index numbers. The first attempt to explain changes in the value of money was the Quantity Theory (*q.v.*), at first in its crude form and then more recently in its form as refined by Irving Fisher, as illustrated in the Equation of Exchange (*q.v.*):

$$MV = PT$$

Lord Keynes attempted to explain the value of money in terms of supply and demand as with other things. For this purpose demand for money was defined as the demand to hold money as distinct from investing it, Lord Keynes indicating three motives for holding money—the transactions, precautionary, and speculative motives (*qq.v.*). This approach to explaining the value of money was illustrated by the equation:

$$p = \frac{M}{kR}$$

The symbol M represents the supply of money, R is the real income or volume of production, k is the proportion of the national income people prefer to hold in the form of money (that is, the demand for money) and p is the price level of consumers' goods.

Valuer. A person who undertakes the valuation of property of all kinds, generally prior to its sale.

Variable Amount Direct Debit. A

type of bank standing order to cover future increases in subscriptions—a consequence of inflation.

Variable Cost. A cost of production which varies with output, though not necessarily proportionately with output. The principal variable costs are wages, the cost of raw materials and power.

Variable Proportions, Law of. *See* Returns, Laws of.

Varig. The Brazilian airline, it is the largest in South America.

V.A.T. Abbreviation of Value-added Tax (*q.v.*).

Velocity of Circulation. The average number of times each unit of money is used during a period, that is, the total amount of money spent during a period divided by the amount of money (cash and bank deposits) in circulation. It is one of the influences on the value of money since a change in the Velocity of Circulation is similar in its effects to similar changes in the quantity of money. In a severe inflation the value of money falls to a greater extent than appears to be warranted by the increase in the quantity of money on account of the great increase which usually takes place in the velocity of circulation. In practice it is difficult to calculate the velocity of circulation but the total bank clearings during a period in relation to the total of bank deposits during that period would give some indication of it, though this ignores cash transactions. *See* Quantity Theory of Money.

Vending Machine. *See* Automatic Selling.

Venture Capital. An alternative term for Risk Capital (*q.v.*).

Vertical Combination. With reference to a combine vertical integration means an amalgamation of firms at different stages of production as was the case with the American Iron and Steel Trust.

Vertical Integration. With reference to the structure of an industry it means that most firms carry out all the main stages in the production of a commodity, as occurs in the woollen section of the Yorkshire wool textile industry, whereas the worsted section of that industry is horizontally integrated.

Vertical Mobility. A change of occupation affects the status of the worker. It tends to increase his mobility if he thinks his status will be improved, but it reduces his mobility if he thinks he will suffer a loss of status. *See* Mobility.

Vertical Structure. *See* Vertical Combination; Vertical Integration.

Villein. A worker on a medieval manor who was allowed the use of a number of strips of land in the three main fields in return for working on the lord's demesne a certain number of days each week and at harvest time.

Vintners' Company. One of the more important of the 82 Guilds or Livery Companies of the City of London whose existence dates back to the gilds of the Middle Ages, it ranks eleventh in the order of civic precedence. The company is known to have been in existence in the thirteenth century, when its members were concerned with the importing of wine. It received letters patent in 1363 but had to wait until 1437 for its charter. It still maintains a connection with its original trade.

Visible Balance. An alternative term for the Balance of Trade (*q.v.*).

Visible Items. In the Balance of Payments (*q.v.*) the terms 'visible items' or 'visibles' has been given in recent times to the value of imports and exports of goods, the term 'invisibles' having long been used of payments for and receipts from services.

Vital Statistics. The birth-rate and death-rate statistics of a country (*qq.v.*).

Vocational Guidance. Advising people—perhaps as a result of vocational or aptitude tests—on the occupations for which they appear to be most suited.

Vocational Tests. When applied to schoolchildren their purpose is to discover the occupations for which the children are most suited.

Vocational Training. That part of technical and commercial education devoted to training students in the skills required in their future occupations.

Volume of Production. *See* National Income.

Voluntary Liquidation. The winding up of a company by a resoluion of its shareholders as distinct from winding up as a result of a Court order (compulsory liquidation).

Vostro Account. (Vostro = Italian for *your*.) An account by foreign banks with banks in London. *Cf.* Nostro Account.

Voyage Charter Party. This occurs when a ship is chartered for a specific voyage as distinct from Time Charter where the charter is for a definite period of time.

W

Wadd Jefferson. One of the two large firms of jobbers on the London stock exchange, they are responsible for half the total business in gilt-edged stocks.

Wage Councils. These are bodies originally set up by the Ministry of Labour after 1945 in industries where there were no adequate arrangements for collective bargaining between employers and employees. Wage Councils replaced Trade Boards (q.v.). The Wages Councils Act (1959) consolidated earlier legislation on the subject. In addition to representatives of employers and employees each Wages Council has up to three independent members.

Wage Differentials. *See* Differential.

Wage Drift. A term used of increases in earnings over and above increases in wages obtained as a result of collective bargaining, for example, overtime (particularly where the working week has been 'reduced'), or payments by employers above national rates, either directly or in the form of bonuses, because of a shortage of labour or as a means of attracting more efficient labour.

Wage Freeze. An attempt to hold wages at their existing level for a period of time. A wage freeze was attempted after the devaluation of sterling in 1949, but in view of rising prices during 1949–50 trade unions were unwilling to accept it. A similar policy was attempted under the name of 'pay pause' in 1961–62, the term 'freeze' appearing too severe, but with no greater success. During 1964–69, and again during 1972–1974, the British Government tried to enforce a Prices and Incomes Policy (q.v.).

Wage-goods. A term first used by Prof. A. C. Pigou for the goods, the prices of which determine the value of real wages as distinct from money wages.

Wage Incentives. *See* Bonus (ii).

Wage Rates. There are a number of methods of calculating wages such as time-rates, piece-rates, and the various bonus systems—premium-bonus and task-bonus (qq.v.).

Wage Restraint. The suggestion that trade unions should moderate their demand for wage increases in order to check inflation. *See* Inflationary Spiral; Pay Pause; Prices and Incomes Policy; Wage Freeze.

Wages. The payment to labour for its assistance to production. Theories put forward to explain the determination of wages include the Subsistence Theory, the Wages Fund Theory, and the Marginal Productivity Theory (qq.v.). Wages can be regarded as a price and, therefore, like other prices, determined in a market, in this case the market for labour. The demand for labour is derived from the demand for the goods and services for the production of which it is required, so that anything that stimulates the demand for goods and services will stimulate the demand for labour. There is, however, the possibility of substitution between factors of production, and this must be related to the marginal productivity of labour and the expectations of entrepreneurs of the future trend of business activity. There is not, however, a single market for labour, but a number of markets, each with its own conditions of demand and supply. Thus, there is a separate market for each kind of specific labour, special training, aptitude, and qualifications restricting the supply of labour available for certain kinds of work. The fact that there are many separate markets for labour is the main cause of differences of wages between different occupations. The various markets for labour are to some extent interrelated, and high wages in one occupation may be expected in time to attract labour from other occupations, though the length of the period of training and the particular qualifications required will tend to counteract this tendency. *See* Bargaining Theory of Wages.

Wages Boards. Bodies established in some industries, agriculture for example, to consider wages.

Wages Fund Theory. An early theory of wages, according to which there is a sort of wages fund out of which wages are paid, so that the total that can be paid in wages at any particular time is limited by the size of the fund at that time. The size of the fund, it was thought, was determined by past accumulations of capital.

Wages of Management. One of the elements of profit. In order to calculate the amount of pure profit accruing to an entrepreneur wages of management and interest on capital must be deducted.

Wages-Prices Spiral. *See* Inflationary Spiral.

Wages Structure. The relation between wages in different occupations *e.g.* between skilled and unskilled workers.

Wagner Act (1935). A U.S. labour relations Act, passed as part of Roosevelt's New Deal policy (*q.v.*) to legalise trade unions and collective bargaining. *See also* Taft-Hartley Act (1947).

Wagon Finance Corporation Ltd. A hire purchase finance company, established in Rotherham, and before the nationalisation of the railways engaged in financing the purchase of private railway wagons, the use of which is no longer permitted by British Rail.

Wagonways. An alternative name for the tramways—wagons on wooden rails pulled by horses—built in the late eighteenth century and early nineteenth century to connect collieries or quarries with rivers or canals. They were forerunners of railways.

Waiter. 1. The scarlet-coated attendants of the Room of Lloyd's of London, the term having its origin in the fact that in the eighteenth century the waiters in Edward Lloyd's Coffee House used to supply shipping information to City merchants.
2. The attendants of the London Stock Exchange.

Waiting. A feature of capital formation. During the period of waiting a sacrifice of consumption has to be made, the reward for which is the greater output that becomes possible when the new capital comes into use.

Waiver Clause. A clause in a contract or treaty which enables an undertaking or obligation to be avoided in certain specified circumstances. Under the Washington Loan Agreement (*q.v.*) Great Britain was permitted to waive (or, this case more correctly, to postpone) the interest payment in any year in which it had difficulty with its balance of payments.

Walk-out. A colloquial term for a strike (*q.v.*).

Walks Clerks. A term formerly applied to London bank clerks who used to meet to clear cheques before the opening in 1770 of the first bankers' clearing house in Lombard Street, London. Walks clearings still take place between London banks which are not members of the London Bankers Clearing House.

Wall Street. A street in New York where the head offices of many banks, insurance companies, and other financial institutions are situated. The New York Stock Exchange is also located there and the term is often used as a synonym for it. The term 'Wall Street' is used in New York in very much the same way as is the word 'City' in London.

Wall Street Crash (1929). The collapse of prices on the New York Stock Exchange in 1929 ushered in the Great Depression in the United States and in the world. Excessive speculation in stocks and shares by a large proportion of the people had pushed up prices to excessive heights.

Want Creation. The stimulation of demand by monetary and fiscal policy in order to keep up the level of employment. In the affluent society producers try to create new wants through mass advertising media.

Wants. People want many things, both goods and services, and it is the aim of production to satisfy those wants. The only wants of economic —as distinct from social—importance are those backed up by the purchasing power necessary to satisfy them, these constituting effective demand.

Wants, Double Coincidence of. A pre-requisite of a barter transaction. *See* Barter.

War Agricultural Committees. Set up during the Second World War to ensure efficiency of farming, they were continued after that war as County Agricultural Committees. *See* Agricultural Committees, County.

War Bonus. A temporary addition to wages given during wartime to offset the rise in prices. It was a common practice during the First World War.

Warburg (S. G.) & Co. Ltd. A London merchant bank, of fairly recent origin, being established only after the Second World War, it also has interests in New York and Frankfurt-am-Main.

Warehouse, Bonded. *See* Bonded Warehouse.

Warehouse Warrant. A negotiable document which entitles its holder to the goods named on it, stored at a specific warehouse. Its production is required before the goods can be removed from the warehouse.

Warehousing. One of the functions of a wholesaler (*q.v.*).

War Loan. A Government stock carrying $3\frac{1}{2}\%$ interest and redeemable at a date after 1952. It is now regarded as an irredeemable stock.

Warrant, Dividend. *See* Dividend Warrant.

Warranty. 1. In marine insurance a clause in a policy which must be strictly complied with for the insurance to be effective.

2. An alternative term for a guarantee that an article is free from defective workmanship.

War Stock. *See* War Loan.

Washington Loan Agreement (1945). An agreement signed in Washington in December 1945, whereby Great Britain was allowed a 'line of credit' of $3,750 million by the United States. The financial terms were not onerous; interest was to be at only 2% and repayment was not to begin until January 1952. In addition the interest payment could be postponed in any year in which Great Britain had difficulties with its balance of payments. The other conditions attached to the loan were astounding: (i) Sterling was to be made freely convertible not later than July 1947, although at Bretton Woods a transition period of five years after the end of the war had been envisaged; (ii) All forms of trade discrimination should be abandoned by Great Britain; (iii) Within one year Great Britain had to end exchange control for current transactions. Only dire necessity made Great Britain accept these conditions. It was expected that the loan would last for five years, but in fact it was exhausted by 1947 after the failure to maintain the convertibility of sterling. Only the financial terms were observed, the others being allowed to lapse. *See* Convertibility Crisis (1947).

Wastes of Imperfect Competition. *See* Imperfect Competition.

Wasting Asset. An asset with a limited life which cannot be replaced as, for example, a coal-mine or an oilwell where the supply is certain to be exhausted at some future time.

Watering of Stock. *See* Stock Watering.

Watkinson Committee. The National Advisory Committee on the Employment of Older Men and Women which published its reports in 1952 and 1955. It found that even when the general level of unemployment was very low the incidence of unemployment increased as people became older.

Ways and Means Advances. This is direct borrowing by the Treasury from the Bank of England. It forms only a very small proportion of Government borrowing.

W.E.A. Abbreviation of Workers' Educational Association.

Wealth. A stock of goods existing at a certain time that conform to the following requirements: (i) they must possess utility, that is, they must yield satisfaction; (ii) they must have a money value; (iii) they must be limited in supply; and (iv) it must be possible to transfer their ownership from one person to another. All wealth must be owned by someone, either by individuals or by groups or by the community as a whole. Thus there is personal wealth, that is, the personal belongings of individuals, business wealth, that is, capital goods such as machinery and factory buildings, and what may be called social wealth such as publicly owned property—schools, libraries, the assets of nationalised industries. All these things comprise real wealth. Money in the form of banknotes and bank deposits or securities such as savings certificates or consols make a country neither richer nor poorer (the securities merely representing Government debt), and must not be included if a calculation is to be made of the total wealth of a country. However, an individual who possesses these things may regard them as personal wealth so long as he can exchange them for real wealth, although they are only claims to wealth.

Wealth Tax. Similar to a capital levy (*q.v.*), a tax on the value of a person's total possessions, probably with exemption below a certain amount. The Special Contribution of 1948 was in effect a wealth tax. In 1968 a special tax was imposed for one year on investment income. Since this tax was additional to income tax and surtax the maximum levy on investment income was at a rate of over 100% so that payment clearly had to be made out of capital. No wealth tax as such has as yet been levied in the U.K., though some politicians favour such a tax in order to reduce inequality of wealth and incomes. In 1974 proposals were made for the imposition of a Wealth Tax in the U.K.

Wear and Tear. The depreciation of the value of a thing as a result of ordinary usage as distinct from damage resulting from negligence or accidental causes.

Weekly Half-holiday. An Act of 1850 granted a half-day holiday on Saturdays to women and children employed in factories and workshops. Though the Act made no specific reference to adult men they also obtained the half-day holiday since production in the mills at that time depended on the women and children workers being employed. For the half-day holiday of those employed in retail shops *see* Early Closing Act; Shops (Early Closing) Acts.

Weekly Return. The weekly balance sheet of the Bank of England. *See* Bank Return.

Week-work. The work which the villeins on medieval manors regularly had to undertake for their lords. In addition, at harvest and some other times they had to do boonwork.

Weighting. The system of giving greater emphasis to certain items in the construction of an index number. For example, in the Index of Retail Prices a weight of 60% was given to food in 1914 but only 31·9% in 1962. *See* Index of Retail Prices.

Weight Note. When a sale is effected at an organised produce exchange the seller supplies the buying broker with a Weight Note showing the amount he has purchased.

Weights and Measures Act (1963). Regulations regarding weights and measures, as revised by the Act of 1873 and later Acts, were consolidated by the Act of 1963. It lays down that some commodities must be sold in particular quantities, as for example, tea in amounts of 2 oz, 4 oz or 8 oz, and not packaged in odd amounts which tend to deceive consumers. Since July 1965 sale in odd amounts has been prohibited for many commodities. Matters affecting weights and measures now fall within the province of the Department of Trade.

Weir System. A premium-bonus system of wage payment. A standard time is attached to each piece of work, the ordinary time-rate being paid for the actual time taken with, in addition, a bonus equal to half the time-rate for the time saved.

Welfare Economics. The study and application of economics to improving the economic welfare of the people. The name of Prof. A. C. Pigou is associated with this view of economics.

Welfare State. A term used—often somewhat derisively—of a comprehensive State system of social insurance against unemployment, sickness, old age, and other similar contingencies, and with other schemes, such as a National Health Service, family allowances, national assistance, etc.

Wells Fargo Bank. With its head office in San Francisco, it is the oldest bank in the western United States. Until 1968 it was the largest State bank in California but in that year it became a National bank, the second largest of this type in that state. It ranks eleventh among American banks. It has an interest in the Western American Bank (*q.v.*).

Wembley Exhibition (1923-24). *See* Exhibition.

Werner Plan. A scheme for a monetary union of the E.E.C. countries.

Westdeutsche Landesbank. The largest commercial bank in West Germany.

Western American Bank. A bank consortium formed in 1968 comprising Detroit National, Hambros, Security Pacific and Wells Fargo.

Westminster Insurance Co. Ltd. Founded in 1717, it is the third oldest fire insurance company in Great Britain. *See* Fire Insurance.

W.F.T.U. Abbreviation of World Federation of Trade Unions (*q.v.*).

Wharfage. A charge made for the use of a wharf for embarking or disembarking goods.

Wheatley Act (1924). A Housing Act which granted local authorities subsidies on the houses they built.

Which? The monthly journal of the Consumers' Association (*q.v.*), it contains reports on consumers' goods. Special issues include *Money Which?* and *Motoring Which?*

'Whisky Money.' Revenue from the excise duty on whisky which under the Local Taxation (Customs and Excise) Act of 1890 was to be devoted to the provision of secondary and technical education.

White Collar Workers. A comprehensive term covering all those engaged in clerical, administrative, professional, or managerial work in industry. Recent developments in industrial techniques have tended to increase the proportion of white collar workers in industry, and in the United States white collar workers now outnumber manual workers. In Great Britain in 1921 white collar workers formed only 21% of the working population; today 40%.

White Paper. An official statement of Government policy on some matter of current economic or social interest, generally as a basis for legislation. One of the most outstanding White Papers was that of 1944 on Employment Policy. White Papers are published regularly on the *Balance of Payments*, *National Income and Expenditure*, the *Economic Survey* and many other matters. *See also* Blue Book; Green Paper.

White Plan. The American scheme put forward at the Bretton Woods Conference in 1943 which with the British Keynes Plan formed the basis of the constitution of the International Monetary Fund. *See* Bretton Woods Agreement (1944).

Whitley Councils. The name given to the Joint Industrial Councils (*q.v.*), set up on the recommendation of the Whitley Committee of 1917, their purpose being to make possible regular consultation between employers and employees in order to improve industrial relations.

W.H.O. Abbreviation of World Health Organisation (*q.v.*).

Whole Life Policy. An assurance policy the payment of premiums continuing until the death of the assured. Contrast Endowment Assurance (*q.v.*).

Wholesaler. An intermediary between the producer and the retailer. His main functions are: (i) 'Breaking of bulk', that is, buying in large quantities from the producer and selling in smaller quantities to retailers. (ii) Warehousing, that is, holding stocks to meet fluctuations of demand. (iii) Helping to finance distribution by allowing credit to retailers although paying his own suppliers promptly. (iv) Sometimes preparing a commodity for sale by grading, packing, and branding the goods.

Wholesaler, Elimination of. Since wholesaling is an essential part of the work of distribution the elimination of the wholesaler simply means that the work of wholesaling must be undertaken by someone else —the manufacturer or the retailers. Large-scale retailers generally buy direct from manufacturers, but in the case of multiple shop organisations this merely means that they themselves must then undertake the business of warehousing and distribution of stock to their branches. Manufacturers of many branded goods too prefer to undertake the distribution of their products to retailers to ensure that they reach the maximum number of retail outlets. Where, however, more than one wholesaler acts between the manufacturer and the retailer this is justified only if the complexity of distribution for that particular commodity requires it.

Wholesaler, Types of. Four types of wholesaler in home trade can be distinguished: (i) The wholesaler who for a period owns and warehouses goods, but carries out no process in connection with them; (ii) The wholesaler who owns and stores goods and prepares them for sale; (iii) The wholesaler who organises the distribution of a commodity but does not actually handle it as, for example, the motor-car distributor; (iv) Middlemen like brokers and agents who work on commission, buying or selling on behalf of other wholesalers.

Who Owns Whom. A publication which lists the subsidiaries of parent companies and shows all the companies controlled by holding companies (i) in Great Britain and the United States, and (ii) on the continent of Europe.

Wide-Range Investment. Until 1961 trust funds could be invested only in gilt-edged and similar securities. Since that date, however, trustees have been permitted to invest up to half their funds in certain ordinary shares and unit trusts. *See also* Trustee Securities.

Wider-Band Exchange Rates. A type of flexible exchange rate similar to the Adjustable Peg (*q.v.*) but allowing wider fluctuation from the declared or middle rate.

Wider Share Ownership. A committee, comprising members of all three political parties of the House of Commons, which aims to encourage a greater number of people to invest in shares.

Widows' Pensions. First introduced in the U.K. in 1925 by Sir Winston Churchill. Under the present system of social security a widow receives an allowance (rather larger than the pension) for the first six months of widowhood. There are additional allowances for children. The widow's pension is at the same rate as the retirement pension for a single person but until 1972 it was payable only to widows over 50 years of age at the time of their husband's death. Since 1972 the pension has been payable to widows aged 40 to 50 on a rising scale according to age.

Wife's Expenditure. *See* Husband's Responsibility for Wife's Expenditure.

Wilberforce Reports. These concerned recommendations for improving the wages of electricity workers (1971) and coal miners (1972). Both reports were characterised by recommendations for increases of pay greatly in excess of what the Government had laid down, thereby hampering the Government in its attempt to control inflation. The 1972 report was to end a disastrous strike and declared the pay of miners to be a special case, a fact which other unions were not likely to concede. *Cf.* Willink Report.

Wildcat Strike. A term of American origin for an Unofficial Strike (*q.v.*).

Williams & Glyn's Bank. Formed in 1970 by a merger of Williams Deacon's Bank (founded in Manchester in 1771), the National Bank and Glyn, Mills & Co., it is associated with the National and Commercial Banking Group (*q.v.*). It has over 300 branches.

Willink Report (1962). The final report of a Royal Commission appointed to inquire into the pay and conditions of the police. It found that most police forces were seriously undermanned and recommended that rates of pay for all grades of police officers should be substantially increased to give them higher rates than in comparable occupations in order to attract a sufficient number of new recruits. In times of over-full employment when there is always a greater demand for labour than the supply such a policy can only encourage still further the inflationary spiral of wages and prices. The immediate consequence of the Willink Report was a demand from the teachers' organisations for increases in pay to maintain the existing pay differential *See* Comparability, Principle of.

'Window-Dressing.' The practice of the English commercial banks prior to 1946 of calling in some of their loans immediately before compiling their weekly statements (on which their monthly statements are based) and immediately before their half-year balance in order to show a cash ratio of 10% when a cash ratio of only 8% was being maintained for most of the time. Since 1946 a cash ratio of 8% has been shown.

Window Envelope. An envelope with a transparent portion through which the addressee's name and address on the enclosed letter can be seen, so that the envelope itself does not have to be addressed.

Window Tax. A former tax on houses based on the number of windows, this being taken as an indication of the relative size of houses. It was not, therefore, a tax on windows as such but on houses approximately according to their size though its effect was to cause property owners to build up windows to reduce the amount of tax payable. It was a much simpler matter to count the windows than to assess rateable values, as became the later practice.

Wind up. To bring a limited company to an end either voluntarily or by order of the Court.

Withholding Tax. The deduction of tax on dividends or other securities at source or in some cases by the bank into which they are paid to enable the tax authorities to ensure that the tax is paid. Those not liable to tax (or who are taxable at a lower rate) must then claim a refund.

Without Recourse. When these words (or 'sans recours') are added to the signatures of the drawers and endorsers of a bill of exchange it is done in order to limit their liability.

Witness Assembly. An alternative term for Field Test (*q.v.*).

Witteveen Facility. An arrangement made in 1977 whereby the fourteen richest nations agreed to provide the I.M.F. with an extra 10,000 million dollars to assist countries in financial difficulties.

Women's Wages. *See* Equal Pay.

Won. The standard unit of the currency of Korea, it is subdivided into 100 jeon.

Wool Exchange. *See* London Wool Exchange.

Wool Futures Market. Dealings in wool 'futures' began in London in 1953. The difficulty of satisfactorily grading wool—sold by auction after sampling—for a long time prevented the establishment in Great Britain of a futures market in wool, though such markets in New York and Antwerp had met with some success. It was the exceptionally wide fluctuations in the price of wool during 1950–52 that led to demands for a wool futures market in Great Britain as a means of insuring against such price fluctuations. *See* Futures.

Wool Market. *See* London Wool Exchange.

Worker Participation. This occurs when representatives of trade unions or employees are given seats on the board of a company. *See* Bullock Report (1976).

Workhouse. Established under the Poor Law of 1601, extended by the Workhouse Act of 1722, and continued by the Poor Law Amendment Act (1834), workhouses were places to which people had to go in order to obtain Poor Law relief, the able-bodied being set to work there. Separate accommodation was provided in the workhouses for the aged and infirm. In 1834 parishes were grouped in unions with one workhouse to each union. Those admitted to the workhouses were not to enjoy a standard of living higher than that of the lowest-paid independent labourers.

Working Capital. An alternative term for Circulating Capital (*q.v.*).

Working Conditions. During the past two hundred years there has been a great improvement in working conditions by the introduction of a shorter working week, the granting of longer paid holidays, the provision of healthier and safer conditions in factories, and work being made less onerous as a result of using more and better machinery, etc. Working conditions today are largely controlled by the Factory Acts, the Shops Acts and the Health and Safety at Work etc. Act (1974).

Working Expenses. Expenses necessarily incurred in the running of a business, such as rent, rates, wages, insurance, etc., and shown in the Profit and Loss Account where they are deducted from gross profit to show net profit.

Working Party. A committee appointed to undertake an inquiry of some kind and report their findings. This term was first used in connection with the groups of people who were appointed by the Government in 1946 to inquire into and report on industries that were not to be nationalised. Each working party comprised representatives of the employers and employees in the industry concerned together with an independent member, often an economist. Reports were published on the wool and cotton textile industries, the manufacture of carpets, pottery, boots and shoes, etc.

Working Population. The number of men, women, boys, and girls employed at a particular time. The proportion that the working population forms of the total population depends on a number of factors, such as the general school-leaving age, the general age of retirement, the extent to which girls and unmarried women work, and the extent to which married women go out to work. *See* Labour, Supply of.

'Working to Rule.' As an alternative to going on strike workers may decide to 'work to rule', that is to say, they would pay such meticulous attention to carrying out rules imposed by their employers that the amount of work accomplished per hour was greatly reduced. Workers in occupations where no such rules are in force now often use the term, which has come to be used euphemistically of any 'go-slow' policy.

Workmen's Compensation Acts. The Acts of 1897 and 1906 made employers liable for accidents to their employees arising in the ordinary course of their employment, whether or not the result of employers' negligence. *See* Employer and Employee; Industrial Injury; National Insurance.

Workmen's Tickets. Formerly railways, passenger tramways, and bus companies issued workmen's return tickets at considerably reduced fares.

This provided an example of discriminating monopoly, the separation of markets being effected by issuing the tickets only before a certain time (usually 8 a.m.) and making the return portions available only after a certain time (usually 5 p.m. on the railways, but earlier on Saturdays).

'Workshop of the World.' A term used of Great Britain in the early nineteenth century, the Industrial Revolution occurring first in this country and giving it a long start over others.

Work Study. *See* Time and Motion Study.

World Bank. The name by which the International Bank for Reconstruction and Development (*q.v.*) is popularly known.

World Economic Conference (1933). An international conference convened by the League of Nations during the Great Depression in order to try to persuade nations to co-operate in order to secure a revival of international trade. No agreement could be reached and during the ensuing years nations pursued even more nationalistic policies than before, tariffs being steeply increased all round.

World Federation of Trade Unions. (W.F.T.U.). An international association of trade unions, founded in 1945 with headquarters in Prague, but since 1949 representing only communist unions. *See also* International Confederation of Free Trade Unions.

World Health Organisation (W.H.O.). A body set up by the United Nations to concern itself with matters affecting health throughout the world.

World Liquidity. *See* Liquidity, International.

World Population Conference (1954). A conference called to consider the problem of a rapidly expanding world population. The western nations considered that some form of family limitation was necessary in those parts of the world like south-east Asia and Latin America where population was increasing most rapidly, but this view was not shared by the representatives of the particular countries concerned.

Write Down (or Off). To reduce the book value of an asset or removing it entirely from the books, as with bad debts which it is found impossible to collect.

Wrongful Dismissal. An employee dismissed without notice would be said to be wrongfully dismissed and would be able to claim damages from the employer. *See* Contracts of Employment Act (1972).

W/W. Abbreviation of Warehouse Warrant (*q.v.*).

X, Y, Z

X.cp. Abbreviation of ex-capitalisation (*q.v.*).
X.d. Abbreviation of ex-dividend. See Ex-div.

Xu. A fractional unit of the currency of Vietnam, 100 xu being equal in value to a dong.

Yaoundé Convention. An agreement whereby the former French colonial territories became associates of the European Economic Community. Similar arrangements were agreed for the Commonwealth countries in Africa, the Caribbean and the Pacific.
Yen. The currency unit of Japan divided into 100 sen.
Yield. The return on a security based on its current earnings in relation to its current price on the stock exchange. In the case of a security with no redemption date it will be a 'flat' yield. If the security is to be redeemed at par at some future date, as is the case with most Government stocks, the redemption yield will also take account of the difference between the current stock exchange price and the future redemption price.
Yield Gap. The difference between the yield on Government stocks and the yield on ordinary shares. At one time, owing to the greater risk, the yield on ordinary shares was higher than the yield on Government stocks, but recently the position has been reversed (*see* Reverse Yield Gap).
York–Antwerp Rules. A code of rules drawn up in 1896 and revised in 1924, relating to General Average in marine insurance.
Yorkshire Bank. Established in Leeds in May 1859 and known for a hundred years as the Yorkshire Penny Bank, it now undertakes ordinary commercial banking business. It is jointly owned by Barclay's, Lloyds, the National Westminster, and Williams & Glyn's Banks. It has 180 branches.
Young Plan. A scheme of 1929 for the reduction of German reparations after the First World War. Payments were suspended in 1931. *See also* Dawes Plan.
Yuan. Also known as renminbi, it is the monetary unit of China, it is subdivided into 10 chiao, the chiao being again subdivided into 10 fen.

Zaire. The standard unit of the currency of the Zaire Republic.
'Z' Chart. A chart relating to the output of a firm and, for purposes of easy comparison, showing graphs of monthly totals, the cumulative monthly total and the moving annual (that is, the total at each month for the previous twelve months), these three graphs together taking the shape of a letter Z.
Zero-Rating. *See* Value-added Tax.
Zip Code. An American term for Postal Code (*q.v.*).

Zloty. The currency unit of Poland, it is divided into 100 grosze.
Zollverein. The customs union of German states established in 1833 under the leadership of Prussia. The motive was as much political as economic.
Zoning. 1. A practice adopted during the Second World War to reduce the cost of distribution in terms of labour, etc., suppliers of some consumers' goods being permitted to sell only to retailers in the zone allotted to them, instead of sup-

pliers being allowed to compete against one another throughout the whole country. Though more efficient, and therefore necessary in wartime, zoning reduces consumers' choice.

2. A term used in town and country planning for areas set aside for particular purposes as, for example, light or heavy industry, green belts, etc.

Z.P.G. Abbreviation of Zero Population Growth, an American term for a rate of growth giving a stable population.

Zurich. The financial centre of Switzerland. Most Swiss banks have their head offices here.

Details of other Macdonald & Evans
Publications on related subjects can be found
in the FREE Macdonald & Evans Business
Studies catalogue available from department
BP1, Macdonald & Evans Ltd., Estover Road
Plymouth PL6 7PZ